CW00970503

Ancient Egyptian
Materials and Industries

A. Lucas
and
J. R. Harris

DOVER PUBLICATIONS, INC.
Mineola, New York

Bibliographical Note

This Dover edition, first published in 1999, is an unabridged republication of the fourth edition, as published by Edward Arnold (Publishers) Ltd., London, in 1962.

Library of Congress Cataloging-in-Publication Data

Lucas, A. (Alfred), 1867–1945.
    Ancient Egyptian materials and industries / A. Lucas and J.R. Harris.
        p.   cm.
    Originally published: 4th ed. London : E. Arnold, 1962.
    Includes index.
    ISBN 0-486-40446-3 (pbk.)
    1. Industrial   arts—History. 2. Egypt—Antiquities.
3. Egypt—Civilization. I. Harris, J. R. (John Richard)
II. Title.
T16.L8   1999
670'.932—dc21   98-43429
                                        CIP

Manufactured in the United States of America
Dover Publications, Inc., 31 East 2nd Street, Mineola, N.Y. 11501

'Is there any thing whereof it may be said,
See, this is new? it hath been already of old
time, which was before us.'
Ecclesiastes, i. 10.

PREFACE TO THE FOURTH EDITION

With the death of Alfred Lucas in December 1945 the science of Egyptology lost one of its most gifted and devoted workers. Through a lifetime of modest and painstaking research he gradually transformed our knowledge of the scientific and technical achievements of the ancient Egyptians, replacing wild conjecture by sober fact, and from the unpretentious beginnings of his *Ancient Egyptian Materials* of 1926 created a standard textbook without parallel in any other branch of archaeology. That a comprehensive work of such detail should in time invite revision was surely inevitable, and it is to the credit of Lucas's publishers that it was they who took the initiative towards this new edition rather than see his monument become a milestone of the past.

The guiding principle of Lucas's work was a courteous objectivity, best expressed in his own words from the preface to the third edition.

'Although I have pointed out what I believe to be certain mistakes that occur in the literature of Egyptology and have expressed definite opinions on various disputed matters, I have endeavoured to bear in mind the precept of Robert Boyle [1] that "a man may be a champion for truth without being an enemy to civility; and may confute an opinion without railing at them that hold it" and I would add in the words of Leeuwenhoek: [2] "As I aim at nothing but Truth, and so far as in me lieth, to point out Mistakes that may have crept into certain Matters; I hope that in so doing those I chance to censure will not take it ill; and if they would expose any Errors in my own Discoveries, I'd esteem it a Service; all the more because 'twould thereby give me Encouragement towards Attaining of a nicer Accuracy." '

This objectivity I have, as far as possible, endeavoured to emulate, and, like Leeuwenhoek, I shall be indebted to any who may bring to my notice errors or omissions in the present revision.

Additions, both of recent work and of older bibliography omitted in previous editions, have been incorporated throughout the book, though certain sections, notably those dealing with leather, cosmetics, fibres, woven fabrics, glass, alloys, niello, bitumen, painting materials, writing materials, wood and woodworking, have required more extensive revision. Of technology in particular much has been added, especially in those chapters where it was only briefly treated, and the Appendix of chemical analyses has been enlarged to include all reliable results, only some few early investigations of undated copper and bronze objects having been consciously omitted. [3] The most consistent modification has, however, been in matters of lexicography, in order to eliminate invalid evidence derived from inaccurate or disputed translations of Egyptian texts. Citations of Breasted's *Ancient Records* have therefore been retained only where the translations are beyond all reasonable doubt and involve materials the Egyptian names for which are well known. Elsewhere, references have been given

---

[1] *The Sceptical Chymist*, 1661.
[2] A. van Leeuwenhoek, *Letters*, 1632–1723.
[3] See p. 487, *n.* 1.

to the standard *Wörterbuch der aegyptischen Sprache* or to other more recent and detailed lexicographical discussions. Dates, the spelling of Egyptian proper names and other details have also been emended, and references to the Tasian period as a chronological entity omitted.[4]

As many references as possible are given in the footnotes, which it is hoped may provide a useful bibliography of all significant studies. In some instances more than one reference to the same or similar articles published simultaneously in different periodicals has been cited for the greater convenience of scholars. Titles of books and periodicals which recur in the notes have been abbreviated, and the relatively few abbreviations which are not immediately obvious or may be unfamiliar to some readers are listed at the beginning of the book.[5]

The majority of conclusions and expressions of opinion remain those of the author, and only where recent research has altered the balance of evidence have I ventured to make the necessary alterations. Wherever the evidence has remained unchanged I have respected Lucas's opinions, though not necessarily agreeing in detail in every instance.

Research in connexion with the present edition was virtually completed by the end of 1960, though some further references were added during the subsequent preparation of the manuscript, and notes of certain important books and articles published, or reaching this country, in recent months (as well as one unfortunately overlooked) are given in the Addenda.[6] That there may be other and more serious omissions I am deeply conscious, since the ever increasing number of articles published in relatively obscure periodicals renders the compilation of any comprehensive bibliography almost impossible.

Certain omissions are, on the other hand, deliberate, and few references will be found either to 'popular' publications, the shortcomings of which are well illustrated in one of Lucas's last articles,[7] or to some recent 'handbooks', notably of ancient technology. Statements in such general works have, wherever possible, been traced to their primary source, while unsupported assertions have been treated with reserve, unless reflecting the results of valuable original research. Similarly, relatively little use has been made of a number of recently published excavation reports in which the identifications of materials and the descriptions of technical details are those of the excavators, unsupported by any expert confirmation. Considerations of space have necessarily restricted the inclusion of comparative material to a minimum.

In reviews of previous editions[8] it was suggested that any revision might be improved by the provision of illustrations, including photomicrographs, and the addition of an index of the Egyptian and Coptic names for the various materials referred to in the text. The continued absence of illustrations is due primarily to the disproportionate expense these would involve, the lack of an index of Egyptian and Coptic words to the practical impossibility of such an undertaking. Very few names of materials are known with any degree of certainty, and a mere list of tentative identifications without any indication of the premises on which they are based would only be misleading.

---

[4] Cf. E. J. Baumgartel, *Cultures of Prehistoric Egypt*, I (1955), p. viii.   [5] See pp. xi–xiv.
[6] See pp. 498–9.   [7] A. Lucas, *Ann. Serv.*, XLI (1942), pp. 135–47.
[8] E.g. J. Leibovitch, *Cahiers d'histoire égyptienne*, I, No. 2 (1948), pp. 208–9.

In preparing this new edition I have enjoyed the facilities of a number of libraries, of which I should like particularly to mention the Patent Office Library, the Radcliffe Science Library, Oxford, and the library of the Griffith Institute, Oxford, whose Librarian, Mr R. F. Ovenell, and staff deserve my sincere thanks. To Mr I. E. S. Edwards and his colleagues I am grateful for their kindness in allowing me to consult offprints in the library of the Department of Egyptian Antiquities in the British Museum, and to Prof. J. Černý for the loan of books and pamphlets from his private library. For valuable comments and helpful suggestions I am indebted to Mr A. F. Shore of the British Museum and Mr J. W. Waterer of the Museum of Leathercraft, while to my wife I owe my thanks for many references from obscure journals and for help in the thankless task of proof correction. Finally I must record my gratitude to the Governing Bodies of Christ Church, Oxford and Worcester College, Oxford for their generous financial support, which alone has made it possible for me to undertake this work.

J. R. HARRIS
Oxford 1962

CONTENTS

LIST OF ABBREVIATIONS

This list is not a bibliography. It is merely intended to facilitate reference, and only includes such abbreviations as may not be immediately clear.

Amenemhēt
   The Tomb of Amenemhēt (N. de G. Davies and A. H. Gardiner)
Ann. Chim. et Phys.
   Annales de chimie et de physique
Ann. Serv.
   Annales du service des antiquités de l'Égypte
Antefoker
   The Tomb of Antefoker, Vizier of Sesostris I, and of his Wife Senet (N. de G. Davies, Nina de G. Davies and A. H. Gardiner)
A.R.
   Ancient Records of Egypt (J. H. Breasted)
Arch.
   Archaeology, Archaeological
Bau- und Denkmalsteine
   Die Bau- und Denkmalsteine der alten Ägypter und ihre Namen. Sitz. Berl. Ak. 1933, pp. 864–912 (K. Sethe)
B.I.F.A.O.
   Bulletin de l'institut français d'archéologie orientale
Boston Bull.
   Bulletin of the Museum of Fine Arts, Boston
Bull.
   Bulletin
Cairo Sc. Journ.
   Cairo Scientific Journal
C.R.Ac.Sci.
   Comptes rendus de l'académie des sciences
Dahchour
   Fouilles à Dahchour, mars-juin 1894; 1894–1895 (J. de Morgan)
Deir el Gebrâwi
   The Rock Tombs of Deir el Gebrâwi (N. de G. Davies)
Drogennamen
   Wörterbuch der ägyptischen Drogennamen: Grundriss der Medizin, VI (H. v. Deines and H. Grapow)
First or Aswan Cataract
   A Description of the First or Aswan Cataract of the Nile (J. Ball)
F.u.F.
   Forschungen und Fortschritte
Fussboden
   Der Fussboden aus dem Palaste des Königs Amenophis IV zu el Hawata (F. W. von Bissing)
Geog.
   Geography, Geographical

Geol.
  Geology, Geological
Glazed Tiles
  Glazed Tiles from a Palace of Ramesses II at Ḳantīr (W. C. Hayes)
Grundriss der Medizin
  Grundriss der Medizin der alten Ägypter (H. Grapow and others)
Hemaka
  The Tomb of Hemaka (W. B. Emery)
History of Technology
  History of Technology (C. Singer, E. J. Holmyard and A. R. Hall)
Huy
  The Tomb of Ḥuy, Viceroy of Nubia in the Reign of Tutʿankhamūn (Nina de G. Davies and
  A. H. Gardiner)
Ind. and Eng. Chemistry
  Industrial and Engineering Chemistry
Inst.
  Institute, Institut
J.A.O.S.
  Journal of the American Oriental Society
J.E.A.
  Journal of Egyptian Archaeology
J.N.E.S.
  Journal of Near Eastern Studies
Journ.
  Journal
Ken-Amūn
  The Tomb of Ken-Amūn at Thebes (N. de G. Davies)
Lavorazione delle pelli
  La lavorazione delle pelli e del cuoio dell'Egitto antico. Bollettino ufficiale, R. Stazione sperimentale
  per l'industria delle pelli e delle materie concianti, XI (1933), pp. 75–94 (G. Bravo)
Leather
  Article 'Leather', in History of Technology, II, pp. 147–90 (J. W. Waterer)
Leather Working
  Leather Working in Ancient Egypt (Russian). Izvestia Gosudarstvennoi Akademii Istorii Materialnoi
  Kulturi, Tom VII, Vipusk I (I. M. Lure)
Lexicographical Studies
  Lexicographical Studies in Ancient Egyptian Minerals (J. R. Harris)
Meir
  The Rock Tombs of Meir (A. M. Blackman)
Mém.
  Mémoires
Menkheperrasonb
  The Tombs of Menkheperrasonb, Amenmosĕ and Another (Nina de G. Davies and N. de G.
  Davies)
Mereruka
  The Mastaba of Mereruka (P. Duell)
Meryet-Amūn
  The Tomb of Queen Meryet-Amūn at Thebes (H. E. Winlock)
Metallkunst
  Die Metallkunst der alten Ägypter (G. Möller)

Minerals of Economical Interest
    Minerals of Economical Interest in the Deserts of Egypt. Congrès Int. de Géog., Le Caire, Avril 1925, III (1926), pp. 163–8 (L. Nassim)
Mitt. Kairo
    Mitteilungen des deutschen Instituts für ägyptische Altertumskunde in Kairo
M.M.A. Bull.
    Bulletin of the Metropolitan Museum of Art, New York
Naga-ed-Dêr
    The Early Dynastic Cemeteries of Naga-ed-Dêr (G. A. Reisner and A. C. Mace)
Nakht
    The Tomb of Nakht at Thebes (N. de G. Davies)
Nefer-hotep
    The Tomb of Nefer-ḥotep at Thebes (N. de G. Davies)
Nefer-ir-ke-rē
    Das Grabdenkmal des Königs Nefer-ir-keꝫ-reꜥ (L. Borchardt)
Ne-user-rē
    Das Grabdenkmal des Königs Ne-user-reꜥ (L. Borchardt)
O.L.Z.
    Orientalistische Literatur-Zeitung
Oud. Med. N.R.
    Oudheidkundige Mededelingen, Nieuwe Reeks
Per-nēb
    The Decoration of the Tomb of Per-nēb (C. R. Williams)
Pflanzenreste
    Ueber Pflanzenreste aus altägyptischen Gräbern. Berichte der Deutsch. Botan. Gesellsch., 1884 (G. Schweinfurth)
Prehistoric and Early Iron
    Notes on Prehistoric and Early Iron in the Old World (H. H. Coghlan)
Prehistoric Metallurgy of Copper and Bronze
    Notes on the Prehistoric Metallurgy of Copper and Bronze (H. H. Coghlan)
Preservative Materials
    Preservative Materials used by the Ancient Egyptians in Embalming (A. Lucas)
P.S.B.A.
    Proceedings of the Society of Biblical Archaeology
Ptahhetep
    The Mastaba of Ptahhetep and Akhethetep at Saqqareh (N. de G. Davies and F. Ll. Griffith)
Puyemrê
    The Tomb of Puyemrê at Thebes (N. de G. Davies)
Rec. Trav.
    Recueil de travaux relatifs à la philologie et à l'archéologie égyptiennes et assyriennes
Rekh-mi-rē
    The Tomb of Rekh-mi-rēꜥ at Thebes (N. de G. Davies)
Reliefs, A.R., M.R., N.R.
    Die Reliefs (und Malereien) *des alten, mittleren, neuen Reiches* (L. Klebs)
Report on the Mineral Industry
    Report on the Mineral Industry of Egypt (Mines and Quarries Dept.) 1922 edition unless otherwise stated
Rev. d'Ég.
    Revue d'Égyptologie

Sahu-rē
    Das Grabdenkmal des Königs Sȝȝḥu-reʿ (L. Borchardt)
Saqqara
    Excavations at Saqqara (J. E. Quibell)
Scepter
    The Scepter of Egypt (W. C. Hayes)
Sculpture and Painting
    A History of Egyptian Sculpture and Painting in the Old Kingdom (W. S. Smith)
Senebtisi
    The Tomb of Senebtisi at Lisht (A. C. Mace and H. E. Winlock)
Servant Statues
    Egyptian Servant Statues (J. H. Breasted (Jr.))
Sheikh Said
    The Rock Tombs of Sheik Saīd (N. de G. Davies)
Slain Soldiers
    The Slain Soldiers of Nēb-ḥepet-rēʿ Mentu-ḥotpe (H. E. Winlock)
Soc.
    Society, Société
Thoutmôsis IV
    The Tomb of Thoutmôsis IV (H. Carter and P. E. Newberry)
Tut-ankh-Amen
    The Tomb of Tut-ankh-Amen (H. Carter)
Two Officials
    The Tombs of Two Officials of Tuthmosis the Fourth (N. de G. Davies and Nina de G. Davies)
Two Sculptors
    The Tomb of Two Sculptors at Thebes (N. de G. Davies)
Unt.
    Untersuchungen zur Geschichte und Altertumskunde Aegyptens (K. Sethe)
Wb.
    Wörterbuch der aegyptischen Sprache (A. Erman and H. Grapow)
Wohlriechende Natron
    Über das wohlriechende Natron bei den alten Ägyptern (R. O. Steuer)
Yuaa and Thuiu
    The Tomb of Yuaa and Thuiu (J. E. Quibell)
Z.Ä.S.
    Zeitschrift für ägyptische Sprache und Altertumskunde
Zeitschr. f. angew. Chemie
    Zeitschrift für angewandte Chemie

CHRONOLOGICAL TABLE

PALEOLITHIC PERIOD

MESOLITHIC PERIOD

NEOLITHIC PERIOD   Ended ? *c.* 5000 B.C.

BADARIAN PERIOD (S.D. 20–29)

PREDYNASTIC PERIOD

Early (Amratian) : Naqada I (S.D. 30–38)   *c.* 5000–*c.* 3000 B.C.
Middle (Gerzean)
Late (Semainean) } Naqada II (S.D. 38–65)

UNION OF UPPER AND LOWER EGYPT   *c.* 3000 B.C. ($\pm$150 yrs)

PROTODYNASTIC PERIOD   { 3000–2778 B.C.[1]
 Dynasty I   { 2850–2650 B.C.[2]
 Dynasty II

OLD KINGDOM

 Dynasty III   { 2778–2723 B.C.[1]
          { 2650–2600 B.C.[2]

 Dynasty IV   { 2723–2563 B.C.[1]
          { 2600–2480 B.C.[2]

 Dynasty V   { 2563–2423 B.C.[1]
          { 2480–2350 B.C.[2]

          { 2423–2263 B.C.[1]
 Dynasty VI   { 2350–? [2]
          { 2314–2190 B.C.[3]

FIRST INTERMEDIATE PERIOD

 Dynasty VII (possibly fictitious)   2190–2163 B.C.[3]

          { 2263–2220 B.C.[1]
 Dynasty VIII   { ?–2190 B.C.[2]
          { 2180–2070 B.C.[3]

          { 2222–2130 B.C.[1]
 Dynasty IX   { 2190–? [2]
          { 2175–2130 B.C.[3]

          { 2130–2070 B.C.[1]
 Dynasty X   { ?–2052 B.C.[2]
          { 2130–2040 B.C.[3]

MIDDLE KINGDOM

 Dynasty XI   { 2160(?)–2000 B.C.[1]
          { ?–1992 B.C.[3]

          { 2000–1785 B.C.[1]
 Dynasty XII   { 1991–1778 B.C.[2]
          { 1991–1786 B.C.[4]
          { 1989–1776 B.C.[5]

SECOND INTERMEDIATE PERIOD

Dynasty XIII ⎱		⎰ 1785–1680 B.C.[1]
Dynasty XIV ⎰		⎱ 1778–1670 B.C.[2]
Dynasty XV ⎱ ('Hyksos')		⎧ 1730–1580 B.C.[1]
Dynasty XVI ⎰		⎨ 1670–1570 B.C.[2]
		⎩ 1720/10–1570/60 B.C.[6]
		⎧ 1680(?)–1580 B.C.[1]
Dynasty XVII		⎨ 1610–1570 B.C.[2]
		⎩ 1630/20–1570/60 B.C.[6]

NEW KINGDOM

Dynasty XVIII   1580–1314 B.C.[1]
   (including the Amarna period)   c. 1370–1350 B.C.
Dynasty XIX   1314–1200 B.C.[1]
Dynasty XX   1200–1085 B.C.[1]

LATE PERIOD

Dynasty XXI   1085–950 B.C.[1]
Dynasty XXII (Libyan)   950–730 B.C.[1,7]
Dynasty XXIII   817–730 B.C.[1]
Dynasty XXIV   730–715 B.C.[1]
Dynasty XXV (Ethiopian)   751–656 B.C.[1]
Dynasty XXVI (Saite period)   664–525 B.C.[1,8]
Dynasty XXVII (Persian domination)   525–404 B.C.[1]
Dynasty XXVIII   404–398 B.C.[1]
Dynasty XXIX   398–378 B.C.[1]
Dynasty XXX   378–341 B.C.[1]
Dynasty XXXI (Second Persian domination)   341–333 B.C.[1]
Dynasty XXXII (Alexander and his heirs)   332–305 B.C.

PTOLEMAIC PERIOD   305–30 B.C.

ROMAN PERIOD   30 B.C.–A.D. 395

BYZANTINE PERIOD   A.D.395–640

---

[1] Dates proposed by E. Drioton and J. Vandier, *Les peuples de l'orient méditerranéen, II, l'Égypte* (3rd ed., 1952).

[2] Dates proposed by A. Scharff, in A. Scharff and A. Moortgat, *Ägypten und Vorderasien im Alterum.*

[3] Dates proposed by H. Stock, *Die erste Zwischenzeit Ägyptens.*

[4] Dates proposed by R. A. Parker, *The Calendars of Ancient Egypt.*

[5] Dates proposed by W. F. Edgerton, *J.N.E.S.*, I (1942), p. 314.

[6] Dates proposed by H. Stock, *Studien zur Geschichte und Archäologie der 13. bis 17. Dynastie Ägyptens.*

[7] A. M. Blackman, *J.E.A.*, xxvii (1941), p. 92, places the beginning of Dynasty XXII in 945 B.C.

[8] The first year of Dynasty XXVI is placed one year earlier in accordance with R. A. Parker, *Mitt. Kairo,* xv (1957), p. 212.

Chapter I

ADHESIVES

The principal adhesives employed, or possibly employed, as cementing materials in ancient Egypt, arranged in alphabetical order for the sake of convenience, were albumin (white of egg), beeswax, clay, glue, gum, gypsum (plaster of Paris), natron, resin, salt, solder and starch, which may now be considered.

ALBUMIN

Albumins are natural nitrogenous bodies of complex composition, containing sulphur in small proportion, that occur both in animals and in plants, the only albumin, however, that need be considered here being egg albumin, or white of egg. This has often been suggested as the adhesive that was employed for the ancient Egyptian paint, thus Spurrell states that he found proof of the use of egg albumin on the Twelfth Dynasty tomb paintings at Kahun.[1] The evidence he gives was that the paint was unaffected both by hot and by cold water and also by soap; that when heated it charred and gave off ammonia; that it was insoluble in dilute hydrochloric acid, but soluble in the strong acid, as the result of which he says 'There can be little doubt that it is albumen. It cannot be gelatine or any resinous gum.' He also says that 'A peculiar condition, somewhat glossy, of the surface of the stone around other paintings was found to be caused by a dressing of this albumen over surfaces now devoid of colour', which he suggests may have been done to fill up the pores of the stone. He states that 'There appears to be no doubt left that all the colours which I have examined having the above characters had egg albumen for a medium and this extends from Senefru's time to that of the Romans . . .' Spurrell also reports egg albumin from some of the Eighteenth Dynasty paintings at El Amarna.[2]

Laurie obtained a positive reaction for both nitrogen and sulphur when testing the adhesive used to fasten ancient Egyptian gold leaf to plaster (gesso), and, therefore, concluded that the adhesive employed was egg albumin.[3]

Ritchie also tested the adhesive used for fixing gold leaf on plaster (gesso) and found that when examined spectroscopically there was evidence of the presence of phosphorus, which he suggested possibly might indicate egg albumin.[4]

While in no way denying that egg albumin may have been employed sometimes in ancient Egypt as an adhesive, I would point out that, although this has been shown

---

[1] F. C. J. Spurrell, *Arch. Journ.*, LII (1895), pp. 229–30.

[2] F. C. J. Spurrell, *Arch. Journ.*, LII (1895), p. 238.

[3] A. P. Laurie, in R. Mond and O. H. Myers, *Bucheum*, I, pp. 68–69; *Technical Studies*, II, (1933–4), pp. 213–16; *Analyst*, LVIII (1933), p. 468.

[4] Private letter, the specimens tested having been supplied by me.

to be probable, it has not been proved. There are considerable difficulties in identifying albumin with certainty in very small specimens of material that have been exposed for hundreds, or even thousands, of years, particularly as there is no specific test for albumin, but also because albumin, even if originally present, may have undergone considerable chemical change. The fact that Spurrell found the material he tested was nitrogenous organic matter is no proof that it was albumin, since glue is also a nitrogenous organic matter that might well have been present. Also, if the stone on which the painting was done had been sized with albumin, as Spurrell suggested, the albumin found may have been present in the size and not in the paint. I have examined a very large number of specimens of ancient Egyptian paint and have always found it to be so very easily removed by water that I cannot think the adhesive was albumin, unless, if originally present, it has perished. Further, although the particular specimens of paint referred to by Spurrell, that were not acted on by water, may have contained albumin, it should not be forgotten that beeswax and resin, both of which were certainly sometimes used during the Eighteenth Dynasty for covering tomb paintings, would also have been unacted upon by water.

With reference to Laurie's work, here again the nitrogenous organic matter found may have been glue and not albumin, and the sulphur may have been derived from glue, which also contains it,[1] and not from albumin.

Ritchie, while suggesting that the presence of phosphorus possibly might indicate albumin, lays no stress on this. The phosphorus, however, might well have been in the form of calcium phosphate, which is not an uncommon constituent of limestone, and, therefore, of the whiting of which the gesso tested was composed.

In my opinion, much more work is required before it can be accepted as satisfactorily proved that the ancient Egyptians employed egg albumin as an adhesive, and the criticisms made are intended to be helpful and not merely destructive. Although the domestic fowl was not introduced into Egypt until a late period, egg albumin was plentiful and easily obtainable, as geese and ducks were abundant. The origin of the present-day barnyard fowl was the Indian jungle fowl (*Gallus banciva*).[2]

BEESWAX

One adhesive used in ancient Egypt for painting and for coating paintings, about which there is no uncertainty, is beeswax, but as these uses are not as an adhesive in the ordinary sense, they will be considered in connexion with painting materials.[3] Other uses of beeswax, also not as an adhesive, were in mummification;[4] for shipbuilding;[5] for making magical figures;[6] for bronze casting;[7] and, at a very late date, for covering the surface of writing tablets;[8] all of which will be dealt with in other connexions. Here the inquiry will be limited to the use of beeswax as an ordinary adhesive only, for which purpose it was employed in considerable amount. Thus it was used for luting on the lids of vases, five of which of alabaster so treated were

---

[1] Sulphur in modern glue may be due to the use of sulphurous acid for bleaching, but this is not the case with the ancient glue.

[2] H. Carter, *J.E.A.*, IX (1923), pp. 1–4.   [3] See pp. 352–3.   [4] See p. 303.

[5] M. Rostovtzeff, *A Large Estate in the Third Century, B.C.*, p. 123.

[6] See p. 337.   [7] See p. 221.   [8] See p. 364.

found in the tomb of Tutankhamūn,[1] and it was also present on several alabaster lids from the same tomb,[1] the vases of which were missing; it was used, too, for fixing at least three alabaster vases to their pedestals[1] and at the back of two uraei,[1] manifestly as an adhesive. Spurrell found beeswax employed for fastening in place the flint teeth of an Eighteenth Dynasty sickle[2] and Winlock gives an example of its use with limestone powder in the Middle Kingdom for cementing on a razor handle.[3] Another use of beeswax was for curling and plaiting wigs, which will be described in connexion with hair.[4]

On the basis of the known melting-points of certain specimens of ancient Egyptian beeswax, Mercier [5] has suggested that different qualities of wax were employed for specific purposes, and that in particular that used as an adhesive and cement was perhaps adulterated with a resinous substance. This may have been either a vegetable resin or propolis intentionally mixed with the wax, though it is also possible that darker waxes containing propolis as a natural impurity were deliberately selected from the hive.

It does not seem to have been the custom to place beeswax in tombs and no record of the finding of it can be traced, but at El Amarna a piece of beeswax was found in a house.[6]

CLAY

The use of clay as mortar with sun-dried bricks will be dealt with in connexion with building materials.[7]

GLUE

This material is one of the earliest, best known and most reliable of adhesives, especially for wood. It is made by extracting certain animal products containing gelatine, such as bones, skins, cartilage and tendons, with boiling water, concentrating the liquid by evaporation and then pouring it into moulds, in which, when cold, it sets into a solid mass.

Glue was used in ancient Egypt for many different purposes, namely, (a) to fasten wood together and to fix ebony and ivory inlay in place; (b) for mixing with whiting to make both plaster and 'stopping'; (c) probably to fasten coarse woven linen fabric to wood and to plaster and to fasten gold foil to plaster; (d) probably as a sizing material for stone and plaster surfaces before painting; and (e) possibly as an adhesive for pigments. These various uses may now be considered.

At what date and for what purpose glue was first employed in Egypt is uncertain, but probably not as an adhesive for wood, since in the Fourth Dynasty tomb of Hetepheres the wood was fastened together by means of mortise and tenon joints and then sometimes bound with strips of hide,[8] which suggests that glue was not

---

[1] Analysed by me.   [2] F. C. J. Spurrell, in W. M. F. Petrie, *Tell el Amarna*, pp. 37–38.
[3] H. E. Winlock, *Treasure of El Lāhūn*, pp. 63, 74.   [4] See pp. 30–31.
[5] M. M. Mercier, *Mémoires de la Société nationale des Antiquaires de France*, 9ᵉ Sér., II (1951), pp. 127–60.
[6] T. E. Peet and C. L. Woolley, *City of Akhenaten*, I, p. 25.   [7] See p. 75.
[8] G. A. Reisner, *Boston Bull.*, XXV (1927), Supplement; XXVI (1928), pp. 76–88; XXVII (1929), pp. 83–90; XXX (1932), pp. 56–60; cf. also *History of the Giza Necropolis*, II.

used, though as practically all the wood had perished, this could neither be proved nor disproved. Several specimens of plaster from this tomb, however, analysed by me consisted of whiting containing nitrogenous organic matter that might have been glue, since so far as could be determined from the small amount of material available for analysis, there was not any other adhesive present, and some adhesive is essential, whiting possessing practically no natural coherence.

Plaster of this nature (i.e. whiting and glue, which is termed 'gesso' by Egypt-ologists) has been identified by me from the Third Dynasty, where it was used for fastening the small blue faience tiles to the walls in the step pyramid at Saqqara and in the great tomb of Djoser adjoining the pyramid, and also from the Fifth Dynasty, where a carved limestone bust was covered with a painted layer of this plaster. Painted and gilded gesso decoration also occurs on a copper diadem of Old Kingdom date,[1] and Winlock states that the wooden models from the tomb of Meketrē (Eleventh Dynasty) were patched with gesso.[2] Gesso was employed on a large scale during the Eighteenth Dynasty and onwards for applying to wood as a ground for painting and gilding, being often worked with designs in low relief before being gilt, and at a later date it was used extensively for making cartonnage mummy masks and coffins, which consist of layers of linen and gesso, or, at a still later date, of old papyrus documents and gesso, with or without linen.[3] Where gesso was on wood, there was sometimes a layer of coarse woven fabric (linen) between the two, and, not only was the canvas probably treated with glue to make it adhere to the wood on one side and to the plaster on the other, but in those instances in which the gold was thick, this was probably also fastened on with glue,[4] though whether glue was used when the gold was only thin leaf has not been determined.

Gesso was also used for architectural decoration in certain temples of the New Kingdom, a thin coat being applied on very fine linen fabric glued to the sandstone. The gesso was carved in low relief and painted, and possibly also gilt.[5]

It is probable that in a very few instances the adhesive present in whiting plaster was other than glue. Thus, of two specimens of plaster of predynastic date, described as gesso, one appeared to have no organic adhesive, the calcium carbonate perhaps containing sufficient clay to act as a binder,[6] while a plaster from the tomb of Yuya and Tuyu, examined by Pollard, seemed to be a form of gesso consisting of calcium carbonate with possibly an albuminoid binder.[7]

A specimen of glue of Eighteenth Dynasty date was found by Carter in a rock chamber over the mortuary temple of Hatshepsut at Deir el Bahari. This, which was examined by me, was in the form of a rectangular piece thirteen centimetres long with a square section of about two centimetres each way, that manifestly had been cast, and, except that it had dried and shrunk, it could not be

---

[1] D. Dunham, *Boston Bull.*, XLIV (1946), pp. 23–29.

[2] H. E. Winlock, *Models of Daily Life*, p. 73.

[3] An earlier example of gesso cartonnage is a small basket-shaped receptacle from Deir el Medineh (B. Bruyère, *Deir el Médineh (1934–1935)*, p. 56).

[4] Very thick foil was fastened on with gold rivets.

[5] Cf. U. Hölscher, *Excavation of Medinet Habu*, IV, pp. 39–42; *Z.Ä.S.*, LXXVI (1940), pp. 41–45.

[6] R. Mond and O. H. Myers, *Cemeteries of Armant*, I, pp. 121–32.

[7] W. B. Pollard, in J. E. Quibell, *Yuaa and Thuiu*, p. 80.

distinguished from modern glue, to all the usual tests for which it responded.[1]

The use of glue is probably shown in a scene on a tomb wall of Eighteenth Dynasty date at Thebes,[2] and also on an ostracon now at Leipzig, of which the date is not given.[3]

Spurrell reports [4] gelatine used as an adhesive in paint from the Fourth Dynasty, and Toch thought he found evidence of glue or gelatine on the mural paintings in the Fifth Dynasty tomb of Perneb.[5] The use of gelatine is also reported by Spurrell in a painted pavement from El Amarna.[6] I have examined a large number of pigments from ancient Egyptian painted objects, including mural paintings, but the specimens of material available have all been too small for any satisfactory determination of the nature of the adhesive to be made, particularly as there is no specific test for glue. Also, it should not be forgotten that the presence of glue in a paint does not neces-sarily mean that it was employed as a binder, since it may have been used in the same manner as modern size, namely, to fill up the pores in the plaster, stone, or other painting ground, before the paint was applied.

Brunton mentions a small painted wooden box of Fifth Dynasty date with mitred joints fastened with some 'resinous material, which was possibly glue'.[7] Mace and Winlock state[8] that a staff from a Twelfth Dynasty tomb was joined with glue, and Carter found glue used as an adhesive on a toilet box and on a game board, both of late Middle Kingdom, or Second Intermediate Period date.[9] Winlock says[10] that glue was used on two of the coffins of Queen Meryetamūn of the Eighteenth Dynasty, and that a wooden box from the same tomb was 'carelessly mended with a mixture of mud and glue'.[11] Glue is present on many of the objects from the tomb of Tutankha-mūn, where it was employed exactly in the manner of the modern joiner to fasten wood together and to fix ebony and ivory veneer and inlay in place. A number of specimens of 'stopping' from the same tomb, used to fill holes and to cover up im-perfections in wood, were found on analysis by me to consist of a mixture of whiting and glue (i.e. gesso), coloured (in one case with yellow ochre) to match the colour of the wood, or of the paint on the wood.[12] Several hundred tiny shawabti figures of uncertain, but late, date, in the Cairo Museum, I examined were found to be com-posed of powdered limestone held together with glue and moulded.[13]

GUM[14]

Gum is obtained at the present day largely from various species of acacia that grow in the Sudan, but as the acacia also grows in Egypt, where it was more plentiful

---

[1] A. Lucas, in H. Carter, *Tut-ankh-Amen*, II, pp. 166–7 (Appendix II).

[2] N. de G. Davies, *Rekh-mi-rē*, Pl. LV.

[3] N. de G. Davies, *M.M.A.Bull.*, Egyptian Exped. 1916–1919, p. 32, Fig. 22.

[4] F. C. J. Spurrell, in W. M. F. Petrie, *Medum*, p. 50; *Arch. Journ.*, LII (1895), p. 226.

[5] M. Toch, *Journ. Ind. and Eng. Chemistry*, X (1918), p. 118.

[6] F. C. J. Spurrell, *Arch. Journ.*, LII (1895), p. 239.   [7] G. Brunton, *Mostagedda*, p. 98.

[8] A. C. Mace and H. E. Winlock, *Senebtisi*, p. 89.

[9] Carnarvon and H. Carter, *Five Years' Explorations*, pp. 56–57.

[10] H. E. Winlock, *Meryet-Amūn*, pp. 16, 18, 21.   [11] H. E. Winlock, *Meryet-Amūn*, p. 44.

[12] A. Lucas, in H. Carter, *Tut-ankh-Amen*, II, pp. 166–7 (Appendix II).

[13] Nos. J. 66773–66774.

[14] Cf. A. Lucas, *Preservative Materials*, pp. 29–30; J. R. Harris, *Lexicographical Studies*, pp. 158–9.

formerly than now, the greater part, if not the whole, of the ancient Egyptian gum may have been obtained locally. Pliny states [1] that in his day the best gum was obtained from Egypt, which, however, may mean from the Sudan through Egypt.

The 'gum of myrrh' mentioned in ancient texts [2] was not gum in the ordinary sense, but an odoriferous gum-resin used as incense, and the 'gum of god's land';[3] the 'gum of Punt';[4] the 'gum' from Genebteyew [5] and other 'gums' [6] were probably similar material, and not gums, since, even in modern commercial practice, many gum-resins are loosely called gum.

According to Herodotus,[7] gum was employed to fasten together the linen bandages in which mummies were wrapped after embalming, with reference to which he states that the Egyptians mostly used it instead of glue. Gum has been identified on mummy bandages in two instances (undated) by Reutter,[8] and in four instances (all Twentieth Dynasty) by me, and Elliot Smith states [9] that 'a sheet of cloth saturated with some gum-like substance was placed in front of the face' of the mummy of Amenhotpe III (Eighteenth Dynasty), and he also mentions 'gum-saturated bandages'.

Spurrell found gum, which he states was gum acacia, used as an adhesive for paint in the Fourth Dynasty [10] and also in the Eighteenth Dynasty.[11] This, he says, had decayed and left the pigment pulverulent and loose. He also states [11] that 'Several pots of paint were found to have a thick layer of gum overlying the colour, which had settled out at the bottom, these had not been exposed and the gum answered all the usual tests. Gum was also used for the painting of Akhenaten and the little princesses. It was used also on parts of the painted pavement.' Laurie found gum in a paint of Nineteenth Dynasty date.[12] Winlock[13] reports the use of 'a water-soluble gum' as a varnish on certain parts of the models from the tomb of Meketrē (Eleventh Dynasty). Another probable use of gum was for binding together the powdered pigments to make the cakes that are found on the scribes' palettes.

Gypsum

The earliest use of gypsum (plaster of Paris) as an adhesive, so far as is at present known, was for repairing a large pottery vessel of predynastic date found by Menghin and Amer at Ma'adi, the material having been analysed by me. Gypsum plaster was also used to repair the sarcophagus recently found in the pyramid of Sekhemkhet at Saqqara (Third Dynasty),[14] and among the objects from the tomb of Tutankhamūn was a pottery jar, the cover of which was fastened on with gypsum.

The most important use of gypsum as an adhesive in ancient Egypt was for mortar, and another important use, though not exactly as an adhesive, was for

---

[1] XVI: 21.   [2] A.R., II, 288; III, 116.   [3] A.R., IV, 29.

[4] A.R., IV, 29, 31.   [5] A.R., II, 474.   [6] A.R., IV, 378.   [7] II: 86.

[8] L. Reutter, De l'embaumement avant et après Jésus-Christ, pp. 52, 96; Sphinx, XVII (1913), p. 113.

[9] G. Elliot Smith, Royal Mummies, p. 48.

[10] F. C. J. Spurrell, in W. M. F. Petrie, Medum, p. 50.

[11] F. C. J. Spurrell, Arch. Journ., LII (1895), p. 238.

[12] A. P. Laurie, Materials of the Painter's Craft, p. 22; Painter's Methods and Materials, pp. 17, 172.

[13] H. E. Winlock, Models of Daily Life, p. 74.

[14] Z. Goneim, Horus Sekhemkhet, pp. 35–36.

plaster, both of which will be dealt with in connexion with building materials.[1]

For whatever purpose gypsum is employed it must first be calcined, as it is only after calcination and subsequent slaking with water that its adhesive property is developed.

NATRON

The use of natron as an adhesive will be described in connexion with the making of faience.[2]

RESIN

Another important adhesive employed in ancient Egypt was resin, the use of which goes back to the neolithic period, when it was employed to fix in place the flint teeth of a sickle,[3] from which time onwards it was in regular use. Thus a narrow-necked jar from the First Dynasty tomb of 'Hemaka' was sealed with a mixture of resin and quartz sand;[4] a cement of resin and powdered limestone was found attached to some diorite paving blocks and also to some tesserae of Third Dynasty date from Saqqara;[5] a mixture of resin and broken alabaster (both coarse fragments and fine dust) was used as an adhesive on a Third Dynasty sarcophagus from Saqqara;[6] resin was used for securing in place the metal bolts of the granite sarcophagus of Khafrē (Fourth Dynasty);[7] a mixture of resin and powdered limestone fastened on the handle of a Middle Kingdom razor,[8] and incidentally it may be mentioned that resin is the principal ingredient of many of the cements employed at the present day to fasten on the handles of knives and forks. The use of resin as an adhesive was well exemplified in the Eighteenth Dynasty tomb of Tutankhamūn,[9] where it was employed to repair the broken lid of the sarcophagus;[10] on the rebated edge of the gold coffin, where apparently it was used to lute on the lid and so to make a tight joint; to lute on the lids of alabaster and limestone vases;[11] to fix an alabaster vase to its stand;[11] to cement in place spouts of some of the faience libation vases,[11] and to fasten inlay of stone, glass and faience into their setting.[11] Occasionally the resin was used alone, but more generally it was mixed with powdered limestone. A similar mixture was also employed for an ancient repair to the alabaster canopic box of Horemheb (Nineteenth Dynasty) now in the Cairo Museum.[11] Resin was also used on a Twenty-sixth Dynasty sarcophagus from Saqqara to support the lid just before it settled into position,[12] and it was present between the lid and the top of the box of a coffin which I examined, but particulars of which now cannot be traced.[12]

When resin, or a resin mixture, was employed in ancient Egypt to fix inlay in

---

[1] See pp. 75, 76–79.   [2] See pp. 162, 175, 177–8.

[3] G. Caton-Thompson and E. W. Gardner, *Desert Fayum*, p. 45.   [4] Analysed by me.

[5] C. M. Firth, J. E. Quibell and J.-P. Lauer, *Step Pyramid*, I, p. 127. Analysed by me.

[6] Submitted by M. J.-P. Lauer and analysed by me.

[7] W. M. F. Petrie, *Pyramids and Temples of Gizeh*, p. 108.

[8] H. E. Winlock, *Treasure of El Lāhūn*, pp. 63, 74.

[9] A. Lucas, in H. Carter, *Tut-ankh-Amen*, II, p. 167 (Appendix II).

[10] This was originally reported by me to consist of gypsum, but the specimen was not taken by me and there must have been some mistake, since a subsequent sample taken by myself was found to consist of a mixture of resin and powdered limestone.

[11] Analysed by me.   [12] Submitted by Mr. C. M. Firth and analysed by me.

place, the effect was often enhanced by the cement being tinted the same colour as the inlay, blue cement being used for blue inlay and red cement for red inlay and so on. Inlay of transparent quartz, or of transparent calcite, was fastened in place with a red cement, which improved the appearance of the stone considerably, imparting to it the semblance of carnelian. Resin was used occasionally as a mortar in building,[1] and Spurrell reports that a resin, which he suggests may have been mastic, was used as a binder in painting of Fourth Dynasty date.[2]

A further use of resin, of resin and powdered limestone and of resin and broken quartz, though not as an adhesive, will be described in connexion with mummification.[3]

SOLDER

Solder is a cementing material used for joining metals, and consists of any metal, or alloy, having a melting-point lower than that of the metal, or metals, joined. Examples of the ancient use of solder will be given when dealing with metals.[4]

STARCH

Pliny states [5] that starch made from the finest wheaten flour, mixed with boiling water, was used in connexion with the manufacture of papyrus. No adhesive except its own juice was necessary to make small sheets of papyrus, if this were used freshly gathered,[6] but since an adhesive was required to fasten the small sheets together to make a roll, the starch was probably for this latter purpose. No identification of starch on papyrus, or on other ancient Egyptian material, can be traced.

SALT

The use of salt as an adhesive will be dealt with in connexion with the making of faience.[7]

MISCELLANEOUS AND UNIDENTIFIED ADHESIVES

There are certain cementing materials that have not yet been sufficiently investigated and the nature of which is still unknown, while others are apparently unique and cannot easily be classified. Thus, the cement used for fixing in place the sickle flints and arrow heads from the First Dynasty tomb of 'Hemaka' at Saqqara has not yet been identified. In each case the cement contains a very large proportion of calcium carbonate (44 per cent in one specimen), and also organic matter, the nature of which, however, it was impossible to determine with the small amount of material available for analysis. Also, some of the plaster and mortar from the Third, Fourth and Eighteenth Dynasties respectively [8] consists essentially of calcium carbonate and contains no adhesive that can be recognized, though, in some cases, there is a very small proportion of clay, organic matter, or gypsum respectively present. The latter (gypsum), however, is probably not the adhesive, as there is not any evidence that the material has been calcined, and gypsum is inert unless so treated.[9] This problem has been discussed by Dr. J. W. Matthews and by Professors Brammall and Briscoe,[10]

---

[1] See pp. 75, 95.   [2] F. C. J. Spurrell, *Arch. Journ.*, LII (1895), pp. 224–6.
[3] See pp. 316–24.   [4] See pp. 215–6.   [5] XIII: 26.   [6] See p. 139.
[7] See p. 178.   [8] See pp. 75–76.   [9] See p. 79.
[10] R. Mond and O. H. Myers, *Cemeteries of Armant*, I, pp. 122–30.

who suggest that a slight degree of adhesion might have been obtained by the solution, on the addition of water, of the calcite present, and its subsequent re-crystallization on drying, or by 'hydraulicking', by which is meant the feeble calcination of a material that contains a small proportion of clay. In the case of plaster, it should not be forgotten that the groundwork (clay or porous limestone) to which the plaster is applied may itself form the adhesive, if the layer of plaster is only thin. Although practically almost any material, even totally inert quartz, will cohere to at least a small extent if sufficiently finely ground and moistened, it will fall apart again on drying; hence fine grinding is not the solution of the problem, and, moreover, the material is not finely ground.

Various cements used to fix inlay have been examined by Kopp, and in each case the nature of the binder has been undetermined. A cement used in the Twelfth Dynasty jewellery from Lahun was a 'ground-lime plaster mixed with some organic adhesive',[1] while two cements from jewellery of the Eighteenth Dynasty were described as (a) 'evidently made by calcining an impure natural gypsum or limestone, or the two together, and grinding to a smooth paste with a mucilaginous solution',[2] and (b) 'a mixture of powdered limestone with a binder of fatty matter, possibly beef tallow'.[3] A brown inlay cement, also of the Eighteenth Dynasty, 'could represent either an original natural plant product or an artificial compound'.[2]

An adhesive used for fixing a sliding panel in the sarcophagus found in the pyramid of Sekhemkhet at Saqqara was examined by Iskander and found to be 'mostly composed of calcium phosphate, traces of calcium sulphate and a very little organic nitrogenous matter' (probably the remains of glue).[4]

---

[1] A. H. Kopp, in H. E. Winlock, *Treasure of El Lāhūn*, p. 31.
[2] A. H. Kopp, in H. E. Winlock, *Treasure of Three Egyptian Princesses*, p. 65.
[3] A. H. Kopp, in H. E. Winlock, *Treasure of Three Egyptian Princesses*, p. 66.
[4] Z. Iskander, in Z. Goneim, *Horus Sekhemkhet*, p. 35.

Chapter II
ALCOHOLIC BEVERAGES
AND SUGAR

The alcoholic beverages of ancient Egypt were of two kinds, namely, beer and wine.

BEER[1]

For an understanding of the nature and mode of preparation of ancient Egyptian beer, some knowledge of the underlying principles of brewing is necessary and, therefore, modern beer and its manufacture will be described very briefly.

Modern beer is essentially an infusion of malt, flavoured with the bitter of hops and fermented with yeast: it contains usually from about 2 to about 6 per cent of alcohol by volume.

When barley, or other farinaceous grain, germinates, an active nitrogen-containing substance termed an enzyme (of which there are many kinds, the particular one now referred to being known as diastase), which is present naturally in the grain in small proportion, increases considerably in amount and converts a small part of the starch of the grain into a particular kind of sugar called maltose and a gummy material termed dextrin, the former of which becomes the food supply for the growing plant in its early stages. Malting is the reproduction of this natural process under conditions that can be controlled, the grain being first exposed to moisture and warmth until it germinates and then being heated to arrest further growth, in order that the sugar (maltose) formed may be conserved: the resulting product is termed 'malt'.

After malting comes brewing, in which there are three main processes, namely, (a) maceration of crushed malted grain, or of a mixture of malted and unmalted grain, in hot water, during which the diastase present converts that part of the starch of the grain, not previously acted upon, into maltose and dextrin; (b) boiling the solution extracted from the grain with hops, so as to flavour it, and (c) fermentation of the solution with yeast, which first of all, by means of an enzyme termed maltase, converts the maltose into another kind of sugar called dextrose (maltose not being directly fermentable by yeast), which is then split up by still another enzyme (zymase) into alcohol and carbon dioxide gas, the alcohol and part of the gas remaining dissolved in the liquid. The essentials of brewing, therefore, are the conversion of the starch of a cereal grain into sugar and the subsequent change of this sugar into alcohol and carbon dioxide.

---

[1] A. Lucas, *Ancient Egypt*, 1928, pp. 1–3. Cf. also L. F. Hartmann and A. L. Oppenheim, *On Beer and Brewing Techniques in Ancient Mesopotamia, J.A.O.S. Supplement* No. 10 (1950).

As a further preliminary to the description of ancient Egyptian beer, a beer called *bouza* made at the present day in Egypt by Nubians may be described. I examined sixteen different specimens of this *bouza*, purchased from retail dealers in Cairo: they were all similar and had the appearance of thin gruel: they contained much yeast, were in a state of active fermentation and had been made from coarsely ground wheat: the amount of alcohol present varied from 6.2 per cent to 8.1 per cent by volume, with a mean of 7.1 per cent.

Inquiries elicited the information that in Cairo *bouza* is prepared as follows, though doubtless there are variants of the method:

1. A good quality of wheat is taken; the dirt and foreign material are picked out and the wheat is ground coarsely.

2. Three-quarters of the ground wheat are put into a large wooden basin or trough and kneaded with water into a dough, yeast being added.

3. The dough is made into thick loaves, which are baked, though only lightly, so as not to destroy the enzymes or to kill the yeast.[1]

4. The remaining quarter of the wheat is moistened with water and exposed to the air for some time, after which, while still moist, it is crushed.

5. The loaves are broken up and put into a vessel with water and the crushed moist wheat added: the mixture ferments on account of the yeast present in the bread, though in order to induce a quicker fermentation a little old *bouza* from a previous brewing is often added.

6. After fermentation, the mixture is passed through a hair sieve, the solid material being pressed well on the sieve with the hands.

Operation No. 4 is manifestly a primitive and very incomplete form of malting, resembling very closely that described by Zosimos.[2] Malting, however, although general at the present day, is not essential, and at one time it was customary in certain parts of Europe to make beer from unmalted rye. But, as starch is not directly fermentable by yeast and requires to be converted into sugar before fermentation can take place (which is usually brought about by the diastase produced during malting), the fermentation of unmalted grain needs explanation. The same problem presents itself in the fermentation that produces the carbon dioxide to which the rising of leavened bread is due. The explanation is simple. Cereal grains contain a small amount of certain sugars (sucrose and raffinose), which, though not directly fermentable, are converted by one of the enzymes of the yeast (invertase) into dextrose, which, as already explained, is fermentable. In addition, however, there is also a small amount of diastase in the grain, which produces maltose from some of the starch present, this maltose subsequently being converted into dextrose, which undergoes fermentation. Sugars also may be formed from the starch of the grain by means of moulds, which are present on the grain and in the air and of which many 'contain . . . diastase in considerable quantity and are consequently possessed of powerful starch-converting activity',[3] and moulds have been utilized in the East from very early times for the

---

[1] Specimens of this beer-bread were obtained and examined.

[2] See p. 14.

[3] A. C. Chapman, *Micro-organisms and some of their Industrial Uses, Royal Society of Arts*, 1921, pp. 8–9.

conversion of starch into sugar and of sugar into alcohol [1] and certain moulds [2] are used for saccharification purposes today on a very large scale in special methods of preparing alcohol.[3]

Lane in 1860 stated [4] that *bouza* 'which is an intoxicating liquor made from barley-bread, crumbled, mixed with water, strained and left to ferment, is commonly drunk by the boatmen of the Nile and by other persons of the lower orders'.

Burckhardt, writing in 1822, states [5] that in Berber (Nubia) *bouza* was made from strongly leavened millet bread, which was broken into crumbs, mixed with water and kept for several hours over a slow fire, after which more water was added and the mixture left for two nights to ferment: he describes the ordinary *bouza* as not being strained and looking more like soup or porridge than a beverage, but mentions a better quality obtained by straining through a cloth: he also says that barley was used sometimes instead of millet and that it produced a superior beer, which was of a pale muddy colour and very nutritious: he says further that in Cairo and in all the towns and larger villages of Upper Egypt there were shops for the sale of *bouza* kept exclusively by Nubians, which is still true today.

Bruce in 1805 gave a similar account of the preparation of *bouza* in Abyssinia.[6]

A similar beer called *merissa* is brewed in the Sudan: [7] 'wherever the dura crop is found . . . there also is merissa made.' [8] A primitive method of malting is performed by the women, who chew the grain and then spit it out and use it.

The making of beer clearly dates back to a very early period, and residues of pre-dynastic date have been found in jars which originally contained beer that has evaporated.[9]

Beer is mentioned frequently in ancient Egyptian texts,[10] as a divine or mortuary offering,[10] as a beverage,[10] and as a constituent of medicines.[11] The earliest reference known to me is from the Third Dynasty,[12] and the next in chronological order are from the Fifth Dynasty, when beer is named as a mortuary offering,[13] and in the Pyramid Texts.[14] Several different kinds of beer are listed in an onomasticon of the New Kingdom, though the exact significance of the terms is not known.[15]

---

[1] In Japan cultures of *Aspergillus oryzae* supply the diastase for the saccharification of the starch of rice and wheat bran used for making alcoholic drinks, and in China a mixture of micro-organisms, of which the predominating one is a fungus (*Amyloces rouxii*) belonging to the group of mucors, is employed, not only for the saccharification of starch, but also for the fermentation of the sugar into alcohol (W. L. Owen, 'Production of Industrial Alcohol from Grain by Amylo Process', *Ind. and Eng. Chemistry*, xxv (1933), pp. 87–89.

[2] *Amyloces rouxii* and certain special mucors such as *Rhizopus delemar*.

[3] The Amylo and Boulad Processes.

[4] E. W. Lane, *Manners and Customs of the Modern Egyptians* (Everyman's Library), pp. 96, 342.

[5] J. L. Burckhardt, *Travels in Nubia*, 1819, pp. 143, 218.

[6] J. Bruce, *Travels to Discover the Source of the Nile*, vii (1805), pp. 65–66, 335.

[7] J. Petherick, *Egypt, the Sudan and Central Africa*, 1861, pp. 157–9; A. J. Arkell, *Sudan Notes*, xxii (1939), pp. 83–84.

[8] C. B. Tracey, *Sudan Notes*, viii (1925), pp. 212–15.   [9] W. M. F. Petrie, *Prehistoric Egypt*, p. 43.

[10] Cf. *A.R.*, v (Index), p. 108; A. Erman, *Literature of the Ancient Egyptians*, trans. A. M. Blackman; *Wb.* iii. 169. 11–20.

[11] H. v. Deines and H. Grapow, *Drogennamen*, pp. 372–83.

[12] M. A. Murray, *Saqqara Mastabas*, i, p. 39.   [13] *A.R.*, i, 252.

[14] S. A. B. Mercer, *Pyramid Texts*, iv (Index), p. 247.

[15] A. H. Gardiner, *Ancient Egyptian Onomastica*, ii, pp. 233–7.

As well as having been made in the country, beer was also imported, though probably only to a small extent and at a comparatively late period, the only references to this that can be found being of New Kingdom date, where beer from Kedi in Asia is referred to.[1]

Egyptian beer is described by several of the classical writers; thus Herodotus says [2] that the Egyptians 'use a drink made of barley'; Diodorus states [3] that they 'make a' drink of barley . . . for smell and sweetness of taste not much inferior to wine'; Strabo says [4] that 'Barley beer is a preparation peculiar to the Egyptians. It is common among many tribes, but the mode of preparing it differs in each' and that it was one of the principal beverages of Alexandria; [5] this same writer also states [6] that the Ethiopians made a drink both from millet and from barley; Pliny says [7] that an intoxicating beverage was made in Egypt from corn; Athenaeus states [8] that the Egyptians, who could not afford wine, used an intoxicating drink made from barley. During the Ptolemaic period brewing was controlled by the State.

The brewing of beer is depicted on a number of tomb walls, for example, in a Fifth Dynasty tomb from Saqqara, now in the Leiden Museum; [9] in another Fifth Dynasty tomb at Saqqara; [10] in a Sixth Dynasty tomb at Deir el Gebrawi; [11] in a Middle Kingdom tomb at Meir;[12] in a Middle Kingdom tomb[13] and in an Eighteenth Dynasty tomb [14] respectively in the Theban necropolis, in each case bread-making and brewing being associated, the former being a preliminary step towards the latter.[15] Among the processes shown are the making and baking of the bread, the mixing and filtering of the beer, and the pouring of the beer into jars. Baking and brewing are also illustrated by various tomb models, and an Eleventh Dynasty wooden model found at Deir el Bahari shows the operations of corn being ground; dough being kneaded; the 'mash' being made; the solution being fermented and the finished beer being poured into jars.[16] Similar models of about the same date are described by Garstang,[17] and by Breasted,[18] who also publishes a number of individual figures engaged in kneading the mash and straining it through a sieve into a vessel. The significance of these scenes and models has been discussed by Borchardt [19] and others, and it is practically certain that both in mode of preparation and in

---

[1] A. Erman, *Literature of the Ancient Egyptians*, trans. A. M. Blackman, pp. 207, 210; *Wb.* III. 169. 19.

[2] II: 77.   [3] I: 3.   [4] XVII: 2, 5.

[5] XVII: 1, 14.   [6] XVII: 2, 2.   [7] XIV: 29.   [8] I: 34; X: 418.

[9] H. T. Mohr, *Mastaba of Hetep-Her-Akhti* (Mededeelingen en Verhandelingen, Ex Oriente Lux, v).

[10] G. Steindorff, *Ti*, Pls. LXXXIII–IV.   [11] N. de G. Davies, *Deir el Gebrâwi*, II, p. 26, Pl. xx.

[12] A. M. Blackman, *Meir*, IV, p. 35, Pl. XIII.

[13] N. de G. Davies and A. H. Gardiner, *Antefoker*, p. 15, Pls. XI, XIa.

[14] N. de G. Davies, *Ken-Amūn*, p. 51, Pl. LVIII.

[15] Cf. H. F. Lutz, *Viticulture and Brewing*; P. Montet, *Scènes de la vie privée*, pp. 242–54.

[16] H. E. Winlock, *M.M.A.Bull., Egyptian Exped. 1918–1920*, p. 26, Fig. 12; *Models of Daily Life*, pp. 25–29.

[17] J. Garstang, *Burial Customs*, pp. 63, 73–76, 86, 94, 126–8, Figs. 50, 61, 62, 75, 84, 124–5.

[18] J. H. Breasted (Jr.), *Servant Statues*, pp. 30–35, 37–42.

[19] L. Borchardt, *Z.Ä.S.*, xxxv (1897), pp. 128–34; L. Klebs, *Reliefs, A.R.*, pp. 91 f.; *M.R.*, pp. 120 f.; *N.R.*, pp. 171 f. Cf. also L. Borchardt, *Z.Ä.S.*, xxxvII (1899), pp. 82–83; H. Schäfer, *Z.Ä.S.*, xxxvII (1899), p. 84.

composition the ancient Egyptian beer approximated closely to the modern Nubian *bouza*.

According to a description attributed to Zosimos of Panopolis in Upper Egypt, who lived about the end of the third century or the beginning of the fourth century A.D., and spent his youth at Alexandria, ancient Egyptian beer was made as follows: [1] 'Take well-selected fine barley, macerate it for a day with water, and then spread it for a day in a spot where it is well exposed to a current of air. Then for five hours moisten the whole once more, and place it in a vessel with handles, the bottom of which is pierced after the manner of a sieve.' The meaning of the next few lines is not clear, but according to Gruner the barley was then probably dried in the sun, in order that the husks, which are bitter and which would have imparted a like taste to the beer, might peel off. Continuing the description of Zosimos: 'The remainder must be ground up and a dough formed with it, after yeast has been added, just as is done in bread-making. Next the whole is put away in a warm place, and as soon as fermentation has set in sufficiently, the mass is squeezed through a cloth of coarse wool, or else through a fine sieve, and the sweet liquid is gathered. But others put the parched loaves into a vessel filled with water, and subject this to some heating, but not enough to bring the water to a boil. Then they remove the vessel from the fire, pour its contents into a sieve, warm the fluid once more, and then put it aside.'

Although Zosimos describes a primitive method of malting, which is almost identical with that used today in Cairo in making *bouza*, no evidence of malting can be identified, either in the tomb scenes or on the tomb models, and how far the practice (which is not essential) dates back is not known. However, a papyrus of Middle Kingdom date mentions a particular kind of grain specially prepared for beer making, which may be malt,[2] and Helbaek [3] states that he has examined malt from tombs of the Old Kingdom.

Statements have been made that the ancient Egyptians used bitter and other flavouring substances for their beer, much as hops are now employed, and that these included lupin;[4] skirret [4] (*Sium sisarum*); the root of an Assyrian plant;[4] rue;[5,6] safflower;[6,7] mandrake fruit;[7] bitter orange peel [8] and resin,[8] but the evidence (much of which is of very late date) is unsatisfactory and in some instances almost certainly refers to the use of beer as a vehicle for medicine and not to the flavouring of beer as a beverage. One authority often quoted is the Roman agricultural writer

---

[1] The translation is that of C. G. Gruner, as given by Arnold (J. P. Arnold, *Origin and History of Beer and Brewing*, 1911). Other translations differ somewhat, for example those of H. F. Lutz (*Viticulture and Brewing*, p. 78) and P. Montet (*Scènes de la vie privée*, pp. 253–4).

[2] C. F. Nims, *J.N.E.S.*, IX (1950), pp. 261–2; *J.E.A.*, XLIV (1958), pp. 60–63. Cf. also A. H. Gardiner, *Ancient Egyptian Onomastica*, II, pp. 223–5.

[3] Quoted by C. F. Nims, *J.E.A.*, XLIV (1958), p. 63, *n.* 6.

[4] J. G. Wilkinson, *The Ancient Egyptians*, (1878), I, pp. 395–6.

[5] H. Schulze-Besse, *Bier u. Bierbereitung bei den Völkern der Urzeit*, I, *Babylonien u. Ägypten*, Geleitwort.

[6] E. Huber, *Bier u. Bierbereitung bei den Ägyptern*, in *Bier u. Bierbereitung bei den Völkern der Urzeit*, p. 43.

[7] M. Philippe, *Die Braukunst der Ägypter im Lichte heutiger Brautechnik*, in *Bier u. Bierbereitung bei den Völkern der Urzeit*, p. 55.

[8] J. Grüss, *Tageszeitung für Brauerei*, XXVII (1929), pp. 277–8.

Columella, who says [1] '. . . the Egyptians made the sweetish taste of their Pelusian beer more palatable by adding to it pungent spices and lupine'. According to Arnold, however,[2] 'This passage . . . must be interpreted differently. What he intends to say is that pungent or bitter substances were eaten with the beer of Pelusium, such as lupine, so as to stimulate the enjoyment, which was a custom likewise in vogue with the Romans who partook of such substances as appetisers.' With respect to the use of the mandrake fruit, both Gauthier [3] and Dawson [4] have shown that the ancient Egyptian word, thought at one time to mean mandrake, has been mistranslated and is the name of a mineral (probably a species of red ochre) and not of a plant.[5] The bitter orange peel and the resin thought to have been used were found on a tray of funerary offerings (Eleventh Dynasty) accompanying some bread which may have been beer-bread, though there is no proof of this, but their use in beer is very improbable. In modern Nubian *bouza* neither flavours nor bitters are employed, though the Abyssinians in Bruce's time added to their *bouza* the powdered bitter leaves of a certain tree called *ghesh*.[6] Montet thinks that sometimes at least a liquid made from crushed dates was added to the beer,[7] and this is confirmed by the Middle Kingdom papyrus already mentioned,[8] and by a scene in a tomb of the Middle Kingdom [9] where a substance made from dates is evidently being added to a special type of beer.[10] However, such an addition might well have been made, not to perfume the beer, as suggested by Montet, but to sweeten it, in the same manner as a special sugar (glucose) is added sometimes by modern English brewers to the fermented wort, the operation being termed 'priming'.

Naturally none of the ancient beer has remained to the present day and therefore it has not been possible to examine it, but dried residues from beer jars [11,12] and also the dried and exhausted grain after 'mashing' [12] (i.e. maceration in water) have been discovered. A number of specimens of the former, ranging in date from the predynastic period to the Eighteenth Dynasty, have been examined by Dr. J. Grüss, of Berlin,[13] who found them to consist of starch grains from the corn used (which was not barley, but a kind of wheat known as Emmer, the only wheat grown in Egypt until a late date); yeast cells; moulds; bacteria and small proportions of various

---

[1] *De re rustica*, X: 114.

[2] J. P. Arnold, *Origin and History of Beer and Brewing*, p. 87.

[3] H. Gauthier, *Revue égyptologique*, XI (1904), pp. 1–15.

[4] W. R. Dawson, *Journ. Royal Asiatic Society*, 1927, pp. 497–503.

[5] Cf. J. R. Harris, *Lexicographical Studies*, pp. 155–7.

[6] J. Bruce, *Travels to Discover the Source of the Nile*, VII (1805), pp. 65–66, 335.

[7] P. Montet, *Scènes de la vie privée*, p. 250.

[8] W. W. Struve, *Mathematischer Papyrus des Staatlichen Museums . . . in Moskau*, pp. 69–71; A. H. Gardiner, *Ancient Egyptian Onomastica*, II, pp. 225–7; C. F. Nims, *J.N.E.S.*, IX (1950), pp. 261–2; *J.E.A.*, XLIV (1958), pp. 60–63.

[9] N. de G. Davies and A. H. Gardiner, *Antefoker*, p. 15, Pl. XI.

[10] R. J. Forbes (*Studies in Ancient Technology*, III, p. 61; in *History of Technology*, I, pp. 266–7) wrongly interprets this scene as showing the making of date wine.

[11] W. M. F. Petrie, *Prehistoric Egypt*, p. 43; H. E. Winlock, *M.M.A. Bull., Egyptian Exped. 1918–1920*, p. 32; C. M. Firth, *Arch. Survey of Nubia, 1909–1910*, p. 17.

[12] W. M. F. Petrie, *Gizeh and Rifeh*, p. 23.

[13] J. Grüss, *Tageszeitung für Brauerei*, XXVI (1928), pp. 1123–4; XXVII (1929), pp. 275–8, 517, 679–82; XXVIII (1930), pp. 98, 774–6; H. E. Winlock, *Meryet-Amūn*, pp. 32–33.

impurities. The yeast was principally a variety of wild yeast, previously unknown, which Dr. Grüss named *Saccharomyces Winlocki* after Mr. H. E. Winlock, who supplied the material for examination. The Eighteenth Dynasty yeast was found to have cells approximating in size to the modern yeast and to be of a more uniform shape and freer from moulds and bacteria than the earlier yeast, from which Grüss concludes that the ancient Egyptian brewer had anticipated the modern brewer by making a pure, or almost pure, yeast culture.[1] The evidence, however, seems inadequate to support such a wide conclusion.

It may be mentioned that yeast is a uni-cellular plant belonging to the fungus family and is distributed abundantly throughout the world, being found wild on many plants (particularly on ripe fruits) and in the air: there are many varieties, two of the principal useful ones being the cultivated beer yeast (*Saccharomyces cerevisiae*) and the wild yeast (*Saccharomyces ellipsoideus*) which occurs on grapes and brings about vinous fermentation: many other yeasts also are known, but as some of them produce a bitter flavour, an objectionable taste or a persistent turbidity in the fermented liquid, these are avoided in modern brewing. On account of the ubiquity of yeast, fermentation is a natural process, and when solutions containing certain kinds of sugar are exposed to the air, after a short time they begin to ferment.

Three Eighteenth Dynasty specimens of exhausted grain from Deir el Medineh [2] were examined by me and found to be barley. These I submitted for more detailed examination to Professor F. W. Oliver, who reported that 'The principal sample was a small form of 2-rowed barley (*Hordeum distichum*).'

WINE[3]

Wine usually denotes the fermented juice of fresh grapes, and this was the principal wine of the ancient Egyptians, though they had also other kinds, namely, palm wine, date wine, according to Pliny [4] a further kind made from the *myxa* fruit, and at a late date occasionally pomegranate wine, all of which may now be considered.

Grape Wine

Wine, meaning grape wine, is referred to frequently in ancient Egyptian texts,[5] the earliest references known to me being of the Second Dynasty,[6] though the winepress hieroglyph was used in the First Dynasty,[7] from which period wine jars also are known.

Wine is frequently mentioned as a divine and mortuary offering,[5] as a beverage,[5] as tribute,[5] and occasionally as a constituent of medicines.[8]

---

[1] J. Grüss, *Tageszeitung für Brauerei*, xxvii (1929), pp. 681–2.

[2] B. Bruyère, *Deir el Médineh (1934–1935)*, p. 110.

[3] A. Lucas, *Ancient Egypt*, 1928, pp. 3–8.   [4] xiii: 10.

[5] *Wb.* I. 115. 5–8; *A.R.*, v (Index), p. 170; A. Erman, *Literature of the Ancient Egyptians*, trans. A. M. Blackman.

[6] Z. Y. Saad, *Ceiling Stelae in Second Dynasty Tombs (Ann. Serv., Cahier xxi)*, pp. 8, 12, 15, 17, 18, 19, 24.

[7] W. M. F. Petrie, *Social Life in Ancient Egypt*, pp. 102, 135; H. Petrie, *Egyptian Hieroglyphs of the First and Second Dynasties*, Pl. xvii.

[8] H. v. Deines and H. Grapow, *Drogennamen*, pp. 47–50.

Vintage scenes are often depicted upon tomb walls, for example, in a Fifth Dynasty tomb at Saqqara;[1] in a Sixth Dynasty tomb at Saqqara;[2] in a Twelfth Dynasty tomb at El Bersheh;[3] in several tombs of the same period at Beni Hasan;[4] in many others of Eighteenth and Nineteenth Dynasty dates respectively in the Theban necropolis,[5] and in a tomb of the Saïte period.[6] The gathering, treading or pressing of grapes, or all three of these processes, are shown, as well as other operations connected with the production of wine.[7]

The preparation of wine is a comparatively simple matter, all that is necessary being to crush the grapes in order to free the juice, which is separated from the stalks, skins and stones and then allowed to ferment, which it does naturally, chiefly by means of the wild yeasts (principally *Saccharomyces ellipsoideus* but also *S. apiculatus*) present on the skins of the grapes, but also to some extent by the action of certain enzymes (largely zymase) present in the juice. The fermentation consists in the conversion of the sugars present in the juice [these being glucose (dextrose) and fructose (levulose)] into alcohol and carbon dioxide.

According to the scenes on the tomb walls already referred to, the grapes were crushed by treading until no more juice could be extracted. This method is still used largely today in France and Spain, because it gives results that are in many ways better than those obtained by mechanical presses, the great advantage of the human foot being that while it crushes the grapes perfectly it does not crush the stalks or stones, which a press tends to do, so liberating undesirable astringent and colouring matters. After treading, the residue was placed in a cloth or bag, which was tightly twisted in order to squeeze out the remaining juice, a method still used in the Fayum at the beginning of the nineteenth century.[8] The juice was then poured into large pottery jars, where it fermented, but there is nothing to show whether the juice from the treading was mixed with that from the squeezing, or whether the two lots were fermented separately. The latter, having been in contact with the stalks, seeds and skins for a longer period, would have been the more astringent and the more highly coloured of the two, as when fermentation had produced alcohol, this would have extracted astringent substances from the stalks and seeds and, if 'black' grapes were used, also considerable colouring matter from the skins.

The colour of wine depends upon the colour of the grapes and whether or not the skins are included in the fermentation. 'White' grapes naturally produce white

[1] N. de G. Davies, *Ptahhetep*, I, Pls. XXI, XXIII. [2] P. Duell, *Mereruka*, II, Pls. CXIV, CXVI.
[3] P. E. Newberry, *El Bersheh*, I, Pls. XXIV, XXVI, XXXI.
[4] P. E. Newberry, *Beni Hasan*, I, Pls. XII, XLVI; II, Pls. VI, XVI.
[5] N. de G. Davies, *Nakht*, Pls. XXII, XXIII, XXVI; *Puyemrê*, Pls. XII, XIII; *Two Officials*, Pl. xxx; *Five Theban Tombs*, Pl. XXXI; *Two Ramesside Tombs*, Pls. XXX, XXXII, XXXIII; *Nefer-hotep*, I, Pl. XLVIII; A. E. P. Weigall, *Guide to the Antiquities of Upper Egypt*, 1913, pp. 115, 123, 139, 160, 178.
[6] A. Lansing, *M.M.A. Bull., Egyptian Exped. 1916–1919*, p. 21.
[7] Cf. P. Montet, *Scènes de la vie privée*, pp. 265–73; *Rec. Trav.*, XXXV (1913), pp. 117–24; C. Desroches Noblecourt, *Revue des arts asiatiques*, I (1954), pp. 40–60; L. Keimer, *Gartenpflanzen*, pp. 62–64; F. Hartmann, *l'Agriculture*, pp. 156–75, 303–6; H. F. Lutz, *Viticulture and Brewing*, pp. 46–61; F. Woenig, *Pflanzen*, pp. 254–76; G. M. Ollivier Beauregard, *Chez les Pharaons*, pp. 113–33; H. v. Minutoli, *Mag.f.d.Rit.d. Auslandes*, 1839, No. 140.
[8] P. S. Girard, *Description de l'Egypte, état moderne*, II, *Mém. sur l'agriculture, l'industrie et le commerce de l'Egypte*, 1812, p. 608.

wine, the juice being colourless, and, as the juice of 'black' grapes is also usually colourless,[1] these, too, will produce white wine, if the skins are separated before fermentation, though if the skins are not removed a red wine is obtained.

No literary reference to the colour of the grapes grown anciently in Egypt can be traced, though there is indirect linguistic evidence pointing to a dark colour.[2] Grapes shown on several tomb walls of the New Kingdom at Thebes are dark-coloured,[3] deep blue or violet, though less frequently they are shown as red, pink, green, or white. Erman states that in the Old Kingdom the wine included white, red and black varieties.[4] Petrie says [5] 'In the Old Kingdom only dark grapes are represented, and the wine must have been red. At El Bersheh in the XIIth dynasty white grapes are seen and the juice is light, such as would make white wine.' In a Middle Kingdom tomb at Meir white wine is mentioned.[6] The colour of the wine is not mentioned in the papyri of the Graeco-Roman period,[7] but Athenaeus refers to the Egyptian wine varying in colour and mentions both white and pale wine.[8] It seems probable, therefore, that both light and dark grapes were used.[9]

The amount of alcohol produced in wine by fermentation is limited by two factors, one being the quantity of sugar present in the grapes and the other being the fact that the yeast is killed (with the consequent gradual slowing down and final arrest of the fermentation) by the alcohol formed when the proportion reaches about 14 per cent,[10] although there may still be fermentable sugar present and, if the grapes used are rich in sugar, the portion that escapes fermentation remains, imparting sweetness to the wine.

In ancient Egypt, on account of the slow method of pressing adopted and the high temperature towards the end of the summer, when the vintage must have taken place, the fermentation would almost certainly have commenced before all the juice was extracted, but it occurred principally in the large jars to which the juice is shown as being transferred while the pressing is still going on. These jars necessarily must have been left open until the fermentation had almost ceased, otherwise they would have burst from the pressure of carbon dioxide generated; but when the fermentation was almost over the jars were stoppered with 'a wad of vine leaves' over which 'was moulded roughly with the fingers to a height of about 10 cm. a tenacious mixture of black earth and chopped straw', as found by Winlock at the Christian Monastery of Epiphanius at Thebes,[11] or with 'a rush bung completely covered over with a clay or mud capsule that enveloped the whole of the mouth and neck of the jar' in the

---

[1] Some few kinds of 'black' grapes give a coloured juice.
[2] Cf. J. R. Harris, *Lexicographical Studies*, p. 226.
[3] N. de G. Davies, *Nakht*, Frontispiece, Pls. xxv, xxvi; *Two Ramesside Tombs*, Pl. xxxiii.
[4] A. Erman, *Life in Ancient Egypt*, 1894, p. 196.
[5] W. M. F. Petrie, Review in *Ancient Egypt*, 1914, p. 38. See also P. Montet, *Rec. Trav.*, xxxv (1913), pp. 117–18.
[6] A. M. Blackman, *Meir*, iii, p. 30.
[7] C. Ricci, 'La Coltura della Vite e la Fabricazione del Vino nell' Egitto Greco-Romano', *Studi della Scuola Papirologica*, iv (1924–6), p. 61.
[8] i: 33.   [9] For the type of grape cf. A. Berget, *Chronique d'Égypte*, ix (1934), pp. 221–4.
[10] The excess of alcohol above about 14 per cent in certain modern wines is due to the addition of extra alcohol.
[11] H. E. Winlock and W. E. Crum, *Monastery of Epiphanius*, p. 79.

manner of those found by Carter in the tomb of Tutankhamūn,[1] or with such variant of the method as the local conditions and the importance of the wine demanded. Wine jars stoppered and sealed are represented in a number of tombs, for example, in one of the Twelfth Dynasty at Beni Hasan [2] and in two of the Eighteenth Dynasty at Thebes, namely, in that of Nakht and in that of Neferhotep.[3] The closing of the jars as soon as possible was essential, since if the wine had been left exposed to the air, another kind of fermentation (the acetous fermentation) caused by a minute organism (*Mycoderma aceti*), always present in the air, would have taken place, which would have converted the alcohol into acetic acid and the wine would have become vinegar. The jars, however, were not all sealed hermetically at this stage, since in some instances slow fermentation was still going on, in which case a small hole was drilled in the neck of the jar, or made in the stopper, as shown in some of those from the Monastery of Epiphanius; [4] in those from the tomb of Tutankhamūn; [5] and in a large number of local ware of Graeco-Roman date from Medum,[6] in order to provide a way of escape for the carbon dioxide being given off in small amount, and, when the fermentation was finished, this hole was sometimes 'stopped with a wisp of straw' [4] and sometimes closed with clay and sealed.[5] At the Monastery of Epiphanius only half the jars had been provided with this small vent.[4] Doubtless occasionally a jar would be sealed finally before fermentation had ceased, and in such a case the internal pressure might be sufficient to break the jar, as appears to have occurred with one of those from the tomb of Tutankhamūn, where the neck seems to have been ruptured and the contents to have flowed down the outside of the jar.

During the Graeco-Roman and Coptic periods wine jars [7] were rendered impermeable by being treated inside with a thin coating of resin, which is always black, the colour probably being due to the charring of a non-black resin by the heat necessary to render it sufficiently liquid to flow as a thin layer over the inside of the jar. A deposit of similar black resin is found often at the apex of the jars that have been treated in this manner.[8] Wine jars blackened inside were discovered at the Monastery of Epiphanius at Thebes by Winlock, who in describing them says, 'Like the Greek wine jars the inside was coated with a black resinous pitch . . .' [4] This practice was known also to the Romans, since Pliny [9] refers to 'The pitch (i.e. blackened resin) . . . for preparing vessels for storing wine . . .' With reference to the wine jars from the tomb of Tutankhamūn, Carter states [5] that 'In all probability the interior of the jars was smeared over with a thin coat of resinous material to counteract the porous nature of the pottery; the broken specimens show a distinct black coating on their inner surface.' I have examined twenty-two wine jars or parts of wine jars

---

[1] H. Carter, *Tut-ankh-Amen*, III, p. 148, Pl. L.

[2] P. E. Newberry, *Beni Hasan*, I, Pl. XII.

[3] N. de G. Davies, *Nakht*, p. 70, Pl. XXVI; *Nefer-hotep*, Pl. XLVIII.

[4] H. E. Winlock and W. E. Crum, *Monastery of Epiphanius*, p. 79.

[5] H. Carter, *Tut-ankh-Amen*, III, pp. 148–9.

[6] Found by Mr. Alan Rowe, to whom I am indebted for the information.

[7] Possibly also jars for containing liquids other than wine, such as oil or honey.

[8] Several specimens of the black coating and the black material from the apex of wine jars of the Graeco-Roman period have been analysed by me and found to be resin in every case. See C. C. Edgar, *Zenon Papyri*, III, No. 59481; IV, No. 59741.

[9] XIV: 25.

from this tomb,[1] of which twenty were broken, ten of them being much broken, thus making the examination a fairly easy matter. The outsides of the jars vary considerably in colour, some being entirely greenish-grey, some entirely red and some partly one colour and partly the other. The insides of the jars are chiefly light-red, though occasionally drab with a reddish tint, but in no instance is there any blackening of the nature of that on the Graeco-Roman wine jars, no resin at the apex and no continuous black coating of any sort, though in some cases there are black spots and small black patches that look very like fungus growths (which they probably are) but in most cases there is not any blackening at all.[2] The edges of the broken surfaces vary in colour from a drab with a slight reddish tint to light-red, mottled in every instance with innumerable white particles, which on testing proved to be calcium carbonate (carbonate of lime). There cannot be any doubt, therefore, that the clay used for these jars was calcareous (i.e. contained calcium carbonate), which explains both the greenish-grey and the red colours, the former being where the jars have been strongly heated and the latter where the heat has been less intense.[3] No evidence of any slip could be found, either inside or outside the jars, and it must be assumed, therefore, that they were sufficiently watertight for the purpose required without either slip or resin coating.[4] That they were not absolutely impermeable seems to be proved by the fact that those of the jars that are unbroken and still stoppered and sealed are empty.

Lutz states [5] that 'The Egyptians, before pouring the wine into the jars, generally smeared the bottoms with resin or bitumen. This was done in order to preserve the wine. It was also thought to improve the flavour of the wine.' No evidence whatever has been found for the use of bitumen in wine jars, nor of the use of resin before the Graeco-Roman period, when the whole of the inside of the jar, not merely the bottom, was coated with resin, which was done to make the jar impermeable and not to preserve the wine (except from evaporation), nor to improve its flavour.

In a Middle Kingdom tomb at Meir wine of eastern Buto, wine of Mareotis and wine of Syene are mentioned; [6] in the Eighteenth Dynasty wine was being obtained from the eastern and western Delta; [7] from the Oasis of Kharga; [8] and as tribute from Asia (Arvad, Djahi and Retenu); [9] in the Twenty-second and Twenty-sixth Dynasties respectively it was obtained from the oases of the western desert [10] and in the Twenty-sixth Dynasty from the western Delta.[10] Wines from various sources are mentioned

---

[1] Five were of the long-necked Syrian type. Fourteen other jars from this tomb were not examined, since nine are still stoppered and sealed, and five, including two additional ones of the Syrian type, are in the Museum show case.

[2] One jar with a broken neck (No. 541) was rinsed with water inside and that it was entirely free from blackening was confirmed. A jar from El Amarna, examined by Mathieu (in J. D. S. Pendlebury, City of Akhenaten, III, pp. 240 f.), was also free from any resinous coating.

[3] See pp. 381–2.

[4] One jar (No. 541) was filled with water and allowed to stand for forty-six hours; there was no leakage of water and the jar was not even damp on the outside.

[5] H. F. Lutz, Viticulture and Brewing, pp. 56–57.

[6] A. M. Blackman, Meir, III, p. 30.   [7] H. Carter, Tut-ankh-Amen, III, p. 147.

[8] H. W. Fairman, in H. Frankfort and J. D. S. Pendlebury, City of Akhenaten, II, p. 105.

[9] A.R., v (Index), p. 170.   [10] A.R., IV, 734, 992.

on jar labels from El Amarna,[1] and several different kinds of wine are listed in the New Kingdom onomasticon already mentioned, though the exact significance of the terms used is not understood.[2]

Herodotus strangely enough says that there were no vines in Egypt,[3] though he mentions that the Egyptian priests drank wine [4] and used it in the temple sacrifices [5] and that wine was consumed at certain festivals,[6] but since he records the importation of wine into Egypt from Greece and Phoenicia,[7] he may have thought that all the wine used in the country was of foreign origin.

Diodorus refers to the vines of Egypt [8] and to the drinking of wine.[9]

Strabo states [10] that Libyan wine, which he says was mixed with sea water, was of poor quality, but that another Egyptian wine, the Mareotic, made in large quantity, was good; he also refers to wine from an oasis in the western desert [11] and to wine from the Fayum province,[12] which latter he says was produced in abundance.

Pliny, in his enumeration of wines foreign to Italy, includes a kind termed Sebennys, made in Egypt, from three different varieties of grapes 'of the very highest quality',[13] namely, the Thasian grape, the 'smoky' grape and the 'pitchy' grape. The Thasian grape, probably so called because it had been introduced into Egypt from Thasos, is described[14] as being 'remarkable for its sweetness and laxative qualities'. Pliny also mentioned an Egyptian wine that he states produced miscarriage.[14]

Athenaeus quotes Hellanicus for the statement that the vine was first discovered in Egypt,[15] and he quotes Dio as saying that the Egyptians were fond of wine and bibulous,[15] and he himself calls them winebibbers:[15] he states,[15] too, that 'The vine is as abundant in the Nile valley as its waters are copious, and the peculiar differences of the wines are many, varying with colour and taste: he says also [16] that the vine was abundant in the Mareotic region in the neighbourhood of Alexandria and that its grapes were 'very good to eat': he mentions several wines,[16] namely the Mareotic (excellent, white, pleasant, fragrant, easily assimilated, thin, does not go to the head, diuretic); the Taeniotic (better than the Mareotic, somewhat pale, has an oily quality, pleasant, aromatic, mildly astringent); the wine of Antylla, a city not far from Alexandria (surpassing all others) and the wine of the Thebaid and especially that from the city of the Copts ('so thin and assimilable, so easily digested, that it may be given even to fever patients without injury'). This same writer states also[15] that the Egyptians used boiled cabbage and cabbage seeds as remedies against drunkenness and subsequent headache. With reference to the mixing of sea water and wine mentioned by Strabo [10] as being practised with the Libyan wine, Athenaeus states[17] that 'Wines which are more carefully treated with sea water do not cause headache; they loosen the bowels, excite the stomach, cause inflation, and assist digestion.' This practice of mixing sea water with wine is mentioned also by Pliny,[13] according to whom, if done sparingly, it was thought to improve the flavour of the wine, though of one wine so treated he states [13] that it 'is far from wholesome'.

---

[1] H. W. Fairman, in J. D. S. Pendlebury, *City of Akhenaten*, III, pp. 165–8.
[2] A. H. Gardiner, *Ancient Egyptian Onomastica*, II, pp. 233–7.   [3] II: 77.
[4] II:37.   [5] II: 39.   [6] II: 60.   [7] III: 6.   [8] I: 3.   [9] I: 4.
[10] XVII: I, 14.   [11] XVII: I, 42.   [12] XVII: I, 35.   [13] XIV: 9.   [14] XIV: 22.
[15] I: 34.   [16] I: 33.   [17] I: 32.

Papyri of the Graeco-Roman period provide information concerning the owner-ship of vineyards, the various operations connected with viticulture, the production of wine, the different qualities of wine, etc.[1]

There is no recorded instance known to me of wine having been discovered in an Egyptian tomb, though wine jars and clay sealings from wine jars are very common. In some of the jars, however, there are the residues left after the evaporation of the liquid and I have analysed three such residues, two from the tomb of Tutankhamūn [2] and one from the Monastery of St. Simeon near Aswan,[3] the potassium carbonate and potassium tartrate found proving that the residues were those from wine. A residue from a jar found at El Amarna was examined by Mathieu,[4] who concluded that the remains were probably those of a fermenting wine.

Palm Wine

A wine-producing palm is mentioned in the Pyramid Texts[5] and both Herodotus [6] and Diodorus [7] state that palm wine was used in Egypt to wash out the abdominal cavity during the process of mummification and Herodotus relates that Cambyses sent a cask of palm wine to Ethiopia.[8] Wilkinson says [9] that palm wine was made in Egypt in his day and that it consisted of the sap of the date palm obtained by making an incision in the heart of the tree, immediately below the base of the upper branches and that, as taken directly from the tree, the liquid was not intoxicating, but acquired this property by fermentation when kept and that the wine resembled in flavour a very light new grape wine: he states also that a palm tapped in the manner described was rendered useless for fruit bearing and generally died. Beadnell states that 'In the oases and other parts of Egypt a fermented liquor . . . is obtained by making a deep incision in the top of the date palm . . .' 'the palm may be bled once or twice a month without sustaining any harm: the operation may, in fact, prove of considerable benefit to a sickly palm'.[10] Oric Bates states [11] that an intoxicant is made in eastern Libya by fermenting the sap of the date palm. In Egypt, too, a similar wine is occasionally prepared, but always from a male tree that is not required, which often dies as the result of the operation and is cut down. The fermentation of the sap is brought about by means of wild yeasts present on the tree and in the air.

Bruijning suggests [12] that the palm wine used anciently in Egypt was obtained, not from the date palm, but from other species of palm, such as the Raphia palm, probably *Raphia monobuttorum*, which he thinks may have grown in Egypt at one time, though it is not now found in the country. It is true that the Raphia palm,

---

[1] C. Ricci, 'La Coltura della Vite e la Fabricazione del Vino nell' Egitto Greco-Romano', *Studi della Scuola Papirologica*, IV (1924–6), Part I.

[2] A. Lucas, in H. Carter, *Tut-ankh-Amen*, III, p. 183 (Appendix II). A second specimen was subsequently examined.

[3] In this Monastery there may still be seen a complete installation for making wine. (U. Monneret de Villard, 'Un Pressoio da Vino dell' Egitto Medioevale', in *Reale Instituto Lombardo di Scienze e Lettere*, LIX, XI–XV, 1926; also 'Descrizione Gen. del Monastero di S. Simeone presso Aswan', in *Ann. Serv.*, XXVI (1926), p. 231.

[4] L. Mathieu, in J. D. S. Pendlebury, *City of Akhenaten*, III, pp. 239–43.

[5] F. F. Bruijning, *Ancient Egypt*, 1922, pp. 1–8.   [6] II: 86.   [7] I: 7.

[8] III: 20.   [9] J. G. Wilkinson, *The Ancient Egyptians* (1878), I, p. 397.

[10] H. J. L. Beadnell, *Egyptian Oasis*, p. 218.   [11] Oric Bates, *Eastern Libyans*, p. 26.

[12] F. F. Bruijning, *Ancient Egypt*, 1922, pp. 3, 7.

which is an African tree, often found growing in forest swamps, does yield a wine and is used for wine making in certain parts of Africa and that it is sometimes called the *Nakhl el Faraoon* (Pharaoh's date palm),[1] but there is no evidence that it ever grew in Egypt and, as the palm wine made at the present time is from the date palm, there is no reason to think that it was otherwise anciently.

Date Wine

Date wine is mentioned occasionally in the ancient Egyptian texts, for example, in the Second Dynasty,[2] in the Sixth Dynasty[3] and on two ostraca of the Nineteenth Dynasty in the Cairo Museum. It is described also by Pliny, who states[4] that it was made 'throughout all the countries of the East', which probably was meant to include Egypt, though Egypt is not specifically named. It was prepared by steeping a certain kind of date in water and pressing out the liquid, which was left to ferment, which it did naturally from the wild yeasts present on the dates. A similar beverage is described by Burckhardt[5] as being made in Nubia by boiling ripe dates with water, straining the liquid and allowing it to ferment. Oric Bates states that in eastern Libya an intoxicant is made by fermenting dates.[6] A date wine, such as that described, was, and still is, made in Egypt sometimes, but instead of being drunk as wine, the liquid *is* distilled and the resulting spirit consumed.

Myxa Wine

With respect to the Myxa wine stated by Pliny[7] to have been made in Egypt, no other mention of it can be traced. The Myxa (*Cordia Myxa*), which is cultivated in gardens in Egypt, bears a mucilaginous fruit, which Theophrastus, who calls it 'the Egyptian plum',[8] describes without referring to any use having been made of it for wine making, although he states that it was made into cakes. Twigs of Middle Kingdom date are reported by Keimer,[9] and some part of the tree, probably the fruit, was identified by Newberry from the Graeco-Roman cemetery at Hawara.[10] Thick layers of the leaves were found by Davies at Sheikh Said which were of late date, probably Coptic,[11] and Griffith found seeds and fruits, probably of similar late date, at Faras in Nubia which are now in the Museum of the Royal Botanic Gardens, Kew.[12]

Pomegranate Wine

The only reference to pomegranate wine in Egypt that can be found is in a late third century A.D. papyrus,[13] although it was known to the Greeks as a medicine.[14] An intoxicating drink first mentioned in texts of the New Kingdom[15] has been identified by Loret[16] as pomegranate wine, and Lutz[17] also states that the Egyptians

---

[1] G. Schweinfurth, *The Heart of Africa*, I, p. 199.

[2] Z. Y. Saad, *Ceiling Stelae in Second Dynasty Tombs* (*Ann. Serv., Cahier* XXI), p. 9.

[3] *A.R.*, I, 336.   [4] XIII: 9; XIV: 19.

[5] J. L. Burckhardt, *Travels in Nubia*, 1819, p. 143.   [6] Oric Bates, *Eastern Libyans*, p. 26.

[7] XIII: 10.   [8] *Enquiry into Plants*, IV: 2, 10.   [9] L. Keimer, *Gartenpflanzen*, pp. 25–26.

[10] P. E. Newberry, in W. M. F. Petrie, *Hawara, Biahmu and Arsinoe*, pp. 48, 53.

[11] N. de G. Davies, *Sheikh Saïd*, p. 4.   [12] No. 86/1913.

[13] A. S. Hunt, *Oxyrhynchus Papyri*, VIII, p. 241.   [14] Dioscorides, V: 34.

[15] *Wb.* IV. 568. 12–17.   [16] V. Loret, *Flore Pharaonique*, 2nd ed., pp. 77–78.

[17] H. F. Lutz, *Viticulture and Brewing*, p. 9.

used this wine. Keimer,[1] however, considered that there was insufficient evidence for the identification, and Peet [2] refers to it as 'a pure guess'. Peet also says [2] that the 'fig wine' mentioned by Lutz is not fig wine, but simply two baskets of figs.

DISTILLED SPIRITS

Distillation is the process of converting a volatile liquid into vapour by heat and then recondensing it again by cooling, and distilled spirits are naturally-flavoured solutions of alcohol in water that have been made by the distillation of certain fermented liquids.

Although the ancient Egyptians made beer and wine, both of which contain alcohol, they were unacquainted with distillation and, therefore, did not know distilled spirits.

When and where the discovery of distillation took place there is no evidence to show, but the first mention of it that can be traced is by Aristotle in the fourth century B.C., who describes the formation of mist and rain [3] (which are caused by natural processes of evaporation and condensation) and who also says,[4] 'Salt water when it turns into vapour becomes sweet and the vapour does not form salt water when it condenses again. This I know by experiment. The same thing is true in every case of the kind: wine and all fluids that evaporate and condense back into a liquid state become water. They are all water modified by a certain admixture, the nature of which determines their flavour.' Evidently Aristotle, although he had distilled wine and made dilute alcohol, did not recognize it as anything other than water 'modified by a certain admixture', the nature of which determined its flavour. Theophrastus (fourth to third century B.C.) had some knowledge of a method of destructive distillation for obtaining wood tar, which he describes,[5] and Pliny (first century A.D.) also knew of this,[6] as well as of a primitive method of obtaining spirits of turpentine by means of distillation.[7]

Zosimos, who is 'the most ancient alchemical author of whom we have genuine writings and can identify',[8] describes and illustrates a variety of retorts and recipients, thus proving that distillation was well known in his time (the end of the third century A.D. or the beginning of the fourth), but he makes no mention whatever of alcohol, and it is highly probable that this was not known until the Middle Ages, its use at first being medicinal and not as a beverage.

SUGAR

In connexion with beer and wine, the use of sugar in ancient Egypt may be dealt with conveniently, as it was from sugar that the alcohol, which imparted the stimulating and intoxicating properties to both these beverages was derived. In the case of beer, sugar, as already described, was produced during the preliminary processes of brewing from the starch present in the grain used, while with wine, the sugar existed ready formed in the grapes, palm juice, dates and other materials employed.

Although sugar is distributed widely in nature, being present as honey, in milk

---

[1] L. Keimer, *Gartenpflanzen*, pp. 51, 152; but cf. in J. D. S. Pendlebury, *City of Akhenaten*, III, p. 164.

[2] T. E. Peet, *Liverpool Annals*, x (1923), p. 53.   [3] *Meteorologica*, I: 9, 11.

[4] *Meteorologica*, II: 3.   [5] *Enquiry into Plants*, IX: 3, 1–3.

[6] XVI: 21–22.   [7] XV: 7.   [8] E. J. Holmyard, *Makers of Chemistry*, p. 35.

and in certain trees, plants, roots, flowers and fruits, it was known anciently only in the form of honey, sugar from the sugar cane being of comparatively late date and that from the beetroot being still more recent.

Cane Sugar

The sugar cane is a native of the Far East and seems to have been first cultivated in India, and the sugar from it was just becoming known to the Roman world in Pliny's time, though only as a medicine.[1] From this same period (first century A.D.) there is a record of sugar or 'honey from the reed called sacchari', as it is termed, having been shipped from India to the Somali coast,[2] and Dioscorides (also first century A.D.) states[3] that there is a kind of 'concreted' honey, called sugar, found in reeds in India and Arabia 'like in consistence to salt, and brittle to be broken between the teeth as salt is'. The bare facts of the existence of sugar cane and the extraction of sugar from it, however, seem to have been known in Greece several centuries earlier than the date mentioned, as Nearchus (fourth century B.C.) is quoted by Strabo[4] (first century B.C. to first century A.D.) for the statement that 'reeds yield honey, although there are no bees . . .'; he also says that there was 'a tree from the fruit of which honey is procured . . .', the identity of which, however, unfortunately is not recorded. Pliny states that Arabia as well as India produced sugar.

So far as can be ascertained there is no mention of sugar from the sugar cane in any ancient Egyptian document, not even in the late Greek papyri, and the only sources of sugar readily available were honey, and such fruits as dates and grapes; but it was honey that took the place in daily life of the modern sugar, the sugar cane, now so largely grown in the country, being a comparatively modern introduction. In the thirteenth century Marco Polo states[5] that certain Egyptians, skilled in the matter, instructed the inhabitants of Un-guen (China) in a method of refining sugar by means of wood ashes.

Honey [6]

Bee-keeping was one of the important minor industries in ancient Egypt and honey is mentioned frequently in ancient texts,[7] the earliest references to it that can be traced being of the Old Kingdom.[8] In the Eighteenth Dynasty it is listed as a funerary offering,[9] and among tribute from the campaigns in Palestine and Syria (e.g. Djahi[10] and Retenu[11]); in the Nineteenth Dynasty it is mentioned as part of the rations of the king's messenger and standard bearer.[12] Honey played an important part in temple ritual, particularly in the cult of the god Min,[13] and in the Harris papyrus of the reign of Ramses III large quantities of honey are included in the temple donations.[14] Honey was also widely used in medicine, and is frequently mentioned in the

[1] XII: 17.   [2] W. H. Schoff, *The Periplus of the Erythraean Sea*, pp. 27, 90, 285.
[3] II: 104.   [4] XV: 1, 20.   [5] Marco Polo, *Travels*, p. 316. (Everyman's Library).
[6] Cf. L. Armbruster, *Archiv für Bienenkunde*, III (1921); XII (1931).
[7] *Wb.* I. 434. 6–12; *A.R.*, V (Index), p. 132; A. Erman, *Literature of the Ancient Egyptians*, trans. A. M. Blackman; R. J. Forbes, *Studies in Ancient Technology*, V, pp. 79–81.
[8] *A.R.*, I, 366; Papyrus in the Cairo Museum, No. J. 15000.   [9] *A.R.*, II, 571.
[10] *A.R.*, II, 462.   [11] *A.R.*, II, 518.   [12] *A.R.*, III, 208.
[13] P. Montet, *J.N.E.S.*, IX (1950), pp. 18–27.   [14] *A.R.*, IV, 151–412.

Edwin Smith surgical papyrus,[1] in the Ebers papyrus,[2] and in other medical texts.[3]

Only four representations of bee-keeping are known, three of which are described by Kuény.[4] In a scene from the Fifth Dynasty sun temple of Neuserrē, now in the Berlin Museum, the taking of honey and other processes are illustrated,[5] in the Eighteenth Dynasty tomb of Rekhmirē at Thebes jars of honey and combs are depicted,[6] and in the tomb of Pabes at Thebes (Twenty-fifth Dynasty) the taking of honey is shown.[7] The fourth scene, now scarcely visible, is in a Theban tomb of the Eighteenth Dynasty.[8] In the Ptolemaic period 'there were royal as well as private bee-farms'.[9]

Two small pottery jars of Eighteenth Dynasty date from the tomb of Tutankhamūn, each marked in hieratic 'honey of good quality', examined by me were practically empty, except for a trace of dried material adhering to the inside. In one case I analysed this, so far as was possible with the very small quantity available, with the result that the chemical tests were negative, the only indication of sugar being a slight smell suggestive of caramel (burnt sugar) when the material was treated with hot water, in which 26 per cent was soluble. Another specimen from the New Kingdom submitted by Dr. L. Keimer as honey was entirely insoluble in water and gave no reaction whatever for sugar. These negative results, however, do not necessarily mean that the specimens had not been honey at one time, but merely indicate that, if honey, they had become so changed that they responded no longer to the usual tests.

A material found in considerable amount in a large alabaster jar in the tomb of Tutankhamūn [10] was black and resinous-looking, with the upper surface covered with the chitinous remains of a very large number of small beetles: there were signs that at one time the substance had been viscous and had run, and throughout the black mass there were innumerable small translucent light-brown crystals. The bulk of the substance could not be identified, but the crystals were sweet, soluble in water and gave all the chemical reactions for sugar, which they undoubtedly were. What the material had been originally it is impossible to say, but honey or a fruit juice, such as grape juice or date extract, is suggested.

It is stated that the Egyptians sometimes preserved their dead in honey;[11] but, if so, this was very exceptional, and the body of Alexander the Great, which is quoted as an example, if so embalmed, was presumably treated in Babylon, where he died, and not in Egypt, and it was the preserved body that was brought to Egypt.

---

[1] J. H. Breasted, *Edwin Smith Surgical Papyrus*, Index, p. 583.   [2] B. Ebbell, *Papyrus Ebers*.
[3] H. v. Deines and H. Grapow, *Drogennamen*, pp. 156–68.
[4] G. Kuény, *J.N.E.S.*, IX (1950), pp. 84–93; L. Armbruster, *Archiv für Bienenkunde*, III (1921), pp. 68–80; G. Jéquier, *B.I.F.A.O.*, XIX (1922), pp. 162–4. Cf. also E. Drioton, *Aesculape*, XXXIX (1956), pp. 44–51.
[5] L. Klebs, *Reliefs, A.R.*, p. 58, Abb. 45.
[6] N. de G. Davies, *Rekh-mi-rē*, pp. 44–45, Pls. XLVIII, XLIX.
[7] A. Lansing, *M.M.A. Bull., Egyptian Exped. 1916–1919*, pp. 21–22.
[8] T. Säve-Söderbergh, *Four Eighteenth Dynasty Tombs*, p. 9, Pl. IX, B.
[9] E. Bevan, *History of Egypt under the Ptolemaic Dynasty*, p. 149.
[10] A. Lucas, in H. Carter, *Tut-ankh-Amen*, III, p. 183 (Appendix II).
[11] E. A. Wallis Budge, *Mummy*, 2nd edition (1925), p. 208; T. J. Pettigrew, *History of Egyptian Mummies*, pp. 85 f.

Date Extract

The use of this as a sweetening material in beer has already been discussed, but there is little evidence for its employment in any other connexion.

Grape Juice

That the Egyptians used unfermented grape juice, probably evaporated to a syrup, as a sweetening material, is proved by the finding in the tomb of Tutankhamūn of part of a pottery jar, similar in size and shape to the wine jars from the same tomb, bearing an inscription in hieratic to the effect that the jar contained unfermented grape juice of very good quality from the temple of Aten.[1] Grape syrup is mentioned in a papyrus of late date [2] and it is still much used in Syria at the present day, where it is called *dibs*. Two specimens of glossy, black, resinous-looking material of Eighteenth Dynasty date found by Bruyère at Deir el Medineh, which I examined, contained 17 per cent and 24.4 per cent respectively of glucose and were probably either honey, as stated by the finder,[3] or grape syrup, and a third specimen of amorphous black material containing tiny white crystals (which were not identified) of the same date and place was probably similar.

On a tomb wall (Twelfth Dynasty) at Beni Hasan, in close connexion with a vintage scene, a man is shown stirring a liquid in a pot on a fire and, adjoining this, a liquid is being strained through a cloth.[4] Several writers have suggested that this may refer to the production of grape syrup.[5] In the first century A.D. the juice of sour grapes,[6] which Dioscorides calls *omphakion*,[7] and Pliny *omphacium*,[8] from Diospolis was exported.

---

[1] Cairo Museum, No. J. 62324.

[2] C. C. Edgar, *Zenon Papyri in the University of Michigan Collection*, 1931, No. 65.

[3] B. Bruyère, *Deir el Médineh (1934–1935)*, p. 109.

[4] P. E. Newberry, *Beni Hasan*, II, Pl. VI.

[5] R. Dage and A. Aribaud, *Le vin sous les pharaons*, p. 50; A. Neuburger, *Technical Arts and Sciences of the Ancients* (trans. H. L. Brose), Fig. 170.

[6] W. H. Schoff, *The Periplus of the Erythaean Sea*, pp. 25, 75.

[7] v: 6.

[8] XII: 60; XXIII: 4.

Chapter III
ANIMAL PRODUCTS

It has been found convenient to group together in the same chapter various products of the animal kingdom, namely, Bone; Feathers; Gut; Hair; Horn; Ivory; Leather; Mother of Pearl; Ostrich Egg-shell; Parchment; Tortoise-shell and Marine and Fresh Water Shells, all of which may now separately be considered.

BONE

Bone was one of the most natural materials for primitive man to use, since generally it was plentiful and was easily splintered and pointed (in the case of certain fish bones it was already pointed) and so, without difficulty, it could be made into small boring implements, such as awls and needles: it was also suitable for carving upon.

Animal bones were used in ancient Egypt from neolithic times [1] through all the subsequent periods, being made into various small objects, principally amulets, arrow heads, awls, beads, bracelets, combs, finger rings, harpoon heads, kohl tubes, needles and pins. Fish vertebrae were occasionally made into beads [2] and pointed fish bones into needles,[3] or awls.[4]

In addition to fresh bone, fossil bone was occasionally also used, a mirror handle made of this material being known.[5]

FEATHERS

In most countries the use of feathers is known from very early times and in Egypt, which is no exception, the custom can be traced back to the Badarian period.[6] The feathers employed were chiefly those of the ostrich, though feathers possibly from the night heron,[7] the crow or raven,[8] and a water-fowl [9] respectively have also been found in tombs, and in one instance pigeon feathers.[10]

Ostrich feathers were used largely for fans and as a head ornament, thus Piankhi (Twenty-fifth Dynasty) received the submission of 'all the chiefs who wore the feather'[11] (probably ostrich feathers); the goddess Maat, various gods, and chariot

---

[1] G. Caton-Thompson, *Journ. Royal Anthrop. Inst.*, LVI (1926), pp. 310, 312; H. Junker *Merimde-Benisalâme*, 1929, p. 237; 1930, pp. 71–72.

[2] G. A. Wainwright, *Balabish*, p. 21.

[3] T. E. Peet and C. L. Woolley, *City of Akhenaten*, I, p. 17.

[4] G. Brunton, *Mostagedda*, pp. 58, 90.

[5] D. E. Derry, *Man*, XXXVII (1937), pp. 109–10.

[6] G. Brunton and G. Caton-Thompson, *Badarian Civilisation*, pp. 28, 38; G. Brunton, *Mostagedda*, p. 29.

[7] G. Brunton, *Mostagedda*, p. 58.

[8] G. A. Wainwright, *Balabish*, p. 12; C. M. Firth, *Arch. Survey of Nubia, 1908–1909*, p. 58.

[9] British Museum, *Guide to the Fourth, Fifth and Sixth Egyptian Rooms*, 1922, p. 87.

[10] J. E. Quibell, *Yuaa and Thuiu*, p. 52.   [11] *A.R.*, IV, 873.

horses are often depicted wearing ostrich feathers; in the Middle Kingdom Egyptian colony at Kerma in the Sudan ostrich feathers were used for making both fans and rugs.[1] Both the water-fowl feathers and the pigeon feathers referred to were employed to stuff cushions.

Although the ostrich is not now found in Egypt, it was fairly common until a very late period in both the eastern and western deserts and in the Eighteenth Dynasty it evidently existed as far north as Heliopolis, since on the handle of a fan from the tomb of Tutankhamūn the king is shown shooting ostriches with a bow and arrow and an inscription states that the hunt took place in 'the eastern desert of Heliopolis'. [2] On the other side of the fan the king has a bundle of ostrich feathers under his arm and the servants are carrying two dead ostriches. On one fan from this tomb the ostrich feathers still remain.

The local ostrich, however, apparently was not plentiful enough to supply all the feathers required, as some were imported, thus on the wall connecting the two pylons of Horemheb at Karnak ostrich feathers are shown being brought from Punt [3] and, on one of the walls of the temple of Beit el Wali in Nubia, Ramses II is depicted receiving Nubian tribute, which includes ostrich feathers.[4]

In several Eighteenth Dynasty tombs at Thebes ostrich feathers are pictured.[5]

GUT

Gut, that cannot be distinguished from modern gut, was employed in ancient Egypt for the strings of musical instruments and for bows.

The earliest example of the use of gut that can be traced is one from the Badarian period, which is described as 'Thong of animal tissue, Gut'.[6] Then, in date order, comes a specimen from the Third Dynasty which was found in the step pyramid at Saqqara, and consists of two small twisted pieces, one about two inches (5 cm.) long, and the other about four inches (10 cm.) long, probably both originally part of the same piece, since they are of the same thickness, about 0.06 inch (1.5 mm.).[7] Several gut bowstrings of Eleventh Dynasty date are known,[8] and one, described as twisted gut, is about 24 cm. long and some 2 mm. thick.[9] After these comes a specimen of the Second Intermediate Period, which is described as 'finely twisted gut, which may have been a bowstring'.[10] The next examples are from the Eighteenth Dynasty and consist of (a) part of a bowstring attached to a bark-covered compound bow from Qurna; [11] (b) a number of twisted pieces of bowstring of different thicknesses, varying from about 0.06 inch (1.5 mm.) to about 0.14 inch (3.5 mm.), all from the tomb of Tutankhamūn (one example of a linen bowstring

---

[1] G. A. Reisner, Kerma, IV–V, pp. 300–1, 315.

[2] H. Carter, Tut-ankh-Amen, II, p. 46.   [3] A.R., III, 37.   [4] A.R., III, 475.

[5] J. G. Wilkinson, The Ancient Egyptians, 1878, III, p. 257; A. E. P. Weigall, Guide to the Antiquities of Upper Egypt, 1913, p. 126; Nina de G. Davies and Norman de G. Davies, Menkheperrasonb, Pl. IX; N. de G. Davies, Puyemrê, I, pp. 87, 103.

[6] G. Brunton, Mostagedda, p. 60.   [7] Now in the Cairo Museum, No. J. 69524.

[8] H. E. Winlock, in Studies Presented to F. Ll. Griffith, p. 388 and n. 3.

[9] H. E. Winlock, Slain Soldiers, p. 10.   [10] G. Brunton, Mostagedda, p. 128.

[11] G. Daressy, Rec. Trav., xx (1898), p. 73. Cairo Museum, No. J. 31389. The string was apparently complete when found. See also G. Brunton, Ann. Serv., XXXVIII (1938), pp. 251–2.

was also found); and (c) portions of three twisted strings still on a lute found at Deir el Bahari.[1]

HAIR

Human nature being fundamentally the same everywhere and at all periods, it is not surprising to find that the women of ancient Egypt, even as early as the First Dynasty at least,[2] used artificial locks of human hair to supplement their own when these had become scanty by reason of old age, or because fashion required it. Human hair, too, was employed for making wigs, though these were also sometimes made of vegetable fibre, but there is no evidence of horsehair or wool having been employed for this purpose, despite the statements in the literature to this effect.[3] I have made a microscopical examination of the fibre of all the wigs in the Cairo Museum (fifteen altogether), the results of the examination of fourteen of which have been published.[3]

Seven of these are large ceremonial wigs of the priests of the Twenty-first Dynasty; they are covered with a mass of small corkscrew curls and have long narrow plaits hanging down behind. Although they have been described as consisting of horsehair,[3] they are all of human hair of a brown or dark brown colour when cleaned, though appearing black before cleaning, and are stuffed (evidently for the sake of economy) with fibres from the reddish-brown fabric-like material that surrounds the base of the branches of the date palm.

A further wig, described as from the same source as the previous seven, is much smaller and consists of small light brown curls without any plaits and without stuffing. This, too, is human hair. Another mass of hair (undated), probably at one time a wig, is very similar, though darker in colour, and is also human hair.

Two other large wigs (undated) are very similar to the seven already mentioned, but without stuffing, and consist of dark brown human hair.

The wig of Queen Isemkhebe (Twenty-first Dynasty), which has been described [3] as 'hair mixed with the wool of a black sheep', is of very large size and is covered with small curls and has long narrow plaits behind, but no stuffing: it consists entirely of human hair, mostly of a dark brown colour.

Yuya's ceremonial wig (Eighteenth Dynasty) which has been described as 'woollen', [3] is similar to that of Queen Isemkhebe and consists entirely of human hair of a very dark brown colour.

Two further wigs of small corkscrew curls on a plaited base, both probably of Roman date, consist of vegetable fibre, one being certainly date palm fibre and the other probably grass.

On all the hair wigs without exception and on one of the fibre wigs there is beeswax, some of which was removed by means of a solvent and identified by its properties, particularly by the melting-point. The present drab colour of many of the curls and plaits is due to dust and dirt that have adhered to the wax. As beeswax

---

[1] A. Lansing and W. C. Hayes, *M.M.A. Bull.*, *Egyptian Exped. 1935–1936*, p. 8. Cairo Museum, No. J. 66248.

[2] Cf. A. Scharff, *Die Altertümer der Vor- und Frühzeit Ägyptens*, II, pp. 12–13.

[3] For references see A. Lucas, *Ann. Serv.*, XXX (1930), pp. 190–6; cf. also E. A. Eisa, *Ann. Serv.*, XLVIII (1948), pp. 9–18.

would be such an eminently suitable material to ensure the permanency of the curls and plaits, there can be little doubt that it was for this purpose that it was employed, and that its presence is not to be explained by any anointing, which would only be possible with a liquid oil, or a solid fat liquefied by heat before use, or one that became liquid at the temperature of the human body, or of the room where the wig was being worn. The melting-point of beeswax, which is slightly more than 60°C. (140°F.), is much too high for it to have melted and flowed over the wig had it been applied in the solid form and, therefore, it is practically certain that it must have been warmed and rubbed into the hair.

Small plaited locks of hair sometimes were treasured in ancient Egypt, as is often done today, and such a lock was found in the tomb of Tutankhamūn,[1] the hair being that of Queen Tiy, who was the grandmother of Tutankhamūn's wife and from whom Tutankhamūn himself was probably descended.

Brunton found three round balls of human hair in predynastic graves [2] and two lots of human hair in tombs of Seventh to Eighth Dynasty date, one of which latter was in the form of a small pad that had been used to apply a red powder, possibly to the face, and the other was associated with eye and face paint.[3] Toilet baskets containing hair were found in the tomb of Queen Meryetamūn [4] and in another tomb of Eighteenth Dynasty date,[5] and two clay balls enclosing human hair were discovered at Kahun in a tomb dated to the Twentieth Dynasty.[6]

Hair was occasionally employed for threading beads, examples being known for bracelets of predynastic [7] and First Dynasty [8] dates respectively. Another bracelet of the First Dynasty was in part composed of hair 'probably from tails of oxen'.[9] From the period Fourth to Tenth Dynasties there are bracelets of fibre and hair [10] and bracelets entirely of hair from 'pan' graves.[10] The nature of the hair in these cases has not been determined. Beads of the Badarian period have been found strung on animal hair.[11] Various objects, too, were made of hair, such as the four from the tomb of Tutankhamūn, which the finder calls fly-whisks.[12] These consist of bunches of long hair fixed in gilt wooden handles having the form of animals' heads, and they are possibly the objects so often shown hanging down at the sides of chariot horses and which are depicted on several pieces of the gold decoration belonging to the harness from this tomb. As pointed out to me by Dr. H. H. Nelson, these objects must have been bundles of fibres, as sometimes they are given a wavy appearance to indicate that they are streaming with the wind. This hair is in so disintegrated a condition that although I examined it microscopically in the usual manner it was impossible to identify it with certainty, but it is probably either horsehair or donkey hair. Fly-whisks of giraffe-tail hair, possibly mixed with a little goat hair, were found by Reisner in the graves of the Middle Kingdom Egyptian colony at Kerma

---

[1] H. Carter, *Tut-ankh-Amen*, III, p. 87.   [2] G. Brunton, *Mostagedda*, p. 90.

[3] G. Brunton, *Qau and Badari*, I, pp. 36, 55.

[4] H. E. Winlock, *Meryet-Amūn*, p. 47; W. C. Hayes, *Scepter*, II, p. 188.

[5] W. C. Hayes, *Scepter*, II, p. 188.   [6] W. F. Crompton, *J.E.A.*, III (1916), p. 128.

[7] G. Brunton, *Mostagedda*, p. 85.   [8] W. M. F. Petrie, *Royal Tombs*, II, p. 19.

[9] W. M. F. Petrie, *Royal Tombs*, II, p. 18.   [10] G. Brunton, *Mostagedda*, pp. 110, 130.

[11] G. Brunton and G. Caton-Thompson, *Badarian Civilisation*, p. 57.

[12] H. Carter, *Tut-ankh-Amen*, II, p. 224, Pl. XLIII (c).

in the Sudan,[1] where there were also a number of armlets of giraffe-tail hair.[1] At Balabish Wainwright found a net bag of giraffe-tail or elephant-tail hair [2] and in Nubia Firth discovered an armlet of elephant-tail hair.[3] A sack of woven goat's hair was discovered at El Amarna,[4] and Brunton found a piece of woven-hair fabric, the hair possibly being goat hair, from the Ptolemaic or early Roman period [5] as well as hair matting of Roman or Coptic date.[6] Hair cords and a piece of very coarse hair cloth of the seventh century A.D. were found by Winlock at Thebes,[7] but the nature of the hair is not stated. A piece of camel-hair cord of Third or early Fourth Dynasty date is known.[8] Cloth made of goat hair is mentioned in 185 B.C.,[9] and a cord of uncertain date was identified by Greiss as human hair.[10]

HORN

Horn was used in ancient Egypt from the earliest periods and objects made from this material have been found in graves. From predynastic times, bracelets,[11,12] combs,[11] harpoon heads,[12] tags,[12] vases or cups [11] and a carved horn adapted for use as a receptacle [13] are known; from the First Dynasty bows,[14] gaming pieces [15] and carved horn [14] and from later periods, miscellaneous objects, including what are possibly strigils, [16] horns used as receptacles and horn handles for tools and weapons. Horn was also employed during the Eighteenth Dynasty as one of the components of compound bows.

IVORY

Ivory, both that from the elephant and that from the hippopotamus, was extensively employed in ancient Egypt from neolithic times [17] onwards, largely because it was dense and fine-grained and well adapted for carving, in which the ancient Egyptians were very skilled. The use of elephant ivory at an early date, although it must mean that the elephant was well known, does not necessarily imply that it was then wild in Egypt, which was probably not so, but merely that being plentiful in the country immediately to the south of Egypt (i.e. in the Sudan and perhaps even as far north as Elephantine), a supply of ivory would be easily accessible. The hippopotamus, on the other hand, was still abundant in Egypt, even as late as several hundred years ago. According to the ancient records ivory was obtained from

[1] G. A. Reisner, Kerma, IV–V, pp. 313–15.   [2] G. A. Wainwright, Balabish, pp. 12, 32, 46.
[3] C. M. Firth, Arch. Survey of Nubia, 1910–1911, p. 84.
[4] J. D. S. Pendlebury, City of Akhenaten, III, p. 246.
[5] G. Brunton, Mostagedda, p. 139.   [6] G. Brunton, Mostagedda, p. 145.
[7] H. E. Winlock and W. E. Crum, Monastery of Epiphanius, pp. 71–72.
[8] G. Caton-Thompson and E. W. Gardner, Desert Fayum, pp. 88, 119, 123.
[9] A. S. Hunt and J. G. Smyly, Tebtunis Papyri, III (Part I), No. 796.
[10] E. A. M. Greiss, Bull. Inst. d'Ég., XXXVI (1955), pp. 228–33.
[11] W. M. F. Petrie, Prehistoric Egypt, pp. 30, 31, 40, 48.
[12] W. M. F. Petrie and J. E. Quibell, Naqada and Ballas, pp. 46–47.
[13] G. Brunton and G. Caton-Thompson, Badarian Civilisation, p. 60.
[14] W. M. F. Petrie, Royal Tombs, II, pp. 26, 38, 39; L. Keimer, Z.Ä.S., LXXII (1936), pp. 121–8.
[15] W. B. Emery, Hemaka, p. 40.
[16] G. A. Wainwright, Balabish, pp. 13, 31, 49.
[17] H. Junker, Merimde-Benisalâme, 1929, p. 237; 1930, pp. 71–72.

Negro Lands (Sixth Dynasty);[1] Punt (Eighteenth Dynasty);[2] God's Land (Eighteenth Dynasty);[3] Genebteyew (Eighteenth Dynasty);[4] Kush (Eighteenth Dynasty)[5] and the South Countries (Eighteenth Dynasty),[6] all of which were situated in Africa to the south of Egypt, but in addition also from Tjehenu (Eighteenth Dynasty),[7] which, too, was in Africa, though to the west, and from Retenu (Eighteenth Dynasty)[8] and Isy (Eighteenth Dynasty),[9] both of which were in Asia.

The ivory objects found in the tombs include anklets, armlets, arrow tips, boxes, bracelets, caskets, castanets, combs, cylinders (carved), dishes (shallow), earrings, ear studs, figures (human and animal), gaming pieces and rods, hairpins, handles for knives, daggers, fans, mirrors and whips, harpoon heads, inlay, legs for articles of furniture, mace heads, pendants, pins, plaques, rings, scarabs (rarely), seals, spoons, vases, veneer, and wands. Numerous ivory objects, chiefly of elephant ivory, and including many of the above categories, were found at Kerma in the Sudan.[10] Among the most notable examples of ivory work are the protodynastic statuette of a king from Abydos,[11] the minute statuette of Khufu,[11] and the boxes and other objects from the tomb of Tutankhamūn.

Carved ivory objects were sometimes artificially stained or painted, generally red, but occasionally very dark brown or black or very rarely green, the nature of which colours, however, it has not been possible to determine, except the red on some First Dynasty arrows, some of which and possibly all was red oxide of iron.[12] Some particularly fine specimens of carved and painted ivory work date from the time of Tutankhamūn.[13]

LEATHER[14]

In a country such as Egypt, where cattle, sheep and goats were domesticated as early as the neolithic period, and where there were many wild animals that were hunted at a still earlier date, namely, during paleolithic times, it is only natural that animal skins should have been made use of as clothing, and, although they have not been found from either the paleolithic or neolithic periods, they have frequently been discovered in Badarian[15] and predynastic[16] graves, having been used both as clothing for the living and wrappings for the dead. The treatment of hides and skins with different substances in order to produce leather was practised at a very early date, and articles of leather are common in tombs of the Badarian[15] and predynastic[17] periods.

[1] A.R., I, 336.　　[2] A.R., II, 263, 265, 272, 486.　　[3] A.R., II, 265.
[4] A.R., II, 474.　　[5] A.R., II, 494, 502, 514.　　[6] A.R., II, 652.
[7] A.R., II, 321.　　[8] A.R., II, 447, 509, 525.　　[9] A.R., II, 493, 521.
[10] G. A. Reisner, Kerma, IV–V, pp. 248–71.　　[11] W. M. F. Petrie, Abydos, II, Pl. XIII.
[12] W. B. Emery, Hemaka, p. 47; R. Macramallah, Un cimetière archaïque . . . à Saqqarah, p. 15.
[13] Cf. J. Capart, L'Art égyptien, IV, Les Arts mineurs, Pls. 704–5; C. Aldred, New Kingdom Art, Figs. 97–98; W. S. Smith, Art and Architecture of Ancient Egypt, Pls. 152–3.
[14] Cf. J. W. Waterer, 'Leather', in History of Technology, II, pp. 147–90; G. A. Bravo, 'La lavorazione delle pelli e del cuoio dell 'Egitto antico', Bollettino ufficiale, R. Stazione sperimentale per l'industria delle pelli e delle materie concianti, XI (1933), pp. 75–94; I. M. Lure, 'Leather Working in Ancient Egypt' (Russian), Izvestia Gosudarstvennoi Akademii Istorii Materialnoi Kulturi, Tom VII, Vipusk I; R. J. Forbes, Studies in Ancient Technology, V, pp. 21–36.
[15] G. Brunton and G. Caton-Thompson, Badarian Civilisation, pp. 19, 40; G. Brunton, Mostagedda, pp. 5–7, 33.
[16] W. M. F. Petrie, Prehistoric Egypt, p. 47.
[17] W. M. F. Petrie, Prehistoric Egypt, pp. 34, 43, 47.

It is probable that in the earliest times hides and skins were treated in a number of different ways,[1] for example by simple drying, by smoke curing, by the application of ochreous earths, by curing with salt, or by softening with fat, urine, dung or brain substance. Bravo found evidence suggestive of the use of an ochreous earth for preserving or colouring a specimen of leather from the predynastic site at Gebelein, and of the use of salt on other specimens from the same site,[2] and the leather rim of a basket of Badarian date examined by Stokar had evidently been prepared by phosphatide tannage.[3]

The process of oil tannage known as 'chamoising' was doubtless known at an early date, and Waterer states that 'Direct evidence of oil-tannage has been found in leather from Egyptian tombs'.[4] Skins were also tawed with alum, which yields a stiff white leather, and Waterer says that 'many objects of tawed leather even of predynastic date have been recovered.'[5] 'Sandals from Mostagedda are made of alumed goatskin', 'a fine pair of Dynasty XIX, from Thebes . . . are of alumed goat-skin leather with brown inner soles of tanned hide', and 'there are play-balls of white and red-dyed alumed leather'.[6] Alum was probably often contaminated with ferric salts and other minerals which would produce a degree of tannage, and may also have been used in conjunction with salt. The use of alum for tawing leather or as a mordant in dyeing leather is suggested by certain linguistic evidence,[7] and Waterer thinks that there is 'a hint of a combination of alum and oil processes' in some of the scenes of leather working depicted on tomb walls.[8]

True tanning with substances containing tannin or tannic acid was certainly known from as early as the predynastic period, and specimens of leather from the remains of a tannery of that period found at Gebelein and now in the Turin Museum were undoubtedly tanned with vegetable substances.[9] The tanning agent used was almost certainly the pods of *Acacia arabica* WILLD. (*Acacia nilotica* DESF.) some of which were found at Gebelein still containing 31.6 per cent of 'tans',[10] though fragments of oak bark were also found and these too may have been employed.[9] Theophrastus (fourth to third century B.C.), after describing the acacia as an Egyptian tree, goes on to say that the fruit is a pod, which the natives . . . "use for tanning hides instead of gall',[11] and Pliny (first century A.D.), no doubt copying from Theophrastus, states that the pods of an Egyptian thorn tree (probably *Acacia arabica*) were 'employed instead of galls in the preparation of leather'.[12] These pods, which contain about 30 per cent of tannin, are still used in the Sudan at the present day for tanning purposes and are also exported.

Leather working is illustrated in a number of tombs,[13] for example in two tombs

---

[1] Cf. A. Gansser, *Ciba Rundschau*, VIII (1949), No. 85, pp. 3156–84; *Ciba Review*, VII (1950), No. 81, pp. 2938–62; M. Levey, *Journ. Chemical Education*, XXXIV (1957), pp. 142–3; *Chemistry . . . in Ancient Mesopotamia*, pp. 64–79; F. Vaughan-Kirby, *Man*, XVIII (1918), pp. 36–40.
[2] G. A. Bravo, *Lavorazione delle pelli*, pp. 85–86.
[3] W. Stokar, *Z.Ä.S.*, LXXII (1936), pp. 135–7.   [4] J. W. Waterer, *Leather*, p. 147.
[5] J. W. Waterer, *Leather*, pp. 149–50.   [6] J. W. Waterer, *Leather*, pp. 162, 163, 164.
[7] J. R. Harris, *Lexicographical Studies*, p. 187.   [8] J. W. Waterer, *Leather*, p. 151.
[9] G. A. Bravo, *Lavorazione delle pelli*, p. 87.   [10] G. A. Bravo, *Lavorazione delle pelli*, p. 86.
[11] *Enquiry into Plants*, IV: 2, 1; IV: 2, 8.   [12] XIII: 19.
[13] L. Klebs, *Reliefs, A.R.*, pp. 95–96; *M.R.*, pp. 121–2; *N.R.*, pp. 166–71.

of the Fifth Dynasty at Giza [1] and Saqqara,[2] in two of the Sixth Dynasty at Saqqara [3] and Deshasheh,[4] in a Twelfth Dynasty tomb at Beni Hasan,[5] in the Eighteenth Dynasty tomb of Rekhmirē at Thebes,[6] and in a Twenty-sixth Dynasty tomb also at Thebes.[7] Among the operations depicted are the treatment of a skin in a large jar (either a preparatory process such as steeping in water or urine for depilation, cleaning and softening, or bating with a dung infusion, or possibly a stage in the tanning proper, the jar containing alum or another tanning substance); the staking of a skin over a trestle to make it pliable (suggesting a stiff alum tawed leather); a process which may represent either the scraping of a skin or more probably the slicking of a skin by working in oil or a feed; the cutting of skins with half-moon knives similar to those used today; the making of sandals [8] and the making of leather rope.[9] Various tools are shown, including the half-moon knife, the awl,[8] and other piercing implements, and in the tomb of Rekhmirē there is illustrated a comb-like tool which was probably used for stripping the flesh side of the hide or skin [10] and not as a multiple piercer as has been suggested. The significance of the scenes, the nature of the operations depicted, and the purpose of the different tools have been discussed by Bravo,[11] Davies,[12] Junker,[8] Lure,[13] Montet,[14] Waterer [15] and others.[16] A single model figure from a tomb shows a leather worker cutting out sandals.[17]

Fragments of leather with painted decoration in red, green, black (or blue) and yellow are known from the predynastic period,[18] and similar painted leather of First Dynasty date was found at Saqqara.[19] Leather was frequently dyed red, yellow or green, and the red colour appears to have been used before either of the other two, though at what period leather dyeing was first practised is uncertain. Petrie refers to examples of predynastic leather 'stained red',[20] and Waterer states that 'Many examples of red-dyed leather have been found in Egypt dating from predynastic times onwards'.[21] Objects dyed red are known from the Eleventh Dynasty [22] and also from 'pan'-graves.[23] The nature of the dyes has not been determined, but the red was possibly kermes or madder, and the yellow pomegranate rind.

---

[1] C. R. Lepsius, *Denkmäler*, II, Pl. XLIX b.   [2] G. Steindorff, *Ti*, Pl. CXXXII.

[3] J. Capart, *Une Rue de Tombeaux*, Pl. XXXIII.   [4] W. M. F. Petrie, *Deshasheh*, Pl. XXI.

[5] P. E. Newberry, *Beni Hasan*, I, Pl. XI; II, Pl. IV.

[6] N. de G. Davies, *Rekh-mi-rē*, Pls. LII–LIV.   [7] N. de G. Davies, *Deir el Gebrâwi*, I, Pl. XXV.

[8] H. Junker, *Weta und das Lederkunsthandwerk im Alten Reich*.

[9] K. Gilbert, in *History of Technology*, I, pp. 451–4.

[10] Cf. I. M. Lure, *Leather Working*; F. Vaughan-Kirby, *Man*, XVIII (1918), pp. 36–40.

[11] G. A. Bravo, *Lavorazione delle pelli*.   [12] N. de G. Davies, *Rekh-mi-rē*, pp. 49–50.

[13] I. M. Lure, *Leather Working*.   [14] P. Montet, *Scènes de la vie privée*, pp. 315–19.

[15] J. W. Waterer, *Leather*.

[16] L. Klebs, *Reliefs, A.R.*, pp. 95–96; *M.R.*, pp. 121–2; *N.R.*, pp. 166–71; W. Wreszinski, *Atlas*, I, p. 312; R. J. Forbes, *Studies in Ancient Technology*, V, pp. 21–36.

[17] J. H. Breasted (Jr.), *Servant Statues*, p. 52; J. Garstang, *Burial Customs*, p. 131.

[18] W. M. F. Petrie and J. E. Quibell, *Naqada and Ballas*, pp. 48–49; W. M. F. Petrie, *Prehistoric Egypt*, p. 43.

[19] W. B. Emery, *Great Tombs*, II, p. 64.

[20] W. M. F. Petrie, *Prehistoric Egypt*, p. 43.

[21] J. W. Waterer, *Leather*, p. 156. Cf. R. J. Forbes, *Studies in Ancient Technology*, V, p. 9.

[22] An object of red leather described as a 'tag from wrists' of Eleventh Dynasty date from Deir el Bahari is in the Cairo Museum (No. J. 51874).

[23] G. A. Wainwright, *Balabish*, p. 26; G. Brunton, *Mostagedda*, p. 130.

Kermes, which consists of the red dried bodies of a female insect (*Coccus ilicis*), is one of the oldest dye substances known, and, as it is stated to be useless without a mordant, but gives a red colour with alum, it was probably used with an alum mordant. The kermes insect feeds on a particular kind of oak tree that grows in south-eastern Europe and north Africa, and the dye has been used for leather in Egypt in modern times.

Madder, prepared from the roots of *Rubia tinctorium* and *Rubia peregrina* both of which are common in the Mediterranean region, has been identified on textiles from the Eighteenth Dynasty and later,[1] and there is textual evidence to suggest that madder used with an alum mordant was also employed in dyeing leather.[2]

Pomegranate rind is sometimes employed in Egypt today for dyeing leather a yellow colour, and possibly therefore it was used anciently, though its use seems unlikely before the Eighteenth Dynasty, the earliest date at which the tree, which is not a native of Egypt but of Western Asia, was certainly known in the country.[3] Pliny states that the skin of the unripe fruit was used for dressing leather.[4]

Leather was used to make a variety of objects including bags, bracelets, bracers (to protect archers' wrists), 'braces' (which were probably a priestly insignia in the late Twentieth, Twenty-first and Twenty-second Dynasties), cushion covers, chariot parts, including parts of the body work, flooring and tyres,[5] dog collars and leashes, harness, quivers, ropes and cords, sandals, seats of chairs and stools, and sheaths for daggers, as well as for writing upon, which was quite common,[6] and for various other purposes. Among notable examples of leather work that may be mentioned are a cylindrical leather bag on a wooden frame found in the tomb of 'Hemaka' (First Dynasty);[7] a painted leather wall hanging of New Kingdom date now in the Metropolitan Museum, New York;[8] the decorated leather covering of a small wooden box described by Schäfer;[9] embossed leather quivers and a dog collar, and another dog collar with punched decoration found by Daressy in the Theban necropolis;[10] the borders of appliqué decoration on the body work of the chariot of Yuya;[11] a fragment of a garment or personal ornament of woven leather found at Thebes and now in Turin;[12] and several 'loincloths' of leather network, made by cutting rows

---

[1] See pp. 152–3.

[2] J. R. Harris, *Lexicographical Studies*, p. 187; V. Loret, *Kémi*, III (1930–35), pp. 23–32; B. Ebbell, *Z.Ä.S.*, LXIV (1929), p. 51.

[3] V. Loret, *Flore Pharaonique*, 2nd ed., pp. 76–77; L. Keimer, *Gartenpflanzen*, pp. 45–51. Keimer cites possible evidence for the occurrence of the pomegranate during the Twelfth Dynasty.

[4] XIII: 33.

[5] Cf. J. E. Quibell, *Yuaa and Thuiu*, pp. 65–67; J. W. Waterer, *Leather*, p. 163. The tyres are described as leather, though rawhide might be expected.

[6] R. Pietschmann, 'Leder und Holz als Schreibmaterialien bei den Aegyptern', *Beiträge zur Kenntnis des Schrift-, Buch- und Bibliothekswesens*, Heft 2 (1895), pp. 105–15; S. R. K. Glanville, *J.E.A.*, XIII (1927), pp. 50–56; *A.R.*, II, 392, *n. a.*

[7] W. B. Emery, *Hemaka*, pp. 41–42.   [8] W. C. Hayes, *Scepter*, II, p. 167.

[9] H. Schäfer, *Z.Ä.S.*, XXXI (1893), pp. 105–7.

[10] G. Daressy, *Fouilles de la vallée des rois*, pp. 32–34. Cf. also H. Carter and P. E. Newberry, *Thoutmôsis IV*, pp. 35–38.

[11] J. E. Quibell, *Yuaa and Thuiu*, pp. 65–67.

[12] E. Schiaparelli, *Relazione sui lavori . . . in Egitto*, I, pp. 14, 17.

of small slits (some as little as 3.5 mm. long) breaking joint with one another.[1] The largest piece of leather work that has survived from ancient Egypt is the funeral 'tent' or canopy of Queen Isemkhebe (Twenty-first Dynasty), now in the Cairo Museum, a mosaic of thousands of pieces of leather (said to be gazelle skin tanned with acacia bark) stitched together and decorated with punched and appliqué work in several colours, including bright pink, deep golden yellow, pale primrose, bluish green and pale blue.[2] Tents of skin are also mentioned in an inscription of the Nineteenth Dynasty.[3] Numerous leather objects including articles of clothing, dating from the Middle Kingdom and Second Intermediate period, were found at Kerma in the Sudan and at Balabish, and have been described by Reisner[4] and Wainwright.[5]

The principal use of rawhide was for binding the blades of tools such as axes and adzes to their wooden handles, and for lashing joints in furniture and other wood-work. Rawhide was also employed in chariot construction to strengthen joints and wheel hubs, and as a bearing for the axle, and, like leather, for the floor, which was composed of a mesh of strips.[6] Whether the tyres of chariots were of leather as usually described or of rawhide is doubtful, but the latter seems more appropriate. Few articles of rawhide have been found intact, but Waterer mentions a rectangular container, possibly of Twelfth Dynasty date, which had been moulded to shape, and a four-string harp of the New Kingdom, the body of which is covered with rawhide.[7] Hides and skins were also used for covering shields, and, as already mentioned, for clothing, and goatskins were commonly employed as water carriers.

Specimens of leather, varying in date from the Eighteenth Dynasty to about the Twenty-third Dynasty, were kindly examined for the author by Sir (then Dr.) R. H. Pickard, F.R.S.,[8] and in several instances goat skin was identified, one example being for the seat of a stool from the tomb of Tutankhamūn,[9] and another being sandals from about the Twenty-second or Twenty-third Dynasty, whereas sandals from the tomb of Tutankhamūn were possibly calf skin.[9] The skins found at Gebelein and examined by Bravo were goat skins,[10] and Waterer refers to sandals made of alumed goat skin.[11] Wainwright states that most of the leather of the 'pan'-grave period found at Balabish was cow hide, though in one instance it was sheep skin.[12] Several of the leather network 'loincloths' mentioned above have been tentatively identified as gazelle skin, and the funeral tent of Queen Isemkhebe is also said to be gazelle skin.

---

[1] Several complete examples and many fragments are known, all dating from the latter half of the Eighteenth Dynasty. Cf. H. Carter, *Ann. Serv.*, IV (1903), pp. 46–47; T. Säve-Söderbergh, *Navy of the Eighteenth Egyptian Dynasty*, pp. 75–78.

[2] Cf. Villiers Stuart, *Funeral Tent of an Egyptian Queen*, pp. 5 f.; the appended plate is inaccurate. For an accurate illustration (in colour) see E. Brugsch, *La Tente funéraire de la princesse Isimkheb*; for a photograph see R. J. Forbes, *Studies in Ancient Technology*, v, p. 43, Fig. 11.

[3] C. R. Lepsius, *Denkmäler*, III, Pl. cxcixa, 19.   [4] G. A. Reisner, *Kerma*, IV–V, pp. 303–11.

[5] G. A. Wainwright, *Balabish*, pp. 24–29.   [6] Cf. J. W. Waterer, *Leather*, p. 163.

[7] J. W. Waterer, *Leather*, p. 147.

[8] At that time Director of the British Leather Manufacturers' Research Association. Special search was also made for both vegetable and mineral tanning substances, but the results were negative.

[9] A. Lucas, in H. Carter, *Tut-ankh-Amen*, II, p. 176 (Appendix II).

[10] G. A. Bravo, *Lavorazione delle pelli*, p. 87.

[11] J. W. Waterer, *Leather*, pp. 162–3.

[12] G. A. Wainwright, *Balabish*, p. 26.

MOTHER OF PEARL

Mother of pearl is the nacrous material lining the shells of the pearl oyster and pearl mussel and is of the same composition as pearl, namely, essentially calcium carbonate.

Mother of pearl seems to have been very little used in ancient Egypt north of Aswan, and, with the exception of the well-known large shells, many of which bear the cartouche of Senwosret I (Twelfth Dynasty),[1] only a few other examples of its use can be traced, these including small oblong strips of 'pan'-grave date for threading as bracelets;[2] a scarab of Eighteenth Dynasty date;[3] a pair of earrings of the Roman period [4] and an amulet on a Coptic necklace.[5] It was employed, however, to a greater extent in Nubia, where it has been found in graves from archaic times onwards, the objects made from it being chiefly bracelets, button-like objects, pendants and rings.

As mother of pearl may be obtained from the Red Sea, this was undoubtedly the source of the ancient supply.

OSTRICH EGG-SHELL

There is abundant evidence, both textual and monumental, to show that at one time the ostrich was fairly plentiful in both the eastern and western deserts of Egypt, though it is now no longer found in the country.

Among the earliest objects of any kind from ancient Egypt are ostrich egg-shells (often broken) and small disk beads and pendants made from them. These beads are very common in the earlier periods (neolithic,[6] Badarian [7] and predynastic [8]), though they occur at all times, except during the Eighteenth Dynasty, at the beginning of which they ceased abruptly; they began to come in again during the Nineteenth Dynasty and were still made in the Twenty-second Dynasty.[9]

PARCHMENT

Parchment is prepared from the skins of animals by first removing the hair and then rubbing the skin smooth with some abrasive material, such as pumice stone. Modern parchment is made from the skins of sheep and goats, but only one identification of the kind of skin used anciently in Egypt for parchment can be traced, and this was gazelle skin.[10]

Parchment is known principally as a material for writing upon, but this was not its earliest use in ancient Egypt, which was for covering drum heads and the sounding boxes of other musical instruments, such as mandolins, lutes and tambourines, the

---

[1] H. E. Winlock, in *Studies Presented to F. Ll. Griffith*, pp. 388–92; A. J. Arkell, *J.E.A.*, xxx (1944), p. 74; C. Aldred, *J.E.A.*, xxxviii (1952), p. 130.

[2] G. A. Wainwright, *Balabish*, p. 20, Pl. iii, 13; W. M. F. Petrie, *Diospolis Parva*, p. 45.

[3] P. E. Newberry, *Scarab-shaped Seals*, p. 368.

[4] W. M. F. Petrie, *Objects of Daily Use*, p. 14, Pl. x (250–1).   [5] Cairo Museum, No. J. 57141.

[6] G. Caton-Thompson, *Journ. Royal Anthrop. Inst.*, lvi (1926), p. 312; G. Caton-Thompson and E. W. Gardner, *Geog. Journ.*, lxxx (1932), p. 371.

[7] G. Brunton and G. Caton-Thompson, *Badarian Civilisation*, pp. 3, 28; G. Brunton, *Mostagedda*, p. 60.

[8] W. M. F. Petrie, *Prehistoric Egypt*, p. 43.   [9] G. A. Wainwright, *Balabish*, p. 22.

[10] B. Bruyère, *Deir el Médineh (1934–1935)*, pp. 116–17, Figs. 53, 61. Cairo Museum, No. J. 63746.

earliest example of this use being possibly of Middle Kingdom date. The objects in the Cairo Museum comprise a lute of which the parchment is coloured pink, which the finders call leather,[1] and an almost rectangular-shaped tambourine, the cover of which the finders call rawhide.[2] Both these, which are from the Eighteenth Dynasty, were found by Lansing and Hayes in the Theban necropolis and in each case the cover is parchment. Bruyère found at Deir el Medineh, a one-stringed instrument, also of Eighteenth Dynasty date, which he calls a lute, but which is termed a mandolin in the Cairo Museum register, the cover of which is stated to be made of gazelle skin.[3] A drum with parchment ends found by Garstang at Beni Hasan is of uncertain date, though the finder thinks it may be from the Middle Kingdom.[4]

TORTOISE-SHELL

Modern tortoise-shell consists of the epidermic plates of a small species of sea turtle, but in ancient times probably the plates of more than one kind of turtle and also of the land tortoise were used. A large turtle is found in the Nile, a sea turtle both on the Mediterranean and Red Sea coasts of Egypt and a small land tortoise in Sinai, and also in both the eastern [5] and western deserts and the remains of very large land tortoises of Eocene times have been found in the Fayum province.

Tortoise-shell was valued in Egypt from a very early date and a large number of objects of this material have been found in graves, particularly in Nubia, among which may be mentioned part of a ring; bracelets; a dish; a comb; a sounding board of a harp;[6] a sounding board of a mandolin;[7] as also several complete shells [8] and parts of shells.[9] The objects range in date from Badarian times onwards.

MARINE AND FRESH WATER SHELLS[10]

Shells are very common in ancient Egyptian graves, especially in those of early date, and their use goes back to neolithic times. The smaller kinds were used chiefly as amulets, pendants, and strung together to form necklaces and girdles, while the larger shells were employed as receptacles for eye paints and other pigments. The

---

[1] A. Lansing and W. C. Hayes, *M.M.A. Bull., Egyptian Exped. 1935–1936*, p. 8, Figs. 10, 11. Cairo Museum, No. J. 66248.

[2] A. Lansing and W. C. Hayes, *M.M.A. Bull., Egyptian Exped. 1935–1936*, p. 13, Fig. 24. Cairo Museum, No. J. 66246. The nature of the cover is now unrecognizable, owing to its having been unwisely soaked in water when it was removed from the frame, which was repaired in the Museum workshop, but fortunately I examined it before it was destroyed.

[3] B. Bruyère, *Deir el Médineh (1934–1935)*, pp. 116–17, Figs. 53, 61. Cairo Museum, No. J. 63746.

[4] J. Garstang, *Burial Customs*, pp. 121, 156, Fig. 155.

[5] W. H. Schoff, *The Periplus of the Erythraean Sea*, p. 22.

[6] British Museum, *Guide to the Third and Fourth Egyptian Rooms*, 1904, p. 173.

[7] Eighteenth Dynasty. B. Bruyère, *Deir el Médineh (1934–1935)*, Figs. 53, 61.

[8] Carnarvon and H. Carter, *Five Years' Explorations*, p. 76; C. Gaillard and G. Daressy, *La faune momifiée*, p. 69; British Museum, *Guide to the Fourth, Fifth and Sixth Egyptian Rooms*, 1922, p. 31.

[9] G. Brunton, *Mostagedda*, pp. 5, 24, 30, 57.

[10] For Bibliography see Dr. Edmond Dartevelle-Puissant, *Chronique d'Égypte*, XII (1937), pp. 50–53.

greater proportion of these shells were from the Red Sea, though shells from the Mediterranean, freshwater shells from the Nile and land shells were also used.[1]

One kind of shell sometimes employed was dentalium, a marine mollusc having a white, narrow, tubular shell that occurs on the shores of the Red Sea,[2] which were occasionally threaded and used as beads. Although this has been reported from both Badarian[3] and predynastic times,[3] the finder now agrees that the material was wrongly identified by the expert consulted and that it is organ coral and not dentalium and the mistake is corrected in a later publication.[4] A small lot of dentalium shells, however, of unknown date, marked 'Mitraheneh' are in the store of the Cairo Museum. Dentalium has been found in mesolithic burials in Palestine.[5]

Shells were also cut to form beads, bracelets, and other objects.

---

[1] W. M. F. Petrie, *Six Temples at Thebes*, pp. 30–31; G. Caton-Thompson, *Journ. Royal Anthrop. Inst.*, LVI (1926), p. 313; G. Brunton and G. Caton-Thompson, *Badarian Civilisation*, p. 38; G. Brunton, *Qau and Badari*, I, p. 71; III, p. 35; G. A. Wainwright, *Balabish*, pp. 17–19; G. A. Reisner, *Kerma*, IV–V, p. 319; D. Randall MacIver and A. C. Mace, *El Amrah and Abydos*, p. 49; L.-C. Lortet and C. Gaillard, *La faune momifiée*, I–II, pp. 191–8; III–IV, pp. 105–22, 307–25; C. Gaillard and G. Daressy, *La faune momifiée*, pp. 75–84; G. Brunton, *Mostagedda*, pp. 29, 52, 57, 107, 109, 126.
[2] T. Barron and W. F. Hume, *Topog. and Geol. of the Eastern Desert*, pp. 127, 137.
[3] G. Brunton and G. Caton-Thompson, *Badarian Civilisation*, pp. 38, 56.
[4] G. Brunton, *Mostagedda*, p. 85.
[5] Dorothy A. E. Garrod, *Man*, XXXI (1931), pp. 145–6.

Chapter IV

BEADS

The use of beads in Egypt dates back to the neolithic period, that is from about 12,000 to 7,000 years ago. The earliest beads are in the form of small, natural objects, such as bones, pebbles, seeds, shells and teeth, which, if not occurring with holes in them, were perforated artificially. These beads were worn round the neck, arm, ankle, or waist.

Although the objects mentioned possibly were sometimes used merely as ornaments, they were more commonly worn as charms. Strictly, therefore, the earliest beads were pendants employed as amulets, but it was from these objects that artificially-shaped, or artificially-made beads were evolved. Blue beads are still common in Egypt as amulets on children, horses, donkeys, and even on motor-cars.

That beads were very highly prized in ancient Egypt is shown by the enormous numbers of them that have been found in graves of all periods: they were used by both sexes and were made of a great variety of materials, both natural and artificial, including bone, faience, blue frit, glass, glazed material (quartz and steatite),[1] ivory, metal (gold, silver, electrum, copper and iron[2]), resin,[3] shell (including ostrich egg-shell), stones,[4] straw and wood (sometimes gilt).

Mrs. C. R. Williams says [5] 'Indeed, the elaboration of bead jewelry was one of the most prominent contributions of Egypt to the development of personal adornment in antiquity. Never was a people fonder of beads or more ingenious and skilful in combining them; compared with Egyptian bead jewelry, modern bead bags seem trivial, and even the present-day necklaces of better materials are usually of less interesting and less organized designs. It was in Egypt that the colourful combining and intricate threading of beads of precious materials reached a high art.'

Carter and Mace say [6] 'The Egyptians were passionately fond of beads, and it is by no means exceptional to find upon a single mummy an equipment consisting of a number of necklaces, two or three collars, a girdle or two, and a full set of bracelets and anklets. In such a case many thousands of beads will have been employed.' On

---

[1] Also a unique example of glazed serpentine (R. Mond and O. H. Myers, *Cemeteries of Armant*, I, p. 72).

[2] See p. 237. Also an alleged instance of iron pyrites (W. M. F. Petrie, *Illahun, Kahun and Gurob*, p. 25).

[3] Also a bead of bituminous material, possibly ozokerite (R. Mond and O. H. Myers, *Cemeteries of Armant*, I, pp. 97–98, 100).

[4] Including agate, alabaster (calcite), amethyst, azurite, breccia, carnelian, chalcedony, felspar, fluorspar, garnet, haematite, jasper, lapis lazuli, limestone, malachite, olivine, wood opal, porphyry, quartz, sard, serpentine, steatite and turquoise.

[5] C. R. Williams, *Gold and Silver Jewelry*, p. 9.

[6] H. Carter, *Tut-ankh-Amen*, I, p. 159.

three men of the Badarian period Brunton found 'masses of beads running round and round the waist'.[1]

In the Eighteenth Dynasty tomb of Tutankhamūn there were thousands of beads of different kinds, calcite, carnelian, coloured faience, gold, green felspar, opaque coloured glass, lapis lazuli (a few only, mostly large), dark red resin (a few only, all large) and gilt wood. These were respectively on collars, necklaces, pectorals, bracelets, earrings, garments, a pair of small sandals, and three footstools.

A large amount of miscellaneous material has been published in a scattered form describing the methods employed anciently for making beads, which may usefully be quoted and is as follows:

STONE BEADS

In his description of the making of stone beads found at Kerma in the Sudan, where there was a Twelfth Dynasty Egyptian colony, Reisner [2] states that '. . . the natural crystals and pebbles were broken up by percussion. Suitable pieces were then roughly shaped by rolling between stones or by bruising . . . The shaped pieces were then smoothed by rubbing, a process which leaves flat places on the visually curving surface, a state which may be seen on many of the finished beads . . . Some of the small glazed crystal beads . . . appear never to have been smoothed at all, but while still in the roughly bruised form they were pierced and glazed. The polished beads were bored after smoothing and before polishing or glazing . . . The boring operation was undertaken either from one side . . . or from two opposite sides. Apparently if the hole begun on one side gave difficulties, owing to the drill working into a slanting position or being diverted, another boring was begun on the opposite side to meet the first hole. The drill-point usually had a diameter of 1–2 mm., allowing for a certain widening of the hole in the drilling, and must have had a length of not less than 14 mm. It has usually been assumed that such holes could be drilled with a copper drill or a hard vegetable stalk using wet emery powder, and this method would seem to have been used at Kerma. Under the number Su 277 is recorded a stick of what appears to be emery, which has been rubbed, perhaps to obtain the emery powder used in such boring. Two bronze points were found . . . one of which was certainly a drill, and three others, possibly drills, two of them with wooden handles . . . It will be noticed that I assume the use of a bow-drill, which was well known to Egyptian craftsmen from the Early Dynastic Period. After the hole was bored, the bead was polished, and, if desired, glazed. The glazed beads usually have the glaze in the hole, and were therefore dipped in the mass, like the faience beads. As the holes were larger and the material glass-like, the glaze entered the holes, although it did not enter the holes of the faience beads.'

It is much to be regretted that the emery-like material found by Reisner was not analysed. It is stated frequently that emery was used as an abrasive in ancient Egypt, but this has never been proved, and is highly improbable. Unless emery occurs in the Sudan near Kerma, for which there is no evidence, it must have been imported, if used, from the Greek islands, since its occurrence in Egypt has never been confirmed, and importation from the Mediterranean to the Sudan is so improbable that

---

[1] G. Brunton and G. Caton-Thompson, *Badarian Civilisation*, pp. 27–28.

[2] G. A. Reisner, *Kerma*, IV–V, pp. 93–94.

it may be ruled out. Also, since fine quartz sand will abrade quartz, which was the hardest stone the Egyptians worked (except beryl at a late date, which could have been done with its own dust) and since quartz sand is very abundant in Egypt, there was no need for emery.[1]

At Hierakonpolis, near El Kab in Upper Egypt, 'an enormous number of exceedingly small pointed flint implements were found; and with them many broken carnelian pebbles, some chipped in the form of rough beads, one or two of which showed signs of the commencement of the boring operations; also chips of amethyst and rock-crystal, and one or two flakes of greenish black obsidian. Other collections of these small flint points, and materials from which beads were made, were found . . . These flint points seem to be drills for boring carnelian, amethyst and other beads, but how this was accomplished is not evident.' [2]

The most recent description of the methods of making stone beads is that of Myers in collaboration with Hart.[3] Myers points out that naturally 'The first process with all hard stone beads was to chip or flake them to rough shape.' The beads were then finished by 'rubbing down', that is by rubbing them on a flat surface by hand; by 'groove-grinding', applied to cylinder beads, or possibly to several disc beads held together on an axis, which consisted in rubbing them 'in a suitable groove in a hard gritty stone, usually sandstone or quartzite'; or by 'turning', which 'was probably done by attaching the bead to the end of the shaft of a drill, and then turning it in a wooden cup or recess (or against a flat surface) by rotating the shaft in the usual way, feeding it, of course, with an abrasive'. Myers suggests that the head of the drill or boring tool used for perforation, which he calls a 'lap',[4] was of flint, or copper (solid or tubular), and that the tool was driven with a bow or with the hand. The points were evidently of different shapes, V-shaped, pointed, round-ended, flat-ended and tubular. The abrasive was probably the finely-ground chips from the beads themselves, though in one instance finely crushed flint or chert was found in a hole in a steatite bead.[5]

A lot of 152 rough spheroids of carnelian (undated) from Mitrahineh in the Cairo Museum [6] manifestly are partly-made beads that have been roughed out from natural carnelian pebbles (which occur abundantly in Egypt), but which were never finished or bored. The diameters vary from about six to twelve millimetres (approximately 0.23 to 0.47 inch).

In a number of tombs of Eighteenth Dynasty date in the Theban necropolis the drilling of beads by means of a bow-drill is shown, the bow frequently being used to drive two or more drills at once.[7] Myers suggests that these scenes may possibly

[1] See pp. 73–74.   [2] J. E. Quibell and F. W. Green, *Hierakonpolis*, II, p. 12.

[3] R. Mond and O. H. Myers, *Cemeteries of Armant*, I, pp. 74–79, Pls. XXXVI–XXXIX.

[4] In my opinion, this name is not very satisfactory, since a lap may be a lead plug carrying emery powder and oil, such as is used for polishing the interior of the barrels of firearms, or it may be a disc of metal rotated in a lathe.

[5] R. Mond and O. H. Myers, *Cemeteries of Armant*, I, pp. 79, 93.   [6] Museum No. J. 46778.

[7] N. de G. Davies, *Rekh-mi-rē*, p. 49, Pl. LIV; *Two Sculptors*, p. 63, Pl. XI; *Puyemrê*, p. 75, Pls. XXIII, XXVII; *Two Officials*, p. 11, Pl. X; *M.M.A. Bull., Egyptian Exped. 1918–1920*, p. 38, Fig. 9 (Tomb No. 75 at Thebes). Cf. also C. R. Williams, *Gold and Silver Jewelry*, p. 200; G. A. Reisner, *Kerma*, IV–V, p. 202; E. Vernier, *Bijouterie et Joaillerie*, pp. 62–66, 137–9; A. Rieth, *Umschau*, LV (1955), pp. 112–13; *Mitt. Inst. Orientforsch.*, VI (1958), pp. 176–86.

represent the process of 'turning' which he describes.[1] In a Sixth Dynasty tomb at Deir el Gebrawi the drilling of pieces of carnelian, not with a bow-drill, is shown.[2]

In the Cairo Museum there are a number of very tiny beads of Middle Kingdom date made respectively of carnelian, lapis lazuli and turquoise, which vary in diameter from about 0.58 to 0.64 millimetre (approximately 0.023 to 0.025 inch). Vernier gives the mean diameter of two lots of these beads as 0.70 to 0.77 millimetre (approximately 0.028 to 0.031 inch).[3] In what manner these beads were bored is not known. Tiny beads of much the same size have been found also in India and Mesopotamia.

Mackay recently found at Chanhu-daro in India a complete beadmaker's outfit, including the raw material in the form of agate and carnelian, chert drills, grooved blocks of sandstone for shaping the beads, and both finished and unfinished beads, all of which he describes in detail.[4]

Beck says [5] of certain Mesopotamian beads that 'The perforation was done with a hollow rotating drill. Another feature is that it was generally drilled straight through from one end, with the result that there is often a large chip where it broke through the second surface.'

Shell Beads

In addition to the natural marine and freshwater shells merely bored and strung together as beads, which have already been mentioned, the Egyptians also made small ring beads and disc beads from shells, and similar beads, too, from ostrich egg-shell, the form being imposed by the character of the material, and it is not always easy to distinguish between them. Such beads date back to the neolithic period. The method of making these beads is described by Reisner,[6] namely, first, the shell was broken up into conveniently-sized pieces, which were roughly trimmed by crushing away the edges, possibly with a blade, then the hole was drilled from both sides with a blunt point, and finally the beads were smoothed on the edges, probably after stringing. During the Eighteenth Dynasty these disc beads went out of use completely and were replaced by similarly-shaped beads of faience, as, for example, in the tomb of Tutankhamūn, in which, although there were many thousands of beads, there were none of shell. These beads, however, began to come into use again during the Nineteenth Dynasty and were still made in the Twenty-second Dynasty.

Faience Beads

In Egypt, faience beads date from the predynastic period. With respect to the faience beads found at Kerma, Reisner states [7] that 'The greater part of the beads have straight smooth threading holes with little or no discoloration of the inner surfaces. Professor Petrie's conclusion that beads were made on threads which were

---

[1] R. Mond and O. H. Myers, *Cemeteries of Armant*, I, p. 75.

[2] N. de G. Davies, *Deir el Gebrâwi*, I, p. 20, Pl. XIII.

[3] E. Vernier, *Bijoux et Orfèvreries*, Nos. 52825–52826.

[4] E. Mackay, *J.A.O.S.*, LVII (1937), pp. 1–15; *Journ. Royal Soc. of Arts*, LXXXV (1937), pp. 527–45; *Illustrated London News*, 14 November 1936, p. 864.

[5] H. C. Beck, *Ancient Egypt*, 1935, p. 26.

[6] G. A. Reisner, *Kerma*, IV–V, p. 94.

[7] G. A. Reisner, *Kerma*, IV–V, pp. 91–92.

burnt out in the firing is doubtless correct; but whether the beads were made on a thread, or on some other axis, the method of forming the ring-beads, the disc-beads and the tubular beads, suggested first, I believe, by Professor Petrie, is the most obvious. The axis was coated with the body-paste to a depth of 1–5 mm., according to the size and type of the beads in hand, and perhaps rolled on a board. While still moist this long cylinder was cut with a knife into sections, short for the ring-beads and the disc-beads, and long for the tubular beads. These were then dried and baked without removing the axis. The barrel-shaped beads, the pendant-beads and the ball-beads were probably made in the same way by coating an axis and cutting the coat of paste into sections. These sections could then be modelled with the fingers to the desired forms and trimmed at the ends, that is around the axis, with a knife. The ends of the tubular beads have clearly been trimmed, and the slight flattening around the two ends of the hole on almost all ball-beads is without doubt also due to trimming with a knife. The amulet-beads could have been made on an axis in much the same way, but for them the paste-coating was thick and was made into a form with rect-angular section. This could have been done very simply by pressing the coat of paste, while on the axis, against a board or other hard, flat surface. Thereafter the ends were trimmed and the details added with a knife.

'Some of the larger ball-beads were not made on an axis but pierced. The best example was a broken faience bead . . . which had been pierced while the paste was still soft by thrusting with a slender point from one side and then from the opposite side. The instrument used may well have been a blunt-ended, stiff wire, or even a bone or bronze awl.

'I have assumed . . . that the beads were fired the first time while still on the axis. This conclusion is deduced from the advantage of handling such small fragile objects while still on the axis, and from the slight scorching of the inside of the hole in some beads. Dipping was the only obviously practical method of applying the mixed blue-glazing solution. Although the glaze covers the ends of the beads without penetrating the threading-hole, it need not be concluded that the beads were restrung for dipping, as liquid does not readily penetrate such small holes. The glaze did pene-trate the holes of the crystal beads, but these holes were larger in diameter and made in a glass-like material. The next step after the glaze was the second firing. It is to be noted that the ball-heads show a spot on one side where the glaze is imperfect, and the tubular beads show a line down one side, but no beads have contact marks at the ends around the threading holes. The contact marks mentioned are most easily ex-plained by the assumption that the beads were glazed in pans, or on the floor of the oven. Many beads, however, show no trace of contact marks whatever, and I am not sure how these were fired. Possibly the contact marks have been removed by rub-bing. Certain lots of small ring-beads were found . . . in which the beads were gathered together in irregular clusters by the interfusing of the glaze. This condition leads to the conclusion that these particular beads were fired *en masse*, in the oven; but it is obvious that this method was not the usual one.

'The tiny ring-beads appear in many cases to be nearly pure coloured glaze, but with a minute opaque or even whitish core. It is possible that for these beads the axis was coated either (*a*) with a very thin coat of paste, or (*b*) with a thick coat of coloured glazing mixture only and that the beads were then fired only once. But it is also possible that the very tiny ring-beads may have been made in the usual manner, and that owing to their small size the cores have been more highly affected by the heat than in the larger beads and may have been fused with the glaze during firing.'

Petrie states [1] that the faience beads from Naucratis 'were commonly made on a thread, dried and the thread burnt out; they were then dipped in glaze-wash and fired. In early times small beads were rolled between the thumb and finger on the thread, producing a long tapering form like a grain of corn.'

Beck describes methods of making faience beads,[2] and also various methods of decorating them.[3]

The use and distribution of faience beads in the ancient East and in prehistoric Europe has been discussed by Beck and Stone,[4] and by Stone and Thomas.[5]

GLASS BEADS

Although it is sometimes stated that glass beads are known in Egypt from the predynastic period, this lacks confirmation, but they were made certainly from the Fifth Dynasty onwards.

Of the manner of making glass beads Petrie says [6] 'The usual mode of bead-making was by winding a thin thread of drawn-out glass around a wire. These wires are actually found with the beads still stuck on them . . . Many beads were imperfectly formed, and left as spirals owing to the tail of glass thread not being united to the body of the bead. These are found on a corkscrew shape. . . . Some flat beads were made by coiling a long bead, flattening it and then cutting it across. . . . The pendant beads . . . show plainly the coils of the thread by which they were built up, in the clear structure of the glass. And every bead of this age shows more or less of the little peak at each end where the glass thread was finally separated from it. On the contrary the Coptic glass beads are all made by drawing out a glass tube, as shown by long bubbly striations; and then the tube was rolled under an edge across it, to nick it, so as to break it up into beads.'

Petrie also says [7] 'The early glass is all wound with lines running around; the Roman glass is all drawn out and nicked off with lines running along . . .' and [7] 'The thread of glass was wound round upon a hot copper wire of the size of the hole required: and after piling on enough, and completing the pattern of colour the wire contracted in cooling and could be withdrawn. The little point where the thread of glass broke off can be seen at each end of the beads.'

Beck describes [8] four principal ancient methods of making glass beads, most, if not all, of which were used in Egypt. These are as follows:

1. *Wire-wound Beads.* 'A thin stick of glass heated until it had much the consistency of toffee was wound round a wire. During the process the glass was pulled out into a

[1] W. M. F. Petrie, *Arts and Crafts*, p. 119.
[2] H. C. Beck, in G. Brunton, *Qau and Badari*, II, pp. 22–25.
[3] H. C. Beck, *Classification and Nomenclature of Beads and Pendants*, pp. 69–70.
[4] H. C. Beck and J. F. S. Stone, *Archaeologia*, LXXXV (1936), pp. 203–52.
[5] J. F. S. Stone and L. C. Thomas, *Proceedings of the Prehistoric Society*, XXII (1956), pp. 37–84.
[6] W. M. F. Petrie, *Tell el Amarna*, p. 27.
[7] W. M. F. Petrie, *Arts and Crafts*, pp. 121, 125.
[8] H. C. Beck, *Classification and Nomenclature of Beads and Pendants*, pp. 60–69.

thread, and there is frequently a projection on the bead showing where this thread was broken off. When, however, as often happens, the bead has been reheated for subsequent decoration, this projection generally disappears.' This method is the same as that described by Petrie.

2. *Cane Beads*. 'To make these the glass was made into a rod or tube which was called a cane. These canes were sometimes made of one glass only; at other times they were made of different coloured glasses arranged in a pattern.

'To make a bead, a cane, usually tubular, was selected of approximately the same diameter as the bead required. A piece the length of the bead was cut off this cane. In some cases this was used as a bead without any further work on it. In other cases it was finished by either grinding or reheating.

'The method of making tubular canes is of some interest . . . small glass tubes have been found . . . in the glass factory at Tel el Amarna . . . which . . . dates from the XVIIIth dynasty. By examining fragments of these I have been able to trace the method of their manufacture. A strip of glass of considerable thickness, and wide enough to fold round a wire, was, whilst in a plastic condition, folded round and the edges fused together so as to make a tube. . . . These were sometimes reheated and pulled out into small tubular canes, such as those found at Tel el Amarna. . . . Pieces broken from these make long cylindrical beads, and a necklace entirely consisting of such beads simply broken off canes has been found in a New Kingdom grave at Abydos.' Petrie attributes cane beads to the Coptic period.

3. *Folded Beads*. 'When, however, the folded cane is not pulled out into a small tube, but beads are cut from it and ground to shape they are called *Folded beads*.' 'Folded beads were made in several other ways. One method was to prepare a slab of glass with a length nearly equal to the circumference of the required bead, and with a width approximately the length of the bead. This was folded round a rod and the two ends pressed together and fused. A slightly different way of making them was to prepare a strip of a similar form, and whilst it was plastic to press a rod through the centre of it perpendicularly to the face and then bend the two ends of the strip up so as to join together, enclosing the rod between them.'

4. *Double Strip Beads*. 'In this method two strips of glass were taken and placed on top of each other with a rod between them. They were then pressed together and cut off at the correct length to form the diameter of the bead, which was finished by rounding it to shape by pressure whilst the glass was still plastic.'

Beck describes also moulded glass beads and blown glass beads (which latter, however, were not made before the Roman period), and also various methods of decorating glass beads.

Chapter V
BUILDING MATERIALS

The nature of the building materials employed in any country depends upon many factors, the principal of which are the climate, the degree of civilization of the people and the kind of materials available.

Diodorus (first century A.D.) states [1] that 'They say the Egyptians in ancient times . . . made their houses of reeds, of which there are some marks amongst the shepherds at this day, who care for no other houses, but such like, which they say serves their turn well enough.' In Egypt, therefore, one may look back in imagination to a period when primitive shelters of dried reeds [2] were erected as a protection from the sun and wind, and one can imagine also the next stage of development when the reeds were plastered with clay in order to keep out the heat and cold more effectually. In two localities the remains of what probably were structures of this nature of pre-dynastic date (in one case reeds plastered with clay [3] and in the other case twigs plastered with clay [4]) have been found.[5]

At a later period the need of something more substantial than clay-plastered reeds or twigs manifestly was felt. The available suitable materials with which to make a more solid habitation were clay and stone, and, as suggested, clay probably had already been used to fortify the original reed shelters and, if so, its properties would have been familiar, whereas the knowledge and tools necessary for quarrying and dressing stone in quantity did not exist, and, therefore, clay, the known and more easily worked material, was chosen and was made into bricks, which were dried in the sun. The use of stone followed later when civilization had advanced sufficiently to provide metal (copper) tools.

Brick and stone will now be considered, as also the auxiliary materials required for building, namely, mortar, plaster and wood.

BRICK [6]

Brick making is one of the oldest of the arts and was known to most of the nations of antiquity, but in few places has it been practised more than in Egypt, where sun-

---

[1] I: 4.

[2] At the present day temporary shelters of maize stalks are common in the fields, maize, how-ever, being a modern importation into Egypt.

[3] G. Brunton and G. Caton-Thompson, *Badarian Civilisation*, pp. 82–83.

[4] J. Garstang, *Mahâsna and Bêt Khallâf*, pp. 6–7.

[5] For the use of reed and rush in early architecture, cf. A. Badawy, *Ann. Serv.*, LI (1951), pp. 4–17.

[6] Cf. J. R. Harris, *Lexicographical Studies*, pp. 207–8; R. Mond and O. H. Myers, *Cemeteries of Armant*, I, pp. 24–25; *Bucheum*, I, pp. 48–52.

dried bricks still are, as they always have been, the characteristic building material of the country, and in the villages and smaller towns of Egypt the houses today are built of bricks similar to those that were used about 6,000 years ago.

The oldest bricks that have been found in Egypt are of predynastic date, examples being at Naqada in Upper Egypt[1] and those lining two royal tombs at Abydos,[2] also in Upper Egypt. In tombs of First and Second Dynasty date at both Saqqara and Abydos bricks are very common and at Abydos, too, there is a ruined brick fort of the Second Dynasty the walls of which are still about 35 feet high.[3] Great brick walls were built as early as the Old Kingdom,[4] and in the Middle Kingdom brick was used in the construction of pyramids.[5]

The bricks are generally made of Nile alluvium, or Nile mud as it is termed, of which all the cultivated land of Egypt consists and which is essentially a mixture of clay and sand, containing small amounts of impurities. The relative proportions of the two principal ingredients vary in different localities, and it is on the clay that the plastic and cohesive properties of the mud depend. When the percentage of clay is high, the mud is sufficiently tenacious to cohere without any extraneous binding material, though if the mixture is too rich in clay it is not satisfactory and bricks made from it not only dry slowly, but during drying, shrink, crack and lose their shape. In order to prevent this, such alluvium is mixed with sand, chopped straw or other material. Chopped straw also is sometimes added as a binder when the proportion of clay is low. The Egyptian practice of using straw in making bricks is mentioned in a papyrus of the New Kingdom,[6] and in the Bible.[7] Chopped straw, however, and also animal (donkey) dung, which latter is employed occasionally, not only act as mechanical binders, but also increase both the strength and plasticity of the clay, especially if well mixed with it and allowed to remain some time before use.[8] Mellor states[9] that 'Clays which have been sodden with ground waters rich in organic matter are usually highly plastic', and that humic acid, peat and other organic materials are added to clay to increase plasticity.

A predynastic tomb at Armant furnished examples of a medium quality yellow brick 'made obviously from the local clay of the low desert, with no Nile mud added to it'.[10]

The method of making bricks is known from tomb models of Middle Kingdom date,[11] and from the famous scene in the tomb of Rekhmirē̆ (Eighteenth Dynasty),[12] and

---

[1] W. M. F. Petrie and J. E. Quibell, *Naqada and Ballas*, p. 54.

[2] W. M. F. Petrie, *History of Egypt*, I (1924), pp. 4–5.

[3] W. M. F. Petrie, *Social Life in Ancient Egypt*, p. 151.

[4] Somers Clarke and R. Engelbach, *Ancient Egyptian Masonry*, pp. 210–11.

[5] Somers Clarke and R. Engelbach, *Ancient Egyptian Masonry*, pp. 211–13.

[6] C. F. Nims, *Biblical Archaeologist*, XIII (1950), pp. 22–28.   [7] *Exodus*, v: 7–18.

[8] E. G. Acheson, *Journ. Soc. of Chemical Industry*, XXIX (1910), p. 246; A. H. Drummond, *op. cit.*, XXXVIII (1919), p. 439 R.

[9] J. W. Mellor, *Inorganic and Theoretical Chemistry*, VI, p. 490.

[10] R. Mond and O. H. Myers, *Cemeteries of Armant*, I, p. 24.

[11] J. H. Breasted (Jr.), *Servant Statues*, p. 52, Pl. XLVI, c; C. F. Nims, *Biblical Archaeologist*, XIII (1950), p. 23, Fig. 2.

[12] N. de G. Davies, *Rekh-mi-rē̆*, pp. 54–55, Pls. LVIII–LIX; *Paintings from the Tomb of Rekh-mi-rē̆*, Pls. XVI–XVII.

is practically identical with that used in Egypt at the present day.[1] The hard mud was broken up with a hoe, mixed with water, and kneaded with the feet until it was of the right consistency. It was then carried to the brickmaker, who placed the mud in a wooden mould or form, which he then lifted, leaving the brick on the ground to dry in the sun. The form of the mould was that of a box open at both top and bottom, with one side extended to provide a handle. Such a mould of Twelfth Dynasty date was found at Kahun,[2] and miniature moulds of similar type have also been discovered.[3]

Since clay is plentiful and widely distributed in Egypt, and since sun-dried bricks do not require highly skilled labour, either for making or using, the houses constructed with them are cheap; also they are warm in winter and cool in summer and, although they would not stand the wet climate of Europe, they are very suitable for Egypt, where rain, except in the extreme north, is rare.

Old Egyptian bricks differ considerably in size, some being much the same dimensions as modern bricks, while others are very large, for example, two in the Cairo Museum each measure approximately $38 \times 21 \times 12$ inches.

With the advent of stone, both tombs and temples, which previously had been built of sun-dried bricks, began to be constructed of the newer material, but the houses, not only those of the poorer classes, but also those of the nobles and even the palaces of the Pharaohs, still continued to be made of brick, and it is for this reason that the houses and palaces have perished, while the tombs and temples remain, sun-dried brick being a much less enduring material than stone and also one that lends itself more readily than large blocks of stone to the building requirements of the modern inhabitants.

Burnt bricks, although used in Mesopotamia [4] and at Mohenjo-daro in India [5] at a very early date, were not employed generally in Egypt, so far as is known, before the time of the Roman occupation of the country. Petrie, however, mentions [6] several most unusual occurrences of burnt bricks for tombs and part of the foundations of a building at Nebesheh and Defenneh, of the Nineteenth and Twentieth Dynasties, though he says that Egyptian bricks 'were very rarely fired until the Roman age'.[7]

STONE

Egypt is the home of stone working and possesses both the oldest and largest stone buildings in the world. This activity in stone on a large scale and at so early a period was due partly to the fact of the country being very rich in stone and partly to the

---

[1] Cf. G. A. Reisner, *Mycerinus*, pp. 72–73; Somers Clarke and R. Engelbach, *Ancient Egyptian Masonry*, p. 208; C. F. Nims, *Biblical Archaeologist*, XIII (1950), pp. 26–27.

[2] W. M. F. Petrie, *Kahun, Gurob and Hawara*, p. 26, Pl. IX.

[3] Carnarvon and H. Carter, *Five Years' Explorations*, p. 31, Pl. XXII; H. Carter and P. E. Newberry, *Thoutmôsis IV*, pp. 3–4; J. E. Quibell, *Yuaa and Thuiu*, p. 61.

[4] L. W. King, *History of Sumer and Akkad*, pp. 3, 21, 22, 89, 91; L. Delaporte, *Mesopotamia*, pp. 175, 177; C. L. Woolley, *Antiquaries Journal*, VII (1927), p. 387.

[5] J. Marshall, *Mohenjo-daro and the Indus Civilisation*, I, p. 15; E. J. H. Mackay, in J. Marshall, *op. cit.*, p. 266; *Journ. Royal Soc. of Arts*, LXXXII (1934), p. 212.

[6] W. M. F. Petrie, *Tanis*, II, *Nebesheh and Defenneh*, pp. 18, 19, 47.

[7] W. M. F. Petrie, *Egyptian Architecture*, p. 3.

further fact that copper tools for working it were available. The earliest examples of the use of stone for building purposes that can be dated accurately are of the First Dynasty, namely, the lining and roofing with roughly cut slabs of limestone of a number of small chambers in a tomb of that date at Saqqara;[1] the limestone portcullis 'which shows a very high standard of the mason's craftmanship' in the First Dynasty tomb of 'Hemaka' at Saqqara;[2] and a pavement of roughly dressed granite slabs in the tomb of Wedimu (Den) at Abydos.[3] Also, 'a great deal of worked limestone in large slabs' was found in the large First Dynasty mastaba of Senir at Tarkhan (about 45 miles south of Cairo),[4] and 'big limestone slabs carefully cut and well dressed' were used in a First Dynasty cemetery at Helwan.[5]

Less exactly dated, but certainly of the archaic period, are the natural blocks of undressed, or only roughly dressed, sandstone employed for walls, pavements, facing work and a tomb chamber at Hierakonpolis near Edfu in Upper Egypt[6] and the limestone lining and flooring of a protodynastic tomb near Qau, also in Upper Egypt.[7]

Of the Second Dynasty there are two inscribed limestone lintels from tombs at Saqqara;[8] a limestone room in the tomb of Khasekhemui at Abydos,[9] an inscribed red granite door jamb[10] and fragments of a similar red granite door jamb or stela[11] from a temple of the same Pharaoh at Hierakonpolis.

Of the Second or Third Dynasty are the rough limestone slabs used for roofing and for portcullises in several tombs at Saqqara.[12]

In the Third Dynasty the increased use of stone for building is very marked, especially in Lower Egypt, where it culminates in the very fine buildings discovered at Saqqara. Examples of stone work of this dynasty that may be mentioned are, in Upper Egypt, a limestone room in the tomb of Neterkhet (Djoser) at Beit Khallaf, not far from Abydos,[13] the stone of which is stated to be 'carefully dressed', and the limestone of the tomb of Sanakht[13] and of three other tombs[13] also at Beit Khallaf. In Lower Egypt there are the large blocks of granite in the unfinished pyramid at Zawyet el Aryan, between Giza and Abusir; the limestone of the pyramid of Djoser (the step pyramid) at Saqqara and its temenos wall; the adjoining limestone colonnade and temples; the pyramid complex of Sekhemkhet; the granite chamber in the step pyramid and the granite chamber in the neighbouring great tomb,[14] all of which date from the early part of the dynasty.

---

[1] J. E. Quibell, *Saqqara, 1912–1914*, pp. 3, 5.   [2] W. B. Emery, *Hemaka*, p. 6.

[3] W. M. F. Petrie, *Royal Tombs*, II, pp. 9–10, Pl. LIVa.

[4] W. M. F. Petrie, G. A. Wainwright and A. H. Gardiner, *Tarkhan, I, and Memphis*, V, p. 15.

[5] Z. Y. Saad, *Ann. Serv.*, XLI (1942), p. 408.

[6] J. E. Quibell and F. W. Green, *Hierakonpolis*, II, pp. 3–7, 14, 51.

[7] G. Brunton, *Qau and Badari*, I, pp. 14–15.

[8] J. E. Quibell, *Saqqara, 1912–1914*, p. 10.

[9] W. M. F. Petrie, *Royal Tombs*, II, p. 13, Pl. LVII.

[10] J. E. Quibell, *Hierakonpolis*, I, p. 6, Pl. II. This is in the Cairo Museum and is coarse-grained red granite and not grey granite as stated by the finders.

[11] A. Lansing, *M.M.A. Bull., Egyptian Exped. 1934–1935*, p. 44, Fig. 11.

[12] J. E. Quibell, *Saqqara, 1912–1914*, pp. 1, 3, 10, 15, 17, 29, 40, 41.

[13] J. Garstang, *Mahâsna and Bêt Khallâf*, pp. 3–15, Pls. VI, VII, XVII.

[14] C. M. Firth, J. E. Quibell and J.-P. Lauer, *Step Pyramid*; J.-P. Lauer, *Pyramide à degrés*.

The Palermo stone states that a temple of stone was erected by an unknown king of the Second Dynasty, but the remains of this have not been found.[1]

From the examples given, it becomes almost certain that the use of stone for building purposes originated in Lower Egypt in connexion with the necropolis of Memphis at Saqqara, where undoubtedly it was perfected, and since there were associations as early as the First Dynasty between Memphis and Abydos and in the Third Dynasty between Memphis and Beit Khallaf, the stone working in the south seems to have been merely a reflection of that from the north.

The principal kinds of stone employed for building in ancient Egypt were limestone, sandstone and, to a much less extent, granite with the occasional use of alabaster, basalt and quartzite, all of which may now be considered.

Limestone [2]

Limestone consists essentially of calcium carbonate (carbonate of lime), but contains varying, though usually small, proportions of other ingredients, such as silica, clay, oxide of iron and magnesium carbonate, and it differs considerably in quality and hardness.[3] It occurs extensively in Egypt, the hills bordering the Nile Valley from Cairo to a little beyond Esna, a distance of about 500 miles, being formed of this material and it occurs also sporadically from Esna to within a short distance of Aswan, for example on the west bank of the river at Faras near Silsila and on the east bank at Rangama near Kom Ombo; it is found also in other localities, as at Mex near Alexandria and in the neighbourhood of Suez.

Examples of the early use of limestone as a building material have been given already, and it continued to be employed for tombs and temples until about the middle of the Eighteenth Dynasty, when, though still occasionally used, as in the temples of Seti I [4] and Ramses II [5] at Abydos, both of the Nineteenth Dynasty, it largely gave place to sandstone. In addition to the use of limestone as a building material, a very large number of tombs of all periods were cut out of the living limestone rock.

Although limestone was quarried generally in the immediate vicinity of where it was required, the better qualities were obtained from special localities, and such quarries often are referred to in the ancient records, for example, those at Tura (Troja), Ma'sara, Ayan (Tura-Ma'sara) and Gebelein,[6] which may be seen today with the ancient inscriptions on the walls.

At Tura the inscriptions date from the Twelfth Dynasty to the Thirtieth Dynasty,[7,8]

---

[1] *A.R.*, I, 134.

[2] Cf. J. R. Harris, *Lexicographical Studies*, pp. 69–71; K. Sethe, *Bau- und Denkmalsteine*, pp. 866–73 (5–12). See also below, p. 414.

[3] Cf. H. Junker, *Giza*, I, pp. 88–90.

[4] Most of the walls are of limestone, as also the pavement and portions of the pillars in the entrance courts, but two of the walls, most of the pillars and the roof are of sandstone.

[5] Sandstone, granite and alabaster were all employed, the sandstone for pillars, the granite for door-frames and the alabaster for the sanctuary.

[6] *A.R.*, v (Index), pp. 73, 78, 87, 101, 154; K. Sethe, *Bau- und Denkmalsteine*, pp. 866–73 (5–12); J. R. Harris, *Lexicographical Studies*, pp. 69–71.

[7] *A.R.*, I, 739; II, 799, 875; W. M. F. Petrie, *History of Egypt*, I (1924), p. 192; II (1924), p. 36; III (1918), pp. 166, 375, 385.

[8] S. Birch, in H. Vyse, *Pyramids of Gizeh*, III, pp. 93–103; G. Daressy, *Ann. Serv.*, XI (1911), pp. 257–68; W. Spiegelberg, *Ann. Serv.*, VI (1905), pp. 219–33.

but there are references to the Tura quarries on the monuments as early as the Fourth Dynasty, and the stone was employed extensively at Saqqara from the Third Dynasty and at Giza from the Fourth Dynasty. In the Cairo Museum there is a letter on papyrus (No. 49623) of the Sixth Dynasty written by an officer in charge of certain Tura quarrymen. The quarries are still being worked on a large scale.

At Ma'sara the inscriptions range from the Eighteenth Dynasty to the Ptolemaic period.[1,2] The quarries are still productive. It has been found recently, when they were explored systematically and the old debris removed, that the ancient quarries are very much more extensive than it was thought. Several previously unknown inscriptions have been discovered.

At Gebelein the inscriptions are from the Nineteenth Dynasty to the Roman period.[3] The quarries are not now worked.

Other limestone quarries in which there are ancient inscriptions also are known, thus at El Bersheh there are quarries in one of which is a cartouche of the Thirtieth Dynasty;[4] in a quarry at El Amarna there is a cartouche of the Eighteenth Dynasty;[5] on the west of the Nile opposite Luxor there are small quarries in which until comparatively recently, when they were destroyed, were three inscriptions, one of the Twenty-sixth Dynasty and two of Roman date;[6] at Abydos there are two ancient quarries, one to the south and the other to the north-west, in the former of which it is stated there are cartouches, and in the latter, cut at one of the entrances, is a sacred eye; near the ancient Ptolemais there are quarries of fine-grained limestone in which are inscriptions dating from the end of the Thirtieth Dynasty to the early part of the Roman imperial epoch;[7] at Qau (Antaeopolis) there are extensive quarries, some of which have a brick causeway leading to them, the bricks of which are stamped with the cartouche [8] of Amenhotpe II (Eighteenth Dynasty). In one of the quarries there is 'a crude painting of the Romanized local deity Antaios . . .'[8] and at Beni Hasan ancient quarries extend for at least three miles along the cliffs.[9]

As an example of stone having been quarried on the spot where it was required, that for the Giza pyramids may be mentioned. The stone of which the greater part of these pyramids is built is very characteristic, being highly fossiliferous and containing innumerable nummulites, and is identical with that of the plateau on which the pyramids stand and several of the large depressions nearby are the quarries from which this stone was obtained, although being now partly buried in sand they are not easily recognizable, the hollow in which the sphinx is, for example, being one of the quarries. It should be mentioned that many years ago (in 1883) Petrie denied this and stated,[10] 'But no quarryings exist on the western side in the least adequate to yield

[1] S. Birch, in H. Vyse, Pyramids of Gizeh, III, pp. 93-103; G. Daressy, Ann. Serv., XI (1911), pp. 257-68; W. Spiegelberg, Ann. Serv., VI (1905), pp. 219-33.

[2] A.R., II, 26; W. M. F. Petrie, History of Egypt, III (1918), p. 375.

[3] A.R., III, 209; IV, 627; G. Daressy, Rec. Trav., X (1888), pp. 133 8.

[4] G. W. Fraser, in P. E. Newberry, El Bersheh, II, p. 56.

[5] W. M. F. Petrie, Tell el Amarna, p. 4.   [6] W. M. F. Petrie, Qurneh, p. 15.

[7] J. de Morgan, U. Bouriant and G. Legrain, Note sur les carrières antiques de Ptolémais, Mém. Miss., VIII, pp. 353-79.

[8] W. M. F. Petrie, Antaeopolis, pp. 15, 16.

[9] Somers Clarke and R. Engelbach, Ancient Egyptian Masonry, p. 15.

[10] W. M. F. Petrie, Pyramids and Temples of Gizeh, p. 209.

the bulk of either of the greater Pyramids; and the limestone of the western hills is different in its character to that of the Pyramid masonry, which resembles the qualities usually quarried on the eastern shore. It seems, therefore, that the whole of the stones were quarried in the cliffs of Tura and Masara and brought across to the selected site.' As Petrie wrote before any of the quarries had been uncovered it is not strange that they should have been overlooked, but it is singular that no mention is made of the very large amount of stone that was removed anciently in levelling the foundation plateau and in cutting back the rock on the north and west sides of the pyramid of Khafrē, which stone almost certainly was used in the construction of the pyramid and would have formed a not inconsiderable proportion of the whole quantity employed. Of the Menkaurē quarry Reisner says [1] '. . . the quarry south-east of the Third Pyramid, which is nearly of sufficient size to have supplied the whole', that is 'the core of the pyramid, the foundation platforms of the temples and the massive core walls', which 'were all of this stone' (i.e. the local nummulitic limestone).

The casing stones of the two larger pyramids, those of Khufu (Cheops) and Khafrē (Chephren), and the casing stone of the upper portion of the third pyramid, that of Menkaurē (Mycerinus), although limestone, were of a different and much finer-grained quality than the rest of the stone and free from fossils, as may be seen from the few blocks that remain, and, as this stone does not occur in the immediate neighbourhood, it must have been brought from elsewhere and almost certainly from the Tura quarries on the opposite side of the river, and the statements of Herodotus,[2] Diodorus,[3] Strabo[4] and Pliny[5] that the stone for the construction of the pyramids was brought across the river from quarries in the Arabian hills is true only of that for the casing. At that time, however, the casing of the first and second pyramids was intact and all that could have been seen was the Tura stone on the outside, and there would have been no indication that the stone underneath was different. The step pyramid of Saqqara, too, is built of stone quarried on the spot and was cased with a better quality of stone, probably also from Tura.

The Old Kingdom tombs and temples, for which limestone was employed, were situated mostly in the neighbourhood of the capital, Memphis, where limestone of good quality, suitable for building, carving and painting upon, was plentiful, whereas when building on a large scale shifted south in the Eighteenth and following Dynasties, immense quantities of stone were required, at first in the vicinity of Thebes, which had succeeded Memphis as the capital, and later at places still farther south.

Although limestone occurs abundantly near Thebes, it is mostly of poor quality and ill adapted for building purposes. To this there are two exceptions, already mentioned, namely, a little north of Elwat el Debban, near the Valley of the Tombs of the Kings, on the west of the Nile opposite Luxor and at Gebelein, almost midway between Luxor and Esna, in both of which places there is a comparatively small amount of better-quality stone that was worked anciently.

In consequence, therefore, of the great scarcity of good-quality limestone near Thebes, when building stone was required in large quantities, the choice was between transporting limestone from a distance or employing a substitute. Whether the

---

[1] G. A. Reisner, *Mycerinus*, p. 69.
[2] II: 8, 124. [3] I: 5. [4] XVII: I, 34. [5] XXXVI: 17.

first of the alternatives was ever adopted is uncertain, but the fine-grained limestone of the walls of the mortuary temple of Mentuhotpe at Deir el Bahari and that of the temple of Amenhotpe I at Karnak appears too good a quality to be local. At Abydos, too, the limestone used in the temples of Seti I and Ramses II respectively, which is of a particularly good quality, may not be local, although there are two ancient quarries of fairly good stone in the neighbourhood.

Sandstone [1]

Sandstone consists essentially of quartz sand derived from the disintegration of older rocks, cemented together by very small proportions of clay, calcium carbonate, oxide of iron or silica.

As already mentioned, the hills bordering the Nile valley from Cairo to near Esna are of limestone, but beyond Esna this limestone is replaced by sandstone, which in turn forms the hills on both sides of the river until near Aswan and again beyond Aswan from Kalabsha to Wadi Halfa.[2] The most northerly occurrence of sandstone is near Sabaia, between Esna and Mahamid. Sandstone also occurs at Aswan.[3]

Although not employed generally until about the middle of the Eighteenth Dynasty, sandstone was not an entirely new and untried material, as already it had been used on a small scale in the form of natural blocks of undressed or only roughly dressed material at Hierakonpolis as early as the archaic period.[4] It was employed also in the Eleventh Dynasty for the foundations, pavements, pillars, architraves, roof slabs and the walls in the hypostyle hall in the mortuary temple of Mentuhotpe at Deir el Bahari,[5] and in the Twelfth Dynasty for the now ruined columned hall of Senwosret I at Karnak,[6] and in the construction of the temple of Amenemhet III and IV at Medinet Mādi.[7] The use of sandstone on a large scale, however, began about the middle of the Eighteenth Dynasty and practically all the existing temples in Upper Egypt are of this material, for example, the following-named (the earliest of which dates from the Eighteenth Dynasty and the latest from the Roman period), Luxor,[8] Karnak, Qurna,[9] the Ramesseum,[10] Medinet Habu, Deir el Medineh, Dendera, Esna, Edfu, Kom Ombo, Philae, those in Nubia (i.e. between Aswan and Wadi Halfa) and those in the oases of the western desert.

---

[1] Cf. J. R. Harris, *Lexicographical Studies*, pp. 71–72; K. Sethe, *Bau- und Denkmalsteine*, pp. 873–6 (12–15). See also below, p. 419.

[2] From Aswan to Kalabsha, a distance of about forty miles, the hills are of granite and other igneous rock.

[3] J. Ball, *First or Aswan Cataract*, pp. 65–66.   [4] See p. 51.

[5] Somers Clarke, in E. Naville, *XIth Dyn. Temple at Deir el Bahari*, II, pp. 13–14.

[6] C. R. Lepsius, *Denkmäler*, Text, III, p. 29.

[7] A. Vogliano, *Secondo Rapporto degli Scavi . . . nella Zona di Madinet Mādi*; R. Naumann, *Mitt. Kairo*, VIII (1939), pp. 185–9. Naumann describes the stone as 'Kalksandstein'.

[8] An inscription in the limestone quarry of Gebelein states that in the reign of Nesbanebded (Smendes) of the Twenty-first Dynasty stone from the quarry was employed to repair a wall round the Luxor temple (*A.R.*, IV, 627).

[9] Limestone was used for the bottom courses of several walls and in a few other places. An inscription in the limestone quarry of Gebelein states that in the reign of Seti I stone from the quarry was employed in Seti's mortuary temple at Qurna (*A.R.*, III, 209).

[10] Limestone was employed for the columns in a side hall and for part of the pavement.

The exceptions to the general use of sandstone are the mortuary temple of Hat-shepsut at Deir el Bahari (Eighteenth Dynasty) and the temples of Seti I and Ramses II respectively at Abydos (Nineteenth Dynasty), the first being almost entirely of lime-stone [1] and the other two containing much limestone. The Cenotaph of Seti I (the Osireion) at Abydos is built largely of sandstone with an outer casing of limestone and granite pillars and architraves.[2]

In addition, however, to the exceptions just mentioned, other temples in Upper Egypt, of which now only a few remains exist, were built in part of limestone, as for instance the mortuary temple of Amenhotpe I [3] (early Eighteenth Dynasty) on the west of the Nile opposite Luxor; the temple of the same pharaoh at Karnak; the temple of Thutmose III [4] (middle Eighteenth Dynasty) situated to the north-east of the Ramesseum; the temple of Amenhotpe II [5] (middle Eighteenth Dynasty) between that of Thutmose III and the Ramesseum; the temple of Thutmose IV [5] (latter part of Eighteenth Dynasty) to the south-east of the Ramesseum and the temple of Meneptah [4] (Nineteenth Dynasty) almost midway between the Ramesseum and Medinet Habu.

The principal ancient sandstone quarries were at Silsila, which is situated on the Nile about forty miles north of Aswan between Edfu and Kom Ombo. The quarries, which are very extensive, bear inscriptions dating from the Eighteenth Dynasty down to Greek and Roman times.[6] It seems probable that the earliest inscriptions, namely those of the Eighteenth Dynasty, represent the date when the quarry was first ex-ploited, since the sandstone of the Eleventh Dynasty temple at Deir el Bahari (the principal example of the earlier use of sandstone), judging from its colour and texture, was not from these quarries. Its place of origin, however, is unknown, though sug-gestions have been made that it was from Aswan,[7] but though sandstone occurs at Aswan,[8] I have not been able to find there the particular quality used in the Mentu-hotpe temple.

Other ancient sandstone quarries are at Sirag [9] about twenty miles south of Edfu and at Qirtas, in Nubia, about twenty-five miles south of Aswan, which latter, as shown by inscriptions in the quarry, was worked from about the Thirtieth Dynasty until Roman times, chiefly for the stone used in the construction of the temples at Qirtas and the temples of Philae.[10]

---

[1] A number of architraves in the north colonnade of the middle terrace are of sandstone which is also present in the foundations of the two lower colonnades and of the south-west sup-porting wall.

[2] E. Naville, *J.E.A.*, I (1914), pp. 160–5; H. Frankfort, *Cenotaph of Seti I*, pp. 3, 10, 11, 14–18, 21, 241.

[3] Sandstone was also employed, but probably only for later additions.

[4] A considerable amount of sandstone was also employed.

[5] Probably largely sandstone.

[6] A. E. P. Weigall, *Guide to the Antiquities of Upper Egypt*, 1913, pp. 358–60; *A.R.*, II, 348, 932; III, 205, 552, 627; IV, 18, 702; W. M. F. Petrie, *History of Egypt*, III (1918), pp. 8, 119, 143, 144.

[7] Somers Clarke, in E. Naville, *XIth Dyn. Temple at Deir el Bahari*, II, p. 14.

[8] J. Ball, *First or Aswan Cataract*, pp. 65–66.

[9] W. F. Hume, *Explan. Notes to the Geol. Map of Egypt*, p. 47.

[10] J. L. Burckhardt, *Travels in Nubia*, pp. 113–16; A. E. P. Weigall, *Guide to the Antiquities of Upper Egypt*, pp. 496–7.

At El Kab much of the sandstone employed for the temples was quarried in the neighbouring hills and is of very poor quality, but that used in the temple of Thutmose III is better and was possibly obtained from elsewhere.[1]

The stone for the temples of Nubia was quarried in the immediate vicinity of where it was required, and there are small ancient quarries at Dabod,[2] Tafa[3] and Beit el Wali.[4] The Nubian sandstone has been described, and specimens analysed, by Andrew[5] and Shukri and Said.[6]

Granite[7]

Granite is the name of a large class of crystalline rocks of igneous origin, that are not homogeneous in structure like limestone and sandstone, but are composed of a number of different minerals, chiefly quartz, felspar and biotite mica, but also sometimes hornblende and occasionally augite, the abundance of the quartz constituting one of the characteristic features of granite. The principal individual minerals readily being visible to the naked eye, the rock has a granular structure, from which its name is derived.

Granite was employed for building from the early dynastic period onwards, generally as a lining material for chambers and passages and for door frames. Examples of its early use have been mentioned already,[8] but to these may be added its employment in the interior of the three large pyramids at Giza; for facing part at least of the lowest course of the pyramid of Khafrē;[9] for facing the greater part (about two-thirds) of the pyramid of Menkaurē, where a considerable portion is still in position; in the interior of the pyramid temples of both Khafrē and Menkaurē and for the construction of the small temple near the sphinx (valley temple of Khafrē), all of which are of Fourth Dynasty date. Examples of its later use are certain door-frames in many of the temples of Upper Egypt.

The use of granite in the pyramid of Khafrē is referred to by Herodotus, who says 'the lowest layer of it is of variegated Ethiopian stone'[10] and the granite facing of the pyramid of Menkaurē is mentioned by several of the classical writers, thus Herodotus states that 'as far as the half of its height it is of Ethiopian stone';[11] Diodorus says, 'The walls for fifteen stories high were of black marble like that of Thebes, the rest was of the same stone with the other pyramids';[12] Strabo writes that, 'from the

[1] Somers Clarke, *J.E.A.*, VIII (1922), pp. 20, 24, 29.
[2] A. E. P. Weigall, *Guide to the Antiquities of Upper Egypt*, p. 492.
[3] A. E. P. Weigall, *Guide to the Antiquities of Upper Egypt*, p. 501.
[4] A. E. P. Weigall, *Guide to the Antiquities of Upper Egypt*, p. 510.
[5] G. Andrew, *Bull. Inst. d'Ég.*, XIX (1937), pp. 93–115.
[6] N. M. Shukri and R. Said, *Bull. Fac. Sci. Cairo*, XXV (1947), pp. 151–68; *Bull. Inst. d'Ég.*, XXVII (1946), pp. 229–64.
[7] Cf. J. R. Harris, *Lexicographical Studies*, pp. 72–74; K. Sethe, *Bau- und Denkmalsteine*, pp. 876–82 (15–21). See also below, p. 412.
[8] See p. 51.
[9] H. Vyse (*Pyramids of Gizeh*, II, p. 115) says 'The two lower tiers, about seven or eight feet in height, have facings of granite as Herodotus has truly described.' W. M. F. Petrie (*Pyramids and Temples of Gizeh*, p. 96) states 'I have seen but one course; Vyse reports finding two courses.' I also have been able to find only one course.
[10] II: 127   [11] II: 134.   [12] I: 5.

foundation nearly as far as the middle, it is build of black stone . . . which is brought from a great distance; for it comes from the mountains of Ethiopia, and being hard and difficult to be worked, the labour is attended with great expense'[1] and Pliny states that 'it is built of Ethiopian stone'.[2]

In most instances the granite used anciently for all purposes was the coarse-grained red variety from Aswan, but grey granite (generally very dark grey, also from Aswan) was employed as well, though only to a comparatively small extent. Thus, in the First Dynasty tomb already mentioned, there is grey granite mixed with the red;[3] but the Second Dynasty temple door jamb from Hierakonpolis stated by the finder to be grey granite is coarse-grained red granite. Judging from the fragments of dark grey granite that lie about the ruins of the pyramid temple of Khafrē this stone was employed in its construction and a few blocks of dark granite are present in Khafrē's valley temple; among the red granite of the pyramid of Menkaurē, both outside and inside, there is an occasional block that is dark grey and in the temple adjoining this pyramid there is a considerable amount of both red granite and dark grey granite; dark grey granite, as well as red granite, was employed also for door frames in some of the Upper Egyptian temples and in the Cenotaph of Seti I at Abydos. Although for Egyptological purposes it is sufficient to call this grey stone 'dark grey granite', strictly it is a hornblende-biotite granite. The *syenites* of Pliny, a name first used by this writer to describe a rock quarried at Syene [4] (the ancient name for Aswan), which stone he states was employed for certain columns in the Egyptian Labyrinth,[5] almost certainly was the ordinary Aswan red granite, as Pliny explains that *syenites* had formerly been called *pyrrhopoecilon* (i.e. spotted with red). The term syenite is now, however, applied to a granitic rock, resembling in appearance dark grey granite, in which mica is partly replaced by hornblende (which gives a dark colour to the stone) and in which quartz is absent or present only in small proportion.

Granite is widely distributed in Egypt and occurs plentifully at Aswan, in the eastern desert and in Sinai and to a small extent in the western desert.

The principal ancient granite quarries are at Aswan in two localities, one about a kilometre south of the town and the other on the east side of the plateau, but other and smaller quarries also exist on the islands of Elephantine and Sehel and in a few other places.[6] Quarries at Aswan,[7] Elephantine [8] and at the First Cataract [9] are all referred to in the ancient records as early as the Sixth Dynasty, also a quarry at Ibhet,[10] which has not been identified. The use of granite for building and other purposes is mentioned constantly.

In addition to the granite of Aswan and neighbourhood, the only other granites known to have been worked anciently are the red granite of Wadi el Fawakhir[11] (a continuation of Wadi Hammamat), between Qena and Quseir, the date of the working of which is unknown, but probably late (Weigall says Roman) [12] and the

---

[1] XVII: 1, 33.   [2] XXXVI: 17.   [3] W. M. F. Petrie, *Royal Tombs*, II, p. 10.
[4] XXXVI: 13.   [5] XXXVI: 19.   [6] J. Ball, *First or Aswan Cataract*, p. 74.
[7] *A.R.*, I, 42.   [8] *A.R.*, I, 322.   [9] *A.R.*, I, 324.   [10] *A.R.*, I, 321, 322.
[11] T. Barron and W. F. Hume, *Topog. and Geol. of the Eastern Desert*, pp. 49, 118, 119, 265.
[12] A. E. P. Weigall, *Travels in the Upper Egyptian Deserts*, p. 50.

black and white granite quarried for export by the Romans at Mons Claudianus in the eastern desert.[1]

Alabaster [2]

Ordinarily alabastar means calcium sulphate (gypsum), but the material employed so extensively in ancient Egypt, which also is called alabaster, and which probably has the prior claim to the name, is an entirely distinct material of very similar appearance, but different chemical composition and consists of calcium carbonate. Geologically, Egyptian alabaster is calcite, of the type known commercially as 'onyx marble', though it is sometimes erroneously called aragonite, which is of the same composition, but of different crystalline form and different specific gravity. Whether aragonite is found in Egypt is not known, but its occurrence has not been reported and all the alabaster examined by me has been calcite.

The name alabaster, therefore, will be used in the present book as always meaning calcite, a compact crystalline form of calcium carbonate, white or yellowish white in colour, translucent in thin sections and frequently banded.

Alabaster was employed as a subsidiary building material chiefly for lining passages and rooms, particularly shrines, from early dynastic times to at least as late as the Nineteenth Dynasty, for example, possibly for a chamber in the step pyramid at Saqqara [3] (Third Dynasty); for a chamber in the valley temple of Khafrē (Fourth Dynasty); judging from the blocks lying about, in the pyramid temple of Khafrē; for the pavements of a corridor, a large court and a passage respectively in the pyramid temple of Unis at Saqqara [4] (Fifth Dynasty); for the pavement of the central part of the pyramid temple of Teti at Saqqara (Sixth Dynasty);[5] for a naos in the Mentuhotpe temple at Deir el Bahari (Eleventh Dynasty);[6] for the sanctuary of a temple of Senwosret I [7] at Karnak (Twelfth Dynasty); for the sanctuaries of the temples of Amenhotpe I,[7,8] Amenhotpe II [9] and Thutmose IV [7,10] respectively (all Eighteenth Dynasty and at Karnak); for lining a corridor leading to the sacred lake at Karnak (Eighteenth Dynasty) and for the sanctuary of the temple of Ramses II at Abydos (Nineteenth Dynasty).

Alabaster occurs in Sinai,[11] where, however, there is not any evidence of its ever having been worked, and in various localities in the desert on the east side of the Nile.

---

[1] W. F. Hume, *Geology of Egypt*, II, Part II, pp. 380–5; K. Fitzler, *Steinbrüche und Bergwerke*, pp. 94–99; G. Schweinfurth, 'Steinbrüche am Mons Claudianus', *Zeitschr. d. Gesellsch. f. Erdkunde zu Berlin*, XXXII (1897), pp. 1–22.

[2] Cf. J. R. Harris, *Lexicographical Studies*, pp. 77–78; K. Sethe, *Bau- und Denkmalsteine*, pp. 882–9 (21–28); G. Jéquier, *B.I.F.A.O.*, XIX (1922), pp. 92–102; A. Lucas, *J.E.A.*, XVI (1930), pp. 202–3. See also below, pp. 406–7.

[3] C. M. Firth, *Ann. Serv.*, XXV (1925), pp. 153–4.

[4] C. M. Firth, *Ann. Serv.*, XXX (1930), p. 186.

[5] J. E. Quibell, *Saqqara, 1907–1908*, p. 19.

[6] E. Naville, *XIth Dyn. Temple at Deir el Bahari*, I, p. 35.

[7] H. Chevrier, *Ann. Serv.*, XXVIII (1928), p. 120.

[8] H. Chevrier, *Ann. Serv.*, XXII (1922), pp. 238–40; XXIII (1923), p. 112; XXIV (1924), p. 56.

[9] H. Chevrier, *Ann. Serv.*, XXIV (1924), p. 57.

[10] H. Chevrier, *Ann. Serv.*, XXIV (1924), pp. 59–60.

[11] H. J. L. Beadnell, *Wilderness of Sinai*, p. 83.

Beginning with the most northerly of these occurrences and proceeding southwards they are situated respectively as follows, (a) in the Wadi Gerrawi near Helwan, where there is a quarry dating from the Old Kingdom;[1] (b) in the Cairo-Suez desert, where the stone was worked for a short period in modern times, but where there is no evidence of ancient working;[2] (c) in the Wadi Moathil (a branch of the Wadi Sennur), almost due east of Maghagha, where there are not any signs of ancient working, but where there was extensive quarrying in the time of Mohammed Ali;[3] (d) in the district extending from about Minia to a little south of Asiut, a distance of nearly ninety miles, where there are signs of working in many places and where the most important of the ancient quarries are situated. These, which are referred to frequently anciently, are at Hatnub, about fifteen miles east of El Amarna, and in them are inscriptions beginning in the Fourth Dynasty and continuing until the New Kingdom.[4,5,6] In one small alabaster quarry near El Amarna there are inscriptions of the Nineteenth Dynasty [5] and in another a rude relief, probably of Roman age.[6] A quarry, also in the same district, but farther south, situated in the Wadi Asiut, was worked at the beginning of the Eighteenth Dynasty and was reopened in the time of Mohammed Ali.[7]

A white translucent alabaster occurs in small amounts and is worked on a small scale for vases (often sold as ancient ones) about three miles behind Wadiyein which branches off Wadi el Muluk, on the west side of the Nile opposite Luxor. There is no evidence of ancient working.

Egyptian alabaster was known to Theophrastus (fourth to third century B.C.), Pliny (first century A.D.) and Athenaeus (second to third century A.D.). Theophrastus states [8] that alabaster was found in Egypt in the neighbourhood of Thebes, where it was dug up in large masses; Pliny writes in one place [9] that alabaster was found in the vicinity of Thebes and in another place [10] that it was obtained from Alabastron, the position of which he refers to elsewhere[11] in a very confused manner; thus after mentioning the mountains that form 'the boundaries of the province of Thebais' he says, 'On passing these we come to the towns of Mercury (i.e. probably Hermopolis), Alabastron, the town of Dogs and that of Hercules. . . .' If Alabastron were anywhere near Hermopolis it cannot have been far from Hatnub and these quarries, therefore, may have been known by repute to Pliny. Athenaeus states[12] that the Egyptians

---

[1] W. M. F. Petric and E. Mackay, *Heliopolis, Kafr Ammar and Shurafa*, pp. 38–39.

[2] T. Barron, *Topog. and Geol. of the District between Cairo and Suez*, pp. 20, 93.

[3] W. F. Hume, *Explan. Notes to the Geol. Map of Egypt*, p. 46; R. Fourtau, *Bull. Soc. khéd. géog.*, Cairo, 1900, p. 548; R. F. Burton, *Gold Mines of Midian*, 1878, p. 89.

[4] R. Anthes, *Felseninschriften von Hatnub (Unt. IX)*; *A.R.*, I, 7, 305, 690; G. W. Fraser, *P.S.B.A.*, XVI (1893–4), pp. 73–82; W. M. F. Petrie, *History of Egypt*, I (1924), pp. 45, 56, 100, 102, 114, 125, 161.

[5] W. M. F. Petrie, *Tell el Amarna*, pp. 3–4.

[6] P. Timme, *Tell El Amarna*, 1917, pp. 45–47.

[7] A. E. P. Weigall, *Ann. Serv.*, XI (1911), p. 176; W. F. Hume, *Cairo Sc. Journ.*, VI (1912), p. 72; R. Lepsius, *Discoveries in Egypt, Ethiopia and the Peninsula of Sinai in the Years 1842–1845*, pp. 112–13.

[8] *On Stones*, XV.   [9] XXXVI: 12.   [10] XXXVII: 54.

[11] V: 11.   [12] V: 26.

sometimes built walls of alabaster. The uses of alabaster for purposes other than for building will be dealt with separately.[1]

Basalt [2]

Basalt is a black,[3] heavy, compact rock, often showing tiny glittering particles: it consists of an aggregate of various minerals, which in true basalt are too fine-grained to be distinguished separately, except by means of a microscope, the coarser varieties of rock where the separate minerals can be recognized with the naked eye being dolerite. There is, however, no hard and fast dividing line between the two, a coarse-grained basalt being a fine-grained dolerite, and the material so largely employed in ancient Egypt, being relatively coarse-grained, though generally called basalt, is strictly a fine-grained dolerite. However, as the name basalt for this stone has become established so firmly in the literature of Egyptology and as it is neither misleading nor entirely wrong, it is suggested that it should be retained and it will be used in the present book.

Basalt was employed largely in the Old Kingdom as a material for pavements, thus in the Third Dynasty step pyramid at Saqqara and in the large tomb adjoining a few basalt paving blocks were found;[4] the pavement in the Fourth Dynasty pyramid temple of Khufu at Giza (all that now remains of the temple) is of basalt; also pavements of a court, a causeway, two small chambers and a small offering place in a Fifth Dynasty mortuary temple at Saqqara [5] and pavements, and possibly other parts of the building, in the mortuary temples of two Fifth Dynasty temple-pyramids at Abusir [6] (between Giza and Saqqara).

Basalt is distributed widely in Egypt and occurs at Abu Za'bal,[7] which is situated about midway between Cairo and Bilbeis; to the north-west of the Giza pyramids [7] (beyond Kirdasa in the Abu Roash area); in the Cairo-Suez desert; [8] in the Fayum; [9] a short distance to the south-east of Samalut in Upper Egypt;[10] at Aswan;[11] in the Baharia Oasis; [7] in the eastern desert and in Sinai.[7]

The basalt employed in such large quantity during the Old Kingdom in the necropolis stretching from Giza to Saqqara was probably local and all the available evidence points to the Fayum as the source. Thus, in the Fayum, within easy reach of this necropolis, there is a basalt quarry[9,12] approached by a made road, and, therefore, manifestly worked on a large scale and, near the quarry, is a small temple probably

---

[1] See pp. 406–7, 421–3.

[2] Cf. A. Lucas, *J.E.A.*, XVI (1930), pp. 203–5. See also below, p. 407.

[3] The colour is brown when the stone is weathered and partly decomposed.

[4] C. M. Firth, J. E. Quibell and J.-P. Lauer, *Step Pyramid*, I, pp. 62 (n. 1), 93.

[5] C. M. Firth, *Ann. Serv.*, XXIX (1929), pp. 65, 68.

[6] L. Borchardt, *Ne-user-rē*, pp. 7, 8, 56, 57, 142, 151; *Sahu-rē*, I, pp. 7, 15, 24, 32, 34, 37, 64, 93, 96.

[7] W. F. Hume, *Explan. Notes to the Geol. Map of Egypt*, pp. 32, 33.

[8] T. Barron, *Topog. and Geol. of the District between Cairo and Suez*, pp. 103–7.

[9] H. J. L. Beadnell, *Topog. and Geol. of the Fayum Province of Egypt*, pp. 15, 28, 34, 53, 56, 62.

[10] The information about the Samalut basalt was kindly given by Mr. O. H. Little, Director, Geological Survey, Cairo.

[11] J. Ball, *First or Aswan Cataract*, p. 88.

[12] G. Caton-Thompson and E. W. Gardner, *Desert Fayum*, pp. 5, 136–8.

of Old Kingdom date and there is no evidence of the ancient quarrying of basalt near Cairo, except in the Fayum, the present quarry at Abu Za'bal being entirely modern. Moreover, the basalt employed in the Old Kingdom is found to be more nearly like that from the Fayum than that from Abu Za'bal.

On this point Miss Caton-Thompson writes [1] 'Microscopical examination of the Fayûm basalt and a specimen from the Fifth Dynasty pavement at Saqqara shows them to be indistinguishable; and although the rock type is a common one, the presence of similar inclusions in both supports their community of origin.'

Dr. John Ball [2] writes 'I return the specimens and slides of basalt. After examining them myself and finding there was nothing apparently distinctive about the rocks from the different localities [3] I passed them to Andrew.' [4] Mr. Andrew reported as follows: 'The rock coming from the temple of the 1st Pyramid could certainly have come from the same locality as that labelled "Shed el Faras". Whether it did so is not so easy to say,' and again, '1st Pyramid rock resembles Shed el Faras.[5] But this character is quite easily met in greater degree by collecting several specimens from one locality in the basalt.'

Also during the Old Kingdom, another material, gypsum, employed for mortar and plaster in the Giza necropolis, was almost certainly procured, in part at least, from the Fayum [6] and probably certain gypsum vases found at Giza were obtained also from the Fayum.[7]

The former Controller, Department of Mines and Quarries (Sir H. Sadek Pasha), informed me that there was no evidence of any working of the Abu Roash basalt, which would have been the nearest source of supply, and that 'the quality is poor and decomposed'.[8]

Quartzite [9]

Quartzite is a hard, compact variety of sandstone that has been formed from ordinary sandstone by the deposition of crystalline quartz between the sand grains, that is to say, it is silicified sandstone; it varies considerably both in colour and in texture and may be white, yellowish or various shades of red and either fine-grained or coarse-grained.

Quartzite occurs in various localities in Egypt, notably at Gebel Ahmar,[10] which is situated close to Cairo in the north-east; between Cairo and Suez;[11] on the Bir

---

[1] Private communication. See A. Lucas, *J.E.A.*, XVI (1930), pp. 204–5.

[2] Director, Desert Survey of Egypt.

[3] The specimens were hand specimens and microscopic slides of (*a*) the Fayum basalt; (*b*) the Abu Zaabal basalt; (*c*) basalt from the pavement of the temple of the great pyramid at Giza; (*d*) basalt vase of predynastic date from Ma'adi and (*e*) basalt from Fifth Dynasty pavement at Saqqara (hand specimen only).

[4] Mr. Gerald Andrew, Department of Geology, Egyptian University, subsequently Geologist, Sudan Government.

[5] This should be Widan el Faras, i.e. the Fayum basalt.

[6] See pp. 78–79.   [7] See p. 413.   [8] Private communication.

[9] Cf. J. R. Harris, *Lexicographical Studies*, pp. 75–76; K. Sethe, *Bau- und Denkmalsteine*, pp. 889–94 (28–33). See also below, pp. 418–9.

[10] T. Barron, *Topog. and Geol. of the District between Cairo and Suez*, p. 56.

[11] T. Barron, *Topog. and Geol. of the District between Cairo and Suez*, pp. 61, 62, 103, 104.

Hammam-Moghara road [1] and at Gart Muluk [1] in the Wadi Natrun depression, both in the western desert, capping the Nubian sandstone on the east of the Nile to the north of Aswan and in Sinai.[2]

Only a few examples are known to me of the use of quartzite as a building material, namely, for the thresholds of several doorways in the pyramid temple of Teti at Saqqara (Sixth Dynasty) [3] and for lining the burial chambers in the Hawara pyramid (Twelfth Dynasty) [4] and in both the north and south pyramids at Mazghuna (Twelfth Dynasty).[5]

The Gebel Ahmar quarries are still worked and until recently there were fragmentary ancient inscriptions in them,[6] but these now no longer exist. This quarry and the stone from it are mentioned several times in the ancient records.[7] The quartzite to the north of Aswan has also been quarried extensively and in one place there is a hieroglyphic inscription, as also an ancient ramp leading down from the quarry.[8]

Quarrying

The quarrying of stone could not, and did not, begin until it was rendered possible by the advent of metal (copper) tools, when for the first time the use of stone on a large scale for building purposes became practicable. The stone used earlier for vases and other comparatively small objects had been procured from blocks that, having been detached from the cliffs by natural processes, were easily accessible, or from boulders found in the ancient dry water courses and at the sides of the river in the cataract areas, and, even after the quarrying of soft stone had become common, one at least of the hard stones, namely granite, was almost certainly obtained for a considerable period from boulders. The method of quarrying stone is inferred from the evidence still to be seen in the ancient quarries, more particularly where there are blocks only partly detached.

Quarrying almost certainly started at Saqqara and developed out of the cutting away of soft limestone rock in order to make tombs, the stone taken out at first probably being in pieces that were both too small and too irregular in shape to be of any use, but later the stone would have been cut out in large pieces that were roughly shaped and used for lining and flooring tombs excavated in the earth or sand. Still later the stone would have been taken out in larger and more regularly shaped blocks suitable for building.

The quarrying of soft stone (alabaster, limestone and sandstone) has been described by Somers Clarke and Engelbach;[9] by Petrie[10] and by Reisner.[11] It was by

---

[1] W. F. Hume, *Explan. Notes to the Geol. Map of Egypt*, p. 16.

[2] T. Barron, *Topog. and Geol. of the Peninsula of Sinai*, pp. 163, 199.

[3] J. E. Quibell, *Saqqara, 1907–1908*, p. 19.

[4] W. M. F. Petrie, *Kahun, Gurob and Hawara*, p. 16; *History of Egypt*, I (1924), p. 196.

[5] W. M. F. Petrie, G. A. Wainwright and E. Mackay, *Labyrinth, Gerzeh and Mazghuneh*, pp. 44–49, 51–54.

[6] L. Borchardt, *Z.Ä.S.*, XLVII (1910), p. 161; G. Daressy, *Ann. Serv.*, XIII (1914), pp. 43–47.

[7] *A.R.*, V (Index), pp. 78, 130.

[8] Information kindly supplied by Mr. G. W. Murray, Desert Survey of Egypt.

[9] Somers Clarke and R. Engelbach, *Ancient Egyptian Masonry*, pp. 12–22.

[10] W. M. F. Petrie, *Arts and Crafts*, p. 70; *Qurneh*, pp. 15–16; *Egyptian Architecture*, p. 26.

[11] G. A. Reisner, *Mycerinus*, pp. 69–70.

isolating a block on four sides by means of trenches cut in the rock and then detaching it from below by the action of wooden wedges or wooden beams wetted with water. The tools employed were chisels of stone and metal (the metal being copper until the Middle Kingdom when bronze was introduced and then either copper or bronze until the advent of iron), wooden mallets and stone hammers,[1] and picks of stone [2] and possibly metal. The stone was removed in steps from the top downwards.

At Beni Hasan, where the tombs are of Middle Kingdom date, Fraser found 'ancient stone chisels with which the surfaces of the walls had been dressed down. They are chipped out of the boulders which abound here, the material being a hard, fine, crystalline limestone. They appear to have been used with both hands, and not to have had any hafts.'[3]

Petrie, writing of the tombs of the same period at Qau (Antaeopolis), says [4] 'other tombs of the same period were cut into the rock by pick-work, probably by pointed stone mauls, as on all the quarry working here; this tomb was bruised out by ball hammers like the granite quarrying at Aswan'.

Carter found at Thebes, of Eighteenth Dynasty date, 'numbers of chert hammers and chisels, and also heaps of flakes, showing that they had been made on the spot. . . . They were probably used for the rougher work when hewing out the rock.'[5]

Flint implements employed in quarrying and for the cutting of rock tombs have also been described by Seton Karr,[6] and the method of cutting and decorating these tombs has been discussed in some detail by Somers Clarke [7] and Mackay.[8]

The apparently rapid development of stone working for building purposes between the early part of the First Dynasty, when stone was first employed on a small scale for tombs, and the beginning of the Third Dynasty, when the step pyramid with the adjoining temples and colonnades, which show a complete mastery of the material, were erected, is not so remarkable as might appear at first sight. Thus the period between the two was at least two centuries, and, also, the stone used was principally, though not entirely, limestone, since a small amount of granite was also used, and limestone is comparatively soft and easily worked. Further, two important fresh factors were present, namely, the development of copper tools at that particular time, and the plentiful occurrence of limestone in the neighbourhood of the capital, Memphis, where the need for something more durable than mud brick would have been felt first. These factors appear ample to account for the local development of stone working without the necessity of attributing it to foreign influences. Also, it should not be forgotten that stone working on a small scale was no new thing in Egypt, as is shown by the making of stone vessels, not only of soft stones (alabaster, breccia, limestone, marble, serpentine and steatite), but also of hard stones (basalt,

[1] Somers Clarke and R. Engelbach, *Ancient Egyptian Masonry*, p. 17; G. A. Reisner, *Mycerinus*, pp. 69, 232, 236.

[2] F. Debono, *Ann. Serv.*, XLVI (1947), pp. 265–85.

[3] G. W. Fraser, *Egypt Exploration Fund, Special Extra Report*, 'The Season's Work at Ahnas and Beni Hasan, 1890–91'.

[4] W. M. F. Petrie, *Antaeopolis*, p. 8.

[5] Carnarvon and H. Carter, *Five Years' Explorations*, p. 10.

[6] H. W. Seton Karr, *Ann. Serv.*, VI (1905), pp. 176–84.

[7] Somers Clarke, *Archaeologia*, LV (1896), pp. 21–32.

[8] E. Mackay, *J.E.A.*, VII (1921), pp. 154–68.

diorite, granite, greywacke (schist) and porphyritic rock), which was practised with great success as early as the predynastic period, and that as far back as the neolithic period, basalt vases had been made.

As already mentioned, it seems highly probable that the quarrying of hard stone from the rock mass was not practised until some considerable time after the quarrying of soft stone had become common, but that granite, the most generally used of the hard stones, was still obtained from large boulders (which are plentiful at Aswan at the present day and which have been used in recent times to supply part of the granite required for the dam) and that it was not until the Middle Kingdom and later, when objects such as huge obelisks and colossal statues were required, that the quarrying of this stone from the living rock was resorted to. The two other hard stones employed for building, namely basalt and quartzite, also may have been obtained at first from fallen or easily detached blocks.

The ancient quarrying of granite and quartzite has been studied in detail by Engelbach,[1] who concludes that the method employed for granite consisted essentially of pounding with balls of dolerite, together with the use of wedges, either of metal or wood, the slots for which were cut with a metal tool. In the case of quartzite, pounding and wedging were likewise usual, but in addition another tool, possibly some sort of metal pick, was employed.[2] The extraction of granite has also been discussed by Pillet,[3] who refers to the cutting of a small groove with mortise holes, and to the use of wedges, but maintains that the process of pounding was a stage in the preliminary dressing of the block rather than in the actual extraction. Somers Clarke [4] has described the use of plugs and heavy wedges in a modern experimental method of detaching a granite block, and also mentions the Indian technique of heating and water chilling. Whether this was ever employed by the ancient Egyptians is not known, but it seems possible that fire and water may have been used to break up the surface layers of granite in order to find a flawless piece.[5] Actual specimens of some of the tools and appliances used in quarrying and stone working and miniature models from foundation deposits have been described by Petrie [6] and others.[7]

As a rule, large monuments such as obelisks, colossal statues and sarcophagi were roughly blocked out before they left the quarry, and some were even given a preliminary dressing, lugs being sometimes left to facilitate transport.

Stone Working

The ancient methods of working stone after it had been quarried may be deduced partly from the tool marks left on objects, particularly on statues, of which a number

---

[1] R. Engelbach, *Problem of the Obelisks*, pp. 23, 26, 34, 36, 42; Somers Clarke and R. Engelbach, *Ancient Egyptian Masonry*, pp. 23–33. Cf., however, below p. 499.

[2] Cf. also A. F. R. Platt, *P.S.B.A.*, xxxi (1909), pp. 172–84.

[3] M. Pillet, *B.I.F.A.O.*, xxxvi (1936–7), pp. 71–84.

[4] Somers Clarke, *Ancient Egypt*, 1916, pp. 110–13.

[5] Cf. F. M. Barber, *Mechanical Triumphs of the Ancient Egyptians*, pp. 71 f.

[6] W. M. F. Petrie, *Tools and Weapons*, pp. 41–46.

[7] J.-P. Lauer, *Pyramide à degrés*, I, pp. 232–5; C. M. Firth, J. E. Quibell and J.-P. Lauer, *Step Pyramid*, I, pp. 124–6; G. A. Reisner, *Mycerinus*, pp. 231–2; Somers Clarke and R. Engelbach, *Ancient Egyptian Masonry*, p. 224; A. Badawy, *Ann. Serv.*, xlvii (1947), pp. 145–57.

of unfinished examples are known, and partly also from illustrations of some of the processes that are depicted on certain tomb walls. The subject has been studied by Somers Clarke,[1] Edgar,[2] Engelbach,[3] Petrie,[4] Pillet,[5] Platt,[6] Reisner [7] and others,[8] and the various stages in the production of statues have been discussed by Anthes,[9] Bille de Mot,[10] Edgar [2] and Reisner.[7]

The ancient Egyptian stone statues, particularly those in such hard materials as diorite, granite, quartzite and 'schist', have long been a source of admiration on account of their excellent workmanship, and of wonder and speculation as to the nature of the tools used. Various methods by means of which it is thought these hard stones were worked have been, and from time to time still are, described, these including the use of steel (a very frequent explanation) or of copper or bronze tools set with diamonds or other hard precious stones, and it is refreshing to read Reisner's statement that 'the technical processes used in carving hard stone statues were of the simplest sort, as must be the case when steel is not available'.[11] The principal operations were:

1. Pounding with a stone. Possibly represented in a Fifth Dynasty tomb at Saqqara,[12] in a Sixth Dynasty tomb at Deir el Gebrawi,[13] and in an Eighteenth Dynasty tomb at Thebes.[14]

2. Rubbing with stones held in the hand, probably accompanied by the use of an abrasive powder.[15] Represented in a Fifth Dynasty tomb at Saqqara [12] and in an Eighteenth Dynasty tomb at Thebes.[14] The final polishing was probably done with a fine abrasive, possibly in the form of a sludge, though Platt [16] suggests that smooth pebbles may also have been used.

3. Sawing by means of a copper blade, with the use of an abrasive powder.[17] No representations of this are known.

4. Boring by means of a tubular drill and an abrasive powder, the drill being a

---

[1] Somers Clarke, *Ancient Egypt*, 1916, pp. 110–13.

[2] C. C. Edgar, *Rec. Trav.*, XXVII (1905), pp. 137–50; *Sculptors' Studies and Unfinished Works*, pp. i–x.

[3] Somers Clarke and R. Engelbach, *Ancient Egyptian Masonry*, pp. 194, 198, 202–4.

[4] W. M. F. Petrie, *Journ. Royal Anthrop. Inst.*, XIII (1884), pp. 88–106; *Pyramids and Temples of Gizeh*, pp. 173–7; *Arts and Crafts*, pp. 69–82; *Egyptian Architecture*, pp. 27–32; *Tools and Weapons*, pp. 41–46.

[5] M. Pillet, *B.I.F.A.O.*, XXXVI (1936–7), pp. 71–84.

[6] A. F. R. Platt, *P.S.B.A.*, XXXI (1909), pp. 172–84.

[7] G. A. Reisner, *Mycerinus*, pp. 115–18, 232.

[8] F. F. Tuckett, 'Notes on Ancient Egyptian Methods of Hewing, Dressing, Sculpturing and Polishing Stone', *Proc. Clifton Antiquarian Club*, II (1893), pp. 115–35.

[9] R. Anthes, *F.u.F.*, XXIV (1948), pp. 169–73; *Mitt. Kairo*, X (1941), pp. 79–121.

[10] E. Bille de Mot, *Chronique d'Égypte*, XIII (1938), pp. 220–33.

[11] G. A. Reisner, *Mycerinus*, pp. 117–18.

[12] G. Steindorff, *Ti*, Pl. CXXXIV.

[13] N. de G. Davies, *Deir el Gebrâwi*, I, Pl. XVI.

[14] N. de G. Davies, *Rekh-mi-rē*, Pl. LX.

[15] Cf. W. C. Hayes, *Royal Sarcophagi of the XVIII Dynasty*, pp. 33–34; A. F. R. Platt, *P.S.B.A.*, XXXI (1909), pp. 172–84.

[16] A. F. R. Platt, *P.S.B.A.*, XXXI (1909), p. 183.

[17] Cf. W. M. F. Petrie, *Tools and Weapons*, pp. 43–44.

hollow tube of copper turned either by rolling between the hands or by means of a bow.[1] A tubular drill was used also for boring out stone vessels, particularly cylindrical jars,[2] and Petrie states [3] that a borer of this kind was used for 'beginning the hollowing out of the great diorite bowls' and also for 'more upright vessels', of which examples in basalt and alabaster are given. No certain representations of this are known, though it may be shown in a Fifth Dynasty tomb at Saqqara.[4]

In this connexion another form of boring tool employed for hollowing out stone vessels may be mentioned, namely, a kind of centre-bit provided with an eccentric handle and two heavy weights, the handle probably being of wood and the drill being flint, often crescent-shaped, of which numerous specimens have been found at Saqqara and elsewhere, as also a large number of holes bored with such flints, some at Abusir [5] and others in blocks of limestone of Third Dynasty date at Saqqara,[6] these latter being probably trials by apprentices learning the use of the drill. This drill is represented in various tomb scenes.

5. Drilling with a copper or stone point with an abrasive powder. In a Fifth Dynasty tomb [7] a drill is being used 'in boring a stone seal',[8] and in a Sixth Dynasty tomb the drilling of carnelian is pictured,[9] and in various other tombs a drill is shown being rotated by means of a bow for drilling beads and in another tomb for drilling some unknown object.[10]

6. Rubbing with a copper (?) point with abrasive powder. The evidence for this is doubtful. The implement is shown in an Eighteenth Dynasty tomb,[11] and on the schist triads of Menkaurē 'some of the signs . . . show slips of a sharp point'.[12]

In addition, there is evidence from reliefs of the Old Kingdom[13] that both the chisel and the adze were used in dressing statues, though it is probable that they were only employed on wood or limestone.

From the nature and position of marks left on certain monuments, Engelbach[14] has argued that the Egyptian sculptors also used an implement akin to a modern mason's pick—a metal hammer pointed at both ends and with a wooden haft. Hayes[15] thinks that some of the royal sarcophagi of the Eighteenth Dynasty were roughly dressed with such an implement, and it may also have been used for cutting wedge slots in quarrying, though none has ever been found and none is known from representations.

---

[1] The tubular drill may also have been turned by means of a weighted crank handle.

[2] G. A. Reisner, *Mycerinus,* p. 118.

[3] W. M. F. Petrie, *Journ. Royal Anthrop. Inst.,* XIII (1884), pp. 93–94.

[4] G. Steindorff, *Ti,* Pl. CXXXIV.

[5] L. Borchardt, *Ne-user-rē,* pp. 142–3, Figs. 123–4.

[6] C. M. Firth, J. E. Quibell and J.-P. Lauer, *Step Pyramid,* I, pp. 124, 126; II, Pl. XCIII.

[7] G. Steindorff, *Ti,* Pl. CXXXIII.   [8] G. A. Reisner, *Mycerinus,* p. 118.

[9] N. de G. Davies, *Deir el Gebrâwi,* I, p. 20, Pl. XIII.

[10] N. and N. de G. Davies, *Menkheperrasonb,* p. 25, Pl. XXX.

[11] N. de G. Davies, *Rekh-mi-rē,* Pl. LX.

[12] G. A. Reisner, *Mycerinus,* p. 118 (6).

[13] P. Montet, *Scènes de la vie privée,* pp. 288–95; W. S. Smith, *Sculpture and Painting,* pp. 105–6.

[14] R. Engelbach, *Ann. Serv.,* XXIX (1929), pp. 19–24. Cf. also A. F. R. Platt, *P.S.B.A.,* XXXI (1909), p. 181.

[15] W. C. Hayes, *Royal Sarcophagi of the XVIII Dynasty,* pp. 33–34.

Other similar marks have been taken to indicate the use of a pointed tool struck by a mallet, and with reference to certain unfinished works Edgar says,[1] 'When dealing with these harder stones the sculptors worked mainly with a pointed instrument or punch . . . the marks become smaller and finer as the work advances.'

'For the soft limestone, of which almost all the models are made, a different treatment was adopted, most of the work being done with the chisel instead of the punch. The saw seems to have been used sometimes in the earlier stages when large pieces were being removed from the block . . . The general form was usually given by long regular strokes of the chisel or gouge . . . The gouge, which leaves a concave mark . . . was used as well as the straight-edged chisel . . . and the claw chisel was probably known also . . . That a pointed instrument was used for soft as well as for hard stones is shown . . . On finished limestone works one often sees marks of a scraper of some sort.'

The sculptors' studies and unfinished works described by Edgar are all of such a late date that the use of iron chisels, or other iron tools, is not only possible but practically certain, as it is known that in the third century B.C. iron tools were being supplied to quarrymen.[2] Edgar says 'Almost all the objects catalogued here are of comparatively late date. The unfinished statues range from the Saïtic period to the Roman annexation . . . It is probable . . . that many of the limestone studies belong to Ptolemaic times.'

I have examined seventeen of these objects[3] made from hard stone (dolerite, greywacke [schist] and grey granite). They are in very different stages of work, and in about half of them the tool marks appear to be those of a chisel, while in other instances a pointed tool has been used.

In connexion with the working of hard stones, too much stress is usually laid upon the use of chisels,[4] and those who think that steel must have been used point out that copper and bronze chisels, no matter to what extent they have been hardened by hammering, will not cut such hard stones as diorite, granite and schist, and that they cannot be used with an abrasive powder. This is admitted freely, and chisels certainly were not employed, except for soft stones. But for the use of saws and drills, including tubular drills, there is ample evidence in the marks that remain on the stones on which they have been used.[5] Thus saw marks exist on the basalt of the pavement of the pyramid temple of Khufu;[6] on the red granite sarcophagi of Khufu and Khafrē respectively;[6] on the red granite sarcophagus of Hordjedef (Fourth Dynasty)[7] found by Reisner at Giza; on the lid of the grey granite sarcophagus of Meresankh;[8] on the back of one of the triads of Menkaurē;[9] on two unfinished alabaster statues of the same Pharaoh[10] and on blocks from the pyramid

---

[1] C. C. Edgar, *Sculptors' Studies and Unfinished Works*, pp. i–viii.

[2] J. P. Mahaffy, *Flinders Petrie Papyri*, II, p. 7.

[3] Nos. 33301–33313, 33321, 33388, 33473, 33476.

[4] Cf. e.g. H. Garland, *Cairo Sc. Journ*, VII (1913), pp. 190–2; E. S. Thomas, *op. cit.*, pp. 193–4.

[5] The evidence was first recognized and published by Petrie.

[6] W. M. F. Petrie, *Pyramids and Temples of Gizeh*, pp. 46, 84, 106.

[7] G. A. Reisner, *Mycerinus*, p. 241; Cairo Museum, No. J. 54938. Owner called Djedefher.

[8] Cairo Museum, No. J. 54935B.   [9] Cairo Museum, No. J. 46499.

[10] G. A. Reisner, *Mycerinus*, pp. 111, 116.

complex of Neuserrē.[1] The marks of tubular drills are found on a block from the
same complex,[1] which has traces of verdigris from the copper of the drill;[2] on an
alabaster statue of Menkaurē [3] and also on an unfinished statue of the same monarch;[4]
on the well-known diorite statue of Khafrē; in four different sizes in the eye sockets
of a Twelfth Dynasty statue in dark grey granite;[5] in the eye sockets of a dark grey
granite head, probably also of Middle Kingdon date;[6] on an obsidian head of Thutmose III from Karnak.[7] Tubular drills were also used for making sockets in the
granite of the pyramid temple of Menkaurē to take the ends of door-posts and for
bolts,[8] and to bore holes in granite for metal pegs,[9] and Petrie gives many additional
examples of tubular drill holes and cores.[10] I examined in the store room at Saqqara
a large drill core about 8 cm. (approx. 3 in.) in diameter, of coarse-grained red granite
with green patches on the outside from the copper of the drill, and a small drill core
about 3.2 cm. (approx. 1.25 in.) in diameter of diorite. Examples of drilling with a
copper or stone point, where the drill holes are still clearly visible and unmistakable,
exist in the nostrils, ears and corners of the mouth of an alabaster statue of Menkaurē;[11]
on a diorite bowl of Khaba (Third Dynasty);[12] and on two pieces of inscribed stone
vases (Third Dynasty) from the step pyramid at Saqqara. The inscriptions have been
described and illustrated by Gunn [13] and the objects are in the Cairo Museum, one
(Gunn's No. 4, Pl. I; Museum No. J. 55257) being part of a diorite vase and the other
(Gunn's No. 1, Pl. III; Museum No. J. 55273) being part of a vase described by Gunn
as diorite, which, however, is not diorite, but probably dolomitic limestone.

The saws and drills, except the 'centre-bit' mentioned, must have been of copper [14]
until the Middle Kingdom (about 2000 B.C.) when bronze tools were first used [15]
and then either of copper or bronze until iron came into general use,[16] and, as neither
copper nor bronze is sufficiently hard to cut such stones as basalt, diorite, granite,
quartzite and schist, a harder material than the metal was required to do the work,
which must have been used either in the form of cutting points (teeth) or as a loose
powder.

The principal advocate of fixed cutting points is Petrie, who stated in 1883 [17] that
'The material of these cutting points is yet undetermined; but only five substances

---

[1] L. Borchardt, Ne-user-rē, p. 142. [2] Cf. also G. A. Reisner, Mycerinus, p. 180.

[3] G. A. Reisner, Mycerinus, pp. 111, 116.

[4] G. A. Reisner, Mycerinus, pp. 117, 118.

[5] L. Borchardt, Statuen und Statuetten, II, No. 382; R. Engelbach, Ann. Serv., XXIX (1929), p. 21.

[6] L. Borchardt, Statuen und Statuetten, II, No. 383: R. Engelbach, Ann. Serv., XXIX (1929), p. 21.

[7] Cairo Museum, No. J. 38248.

[8] G. A. Reisner, Mycerinus, p. 86.

[9] W. M. F. Petrie and F. Ll. Griffith, Tanis, II, Nebesheh and Defenneh, p. 10.

[10] W. M. F. Petrie, Journ. Royal Anthrop. Inst., XIII (1884), pp. 88–106; Pyramids and Temples of
Gizeh, pp. 173–7; Tools and Weapons, pp. 44–45.

[11] G. A. Reisner, Mycerinus, pp. 117, 118.

[12] A. J. Arkell, J.E.A., XLIV (1958), p. 120.

[13] B. Gunn, Ann. Serv., XXVIII (1928), pp. 159, 162.

[14] The hardening of copper is discussed on pp. 213–4.

[15] For bronze and the date of its introduction into Egypt, see pp. 217–20.

[16] The use of iron in Egypt is discussed on pp. 235–43.

[17] W. M. F. Petrie, Pyramids and Temples of Gizeh, p. 173; cf. Journ. Royal Anthrop. Inst., XIII
(1884), p. 91.

are possible: beryl, topaz, chrysoberyl, corundum or sapphire, and diamond. The character of the work would certainly seem to point to diamond as being the cutting jewel, and only the considerations of its rarity in general, and its absence from Egypt, interfere with this conclusion, and render the tough uncrystallized corundum the more likely material.' In 1925, however, Petrie wrote,[1] 'The cutting of granite was done by means of jewelled saws . . . and jewelled tubular drills. What cutting points were used is unknown, but it seems impossible for corundum to do such cutting through quartz.' In 1937 Petrie stated [2] 'that a slicing tool was used, set with fixed emery points . . .'

With respect to the tubular drills, Petrie states [3] that '. . . not only did the Egyptians set cutting jewels round the edge of the drill tube . . . but . . . they also set cutting stones in the sides of the tube, both inside and out. . . .'

The hardest rock that the ancient Egyptians cut was quartz, either as quartzite (which is wholly quartz) or as quartz crystals in granite and other rocks.[4] The hardness of quartz on the Mohs scale is 7. The five stones mentioned by Petrie, as alone being possible to use for cutting the Egyptian rocks, all have a hardness greater than that of quartz, beryl being 7.5 to 8; topaz, 8; chrysoberyl, 8.5; the gem forms of corundum (ruby, sapphire), 9, and diamond, the hardest of all stones, 10.[5]

Although beryl occurs in Egypt, there is no evidence that it was known before the Greek epoch, it is highly improbable that it was ever obtained in the large quantity that would have been required had it been used for cutting hard stones. The other stones enumerated are not found in Egypt and there is neither evidence nor probability that they were used in ancient Egypt for any purpose, or even that they were known, if at all, until a very late period. The topaz (topazos) of Strabo [6] and Pliny [7] (which they state was obtained from an Island in the Red Sea) was probably the modern peridot, which has a hardness of only 6.5 and which, therefore, is much softer than topaz and too soft to cut quartz.

In my opinion, to suppose the knowledge of cutting these gem stones to form teeth and of setting them in the metal in such a manner that they would bear the strain of hard use, and to do this at the early period assigned to them, would present greater difficulties than those explained by the assumption of their employment. But were there indeed teeth such as postulated by Petrie? The evidence advanced to prove their presence is as follows:[8]

---

[1] W. M. F. Petrie, *Ancient Egyptians, Descriptive Sociology*, p. 58.

[2] W. M. F. Petrie, *Syro-Egypt*, No. 2, 1937, p. 13.

[3] W. M. F. Petrie, *Journ. Royal Anthrop. Inst.*, XIII (1884), p. 95.

[4] This refers to working on a large scale, but even on a small scale the hardest stone was quartz in the form of amethyst and rock crystal. Such stones as agate, carnelian, chalcedony, flint and jasper, which also were worked, consist of silica (of which quartz is the crystalline form) and have much the same hardness as quartz. The beryl, which is slightly harder than quartz, was not used until very late and at first it was not cut, but left in the natural (hexagonal) crystalline form.

[5] *N.B.*—The intervals in the Mohs scale are not of equal value, the diamond, for example, being so much harder than all other minerals that the difference between it and corundum is very much greater than that between any of the other minerals on the scale.

[6] XVI: 4, 6.   [7] VI: 34; XXXVII: 32.

[8] W. M. F. Petrie, *Journ. Royal Anthrop. Inst.*, XIII (1884), pp. 90, 103–4; *Pyramids and Temples of Gizeh*, pp. 173–4; *Arts and Crafts*, p. 73; *Tools and Weapons*, pp. 44–45.

(*a*) A cylindrical core of granite grooved round and round by a graving point, the grooves being continuous and forming a spiral, with in one part a single groove that may be traced five rotations round the core.

(*b*) Part of a drill hole in diorite with seventeen equidistant grooves due to the successive rotation of the same cutting point.

(*c*) Another piece of diorite with a series of grooves ploughed out to a depth of over one-hundredth of an inch at a single cut.

(*d*) Other pieces of diorite showing the regular equidistant grooves of a saw.

(*e*) Two pieces of diorite bowls with hieroglyphs incised with a very free-cutting point and neither scraped nor ground out.

But if an abrasive powder had been used with soft copper saws and drills, it is highly probable that pieces of the abrasive would have been forced into the metal, where they might have remained for some time, and any such accidental and temporary teeth would have produced the same effect as intentional and permanent ones. This possibility is not admitted by Petrie, who states [1] that 'it seems physically impossible that any particle of a loose powder could become so imbedded in a soft metal by the mere accidents of rubbing that it could bear the immense strain . . . needed to plough out a groove of any considerable depth in such a hard material as quartz'. Judging, however, from the analogy of modern 'lapping', in which a fine abrasive powder is employed with a soft metal (copper, lead or soft alloy), and some of which becomes embedded in the metal during use,[2] it is believed that in the ancient method of working some of the abrasive would have been forced into the metal, which was the softest of the three substances present (the copper, the abrasive and the stone).

In the discussion that followed Petrie's paper, Mr. (afterwards Sir) John Evans stated [3] that in his opinion the grooves were caused by the drilling tool having been a tube of soft material employed with some hard gritty substance, and that 'it was not improbable that the spiral grooves on the cores were made either in introducing the tube charged with fresh grinding material into the recess or in withdrawing it when clogged'.[4]

In Petrie's discussion of the evidences (*c*) and (*e*), the expressions used 'ploughing out one-hundredth inch thick of quartz at a single cut',[5] and 'As the lines are only one-one-hundred-and-fiftieth inch wide . . . it is evident that the cutting point must have been harder than quartz',[6] are somewhat misleading since the material referred to by Petrie was not quartz, but diorite, which is not quite so hard; and since diamond dust is used for cutting diamonds, presumably, therefore, quartz powder might be employed for cutting quartz.

In my opinion the abrasive material was a loose powder used wet, and Petrie

---

[1] W. M. F. Petrie, *Journ. Royal Anthrop. Inst.*, XIII (1884), p. 91.

[2] In certain cases the abrasive powder is rubbed into the 'lap' (a disc of soft metal) by means of a hard pebble.

[3] W. M. F. Petrie, *Journ. Royal Anthrop. Inst.*, XIII (1884), pp. 106–7.

[4] Petrie's idea of fixed cutting points is refuted by J. D. McGuire, *Study of the Primitive Methods of Drilling*, 1896; reprinted from *Report of the U.S. National Museum*, 1894, pp. 623–756 (pp. 738 f.).

[5] W. M. F. Petrie, *Journ. Royal Anthrop. Inst.*, XIII (1884), p. 90.

[6] W. M. F. Petrie, *Pyramids and Temples of Gizeh*, pp. 173–4.

states [1] that 'There is no doubt that sawing and grinding with loose powder was the general method'.

That a hard abrasive powder embedded in or used with a soft material will cut hard stones is well known. Prescott and others [2] state that the Aztecs worked granite with copper implements fed with siliceous sand, and it is said that in South America a certain tribe of Indians at one time were in the habit of drilling rock crystal by means of a shoot of the wild plantain fed with quartz sand and water.[3] Moreover, in one of the museums at Kew Gardens there is a cylinder of quartz, about two to three inches long with a hole through, which is stated to have been bored by means of 'slender strips of the skin of the stem of a species of *Alpinia* twisted rapidly between the palms of the hands, with the addition of a little fine sand',[4] which only illustrates the fact that an abrasive powder can cut a substance as hard as itself, as is proved in the case of the diamond, which as already mentioned is abraded by its own dust.

Respecting the nature of the abrasive powder there is much difference of opinion, Borchardt,[5] Hölscher,[6] Junker,[7] Petrie,[8] Vernier [9] and others maintaining that it was emery and Reisner supposing it to have been either emery [10] or pumice,[10] while I venture to suggest that it was neither, but was generally finely-ground quartz sand.

The manner of working stone depicted on certain tomb walls has been referred to already, and beyond the scenes mentioned the Egyptian records are silent on the matter. The classical writers, however, give some little information on the subject.

Theophrastus,[11] after enumerating the precious and semi-precious stones known in his day, states that 'some of the stones . . . are of so firm a texture, that they . . . are not to be cut by instruments of iron, but only by other stones', This author makes no mention of emery, but he describes pumice,[12] though he does not refer to any use of it as an abrasive.

Vitruvius [13] mentions the cutting of stone with a toothed saw, but gives no details of the operation.

Pliny devotes two chapters [14] to the cutting and polishing of stone, chiefly 'marble', and manifestly the use of an abrasive powder was well known in his day, as also the nature of the function it performed, since he says that the cutting of the stone 'though

---

[1] W. M. F. Petrie, *Arts and Crafts*, pp. 73–4.

[2] W. H. Prescott, *History of the Conquest of Mexico* (ed. J. F. Kirk), Appendix I; F. F. Tuckett, 'Notes on Ancient Egyptian Methods of Hewing, Dressing, Sculpturing and Polishing Stone', *Proc. Clifton Antiquarian Club*, II (1893), pp. 115–35, Appendix III.

[3] See discussion on Petrie's paper, *Journ. Royal Anthrop. Inst.*, XIII (1884), p. 108; also J. D. McGuire, *Study of the Primitive Methods of Drilling*.

[4] Royal Botanic Gardens, Kew, *Official Guide to the Museums of Economic Botany*, No. 2, 2nd ed., 1928, p. 49, No. 116.

[5] L. Borchardt, in F. W. von Bissing, *Das Re-Heiligtum des Königs Ne-woser-rē*, I, p. 44; *Ne-user-rē*, p. 142.

[6] U. Hölscher, *Das Grabdenkmal des Königs Chephren*, p. 78.

[7] H. Junker, *Giza*, X, pp. 82–83.

[8] W. M. F. Petrie, *Arts and Crafts*, pp. 74, 79.

[9] E. Vernier, *Bijouterie et Joaillerie*, p. 50.

[10] G. A. Reisner, *Mycerinus*, pp. 116, 117, 118, 180.

[11] *On Stones*, LXXII, LXXV–LXXVII.

[12] *On Stones*, XXXIII–XL.   [13] II: 7, 1.   [14] XXXVI: 9–10.

apparently effected by the aid of iron, is in reality effected by sand; the saw acting only by pressing upon the sand . . .' Among the materials he mentions as being employed for cutting stone are emery (sand of Naxos); 'sand' from India, Egypt and Nubia and certain stones from Cyprus and Armenia and, for putting the final polish on 'marbles', a material from Egypt (Thebaic stone) and pumice are both recommended.

Emery is an impure variety of corundum, its abrasive power depending largely upon the proportion of crystalline aluminium oxide present, but partly also on its physical condition; its hardness is about 8 and the principal constituent, other than aluminium oxide, is iron oxide. It was obtained originally from several of the islands in the Grecian archipelago, notably Naxos, but it is mined at the present day on a very large scale on the mainland of Asia Minor. Beyond statements, which have not been confirmed, that some of the sand at Aswan contains 15 per cent of emery,[1] and that emery is found in Nubia,[2] there is no evidence of its occurrence in Egypt.

Pumice is a light spongy lava with a cellular structure, composed chiefly of aluminium silicate. It is obtained principally from the Lipari islands in the Mediterranean, but may be picked up in small quantity on the northern shore of Egypt. Its hardness is $5\frac{1}{2}$ and, therefore, it could not be used to cut quartz. No evidence can be found of the use of pumice in connexion with stone working, though it may have been employed for polishing glass sculptures, and as an abrasive for cleansing the skin. A piece of Sixteenth Dynasty date, possibly for toilet use, was found at Sedment,[3] and another piece was included among cosmetics in a toilet box of Seventeenth Dynasty date;[4] two lumps of Nineteenth Dynasty date were found at Gurob[5] and some undated pieces at Coptos.[6]

In the absence of any direct positive evidence respecting the nature of the abrasive powder employed anciently in Egypt, the negative evidence may be considered and is as follows:

A few objects[7] (a plummet; a vase; a tool; three small blocks; a piece; a stick; and several hones), mostly of early date, found in Egypt, have been stated to consist of emery, but that the material is emery in any case is very doubtful, and that in several instances it is not emery has been proved.[8]

It is much more likely that any abrasive used should have been a local product, rather than an imported material, provided that a substance existed in the country capable of doing the work required, and quartz sand, which occurs in great abundance almost everywhere in Egypt, will abrade and cut diorite and quartz,[9] which were the hardest stones the ancient Egyptians worked.

If emery were the abrasive employed, this can only mean that its properties were familiar at the time of the Third and Fourth Dynasties (nearly 3000 B.C.), not only in Egypt, where stone working on a large scale was only just beginning, but also in its

---

[1] G. A. Wainwright, *Balabish*, p. 38, *n.* 3, quoting Schweinfurth.

[2] E. Quatremère, *Mémoires géographiques et historiques sur l'Égypte*, II, p. 11.

[3] W. M. F. Petrie and G. Brunton, *Sedment*, I, pp. 16, 19.

[4] W. C. Hayes, *Scepter*, II, p. 22.

[5] W. M. F. Petrie, *Illahun, Kahun and Gurob*, p. 23; *Kahun, Gurob and Hawara*, p. 38.

[6] W. M. F. Petrie, *Koptos*, p. 26.

[7] See pp. 260–1.   [8] See p. 261.   [9] See p. 43.

country of origin (Greece), where stone working was then unknown, which seems most improbable.

Whatever abrasive was employed, it must have been used on a very large scale and vast quantities of it must have been consumed, and hence it must have been very plentiful and cheap, which would hardly have been the case had it been imported.

The Egyptians had been working hard stones on a small scale for amulets, beads, mace heads, palettes, vases and other purposes for at least several hundred years before stone was employed for building and it seems reasonable to suppose that the use of sand as an abrasive would have been familiar to them [1] and that when an abrasive was required on a large scale the same material would have been employed. That sand was sometimes used as an abrasive is proved by the finding by Quibell and Green in a vase grinder's workshop of Old Kingdom date 'a quantity of sand that had been used as an abrading material'.[2] Also at the bottom of a hole made by a tubular drill in a fragment of alabaster of Third Dynasty date from the step pyramid at Saqqara [3] there was a compact mass of what was almost certainly the abrasive powder of a light green colour. The powder consisted of naturally-rounded, very fine grains of quartz sand and the colour was due to a copper compound, evidently from the drill used. Myers reports [4] the use of crushed chert or flint for boring a steatite bead.

In all discussions respecting the manner of cutting hard stones in ancient Egypt it should be remembered that the large number of workmen, the long hours worked in the day, the time occupied in the work and particularly the skill, practice and infinite patience of the workmen are all important factors that should be taken into account.

The much-debated questions of the hardening of copper [5] and of the possible use of steel at an early date [6] will be discussed in connexion with the metals.

MORTAR

The mortar employed in ancient Egypt before Graeco-Roman times was of two kinds, depending upon the nature of the construction, namely, clay for use with sun-dried bricks and gypsum for use with stone. The former is still used for sun-dried bricks at the present day and is the most suitable material for the purpose, but gypsum is not now employed as a mortar, having given place to the more recent lime-sand mixture or to the still more modern cement.

No instance of the use of lime mortar in Egypt, or of lime in any form, is known to the author as occurring before the time of Ptolemy I (323 to 285 B.C.).[7] From this period and from later periods it has, however, been found and, from the few specimens analysed,[7,8] it appears to have been, as is only to be expected, of much the same composition as the lime mortar of today.

---

[1] Possibly in the case of the harder stones, such as opaque quartz, rock crystal and greywacke ('schist'), the chippings from the roughing-out of the vase or other object may have been ground finely and used as the abrasive.

[2] J. E. Quibell and F. W. Green, *Hierakonpolis*, II, p. 17.   [3] Cairo Museum, No. J. 65402.

[4] R. Mond and O. H. Myers, *Cemeteries of Armant*, I, pp. 79, 93.

[5] See pp. 213-4.   [6] See pp. 241-2.

[7] R. Salmoni, 'Sulla Composizione di alcune antiche malte egiziane', *Atti e Memorie della Reale Accad. di Scienze . . . in Padova*, XLIX (1933), pp. 251-6.

[8] See p. 469.

The reason for preferring gypsum to lime, although limestone is very plentiful in the country, even more plentiful than gypsum and also more accessible, was doubtless owing to the scarcity of fuel, lime, as will be shown later when dealing with plaster, requiring a very much higher temperature for burning, and hence more fuel than gypsum, and it was not until the advent of the Greeks and Romans, both of whom knew lime in Europe, where gypsum is useless for outdoor work on account of the wet climate, that lime-burning was practised in Egypt.

Clay Mortar

Clay mortar is simply the ordinary Nile alluvium, consisting of clay and sand, which for use is mixed with sufficient water to bring it to the required consistency, with sometimes the addition of a little chopped straw. Early instances of the use of clay mortar occur in the step pyramid complex at Saqqara. In seven specimens of this mortar analysed by me there was a relatively high percentage of powdered limestone, though the adhesive properties were undoubtedly due to the clay, which varied in proportion from 3 per cent to 55 per cent.[1] Similar mortars have also been found at Giza.[2]

Gypsum Mortar [3]

The mortar employed in ancient Egypt for stone, as already stated, was of gypsum, which necessarily was burnt and slaked before use; in a few samples the gypsum had become dead-burnt, i.e. anhydrous.[4] In much of the stone work, however, the individual blocks were so large, and many, especially the facing stones, were dressed so truly that mortar as a binding or pointing material was not necessary and, although employed, it was largely as a cushion between the stones to prevent the edges from being damaged while they were being placed in position and as a suitable material on which the large unwieldy blocks of stone could slide and by means of which, therefore, in the absence of pulleys and cranes, they could be adjusted and placed accurately in position.

Resin Mortar

Resin apparently was employed occasionally as mortar, and Montet mentions '. . . murs cimentés avec de la résine . . .' in a building of late Persian or early Ptolemaic date at Tanis.[5]

Other Mortars

A mortar consisting of fairly pure powdered limestone and an unidentified organic adhesive (i.e. a species of gesso) was used in the enclosure wall of the unfinished pyramid of Sekhemkhet at Saqqara (Third Dynasty),[6] and a specimen of mortar

---

[1] J.-P. Lauer, Pyramide à degrés, I, pp. 210, 211, 215–17.

[2] H. Junker, Giza, I, p. 90.

[3] Cf. A. Lucas, Ann. Serv., VII (1906), pp. 4–7; H. Junker, Giza, I, p. 90.

[4] Z. Iskander, Ann. Serv., LII (1954), pp. 272–4. Cf. also J. D. S. Pendlebury, City of Akhenaten, III, pp. 243–5.

[5] P. Montet, Ann. Serv., XXXIX (1939), p. 530. Cf. also M. Pillet, Ann. Serv., XXIV (1924), p. 65.

[6] Z. Goneim, Horus Sekhemkhet, p. 36.

or plaster of Old Kingdom date from Armant was almost entirely of calcium carbonate (limestone).[1]

PLASTER

The ancient Egyptian wall plaster was similar in composition to the mortar and consisted of the same two materials, namely, clay and gypsum, and, although both kinds doubtless were employed in house decoration, the houses have largely perished; and except fragments of painted plaster found among the ruins of the palace of Amenhotpe III,[2] situated to the south of the temple of Medinet Habu, and among the ruins of the palaces and houses at El Amarna,[3] practically all the plaster that now remains is that to be found in tombs and temples. A third kind of plaster, used, not for walls, but for covering wood before gilding and painting, will be described later.[4]

Clay Plaster

The use of clay plaster dates from predynastic [5] and early dynastic [6] times. The quality of the plaster varies considerably, but in the main two principal kinds may be recognized, one coarse and generally, if not always, mixed with straw and the other, possibly limited to the Theban necropolis, of better quality, employed both with and without straw, often as a finishing coat to the coarser kind. Both qualities were usually covered with gypsum plaster in order to provide a more suitable surface for painting, a notable exception, however, being at El Amarna, where not only in the private houses, but also in the palaces, the painting was done directly on the clay plaster.

The coarse quality consists of ordinary Nile alluvium, which is essentially a mixture of clay and sand in varying proportions, with generally a small natural admixture of calcium carbonate (carbonate of lime) and occasionally a small proportion of gypsum, which latter, however, is purely accidental and has no binding property, as it has not been burnt.

The better quality is a natural mixture of clay and limestone, both in a very fine state of division, found in hollows and pockets at the foot of the hills and plateaux, from which it has been washed out by the occasional rainstorms that occur. This is still employed locally at the present day, under the name of *hîb*, as a finishing coat to sun-dried brick and to coarse clay plaster.

Gypsum Plaster

This is the characteristic wall plaster of ancient Egypt and is known from early dynastic times and no evidence whatever can be found of the use of lime before the Ptolemaic period,[7] the plaster frequently termed 'lime plaster' being always gypsum until a late date.

---

[1] R. Mond and O. H. Myers, *Cemeteries of Armant*, I, pp. 141, 142.

[2] A. E. P. Weigall, *Guide to the Antiquities of Upper Egypt*, 1913, pp. 290-1; Robb de P. Tytus, *Preliminary Report on the Re-excavation of the Palace of Amenhotep III*; G. Daressy, *Ann. Serv.*, IV (1903), pp. 165-70.

[3] T. E. Peet and C. L. Woolley, *City of Akhenaten*, I; H. Frankfort and J. D. S. Pendlebury, *City of Akhenaten*, II; J. D. S. Pendlebury, *City of Akhenaten*, III; F. G. Newton, *J.E.A.*, X (1924), pp. 289-98; H. Frankfort, *J.E.A.*, XIII (1927), pp. 209-18; *J.E.A.*, XV (1929), pp. 143-9; J. D. S. Pendlebury, *J.E.A.*, XVII (1931), pp. 233-43.

[4] See p. 354.   [5] J. E. Quibell and F. W. Green, *Hierakonpolis*, II, p. 21.

[6] W. M. F. Petrie, *Royal Tombs*, I, p. 9.   [7] See p. 74.

The great use of gypsum plaster was to provide for the walls and ceilings of houses, palaces, tombs and temples a suitable surface for painting upon. Where the wall was plastered with clay, this generally was coated with gypsum plaster, and where clay plaster was not used gypsum plaster was employed for the purpose of covering up faults and irregularities in the stone and of smoothing the surface before painting.

Defects in walls intended for relief decoration were also repaired with gypsum, which was then carved like the stone, and any faults in the reliefs themselves were made good in the same way.[1] Stone statues were occasionally surfaced or repaired with gypsum plaster,[2] the coating on the head of Nefertiti being as much as 2 cm. thick on parts of the crown.[3] The well-known portrait masks of the Amarna period were moulded in gypsum plaster,[4] and other examples of this technique are known,[5] the largest being the head of a young hippopotamus found at Memphis.[6] Gypsum was also used for a variety of other purposes, for example for covering bodies and modelling masks on bodies during the Old Kingdom,[7] for making moulds,[8] as a backing for glass inlay, and occasionally for coating basketwork.[9]

Gypsum, being a natural material, varies considerably both in colour and in composition. The colour may be white, different shades of grey, light brown, or even occasionally pink, examples of pink plaster being in the Twelfth Dynasty tomb of Imhotep at Lisht [10] and in the Eighteenth Dynasty tomb of Tutankhamūn at Thebes.[11] This latter, however, is merely a surface coloration and is adventitious, being due to chemical changes that have taken place in the iron compounds of the plaster in the course of thousands of years. When the colour is grey, this generally is owing to the presence of small particles of unburnt fuel.

Occasionally the plaster used as a finishing coat, which is white or practically white, contains a very large proportion of calcium carbonate and very little gypsum and, although this may be a poor-quality gypsum containing the calcium carbonate naturally, it may be an artificial mixture, additional calcium carbonate possibly having been added in order to produce a lighter colour in plaster that was not white enough for the purpose required. Sometimes the surface coating is so thin as to be merely a distemper or whitewash and consists essentially of calcium carbonate, which may or may not contain a trace of gypsum, which, however, is probably simply an impurity and not the binding material, since whitewash adheres fairly well to limestone and very well to clay without a binder.

---

[1] C. R. Williams, *Per-nēb*, pp. 4, 16, 19, 20; W. S. Smith, *Sculpture and Painting*, pp. 245–6; E. Mackay, *J.E.A.*, VII (1921), pp. 159–63, 166–8.

[2] Cf. H. Junker, *Giza*, V, p. 120.

[3] R. Anthes, *Nofretete*, pp. 6–7.

[4] G. Roeder, 'Lebensgrosse Tonmodelle aus einer altägyptischen Bildhauerwerkstatt', *Jahrbuch der Preussischen Kunstsammlungen*, LXII (1941), Heft 4, pp. 145–70; C. de Wit, *Statuaire de Tell el Amarna*.

[5] W. M. F. Petrie, *Arts and Crafts*, pp. 142–6.

[6] W. M. F. Petrie, E. Mackay and G. A. Wainwright, *Meydum and Memphis*, III, p. 40, Pl. XXXIX (3).

[7] Cf. H. Junker, *J.E.A.*, I (1914), p. 252.

[8] C. C. Edgar, *Greek Moulds*, pp. iii–vi.   [9] Cf. H. Junker, *Giza*, VIII, p. 54, *n.* 2.

[10] A. M. Lythgoe, *M.M.A. Bull., Egyptian Exped. 1914*, p. 16.

[11] A. Lucas, in H. Carter, *Tut-ankh-Amen*, II, p. 164 (Appendix II).

Lumps of gypsum with hieratic inscriptions, found at El Amarna,[1] were evidently specimens of plaster preparations moulded from a fluid mixture and submitted for inspection to ensure that they reached a required standard. Five examples were examined [2] and appeared to be mixtures of overburnt and slow-setting gypsum plaster and ordinary lime plaster with traces of iron oxide and sand. That the samples were, in fact, mixtures of lime and gypsum plasters is improbable, and it is more likely that they represent gypsum plasters with calcium carbonate as a natural impurity or deliberately added for greater whiteness. The overfiring of the gypsum is difficult to explain.

Gypsum occurs plentifully in Egypt in two conditions, one a rock-like formation, which is found in the Mariout region to the west of Alexandria;[3] in the district between Ismailia and Suez;[4] in the Fayum;[5] and near the Red Sea coast;[4] the other in scattered masses of loosely-aggregated crystals, which merely have to be dug up from just below the surface of the limestone desert; and it is this latter that was, and still is, used so largely for making plaster. At the present time it is worked in the vicinities of both Cairo and Alexandria and in the district stretching south from Cairo to Beni Suef, but there are small local deposits in other places, for example in the oases of the western desert.[6] As found thus, gypsum is never pure, but contains varying proportions of calcium carbonate and quartz sand, together with small amounts of other ingredients. The presence of the calcium carbonate, which is disclosed readily by chemical analysis, has led those who are not familiar with Egyptian gypsum and who only know the purer European article, to imagine that it is due to an intentional admixture with lime, which in course of time has become converted into carbonate by natural processes, as happens in the case of lime mortar. In the same manner the presence of quartz sand to those who only know of sand in this connexion as a deliberate addition to mortar and plaster is equally confusing and conveys a wrong impression. Ancient Egyptian plaster of the kind under consideration is crude gypsum that has been burnt, powdered and slaked, and any calcium carbonate and sand it contains are not artificial additions, but impurities derived from the raw material in which they occur naturally.

At what date gypsum was first used in Egypt is not known, but a white plaster employed to mend a large red pottery vessel found by Menghin and Amer in the predynastic site at Ma'adi near Cairo, which was analysed by me, was gypsum.

Some little of the gypsum mortar and much of the plaster used in the Giza pyramids and adjacent tombs and in the tombs at Saqqara are of particularly good quality, one specimen analysed by me being 99.5 per cent pure and another 97.3 per cent pure, and in view of Miss Caton-Thompson's discovery in the Fayum of an outcrop

---

[1] W. Spiegelberg, *Z.Ä.S.*, LVIII (1923), pp. 51–52; J. D. S. Pendlebury, *City of Akhenaten*, III, pp. 180–1.

[2] J. D. S. Pendlebury, *City of Akhenaten*, III, pp. 243–5. Examination by A. F. Hallimond and H. E. Cox.

[3] M. Pachundaki, *Bull. Inst. Ég.*, V (1911), pp. 36–40; W. F. Hume, *Cairo Sc. Journ.*, VI (1912), pp. 43–45.

[4] T. Barron and W. F. Hume, *Topog. and Geol. of the Eastern Desert*, pp. 192–7.

[5] H. J. L. Beadnell, *Topog. and Geol. of the Fayum Province*, pp. 77–78.

[6] J. Ball and H. J. L. Beadnell, *Baharia Oasis*, pp. 21, 49; J. Ball, *Kharga Oasis*, p. 84.

of pure gypsum that had been worked in early dynastic times,[1] it is almost certain that the better-quality gypsum employed at Giza and Saqqara was from this source.

Chemically, gypsum is calcium sulphate (sulphate of lime) containing water in intimate combination. On being heated to a temperature of about 100° C. (212° F.) gypsum loses about three-fourths of its water and forms a substance which has the property of recombining with water to produce a material that sets and finally becomes very hard. The temperature usually employed for burning gypsum varies from about 100° C. (212° F.) to about 200° C. (392° F.), but is generally kept at about 130° C. (268° F.), which is a heat readily obtained. This temperature is not sufficiently high to convert any calcium carbonate present into quicklime. The calcined material in the pure form as made in Europe is known as 'plaster of Paris'.

In order that the difference of temperature required to produce lime by burning limestone as compared with that needed to calcine gypsum may be appreciated, it may be mentioned that to convert calcium carbonate into quicklime a temperature of about 900° C. (1,652° F.) is required.

WOOD

The principal use of wood in building in ancient Egypt was for the doors, sometimes for the roofs [2] and occasionally for the columns [2] and architraves [3] of temples; for the doors and roofs of houses and in certain predynastic and early dynastic burials for roofing, flooring and lining graves.[4] In addition, certain architectural forms used in stone construction may perhaps be based on wooden originals.[5] The employment of wood as a building material, however, was not its only, nor its greatest use, and its consideration, therefore, will be deferred to a special chapter.

---

[1] G. Caton-Thompson and E. W. Gardner, *Desert Fayum*, pp. 103–23.

[2] G. A. Reisner, *Mycerinus*, pp. 40, 47, 67, 92.

[3] P. Barguet and J. Leclant, *Karnak-Nord*, IV, p. 105, *n.* 2.

[4] Cf. H. Balcz, *Mitt. Kairo*, I (1930), pp. 73–83; W. M. F. Petrie, *Egyptian Architecture*, pp. 17–21.

[5] Cf., however, A. Badawy, *Ann. Serv.*, II (1951), pp. 17–21.

Chapter VI
COSMETICS, PERFUMES AND INCENSE [1]

COSMETICS

Cosmetics are as old as vanity. In Egypt their use can be traced back almost to the earliest period from which burials have been found, and continues to the present day. Among the prescriptions in the medical papyri are several for making the hair grow, preventing the hair from going grey, removing unwanted hair, preventing wrinkles and spots, improving the skin, and preventing body odour.[2]

The ancient Egyptian cosmetics included eye-paints, face-paints and oils and solid fats (ointments), all of which are here considered.

Eye-paints

The two commonest eye-paints were malachite (a green ore of copper) and galena (a dark grey ore of lead), the former being the earlier of the two, but being ultimately largely replaced by the latter, which became the principal eye-paint of the country. Both malachite and galena are found in the graves in several conditions, namely, as fragments of the raw material, as stains on palettes and stones on which this was ground when required for use and in the prepared state (*kohl*), either as a compact mass of the finely ground material made into a paste (now dry) or more frequently as a powder. Malachite is known from the Badarian and predynastic periods [3,4] until at least the Nineteenth Dynasty,[5] while galena, although it has once been found from the Badarian period,[6] does not appear generally until a little later [4,7] but it continues until the Coptic period.[5]

The crude form of both malachite and galena was often placed in the graves in small linen or leather bags. The prepared form has been found contained in shells,[8] in segments of hollow reeds, wrapped in the leaves of plants and in small vases, sometimes reed-shaped.

---

[1] Cf. A. Lucas, *J.E.A.*, XVI (1930), pp. 41–53.

[2] Cf. H. v. Deines, H. Grapow and W. Westendorf, *Übersetzung der Medizinischen Texte* (*Grundriss* IV, i), pp. 296–304.

[3] G. Brunton, *Mostagedda*, p. 30; *Qau and Badari*, I, p. 63; G. Brunton and G. Caton-Thompson, *Badarian Civilisation*, pp. 31, 41, 85–87, 99, 102, 103, 109.

[4] W. M. F. Petrie, *Prehistoric Egypt*, p. 43; E. J. Baumgartel, *Cultures of Prehistoric Egypt*, II, pp. 57–59, 81–85, etc.

[5] A. Wiedemann, in W. M. F. Petrie, *Medum*, pp. 42, 43.

[6] G. Brunton, *Mostagedda*, pp. 54, 57.

[7] G. Brunton, *Qau and Badari*, I, pp. 13, 31, 63, 70; R. Mond and O. H. Myers, *Cemeteries of Armant*, I, p. 12.

[8] Shells were also employed as receptacles for pigment other than eye-paint.

When *kohl* is found as a mass, as distinct from a powder, this has often manifestly shrunk [1,2] and has also sometimes acquired markings from the interior of the receptacle,[1] from which it is evident that such preparations were originally in the condition of a paste, which has dried. With what the fine powder was mixed to form the paste has not been determined, though, since fatty matter is absent [1] the use either of water or gum and water seems probable. Fatty matter, however, may have been used in applying the *kohl* to the face.

The composition of the ancient Egyptian *kohl* has been examined by several authorities, including Baeyer (quoted by Ebers),[3] Virchow,[4] Fischer,[5] Wiedemann [6] (quoting Fischer's analyses), Hofmann,[7] Florence and Loret[8] (quoting all the earlier analyses and two of their own), Barthoux [9] (who examined various specimens thought to be *kohl*), Kopp,[10] Brittner,[11] and the present writer, who has analysed a large number of specimens, the results of a few of which have been published.[12] To these must be added some identifications recently referred to by Zaki Saad.[13]

The results of the above analyses, omitting those of Barthoux, which will be dealt with separately, show that the material was galena in 45 cases out of 74 (just over 60 per cent),[14] while the rest consisted respectively of oxide of manganese (10); brown ochre (7);[15] carbonate of lead (2);[16] magnetic oxide of iron (2);[17] black oxide of copper (1); sulphide of antimony (1);[18] malachite (5),[19] and chrysocolla, a greenish-blue ore of copper (1).

---

[1] A. Wiedemann, in W. M. F. Petrie, *Medum*, p. 42.

[2] Particularly noticeable in the case of dry pastes in shells.

[3] G. Ebers, *Papyrus Ebers, die Maasse und das Kapitel über die Augenkrankheiten*, pp. 207–8, 332–3.

[4] R. Virchow, *Zeitschrift für Ethnologie*, xx (1888), *Verh. Berl. Gesellsch.*, pp. 210–13, 340–1, 417–18, 577–8.

[5] X. Fischer, 'Ueber altägyptische Augenschminken', *Archiv für Pharmacie*, ccxxx (1892), pp. 9–38.

[6] A. Wiedemann, *Die Augenschminke mestem, Aegyptologische Studien* (1889); in W. M. F. Petrie, *Medum*, pp. 41–44.

[7] K. B. Hofmann, 'Ueber mesdem', *Mittheilungen des Vereines der Aerzte in Steiermark* (1894), Nos. 1–2.

[8] A. Florence and V. Loret, in J. de Morgan, *Dahchour, mars-juin 1894*, pp. 153–64.

[9] J. Barthoux, 'Les fards, pommades et couleurs dans l'antiquité', *Congrès Int. de. Géog.*, Le Caire, *Avril 1925*, IV (1926), pp. 251–67.

[10] Quoted by H. E. Winlock, *Treasure of El Lāhūn*, pp. 67, 74–75; W. C. Hayes, *Scepter*, II, p. 191.

[11] Quoted by R. Anthes, *Mitt. Kairo*, XII (1943), pp. 11–12.

[12] G. Brunton, *Qau and Badari*, I, p. 70; III, p. 34; J. E. Quibell, *Ann. Serv.*, II (1901), p. 143. Both oxide of manganese and galena, of Eleventh Dynasty date, were found by the Department of Antiquities at Kom el Hisn (delta), and these I have examined.

[13] Z. Y. Saad, *Egyptian Travel Magazine*, 58, pp. 9–10.

[14] Two with trace of sulphide of antimony and five with carbon; one mixed with gypsum to give a grey *kohl*; one analysis uncertain (possibly white lead).

[15] Including a specimen of limonite reported by Myers (R. Mond and O. H. Myers, *Cemeteries of Armant*, I, pp. 12, 141).

[16] One with trace of sulphide of antimony.

[17] One mixed with earthy matter.

[18] Of Nineteenth Dynasty date.

[19] One specimen was mixed with resin, but Florence and Loret (*op. cit.*, p. 161) contend that this was a medicinal preparation and not *kohl*.

It will be seen that only one of the specimens consisted of an antimony compound and only three others contained any antimony compound and those only a trace, manifestly present as an accidental impurity. The general idea, therefore, that ancient Egyptian *kohl*, except when it was the green malachite or chrysocolla, always either consisted of or contained antimony or an antimony compound is wrong, and hence it is most misleading to term it *stibium* (an early Latin name for sulphide of antimony, transferred later to the metal), as is sometimes done. The mistake undoubtedly arose from the fact that both the Greek στίμμι and the Latin *stibium*, which do refer to antimony compounds, are derived from the Egyptian *msdmt*, the term for eye-paint in general, and the black eye-paint in particular. However, in view of the clear evidence of the analyses, there can be no doubt that this word referred primarily to galena.[1]

Lane states [2] that the ordinary Egyptian *kohl* of his day consisted of smoke-black (soot) made by burning either a cheap kind of frankincense or the shells of almonds and that the special quality used on account of its supposed medicinal properties contained, besides carbon, a variety of other ingredients, which he enumerates, and which include lead ore, but among which there is no mention of any antimony compound. The present-day Egyptian *kohl* also consists of soot, made, according to Brunton,[3] by burning the safflower plant (*Carthamus tinctorius*), and is applied by means of a small wooden, bone, ivory or metal rod, the tip of which is moistened with water and dipped into the powder. These rods only began to appear in the Eleventh Dynasty, before which time the *kohl* was probably put on with the finger. Budge found [4] that certain specimens of modern *kohl* from the Sudan consisted of black oxide of manganese. Sonnini in 1780 said that in Egypt a mixture of blacklead (galena) and lamp black was used.[5]

Barthoux's account of the composition of ancient Egyptian *kohl* [6] is disappointing, as the dates and particulars of origin of the specimens, as well as the number of each kind examined, are omitted. Although the correctness of the analytical results is not questioned, it is probable that several of the specimens were not eye-paints and that others were not even cosmetics of any sort. The greater proportion consisted wholly or partly of galena; the rest included carbonate of lead; a compound of antimony and lead (the only one in which any antimony compound occurred); vegetable black (i.e. soot obtained by burning vegetable matter); compounds of arsenic (both with and without admixed iron pyrites, some being orange-coloured and probably none of them cosmetics) and chrysocolla. Another of the specimens Barthoux suggests may have been composed of bitumen impregnated with aromatic essences. This is described as being chestnut-brown, which is not the colour of bitumen, and apart from the improbability of bitumen having been employed for such

---

[1] Cf. J. R. Harris, *Lexicographical Studies*, pp. 174–6; F. Jonckheere, *Histoire de la Médecine*, 1952, No. 7, pp. 2 f. The point was made long ago by Wiedemann, Hofmann, Florence and Loret and others, but the error has persisted. For the Egyptian names of other substances used as eye-paint cf. J. R. Harris, *op. cit.*, pp. 176–8, 183–4 (black), 143–5 (green).

[2] E. W. Lane, *Manners and Customs of the Modern Egyptians* (Everyman's Library), p. 37.

[3] G. Brunton, *Qau and Badari*, I, p. 63.

[4] E. A. Wallis Budge, *Mummy*, 2nd ed., p. 259.

[5] C. S. Sonnini, *Travels in Upper and Lower Egypt*, trans. H. Hunter, I, p. 263.

[6] The word employed is '*fards*', which is used apparently to mean eye-paints and not cosmetics generally.

a purpose, for which it would be most unsuitable, aromatic essences as separate entities, that could be employed for impregnating other substances, were unknown to the ancient Egyptians, since to obtain them a knowledge of distillation would have been necessary, and this process was not discovered until a very late date.[1] A further specimen was rose-coloured and consisted of a mixture of common salt, sodium sulphate, haematite and organic matter, but the composition makes it doubtful whether it was a cosmetic of any sort, and it was almost certainly not an eye-paint. Wax and fatty matter occurred in several instances, but these specimens, although they may have been cosmetics, were probably not eye-paints, since all the specimens of kohl analysed by Fischer,[2] Florence and Loret,[3] and myself have been free from these substances. In a few cases, too, resin (sometimes aromatic) was present, but these also are unlikely to have been eye-paints, since all the specimens of kohl analysed by others have been free from resin. In one case it is true that a powder examined by von Baeyer consisted of malachite and resin, but Florence and Loret consider this to have been a medicament and not an eye-paint on account of the inscription on the receptacle.[4] Although resin is frequently found in graves, particularly in those of early date, close to or associated with the eye-paint materials malachite and galena, there is no evidence to show that it was used with them, and, as already mentioned, all the prepared eye-paints analysed have been free from resin, except the few specimens reported by Barthoux, and that these were indeed eye-paint needs confirmation. In view of Elliot Smith's statement [5] that the malachite and resin were ground together on the slate palettes (also frequently found in the graves), a number of experiments were made by me with specimens of ancient malachite and ancient resin and also with ancient malachite and modern resin (colophony) which were ground together to a very fine powder and applied to the face and in no instance was there any satisfactory adhesion to the skin.

The contents of a small greenish-blue glass bottle, one of about a dozen in the possession of an antiquity dealer in Cairo and probably of Roman date, analysed by me proved to be haematite (oxide of iron) in fine powder.

The materials of the early eye-paints, malachite and galena, are both products of Egypt, malachite being found in Sinai and in the eastern desert and galena near Aswan, and on the Red Sea Coast. The additional materials occasionally employed later, namely carbonate of lead, oxide of copper, ochre, magnetic oxide of iron, oxide of manganese and chrysocolla are also all local products, the only exceptions being compounds of antimony, which, so far as is known, do not occur in Egypt, but which are found in Asia Minor, Persia and possibly also in Arabia.[6]

It is known from historical texts that eye-paint was obtained in the Twelfth Dynasty from the Asiatics,[7] in the Eighteenth Dynasty from Naharin in western

---

[1] See p. 24.

[2] X. Fischer, 'Ueber altägyptische Augenschminken', Archiv für Pharmacie, ccxxx (1892), pp. 9–38.

[3] A. Florence and V. Loret, in J. de Morgan, Dahchour, mars–juin 1894, pp. 153–64.

[4] A. Florence and V. Loret, in J. de Morgan, Dahchour, mars–juin 1894, p. 161.

[5] G. Elliot Smith, In the Beginning, p. 57.

[6] R. F. Burton, Gold Mines of Midian, pp. 168, 375, 390; Land of Midian, I, pp. xxii, 194.

[7] A.R., I, p. 281, n. d.

Asia [1] and from Punt,[2] and in the Nineteenth Dynasty from Coptos.[3] Although there was no necessity for the Egyptians to import eye-paint from abroad, since all the materials employed, except the very rarely used antimony compounds, occur naturally in the country, there would not have been any difficulty in obtaining it from Asia, where the various materials also occur. The eye-paint from Coptos that so puzzled Max Müller [3] may well have been galena from the Red Sea coast, but what eye-paint could have been brought from Punt is a question not easily answered. Punt is chiefly associated with odoriferous gum-resins used as incense (which in the list of articles obtained are enumerated separately), but these are not eye-paints, though they were sometimes employed to impart a fragrance to ointments used as cosmetics. It is certainly possible, however, although it seems unlikely, that some mineral substance, not native to Punt (since none likely to have been sent to Egypt is known to occur there) may have reached Egypt by way of Punt, in the same manner as in Roman times produce from India was carried to ports on the African coast and thence transshipped to Italy. If this were so, the material referred to may have been malachite or galena, which were the principal eye-paints of ancient Egypt and both of which occur in Arabia.[4]

Lip-paint

In the Turin erotic papyrus,[5] a woman is shown in the act of painting her lips, apparently with a brush. The nature of the cosmetic used for this purpose is unknown, but it seems likely to have been a preparation of red ochre, possibly with a base of fat or oil.

Face-paints

A relief of Middle Kingdom date now in the British Museum [6] shows an Egyptian lady applying powder or rouge to her face with a pad, and this is the most reasonable explanation of certain red pigment found in graves in association with palettes [7,8] and as stains on palettes [8,9] and stones,[10] on which it was ground for use. The pigment is a naturally occurring red oxide of iron, generally termed haematite, but which would more conveniently be described as red ochre.[11] Material from a cosmetic jar

---

[1] *A.R.*, II, 501.

[2] *A.R.*, II, 265, 272.

[3] W. Max Müller, *Egyptological Researches*, II, pp. 88–89.

[4] R. F. Burton, *Gold Mines of Midian*, pp. 141, 204, 219, 228, 390 (malachite); pp. 11, 204, 390 (galena); *Land of Midian*, I, pp. xi, xxi, xxiii, 55, 66, 75, 76, 267, 269; II, p. 53 (malachite); I, pp. xxii, 266, 269; II, pp. 191, 242 (galena).

[5] W. Pleyte and F. Rossi, *Papyrus de Turin*, Pl. CXLV.

[6] I. E. S. Edwards, *J.E.A.*, XXIII (1937), p. 165, Pl. XX.

[7] C. M. Firth, *Arch. Survey of Nubia, 1910–1911*, p. 157.

[8] G. Brunton, *Mostagedda*, pp. 30, 57, 109.

[9] W. M. F. Petrie, *Prehistoric Egypt*, p. 37; W. M. F. Petrie and J. E. Quibell, *Naqada and Ballas*, p. 43; W. M. F. Petrie and E. Mackay, *Heliopolis, Kafr Ammar and Shurafa*, p. 18; G. Brunton and G. Caton-Thompson, *Badarian Civilisation*, p. 31; J. E. Quibell, *Archaic Objects*, pp. 226, 227.

[10] G. Brunton, *Qau and Badari*, I, p. 62; E. J. Baumgartel, *Cultures of Prehistoric Egypt*, II, p. 81.

[11] Red ochre, which was the only red pigment known in ancient Egypt until very late, was also much employed for painting tombs and other objects, as also by the scribes in writing, and it is found in graves, apart altogether from palettes and from any suggestion of its use in personal adornment.

of Middle Kingdom date was found by Kopp to be organic matter containing 26.8 per cent of iron oxide (red ochre). The base had probably been a vegetable or tallow grease with perhaps a little gum-resin, and the substance was evidently a form of rouge.[1] Similar cosmetics found at Helwan (First Dynasty) were composed of fatty matter mixed with red oxide of iron and calcium carbonate, with the possible addition of some volatile oil.[2]

Cleansing Cream

The contents of two out of ten large cosmetic jars found in the tomb of three princesses of the Eighteenth Dynasty were examined by H. T. Clarke and found to consist of animal or vegetable oils and lime, or possibly chalk. The substance was probably intended as a cleansing cream for the skin.[3] A somewhat similar substance, largely composed of fatty matter, wax and powdered limestone was found among refuse embalming materials of Saite or Persian date, and had evidently been used to anoint the body.[4]

Oils and Fats

As oils and fats used as cosmetics were frequently scented, except when employed by the poorer classes, they will be dealt with as perfumes.

PERFUMES

The perfumes of ancient Egypt consisted chiefly of fragrant oils and fats (ointments), the use of which is mentioned frequently in ancient texts [5] and by several of the Greek and Roman writers. That in a hot, dry climate, such as that of Egypt, oils and fats should have been applied to the skin and hair was only natural, and the practice is common in Nubia, the Sudan and other parts of Africa at the present day. The oil was of more than one kind, that used by the poorer classes, according to Strabo,[6] being castor oil, which is still used for this purpose in Nubia. Of solid fats the choice was small, being limited to animal fats.

From purely theoretical considerations alone it is exceedingly probable that fragrant substances were sometimes added to these oils and fats, not only to render them more pleasing, but also to mask the tendency of such materials to become rancid and disagreeable. Fortunately, however, it is not necessary to rely on conjecture, as there is definite evidence that such indeed was the case, as will now be shown.

The modern liquid scents and perfumes are solutions in alcohol of various odoriferous principles derived from the flowers, fruits, wood, bark, leaves or seeds of plants, but more generally from flowers. Such perfumes cannot have been known in ancient Egypt, since to produce many of them, as well as to produce the alcohol to dissolve them, a knowledge of the process of distillation is essential, and this was almost certainly not discovered until a late period, the earliest reference to it that can

---

[1] A. H. Kopp, in H. E. Winlock, *Treasure of El Lāhūn*, pp. 67, 74–75.

[2] Z. Y. Saad, *Egyptian Travel Magazine*, 58, pp. 10–11.

[3] H. T. Clarke, in H. E. Winlock, *Treasure of Three Egyptian Princesses*, pp. 53, 67.

[4] Z. Iskander, *Ann. Serv.*, LIII (1956), pp. 189–90.

[5] *A.R.*, v (Index), pp. 123, 149; A. Erman, *Literature of the Ancient Egyptians*, trans. A. M. Blackman, pp. 8, 61, 99, 102, 156, 202, 207, 209, 244, 246, 249.

[6] XVII: 2, 5.

be traced being one by Aristotle [1] in the fourth century B.C. Both Theophrastus [2] (fourth to third century B.C.) and Pliny (first century A.D.)[3] also mention distillation, and from the methods described it seems clear that the process was then in a primitive and, therefore, presumably early stage.[4]

After alcohol, the next best medium for absorbing and retaining odours is fat or oil, a fact that is largely made use of at the present day to abstract the scent from flowers, the petals of which are placed in layers of solid fat or soaked in oil, the perfume being afterwards removed by means of alcohol, in which condition it is used. This method, at least in its entirety, must have been unknown until the process of separating alcohol by distillation from fluids containing it was discovered, though a partial application of it would have been possible without alcohol, since after the fat or oil had become thoroughly impregnated with the perfume, if the exhausted petals had been picked out, strained out or otherwise removed, a scented fat or oil would have remained. A method of this kind was practised by the Greeks in the time of Theophrastus,[5] the oil most used being that from the Egyptian or Syrian *balanos* [6] (*Balanites aegyptiaca*), though olive oil and almond oil were also employed; it is described by Dioscorides [7] in connexion with oil of lilies, the Egyptian make of which he says was one of the best. A similar method was also in use by the Romans of Pliny's day,[8] various plants and plant products being left to steep in oil and then pressed, or sometimes boiled in oil. That a corresponding process was also employed in Egypt seems indicated by Pliny's enumeration of various oils among the constituents of Egyptian unguents.[9]

The method of extracting perfume from flowers and seeds or from the exhausted material of flowers, gum-resins and other fragrant substances steeped in oil was by wringing or squeezing in a cloth or sack, exactly in the same manner as the skins and stalks of grapes were pressed. This is illustrated by several representations from tomb walls, for example, one in a Middle Kingdom tomb at Beni Hasan, now detroyed, but copied by Cailliaud in 1831,[10] a relief of Saite date in the Turin Museum,[11] two others of 'neo-memphite' (i.e. Saite) date in the Louvre,[12] and a fifth, of the Ptolemaic period, in the Museum Scheurleer, Holland.[13] The perfume in each case is that extracted from lilies. A painting from a tomb of the Eighteenth Dynasty appears to show the actual preparation of perfumes or cosmetics.[14]

Egyptian perfumes are described by both Theophrastus and Pliny [15] and are mentioned by Athenaeus,[16] who calls them the best, and expensive. Theophrastus states that one was made from several ingredients, including cinnamon and myrrh [17] (the

---

[1] *Meteorologica*, I: 9, 11; II: 3.   [2] *Enquiry into Plants*, IX: 3, 1–3.

[3] XV: 7; XVI: 21–22.   [4] See pp. 24, 325.

[5] *Concerning Odours*, IV: 14.   [6] *Concerning Odours*, IV: 15, 16, 19.

[7] I: 62.   [8] XIII: 2; XV: 7.   [9] XIII: 2.

[10] F. Cailliaud, *Recherches sur les arts et métiers*, 1831, Pl. 15A.

[11] G. Farina, *Il R. Museo di Antichità di Torino, Sezione Egizia*, p. 54.

[12] G. Bénédite, *Monuments Piot*, XXV (1921–2), pp. 1–28, Pls. IV–VI.

[13] F. W. von Bissing, *Bull. van de Vereeniging tot Bevordering der Kennis van de anticke Beschaving*, IV (1939), pp. 9–14. Now in the Allard Pierson Museum, Amsterdam.

[14] W. Wreszinski, *Atlas*, I, p. 356.

[15] XIII: 2, 6.   [16] I: 66; III: 124; XII: 553.

[17] *Concerning Odours*, VI: 28, 30, 31; IX: 38; X: 42, 44; XI: 55.

other ingredients not being named) and that a certain perfumer 'had had Egyptian perfume in his shop for eight years . . . and that it was still in good case, in fact better than fresh perfume.' Pliny says that Egypt was the country best suited of all for the production of unguents, and that at one time those most esteemed in the Roman world were from Mendes, and he describes the Mendesian unguent as being of a very complex composition, consisting originally of oil of *balanus*,[1] resin and myrrh, but at a later period containing an Egyptian oil extracted from bitter almonds (*metopium*), oil of unripe olives (*omphacium*),[2] cardamoms, sweet rush, honey, wine, myrrh, seed of *balsamum*, galbanum and turpentine resin. A Mendesian unguent made from *balanos* oil, myrrh, cassia and resin is also mentioned by Dioscorides.[3] Pliny also states that the *myrobalanum*, which grew in the country of the Troglodytae, in the Thebaid and in the parts of Arabia that separate Judea from Egypt, yielded an oil particularly suitable for unguents;[4] also that Egyptian *elate*[5] or *spathe*[5] and the fruit of a palm called *adipsos*[6] were all used in making unguents; he also mentions another Egyptian unguent made from *cyprinum* which he states was an Egyptian tree[7] and which was probably henna, the flowers of which are odoriferous.

Bitter almond oil (*metopium*) is mentioned by Dioscorides,[8] but this writer also describes[9] an Egyptian ointment called *metopion*, which was made from bitter almonds, *omphakine* oil, cardamoms, *schoinos*, *kalamos*, honey, wine, myrrh, *balsamon* seed, galbanum and resin.

In connexion with henna it may be mentioned that the leaves were possibly used in ancient Egypt, much as they are today, in the form of a paste to colour the palms of the hands, the soles of the feet, the nails and the hair.[10] Thus, the Romans certainly employed henna, an Egyptian shrub, for colouring the hair,[11] and probably therefore also the Egyptians,[12] and Borchardt has pointed out that the colouring of certain Old Kingdom statues provides indirect evidence for the use of henna on the nails.[13] Maspero found flowers and leaves of henna, of uncertain but probably late date,[14] and Newberry identified twigs of henna from the Ptolemaic cemetery at Hawara.[15]

Besides the perfumes from plants already dealt with and in the absence of animal perfumes (the principal being ambergris, civet and musk), for the use of which in ancient Egypt there is no evidence, the only other likely odoriferous substances that remain for consideration are the plant products, resins and gum-resins, for the use of which to perfume oils and fats there is a certain amount of positive evidence, that may now be considered.

---

[1] See p. 331.

[2] XII: 60; XXIII: 39. The same name was also given to the juice of unripe grapes; cf. Dioscorides, I: 29.

[3] I: 72.

[4] XII: 46. The *myrobalanum* of the ancients was *Moringa aptera* or *M. oleifera*, and the oil was ben oil. See pp. 331–2.

[5] XII: 62.   [6] XII: 47.   [7] XII: 51.   [8] I: 39.   [9] I: 71.

[10] For possible evidence of the use of henna in colouring the nails and hair of mummies, see p. 310.

[11] Pliny, XXIII: 46.   [12] See p. 310.

[13] L. Borchardt, *Z.Ä.S.*, xxxv (1897), pp. 168–70.

[14] G. Schweinfurth, *Pflanzenreste*, p. 360. Cf. also L. Keimer, *Gartenpflanzen*, pp. 51–55.

[15] P. E. Newberry, in W. M. F. Petrie, *Hawara, Biahmu and Arsinoe*, p. 50.

The statement of Theophrastus that a certain Egyptian unguent contained myrrh has already been quoted, as also that of Dioscorides that one Egyptian unguent contained myrrh, galbanum and resin, and that the Mendesian unguent contained myrrh and resin, and that of Pliny that resin, turpentine resin, myrrh and galbanum entered into the composition of the Mendesian unguent, and to these may be added some slight evidence from the Egyptian records and from the tombs. Although as a rule there is little to suggest that any of the oils, fats and ointments, so frequently mentioned in the texts, were scented (there being usually either no description of the material or merely a statement of the purpose for which it was employed), there are several exceptions, namely one instance in which the 'smell of unguents' is referred to,[1] two others in which 'sweet oil of gums'[2] and two in which 'ointment of gums'[3] respectively are named and, since gums are not odoriferous, but since resins and gum-resins are even today often wrongly termed gums, the names suggest a possibility that the oil and ointment referred to may have been perfumed by means of fragrant resins or gum-resins.

From the tombs the evidence leaves much to be desired, but definite facts are gradually being accumulated. Fatty matter has often been found in graves, and this frequently possesses a strong smell,[4] but probably in no instance is the smell the original one, nor can it reasonably be called a perfume; in all the cases known to me it has always been a secondary smell due to chemical changes that have taken place in the fat, often being suggestive of rancid coconut oil and occasionally of valeric acid.[5] Very few examples of this fatty matter have been analysed, and there is no definite proof that any of the specimens were cosmetics, though in one instance this is very probable. Sometimes the fatty matter consists largely of mixed palmitic and stearic acids,[6] probably representing an original animal fat. Four specimens examined have been mixed with solid material that has not been identified,[7] but which in one instance was possibly a balsam.[8] According to Pliny,[9] however, the Roman perfumers of his day (and possibly, therefore, the Egyptian perfumers also) thought that gum or resin added to a cosmetic fixed the perfume, and it seems possible that the solid matter referred to may have been, not a fragrant resin or gum-resin added to perfume the fat, but a non-odoriferous gum or resin used to fix a perfume obtained from some other source.

Specimens of what had probably been perfumes from jars of Middle Kingdom date were examined by Kopp. One example consisted of a gum resin similar to myrrh, with small splinters of (aromatic) wood, and another was a practically pure resin, apparently akin to copal.[10] Residues from jars of ritual oil of the same date were

---

[1] A. Erman, *Literature of the Ancient Egyptians*, trans. A. M. Blackman, p. 156.

[2] *A.R.*, IV, 497, 498.   [3] *A.R.*, IV. 476, 477.

[4] W. M. F. Petrie, *Royal Tombs*, I, p. 14; G. A. Wainwright, *Balabish*, p. 14; W. M. F. Petrie and J. E. Quibell, *Naqada and Ballas*, pp. 27, 39, 40.

[5] See Chapter XIII, Oils, Fats and Waxes.   [6] See p. 328.

[7] A. Lucas, in H. Carter, *Tut-ankh-Amen*, II, pp. 176, 177 (Appendix II). These included the specimen examined by Chapman and Plenderleith and previously by me, together with three apparently somewhat similar specimens examined by me.

[8] A. C. Chapman and H. J. Plenderleith, *Journ. Chem. Soc.*, CXXIX (1926), pp. 2614–19; in H. Carter, *Tut-ankh-Amen*, II, pp. 206–10 (Appendix IV).

[9] XIII: 2.   [10] A. H. Kopp, in H. E. Winlock, *Treasure of El Lāhūn*, pp. 67, 74–75.

also analysed and found to be resins or gum resins, in one case similar to frankincense.[1] Another lump of what may have been perfume, also of Middle Kingdom date, examined by Berthelot,[2] appeared to be a coniferous resin, while a sample of liquid from a small jar of uncertain date, examined by Pollard,[3] probably consisted of an infusion of some plant containing a volatile aromatic oil, and had possibly been employed as a perfume or toilet preparation.

Five specimens of material, all very much alike, from different compartments of a toilet box of unknown date, examined by Gowland, gave results from which he concluded that the material consisted of beeswax mixed with an aromatic resin and a small proportion of vegetable oil.[4] A similar substance from a cosmetic jar of New Kingdom date, analysed by Lijnst Zwikker, was also found to be a mixture of beeswax and resin,[5] and Zwikker has suggested that both it and the specimens examined by Gowland may have been propolis.[6] The purpose of these preparations is uncertain, though it is possible that they were employed for fixing the hair.

According to Dioscorides, the Egyptians knew the root of the iris as a perfume; [7] he says, too, that Balsamon (Balsamodendron opobalsamum) grew in a certain valley in Judea (the Jordan Valley) and in Egypt.[8] This is probably the modern Mecca balsam, but that it ever grew in Egypt is most unlikely. Schweinfurth, however, states that it grew in south Nubia.[9] The incense Kyphi used in ancient Egypt, of which so much has been written, was a very composite material. Plutarch [10] says that it consisted of sixteen ingredients, which agrees with the Egyptian texts, but Dioscorides [11] gives only ten. Various attempts have been made to identify the ingredients,[12] but the precise nature of several of them remains uncertain.

Eight specimens of materials of unknown date, thought to be perfumes, examined by Reutter, are stated to have consisted generally of a mixture of all or most of the following named substances: storax, incense, myrrh, turpentine resins, bitumen of Judea perfumed with henna, aromatic vegetable material mixed with palm wine or the extract of certain fruits (such as cassia or tamarind) and grape wine.[13] These analyses were made on very small quantities of materials (from 0.498 gram to 2.695 grams), and the conclusions are much too definite for the chemical results obtained. Thus, that a very minute residue of black material, suggestive of bitumen and containing sulphur, was obtained from each specimen is not questioned, but the evidence is not sufficient to prove that this was bitumen of Judea.[14] Such a residue is not infrequent in the case of organic substances of the nature of those examined, especially

---

[1] A. H. Kopp, in H. E. Winlock, Treasure of El Lāhūn, p. 75.

[2] M. Berthelot, Ann. Serv., II (1901), p. 161.

[3] W. B. Pollard, Ann. Serv., XIII (1914), pp. 253–4.

[4] W. Gowland, P.S.B.A., XX (1898), pp. 268–9.

[5] J. J. Lijnst Zwikker, Oud. Med. N.R., XXIV (1943), pp. 97–105. Zwikker found no trace of resin in five other specimens he examined.

[6] Cf. M. M. Mercier, Mémoires de la Société nationale des Antiquaires de France, 9ᵉ Sér., II (1951), pp. 127–60.

[7] I: I.   [8] I: 18.   [9] G. A. Wainwright, Balabish, p. 14, n. 2.

[10] Plutarch, De Iside et Osiride, § 80.   [11] I: 24.

[12] V. Loret, Le Kyphi, parfum sacré des anciens Égyptiens; L. Reutter, Bull. de la Soc. fr. d'histoire de la médecine, XII (1913), pp. 167–75.

[13] L. Reutter, Ann. Serv., XIII (1914), pp. 49–78.   [14] See pp. 304–5

when they are several thousands of years old. That bitumen was added to perfumes and in such very small proportions as the black residue represented is not only not warranted by the evidence, but is most improbable. The correctness, too, of the identification of so many different substances in the one mixture, particularly when dealing with such small quantities as were examined, needs confirmation.[1]

INCENSE

Since the word incense (Latin *incendere*, to burn or kindle) has the same literal meaning as the word perfume, which is the aroma given off with the smoke (*per fumum*) of any odoriferous substance when burned, incense, therefore, should be included in any description of ancient Egyptian perfumes.

That incense was employed in ancient Egypt there can be no doubt. Both incense [2] and incense burners (censers) [3] are mentioned in the ancient records, and the offering of incense is shown in the illustrations to the Book of the Dead and is one of the commonest subjects pictured in temples and tombs, and incense [4] and incense burners [5] have been found in graves.

At what date incense was first used in Egypt is uncertain, but the earliest references that can be traced are of the Fifth [6] and Sixth [7] Dynasties respectively, and an incense burner of the Fifth Dynasty [8] has recently been discovered. The earliest certain incense of which I have any knowledge is from the end of the Eighteenth Dynasty, which was in the shape of small balls similar to those so frequently depicted on monuments.[9] Incense of the Ptolemaic period from the graves of the priests of Philae found by Reisner was also partly in the form of balls and partly as discs.[10] It is recorded, too, that incense was among the foundation deposits of the tomb of Ahmose I,[11] but that this was prepared incense, such as that just mentioned, needs confirmation. It is described as being in 'pieces' and is much more likely to have been the dark brown resin, lumps of which so frequently occur in graves, particularly, but not exclusively, in those of early date, and although it may have been incense, this is not certain. Two small balls of incense from the Graeco-Roman cemetery at Hawara are in the Kew Museum.[12]

---

[1] See p. 318. Cf. also R. J. Forbes, *Studies in Ancient Technology*, III, p. 2.

[2] *A.R.*, v (Index), p. 134; A. Erman, *Literature of the Ancient Egyptians*, trans. A. M. Blackman, pp. 28, 33, 34, 40, 91, 102, 103, 105, 133, 209, 235, 239, 247, 287, 293.

[3] *A.R.*, v (Index), p. 113.

[4] E. R. Ayrton, C. T. Currelly and A. E. P. Weigall, *Abydos*, III, p. 34; A. Lucas, in H. Carter, *Tut-ankh-Amen*, II, p. 184 (Appendix II); III, p. 181 (Appendix II); G. A. Reisner, *Arch. Survey of Nubia, 1907–1908*, I, p. 85.

[5] G. Brunton, *Qau and Badari*, I, p. 35; II, p. 6, Pl. LXXXVIII, 98 d; G. A. Reisner, *Arch. Survey of Nubia, 1907–1908*, I, pp. 78, 82, 83, 85, 86, 87, 89, 90, 91, 92; C. M. Firth, *Arch. Survey of Nubia, 1909–1910*, p. 112; *1910–1911*, pp. 52, 53, 57, 59, 60, 61, 65, 66, 73, 78, 199; W. M. F. Petrie, *Dendereh*, p. 34; H. Frankfort, *J.E.A.*, XVI (1930), p. 217; G. Brunton, *Mostagedda*, p. 124.

[6] *A.R.*, I, 161.

[7] *A.R.*, I, 336, 369.

[8] H. Frankfort, *J.E.A.*, XVI (1930), p. 217.

[9] A. Lucas, in H. Carter, *Tut-ankh-Amen*, II, p. 184 (Appendix II); III, p. 181 (Appendix II).

[10] G. A. Reisner, *Arch. Survey of Nubia, 1907–1908*, I, p. 85.

[11] E. R. Ayrton, C. T. Currelly and A. E. P. Weigall, *Abydos*, III, p. 34.

[12] Museum No. 1, No. 155/1888.

The two best known and most important incense materials are frankincense and myrrh, which may now be described.

Frankincense (Olibanum)

This has been regarded from a very early period, and is still regarded, as true or genuine incense. It is a fragrant gum-resin occurring in the form of large tears, generally of a light yellowish-brown colour, though the purer varieties are almost colourless or of a slight greenish tint.[1] It is translucent when fresh, but after transport (which is necessarily the condition in which it comes into commerce) it becomes covered with its own fine dust, produced by friction between the pieces, and the outside is then semi-opaque. Most other incense materials are more definitely coloured, many of them being dark yellow, dark yellowish-red, yellowish-brown, or, in a few cases, grey or black. The white incense, therefore, mentioned in the Papyrus Harris [2] (Twentieth Dynasty) suggests frankincense, since this is more nearly white than any other incense material. Pliny states that whiteness was one of the features whereby a good quality of frankincense (Latin, *thus*) might be recognized,[3] and its name in Hebrew, Greek and Arabic signifies milk-white. The Egyptian word *sntr*,[4] generally translated 'incense', is thought by Steuer [5] to have referred specifically to frankincense, at least during the early part of the Eighteenth Dynasty (reign of Hatshepsut), though Loret [6] prefers to regard it as turpentine resin (from *Pistachia terebinthus*).

Frankincense is yielded by certain small trees of the genus *Boswellia*, growing principally in Somaliland and southern Arabia. A variety of frankincense, however, is obtained from *Commiphora pedunculata*, which grows in the eastern Sudan near Gallabat [7] and also in the adjoining parts of Abyssinia. The statements in ancient texts, therefore, that 'incense' reached Egypt from Negro tribes in the Sixth Dynasty [8] and from Punt in the Eighteenth [9] and Twentieth [10] Dynasties in no way conflict with its having been frankincense, since Punt (whether Somaliland or southern Arabia) is the home of frankincense, while the Negro tribes dwelt to the south of Egypt, and a product of Punt or of the eastern Sudan might easily have passed through their country on its way to Egypt. Even the incense obtained from Retenu,[11] Djahi[12] and Naharin [13] in the Eighteenth Dynasty may have been, at least in part, frankincense, since there would not have been any great difficulty in a product of southern Arabia reaching western Asia, though, on the other hand, this source suggests some other kind of incense material.

Pliny quotes King Juba for the statement that the frankincense tree (*thus*) grew in Carmania and Egypt, 'where' (apparently Egypt is meant) it was introduced by the Ptolemies,[14] but in another place [15] he says that it was ladanum that was found

---

[1] Bertram Thomas, *Arabia Felix*, p. 122; R. H. Kiernan, *The Unveiling of Arabia*, 1937, p. 213.

[2] *A.R.*, IV, 233, 239, 299, 344, 376.

[3] XII: 32.   [4] *Wb.* IV. 180.18–181.17.

[5] R. O. Steuer, *Wohlriechende Natron.*   [6] V. Loret, *Résine de Térébinthe.*

[7] Through the courtesy of the District Commissioner, Gallabat, I have been able to obtain some of this incense for examination. There are specimens of it in the Imperial Institute Museum, London.

[8] *A.R.*, I, 336, 369.   [9] *A.R.*, II, 265.   [10] *A.R.*, IV, 130.

[11] *A.R.*, II, 447, 472, 473, 491, 518, 525, 616.   [12] *A.R.*, II, 462, 509, 510, 519.

[13] *A.R.*, II, 482.   [14] XII: 31.   [15] XII: 37.

originally in Carmania, and that was planted by order of the Ptolemies 'in the parts beyond Egypt'.

The trees brought by Hatshepsut's expedition from Punt, which are depicted on the walls of the queen's mortuary temple at Deir el Bahari, are termed myrrh by Breasted [1] and frankincense by Naville [2] and are stated by Schoff [3] to be *Boswellia Carteri*, the frankincense tree of Dhofar in southern Arabia, though Steuer [4] insists that they are in fact myrrh. Representations of about thirty trees, or parts of trees, still exist on the walls of the temple, two forms being shown, one having luxuriant foliage and the other being quite bare, but whether they are the same tree depicted differently or at different seasons of the year, or whether they are two entirely different trees there is nothing to indicate. In any case, however, they are drawn in so conventional a manner that there cannot be any certainty about their identity. Schoff takes note only of the trees with foliage (which are those usually copied) ignoring altogether those without foliage, and says that the rich foliage cannot be meant to represent 'the bare, thorny, trifolite, but almost leafless myrrh tree, nor the almost equally leafless varieties of Somaliland frankincense'. It is possible, however, that the trees without foliage may be intended for one of these, and Steuer maintains that both the leafless trees and those with foliage represent myrrh trees shown in different conditions.[5]

Among the imports into Egypt in the Roman period on which duty was levied was frankincense [6] (both African and Arabian), and Pliny states [7] that this material was prepared for sale (presumably by cleaning and sorting) at Alexandria.

Lane says [8] that the Egyptian women of his day chewed frankincense in order to perfume their breath, which is still a custom.

The incense from the tomb of Tutankhamūn already mentioned, which has been examined by me, is possibly frankincense. It is of a light yellowish-brown colour, brittle, slightly resinous-looking, burns with a smoky flame, giving off a pleasant aromatic odour and has a solubility of approximately 80 per cent in alcohol and 20 per cent in water and is therefore a gum-resin and so cannot be ladanum, Mecca balsam or storax, and the colour is not that of myrrh, bdellium or galbanum, and altogether it is very suggestive of frankincense that has been powdered and made into balls.[9]

Myrrh [10]

Myrrh, like frankincense, is a fragrant gum-resin and is obtained from the same countries as frankincense, namely, Somaliland and southern Arabia. It is derived from various species of *Balsamodendron* and *Commiphora*, and occurs in the form of yellow-

---

[1] *A.R.*, II, 264, 265, 272, 288.

[2] E. Naville, *Temple of Deir el Bahari*, III, p. 12.

[3] H. Schoff, *The Periplus of the Erythraean Sea*, p. 218.

[4] R. O. Steuer, *Myrrhe und Stakte; J.A.O.S.*, LXIII (1943), pp. 279–84.

[5] R. O. Steuer, *J.A.O.S.*, LXIII (1943), pp. 279–84.

[6] H. Schoff, *The Periplus of the Erythraean Sea*, p. 289.   [7] XII: 32.

[8] E. W. Lane, *Manners and Customs of the Modern Egyptians* (Everyman's Library), p. 194.

[9] A. Lucas, in H. Carter, *Tut-ankh-Amen*, III, pp. 181–2 (Appendix II).

[10] Cf. R. O. Steuer, *Myrrhe und Stakte*; G. A. Wainwright, *J.E.A.*, XXI (1935), pp. 254–5 (review of Steuer); A. Lucas, *J.E.A.*, XXIII (1937), pp. 27–33; R. O. Steuer, *J.A.O.S.*, LXIII (1943), pp. 279–84.

ish-red masses of agglutinated tears, often covered with its own fine dust; it is never white or green and so cannot be either the white [1] or 'green' [2] incense referred to in Egyptian texts. In Breasted's translations it is stated that myrrh was obtained from Punt (Fifth,[3] Eleventh,[4] Eighteenth,[5] Twentieth [6] and Twenty-fifth [7] Dynasties) and from Genebteyew [8] (Eighteenth Dynasty), which is in agreement with its known origin. Even the receipt of myrrh from Retenu [9] in western Asia (Eighteenth Dynasty) is not impossible, since it might readily have reached Retenu from Arabia. The Egyptian word translated 'myrrh' is ʿntyw,[10] which has, however, been interpreted as frankincense by some, and by others as a general term embracing several different aromatic resins. The large red lumps of ʿntyw shown in the Deir el Bahari reliefs are certainly suggestive of myrrh,[11] and Steuer has collected evidence to show that ʿntyw was myrrh, perhaps a special variety, and that mḏt, the oil prepared from it, was stacte.[12] On the other hand, a Ptolemaic text at Edfu mentions several different species of ʿntyw, some of them identified by Ebbell,[13] which would imply that in the Graeco-Roman period at least the word had a somewhat wider range of meaning.

Theophrastus, Dioscorides and Pliny have already been quoted for the statements that myrrh entered into the composition of certain Egyptian unguents, and Plutarch refers to the use of myrrh as incense in Egypt.[14] A late papyrus (257 B.C.) mentions Mendesian myrrh in small lead vessels.[15]

Myrrh has been identified by Reutter in ancient Egyptian perfumes [16] (undated), a specimen of gum-resin from a jar found in a tomb of Nineteenth or Twentieth Dynasty date was identified as myrrh by Coremans,[17] and specimens of gum-resin from certain royal and priestly mummies of the Eighteenth, Nineteenth, Twentieth and Twenty-first Dynasties respectively examined by the author were probably myrrh.[18] This identification was confirmed in one instance by Launoy.[19]

Satisfactory incense materials other than frankincense and myrrh are very few and must have been still fewer in ancient Egypt, since such substances as benzoin and camphor from the Far East and, in the earlier periods, the products of India were probably not then available. Speculation, however, as to what might have been employed is of little value and may be misleading, and only those materials will be

---

[1] *A.R.*, IV, 233, 239, 299, 344, 376.   [2] *A.R.*, II, 572; but see p. 94.

[3] *A.R.*, I, 161.   [4] *A.R.*, I, 429.   [5] *A.R.*, II, 265, 274, 276, 277, 321, 486.

[6] *A.R.*, IV, 130, 210, 407.   [7] *A.R.*, IV, 929.

[8] *A.R.*, II, 474.

[9] *A.R.*, II, 491.

[10] *Wb.* I. 206. 7–207. 3.

[11] A. Lucas, *J.E.A.*, XXIII (1937), p. 29; R. O. Steuer, *J.A.O.S.*, LXIII (1943), p. 282.

[12] R. O. Steuer, *Myrrhe und Stakte* (reviewed by G. A. Wainwright, *J.E.A.*, XXI (1935), pp. 254–5); R. O. Steuer, *J.A.O.S.*, LXIII (1943), pp. 279–84. See, however, Lucas's objections (*J.E.A.*, XXIII (1937), pp. 27–33).

[13] B. Ebbell, *Acta Orientalia*, XVII (1939), pp. 88–111.

[14] *De Iside et Osiride*, § 52.

[15] C. C. Edgar, *Zenon Papyri*, I, No. 59089.

[16] L. Reutter, *Ann. Serv.*, XIII (1914), pp. 49–78.

[17] P. Coremans, *Chronique d'Égypte*, XVI (1941), pp. 101–4.

[18] A. Lucas, *Preservative Materials*, pp. 26–29.

[19] R. Pfister, *Nouveaux textiles de Palmyre* (1937), p. 10.

mentioned for the use of which in Egypt there is some probability, and these are limited to galbanum, ladanum, and storax, which may now be described.

Galbanum

This is a fragrant gum-resin generally occurring in masses of agglomerated tears and is of a light brownish-yellow to a dark brown colour, with often a greenish tint; it has a greasy appearance and, though usually hard, it may occasionally be of semi-solid consistency; it is a native of Persia and a product of various species of the umbelliferous plant *Peucedanum*, of which *P. galbaniflorum* is the most important. This is the only green incense material known to me, except that frankincense is green when freshly gathered [1] and even as found in commerce it may occasionally have a slight greenish tint. As there would not have been any difficulty in galbanum reaching Egypt from Persia in the Eighteenth Dynasty, this may well have been the 'green' incense mentioned in ancient texts,[2] though the translation 'green' as uncertain, since the Egyptian word also means 'fresh'. According to Dioscorides [3] and Pliny,[4] galbanum was one of the constituents of the Mendesian unguent, and it is mentioned in the Bible as entering into the composition of Jewish incense.[5] There is no record of galbanum having been found in ancient Egyptian graves.

Ladanum

This, unlike the other incense materials described, is a true resin and not a gum-resin; it occurs in commerce as dark brown or black masses, which are often viscid or easily softened by handling: it exudes naturally from the leaves and branches of various species of *Cistus* that grow in Asia Minor, Crete, Cyprus, Greece, Palestine, Spain and other parts of the Mediterranean region, though not at the present time in Egypt. Pliny states [6] that the Ptolemies introduced ladanum into 'the parts beyond Egypt', the meaning of which is obscure.[7]

Newberry has suggested (on very dubious grounds) that the ancient Egyptians were acquainted with ladanum as early as the First Dynasty.[8] From purely theoretical considerations this might be expected, since, even if ladanum were not an Egyptian product, it was abundant in countries bordering the Mediterranean with which Egypt had intercourse and from which it might easily have been obtained. No positive evidence, however, can be found for this early use. The earliest literary references known to me for the use of ladanum in Egypt are in the Bible, where it is stated that certain merchants carried ladanum into Egypt from Gilead [9] and that Jacob sent ladanum to Egypt as a present to his son Joseph.[10] The date of this record is probably not earlier than the tenth century B.C. and possibly as late as the eight century B.C. Incidentally it may be noted that the sending of ladanum from Palestine to Egypt suggests that ladanum at that time was either not a product of Egypt or that it was not very plentiful. The next literary reference in date order that can be traced is the one already quoted from Pliny in the first century A.D. In modern times Lane states

---

[1] Bertram Thomas, *Arabia Felix*, p. 122.   [2] *A.R.*, II, 572.
[3] I: 71.   [4] XIII: 2.   [5] *Exodus*, XXX: 34 (Revised Version).
[6] XII: 37.   [7] See pp. 91–92.   [8] P. E. Newberry, *J.E.A.*, XV (1929), p. 94.
[9] *Genesis*, XXXVII: 25 (Revised Version).   [10] *Genesis*, XLIII: 11 (Revised Version).

that it was customary for the Egyptian women of his day to chew ladanum to perfume their breath.[1]

So far as is known, the only instance of ladanum having been found in connexion with ancient Egypt is a specimen of Coptic incense of the seventh century from Faras near Wadi Halfa, which was examined by me and the results published some years ago.[2] This was a fragrant, black resin containing 31 per cent of mineral matter and is probably ladanum. A genuine specimen of ladanum of good quality analysed for comparison purposes yielded 80 per cent of resinous matter and 20 per cent of matter insoluble in alcohol.

Storax

Storax (Styrax) is a balsam obtained from the tree *Liquidambar orientalis*, belonging to the natural order *Hamamelideae*, indigenous to Asia Minor. It is a turbid, viscid greyish liquid having an odour like benzoin and belongs to the same class of bodies, the distinguishing feature of which is that they contain either cinnamic or benzoic acid, storax containing the former. At one time, however, the name storax was applied to the solid resin obtained from *Styrax officinalis*, which somewhat resembles benzoin. Reutter has identified storax in Egyptian mummy material [3] and in ancient Egyptian perfumes,[4] both unfortunately undated. There is no evidence that 'gum-styrax, modern storax, was taken from trees in upper Egypt', as stated by Rostovtzeff,[5] and the word translated by him as styrax is rendered as 'vegetable juice' by Edgar, who says [6] that Rostovtzeff's note on this word 'is based upon a misapprehension'.

Miscellaneous Incense Materials

Specimens of various miscellaneous materials of ancient Egyptian origin submitted as incense have been examined by me from time to time and may now be described. One of these was Coptic incense of the same date and from the same place as the ladanum already mentioned. This second specimen, however, was very different; it was in irregular-shaped pieces of a dark reddish-brown colour, translucent when freshly fractured, very resinous-looking and possessed a fragrant smell. On analysis it proved to be a true resin, as distinguished from a gum-resin, and therefore could not be frankincense, myrrh, galbanum or storax, and its colour was not that of ladanum; it was not identified.[2] A specimen of material found by Legrain at Karnak was dull and opaque in appearance, and on analysis proved to be a true resin mixed with 76 per cent of limestone dust. Although described by the finder as incense, it is suggested that it was a cementing material similar to that discovered at Karnak a few years later by Pillet,[7] and to that found by Montet at Tanis.[8]

---

[1] E. W. Lane, *Manners and Customs of the Modern Egyptians* (Everyman's Library), p. 194.

[2] A. Lucas, *Preservative Materials*, pp. 31–32.

[3] L. Reutter, *De l'embaumement avant et après Jésus-Christ*, pp. 49, 59.

[4] L. Reutter, *Ann. Serv.*, XIII (1914), pp. 49–78.

[5] M. Rostovtzeff, *A Large Estate in Egypt in the Third Century, B.C.*, p. 178.

[6] C. C. Edgar, *Zenon Papyri*, III, No. 59368, p. 113.

[7] M. Pillet, *Ann. Serv.*, XXIV (1924), pp. 64–65.

[8] P. Montet, *Ann. Serv.*, XXXIX (1939), p. 530.

A mixture of resin (or gum-resin) and natron was found in the tomb of Tut-ankhamūn, which may have been incense, natron being sometimes used in incense.[1] The resin (or gum-resin, there was too little of the specimen available for this point to be determined) is in the form of very small tears and rods, the latter being 2 to 5 mm. long and 0.5 mm. in diameter; it is white on the outside from adhering natron and its own fine dust, but light yellowish-brown in the interior; it is largely, though not entirely, soluble in alcohol: it has not been identified, but it is certainly not myrrh and the appearance is not that of frankincense.[2]

That frankincense occurs in the Sudan has already been stated, but in addition there are also other materials that might be employed as incense, though whether they have been so used is unknown. I have examined two of these, one *Gafal* resin stated to be obtained from *Balsamodendron africanum* and the other the product of *Gardenia Thunbergia*. The *Gafal* resin was in the form of irregular-shaped masses, yellowish, light brown or dark brown in colour and generally translucent and very resinous-looking. The *Gardenia Thunbergia* product was also in irregular lumps, but very different in appearance from the *Gafal* resin; it varied in colour from a light yellowish-brown to black and was entirely opaque. Both materials are fragrant gum-resins and seem very suitable for incense purposes.

As already mentioned, resin is a very common material in ancient Egyptian graves of all periods, being a marked feature of Badarian and predynastic burials long before mummification was practised and also of early dynastic burials in cases where the body had not been mummified, either because the practice was not yet known, or because it had not become general.

This resin is always a true resin, as distinguished from gum-resins such as frankincense and myrrh, which latter are products of countries that are farther south and hotter than Egypt, whereas most true resins, and probably all those under discussion, are either from coniferous trees (cedars, pines, firs and spruces), or from species of *Pistacia* (chiefly *P. terebinthus*) that grow in countries more northerly and colder than Egypt and, considering the early connexions of Egypt with western Asia, where such trees are plentiful, this would seem a likely source from which these resins might have been obtained.

These resins, many of which are very similar in appearance, are usually without smell, though occasional specimens are fragrant: they are generally opaque and of a dull brown colour on the outside, but bright and resinous-looking in the interior: they give similar results on analysis and are probably largely, though not entirely, of one kind, the botanical source of which it has not been possible to determine. As these resins are of a date before mummification and also before the use of resin for varnish or as an adhesive or for making into personal ornaments and other objects,[3] except occasional small beads which have been found from predynastic times,[4] the most likely use seems to have been as incense,[5] more particularly as there is no evidence that frankincense and myrrh were known before the dynastic period. As a rule, however,

---

[1] British Museum, *Introductory Guide to the Egyptian Collections*, 1930, p. 5.
[2] A. Lucas, in H. Carter, *Tut-ankh-Amen*, III, p. 181 (Appendix II).
[3] See p. 388, where a list is given of resin objects found in the tomb of Tutankhamūn.
[4] E. R. Ayrton and W. L. S. Loat, *Predynastic Cemetery of El Mahasna*, pp. 11, 17, 27, 31.
[5] Cf. H. Junker, *El-Kubanieh-Sud*, pp. 92–93.

the smell produced when this resin is burned is not fragrant according to modern ideas, being very like burning varnish, though occasionally specimens have been examined that are aromatic.[1] If incense, this was the forerunner of the more sweet-smelling and probably much more rare and expensive frankincense and myrrh and, if not incense, then the almost entire absence in graves of one of the most commonly employed materials in the religion and magic of ancient Egypt remains unexplained. Possibly, too, even after frankincense and myrrh became known their use was re-stricted to special occasions on account of their rarity and price, a more easily obtained and cheaper material being employed for ordinary purposes and by the poorer people, which would explain the occurrence of this brown resin in the graves of all periods and of all ranks. The discussion of the botanical sources of these resins will be con-sidered when dealing with the true resins employed at a later date and principally in connexion with mummification.[2]

FRAGRANT WOODS

In connexion with perfume and incense the use of fragrant woods in ancient Egypt may be mentioned.

In the tomb of Tutankhamūn there was a small red pottery jar containing cut pieces of plant stalks, which was inscribed 'perfume' or 'substance used for perfum-ing'.[3]

Winlock reports 'small splinters of wood, which was doubtless originally aromatic' of Eleventh Dynasty date from El Lahun,[4] and of the same date from Thebes he found 'little sticks of sweet-scented wood for perfumes'.[5]

The origin of this aromatic wood is not known, but scented woods occur in East Africa (Uganda and Kenya). [6]

---

[1] Ure (quoted by J. G. Wilkinson, *The Ancient Egyptians,* 1878, III, pp. 398–9) examined two specimens of resin, both of which were soluble in alcohol, but only one was soluble in turpentine.

[2] See pp. 319–22.

[3] Kindly translated by Prof. Černý.

[4] H. E. Winlock, *Treasure of El Lāhūn,* p. 67.

[5] H. E. Winlock, *M.M.A. Bull., Egyptian Exped. 1930–1931,* pp. 32, 35–36, Fig. 34.

[6] C. R. Metcalfe, *Bull. of Misc. Information,* No. 1, 1933, Royal Botanic Gardens, Kew.

Chapter VII

INLAID EYES[1]

Inlaid eyes were used in ancient Egypt for coffins, mummies, mummy masks, statues and statuettes, and also occasionally in reliefs,[2] but no evidence has been found that they were ever used by the living. Dr. M. A. Murray, however, describing one particular eye in the Museum of University College, London, states [3] that 'The shape and size of the eye, as well as the fact that the edges are carefully rounded, show that it was for human use. Eyes for insertion in statues and coffins have sharp edges totally unlike this example.' This eye is glass and is all one piece; the eyeball is white with a blue border and the pupil black; there is no iris. The blue border, the absence of an iris and the poor workmanship make it most improbable that the eye was intended for a living person, as it would not match any human eye, and it seems much more likely that it is from a mummy.

Before the ancient eyes are described, the visible parts of the human eye may be mentioned, and are as follows:

Eyelids: the covers of the eyes formed of movable membrane which permits the eyes to be covered or uncovered at will. There are two eyelids, an upper and a lower one, to each eye.

Eyelashes: the fringes of hair that edge the eyelids.

Eyeball: the whole eye, or sphere, contained within the orbit, the white being that part of the outer, or sclerotic, coat of the eyeball that is usually seen.

Cornea: the circular, transparent, colourless front of the eye, through which the light enters, and which is continuous with the sclerotic coat, but projects a little beyond it, since it has a slightly greater convexity than the rest of the eyeball.

Iris: the coloured annular curtain behind the cornea which expands and contracts, causing the pupil to dilate or narrow as the case may be.

Pupil: a circular opening in the middle of the iris that appears to be black because beyond it is the dark interior of the eye.

Canthus: the angle between the upper and lower eyelids; therefore there are two canthi to each eye.

---

[1] This chapter has been taken in part from an article 'Inlaid Eyes in Ancient Egypt, Mesopotamia and India', published by me in *Technical Studies*, VII (1938), pp. 3–32, and from a previous article 'Artificial Eyes in Ancient Egypt', in *Ancient Egypt*, 1934, pp. 84–98, but considerable alterations and additions have been made. For an earlier study of artificial eyes, both human and animal, see E. Pergens, 'Über Kunstaugen aus dem alten Ägypten', in P. Diergart, *Beiträge aus der Geschichte der Chemie, 1909*, pp. 201–11. A recent article by R. P. Wilson, 'Artificial Eyes in Ancient Egypt', in *New Zealand Medical Journal*, Oct. 1951, Supplement, pp. 27–42, is largely taken from this chapter.

[2] L. Borchardt, *Ne-user-rē*, p. 39; W. S. Smith, *Sculpture and Painting*, p. 202.

[3] *Ancient Egypt, 1934*, pp. 98–99.

Caruncle: a small red swelling at the inner angle only of the eyelids, just within the inner canthus. There is no caruncle in the outer canthus.

With very few exceptions, all the eyes in the Cairo Museum have been examined by me, as also many others. Naturally, it was not convenient to remove large objects from their cases for examination, but occasionally it was possible to get inside a case, or even to remove the case, leaving the object on the stand. Naturally, too, the eyes could not be taken out of the sockets and separated into their component parts and, therefore, a partial examination was all that was possible. Fortunately, however, there were many loose eyes that could be taken apart and examined in detail.

Much thought has been devoted to finding a good and simple system of classification with the minimum number of classes, and the course adopted has been to take as a guiding principle the technique and not the materials. Slight differences in technique, as well as differences in materials with the same technique, are regarded as variants of a class and not as separate classes; otherwise the number of classes would have been very large.

PREDYNASTIC PERIOD

Simple inlaid eyes date from the predynastic period and often consist of white shell, ring beads.[1] Objects of this date in the Cairo Museum having inlaid eyes are: (a) a human figure with eyes inlaid in black material;[2] (b) a fish palette with one white inlaid eye, probably not a bead;[3] (c) a human figure in ivory with inlaid eyes of white ring beads;[4] and (d) a vase in the form of a gazelle with a white ring bead for one eye, the other eye being missing.[5] In the British Museum there is a predynastic figure of a woman carved in bone with inlaid eyes of lapis lazuli.[6] Similar simple eyes were also used at later periods, for example, there is in the Cairo Museum a small ivory fish of Tenth or Eleventh Dynasty date, the eyes of which consist of small blue ring beads.[7]

CLASS I

This kind of eye is known from the Fourth Dynasty[8] to the Thirteenth Dynasty: it is an admirable imitation of the natural eye, of which it reproduces all the essential features (eyelids, eyeball, cornea, iris, pupil and caruncle) and is very much better than the eyes made at any other period, or by any other ancient people.

Eyelids: the outer edge of a narrow frame surrounding the eyeball, generally metal (copper or silver), but very occasionally faience or blackened limestone.

Eyelashes: none.

Eyeball: wedge-shaped with a rounded front for statues, statuettes, masks and anthropoid coffins, and flat for non-anthropoid coffins. The material is generally polished opaque quartz, but sometimes polished crystalline limestone, often Egyptian

---

[1] W. M. F. Petrie, *Prehistoric Egypt*, p. 6, Pl. II; W. M. F. Petrie and J. E. Quibell, *Naqada and Ballas*, p. 10.

[2] No. J. 52839.   [3] No. J. 57562.   [4] No. J. 41228.   [5] No. J. 66628.

[6] British Museum, *Introductory Guide to the Egyptian Collections*, 1930, p. 21, Fig. 6.

[7] No. J. 54343.

[8] The Third Dynasty statue of Djoser in the Cairo Museum originally had inlaid eyes which have been gouged out.

alabaster (calcite) [1] with a shallow circular depression drilled in the middle of the front to receive the cornea, which is fastened in place with an adhesive, sometimes resin.

Cornea: transparent rock crystal, rounded and polished at the front, but matt (like ground glass) at the back and edges.

Iris: there is no separate iris, but the effect of a brown iris is produced by a disc of dark brown resin placed behind the cornea, as dimly seen through the matt surface at the back. Sometimes the iris is grey, or partly grey and partly brown, and I have found by experiment that when the cornea is merely placed in the resin, and is not in absolute contact with it at every point, but is separated from it by a thin film of air, the appearance, as seen from the front, is grey, and is due almost entirely to the optical effect of the matt surface at the back of the cornea, but when the resin is in absolute and intimate contact with the cornea, the colour, as seen from the front, is brown. The majority of present-day Egyptians have brown irides, and it seems probable, therefore, that this also was the case anciently, hence brown irides are more likely than grey ones. If the original colour were brown, the cornea must have been placed in position when the resin was still in the viscous condition, before it cooled and became solid, since only in this manner could absolute contact between the cornea and the resin have been produced. If so, then the grey, or patches of grey, may be explained by assuming that in these cases the resin has shrunk, so that it no longer makes absolute contact with the cornea.

Pupil: a small circular recess drilled in the middle of the back of the cornea and filled with a plug of very dark brown or black resin, or sometimes a circular black spot painted on the resin behind the cornea; occasionally the pupil is absent.

Caruncle: a small red patch painted on the inner canthus, but sometimes on both the inner and outer canthi. That the Egyptians, who were usually such faithful copyists of nature, should have made the mistake of putting two caruncles, instead of only one, is extraordinary. Occasionally the caruncle is absent.

Examples

Squatting Scribe (Fourth Dyn.). Painted limestone; Cairo Museum.
  Eyelids: copper, much corroded.
  White: [2] quartz.
  Cornea: rock crystal.
  Iris: grey and blistered.
  Pupil: a recess at the back of the cornea filled with very dark material.
  Caruncle: none visible.

Maspero states [3] that 'the eyes are inlaid, the alabaster and crystal composing them are set in copper lids; a small splinter of ebony behind the crystal imitates the pupil . . .' It is most improbable that the cornea was taken out for the pupil to be

---

[1] Sometimes the limestone is banded like alabaster (calcite), in which case undoubtedly it is alabaster, but sometimes it is without any special distinguishing mark, when it may be either alabaster or white marble, though generally alabaster. Since both these materials are crystalline limestone, this name may be applied correctly to either and is particularly appropriate when there is any uncertainty which of the two it is.

[2] The word 'white' is used instead of 'eyeball' when the eye is in position and only the front portion can be seen.

[3] G. Maspero, *Guide to the Cairo Museum*, trans. J. E. and A. A. Quibell, 5th ed., 1910, p. 54.

examined, and, if not, there cannot be any evidence of the nature of the pupil, and it is much more probable that it is the dark-coloured resin such as was employed in the Middle Kingdom and not ebony.

Borchardt says [1] that the eyes are inlaid like those of the small seated statue described below, which represents the same person.

Small Seated Statue (Fourth Dyn.). Painted limestone; Cairo Museum.

Eyelids: copper, much corroded.
White: quartz.
Cornea: rock crystal.
Iris: grey.
Pupil: a recess at the back of the cornea filled with very dark material.
Caruncle: none.

Borchardt says [2] that the eyelashes (*Wimpern*), meaning the eyelids (*Augenlider*), are metal, possibly copper; the eyeballs quartz; the iris, meaning the cornea, rock crystal and the pupil a dark-coloured wooden nail.

Rahotpe and Nofret (Fourth Dyn.). Painted limestone; Cairo Museum.

Eyelids: copper.
White: quartz.
Cornea: rock crystal.
Iris: partly brown and partly grey.
Pupil: recess at the back of the cornea filled with very dark material.
Caruncle: present in both canthi of both eyes.

Borchardt states [3] that the eyelashes (*Wimpern*), meaning the eyelids (*Augenlider*), are metal, probably copper; that the white is alabaster or bone; that the iris, meaning the cornea, is rock crystal, with apparently a brownish material underneath, and that the pupil is a dark brown wooden peg.

Daninos Pasha, the finder of the statues, states [4] that the eyelids are bronze, which is most improbable at this date; that the eyeballs are white quartz with rose-coloured veining, evidently mistaking the painted caruncles for natural markings; and that the cornea is rock crystal with a shining nail underneath to represent the pupil.

Dr. M. Murray says [5] that the eyelids are copper; the white is polished limestone and the iris 'clear quartz painted at the back'.

Sheikh el Beled (Fifth Dyn.). Wood; Cairo Museum.

Eyelids: copper.
White: quartz.
Cornea: rock crystal.
Iris: grey.
Pupil: recess at the back of the cornea filled with very dark material.
Caruncle: none.

---

[1] L. Borchardt, *Statuen und Statuetten*, No. 36.
[2] L. Borchardt, *Statuen und Statuetten*, No. 35.
[3] L. Borchardt, *Statuen und Statuetten*, Nos. 3 and 4.
[4] Daninos Pasha, *Rec. Trav.*, VIII (1886), pp. 69–72.
[5] M. A. Murray, *Egyptian Sculpture*, p. 52.

Maspero states [1] that 'The eyes were inlaid . . . They are made of a piece of opaque white quartz, with a frame of bronze surrounding it to imitate the lid; a small disc of transparent rock-crystal forms the iris, while a tiny spangle of polished ebony——not silver, as has been said too often—fixed behind the crystal imparts to it a life-like sparkle.' The eyelids are copper and not bronze; the rock crystal forms the cornea and not the iris and, although the eyes have not been taken apart for the examination of the pupil, it is most improbable that the dark material is ebony, for which no evidence is given.

Borchardt says [2] that the eyelashes (*Wimpern*), meaning the eyelids (*Augenlider*), are metal, probably copper; that the white is a white stone; that the iris, meaning the cornea, is rock crystal; and that the pupil is a wooden nail.

Baedeker rightly says [3] that 'the eyes consist of pieces of opaque white quartz with copper frames to imitate lids', but is wrong when he states that 'small discs of rock-crystal form the pupil', the rock crystal being the cornea.

Petrie refers to the 'eyeball of stone and crystal in a copper frame'.[4]

Bust of a Man (Fifth Dyn.). Wood; Cairo Museum.
  Eyelids: copper.
  White: crystalline limestone.
  Cornea: rock crystal.
  Iris: grey.
  Pupil: none.
  Caruncle: none.
Borchardt says [5] that the eyelashes (*Wimpern*), meaning the eyelids (*Augenlider*), are metal, probably copper; that the white is bone; that the iris, meaning the cornea, is rock crystal; and that the pupil is not visible.

Squatting Scribe (Old Kingdom).[6] Wood coated with painted plaster, in very bad condition. Store Room at Saqqara.
  Eyelids: copper.
  White: quartz.
  Cornea: rock crystal.
  Iris: light grey, but surface irregular with irregular brown lines.
  Pupil: dark grey, consisting of a projection of the material behind the cornea that fits into a recess at the back of the cornea.
  Caruncle: none.

Four Small Statues (Fourth Dyn).[7] Limestone; Cairo Museum.
  There are four similar statues, all of which have sockets for inlaid eyes. In two cases the sockets are empty; in a third case one socket is empty, but the other contains

[1] G. Maspero, *Guide to the Cairo Museum*, 1910, p. 52.
[2] L. Borchardt, *Statuen und Statuetten*, No. 34.
[3] K. Baedeker, *Egypt and the Sudan*, 1929, p. 90.
[4] W. M. F. Petrie, *Arts and Crafts*, p. 33.
[5] L. Borchardt, *Statuen und Statuetten*, No. 32.
[6] No number.
[7] Nos. J. 72214–72217.

a corroded copper rim; the fourth statue has inlaid eyes, but as they are fastened in place with modern plaster, and as there are no copper rims, manifestly they are not in their original condition, and no record can be traced of what they were like when found. As they now are, the eyes consist of cornea and pupil only, the cornea being a disc of rock crystal, rounded and polished at the front and matt at the edges. Through this can be seen a small black pupil, which probably is painted at the back of the cornea.

Anthropoid Coffin of Sepa from El Bersheh (Twelfth Dyn.). Cairo Museum.
Eyelids: limestone, artificially blackened.
White: crystalline limestone.
Cornea: rock crystal.
Iris: brown.
Pupil: recess at the back of the cornea filled with very dark material.
Caruncle: present in both canthi of both eyes.
Lacau [1] calls the eyeball white alabaster; the cornea rock crystal; the iris *un mastic brun*; and the pupil black.

Fifteen Loose Eyes (Middle Kingdom).
Three pairs of these eyes, from mummy masks, are all alike and are in the Cairo Museum.[2]
Eyelids: silver.
Eyeball: [3] wedge-shaped, opaque, white quartz with a circular depression drilled in the front to receive the cornea.
Cornea: rock crystal.
Iris: see below.
Pupil: a small circular recess in the middle of the back of the cornea filled with dark-coloured resin; see below.
Caruncle: Nos. 52945–52946, no caruncle visible, but the eyeballs are blackened by silver compounds from the corroded eyelids, which might mask the red of the caruncles. No. 52947 has no caruncle. No. 52948, caruncle in both canthi. No. 52949, no caruncle visible, but the eyeball is blackened by silver compounds, which might mask the red of the caruncle. No. 52950, possible trace of red in the inner canthus.
No. 52945. The iris is partly grey and partly brown. The cornea was not removed, but behind it there is almost certainly a dark brown resin, such as is present in No. 52948.
The pupil is a small cylindrical projection arising from, and forming part of, the flat surface of the resin behind the cornea, and it fills the recess at the back of the cornea: it has generally a very dark, or black, top and what looks like a white circumference. Vernier explains this [4] by supposing that the whole surface of the dark brown resin, except the top of the projection forming the pupil, was coated with a white material, which he states was undoubtedy plaster (i.e. gypsum plaster), that he thinks

---

[1] P. Lacau, *Sarcophages*, I, No. 28084, p. 199.
[2] E. Vernier, *Bijoux et Orfèvreries*, Nos. 52945–52950.
[3] The word 'eyeball' is used instead of 'white' when the eye is loose and the whole or the greater part, of the eyeball can be seen.
[4] E. Vernier, *Bijoux et Orfèvreries*, p. 313.

has decomposed and largely disappeared. Gypsum plaster, however, is a very permanent material and does not easily decompose and disappear and the few tiny white particles now to be seen in some of the small cavities of the resin of No. 52948 may be merely limestone dust that has accidentally found its way in since the cornea was lost, and no white particles can be found in any of the other eyes. In my opinion, the apparent white of the circumference of the projection forming the pupil is merely an optical effect due to the manner in which the light is reflected from the sides of the recess.

No. 52946. The iris is grey; the pupil has a grey top and apparently a white circumference. The material fastening in the cornea manifestly is modern.

No. 52947. The iris is grey with patches of brown; the pupil is black.

No. 52948. The cornea is missing and the cavity in the eyeball originally covered by the cornea is very deep, much more than usual, and is filled with dark brown resin. Vernier points out [1] that this filling is friable (*sans beaucoup de résistance*) and that it must have been introduced in a viscous (*malléable*) condition. In the absence of the cornea, the iris and pupil are also necessarily missing.

No. 52949. The cornea is loose and can be removed for examination, which was done. The sides and bottom of the depression in the eyeball, which is not nearly so deep as in No. 52948, are very irregular and show that the quartz has been drilled and chipped out, the marks of a tubular drill being visible. It is practically certain that a filling of dark brown resin similar to that present in No. 52948 originally existed in this case also (and probably exists, too, in the other four eyes, though its presence cannot be proved without taking the eyes to pieces), having been put into the cavity to hide the uneven surface of the quartz and to form the coloured iris, but the only evidence of this resin that now remains is a little (forming the pupil) in the hole in the recess in the cornea, and a patch adhering to the back of the cornea round the mouth of the recess.

No. 52950. The iris is grey with patches of brown, and the pupil is black. Vernier wrongly identifies the opaque quartz eyeballs in these eyes as the cornea and says [2] *C'est la pierre blanche qui joue le rôle de cornée.*

One Loose Eye. No. 52848. Cairo Museum.

This is stated by Vernier to be from Dahshur; [3] it is probably from the tomb of Princess Nubheteptikhered.

Eyelids: faience, probably once blue, but now much deteriorated and discoloured.

Eyeball: wedge-shaped quartz.

Cornea: rock crystal.

Iris: grey.

Pupil: circular black spot below the cornea, but whether painted or the usual recess filled with black material cannot be determined without removing the cornea, though probably painted.

Caruncle: present in the inner canthus and probably also in the outer canthus.

Vernier says [3] that the eyelids are *céramique vert brun*; the eyeball *céramique d'un*

---

[1] E. Vernier, *Bijoux et Orfèvreries*, p. 313.

[2] E. Vernier, *Bijoux et Orfèvreries*, pp. 312–3.

[3] E. Vernier, *Bijoux et Orfèvreries*, p. 284.

blanc ivoirin; the *prunelle* rock crystal; and that the depression in the centre of the eyeball for the insertion of the cornea *joue le rôle d'iris.*

Six Loose Eyes. These are two pairs and two single eyes from Lisht kindly given to me by Mr. Ambrose Lansing of the Metropolitan Museum of Art, New York, and are of Old Kingdom date.

The Two Pairs. Identical except in size, one pair being smaller than the other.

Eyelids: missing.

Eyeball: wedge-shaped alabaster, in the front of which a circular depression has been drilled with a tubular drill to receive the cornea, and in this depression there is a disc of dark brown resin, which from the manner in which it fits must have been introduced in the molten condition.

Cornea: a disc of transparent rock crystal, slightly convex and polished on the outer surface and flat and matt on the inner surface and matt round the edges.

Iris: grey with brown patches in one pair of eyes and entirely grey in the other pair, the brown in one eye, in which the cornea was removed for examination, being due to a little resin from the disc behind the cornea adhering firmly to the back of the cornea and doubtless a similar condition accounts for the brown patch in the other eye.

Pupil: a circular spot painted in black on the disc of resin, a little to one side of the middle.

Caruncle: remains of caruncles are present in both canthi of both pairs of eyes.

Single Eye.

Eyelids: missing.

Eyeball: wedge-shaped alabastar in the middle of the front of which a depression has been drilled by means of a tubular drill to receive the cornea.

Cornea: a disc of transparent rock crystal, slightly convex and polished on the upper surface; flat and matt on the under side and matt round the edges.

Iris: grey; there is a disc of dark brown resin behind the cornea.

Pupil: a small circular recess drilled in the middle of the back of the cornea and filled with resin projecting from the surface of the disc.

Caruncle: present in the inner canthus.

Single Eye: This is very tiny and probably from a small statuette.

Eyelids: silver.

Eyeball: wedge-shaped crystalline limestone.

Cornea: rock crystal.

Iris: grey.

Pupil: none.

Caruncle: none.

Pair of Eyes (*Middle Kingdom*). Probably from non-anthropoid coffin; Cairo Museum.[1]

Eyelids: missing.

Eyeball: flat crystalline limestone with a circular depression drilled in the middle of the front to receive the cornea, at the bottom of which there is a small amount of

---

[1] Nos. $\frac{21}{25}|\frac{11}{2}$ A and B.

brown powder (not nearly filling the depression), which is not resin, but contains organic matter and has not been identified.

Cornea: rock crystal.

Iris: brown from the brown powder as seen through the matt surface at the back of the cornea.

Pupil: the usual recess for the pupil has been drilled in the middle of the back of the cornea, but is empty.

Caruncle: present in both canthi of both eyes.

Hathor Heads (Middle Kingdom). Cairo Museum.

Two mirror handles having Hathor heads with inlaid eyes.

Eyelids: silver.

White: not determined.

Cornea: rock crystal.

Iris: grey.

Pupil: recess at the back of the cornea filled with dark material.

Caruncle: none.

No. 52663. The eyes on one side of the mirror have only the white left, which Vernier says [1] is white quartz and the *prunelle* rock crystal. Brunton, who found the mirror, states [2] that 'The eyes are of white paste, in two pieces, set in silver sockets with pupils of crystal.'

No. 53105. One eye is missing and the other is very corroded. Vernier gives no details,[3] but Bénédite says [4] that the eyelids are silver, the white (which he calls the cornea) ivory, and the *prunelle* transparent quartz with a small hole at the bottom to represent the pupil.

Statue of King Hor (Thirteenth Dyn.). Wood; Cairo Museum.

Eyelids: the eyelids (if any) of both eyes are covered thickly with a soft black material, certainly modern, probably used for fixing the eyes into the sockets, which prevents the nature of the eyelids from being determined; de Morgan says that they are gilt.[5]

White: quartz.

Cornea: rock crystal.

Iris: the colour of the right iris is brown with horizontal markings, possibly being the wood at the back of the socket seen through the cornea; the left is grey.

Pupil: the right is missing; the left pupil is a black spot probably painted on the material behind the cornea.

Caruncle: none.

One plate in de Morgan's report [6] describing the finding of this statue shows it with certainly the right eye missing and possibly also the left, while another plate [7]

---

[1] E. Vernier, *Bijoux et Orfèvreries*, No. 52663.

[2] G. Brunton, *Lahun*, I, p. 36.

[3] E. Vernier, *Bijoux et Orfèvreries*, No. 53105. [4] G. Bénédite, *Miroirs*, No. 44089.

[5] J. de Morgan, *Dahchour, mars-juin 1894*, p. 91.

[6] J. de Morgan, *Dahchour, mars-juin 1894*, Pl. xxxiii.

[7] J. de Morgan, *Dahchour, mars-juin 1894*, Pl. xxxv.

shows both eyes. At the present time there are two eyes, but the right eyeball is slightly whiter than the left, which suggests a modern addition, and one of the Museum employees told me that the right eye was put in by the late Mr. A. Barsanti. If so, I suggest that possibly an ancient eyeball and cornea, not belonging to the statue, may have been used.

Borchardt says [1] that the right eye is modern and that only the white and the transparent iris (meaning the cornea) of the left eye are ancient.

Statuette of King Hor (Thirteenth Dyn.). Wood, much broken; Cairo Museum.
  Eyelids: silver, corroded and blackened, not copper as previously stated by me.[2]
  White: crystalline limestone.
  Cornea: rock crystal.
  Iris: grey and blistered.
  Pupil: none.
  Caruncle: none.
  The finder, de Morgan, says [3] that the eyelids are silver and that the eyes are quartz. Borchardt states [4] that the eyelashes (*Wimpern*), meaning the eyelids (*Augenlider*), are metal; that the white is white quartz and that the pupil, meaning the cornea, is transparent.

Mask of King Hor (Thirteenth Dyn.). Wood; Cairo Museum. The eyes are in very bad condition.
  Eyelids: metal, probably copper; now much corroded.
  White: crystalline limestone.
  Cornea: rock crystal (one is missing).
  Iris: grey.
  Pupil: none visible.
  Caruncle: none visible.
  The finder, de Morgan, says [5] *yeux de pierre, sertis de bronze.* Lacau calls the white of the eye alabaster, and the rock crystal *le cristallin,*[6] i.e. the crystalline lens, whereas it is the cornea.

CLASS II

This is the largest and most usual class of eye and it is neither so elaborate nor so effective as that of Class I. It consists generally of eyelids, eyeball, pupil and caruncle only, with occasionally eyelashes, and dates certainly from as early as the Fifth Dynasty to as late as Roman times though the nature of the materials used varied considerably at different periods.

The pupil of these eyes, which generally is very large, is often called the iris, or iris and pupil combined, but in ancient Egypt, although the iris of the natural eye occasionally may have been black, probably it was usually brown, like the majority

---

[1] L. Borchardt, *Statuen und Statuetten,* No. 259.
[2] A. Lucas, *Ancient Egypt,* 1934, p. 90.   [3] J. de Morgan, *Dahchour, mars-juin 1894,* p. 95.
[4] L. Borchardt, *Statuen und Statuetten,* IV, No. 1163.
[5] J. de Morgan, *Dahchour, mars-juin 1894,* p. 98, Fig. 229 (p. 99).
[6] P. Lacau, *Sarcophages,* II, No. 28107, p. 85.

of the present-day Egyptian irides, and when a definite and separate iris is represented in an artificial eye, whether inlaid or painted, it is never black, so far as is known, but always either brown [1] or grey.[2] The grey, except when painted, most probably was brown originally, and when painted it is always of very late date, namely of the Graeco-Roman period, and hence may represent the iris of someone who was not an Egyptian, or not wholly Egyptian. Since, therefore, it was the pupil only of the Egyptian eye that was black, to call the black disc in the middle of the eyeball the iris is wrong.

Eyelids: the outer edge of a thin frame surrounding the eyeball, which is usually copper, though occasionally silver, until the Eighteenth Dynasty, during which period it may be copper, bronze,[3] or glass, with sometimes gold for royal eyes, after which date glass was the usual material employed.

Eyelashes: only rarely represented and then always a prolongation of copper eyelids having the edges serrated.

Eyeball: generally wedge-shaped with convex front for statues, statuettes, mummies, masks and anthropoid coffins until the Graeco-Roman period, during which time the white [4] was often no longer part of a sphere, but a flat inlay with a slightly rounded outer surface, a technique similar to that used for non-anthropoid coffins of all periods. The material of the eyeball was usually crystalline limestone until the Graeco-Roman period, though occasionally white opaque quartz, glass, bone or other substance; and glass during the Graeco-Roman period. There is a hole, or flattened area, in the middle of the front of the eyeball, or white, to receive the pupil, which was fastened in place with an adhesive.

Cornea: usually none.

Iris: usually none.

Pupil: a large disc of black material attached to the front of the eyeball, or white,[4] usually obsidian, with the occasional use of black resin, black limestone (either naturally black or artificially blackened), black glass, or other black material until the Graeco-Roman period, during which generally it was black glass, but occasionally painted. Although the nature of the earlier material has not been proved by analysis to be obsidian, there is a considerable amount of circumstantial evidence that it is. Thus, it has all the appearance of obsidian, which was well known in ancient Egypt and had been employed for various purposes from predynastic times, and the alternative would be black glass, the use of which before the New Empire would be most improbable. Further, in those pupils which it has been possible to examine closely, the numerous small air bubbles that are such a constant feature of ancient Egyptian glass, are absent as are also all signs of the surface corrosion that is so fre-

---

[1] Examples of painted eyes in the Cairo Museum with brown irides are No. 28073 (P. Lacau, *Sarcophages*, I, p. 165); Nos. 33132, 33133, 33134, 33272 (C. C. Edgar, *Graeco-Egyptian Coffins*), and Nos. $\frac{20|8}{19|4}$ and $\frac{18|8}{19|4}$

[2] Painted grey irides occur in No. 33026 (Edgar, *Graeco-Egyptian Coffins*) and in Nos. $\frac{20|8}{19|2}$ and J. 41097.

[3] It is usually impossible to distinguish between copper and bronze without a chemical analysis, which, of course, frequently cannot be made.

[4] The word 'white' is used instead of 'eyeball' when the eye is in position and only the front portion can be seen.

quently found in ancient Egyptian glass and in some of the glass eyes of Graeco-Roman date. The surface also bears fine lines caused by the abrasive powder used for grinding and polishing, whereas similar pupils of black glass are generally, if not always, moulded.

Caruncle: usually a small red patch painted in the inner canthus, but sometimes in both canthi.

Examples

Kneeling Statuette (Fifth Dyn.). Limestone painted; Cairo Museum.
  Eyelids: copper.
  White: crystalline limestone.
  Pupil: obsidian.
  Caruncle: none.
Borchardt says [1] that the eyelashes (*Wimpern*), meaning the eyelids (*Augenlider*), are metal, probably copper; the white a white stone and the pupil black stone.

Pepi Statues (Sixth Dyn.). Copper; Cairo Museum.
  Eyelids: none.
  White: crystalline limestone.
  Pupil: obsidian.
  Caruncle: no evidence.
Quibell and Green state [2] that 'The pupil, a disc of black stone, probably obsidian, is set in an eyeball of white limestone.' Petrie refers to the 'white limestone eye of the statue',[3] probably meaning the large statue, and Wainwright says [4] that 'The use of obsidian as an inlay representing the pupil and iris of the human eye began with the Pepi statues of the VIth. dynasty'. [5]

Figure of Teti (Sixth Dyn.) [6] in a fragment of low relief sculpture (limestone) from his mortuary chapel at Saqqara; Cairo Museum.
  Eyelids: copper.
  White: crystalline limestone.
  Pupil: almost certainly obsidian.
  Caruncle: none.
Two Loose Eyes (Old Kingdom). [7] From a non-anthropoid coffin found at Zawyet el Amwat; Cairo Museum.
  Eyelids: copper.
  Eyeball: flat, hard, crystalline limestone.
  Pupil: obsidian.
  Caruncle: none.

---

[1] L. Borchardt, *Statuen und Statuetten*, No. 119.
[2] J. E. Quibell and F. W. Green, *Hierakonpolis*, II, p. 46.
[3] W. M. F. Petrie, *Ancient Egypt*, 1915, p. 48.
[4] G. A. Wainwright, *Ancient Egypt*, 1927, p. 89.
[5] The Fifth Dynasty eyes mentioned above are earlier.
[6] No. J. 39924.   [7] No. J. 51922.

Non-anthropoid Coffin (Ninth to Eleventh Dyns.).[1] From Asyut; Cairo Museum.
   Eyelids: copper.
   White: banded alabaster.
   Pupil: obsidian.
   Caruncle: none.

Inner Coffin (non-anthropoid) of Amenemhet, Prince of Hermopolis; Cairo Museum.
   One of the eyes is in place,[2] but the other is loose and is exhibited separately.[3]
   Eyelids: copper (one missing).
   Eyeball: flat crystalline limestone.
   Pupil: obsidian.
   Caruncle: present in both canthi.

Outer Coffin (non-anthropoid) of Amenemhet; Cairo Museum. The eyes are not in
   position, but are exhibited separately.[4]
   Eyelids: missing.
   Eyeball: flat, crystalline limestone.
   Pupil: plano-convex discs of limestone covered on both sides with a layer of black
resin, which is called 'bitumen' in the Museum register, but I have tested it and it is
resin and not bitumen. Lacau says [5] that the eyelids are metal; the eyeballs are alabaster
and the iris and pupil combined are polished black stone.
   Caruncle: present in both canthi.

Inner and Outer Coffins (non-anthropoid) of Prince Mesehti from Asyut (Middle King-
   dom); Cairo Museum.
   Eyelids: copper.
   White: almost flat crystalline limestone.
   Pupil: black limestone.
   Caruncle: none visible.
   Lacau says [6] that the eyelids are metal; the eyeballs alabaster; and the *'prunelle'*
black stone.

Two Statues from Asyut (Middle Kingdom).[7] Wood; Cairo Museum.
   Eyelids: copper.
   White: crystalline limestone.
   Pupil: black limestone.
   Caruncle: none.

Small Bust from Karnak (Middle Kingdom).[8] Limestone; Cairo Museum.
   Eyelids: copper.
   White: crystalline limestone.
   Pupil: obsidian.
   Caruncle: none.

---

[1] No. J. 36318.   [2] P. Lacau, *Sarcophages,* II, No. 28091, Pl. XIII.
[3] No. $\frac{21}{25}|\frac{11}{7}$; No. J. 34289.   [4] No. J. 34310.
[5] P. Lacau, *Sarcophages,* II, No. 28092, p. 63.
[6] P. Lacau, *Sarcophages,* II, Nos. 28118–28119, pp. 128, 133.
[7] Nos. J. 36283, 36284.   [8] No. J. 64911.

Twenty-two Loose Eyes (*Middle Kingdom*), as follows:

Seven Eyes (three pairs and one single)[1], mostly, if not all, from El Bersheh;[2] Cairo Museum.

Eyelids: missing in two pairs; metal, probably copper, in one pair and in the single eye, the metal being much corroded in one case.

Eyeball: wedge-shaped crystalline limestone in all cases.

Pupil: obsidian in all cases. In two pairs one pupil is missing in each case; in one pair and in the single eye the pupils probably do not belong.

Caruncle: in one pair there are the remains of a caruncle in the outer canthus of one eye; in the other two pairs and in the single eye a caruncle is present in both canthi.

Single Eye.[3] Probably from El Bersheh. Cairo Museum.

Eyelids: missing.

Eyeball: almond-shaped with rounded edges. The material is almost certainly odontolite (bone-turquoise) and not crystalline limestone, as previously reported by me,[4] although, like limestone, it is readily and entirely soluble with effervescence in hydrochloric acid. It gives a negative result when tested for copper, has a specific gravity of 2.8 and agrees in appearance with genuine odontolite, with which I have directly compared it. The Museum register describes it as green-coloured ivory (*ivoire verdi*).

Pupil: obsidian, which does not fit well, and may not belong.

Caruncle: none.

Single Eye from Abusir el Meleq.[5] Cairo Museum.

Eyelids: metal, probably copper.

Eyeball: wedge-shaped banded alabaster.

Pupil: black resin.

Caruncle: none.

Eleven Loose Eyes from Lisht.[6] These were kindly given to me by Mr. Ambrose Lansing, of the Metropolitan Museum of Art, New York.

These eyes are all practically alike, both in technique and also in respect to materials, and differ only in size. There are three pairs and five single eyes, one of which is larger than the rest and is probably from an anthropoid coffin, and another is very small and manifestly from a small statuette.

Eyelids: missing, except in the small eye, in which they are copper.

Eyeball: wedge-shaped alabaster (calcite).

Pupil: eight are obsidian and three are missing. Underneath the pupil in seven cases

[1] Nos. $\frac{21|11}{25|3}$, $\frac{21|11}{25|4}$, $\frac{21|11}{25|5}$, $\frac{21|11}{25|8}$, $\frac{21|11}{25|6}$.

[2] Ahmed Kamal, *Ann. Serv.*, II (1901), pp. 17, 32, 212, 217.

[3] No. J. 34317.

[4] A. Lucas, *Ancient Egypt*, 1934, p. 91.

[5] No. J. 49474.

[6] These were previously stated by me to consist of four pairs and three single eyes (A. Lucas, *Ancient Egypt*, 1934, p. 92), but on further examination it is now believed that there are only three pairs, the rest being single eyes.

certainly and probably in nine, there is a black material composed of a mixture of whiting and resin coloured with carbon, and used evidently partly as an adhesive and partly to enhance the black of the translucent obsidian. The two exceptions are the large coffin eye and the small statuette eye, the former having no trace of this black material, the cavity for the pupil being a hole through the eyeball without any bottom, and the latter not having been taken to pieces for examination.

Caruncle: three pairs and three single eyes have caruncles in both canthi; one single eye has a caruncle only in the inner canthus, and one single eye (the very tiny one) has not any caruncle.

Two Loose Eyes from Dahshur (Middle Kingdom).[1] Cairo Museum.
   Eyelids: none.
   Eyeball: wedge-shaped alabaster.
   Pupil: obsidian: in one case (No. 52850) there is a layer of dark brown resinous material under the pupil.
   Caruncle: none.

Coffins of Senebtisi (Twelfth Dyn.).
   These are in the Metropolitan Museum of Art, New York, and have not been examined by me. Mace and Winlock state [2] that the eyes of the outer coffin are of 'stone'; that those of the middle coffin 'were made up of almost flat sheets of stone, obsidian for the pupils and opaque calcareous stone for the whites, the latter stippled red in the corners. The pieces were fastened together with a blackish gum and set in tray-like wooden frames . . . the edges of which represented the eyelids' and that the eyes of the anthropoid coffin had 'polished obsidian pupils, whites of calcareous stone stippled red in the corners and silver frames of which the edges project to represent the eyelids'.

Hathor Head (Middle Kingdom). Cairo Museum.
   The head is on a mirror handle and has a double face with inlaid eyes.
   White: probably crystalline limestone.
   Pupil: in one pair of eyes the pupils are missing; in the other pair the nature of the material was not determined, but it is dull black and not either obsidian or glass.
   Caruncle: none.
   Bénédite says [3] that the white is crystalline limestone and that the pupils are *pastilles noires.*

Non-anthropoid Coffin of King Hor (Thirteenth Dyn.). Cairo Museum.
   Eyelids: copper.
   White: flat crystalline limestone.
   Pupil: obsidian.
   Caruncle: none.

---

[1] E. Vernier, *Bijoux et Orfèvreries*, Nos. 52849 and 52850.
[2] A. C. Mace and H. E. Winlock, *Senebtisi*, pp. 23, 30, 40.
[3] G. Bénédite, *Miroirs*, No. 44035.

Lacau states [1] that the eyeballs are alabaster, very white and polished, and that the pupils are black stone, possibly obsidian.

Anthropoid Coffin of Queen Ahhotpe [2] (*Eighteenth Dyn.*). Cairo Museum.
   Eyelids: gold.
   White: crystalline limestone.
   Pupil: obsidian.
   Caruncle: none.

Anthropoid Coffins of Yuya (*Eighteenth Dyn.*). Cairo Museum.
   There are three coffins, the eyes of all of which appear similar, though the materials are not alike.
   Eyelids: blue glass.
   White: innermost coffin, white opaque quartz; middle and outermost coffins, crystalline limestone. [3]
   Pupil: obsidian.
   Caruncle: inner and outer coffins, caruncle in inner canthus only; middle coffin, no caruncle.
   Quibell states [4] that the eyelids are blue glass, the eyeballs marble and the pupils black glass.

Anthropoid Coffins and Mask of Tuyu (*Eighteenth Dyn.*). Cairo Museum.
   There are two coffins only.
   Eyelids: blue glass.
   White: crystalline limestone. [3]
   Pupil: obsidian.
   Caruncle: present in inner canthus only.
   Quibell states [5] that the eyelids are blue glass; the whites white marble and the pupils black glass. With reference to the mask he says 'a curious point is that there is a green faience backing to the white of the eye, invisible outside, inside nearly filling the space inside the blue glass.' This I have not examined.

Anthropoid Coffins and Mask of Tutankhamūn (*Eighteenth Dyn.*). Cairo Museum, except the outermost coffin, which is in the tomb. The appearance of the eyes of all three coffins and the mask is similar, though the materials are different.
   Eyelids: coffins, blue glass; mask, lapis lazuli.
   White: when the innermost coffin was first uncovered the eyeballs were seen to be badly decomposed and they fell to pieces when the coffin was moved. They were crystalline limestone, which probably had been acted upon by the volatile acids derived from the fatty matter forming part of the black anointing material that had

---

[1] P. Lacau, *Sarcophages*, II, No. 28100, p. 77.

[2] No. J. 4663.

[3] Tested since last described (A. Lucas, *Ancient Egypt*, 1934, pp. 92–93).

[4] J. E. Quibell, *Yuaa and Thuiu*, Nos. 51002, 51003, 51004, 51006, 51007, 51009, pp. 4, 5, 10, 20, 23, 28.

[5] J. E. Quibell, *Yuaa and Thuiu*, p. 28.

been poured in large amount over the coffin, though not on the face. I believe that I tested the white of the eyes of the other two coffins and found that they were crystalline limestone, but no note of this can be traced, and they cannot now easily be examined. The whites of the eyes of the mask are quartz.[1]

Pupil: obsidian.

Caruncle: innermost (gold) coffin, no caruncle noticed; middle and outermost coffins, not noted, and cannot now easily be examined; mask, caruncle in both canthi of both eyes.

Carter states in one place [2] that the eyeballs of the outermost coffin are aragonite, and in another place [3] that they are calcite and that the pupils are obsidian.

Anthropoid Canopic Coffins of Tutankhamūn. Cairo Museum.

Eyelids: blue glass.

White: the eyes of one coffin are missing; the nature of the material of the other three has not been determined.

Pupil: the eyes of one coffin are missing and those of the other three are probably obsidian.

Caruncle: none.

Two Large Statues of Tutankhamūn. Cairo Museum.

Eyelids: gold.

White: crystalline limestone.

Pupil: obsidian.

Caruncle: present in both canthi of both eyes.

Small Statuettes of Human Figures from the Tomb of Tutankhamūn.[4] Cairo Museum.

There are altogether twenty-six statuettes with inlaid eyes, one being alabaster and the rest wood gilt. It was previously stated by me [5] that the eyeballs of six of these statuettes were crystalline limestone and the pupils almost certainly obsidian. I have now examined the eyes of all the statuettes, so far as was possible, with the result that in twenty-five instances the white is believed to be opaque white glass and probably in many, if not in all, there is no eyeball, the white being represented by two flat triangular pieces of glass, slightly rounded at the front and inlaid in the corners of the sockets. The pupils are probably obsidian, though black glass is not entirely excluded. The eyelids are metal, either copper or bronze, with one example of gold.[6] In one instance [7] the technique is entirely different and this, therefore, falls into another class. In eighteen cases there are caruncles in both canthi of both eyes; in one case there is a caruncle in the inner canthus only; in three cases the caruncle is

---

[1] Tested since last described (A. Lucas, *Ancient Egypt*, 1934, p. 93).

[2] H. Carter, *Tut-ankh-Amen*, II, p. 52.

[3] H. Carter, *Tut-ankh-Amen*, II, p. 247.

[4] Including gods and goddesses in human form.

[5] A. Lucas, *Ancient Egypt*, 1934, p. 93.

[6] No. J. 60731.

[7] Ahi holding Hathor emblem (No. J. 60732); this is one of a pair, the other (No. J. 60731) having normal Class II eyes.

absent, and in three cases the eyes are too dirty for the presence or absence of caruncle to be ascertained. Carter states [1] of some of these statuettes that 'their eyes are inlaid with obsidian, calcite, bronze, and glass'.

Chariot of Tutankhamūn. Cairo Museum.

There are four small inlaid eyes on one of the chariots, two being inside the body of the chariot and two outside.

Eyelids: blue glass.
White: white opaque glass.
Pupil: black glass.
Caruncle: none.

Canopic Jars from the so-called Tomb of Queen Tiy (Eighteenth Dyn.). Cairo Museum.

There are three jars only (alabastar), the eyes of two of which are missing; those of the third jar are as follows:

Eyelids: blue glass.
White: white opaque glass.
Pupil: black glass.
Caruncle: present in both canthi of both eyes.

Anthropoid Coffin of Hatiay (Eighteenth Dyn.).[2] Cairo Museum.

Eyelids: copper.
White: crystalline limestone.
Pupil: obsidian.
Caruncle: present in inner canthus.
Daressy states [3] *yeux incrustés en pierre, sertis en bronze.*

Three Anthropoid Coffins of Maiherperi (Eighteenth Dyn.).[4] Cairo Museum.

Eyelids: one pair not examined; one pair metal (probably copper) and one pair black, or blackened, limestone.

White: one pair not examined; two pairs crystalline limestone, one being banded alabaster (calcite).

Pupil: one pair not examined; two pairs obsidian.

Caruncle: one pair not examined; one pair has a trace of a caruncle in the inner canthus, and one pair is without caruncle.

Daressy says [5] of one of the coffins *les yeux incrustés de jaspe blanc et noir*; of another *les yeux en pierre noire et blanche sertis du bronze* and of the third *les yeux sont en jaspe blanc et noir et enchassés dans du bronze.*

Two Anthropoid Coffins of Queen Meryetamūn (Eighteenth Dyn.). Cairo Museum.

Winlock, who found these coffins, describes the eyeballs as alabaster and the pupils as obsidian,[6] which, as seen through the glass of the case, they appear to be;

---

[1] H. Carter, *Tut-ankh-Amen,* III, p. 52.   [2] No. J. 31378.
[3] G. Daressy, *Ann. Serv.,* II (1901), p. 3.   [4] Nos. J. 33830, 33831, 33833.
[5] G. Daressy, *Fouilles de la Vallée des Rois,* pp. 4–7.
[6] H. E. Winlock, *Meryet-Amūn,* pp. 18, 20.

the eyelids are blue glass much corroded. Winlock makes no mention of the eyelids of the outer coffin, but those of the inner coffin he says [1] are blue glass 'restored after the robbery'. No caruncles can be seen.

Anthropoid Coffin of Seti I (*Nineteenth Dyn.*).[2] Cairo Museum.
    Eyelids: blue glass.
    White: crystalline limestone.
    Pupil: obsidian.
    Caruncle: present in inner canthus.
    Daressy says [3] *Les yeux incrustés d'émail blanc et noir.*

Upper Part of Wooden Statue of Woman (*Nineteenth Dyn.*). British Museum.
    This has been described by Shorter,[4] who kindly allowed me to examine it. The interest is in the use of bone for the white.
    Eyelids: none.
    White: bone.
    Pupil: missing.
    Caruncle: none.

Three Bronze Statuettes of Divinities (*Late Egyptian period*). Cairo Museum.
    Eyelids: remains of blue glass in two cases; no eyelids in third case.
    White: crystalline limestone.
    Pupil: missing in all three cases.
    Caruncle: none.
    Daressy calls [5] the material of one pair stone or enamel, that of another pair jasper, and says of the third pair merely that they are inlaid.

Single Loose Eye (*Late Egyptian period*).[6] Cairo Museum.
    Eyelids: dark grey, fine-grained, soft stone, probably steatite.
    Eyeball: white opaque glass.
    Pupil: black glass.
    Caruncle: none.

Three Loose Eyes (*Late Egyptian period*).[7] From Abusir el Meleq; Cairo Museum.
    Eyelids: metal, either copper or bronze.
    Eyeball: banded alabastar (calcite).
    Pupil: two missing, the third being dark brown resin fastened to the flattened front of the eyeball.
    Caruncle: not noted.

---

[1] H. E. Winlock, *Meryet-Amūn*, pp. 18, 20.   [2] No. J. 26213.
[3] G. Daressy, *Cercueils des cachettes royales*, No. 61019.
[4] A. W. Shorter, *B.M. Quarterly*, IX (1935), p. 92.
[5] G. Daressy, *Statues de divinités*, I, No. 38260 (25th Dynasty); No. 38319 (25th to 26th Dynasties); No. 38422 (Ethiopian period).
[6] No. J. 34462 (22nd to 25th Dynasties).   [7] Not numbered (23rd to 25th Dynasties).

Two Anthropoid Coffins of Petosiris (Late Egyptian period). Cairo Museum.
Outer Coffin: the eyes are loose [1] and not on the coffin, which is not in the Museum.
    Eyelids: metal, copper or bronze.
    Eyeball: opaque white quartz.
    Pupil: missing.
    Caruncle: none.
Inner Coffin.[2]
    Eyelids: blue glass, much decayed.
    White: opaque white quartz.
    Pupil: obsidian.
    Caruncle: none.

Five Anthropoid Coffins (Late Egyptian period).[3] Cairo Museum.
    Eyelids: two pairs, blue glass; three pairs, black glass.
    White: four pairs, crystalline limestone; one pair, opaque white glass.
    Pupil: one pair, obsidian or black glass; two pairs, black glass; two pairs, neither obsidian nor black glass, but possibly painted.

INLAID EYES IN MUMMIES (CLASS II)

The practice of inlaying artificial eyes in mummies did not begin until a late period. According to Elliot Smith and Warren Dawson [4] it 'was already coming into vogue in the XXth. dynasty' and Elliot Smith gives a number of examples; thus he says of the mummy of Queen Nedjmet [5] (Twenty-first Dynasty), 'Artificial eyes, made of white and black stone, were inserted under the eyelids. This is the earliest instance of the use of stone eyes or of the attempt to represent the pupil in an artificial eye in a mummy, although in statues such objects had been in use more than fifteen centuries.' This writer, however, makes the same statement about Ramses III (Twentieth Dynasty), namely [6] 'The mummy of Ramesses III is I believe the earliest in which this device has been found.' Other examples of similar inlaid eyes in mummies mentioned by this writer are those of Queen Makarē (Twenty-first Dynasty) and of five other mummies of the Twenty-first and Twenty-second Dynasties respectively.[6] I have not examined these eyes, but from the description they all appear to be of Class II.

In this connexion may be mentioned the mummy of a certain Horsiese, priest of Amūn at Thebes (the date is not given), which was unwrapped by Pettigrew. According to Clift [7] it has 'a pair of artificial eyes, apparently of enamel'. Enamel, however, was not used in ancient Egypt, and the eyes were probably similar to those described by Elliot Smith; if so, they would be Class II.

---

[1] No. J. 48065.
[2] No. J. 46592.
[3] Nos. $\frac{21|11}{16|5}$, $\frac{6|11}{16|1}$, $\frac{5|11}{16|9}$, $\frac{27|9}{16|2}$; J. 35055.
[4] G. Elliot Smith and W. R. Dawson, *Egyptian Mummies*, p. 113.
[5] G. Elliot Smith, *Royal Mummies*, p. 96.
[6] G. Elliot Smith, *Royal Mummies*, pp. 87, 99, 103, 105, 108–9, 111, 114.
[7] W. R. Dawson, *J.E.A.*, xx (1934), p. 174.

Budge states [1] that 'In the case of women of quality eyes made of obsidian and ivory were inserted in the eye-sockets.'

Inlaid Eyes in Mummy Masks and Coffins (Class II)

All the mummy masks and coffins of the Graeco-Roman period in the Cairo Museum that are easily accessible, having inlaid eyes (sixty-six masks and eight coffins),[2] have been examined by me, the eyes of forty-one of the masks and of all the coffins being found to be Class II.

Eyelids: occasionally metal, copper or bronze, but usually glass; generally blue, though sometimes black, or such a dark blue that by mere inspection it is impossible to be sure of the colour.

Eyelashes: there is only one instance of eyelashes, these being in the usual form of serrated edges to a prolongation of copper eyelids.

White: usually opaque white glass, but occasionally crystalline limestone. Whether any of the eyeballs are wedge-shaped could not be determined, since they could not be taken out of the sockets for examination. In one instance, however, an eye was loose and this was examined and refixed in the socket, and in another instance an eye was broken and its construction was evident. In both cases the white was a flat piece of glass with a slightly rounded upper surface and a hole in the middle for the insertion of the pupil.

Cornea: none.

Iris: usually none, but in two instances there are irides, one pair brown and one pair grey. The brown irides consist of brown glass, in the middle of which is a small circular pupil of blue glass. The grey irides appear to be a narrow edge of white paint under the outer edge of the black pupil.

Pupil: generally opaque black glass, but possibly obsidian in one instance; in one instance brown glass and, as already stated, in one instance blue glass.

Caruncle: only occasionally present and then red paint.

These eyes have been described in detail by Edgar [3] and summarily by Petrie.[4] Edgar, summarizing his detailed description, says 'On the 1st century masks . . . if inlaid it is made of opaque material, stone or glass', and he adds 'So far as I have had them examined and tested, they seem to be usually, if not always, of glass.' Petrie, referring to the eyes of certain Ptolemaic mummies, writes 'they were made by bending and cutting a piece of opaque white glass to the form, inserting a disc of black glass for the iris and surrounding it with a neatly curved border of blue glass, always polished on the upper surface . . .' He also states that 'The gilt busts of more substantial form, about 50 A.D., required more solid work; and the eyes are then cut in white marble, tapering wedge-shaped behind and with a hole drilled in the middle to receive an iris plug of black glass, or obsidian. The finest portrait busts demanded higher work, and then the iris was of clear brown glass or stone, with a pupil of black glass inserted, giving a still more lifelike expression, heightened by the corners of the white being touched with red.'

---

[1] British Museum, *Guide to the First, Second and Third Egyptian Rooms*, 1924, p. 17.

[2] For the Museum numbers see A. Lucas, *Technical Studies*, VII (1938), p. 18.

[3] C. C. Edgar, *Graeco-Egyptian Coffins*, p. vi.

[4] W. M. F. Petrie, *Hawara, Biahmu and Arsinoe*, p. 17.

Other Examples of the Graeco-Roman Period

Three Statuettes of Divinities.[1] Limestone; Cairo Museum.

Eyelids: in one case, none; in one case, blue glass; in the third case, a black border as part of the white glass eyeball.

White: opaque white glass.

Pupil: black glass.

Caruncle: none.

Small Wooden Bust.[2] Cairo Museum.

Eyelids: none.

White: crystalline limestone.

Pupil: obsidian or black glass.

Caruncle: none.

Four Silver-gilt Statuettes.[3] Cairo Museum.

Eyelids: two blue glass; two very dark blue, or black, glass.

White: opaque white glass.

Pupil: black glass.

Caruncle: none.

Pair of Loose Eyes.[4]

Eyelids: none.

White: thin, slightly concavo-convex, eye-shaped pieces of bone, having in the middle of the front a flattened area to which the pupil has been attached.

Pupil: missing.

Caruncle: none.

Single Loose Eye.[5] Cairo Museum.

Eyelids: blue glass.

White: a thin, slightly curved piece of opaque white glass flattened in the middle of the convex side where the pupil is attached.

Pupil: a thin circular piece of glass, now white and much corroded, but probably black originally.

Caruncle: none.

Examples Undated

Five Anthropoid Coffins.[6] Cairo Museum.

Eyelids: three blue glass; one probably black glass; one without eyelids.

White: three crystalline limestone; two opaque white glass.

Iris: present in one instance only and consists of a grey ring round the black pupil, probably white paint under the thin edge of the translucent black glass.

Pupil: two black glass; one transparent glass with black paint under; one obsidian, or black glass; and one neither obsidian, nor black glass, but probably painted.

Caruncle: none.

---

[1] Nos. 38413, 38902, 38903. [2] No number. [3] Nos. J. 46380–46383; 1st century B.C.
[4] Private collection. [5] No. J. 63031. [6] Nos. J. 33618; J. 41097; $\frac{17|1}{26|5}$, $\frac{23|1}{27|1}$, $\frac{21|11}{16|3}$

Small Gilt Wooden Statuette.[1] Cairo Museum.
    Eyelids: blue glass.
    White: opaque white glass.
    Pupil: black glass.
    Caruncle: none.

Seventeen Loose Eyes.
    These consist of five pairs and seven single eyes, as follows:

Three Pairs of Huge Eyes.[2] Cairo Museum.
    These vary in length from about nine inches to about eighteen inches.
    Eyelids: metal, copper or bronze.
    Eyeball: two limestone; one largely, or wholly, modern plaster.
    Pupil: one probably black glass much corroded on the surface, which is now matt;
two pairs are without pupils.
    Caruncle: none.

Pair of Coffin Eyes.[3] Cairo Museum.
    Eyelids: copper corroded.
    Eyeball: crystalline limestone.
    Pupil: obsidian.
    Caruncle: present in both canthi of both eyes.

Pair of Very Small Eyes.[4]
    Eyelids: none.
    Eyeball: crystalline limestone.
    Pupil: probably obsidian (one missing).
    Caruncle: none.

Seven Single Eyes. Three Cairo Museum;[5] four private collection.
    Eyelids: two blue glass; one steatite;[6] four missing.
    Eyeball: four crystalline limestone; three opaque white glass.
    Pupil: three probably obsidian; three black glass; one missing.
    Caruncle: present in one instance only and in both canthi.

CLASS III

These eyes were included at first with those of Class II. The total number known to me is very small, namely, five pairs and four single ones in my private collection and one single one shown to me by the late Mr. R. H. Blanchard of Cairo. I have also parts of two others, one being an iris with pupil attached and the other only the pupil.

---

[1] No. J. 35215.   [2] Nos. (a) $\frac{20|11}{24|15}$, $\frac{20|11}{24|5}$, (b) J. 37052 and $\frac{20|11}{24|16}$ (c) No number.
[3] No. $\frac{26|3}{25|3}$.   [4] Private collection.   [5] Nos. $\frac{21|12}{26|16}$; J. 36218; $\frac{11|5}{34|1}$.
[6] The eyelids are fastened to the eyeballs by means of black resin, which is also used to fasten in the pupils.

This type of eye is known to me only from Roman mummy masks from the Fayum province; it is anatomically better, and hence more effective, than the Class II eye, because there is always an iris.

Eyelids: copper.

Eyelashes: the usual prolongation of copper eyelids with serrated edges. Whether there were eyelashes in all cases it is impossible to say, but, although they now remain in only two instances, there is evidence that there have been others.

Eyeball: crystalline limestone, all more or less wedge-shaped, which vary in depth from back to front from 1.5 to 2.3 centimetres (approximately one half to one inch), the deeper eyeballs being true wedges tapering almost to a point behind, and the shallower ones having a flat surface at the back. In the middle of the front of the eyeball there is a deep, circular, and generally conical, hole for the insertion of the iris and pupil.

Cornea: none.

Iris: this consists of a conical glass plug having an outer diameter of from 10 to 15 millimetres (approximately 0.4 to 0.6 inch), with a circular hole in the middle for the insertion of the pupil. In one instance, the iris is very light greenish-brown in colour; in another instance it is light green; in two instances it is partly light green and partly black and in the remaining cases it is black. It was suggested previously [1] that these irides probably were black originally and that the present lighter colours of several of them were due to decomposition and chemical change, since in most there is a definite decomposition of the glass. It is now thought, however, that the original colour was brown, or greenish-brown, and that the black is the result of decomposition. The evidence for this is twofold: first, that the one specimen that shows no decomposition is a light greenish-brown colour; and, second, that had the original colour been black, there would not have been any reason for a separate iris, since it would have been indistinguishable from the pupil, and, therefore, a large black pupil similar to that of Class II eyes would have done equally well.

Pupil: a small cone-shaped plug of black glass fitting into the hole in the iris. Between the pupil and the iris there is generally, though not always, a very thin piece of copper foil, so thin that it hardly shows at the surface.

Caruncle: none.

CLASS IV

Reisner found in the Menkaurē pyramid temple at Giza [2] four loose eyes and parts of the frame of a fifth 'probably from one wooden statue and three statuettes', which he describes as 'Five crystal eyes set in copper.' They are all of Fourth Dynasty date.

As these eyes are now in the Museum of Fine Arts, Boston, I have not been able to examine them, but the description given by the finder is as follows:

Eyelids: copper. In one place the material is given as bronze, but this is most improbable at such an early date.

White: there is no eyeball: the whole front of the eye is one piece of transparent rock crystal, the outer surface of which is polished. In one instance the back is matt

---

[1] A. Lucas, *Ancient Egypt*, 1934, p. 96.
[2] G. A. Reisner, *Mycerinus*, p. 114.

and convex, while in another instance it is flat. On the back of the rock crystal the white of the eye is shown by means of white paint.

Cornea: there is no separate cornea, though that part of the rock crystal covering the iris and pupil represents the cornea.

Iris: painted in dark red at the back of the rock crystal.

Pupil: shallow, circular hole in the rock crystal (presumably at the back, though this is not expressly stated), filled with black material.

Caruncle: painted at the back of the rock crystal.

Part of what probably was originally a similar eye of Middle Kingdom date in the Cairo Museum [1] consists of a curved piece of transparent rock crystal of the 'almond' shape of the conventional eye, polished at both sides and with rounded edges. This has a small, circular recess at the middle of the back for the insertion of the pupil, which is missing.

What is also probably a somewhat similar eye is that of the celebrated bust of Nefertiti now in the Berlin Museum. The description of this eye (there is only one), which I owe to the kindness of Professor Alexander Scharff, is that of Professor Rathgen, who examined it, and which is as follows: *Der Grund der Augen (das Weiss im Auge) ist der Kalkstein der Buste, die Pupille ist eine schwarze Scheibe aus Wachs, die äussere Fläche des erhaltenen Auges ist aus Bergkristall.*

Some of the eyes from mummy masks of the Graeco-Roman period are of almost the same technique as that just described, though much inferior both in material and workmanship. I have examined the eyes of twenty-three of these masks in the Cairo Museum,[2] with the following results:

Eyelids: painted.

White: the white plaster of the mask, the colour possibly enhanced in some instances by means of white paint.

Cornea: none.

Iris: none.

Pupil: black paint.

Caruncle: none.

The whole front of the eye is covered with a thin, curved piece of transparent glass which sometimes is now iridescent, owing to surface decay. This glass cover often is of very irregular shape and badly fitted into the socket, but since the edges are buried in the plaster of the socket, they do not show unless the eye is damaged.

Edgar says [3] of these eyes 'But on the heads of the present class the eye is usually inlaid in a different way; a small, convex sheet of transparent glass or mica is laid over a plaster ground on which the iris is painted in black.' With further respect to the mica mentioned, Edgar states [3] that 'On some of the specimens which I have seen the material looked like mica, but in most cases it seems to be artificial glass, sometimes iridescent and sometimes full of small air bubbles.' I have examined carefully the eyes of all these masks and cannot find any in which the material is mica.

A statuette from the tomb of Tutankhamūn [4] has eyes of this type with gold

[1] A. Lucas, *Ancient Egypt*, 1934, p. 89. Museum No. J. 60261.
[2] For the Museum numbers see A. Lucas, *Technical Studies*, VII (1938), pp. 3–32.
[3] C. C. Edgar, *Graeco-Egyptian Coffins*, p. vi.
[4] Museum No. J. 60732.

eyelids: the nature of the white was not determined; the pupil is black paint; there is a caruncle in both canthi of both eyes and the whole of the front of the eyes is covered with transparent, colourless glass.

CLASS V

This type of eye is a very poor imitation of the natural eye and consists of eyelids, eyeball and pupil only, all made in one piece. The material may be limestone, fine-grained white sandstone, faience, glass, or painted wood.

Examples

Single Eye [1] (*Nineteenth to Twentieth Dyn.*). Cairo Museum.

This was found at Qantir and consists of an eye-shaped tray with raised border, which latter represents the eyelids, the eyeball being the bottom of the tray, in the middle of which a large pupil has been painted in deep black. The material of the eye is a very-fine-grained white sandstone, which is artificially coloured slightly black on the surface.

Two Stone Statuettes [2] (*Roman period*). Cairo Museum.

The eyelids, eyeball and pupil are all one piece of glass, the eyelids being represented by a black border to the eyeball, which is opaque white; the pupil is black.

Pair of Eyes [3] (*undated*). Cairo Museum.

The eyelids, eyeball and pupil are all one piece of glass, the eyelids being blue, the eyeball opaque white and the pupil black.

Single Eye [4] (*undated*). Cairo Museum.

The eyelids, eyeball and pupil are all one piece of faience, the eyelids and eyeball being coated with blue glaze and the pupil with black glaze, the latter being slightly corroded on the surface.

Four Single Eyes [5] (*undated*). Cairo Museum.

These eyes are all of slightly different sizes. Three consist of an eye-shaped framework, or tray, with a raised border to represent the eyelids, the bottom of the tray representing the eyeball, in the middle of which is a raised oval-shaped pupil with a convex upper surface. The whole is one piece of limestone, blackened superficially. The fourth eye consists of an eye-shaped tray with raised border without pupil, the whole being one piece of limestone blackened superficially.

Two Single Eyes [6] (*undated*). Cairo Museum.

These, which are not a pair, are from coffins and consist of painted wood. They differ both in size and in technique and are as follows:

Eyelids: painted black directly on the wood in each case.

White: in one case, painted white directly on the wood; in the other case the wood is covered with a thin coat of white plaster.

---

[1] No. J. 64085. [2] L. Borchardt, *Statuen und Statuetten*, IV, Nos. 1190, 1191.
[3] No. J. 25034. [4] No. $\frac{21}{26}|\frac{12}{17}$.
[5] Nos. J. 64767–64769, one without number. [6] Nos. $\frac{2}{27}|\frac{9}{2}$ a, $\frac{2}{27}|\frac{9}{2}$ b.

Iris: in one case, none; and in the other, painted red on the white plaster.

Pupil: painted black directly on the wood in one case and painted black on the white plaster in the other case.

Caruncle: painted red on the white plaster in one case, and painted red on white paint in the other. There is a caruncle in each canthus of each eye.

CLASS VI

This type of eye is only partly inlaid and is confined to bronze statuettes. The eye sockets are part of the bronze casting and in each corner of each socket is inlaid a small triangular piece of gold, or occasionally silver or electrum, leaving a circular area of bronze uncovered in the middle to represent the pupil. Thirty-one of these statuettes in the Cairo Museum [1] have been examined by me, the dates, where they are known, ranging from the late Egyptian period to Ptolemaic times. Daressy, who has described a large proportion of these statuettes, calls most of the examples of gold inlay, silver.[2]

NOT CLASSIFIED

A grotesque figure in wood of unknown date in the Cairo Museum [3] has eyes consisting of translucent red material, which is called carnelian in the register, but which is either red glass, or garnet, but probably glass. A loose eye of similar material was shown to me by the late Mr. R. H. Blanchard of Cairo, who thought it was from a pottery figure of Roman date.

NON-HUMAN EYES

A large number of non-human eyes in the Cairo Museum have been examined by me and are as follows:

Two Leopards' Heads (Twelfth Dyn.).

These are on mirror handles, each of which has a double face with inlaid eyes. The eyelids are silver and the whole eye is covered with a thin curved plate of rock crystal, under which the pupils are painted, the white of the eye probably being plaster. In one case,[4] one eye is missing. Vernier says [5] of one head that the eyes are rock crystal, and of the other that they are of felspar and rock crystal. Bénédite says [6] of one that the cover is glass or quartz, the white (which he calls the cornea) perhaps ivory, the iris painted and the pupil (which he calls *le cristallin*) *un point gravé en creux et enduit de noir.*

Tomb of Tutankhamūn

Lions' Heads: (a) on throne; (b) on couch; (c) on bow case; (d) *Leopards' Heads*; (e) *Lion-headed god;* (f) *Ibex.*

Eyelids: (a), (c), (e), not determined; (b) black glass; (d) blue glass; (f) metal, copper or bronze.

---

[1] For the Museum numbers see A. Lucas, *Technical Studies*, VII (1938), p. 26.

[2] G. Daressy, *Statues de divinités*, I.

[3] No. $\frac{9}{27}|\frac{8}{9}$.

[4] No. 53104.

[5] E. Vernier, *Bijoux et Orfèvreries*, Nos. 53161 and 53104.

[6] G. Bénédite, *Miroirs*, Nos. 44087 and 44088.

White: painted except in (*e*) and (*f*), which have no white.
Iris: (*a*) gold leaf; (*b*), (*c*), (*d*), (*e*) yellow paint; (*f*) brown paint.
Pupil: painted black in all cases.
Caruncle: none.

Cow's Head.
   Eyelids: black glass.
   White: probably white opaque glass, not crystalline limestone, as previously stated
by me.[1]
   Iris: none.
   Pupil: obsidian or black glass.
   Carter refers to the 'inlaid eyes of lapis lazuli glass'.[2]

Anubis.
   Eyelids: gold.
   White: crystalline limestone.[3]
   Pupil: probably obsidian.
   Caruncle: present in both canthi of both eyes.
   Carter states [2] that the eyes 'are inlaid with gold, calcite and obsidian'.

Cobras: (*a*) two on arms of throne; (*b*) six on back of throne; (*c*) large cobra on
      stand; (*d*) two serpent standards.
   Iris: (*a*) probably gold leaf; (*b*) yellowish calcite; (*c*) red, painted; (*d*) brown,
painted.
   Pupil: (*a*), (*c*), (*d*), painted black; (*b*) probably painted, but now almost entirely
disappeared.
   The whole eye in (*a*), (*c*), (*d*) is covered with colourless, transparent glass; (*b*) no
cover.

Birds.
   Many of the birds' eyes are probably obsidian.

Horse Blinkers.
   There are inlaid eyes on two of the blinkers.
   Eyelids: blue glass.
   White: crystalline limestone.
   Pupil: probably obsidian.
   Caruncle: none.

Other Non-Human Eyes

Bulls and Cows.
   An excellent and detailed account of the inlaid eyes of mummies of bulls and
cows from Armant has been published by Myers.[4] In these eyes the eyelids, when
present, are metal, either copper or bronze, and in one case certainly bronze; the
white is usually opaque white glass, but occasionally limestone, with one example of

---

[1] A. Lucas, *Ancient Egypt*, 1934, p. 94.   [2] H. Carter, *Tut-ankh-Amen*, III, p. 41.
[3] Tested since last described.   [4] R. Mond and O. H. Myers, *Bucheum*, I, pp. 65–67.

chert and one of ivory; the pupil is generally black glass, but occasionally obsidian, with two examples of red glass, one of yellow glass and one of black paint, and the caruncle, wrongly called the canthus, when present, instead of being painted as in the human eyes described, and in Tutankhamūn's cow's eyes, is inlaid in red glass.

Head of Anubis from Armant[1] (*Fourth Century* B.C. *to Fourth Century* A.D.). Cairo Museum.
   Eyelids: blue glass.
   White: opaque white glass.
   Pupil: black glass.
   Caruncle: none.

Hawk from Hierakonpolis (*Sixth Dyn.*). Cairo Museum.
   The eyes 'are formed by a single rod of obsidian polished in a spherical curve at each end . . .'[2] There are no eyelids. I had the good fortune to be able to examine this rod of obsidian on one occasion when it was removed temporarily from the head. Wainwright refers to the use of obsidian for the eyes of a very large bird statue of the same provenance and date, which is now in the Museum of University College, London.[3]

Two Hawks in a Pectoral (*Middle Kingdom*). Cairo Museum.
   These have amethyst eyes, and two hawks' heads of the same date have garnet eyes, both of which are described by Vernier.[4] The finder of the hawks' heads, de Morgan, says[5] that the eyes are of such a good colour that they must be ruby and not carnelian. The eyes of the hawks in a pectoral of the same date in New York are also of garnet.[6]

Cobras (*Middle Kingdom*). Cairo Museum.
   Three uraei belonging to jewellery have garnet eyes. These are:
   No. 52641. Uraeus in crown. Vernier calls the eyes obsidian,[7] although the finder, Brunton, states that they are garnet.[8]
   No. 52702. Uraeus. One eye is missing. Vernier calls the other eye obsidian.[7]
   No. 52915. Head of Uraeus. Vernier correctly describes the eyes as garnet.[7]

Fish.
   Miss Caton-Thompson[9] found an amuletic fish of Twelfth Dynasty date, which had eyes of lapis lazuli.

---

[1] No. J. 55620.   [2] J. E. Quibell, *Hierakonpolis*, I, p. 11.
[3] G. A. Wainwright, *Ancient Egypt*, 1927, p. 88.
[4] E. Vernier, *Bijoux et Orfèvreries*, Nos. 52712, 52861, 52862.
[5] J. de Morgan, *Dahchour, 1894–1895*, p. 58.
[6] G. Brunton, *Lahun*, I, p. 28.
[7] E. Vernier, *Bijoux et Orfèvreries*.
[8] G. Brunton, *Lahun*, I, p. 27.
[9] G. Caton-Thompson and E. W. Gardner, *Desert Fayum*, p. 138.

Loose Eyes. Cairo Museum.

Two non-human eyes of Middle Kingdom date described by Vernier [1] as those of a falcon, but which Brunton tells me are from a goose, or swan,[2] are small, almost round, and so corroded that, until they have been cleaned, their nature cannot be determined with certainty. The eyelids are copper and the whole eye is covered with what is probably rock crystal.

Montet found at Tanis [3] a pair of animal eyes of late date, of which the eyelids are metal, either copper or bronze, the front of the eye being an almond-shaped, convaco-convex piece of rock crystal, on the under side of which is an inverted pear-shaped, vertical pupil painted in black, behind which is thin gold leaf for the iris.

Two Pairs of Eyes [4] (*undated*).

From their shape, these are almost certainly from mummies of bulls or cows.

Eyelids: blue glass, but present only in one eye.

Eyeball: missing in one pair of eyes and partly missing in the other pair. The nature of the material cannot be determined without chemical analysis, but probably both the remaining parts are corroded glass.[5]

Pupil: probably obsidian.

Caruncle: none.

It seems highly probable that a mistake has been made in pairing these eyes, since one pupil of each pair is thick and deeply grooved all round the edges, except the top, so that it might be keyed into the eyeball or white; one pupil is much thinner and has no groove, and one pupil has a tenon at the back for fixing it into a socket.

---

[1] E. Vernier, *Bijoux et Orfèvreries*, Nos. 52951–52952.

[2] G. Brunton, *Lahun*, I, p. 38.

[3] No. J. 63151.

[4] Nos. $\frac{22|12}{26|12}$, $\frac{22|12}{26|13}$, $\frac{22|12}{26|14}$, $\frac{22|12}{26|15}$.

[5] One of the eyeballs was previously reported by me (A. Lucas, *Ancient Egypt*, 1934, pp. 96–97) as crystalline limestone because it effervesced considerably with acid, and the other eyeball was reported as probably magnesite, or magnesian limestone, of which it has all the appearance. It is covered with white powder and does not effervesce. See R. Mond and O. H. Myers, *Bucheum*, I, pp. 70–71.

Chapter VIII
FIBRES: WOVEN FABRICS
AND DYEING

Under the head of fibres it is proposed to deal with, not only the fibres employed for making Woven Fabrics, but also those used for Basketry, Brushes, Cordage, Matting and Paper, which may conveniently be done in alphabetical order.

BASKETRY

The making of baskets, or plaiting, was one of the first arts practised by primitive man, being earlier than weaving, of which, as pointed out by Lucretius, it is but the first step, and manifestly it is the simpler of the two, since in basketry no other preparation of the fibre is necessary beyond the selection and cutting into lengths, with sometimes, as in the case of palm leaves, the splitting into suitable widths, whereas before weaving is possible there must always be some preliminary treatment. Thus all fibres must be spun before they can be woven and certain stems (i.e. flax), which are composed of bundles of fibres enclosed in woody tissue, must not only be separated into their component parts, but these must be cleaned from adherent material before they can be employed. Also, baskets are made without the use of any kind of machinery, whereas the appliances of distaff, whorl and spindle are required for spinning and and a machine (the loom) for weaving, before woven fabrics can be produced.

In Egypt, the making of baskets dates back to neolithic times,[1] which probably came to an end about 7,000 years ago.

The subject of basket making in ancient Egypt is one that has been comparatively little studied, either with regard to the materials or to the technique of the methods employed, and although numerous references can be found to materials stated to have been used, these statements are of such different value, and some are of such doubtful worth, that any list of them would be misleading. Recently, however, an important series of identifications has been published by Greiss,[2] many of whose results are incorporated in the present discussion.

The principal materials employed were the leaves of the date palm both for coil and wrapping (the whole leaf being used for coarse work, but being split into narrow strips for finer work), with sometimes the split mid-rib of the branches of the date palm for foundations.[3] In the south, the leaves of the dom palm were often substituted for those of the date palm, but the argun palm does not appear to have been used for

---

[1] G. Caton-Thompson and E. W. Gardner, *Desert Fayum*, pp. 43, 44, 46, 89.
[2] E. A. M. Greiss, *Bull. Inst. d'Ég.*, XXXI (1949), pp. 262–73; XXXVI (1955), pp. 228–33; XXXVII (1956), pp. 252–4; *Mém. Inst. dÉ'g.*, LV (1957), pp. 106–22.
[3] W. S. Blackman, *Fellahin of Upper Egypt*, p. 304.

any purpose. Seven large baskets made from split palm leaf, alone and in conjunction with grass, were found in the Eighteenth Dynasty tomb of Queen Meryetamūn,[1] and the leaf lobes and split midribs of the leaves of both date and dom palm were identified in baskets and lids of various dates examined by Greiss.[2] Sandals were also frequently made of palm fibres.[2] The use of both date palm leaf and dom palm leaf by the Egyptians for plaiting is mentioned by Theophrastus,[3] and these materials are still employed for basketry at the present day.[4]

Less frequent materials were grasses and other plant stems. Grass is recorded as having been used for basketry of neolithic age [5] and at various periods since, among which specimens of Badarian,[6] Eleventh Dynasty,[7] Eighteenth Dynasty [8] and Christian [9] date respectively may be mentioned, but unfortunately the particular kind of grass has not always been identified. Ropes and mats, however, found with the Christian baskets were made of halfa grass (a strong, tough, wild grass that grows abundantly in north Africa, including Egypt) and possibly, therefore, the baskets too may have been made of this material. Four baskets and a tray of Eighteenth Dynasty date from Thebes were made of halfa grass, the 'bottoms, inner rims and other parts which were required to stand special wear or strain are whipped with palm-leaf strip'.[10] Newberry states [11] that 'Two species of grass were used in the manufacture of basket-work', but the species are not named. Sometimes the coil of a basket is of grass and the wrapping of split palm leaf.

The use of halfa grasses in basketry has been discussed by Keimer,[12] and more recently by Greiss,[13] who distinguishes the two species *Desmostachya bipinnata* (=*Eragrostis cynosuroides*) and *Imperata cylindrica*. Both have been definitely identified in ancient Egyptian work,[14] though the former was more extensively used, alone or in conjunction with other fibres, for baskets, brushes, cordage and matting.[15] Esparto grass (*Stipa tenacissima*) and other grasses are sometimes improperly referred to as 'halfa'.[16]

---

[1] H. E. Winlock, *Meryet-Amūn*, pp. 34–35, 76–77.

[2] E. A. M. Greiss, *Bull. Inst. d'Ég.*, XXXI (1949), pp. 262–73; *Mém. Inst. d'Ég.*, LV (1957), pp. 106–22.

[3] *Enquiry into Plants*, IV: 2, 7.

[4] W. S. Blackman, *Fellahin of Upper Egypt*, pp. 155–61.

[5] G. Caton-Thompson, *Antiquity*, I (1927), p. 335.

[6] G. Brunton and G. Caton-Thompson, *Badarian Civilisation*, pp. 62–63.

[7] H. E. Winlock, *M.M.A. Bull., Egyptian Exped. 1925–1927*, p. 8, Fig. 7.

[8] H. E. Winlock, *Meryet-Amūn*, pp. 73, 75, 77.

[9] H. E. Winlock and W. E. Crum, *Monastery of Epiphanius*, p. 74.

[10] A. Lansing and W. C. Hayes, *M.M.A. Bull., Egyptian Exped. 1935–1936*, p. 26. Cf. W. C. Hayes, *M.M.A. Bull., Egyptian Exped. 1934–1935*, p. 27.

[11] P. E. Newberry, in W. M. F. Petrie, *Hawara, Biahmu and Arsinoe*, p. 52.

[12] L. Keimer, *O.L.Z.*, XXX (1927), pp. 76–85, 145–54; *Revue de l'Égypte ancienne*, III (1930) p. 152.

[13] E. A. M. Greiss, *Mém. Inst. d'Ég.*, LV (1957), pp. 5–30.

[14] E. A. M. Greiss, *Mém. Inst. d'Ég.*, LV (1957), pp. 144–5.

[15] For examples of both see E. A. M. Greiss, *Bull. Inst. d'Ég.*, XXXI (1949), pp. 262–73; XXXVI, (1955), pp. 228–33; *Mém. Inst. d'Ég.*, LV (1957), pp. 106–22; V. Täckholm and M. Drar, *Flora of Egypt*, I, pp. 181–3, 485–6.

[16] Cf. L. Keimer, *Revue de l'Égypte ancienne*, III (1930), p. 152; V. Täckholm and M. Drar, *Flora of Egypt*, I, p. 356.

But grass was not the only plant stem employed, the stems of a dicotyledonous plant having been used in neolithic [1] and Badarian [2] times. The Badarian specimen was possibly a species of flax, and flax fibres have also been identified in basketry and matting of dynastic date.[3] Coiled straw was used to line grain silos of the neolithic period,[4] a comb case of protodynastic date was made of straw,[5] and a tray (Eighteenth Dynasty) of straw and palm leaf.[6] Ceruana pratensis FORSK., a small plant well known in Egypt,[7] was also employed in basketry, for example in several vase covers of pre-dynastic date, and in basket coffins of the protodynastic period.[8]

Papyrus, though it was extensively utilized for other purposes, was rarely, if ever, employed for basket making in ancient Egypt. It was undoubtedly used, often in association with reeds, for making certain receptacles, which are, however, better described as boxes rather than baskets, since basketry, as the term is here used, means a simple kind of weaving necessitating the plaiting or interlacing of the fibres, whereas these objects are not plaited. Petrie says [9] that 'Flat papyrus slices of the outer brown skin were greatly used for making boxes for food, framed on lengths of reed lashed together.' He records the finding of a papyrus box of predynastic date,[10] 'papyrus or reed boxes' [11] and 'four boxes of papyrus stems bound with palm rope', [11] though an illustration of what is probably one of the 'boxes' just mentioned is called a 'papyrus basket'.[11] Quibell, recording an object of this nature from the tomb of Yuya and Tuyu, calls it a basket:[12] it consists of a large oblong receptacle for wigs in the form of a dwelling-house and is described as being made of papyrus stems, papyrus pith and reeds. A papyrus box found in the tomb of Tutankhamūn, described by Carter as 'a papyrus basket belonging to the King's writing outfit',[13] so far as can be seen, appears to be made of thin slices of papyrus pith on a framework of reeds: it is lined with linen and is decorated on the top and front with narrow strips of a glossy vegetable material, probably straw, and two small gilt and painted pictures. Another box from the same tomb, which is divided into six compartments, is made of a frame-work and panels of reeds lined with slices of papyrus pith. Bruyère illustrates small papyrus boxes of New Kingdom date,[14] and Greiss refers to 'square boxes' of the Twentieth Dynasty made of papyrus.[15] Greiss also describes two protodynastic

[1] G. Caton-Thompson, Antiquity, I (1927), p. 335.
[2] G. Brunton and G. Caton-Thompson, Badarian Civilisation, pp. 62–63.
[3] E. A. M. Greiss, Bull. Inst. d'Ég., XXXI (1949), pp. 262–73; Mém. Inst. d'Ég., LV (1957), pp. 106–22, 154.
[4] G. Caton-Thompson and E. W. Gardner, Desert Fayum, p. 42.
[5] Z. Y. Saad, Royal Excavations at Helwan 1945–7 (Ann. Serv., Cahier 14), Pl. XLIV (c).
[6] H. E. Winlock, Meryet-Amūn, p. 73.
[7] L. Keimer, Ann. Serv., XXXII (1932), pp. 30–37; E. A. M. Greiss, Mém. Inst. d'Ég., LV (1957), pp. 100–1.
[8] L. Keimer, Ann. Serv., XXXII (1932), pp. 30–37; E. A. M. Greiss, Bull. Inst. d'Ég., XXXVI (1955), pp. 228–33; Mém. Inst. d'Ég., LV (1957), pp. 99, 108, 113, 153.
[9] W. M. F. Petrie, Social Life in Ancient Egypt, p. 143.
[10] W. M. F. Petrie and J. E. Quibell, Naqada and Ballas, p. 26.
[11] W. M. F. Petrie, Deshasheh, pp. 34–35, Pl. XXXIV.
[12] J. E. Quibell, Yuaa and Thuiu, pp. 57–58, Pl. XLVIII.
[13] H. Carter, Tut-ankh-Amen, III, p. 215, Pl. LXVI.
[14] B. Bruyère, Deir el Médineh (1934–1935), pp. 56–57.
[15] E.A.M. Greiss, Bull. Inst. d'Ég., XXXI (1949), pp.257–8.

basket coffins, one made entirely of papyrus culms, the other of papyrus culms together with leaves and culms of *Desmostachya bipinnata* and stem splits of *Ceruana pratensis*,[1] though the technique of construction is more akin to matting than basketry. However, split culms of papyrus and leaf lobes of date palm were used to make a basket lid of uncertain date examined by Greiss,[2] and it is possible that there may be other examples of the use of papyrus in basketry. Papyrus was also employed in making small stools,[3] ring stands for pottery vessels,[4] and sandals.[5]

Greiss states that another species of *Cyperus*, *Cyperus Schimperianus*, was occasionally used in basket making.[6]

Reeds,[7] which are special kinds of water-loving grasses, are generally firm-stemmed and, therefore, although admirably adapted for the framework of boxes, they are not suitable for basketry, since they do not possess the required pliability, though several examples of reed baskets are known from the Badarian period and later.[8] Reeds were sometimes used for making coffins [9] and a particular species, *Phragmites communis*, was employed for making arrows and at a late date for pens. An arrow from the First Dynasty tomb of 'Hemaka' at Saqqara has been identified as *P. communis*, var. *stenophylla*, and others from the Eighteenth Dynasty tomb of Tutankhamūn as *P. communis*, var. *isiaca*.[10] Garstang mentions flutes of *Arundo donax*,[11] and Junker states that plaited basketwork of *Arundo donax* was used to line cereal silos at Merimda, though the identification requires confirmation.[12]

Rushes[13] were also occasionally employed in basketry, and Greiss has identified *Juncus arabicus* in two basket lids of unknown date and *Juncus acutus* in a basket of the Eighteenth Dynasty from Deir el Medineh, another basket probably of the New Kingdom, and four basket covers of uncertain date.[14]

The principal techniques used in ancient basketry and matting have been discussed by Mrs. Crowfoot,[15] who distinguishes them as follows:

---

[1] E. A. M. Greiss, *Bull. Inst. d'Ég.*, XXXVI (1955), p. 231; *Mém. Inst. d'Ég.*, LV (1957), pp. 108–9, 151.

[2] E. A. M. Greiss, *Bull. Inst. d'Ég.*, XXXI (1949), p. 273; *Mém. Inst. d'Ég.*, LV (1957), p. 112.

[3] B. Bruyère, *Deir el Médineh (1934–1935)*, pp. 56–57.

[4] H. E. Winlock, *Meryet-Amūn*, pp. 74, 79.

[5] V. Täckholm and M. Drar, *Flora of Egypt*, II, pp. 118–19.

[6] E. A. M. Greiss, *Mém. Inst. d'Ég.*, LV (1957), p. 85.

[7] E. A. M. Greiss, *Mém. Inst. d'Ég.*, LV (1957), pp. 57–75, 148–50; V. Täckholm and M. Drar, *Flora of Egypt*, I, p. 207 (*Arundo*), pp. 213–15 (*Phragmites*).

[8] G. Brunton, *Mostagedda*, p. 63.

[9] G. Brunton, *Qau and Badari*, I, pp. 13, 22, 31, 32, 47; W. M. F. Petrie, *Deshasheh*, p. 34; A. Rowe, *The Mus. Journ.*, Philadelphia, XXII (1931), p. 27; R. Macramallah, *Un cimetière archaïque . . . à Saqqarah*, p. 3.

[10] E. A. M. Greiss, *Bull. Inst. d'Ég.*, XXXI (1949), p. 270.

[11] J. Garstang, *Burial Customs*, pp. 154–5. Cf. also V. Loret, *Journal asiatique*, 8e sér., XIV (1889), pp. 111–42, 197–237.

[12] Cf. E. A. M. Greiss, *Mém. Inst. d'Ég.*, LV (1957), pp. 148–9.

[13] E. A. M. Greiss, *Mém. Inst. d'Ég.*, LV (1957), pp. 90–98, 152–3; V. Täckholm and M. Drar, *Flora of Egypt*, II, pp. 451 f.

[14] E. A. M. Greiss, *Bull. Inst. d'Ég.*, XXXI (1949), pp. 262–73; *Mém. Inst. d'Ég.*, LV (1957), pp. 106–22, 152–3. Cf. also V. Täckholm and M. Drar, *Flora of Egypt*, II, pp. 473–7.

[15] G. M. Crowfoot, in *History of Technology*, I, pp. 415–18.

(a) Coiled basketry, in which a core consisting of a bundle of fibres is coiled spirally, the different layers being fastened together by a sewing strip. Three distinct types of centre and four main variations in the method of wrapping are described and illustrated.

(b) Twined work, in which single rushes or bundles of fibres are laid side by side and interlaced by two threads. This technique, of which five variations are noted, is most commonly used for matting.

(c) Wrapped work, akin to weaving, and also used for matting, in which a single wrapping strand passes round bundles of fibres.

(d) Matting work, also akin to weaving, in which one series of fibres forms the warp and another the weft.

(e) Plaited work, in which plaits are made separately and sewn into the required shape.

(f) Wickerwork, in which strands are woven in and out of a stake-frame.

So far as can be ascertained, all ancient Egyptian baskets were of the coiled type, though twined work was used for hamper coffins, bags and matting, and different forms of matting work have survived. Wickerwork, the most common technique in modern basketry, was apparently not known.

Many individual specimens of Egyptian basketwork from the neolithic period onwards are described in Mrs. Crowfoot's article.[1] with particular reference to the variations of technique that were employed, and both Miss Blackman [2] and Wainwright [3] have also described a few ancient baskets, comparing them with modern Egyptian examples with which they are almost identical. Seven types of basket of New Kingdom date from Deir el Medineh are illustrated by Bruyère, who notes the use of vertical bindings or ribbings for strengthening, and the frequent presence of an internal flange to support the lid.[4]

The ancient baskets were often decorated, thus Wainwright says [5] that '. . . many XVIIIth dynasty baskets show regular patterns carried out in colours', and again that 'small or finely made ones . . . are quite commonly decorated in colour, while larger ones . . . often have seams of ornamental stitching running up their sides'. Carter points out that some of the baskets from the tomb of Tutankhamūn have patterns formed by interweaving dyed fibres with undyed fibres.[6] Petrie describes certain baskets of Twelfth Dynasty date as having woven patterns on the sides; [7] one from the Eighteenth Dynasty as being red and black [8] and one of the Roman period as red and white.[8] Four baskets and a tray decorated with designs in red and black of Eighteenth Dynasty date were found at Thebes,[9] and a coloured grass basket of the Eleventh Dynasty.[10]

[1] G. M. Crowfoot, in *History of Technology*, I, pp. 418–24.

[2] W. S. Blackman, *Fellahin of Upper Egypt*, p. 304.

[3] G. A. Wainwright, *Ann. Serv.*, XXIV (1924), pp. 108–11; *Bull. Soc. sult. de géog.*, Cairo, IX (1919), pp. 177–9.

[4] B. Bruyère, *Deir el Médineh (1934–1935)*, pp. 52–56.

[5] G. A. Wainwright, *Ann. Serv.*, XXIV (1924), pp. 108–11.

[6] H. Carter, *Tut-ankh-Amen*, III, p. 149.   [7] W. M. F. Petrie, *Illahun, Kahun and Gurob*, p. 21.

[8] W. M. F. Petrie, *Objects of Daily Use*, pp. 48–49.

[9] A. Lansing and W. C. Hayes, *M.M.A. Bull., Egyptian Exped. 1935–1936*, p. 26.

[10] H. E. Winlock, *M.M.A. Bull., Egyptian Exped. 1925–1927*, p. 8, Fig. 7.

Basketry work was also employed for sieves, which 'are well known from dynastic times'.[1] A specimen of Eighteenth Dynasty date had a 'mesh with web of palm fibre crossed by warp of palm leaf', the edging being of palm fibre bound with palm leaf,[2] and other sieves made wholly or partly of the fibre and leaf of both date and dom palm have been examined by Greiss.[3] Petrie found 'part of a strong sieve of rush'[4] of the Twentieth Dynasty, two sieves of unknown date examined by Greiss were of *Saccharum biflorum*,[5] and a large sieve of Roman date was made of the culms of *Cyperus Schimperianus*, the split midrib of *Phoenix dactylifera*, and leaves of *Saccharum biflorum*.[6] A sieve of the New Kingdom from Deir el Medineh was made of halfa grass (*Desmostachya bipinnata*) and dom palm leaf,[7] and an example found by Winlock from a Christian Monastery at Thebes 'had a rim made of two cords of grass wrapped around and bound together with palm leaf and a mesh made of small reeds laced together with grass and reinforced at the back with two palm sticks. . . .'[1]

BRUSHES

Brushes were in common use in ancient Egypt and have often been found: they were all made of vegetable fibre, though not always of the same sort of fibre, and were essentially of three kinds, namely, (*a*) bundles of coarse fibre or twigs bound together at the top with thin rope, string or palm leaf, so as to form a handle, separate wooden handles not being used; (*b*) bundles of finer fibre though of different degrees of fineness, doubled into half their length and lashed together at the doubled end, and (*c*) pieces of fibrous wood bruised at one end until the fibres separated and formed bristles.

As examples of the first kind may be mentioned the fan-shaped brushes of split reeds used both for sweeping the floor and for fanning the charcoal used for cooking, referred to and illustrated by Petrie;[8] the brush made of the fruit-stalks of dates found by Quibell[9] and the brushes formed of the twigs of *Ceruana pratensis* mentioned by Keimer.[10] Muschler, in his description of this plant, says,[11] 'Generally used for making little brooms, found . . . in old Egyptian tombs', and it is still largely used for brush making in Egypt at the present day.[10] Greiss examined three 'brooms' of this type, two of which were of *Desmostachya bipinnata*, and one of date palm leaf.[12]

Examples of the second kind are a brush of New Kingdom date from Deir el Medineh and two others of uncertain date, identified by Greiss as *Desmostachya bipinnata*,[12] brushes found by Naville at Deir el Bahari,[13] five brushes of palm fibre

---

[1] H. E. Winlock, and W. E. Crum, *Monastery of Epiphanius*, p. 63.

[2] T. E. Peet and C. L. Woolley, *City of Akhenaten*, I, p. 74.

[3] E. A. M. Greiss, *Bull. Inst. d'Ég.*, XXXI (1949), pp. 262–73; *Mém. Inst. d'Ég.*, LV (1957), pp. 106–22. Cf. also Carnarvon and H. Carter, *Five Years' Explorations*, p. 31.

[4] W. M. F. Petrie, *Kahun, Gurob and Hawara*, p. 32.

[5] E. A. M. Greiss, *Mém. Inst. d'Ég.*, LV (1957), p. 149.

[6] E. A. M. Greiss, *Mém. Inst. d'Ég.*, LV (1957), p. 116.

[7] E. A. M. Greiss, *Mém. Inst. d'Ég.*, LV (1957), p. 115.

[8] W. M. F. Petrie, *Social Life in Ancient Egypt*, p. 143; *Objects of Daily Use*, p. 49, Pl. XLII (178).

[9] J. E. Quibell, *Monastery of Apa Jeremias*, p. 17.

[10] L. Keimer, *Ann. Serv.*, XXXII (1932), pp. 32–33.

[11] R. Muschler, *Manual Flora of Egypt*, II, p. 969.

[12] E. A. M. Greiss, *Bull. Inst. d'Ég.*, XXXI (1949), pp. 269, 273.

[13] E. Naville and H. R. Hall, *XIth Dynasty Temple at Deir el Bahari*, III, p. 30, Pl. XXXIII.

of Roman date illustrated by Petrie,[1] and those from the Monastery of Epiphanius described by Winlock,[2] some of which were made of halfa grass and some of split palm leaf, the first-named material being used for the smaller brushes and the second for the larger ones. Small stumpy brushes of this sort were employed for painting and one such was found by Davies as part of a tomb painter's outfit,[3] two by Peet and Woolley [4] and two others by Pendlebury,[5] several being still clogged with the ancient paint. These paint brushes resemble very much in general appearance a certain kind of modern shaving brush.

The wooden brushes of the third kind described were used exclusively for painting, and ten specimens were among the tomb painter's outfit mentioned.[3] These, as already explained, consist of pieces of fibrous wood of different thicknesses, probably all portions of the mid-rib of the branches of the date palm, which have been bruised at one end until the fibres have separated and formed coarse bristles. They still have on them the ancient paint, from which it is evident that separate brushes were kept for different colours.[6] The marks of brushes of two different thicknesses (2–7 mm. and 10–15 mm.) have been noted on paintings of the Amarna period.[7]

CORDAGE

Although no detailed study of the ropes and twines of ancient Egypt had been made, a certain number of facts relating to them are known, which may now be considered.

Rope making consists in spinning or twisting separate fibres into a yarn, and then twisting the yarns into strands and the strands into rope, the sense of twist being reversed each time.[8] The use of a weighted whirling tool for twisting a leather rope, and the laying of two strands into a rope are depicted in tombs of the Eighteenth Dynasty.[8]

Specimens of rope and cord have been found from the Badarian and predynastic periods, the former being of reed,[9] the latter of flax,[10] grass,[11] esparto grass (*Stipa tenacissima*)[12] and halfa grass (*Desmostachya bipinnata*).[13] From the First Dynasty, flax,[14] and papyrus [15] were used, and a rope of Third Dynasty date was also identified as papyrus.[16] Ropes of palm fibre were employed to secure coffins of Old Kingdom

---

[1] W. M. F. Petrie, *Hawara, Biahmu and Arsinoe*, p. 11, Pl. XIII (24, 25); *Objects of Daily Use*, p. 49, Pl. XLII (179–84).

[2] H. E. Winlock and W. E. Crum, *Monastery of Epiphanius*, p. 75.

[3] N. de G. Davies, *Five Theban Tombs*, pp. 5–6, Pl. XVII.

[4] T. E. Peet and C. L. Woolley, *City of Akhenaten*, I, p. 76.

[5] J. D. S. Pendlebury, in *Illustrated London News*, 19th March 1933.

[6] N. M. Davies and A. H. Gardiner, *Ancient Egyptian Paintings*, III, pp. xxxii–xxxiii.

[7] F. W. von Bissing and M. Reach, *Ann. Serv.*, VII (1906), p. 67; F. W. von Bissing, *Fussboden*, p. 14.

[8] K. Gilbert, in *History of Technology*, I, pp. 451–4.   [9] G. Brunton, *Mostagedda*, p. 63.

[10] G. Brunton and G. Caton-Thompson, *Badarian Civilisation*, p. 67.

[11] E. R. Ayrton and W. L. S. Loat, *Predynastic Cemetery at El Mahasna*, p. 17.

[12] O. Menghin and M. Amer, *Excavations of the Eg. University . . . at Ma'adi, Second Prelim. Report*, pp. 49, 67–68. Cf., however, V. Täckholm and M. Drar, *Flora of Egypt*, I, p. 356.

[13] E. A. M. Greiss, *Mém. Inst. d'Ég.*, LV (1957), pp. 106–7.

[14] W. B. Emery, *Hemaka*, pp. 43–44; E. A. M. Greiss, *Bull. Inst. d'Ég.*, XXXI (1949), p. 269.

[15] E. A. M. Greiss, *Bull. Inst. d'Ég.*, XXXI (1949), p. 265.

[16] E. A. M. Greiss, *Bull. Inst. d'Ég.*, XXXI (1949), p. 273.

date from Kafr Ammar,[1] and a two-strand rope of camel hair of similar date is also known.[2] A rope of Sixth Dynasty date was composed of the fibres of a monocotyledonous plant, possibly halfa grass.[3] Of the Eleventh Dynasty is a piece of plaited linen cord 67 cm. long and 3–4 mm. wide,[4] and a rope of flax fibre has also been found from the Twelfth Dynasty.[5] A grass rope about 250 cm. long, probably dating from the Twenty-first Dynasty, was discovered in the tomb of Queen Meryetamūn.[6]

The material most commonly used for making ropes or cords in ancient Egypt was, however, date palm fibre, which consists of the fibres from the naturally-reticulated fabric-like material which at first envelops the leaf and is found at the crown of the trunk of the date palm, surrounding the base of the branches. Many instances of its use in dynastic times may be quoted,[7] and in a papyrus document of unknown, but late, date 200 bundles of palm fibre for making ropes are mentioned.[8] Both date palm fibre and halfa grass were being used as late as the sixth or seventh century A.D.,[9] and date palm fibre is still employed for rope making at the present day.

Theophrastus[10] and Pliny[11] both state that the Egyptians made ropes of papyrus, and in two rope making scenes depicted on tomb walls, one of the Fifth Dynasty[12] and the other probably of the Eighteenth Dynasty,[13] the material being employed is apparently papyrus. Petrie refers to 'papyrus cord',[14] and the use of papyrus for ropes is recorded by Greiss.[15] In May 1942 seven very thick ropes were found buried in debris in one of the Tura caves, which are old stone quarries. These ropes were of papyrus and consisted of three strands, each of which had about forty yarns and each yarn about seven fibres. The circumference was about eight inches and the diameter about two and a half inches. They are not modern, but the date is uncertain. In October 1944 in another of the Tura caves a further rope of papyrus was found, which was about half the thickness of the previous one, with two strands, eight yarns per strand and three fibres per yarn.[16]

A number of specimens of string of Eighteenth Dynasty date examined by me were all made of flax fibre, and Greiss identified a cord of uncertain date as human

---

[1] W. M. F. Petrie and E. Mackay, *Heliopolis, Kafr Ammar and Shurafa*, p. 28.

[2] G. Caton-Thompson and E. W. Gardner, *Desert Fayum*, pp. 88, 119, 123.

[3] G. Brunton, *Qau and Badari*, I, p. 71.

[4] H. E. Winlock, *Slain Soldiers*, p. 10.

[5] W. M. F. Petrie, *Kahun, Gurob and Hawara*, pp. 28, 35.

[6] H. E. Winlock, *Meryet-Amūn*, pp. 47, 79.

[7] E.g. W. M. F. Petrie and E. Mackay, *Heliopolis, Kafr Ammar and Shurafa*, p. 28; W. M. F. Petrie, *Deshasheh*, p. 35; E. Naville and H. R. Hall, *XIth Dynasty Temple at Deir el Bahari*, III, p. 30; Carnarvon and H. Carter, *Five Years' Explorations*, p. 71; H. E. Winlock, *Meryet-Amūn*, p. 74; E. A. M. Greiss, *Bull. Inst. d'Ég.*, XXXI (1949), pp. 271–2.

[8] C. C. Edgar, *Zenon Papyri*, III, No. 59438.

[9] H. E. Winlock and W. E. Crum, *Monastery of Epiphanius*, p. 72.

[10] *Enquiry into Plants*, IV: 8, 4. [11] XIII: 22.

[12] N. de G. Davies, *Ptahhetep*, I, Pl. xxv.

[13] E. Mackay, *J.E.A.*, III (1916), pp. 125–6, Pl. xv.

[14] W. M. F. Petrie, *Deshasheh*, p. 33.

[15] E. A. M. Greiss, *Bull. Inst. d'Ég.*, XXXI (1949), pp. 265, 271–3; *Mém. Inst. d'Ég.*, LV (1957), p. 151.

[16] Cf. E. A. M. Greiss, *Bull. Inst. d'Ég.*, XXXI (1949), pp. 271–2.

hair.[1] String was employed for the making of nets, with knots similar to modern examples, and ancient netting needles have been found.[2]

MATTING

The making of mats has always been, as it still is, one of the important minor industries of Egypt, and mats have been found in graves from the Badarian and predynastic periods onwards, the body frequently resting on a mat, or being covered with, or wrapped in, a mat. Mat-making is illustrated in a Twelfth Dynasty tomb at Beni Hasan,[3] though there are discrepancies in the published copies of the scene which make detailed interpretation somewhat difficult.[4]

The materials principally used for the ancient mats are generally stated to have been either reeds or rushes,[5] but these terms are often employed loosely and incorrectly and the subject of ancient Egyptian mat making needs further work.

Greiss has recorded the identification of the leaf lobes of the dom palm in a fragment of matting of Badarian date,[6] and of *Phragmites communis*, var. *mauritianus*, and *Juncus arabicus* as well as the culms of a species of *Cyperus* in matting of predynastic date.[7] Some of the Badarian and predynastic matting was made of reeds,[8] some of rushes and some of grass. Certain First Dynasty mats were made of halfa grass and others of reeds (*Phragmites communis*)[9] and matting from the First Dynasty examined by me was probably grass bound with flax string.[10] Matting of the Fourth Dynasty, found with the funerary boats of Khufu, was of cattail (*Typha australis*), common rush (*Juncus sp.*) and reed (*Phragmites communis*),[11] some from the Fifth Dynasty at Abusir was composed of palm ribs and palm fibre[12] and matting of Sixth Dynasty date from the Qau-Badari district of Upper Egypt was of rushes.[13] Petrie states that very thin grass was used for mats in the Hyksos period;[14] a large mat from El Amarna was of palm fibre tied with hemp cords[15] and another Eighteenth Dynasty mat was of papyrus.[16] Petrie also records mats of papyrus of predynastic date.[17] Greiss has examined two mats, probably of Eighteenth Dynasty date, from Deir el Medineh and identified the materials as flax fibres, leaves of *Desmostachya bipinnata*, and culms

[1] E. A. M. Greiss, *Bull. Inst. d'Ég.*, XXXVI (1955), pp. 228–33.
[2] W. M. F. Petrie, *Kahun, Gurob and Hawara*, p. 28; *Tools and Weapons*, p. 53.
[3] P. E. Newberry, *Beni Hasan*, II, Pl. XIII.
[4] Cf. G. M. Crowfoot, *Ancient Egypt*, 1933, pp. 93–99; C. H. Johl, *Altägyptische Webestühle*, pp. 31–35.
[5] For references to rush mats see V. Täckholm and M. Drar, *Flora of Egypt*, II, pp. 470–3.
[6] E. A. M. Greiss, *Bull. Inst. d'Ég.*, XXXI (1949), p. 271.
[7] E. A. M. Greiss, *Mém. Inst. d'Ég.*, LV (1957), pp. 107, 149, 152.
[8] G. Brunton, *Mostagedda*, pp. 6–7, 33, 36, 62–63, 93; G. Brunton and G. Caton-Thompson, *Badarian Civilisation*, p. 67; D. Randall MacIver and A. C. Mace, *El Amrah and Abydos*, p. 31, Pl. XI (5, 6).
[9] R. Macramallah, *Un cimetière archaïque . . . à Saqqarah*, pp. 3, 40–42, 47–50.
[10] W. B. Emery, *Hemaka*, p. 43.
[11] Anon., *Archaeology*, IX (1956), pp. 208–9.
[12] H. Schäfer, *Priestergräber vom Totentempel des Ne-user-rê*, p. 114.
[13] G. Brunton, *Qau and Badari*, I, p. 71.
[14] W. M. F. Petrie, *Social Life in Ancient Egypt*, p. 143.
[15] T. E. Peet and C. L. Woolley, *City of Akhenaten*, I, p. 81.
[16] J. E. Quibell, *Yuaa and Thuiu*, p. 65.
[17] W. M. F. Petrie and J. E. Quibell, *Naqada and Ballas*, pp. 23, 25.

of *Juncus maritimus*, var. *arabicus*.[1] Winlock mentions grass mats of the Nineteenth Dynasty, the Twenty-sixth Dynasty and the sixth or seventh century A.D.,[2] respectively, which latter 'were all made of halfa grass bundles on 5 mm. cords of the same grass usually, but sometimes of palm fibre'. Wainwright states [3] that a mat of late New Kingdom date (Twenty-third to Twenty-fifth Dynasties) was made of soft rush, Keimer [4] says that *Saccharum biflorum* was also used for matting, and Greiss [5] states that both *Cyperus Schimperianus* and *Cyperus alopecuroides* (foxtail sedge) were employed in mat making, the latter from as early as the Badarian period.[6]

As already mentioned, the variations of matting technique and the system of twined work used in matting have been described by Mrs. Crowfoot with reference to individual examples,[7] and the same author has also discussed the ancient method of mat making in the light of modern Egyptian practice.[8]

PAPYRUS [9]

The papyrus plant (*Cyperus Papyrus*), a plant belonging to the sedge family (which at one time grew abundantly in the marshy districts of Lower Egypt, where, however, it is no longer found, though it still flourishes in the Sudan), was employed by the Egyptians for many purposes, some of which have been enumerated by Herodotus,[10] Theophrastus[11] and Pliny.[12] The rhizome was eaten,[13] and used as fuel, and the flowers and culms were incorporated in floral decorations. The stem was employed in making light boats, and from the outer pith were made numerous objects, including baskets, boxes, cordage, matting, ring stands, sandals, sieves, stools, etc.[14] Papyrus was also employed medicinally,[15] and the whole plant or parts of it were used in early architecture.[16] Its principal value was, however, for making sheets of material for writing upon, which was the forerunner of modern paper, to which it gave its name.

Specimens of papyrus from the Sudan measured by me varied from seven feet to ten feet in length, excluding the flowering top and the root, and the maximum diameter was nearly an inch and a half (1.4 inch).[17] The stem is triangular in section

---

[1] E. A. M. Greiss, *Mém. Inst. d'Ég.*, LV (1957), pp. 152, 154.

[2] H. E. Winlock and W. E. Crum, *Monastery of Epiphanius*, pp. 72–74.

[3] G. A. Wainwright, in W. M. F. Petrie and E. Mackay, *Heliopolis, Kafr Ammar and Shurafa*, p. 37; *Bull. Soc. sult. de géog.*, Cairo, IX (1919), p. 179.

[4] L. Keimer, *O.L.Z.*, XXX (1927), pp. 76–85, 145–54.

[5] E. A. M. Greiss, *Mém. Inst. d'Ég.*, LV (1957), pp. 85, 87, 152.

[6] For examples see also V. Täckholm and M. Drar, *Flora of Egypt*, II, pp. 95–96.

[7] G. M. Crowfoot, in *History of Technology*, I, pp. 415–24. Cf. also H. E. Winlock and W. E. Crum, *Monastery of Epiphanius*, pp. 72–74.

[8] G. M. Crowfoot, *Ancient Egypt*, 1933, pp. 93–99.

[9] Cf. V. Täckholm and M. Drar, *Flora of Egypt*, II, pp. 102 f., in particular pp. 126–33.

[10] II: 37, 92, 96; VII: 25.   [11] IV: 8, 3, 4.   [12] XIII: 21–26; XXIV: 51.

[13] M. A. Ruffer, *Mém. Inst. d'Ég.*, I (1919), pp. 67–69; L. Keimer, *Journ. Soc. Oriental Research*, XI (1927), pp. 142–5; V. Täckholm and M. Drar, *Flora of Egypt*, II, pp. 104–6.

[14] Cf. E. A. M. Greiss, *Bull. Inst. d'Ég.*, XXXI (1949), pp. 257–9; *Mém. Inst. d'Ég.*, LV (1957), pp. 77–78, 150–1; V. Täckholm and M. Drar, *Flora of Egypt*, II, pp. 114–25; C. Desroches Noblecourt, *Le Papyrus*, part I, pp. 6–7; N. Lewis, *l'Industrie du Papyrus*, pp. 23–45.

[15] V. Täckholm and M. Drar, *Flora of Egypt*, II, pp. 104–6.

[16] A. Badawy, *Ann. Serv.*, LI (1951), pp. 4–17; W. M. F. Petrie, *Egyptian Architecture*, pp. 16–17.

[17] Kindly supplied by Mr. G. W. Grabham, Sudan Government Geologist.

and consists of two parts only, a thin tough outer rind and an inner cellular pith, and it was this latter that was employed as a writing material. The method of making sheets suitable for writing upon from this very unpromising-looking material is described by Pliny,[1] according to whom the stem of the plant was sliced into thin strips, which were placed side by side upon a table and across them at right-angles another series of similar strips; they were then moistened with Nile water, pressed and dried in the sun, Pliny adding that Nile water 'when in a muddy state has the peculiar qualities of glue'. This account is both obscure and wrong. Thus there is no mention of whether the outer rind of the papyrus was removed or not before the material was sliced, though that it was removed is possibly to be inferred from a subsequent statement that the rind was 'solely used for making ropes'. Also, although the Nile water during flood is muddy, it does not contain anything that could possibly act as an adhesive. A later allusion to paste 'made of the finest flour of wheat mixed with boiling water' is far from clear, but probably refers to the fastening of a number of sheets of papyrus together to make one long sheet.[2]

Bruce [3] 'made several pieces of this paper, both in Abyssinia and Egypt', of which he says that 'some were excellent', though this is qualified by the further statement that 'even the best of it was always thick and heavy, drying very soon, then turning firm and rigid and never white'. Bruce is as unsatisfactory as Pliny on the point of whether the rind was removed or not before the papyrus was sliced, though apparently not, since he says, 'There seemed to be an advantage in putting the inside of the pellicle in the situation in which it was before being divided, that is, the interior parts face to face, one long-ways and one cross-ways, after which a thin board of the cover of a book was laid first over it and a heap of stones piled upon it.' This was done, as expressly stated, 'while moist', after which 'they were suffered to dry in the sun'. Bruce adds that it appeared to him 'that the sugar or sweetness, with which the whole juice of this plant is impregnated, is the matter that causes the adhesion of these strips together'.

I tried to make papyrus paper by peeling off the rind, slicing the pith and strongly pressing the slices together, but was unsuccessful, because the papyrus was not fresh, but consisted of plants that had been sent to Cairo from the Sudan, the pith of which had become dry.

Papyrus was successfully reproduced by H. Ibscher, and Battiscombe Gunn, who made excellent papyrus paper,[4] from plants grown in his garden at Ma'adi, according to a method worked out by Miss E. Perkins, was good enough to demonstrate the method employed, as a result of which I have been able to produce similar material.

The method is to cut a number of sections of the fresh green papyrus stems into lengths that can easily be manipulated; strip off the outer rind; separate the inner pith into thick slices (not necessarily all of exactly the same thickness) by making a cut with a knife at one end and then pulling off the slices; place an absorbent cloth on a table and on this arrange a number of slices of the pith parallel to and slightly over-

---

[1] XIII: 21–26; XXIV: 51.

[2] Pliny's account is described by A. J. C. A. Dureau de la Malle, *Mémoire sur le papyrus et la fabrication du papier chez les anciens*, 1850.

[3] J. Bruce, *Travels to Discover the Sources of the Nile*, 1805, VII, pp. 117–31.

[4] Now exhibited in the Cairo Museum.

lapping one another and across them at right angles a further lot, also slightly over-lapping; cover with a thin absorbent cloth and beat the whole for an hour or two with a rounded stone of a size that can be held comfortably in one hand or with a wooden mallet and finally place the material in a small press for several hours or overnight. The slices become welded together, adhering firmly to one another and forming one homogeneous sheet of thin paper suitable for writing upon,[1] the surface of which may be improved by burnishing.[2] The colour of the paper produced, although almost white,[3] was unfortunately marred by being spotted with numerous small light-brown coloured specks, which doubtless could be avoided if special precautions were taken. Any holes or thin places are easily patched before the sheet is pressed and dried by putting a small piece of fresh pith on the defective place and beating until it becomes merged into the rest.

Substantially similar accounts of the fabrication of papyrus are given by Mme. Noblecourt [4] and Černý,[5] both of whom agree that no extraneous adhesive was used in the manufacture, though the individual sheets were subsequently stuck together.[6] More recently, however, papyrus specimens of very high quality have been reproduced by Mr. S. Baker of the British Museum, following a method in some respects different from that of Gunn, and I am most grateful to Mr. Baker for explaining the details to me and allowing me to publish them here.

The papyrus was cut low down, just above the water level, and the lower part of the stem only was used. The outer rind was first removed by making a cut at one end and stripping it off, and the inner pith was similarly separated into strips one-eighth to one-quarter inch in thickness,[7] each stem dividing into seven or eight strips. The strips were then laid side by side,[8] but *not* overlapping, with a similar layer at right angles on top of them, and the whole was beaten together with a wooden mallet,[9] no adhesive being used. The resulting product was then polished with a pebble or a a piece of hard wood. For joining together the separate sheets Baker found that an adhesive was essential, since, although a join could be made using only the natural juice of the pith, it was not satisfactory and tended to fall apart again.

The subsequent making of the papyrus roll, its use and the method of writing

---

[1] Without the addition of any extraneous adhesive.

[2] This was probably done with a smooth pebble or with a special implement of hard wood or ivory.

[3] It is evident from the representations of papyrus rolls in Egyptian wall paintings that new papyrus was white, or nearly so, though old papyrus was conventionally coloured yellow. Cf. J. Černý, *Paper and Books in Ancient Egypt*, pp. 6–7.

[4] C. Desroches Noblecourt, *Le Papyrus*, part I, pp. 9–11.

[5] J. Černý, *Paper and Books in Ancient Egypt*, pp. 5–6.

[6] Cf. also W. Schubart, *Papyruskunde*, pp. 37–39, 45; N. Lewis, *l'Industrie du Papyrus*, pp. 46–58. Schenk, in G. Ebers, *Papyros Ebers*, p. 3, and G. Möller, *Hieratische Paläographie*, I, p. 4, thought that an adhesive was used in the actual fabrication.

[7] The final product was, of course, much thinner. Two specimens of New Kingdom papyrus measured with a micrometer by Černý were 0.10 mm. and 0.15 mm. thick respectively.

[8] In cases where the stem had a marked taper the slices of pith were laid alternately top to bottom.

[9] The actual implement used was a lead-beater's tool, though the layers could be beaten together equally well with a round stone, or rolled with a roller.

upon it have been discussed by several authorities,[1] and in particular by Černý,[2] who has also collected much detailed information regarding the dimensions of papyri.

There are no representations of the making of papyrus paper on tomb walls, but the gathering of the plant, the transport of the bundles, the stripping and cleaning of the stems and the making of boats and ropes are shown.[3]

The date when papyrus was first made is not known, but in the Cairo Museum there are small papyrus documents from both the Fifth[4] and Sixth Dynasties,[5] and a find of ten documents of Sixth Dynasty date was made at Gebelein.[6] Earlier still, however, is an unused roll from the First Dynasty,[7] and the hieroglyph representing a roll of papyrus is also known from this date.[8] During the Roman period various different qualities of papyrus were produced, and the papyrus industry of Graeco-Roman Egypt has been described in detail by Lewis.[9]

WOVEN FABRICS

The woven fabrics, like most other objects that have survived from ancient Egypt, are those that have been found in tombs, which are largely confined to wrappings for the dead. Occasionally, however, a garment worn during life, such as a shirt, is discovered on a body, or fabrics other than those on the body have been placed in the tomb. Spinning and weaving were among the oldest of the crafts practised in Egypt, and woven fabrics from as early as the neolithic period have been found.[10]

Various stages in the processes of spinning and weaving are represented on the walls of tombs of the Twelfth Dynasty at Beni Hasan[11] and El Bersheh[12] respectively, and in Eighteenth Dynasty tombs at Thebes,[13] and are further illustrated by a number of tomb models of Middle Kingdom date,[14] the most elaborate being one in the Metropolitan Museum (restored)[15] and that from the tomb of Meketrē, now in

---

[1] Cf. G. Möller, *Hieratische Paläographie*, I, pp. 4–8; II, pp. 4–6; III, pp. 4–6.

[2] J. Černý, *Late Ramesside Letters*, pp. xvii–xx; *Paper and Books in Ancient Egypt*.

[3] P. Montet, *Scènes de la vie privée*, pp. 74–81; L. Klebs, *Reliefs, A.R.*, pp. 100, 101–2; *M.R.*, pp. 134–5, 136–7; *N.R.*, pp. 42–44, 191; N. de G. Davies, *Puyemrê*, Pls. xviii–xix.

[4] Nos. C.G. 58063, 58064.

[5] Nos. J. 49623, C.G. 58043.

[6] *Chronique d'Égypte*, xi (1936), pp. 57–58.

[7] W. B. Emery, *Hemaka*, p. 14.

[8] H. Petrie, *Egyptian Hieroglyphs of the First and Second Dynasties*, Pl. xli.

[9] N. Lewis, *l'Industrie du Papyrus*, pp. 94 f.

[10] G. Caton-Thompson and E. W. Gardner, *Desert Fayum*, pp. 46, 49, 88, 90.

[11] P. E. Newberry, *Beni Hasan*, I, Pls. xi, xxix; ii, Pls. iv, xiii; F. Ll. Griffith, *Beni Hasan*, iv, Pl. xv.

[12] P. E. Newberry, *El Bersheh*, I, Pl. xxvi.

[13] N. de G. Davies, *Five Theban Tombs*, Pl. xxxvii; *Nefer-hotep*, Pl. lx.

[14] (a) J. Garstang, *Burial Customs*, pp. 132–3; J. H. Breasted (Jr.), *Servant Statues*, p. 55; H. Ling Roth, *Ancient Egyptian and Greek Looms*, p. 11; C. H. Johl, *Altägyptische Webestühle*, p. 10; G. M. Crowfoot, *Methods of Hand Spinning*, Pl. 17. (b) J. E. Quibell and A. G. K. Hayter, *Saqqara, Teti Pyramid North Side*, pp. 42–43, Pl. xxvi; J. H. Breasted (Jr.), *Servant Statues*, p. 53. (c) C. M. Firth and B. Gunn, *Teti Pyramid Cemeteries*, p. 53, Pl. xxxi; J. H. Breasted (Jr.), *Servant Statues*, pp. 52–53. (d) J. H. Breasted (Jr.), *Servant Statues*, pp. 53–54; H. E. Winlock, *Ancient Egypt*, 1922, p. 74.

[15] C. R. Clark, *M.M.A. Bull.*, iii (1944–5), pp. 24–29; J. H. Breasted (Jr.), *Servant Statues*, pp. 54–55, Pl. 48a.

Cairo.[1] The Meketrē model deserves particular attention, since it illustrates each process very clearly. Three women seated on the ground have before them piles of flax fibres from which they prepare loosely twisted slivers or roves by rolling the fibres on the left knee. The rove is then wound into balls and placed in tension pots from which threads are drawn by three spinners who hold a spindle in each hand and appear to be spinning or doubling the thread, twisting it on to the left-hand spindle and spinning it with the right on which the spun thread is also collected. Two women arrange the spun thread into warps on pegs on the wall, winding it in a figure of eight. The weaving is done on two ground looms with the beams fastened to pegs in the floor; these looms are of solid wood, but the heddle rods, heddle jacks, shed sticks, weavers' swords or beaters in, and shuttles are all clearly indicated.

Spinning

Spinning is the forming of threads by drawing out and twisting fibres, the twist in all Egyptian spinning being in the S direction (i.e. to the left), doubtless because flax naturally rotates in this direction when drying. The various methods of spinning employed in ancient Egypt have been described by Mrs. Crowfoot,[2] who has studied the tomb scenes and models already mentioned, comparing them with modern technique. In addition to simple hand spinning, three types of spindle spinning are represented, grasped spindle, supported spindle, and suspended spindle, the last being the most common. Winlock regards the use of two or more suspended spindles as an innovation of the Hyksos.[3] Spindles and spindle whorls are quite common in museum collections,[4] and tension buckets of stone and pottery are known.[5] Balls of thread have also been found.[6]

Weaving

The preliminary process of warping and setting up the warp, already mentioned in describing the Meketrē tomb model, has been described by Johl,[7] while the actual technique of weaving has been discussed by Braulik,[8] Miss Clark,[9] Johl,[10] Ling Roth,[11] Winlock[12] and others.[13] Egyptian looms were hand operated and of two types, a

---

[1] H. E. Winlock, *M.M.A. Bull., Egyptian Exped. 1918–1920*, p. 22; *Models of Daily Life*, pp. 29–33; J. H. Breasted (Jr.), *Servant Statues*, p. 54, Pl. 48b; H. Ling Roth and G. M. Crowfoot, *Ancient Egypt*, 1921, pp. 97–101; G. M. Crowfoot, in *History of Technology*, I, p. 437; C. H. Johl, *Altägyptische Webestühle*, pp. 10–15.

[2] G. M. Crowfoot, *Methods of Hand Spinning*, pp. 7–32; in *History of Technology*, I, pp. 424–5, 437–8. Cf. also A. Braulik, *Altägyptische Gewebe*, pp. 54–57; R. J. Forbes, *Studies in Ancient Technology*, IV, pp. 152–4; G. M. Crowfoot, *Ancient Egypt*, 1928, pp. 110–17.

[3] H. E. Winlock, *Rise and Fall of the Middle Kingdom*, p. 166.

[4] W. C. Hayes, *Scepter*, II, p. 411; W. M. F. Petrie, *Tools and Weapons*, pp. 53–54, Pl. LXVI; E. J. Baumgartel, *Cultures of Prehistoric Egypt*, II, pp. 120–1.

[5] W. C. Hayes, *Scepter*, II, p. 411; G. Nagel, *La Céramique du nouvel empire à Deir el Médineh*, pp. 183–8.

[6] B. M. Cartland, *J.E.A.*, V (1918), p. 139.   [7] C .H. Johl, *Altägyptische Webestühle*, pp. 15–22.

[8] A. Braulik, *Altägyptische Gewebe*, pp. 74–87.

[9] C. R. Clark, *M.M.A. Bull.*, III (1944–5), pp. 24–29.

[10] C. H. Johl, *Altägyptische Webestühle*, passim.

[11] H. Ling Roth, *Ancient Egypt and Greek Looms*, passim.

[12] H. E. Winlock, *Models of Daily Life*, pp. 29–33.

[13] T. Midgley, in G. Brunton and G. Caton-Thompson, *Badarian Civilisation*, p. 64.

horizontal ground loom, known from the Badarian period [1] and used exclusively until the end of the Middle Kingdom [2] and sporadically after,[3] and a vertical loom, first employed during the New Kingdom,[4] which Winlock thinks was introduced by the Hyksos.[5] The former is illustrated by the Middle Kingdom tomb scenes and models mentioned above, and the latter in tomb paintings of the Eighteenth Dynasty. Heddle jacks and warp weights from ancient Egyptian looms have been described by Winlock [6] and Mace [7] respectively, and these and other articles of the weaver's equipment, including combs, beaters in (weavers' swords) heddle rods, pegs for setting out the loom, shuttles and warp spacers, are discussed by Johl [8] and Ling Roth [9] and are fairly common in museum collections.[10] Whether the Egyptians ever made use of the reed in weaving is doubtful, though the greater warp density characteristic of Egyptian textiles and the great irregularity in the spacing of the warp threads as compared with modern fabrics would suggest that there was no reed to keep the threads apart. Such examples as have been found are almost certainly of late date,[11] but Spiegelberg maintains that the reed is represented in the hieroglyphic script.[12]

The woven fabrics found in Egyptian tombs until a late date are principally of linen, though fabrics of grass and of reed fibre have also been discovered. Wool, though probably always used for clothing to at least some extent and certainly at a late date, was accounted ceremonially unclean and so, as Herodotus, referring to the Egyptians, says,[13] 'nothing of wool is taken into their temples or buried with them, for their religion forbids it'. At a very late period the knowledge, first of cotton and then of silk, reached Egypt. All of these materials may now be separately described in order of importance.

Linen

Flax (originally *Linum humile*, but now *Linum usitatissimum*) has been grown in

---

[1] G. Brunton and G. Caton-Thompson, *Badarian Civilisation*, Pl. XLVIII (6); G. M. Crowfoot in *History of Techonology*, I, p. 432.

[2] C. H. Johl, *Altägyptische Webestühle*, pp. 8–39; H. Ling Roth, *Ancient Egyptian and Greek Looms*, pp. 3–14; G. M. Crowfoot, in *History of Technology*, I, pp. 427, 438–9; C. R. Clark, *M.M.A. Bull.*, III (1944–5), pp. 24–29; H. E. Winlock, *Models of Daily Life*, pp. 29–33; A. Braulik, *Altägyptische Gewebe*, pp. 57–73.

[3] C. H. Johl, *Altägyptische Webestühle*, pp. 39–58.

[4] C. H. Johl, *Altägyptische Webestühle*, pp. 47–57; H. Ling Roth, *Ancient Egyptian and Greek Looms*, pp. 14–18; G. M. Crowfoot, in *History of Technology*, I, pp. 427, 438–9; A. Braulik, *Altägyptische Gewebe*, pp. 57–73. Cf. also L. M. Wilson, *Ancient Textiles from Egypt in the University of Michigan Collection*, pp. 4–8.

[5] H. E. Winlock, *Rise and Fall of the Middle Kingdom*, p. 166.

[6] H. E. Winlock, *Ancient Egypt*, 1922, pp. 71–74.

[7] A. C. Mace, *Ancient Egypt*, 1922, pp. 75–76. Cf. also C. H. Johl, *Altägyptische Webestühle*, pp. 36–39.

[8] C. H. Johl, *Altägyptische Webestühle*, pp. 35–36, 39–45, 45–47.

[9] H. Ling Roth, *Ancient Egyptian and Greek Looms*, pp. 18–23.

[10] W. C. Hayes, *Scepter*, II, pp. 218–19; W. M. F. Petrie, *Tools and Weapons*, pp. 53–54, Pl. LXVI.

[11] Cf. J. Garstang, *Burial Customs*, pp. 133–6; H. Ling Roth, *Ancient Egyptian and Greek Looms*, pp. 22–23.

[12] W. Spiegelberg, *Z.Ä.S.*, XLV (1908), pp. 88–89.   [13] II: 81.

Egypt from very remote times, and was used for the production of linen fabrics as early as the neolithic period,[1] as well as for a number of other purposes, some of which have been described in connexion with basketry, cordage and matting.[2] Flax is normally harvested at different times according to the use to which it is to be put. When the stems are green the fibres are soft enough for very fine thread, when they are yellow the fibres are stronger and suitable for good linen cloth, while when the flax is dead ripe the fibres are tough and can be made into ropes and mats. Once pulled, the flax is rippled by drawing it through a comb-like tool and then retted, i.e. soaked to separate the woody parts from the bast fibres. These fibres are then further treated by beating and scraping (scutching) to remove any remaining bits of stem, and are finally combed out (hackled), after which they are ready to be roved and spun. The cultivation and preliminary processing of flax are illustrated in a number of tomb scenes,[3] and the commercial side of flax growing in Egypt is referred to by Pliny,[4] who says that 'by its aid . . . she imports the merchandise of Arabia and India' and that it was from Egyptian flax that 'the greatest profits are derived'. There is still a considerable flax cultivation in the country at the present day.

Ancient Egyptian linen varies considerably in texture, from the finest gauze to a canvas-like coarseness, and several different kinds of linen are distinguished in the linen lists of the Old Kingdom.[5] Many specimens of Egyptian textiles have been examined by experts, notably Braulik,[6] Mrs. Crowfoot,[7] Miss Hald,[8] van Henneberg,[9] T. Midgley[10] and W. W. Midgley.[10] These include examples from the Badarian[11] and predynastic[12] periods, from the protodynastic period,[13] from the Old Kingdom and First Intermediate period,[14] from the Middle Kingdom and Second

---

[1] G. Caton-Thompson and E. W. Gardner, *Desert Fayum*, p. 46.

[2] Cf. E. A. M. Greiss, *Mém. Inst. d'Ég.*, LV (1957), pp. 106–22, 154.

[3] P. Montet, *Scènes de la vie privée*, pp. 192–9; F. Hartmann, *l'Agriculture*, pp. 146–52; H. F. Lutz, *Textiles and Costumes*, pp. 3–18; L. Klebs, *Reliefs, A.R.*, pp. 53–54; *M.R.*, pp. 75–76; *N.R.*, pp. 21–22.

[4] XIX: 2.

[5] W. S. Smith, *Z.Ä.S.*, LXXI (1935), pp. 134–49.

[6] A. Braulik, *Altägyptische Gewebe*, pp. 5–53.

[7] G. M. Crowfoot, in *History of Technology*, I, pp. 431f.

[8] M. Hald, *Acta Archaeologica*, XVII (1946), pp. 50–78.

[9] A. van Henneberg, *Bull. du Musée d'ethnographie du Trocadéro*, July 1932, pp. 3–17.

[10] In various excavation reports.

[11] T. Midgley, in G. Brunton, *Mostagedda*, pp. 33, 61–62; in G. Brunton and G. Caton-Thompson, *Badarian Civilisation*, pp. 64–67.

[12] T. Midgley, in G. Brunton, *Mostagedda*, pp. 92–93; *Matmar*, p. 23; in G. Brunton and G. Caton-Thompson, *Badarian Civilisation*, pp. 64–67; W. W. Midgley, in W. M. F. Petrie, G. A. Wainwright and E. Mackay, *Labyrinth, Gerzeh and Mazguneh*, p. 6.

[13] T. Midgley, in G. Brunton, *Matmar*, p. 29; *Qau and Badari*, I, pp. 70–71; W. W. Midgley, in W. M. F. Petrie and E. Mackay, *Heliopolis, Kafr Ammar and Shurafa*, pp. 48–50; A. Lucas, in W. B. Emery, *Hemaka*, pp. 43–44.

[14] T. Midgley, in G. Brunton, *Mostagedda*, pp. 112–13; *Matmar*, p. 54; W. W. Midgley, in W. M. F. Petrie and E. Mackay, *Heliopolis, Kafr Ammar and Shurafa*, pp. 50–51; in *Historical Studies*, II, pp. 37–39; M. Hald, *Acta Archaeologica*, XVII (1946), pp. 50–52; W. M. F. Petrie, *Deshasheh*, pp. 31–32.

Intermediate period,[1] from the New Kingdom [2] and the late period,[3] and many of Ptolemaic, Roman and Coptic date,[4] as well as mummy wrappings of various dates, but chiefly of the late period.[5] Braulik,[6] Miss Bellinger,[7] Mrs. Crowfoot [8] and Miss Riefstahl [9] have studied the different textile techniques used by the ancient Egyptians, including tapestry weave, warp weave, pile and loop techniques, embroidery and the controversial tablet weaving.

A few small fragments of coloured tapestry woven linen were found in the tomb of Thutmose IV,[10] and a number of coloured tapestry woven linen objects (a tunic, gloves and girdles) in the tomb of Tutankhamūn.[11] Two other fragments of tapestry weave from the Theban necropolis are mentioned by Daressy,[12] and two possible examples from the tomb of Kha are discussed by Miss Riefstahl [13] who also refers to a fragment of Twenty-second Dynasty date.[14] The process of tapestry weaving is described by Kendrick.[15]

---

[1] T. Midgley, in G. Brunton, *Mostagedda*, pp. 132–3; *Qau and Badari*, III, p. 34; T. W. Fox, in M. A. Murray, *Tomb of Two Brothers*, pp. 65–71; H. E. Winlock, *Slain Soldiers*, p. 32; E. Riefstahl, *Patterned Textiles*, p. 17; W. M. F. Petrie, *Kahun, Gurob and Hawara*, pp. 27–28.

[2] M. Hald, *Acta Archaeologica*, XVII (1946), pp. 53–54; E. Schiaparelli, *La Tomba intatta dell' Architetto Cha*, pp. 90–100; W. G. Thomson, in H. Carter and P. E. Newberry, *Thoutmôsis IV*, pp. 143–4; H. E. Winlock, *Materials used at the Embalming of King Tūt-ankh-Amūn*, pp. 8–10; R. Pfister, *Revue des arts asiatiques*, XI (1937), pp. 207–18; G. M. Crowfoot and N. de G. Davies, *J.E.A.*, XXVII (1941), pp. 113–30; B. H. Stricker, *Oud. Med. N.R.*, XXIV (1943), pp. 89–91.

[3] T. Midgley, in G. Brunton, *Matmar*, p. 90.

[4] E.g. J. Beckwith, *Ciba Review*, XII (1959), pp. 2–27; G. M. Crowfoot and J. Griffiths, *J.E.A.*, XXV (1939), pp. 40–47; S. Donadoni, *Stoffe decorate da Antinoe*; I. Errera, *Collection d'anciennes étoffes égyptiennes*; L. Guerrini, *Stoffe Copte del museo archeologico di Firenze*; M. Hald, *Acta Archaeologica*, XVII (1946), pp. 54, 67, 67–78; A. F. Kendrick, *Catalogue of Textiles from Burying Grounds in Egypt*, I–III; C. J. Lamm, *Bull. Soc. Arch. Copte*, IV (1938), pp. 23–28; C. J. Lamm and R. J. Charleston, *Bull. Soc. Arch. Copte*, V (1939), pp. 193–9; T. Midgley, in G. Brunton, *Mostagedda*, pp. 138–9, 142–5; L. Start, *Coptic Cloths*; W. F. Volbach, *Koptische Stoffe*; L. M. Wilson, *Ancient Textiles from Egypt in the University of Michigan Collection*.

[5] J. Thomson, *London and Edinburgh Phil. Mag.*, V (1834), pp. 355–65; A. Macalister, *Journ. Royal Anthrop. Inst.*, XXIII (1894), pp. 102–15; A. C. Mace and G. Elliot Smith, *Ann. Serv.*, VII (1906), pp. 166–82; W. W. Midgley, in H. Ling Roth, *Ancient Egyptian and Greek Looms*, pp. 26–29; T. W. Fox, in M. A. Murray, *Tomb of Two Brothers*, pp. 65–71; T. Midgley, in R. Mond and O. H. Myers, *Bucheum*, I, pp. 71–73; M. Hald, *Acta Archaeologica*, XVII (1946), pp. 54–60; A. van Henneberg, *Bull. du Musée d'ethnographie du Trocadéro*, July 1932, pp. 3–17; A. Braulik, *Altägyptische Gewebe*, pp. 5–53.

[6] A. Braulik, *Altägyptische Gewebe*, pp. 5–38.

[7] L. Bellinger, *Textile Museum, Workshop Notes*.

[8] G. M. Crowfoot, in *History of Technology*, I, pp. 429–45.

[9] E. Riefstahl, *Patterned Textiles*.

[10] W. G. Thomson, in H. Carter and P. E. Newberry, *Thoutmôsis IV*, pp. 143–4; E. Riefstahl, *Patterned Textiles*, pp. 20–21; G. M. Crowfoot, in *History of Technology*, I, pp. 439–40; H. Carter, *Embroidery*, Dec. 1932, p. 9.

[11] H. Carter, *Tut-ankh-Amen*, I, pp. 171, 172; III, pp. 124–6; R. Pfister, *Revue des arts asiatiques*, XI (1937), pp. 211–15; E. Riefstahl, *Patterned Textiles*, pp. 24–26; H. Carter, *Embroidery*, Dec. 1932, p. 10.

[12] G. Daressy, *Fouilles de la vallée des rois*, pp. 302–3; E. Riefstahl, *Patterned Textiles*, pp. 22–23.

[13] E. Riefstahl, *Patterned Textiles*, pp. 21–22; G. M. Crowfoot, in *History of Technology*, I, p. 440.

[14] E. Riefstahl, *Patterned Textiles*, p. 27.

[15] A. F. Kendrick, *Catalogue of Textiles from Burying Grounds in Egypt*, I, p. 21.

Among examples of warp weave, either simple or with floating threads, may be mentioned the braid on a saddle cloth from the tomb of Senmut,[1] the bands on a tunic from the tomb of Tutankhamūn,[2] a braided textile from the tomb of Kha,[3] a textile from a tomb of the Eighteenth Dynasty now in the Victoria and Albert Museum,[4] a textile of uncertain date in the Hood collection,[5] and bands in the Graf collection, possibly of the Twenty-second Dynasty.[6]

Pile textiles of Middle Kingdom date have been found at Kerma,[7] and others, chiefly of the Graeco-Roman and Coptic periods, are described by Bellinger.[8] Textiles with a loop technique akin to tufted towelling are known from the Eleventh Dynasty.[9] Mackay has suggested that a rippled fabric was also known to the Egyptians,[10] but the representations he adduces may, in fact, indicate elaborate pleating. Reisner found a pleated linen garment in a Sixth Dynasty tomb at Naga ed Der [11] and one of similar date was discovered at Deshasheh,[12] several examples of pleated linen are known from the Middle Kingdom,[13] and in the Cairo Museum there are three specimens of pleated linen of the Eighteenth Dynasty, one 'showing two series of accordion-pleatings at right-angles to each other being specially remarkable'.[14] Pleated linen has been discussed by Spiegelberg [15] and Miss Riefstahl.[16]

Specimens of embroidery were found in the tomb of Thutmose IV,[17] and on tunics [18] and other objects [19] in the tomb of Tutankhamūn. Embroideries of late date are described by Lamm.[20]

---

[1] E. Riefstahl, *Patterned Textiles*, p. 20; G. M. Crowfoot, in *History of Technology*, I, p. 441.

[2] G. M. Crowfoot and N. de G. Davies, *J.E.A.*, XXVII (1941), pp. 117–25; R. Pfister, *Revue des arts asiatiques*, XI (1937), pp. 212–13; E. Riefstahl, *Patterned Textiles*, pp. 24–26.

[3] G. M. Crowfoot, in *History of Technology*, I, p. 440; E. Riefstahl, *Patterned Textiles*, pp. 21–22.

[4] G. M. Crowfoot and N. de G. Davies, *J.E.A.*, XXVII (1941), p. 122; R. Pfister, *Revue des arts asiatiques*, XI (1937), p. 218; E. Riefstahl, *Patterned Textiles*, p. 26.

[5] G. M. Crowfoot, *Ancient Egypt*, 1933, pp. 43–45; G. M. Crowfoot and N. de G. Davies, *J.E.A.*, XXVII (1941), p. 122; E. Riefstahl, *Patterned Textiles*, p. 26.

[6] E. Riefstahl, *Patterned Textiles*, p. 28. Cf. A. van Gennep and G. Jéquier, *Tissage aux Cartons*, pp. 101–5.

[7] E. Riefstahl, *Patterned Textiles*, p. 35; G. M. Crowfoot, in *History of Technology*, I, p. 435.

[8] L. Bellinger, *Textile Museum, Workshop Notes*, No. 12.

[9] H. E. Winlock, *Slain Soldiers*, p. 32; E. Riefstahl, *Patterned Textiles*, p. 17; G. M. Crowfoot, in *History of Technology*, I, p. 435. Cf. also E. Riefstahl, *op. cit.*, p. 22.

[10] E. Mackay, *J.E.A.*, X (1924), pp. 41–43.

[11] W. S. Smith, *Z.Ä.S.*, LXXI (1935), pp. 138, 139, Fig. 1; E. Riefstahl, *Patterned Textiles*, p. 8.

[12] W. M. F. Petrie, *Deshasheh*, Pl. XXXV.

[13] W. Spiegelberg, *Ann. Serv.*, XXVII (1927), pp. 154–5 (Cairo No. J. 43684); H. E. Winlock, *M.M.A. Bull., Egyptian Exped. 1924–1925*, p. 7, Fig. 3; E. Chassinat and C. Palanque, *Nécropole d'Assiout*, pp. 163–4, Pl. XXXIII; Ahmed Bey Kamal, *Ann. Serv.*, XIII (1914), pp. 171–2, Fig. 21.

[14] Eg. Museum Cairo, *A Brief Description of the Principal Monuments*, 1932, p. 98 (No. 6094); W. Spiegelberg, *Ann. Serv.*, XXVII (1927), pp. 155–6.

[15] W. Spiegelberg, *Ann. Serv.*, XXVII (1927), pp. 154–6.   [16] E. Riefstahl, *Patterned Textiles*, p. 8.

[17] W. G. Thompson, in H. Carter and P. E. Newberry, *Thoutmôsis IV*, p. 144; E. Riefstahl, *Patterned Textiles*, pp. 20–21 (Nos. 46526, 46529).

[18] G. M. Crowfoot and N. de G. Davies, *J.E.A.*, XXVII (1941), pp. 125–6; R. Pfister, *Revue des arts asiatiques*, XI (1937), pp. 212–13; H. Carter, *Embroidery*, Dec. 1932, p.10.

[19] R. Pfister, *Revue des arts asiatiques*, XI (1937), pp. 214, 216–17.

[20] C. J. Lamm, *Bull. Soc. Arch. Copte*, IV (1938), pp. 23–28.

It has been asserted by van Gennep and Jéquier,[1] Johl,[2] and others that the ancient Egyptians were conversant with tablet weaving, though Miss van Reesema[3] attributes all the alleged examples to the 'sprang' technique of plaiting with stretched threads,[4] and Mrs. Crowfoot and Ling Roth[5] deny that tablet weaving was known before the Coptic period, the earliest certain instance being of that date.[6] The most controversial of the supposed examples of tablet weaving is the so-called 'girdle' of Ramses III,[7] in fact a kind of loose jacket.[8] This was originally described by Lee[9] as having been woven on a complicated loom, though Ling Roth[10] maintained that a simple loom would have sufficed. Lehmann-Haupt,[11] however, suggested that the girdle was the product of tablet weaving, and this view was strongly supported by van Gennep and Jéquier[12] and by Johl,[13] though rejected by Miss van Reesema,[14] who tried to show that it could have been made by plaiting with stretched threads. In fact, there can be little doubt that Mrs. Crowfoot[15] and Miss Riefstahl[16] are right in describing the technique as a species of warp-weave, a warp-face double weave with floating threads.

Wool

Although there are very few instances of wool having been found in Egyptian tombs until a late date, there cannot be any doubt that the Egyptians, who possessed large flocks of sheep, made use of wool as a covering. Herodotus mentions the wearing of loose, white woollen mantles over linen tunics but adds that the Egyptians did not allow anything of wool to be taken into their temples or buried with the dead,[17] while Diodorus states that the Egyptian sheep yielded wool 'for clothing and ornament'.[18]

Woollen garments have been found in graves of the early Christian period,[19] and

[1] A. van Gennep and G. Jéquier, Tissage aux Cartons, in particular pp. 61–105.
[2] C. H. Johl, Altägyptische Webestühle, pp. 59–61.
[3] E. S. van Reesema, Contribution to the Early History of Textile Technics, pp. 26–50.
[4] M. Hald, Acta Archaeologica, XVII (1946), p. 89, says that the 'sprang' technique first appeared in Egypt in the fourth to fifth century A.D.
[5] G. M. Crowfoot and H. Ling Roth, Liverpool Annals, X (1923), pp. 7–20. Cf. A. van Gennep and G. Jéquier, Tissage and Cartons, pp. 111–14.
[6] G. M. Crowfoot, Ancient Egypt, 1924, pp. 98–100.
[7] T. E. Peet, J.E.A., XIX (1933), pp. 143–9.
[8] L. Borchardt, Allerhand Kleinigkeiten, pp. 13–18.
[9] T. D. Lee, Liverpool Annals, V (1913), pp. 84–96.
[10] H. Ling Roth, Ancient Egyptian and Greek Looms, pp. 24–25.
[11] C. F. Lehmann-Haupt, Liverpool Annals, VII (1914–16), p. 50.
[12] A. van Gennep and G. Jéquier, Tissage aux Cartons, pp. 93–100.
[13] C. H. Johl, Altägyptische Webestühle, pp. 61–70.
[14] E. S. van Reesema, Contribution to the Early History of Textile Technics, pp. 47–50.
[15] G. M. Crowfoot and H. Ling Roth, Liverpool Annals, X (1923), pp. 12–19; G. M. Crowfoot, J.E.A., XXVII (1941), p. 122; in History of Technology, I, p. 441.
[16] E. Riefstahl, Patterned Textiles, pp. 26–27.
[17] II: 81.   [18] I: 87.
[19] G. A. Reisner, Arch. Survey of Nubia, 1907–1908, I, p. 107; C. M. Firth, Arch. Survey of Nubia, 1908–1909, pp. 36, 91, 96; 1910–1911, pp. 98, 124, 190; G. Brunton, Qau and Badari, III, p. 26. See also A. Roscio, Atene e Roma, XXI (1918), pp. 207–14; M. Dimand, Die Ornamentik der ägyptischen Wollwirkereien.

the use of coloured wool at this date for the decoration of linen fabrics is fairly common. The few finds of wool of earlier dates that can be traced include, in chronological order, one predynastic example of 'brown and white woollen knitted stuff',[1] a woollen cloth wrapped round the remains of a male skeleton of First Dynasty date,[2] a specimen found in the pyramid of Menkaurē at Giza, recorded as 'part of a skeleton . . . enveloped in coarse woollen cloth of a yellow colour',[3] which was almost certainly an intruded burial of much later date than the pyramid, and a specimen from the Twelfth Dynasty found by Petrie,[4] who says regarding it, 'wool was also spun; a handful of weaver's waste is mainly made up of blue worsted ends and blue wool, with some red and some green ends. A lump of red dyed wool, not yet spun, was found'. Brunton found yellow wool from the Second Intermediate period,[5] and a sack of woven goat's hair excavated at El Amarna contained a mass of goat's wool, five large balls of wool each consisting of several hundred metres of spun wool, and a square garment of woven wool.[6] Braulik records a woollen textile from Saqqara, dating from not earlier than 300 B.C.,[7] and there is a woollen netted turban of pre-Christian Roman date,[8] with reference to which, Winlock, the finder, says, 'Apparently it was the style in Thebes just before the Christian era to swathe the hair in fine linen veils until the head was twice its natural size, and then over that to pull such a netted brown and red turban, tied behind with drawing-strings'; and woollen fabrics were found by Brunton at Mostagedda of early Roman, later Roman and Coptic dates.[9] The reported use of wool for wigs is unlikely and requires confirmation, since none was detected in any of the wigs in the Cairo Museum.[10] A word which has been translated as wool occurs in a papyrus of the New Kingdom, though the meaning is doubtful.[11]

Cotton [12]

The home of the cotton industry is undoubtedly India, from which it spread westwards, and woven cotton fabric has been found at Mohenjo-daro in India which is dated between 3250 B.C. and 2750 B.C.[13]

Schoff states[14] that 'Cotton thread and cloth are repeatedly mentioned in the laws of Manu, 800 B.C.'

Herodotus (fifth century B.C.) states that in India 'there grows on wild trees wool

---

[1] W. M. F. Petrie and J. E. Quibell, *Naqada and Ballas*, p. 24.

[2] Z. Y. Saad, *Royal Excavations at Helwan, 1945–7 (Ann. Serv., Cahier, 14)*, p. 44.

[3] H. Vyse, *Pyramids of Gizeh*, II, p. 86.

[4] W. M. F. Petrie, *Kahun, Gurob and Hawara*, p. 28.

[5] W. M. F. Petrie and G. Brunton, *Sedment*, I, pp. 17–20.

[6] J. D. S. Pendlebury, *City of Akhenaten*, III, p. 246. The position in which the sack was found suggests that it is to be dated to the Eighteenth Dynasty.

[7] A. Braulik, *Altägyptische Gewebe*, p. 53, No. 217.

[8] H. E. Winlock, *M.M.A. Bull., Egyptian Exped. 1924–1925*, pp. 31–32.

[9] G. Brunton, *Mostagedda*, pp. 138, 139, 142, 143.

[10] A. Lucas, *Ann. Serv.*, XXX (1930), pp. 190–6.

[11] *Wb.* IV.49.2.

[12] Cf. L. Keimer, *Gartenpflanzen*, pp. 59–61.

[13] J. Marshall, *Mohenjo-daro and the Indus Civilization*, pp. VI, 33, 194. E. Mackay, *Indus Civilisation*, pp. 103, 107, 137–8.

[14] W. H. Schoff, *The Periplus of the Erythaean Sea*, p. 71.

more beautiful and excellent than the wool of sheep; these trees supply the Indians with clothing'.[1] Also 'The Indians wore garments of tree-wool'.[2]

On an Assyrian cylinder of the time of Sennacherib (seventh century B.C.) 'trees that bear wool' are mentioned.[3]

Theophrastus (fourth to third century B.C.) states that the island of Tylos (i.e. Bahrein) in the Arabian (i.e. Persian) Gulf 'produces the wool-bearing tree in abundance' and refers to fabrics being woven from it:[4] he also says that 'This tree is also found in India as well as in Arabia.' Pliny (first century A.D.) copies this description of cotton from Theophrastus, but contrasts the trees that bear 'wool' (cotton) with those that bear 'Seres' (i.e. mulberry trees with silk cocoons on them).[5]

Herodotus (fifth century B.C.) relates that two linen corslets given by the Egyptian king Amasis of the Twenty-sixth Dynasty (about 569 to 525 B.C.), one to the Samians or Lacedaemonians and the other to a temple in Lindus, were embroidered in cotton.[6]

Pliny (first century A.D.) states that 'The upper part of Egypt, in the vicinity of Arabia, produces a shrub known by the name of *gossypium*'[7] and that 'the most esteemed vestments worn by the priests of Egypt are made of it'.[7] This same author also says that 'Ethiopia, which borders Egypt, has in general no remarkable trees with the exception of the wool-bearing ones . . .'[8] Pliny, however, is by no means a paragon of detailed accuracy.

Cotton is mentioned in papyri as early as the second century A.D.[9]

The earliest cotton fabrics that can be traced in Egypt are of the Roman period from Karanog in Nubia. These were originally reported as linen,[10] but they have since been examined by experts and are undoubtedly cotton.[11] It is thought that they may have been of Sudanese origin, more particularly because Reisner discovered cotton fabrics at Meroe in the Sudan of Graeco-Roman date,[12] and because there are early literary references to the use of cotton in Nubia, one about A.D. 250 and the other about eight centuries later.[11] Recently, however, fragments of cotton fabrics dated to the fourth century A.D. have been found in the monastery of Apa Phoebammon,[13] and since there is a strong probability that these were of local manufacture one may doubt Pfister's statement that cotton fabrics were not produced in Egypt until several centuries after the Arab conquest (A.D. 640).[14]

Silk

The silk industry had its origin in China and probably the material first reached the Mediterranean countries by way of Persia. Silk was not used in Egypt until late,

[1] III: 106.   [2] VII: 65.   [3] L. W. King, *P.S.B.A.*, XXXI (1909), pp. 339–43.

[4] *Enquiry into Plants*, IV: 7, 7, 8.   [5] XII: 21

[6] III: 47.   [7] XIX: 2.   [8] XIII: 28.

[9] J. G. Winter and H. C. Youtie, *American Journal of Philology*, LXV (1944), pp. 249–58.

[10] C. L. Woolley and D. Randall MacIver, *Karanog, The Roman-Nubian Cemetery*, pp. 27, 28, 245 (G. 394, G. 531, G. 7511), Pl. 108, Fig. 1.

[11] F. Ll. Griffith and G. M. Crowfoot, *J.E.A.*, XX (1934), pp. 5–12.

[12] R. E. Massey, *Sudan Notes*, VI (1923), pp. 231–3; Royal Botanical Gardens, Kew, *Bulletin*, 1924, pp. 76–77, 267–70. Mr. Massey kindly gave me his specimens and microscope slides when he was leaving the Sudan and I was able to confirm his conclusions.

[13] E. A. M. Greiss, *Bull. Soc. Arch. Copte*, XIII (1951), pp. 193–5; *Chronique d'Égypte*, XXVII (1952), pp. 321–3; *Mém. Inst. d'Ég.*, LV (1957), pp. 155–6.

[14] R. Pfister, *Revue des arts asiatiques*, XI (1937), pp. 167–72.

and the earliest example that can be traced is of Ptolemaic date from Mostagedda, a woollen tunic having decorative stripes with weft of white silk.[1] Lucan, writing in the middle of the first century A.D. describes Cleopatra, 'her white breasts resplendent through the Sidonian fabric, which, wrought in close texture by the skill of the Seres, the needle of the workman of the Nile has separated, and has loosened the warp by stretching out the web'.[2] A portion of a coloured silk fabric was found at Qustul, south of Abu Simbel, the exact date of which is not yet certain, though probably not earlier than the fourth century A.D.[3] This, which was examined by me, was not a mulberry silk (i.e. the fibres were not those of the caterpillar *Bombyx mori*) but a 'wild silk' of the nature of Tussah silk. A blue and red coloured silk border to a garment of Roman date was found by Brunton in Upper Egypt.[4] From the fourth century A.D. onwards silk becomes more common.

Grass and Reed

The use of grass and reed for matting has already been mentioned, but these materials were used also for woven fabrics other than matting. Midgley states [5] that some of the predynastic woven fabrics, thought at first to be linen, were probably not linen, and of some material found at Armant he says [6] 'The microscopic structure of the fibre is similar to that used in some Badarian cloths.' 'It is apparently some fibrovascular tissue not in any way related to flax.' Some of the specimens he says [6] were 'spun from reed fibre . . .' and again others 'are made from yarns of grass or reed fibre . . .' Also, 'The fibres from Mostagedda show quite conclusively that from Badarian until early Roman times vegetable fibres other than flax had been used . . .' [6] Manifestly much more work is required before the whole history of the fibres employed in ancient Egypt for weaving is known.

Hemp

With respect to the use of hemp for woven fabrics in ancient Egypt, Midgley says [7] 'Hemp is the type "A" fibre which is found in the Badarian, Predynastic, and Pan-grave clothes, and I find it in the Dynastic fabrics from the Badarian sites also.' Again, of certain woven fabrics of Roman date, he says [7] that 'it is certain that the yarn is made from hemp'. The botanical source of the hemp is not specified, but the name is applied to a large number of bast fibres from different plants, one at least of which, for instance Deccan hemp (*Hibiscus cannabinus*), grows in Egypt.

Ramie

Midgley reports ramie fibre in fabrics of predynastic [8] and protodynastic [9] date,

---

[1] G. Brunton, *Mostagedda*, pp. 139, 145 (identification by Midgley).

[2] *Pharsalia*, x: 141, quoted by W. H. Schoff, *The Periplus of the Erythraean Sea*, p. 265.

[3] W. B. Emery, *Royal Tombs of Ballana and Qustul*, p. 385.

[4] G. Brunton, *Qau and Badari*, III, p. 26.

[5] G. Brunton and G. Caton-Thompson, *Badarian Civilisation*, p. 67; G. Brunton, *Mostagedda*, pp. 145–6.

[6] R. Mond and O. H. Myers, *Bucheum*, I, pp. 71–73. Cf. also R. Mond and O. H. Myers, *Cemeteries of Armant*, I, pp. 139–41.

[7] G. Brunton, *Mostagedda*, p. 145.

[8] W. W. Midgley, in W. M. F. Petrie, G. A. Wainwright and E. Mackay, *Labyrinth, Gerzeh and Mazguneh*, p. 6.

[9] W. W. Midgley, in W. M. F. Petrie and E. Mackay, *Heliopolis. Kafr Ammar and Shurafa*, p. 50, Pl. LVIII.

but the copy of the photomicrograph published is far from convincing. Täck-holm and Drar,[1] who had the material re-examined, state that it is not ramie, because the fibres are not those of a dicotyledenous plant, and suggest that it may be an un-known species of *Ensete*. That ramie, which is a native of China, should be found in Egypt at an early date is most improbable.

DYEING

The art of dyeing was known in Egypt as early as the predynastic period, as matting of that date dyed red at the edges has been found.[2] Very little is known about either the nature of the dyes used or their methods of use, though, since artificial dyes are modern, the ancient Egyptian dyes must have been natural colours, and probably they were largely, if not wholly, of local origin.

Two Greek papyri, dating from about the third or fourth century A.D., which were found in Egypt, probably at Thebes, describe the process of dyeing and the nature of the colours used at that period. These are Papyrus X, now in Leyden, translated by Berthelot,[3] and Papyrus Holm, now in Stockholm, published by Lager-crantz.[4] These two papyri, so far as they deal with dyes and dyeing, have been made the subject of a special study by Pfister.[5]

Five principal dyes are mentioned, which have been identified as archil (orchil), a purple colour derived from certain marine algae found on rocks in the Mediterranean Sea;[6] alkanet, a red colour prepared from the roots of *Alkanna tinctoria*; madder, a red colour extracted from the roots of *Rubia tinctorium* and *Rubia peregrina*, both Alkanna and Rubia being common in the Mediterranean region and, according to Muschler,[7] both having been found growing in Egypt, while Oliver mentions *Alkanna tinctoria* as growing in the desert west of Alexandria;[8] kermes, a red colour from the dried bodies of a certain female insect, *Coccus ilicis*, found on an evergreen oak that grows in north Africa and south-east Europe, and woad, a blue colour obtained by a process of fermentation from the leaves of *Isatis tinctoria*.[9]

Herodotus states[10] that 'Libyan women wear hairless tasselled goat-skins over their dress, coloured with madder'.

The ancient Egyptian names for alkanet and madder have been identified with some degree of certainty by Loret.[11]

The different dyes may conveniently be considered in alphabetical order of colour.

---

[1] V. Täckholm and M. Drar, *Flora of Egypt*, III, pp. 539–41.

[2] G. A. Reisner, *Arch. Survey of Nubia, 1907–1908*, I, p. 124, No. 81.

[3] M. Berthelot, *Collections des anciens alchimistes grecs*, 1887.

[4] O. Lagercrantz, *Papyrus Graecus Holmiensis: Recepte für Salber, Steine und Purpur*.

[5] R. Pfister, 'Teinure et alchimie dans l'orient hellénistique', *Seminarium Kondakovianum*, VII (1935).

[6] Modern archil is obtained from lichens growing on trees in Florida.

[7] R. Muschler, *Manual Flora of Egypt*, II, pp. 798, 919. See also G. Schweinfurth, *Bull. Inst. Ég.*, VIII (1887), p. 327.

[8] F. W. Oliver, 'The Flowers of Mareotis', *Trans. Norfolk and Norwich Naturalists' Society*, XIV (1938).

[9] Pfister calls this indigo.

[10] IV: 189.

[11] V. Loret, *Kêmi*, III (1930–35), pp. 23–32; cf. also B. Ebbell, *Z.Ä.S.*, LXIV (1929), p. 51.

Blue

The ancient Egyptian blue has always been called indigo, meaning *Indigofera tinctoria*, imported from India, and over a hundred years ago Thomson[1] and Herapath[2] identified it on ancient Egyptian fabrics, though unfortunately the date of the material is not stated. I, too, found what I thought at the time was Indian indigo on an ancient Egyptian fabric (undated) and others also have reported Indian indigo from Egyptian fabrics. Indigo, however, is produced from a great variety of plants of which the two principal are Indian indigo from the leaves of *Indigofera tinctoria*, and woad, from the leaves of *Isatis tinctoria*, the colouring matter of both of which, if not absolutely identical, is so much alike that it is difficult, if not impossible, to distinguish between them. The dye does not occur ready formed in the plant, but is obtained by the artificial fermentation of the leaves, which contain a constituent that becomes converted into indigo.

Indigo was cultivated in Egypt during the last century, but this cultivation probably does not date back earlier than the Middle Ages.[3] Maqrisi (fourteenth century A.D.) says[4] that indigo was cultivated in Egypt in his day. The locally-made dye has now been replaced by imported artificial indigo. The former cultivated indigo was *Indigofera argentea*,[3] a species that grows wild in Nubia, Kordofan, Sennar and Abyssinia, though sometimes it is said to have been the Indian indigo *Indigofera tinctoria*.[5]

With respect to a blue colour on a tunic from the tomb of Tutankhamūn, Mrs. Crowfoot writes[6] 'The blue, which was not examined, is as he (i.e. Pfister) says, undoubtedly indigo, but I do not agree with him that the plant used was woad, *Isatis tinctoria*, L. I suggest that a more probable source was *Indigofera argentea*, L. (. . .) which is cultivated and sub-spontaneous in Lower Egypt and indigenous in Upper Egypt and the Sudan, unless indeed *Indigofera tinctoria*, L., so widely exported later, had already been brought from India.' Although *Indigofera argentea* is sub-spontaneous in Lower Egypt and indigenous in Upper Egypt, it is not likely to have been used as a dye until it was cultivated, for which there is no evidence before the Middle Ages.

Woad was certainly cultivated in the Fayum province of Egypt in early Christian times, that is from the first to the fourth century A.D.,[7] and probably earlier, and, therefore, what has been assumed to have been Indian indigo on ancient Egyptian fabrics may have been woad, more particularly since Indian indigo, although known to the Romans of Pliny's time,[8] was only used as a pigment for painting and not as a dye. Vitruvius (first century B.C.) mentions the scarcity of indigo and the use of woad as a substitute in painting.[9]

---

[1] J. Thomson, *London and Edinburgh Phil. Mag.*, v (1834), pp. 361–2.

[2] W. Herapath, *London and Edinburgh Phil. Mag.*, III (1852), p. 528.

[3] G. P. Foaden and F. Fletcher, *Text-Book of Egyptian Agriculture*, II, 1910, p. 513. V. Loret, *Flore Pharaonique*, 2nd ed., p. 90.

[4] U. Bouriant, *Mém. Miss.*, XVII (1900), p. 201.

[5] P. S. Girard, *Description de l'Égypte, état moderne*, II, 1812, p. 545.

[6] G. M. Crowfoot and N. de G. Davies, *J.E.A.*, XXVII (1941), p. 116, *n.2*.

[7] B. P. Grenfell and A. S. Hunt, *Oxyrhynchus Papyri*, I, pp. 164, 166; II, pp. 270, 271; III, p. 282; IV, pp. 215–21; X, pp. 221–2; XIV, pp. 147–8; A. S. Hunt, *op. cit.*, VII, pp. 205–6.

[8] XXXIII: 57; XXXV: 25, 27.   [9] VII: 14, 2.

Pfister examined a large number of dyed woven woollen fabrics chiefly from Antinoë in Upper Egypt, ranging in date from the third century A.D. to the seventh century A.D., on which he identified the blue colour as woad, which, however, he calls indigo.[1] Schunck also identified what he calls indigo on fabrics from Gurob dating from 400–500 A.D.[2]

Winlock, writing of a blue dye of late Eighteenth Dynasty date, says [3] that it 'was probably the juice of the sunt berry (*Acacia nilotica*),' but the evidence is not given, and the sunt has a pod with seeds and not berries.

Black

Although on several of the dyed fabrics from the tomb of Thutmose IV (Eighteenth Dynasty) there is a colour that appears to be black, yet from a careful examination of these fabrics it appears probable that the original colour may have been dark brown. The nature of the colour was not determined, but it may possibly have been made by imposing red on blue. A similar colour was noted by Schunck, who suggests that it may have been produced by imposing madder on indigo.[4]

Brown

Pfister suggests [5] that perhaps the brown colour on some of the Antinoë fabrics may be catechu (cutch), which is prepared from the Mimosa catechu grown in India and there used for dyeing cotton, but this seems most unlikely.

Green

In one instance,[6] Pfister found a green colour to be due to indigo (woad) together with a yellow colour, and a similar green was also examined by Schunck.[7] I found that a green colour on thin plaster on a stick from the tomb of Tutankhamūn consisted of a mixture of blue (blue frit) and a yellow. In none of these instances could the nature of the yellow colour be determined.

Purple

Pfister found [8] that the purple colour on the Antinoë fabrics was madder on indigo (woad), and Schunck records a purple made by mixing red and blue threads.[9]

Red

On the Antinoë fabrics this was generally madder, but occasionally kermes,[10] with two instances of what Pfister calls cochineal or sometimes Persian cochineal.[11] It can-

[1] R. Pfister, *Seminarium Kondakovianum*, VII (1935), pp. 40–41; *Tissus Coptes du Musée du Louvre*.

[2] E. Schunck, 'Notes on Some Ancient Dyes', *Mem. and Proc. Manchester Lit. and Phil. Soc.*, V (1892), p. 158.

[3] H. E. Winlock, *Materials used at the Embalming of King Tūt-ankh-Amūn*, p. 10.

[4] E. Schunck, *Mem. and Proc. Manchester Lit. and Phil. Soc.*, V (1892), p. 161.

[5] R. Pfister, *Seminarium Kondakovianum*, VII (1935), pp. 41–42; *Tissus Coptes du Musée du Louvre*.

[6] R. Pfister, *Seminarium Kondakovianum*, VII (1935), p. 42.

[7] E. Schunck, *Mem. and Proc. Manchester Lit. and Phil. Soc.*, V (1892), p. 159.

[8] R. Pfister, *Seminarium Kondakovianum*, VII (1935), pp. 39–40; *Tissus Coptes du Musée du Louvre*.

[9] E. Schunck, *Mem. and Proc. Manchester Lit. and Phil. Soc.*, V (1892), p. 161.

[10] R. Pfister, *Seminarium Kondakovianum*, VII (1935), pp. 37–39; *Tissus Coptes du Musée du Louvre*.

[11] R. Pfister, *Seminarium Kondakovianum*, VII (1935), p. 46.

not, of course, have been the modern cochineal, since this originally came from Mexico and was not known in Egypt at the time. A 'full deep red' and a 'dull chestnut brown' were found by Schunck to be due to madder,[1] and a red-brown colour on one of the fabrics from the tomb of Tutankhamūn was identified as madder [2] by Pfister. An orange-red colour on mummy wrappings of Twenty-first Dynasty date [3] Pfister found to be due to henna,[4] probably mixed with a red colour obtained from the flowers of *Carthamus tinctorius*.[5] This latter plant grew abundantly in ancient Egypt and is still plentiful, and from the flowers both a red and a yellow dye are obtained. The yellow is not now used, as it is soluble in water and, therefore, not permanent, but the red is insoluble in water though soluble in dilute solutions of alkali, such as natron, and has been employed in modern times for dyeing silk, as also for colouring starch to make rouge for toilet purposes, and the deep-red flower petals are used sometimes for colouring soup. Girard states [6] (1812) that the flowers were employed for dyeing, and Thomson thought that a red dye on some fabrics examined by him was due to safflower.[7]

Yellow

Many years ago Thomson suggested that the yellow dye of the ancient Egyptians was derived from the safflower, but he was unable to prove this,[7] though it has since been established definitely by Hübner,[8] who identified it on fabrics of Twelfth Dynasty date. Hübner found also that another and slightly different shade of yellow of the same date was iron buff.[8]

Mordants

In the process of dyeing generally two mediums are necessary, one being the colour and the other an agent, or mordant, as it is called, to fix the dye to the fabric, and in Egypt, although probably at first mordants were not used, by Pliny's time (first century A.D.) a mordant was certainly employed and is referred to by that author, who states [9] that 'In Egypt, too, they employ a very remarkable process for the colouring of tissues. After pressing the material, which is white at first, they saturate it, not with colours, but with mordants that are calculated to absorb colour. This done, the tissues, still unchanged in appearance, are plunged into a cauldron of boiling dye, and are removed the next moment fully coloured. It is a singular fact, too, that although the dye in the pan is of one uniform colour, the material when taken out of it is of various colours, according to the nature of the mordants that have been

---

[1] E. Schunck, *Mem. and Proc. Manchester Lit. and Phil. Soc.*, v (1892), pp. 159–61.

[2] R. Pfister, *Revue des arts asiatiques*, XI (1937), p. 209.

[3] G. Maspero, *Les momies royales de Deir el Bahari*, Mém. Miss., I (1889), pp. 537, 539, 563, 768.

[4] Descotiles and Berthelot, *Memoirs relative to Egypt*, stated that henna was employed for dyeing mummy wrappings.

[5] R. Pfister, *Revue des arts asiatiques*, XI (1937), p. 210; cf. also G. Schweinfurth, *Bull. Inst. Ég.*, III (1882), pp. 70–71; L. Keimer, *Gartenpflanzen*, pp. 7–8.

[6] P. S. Girard, *Description de l'Égypte, état moderne*, II, 1812, pp. 538–9.

[7] J. Thomson, *London and Edinburgh Phil. Mag.*, v (1834), pp. 362–3.

[8] J. Hübner, in M. A. Murray, *Tomb of Two Brothers*, pp. 72–79; *Journ. Soc. Dyers and Colourists*, XXV (1909), pp. 223–6. Cf. also R. Pfister, *Tissus Coptes du Musée du Louvre*.

[9] XXXV: 42.

respectively applied to it: these colours, too, will never wash out.' Unfortunately
the nature of the mordants is not mentioned, though the principal one was almost
certainly alum, which occurs in Egypt and which was worked anciently.[1] No certain
instance of its use can be quoted, though it has been suggested that it was employed
on fabrics of Twelfth Dynasty date,[2] and there is textual evidence which may indicate the use of alum as a mordant with madder during the New Kingdom.[3]

According to the two papyri already mentioned the mordants used in Egypt in
early Christian times included alum, but also salts of iron, such as the acetate, specially
prepared from iron and vinegar, and the sulphate, which occurs frequently as an
impurity in the alum.[4]

The remains of a dye-house of Roman date were found by Petrie at Athribis, near
Sohag, who states [5] 'These vats . . . most of them are blue-black with indigo and some
red.' The Italian archaeological Mission found at Tebtunis (Kom el Breigat) 'a Roman
fullonica, or dyeing and cleaning works, very similar to the modern Egyptian ones'.[6]

---

[1] See pp. 257-9.
[2] M. A. Murray, *Tomb of Two Brothers*, p. 74.
[3] Cf. J. R. Harris, *Lexicographical Studies*, p. 187.
[4] R. Pfister, *Tissus Coptes du Musée du Louvre*.
[5] W. M. F. Petrie, *Athribis*, p. 11.
[6] *Egyptian Gazette*, April 23rd, 1935.

Chapter IX
GLAZED WARE[1]

The sequence which at present obtains for glazed ware from ancient Egypt is—first, glazed steatite from the Badarian civilization;[2] second, glazed powdered quartz (faience) from the predynastic period, sequence date 31,[3] a number of variants of which came in later; third, glazed solid quartz, also from the predynastic period, but sequence date 48,[3] and fourth, glazed pottery from the Arab period. This sequence. however, is liable to be upset at any time by fresh discoveries, and the natural sequence would seem to be—first, glazed solid quartz, which is the most likely to have been discovered accidentally and to have formed the starting-point for glazed ware; second, glazed quartz powder, the powdering and moulding, or other shaping, of quartz being an ingenious method of avoiding the cutting of such a hard stone; third, glazed steatite, which is merely the substitution of a natural soft stone, that can easily be carved, for a hard stone that can only be cut with difficulty; and fourth, glazed pottery. It seems highly probable, however, that at a very early date attempts were made to glaze pottery, which would have made it not only decorative but also impermeable to liquids, a very desirable property, but any such attempts must have ended in failure, since the only glaze known was an alkaline one, which will not adhere to ordinary clay ware, the lead glaze that will adhere not having been discovered until much later.[4]

The various kinds of glazed ware enumerated will now be described in order of sequence.

A. GLAZED STEATITE

The earliest glazed material of any kind known from ancient Egypt is steatite, beads of which were very plentiful in the Badarian civilization. Brunton, who found them, suggests that they 'can hardly have been made locally'.[5] This, of course, may be so, but it should not be forgotten that steatite is found in Egypt, and that there is a deposit at Gebel Fatira less than 100 miles from Badari, slightly to the south-east between the Nile and the Red Sea. Another occurrence of steatite is at Hamr, near

---

[1] Since the materials are being dealt with in alphabetical order, glazed ware should come after glass, but, as it was from glazed ware that glass developed, the natural order is being used in this instance. This chapter is taken in part from an article by me published in *J.E.A.*, XXII (1936), pp. 141–64.

[2] G. Brunton and G. Caton-Thompson, *Badarian Civilisation*, pp. 27, 28, 41.

[3] W. M. F. Petrie, *Prehistoric Egypt*, p. 42.

[4] Occasionally pottery was coated with an ordinary resin varnish. The few specimens examined have all been from the Eighteenth Dynasty.

[5] G. Brunton and G. Caton-Thompson, *Badarian Civilisation*, p. 41.

Aswan, where there is evidence of ancient working, and a third in Wadi Gulan, opposite Gulan Island, north of Ras Benas on the Red Sea coast.

Steatite is a massive form of talc, and consists of hydrated magnesium silicate; it can easily be cut with a knife, or scratched with the finger-nail, its hardness on Mohs' scale being only 1. Its specific gravity is 2.7 to 2.8; it is usually white or grey in colour, though occasionally smoke-black.

Steatite is a very suitable material for carving into small objects such as amulets, beads, scarabs (the greater proportion of which are of steatite), small statuettes, and small vases, not only on account of its softness and the consequent ease with which it can be cut, but also because it is fine-grained. It possesses a further quality that makes it satisfactory as a base for glazing, namely, infusibility, and not only may it be heated without decomposition or fracture, but the heating, by dehydrating it, causes it to become hard enough to scratch glass.

Some interesting objects of glazed steatite have been discussed by Beck,[1] who has also studied the glaze of Badarian and predynastic beads.[2] He notes 'a very real difference' between the two, the Badarian glaze being crystalline, the predynastic completely vitreous. Beck suspects a real variation in technique, but it seems probable that the difference is due either to the presence of more alumina in the raw materials or to a change in the temperature at which the glaze was melted or maintained.[3]

Glazed steatite continued in use until the 'Arab age',[4] but glazed scarabs of this material are still being made by the modern forgers of antiquities at Qurna near Luxor.

B. FAIENCE

Egyptian faience is a ware made from glazed quartz frit (powdered quartz). It is not true 'faience', a name reserved for the tin-glazed earthenwares such as *maiolica* or delftware, nor is it either 'porcelain' or 'glazed pottery'. These two terms, often used to describe Egyptian faience, are entirely wrong and misleading, porcelain being a hard translucent glazed ware made from kaolin, and pottery a ware made from clay, shaped while wet and then hardened by baking. The alternative name 'glazed siliceous ware', suggested by Burton,[5] is too vague, since it would include glazed siliceous pottery. Egyptian faience has also frequently been referred to as 'glaze', notably by Petrie. This is quite wrong, and it would be just as reasonable to call a varnished object 'varnish' as to call a glazed object 'glaze'.[6]

Faience was extensively employed for making a wide variety of objects, notably small pieces such as amulets, beads, scarabs and inlay for jewellery, statuettes and particularly shawabti figures, bowls, chalices and other vessels, and tiles and other sizeable pieces of architectural inlay. Great quantities of faience fragments were found on the site of the Middle Kingdom Egyptian colony at Kerma in the Sudan

---

[1] H. C. Beck, *Ancient Egypt*, 1934, pp. 70–76. Cf. also F. A. Bannister and H. J. Plenderleith, *J.E.A.*, XXII (1936), pp. 2–6.

[2] H. C. Beck, in G. Brunton, *Mostagedda*, pp. 60–61.

[3] A. Lucas, in G. Brunton, *Mostagedda*, pp. 60–61.

[4] W. M. F. Petrie, *Prehistoric Egypt*, p. 42.

[5] W. Burton, *Journ. Royal Soc. of Arts*, LX (1912), p. 596.

[6] The term may possibly be justified when used to describe small pieces of 'faience' inlay, from the back of which the core material has been deliberately ground away. See U. Hölscher, *Excavation of Medinet Habu*, IV, p. 40, n. 64.

and are described by Reisner,[1] and numerous specimens of architectural inlay have been discovered at El Amarna,[2] Tell el Yahudiyeh,[3] Qantir,[4] Medinet Habu [5] and elsewhere.[6] Of particular interest are the well-known faience tiles with figures of foreign prisoners in relief, mainly from Medinet Habu and Qantir,[7] and the statues of lions, also from Qantir,[8] which, with a huge *uas*-sceptre found by Petrie,[9] are the largest faience objects yet discovered. The principal stages in the making of faience have been described by von Bissing [10] and Reisner.[11]

Faience may be classified into ordinary faience and a number of variants, all of which may now be discussed.

Ordinary Faience

Typical Egyptian faience consists of a body material (core) coated with a vitreous, alkaline glaze, and ranges in date from predynastic times [12] to as late as the fourteenth century A.D.[13]

Body Material

This is always granular, generally friable and often very friable, though sometimes hard, and usually very finely divided, but occasionally comparatively coarse. It is frequently white, or practically white, in colour, but sometimes tinted brown, grey or yellowish and occasionally very slightly blue or green.[14]

Many hundreds, and probably thousands, of specimens of ordinary faience have been examined, but no useful purpose would be served by giving the details of them all, though the colour of the body material of a few may be recorded. Thus, forty-one specimens from the First and Second Dynasties, now in the Cairo Museum, which are important because they belong to a comparatively early period in the history of the material, are as follows:

Colour of Core	Number	Per cent
Very white	8	20
Grey	3	7
Slightly yellow	11	27
Light to dark brown [15]	19	46
	41	100

[1] G. A. Reisner, *Kerma*, IV–V, pp. 134–75.   [2] W. M. F. Petrie, *Tell el Amarna*, pp. 12, 28–30.
[3] W. M. F. Petrie, *Hyksos and Israelite Cities*, p. 17, Pl. XVIA.
[4] W. C. Hayes, *Glazed Tiles*; M. Hamza, *Ann. Serv.*, XXX (1930), pp. 51–52.
[5] R. Anthes, in U. Hölscher, *Excavation of Medinet Habu*, IV, pp. 44–47; U. Hölscher, *op. cit.*, pp. 38–42; *Z.Ä.S.*, LXXVI (1940), pp. 41–45.
[6] Cf. U. Hölscher, *Excavation of Medinet Habu*, IV, p. 39, n. 62.
[7] G. Daressy, *Ann. Serv.*, XI (1911), pp. 49–63; R. Anthes, in U. Hölscher, *Excavation of Medinet Habu*, IV, pp. 42–44, Pls. XXX–XXXIV; W. C. Hayes, *Glazed Tiles*; cf. also W. M. F. Petrie, *Hyksos and Israelite Cities*, p. 17, Pl. XVIA.
[8] M. Hamza, *Ann. Serv.*, XXX (1930), pp. 46–51; W. C. Hayes, *Glazed Tiles*, pp. 19–21.
[9] W. M. F. Petrie and J. E. Quibell, *Naqada and Ballas*, p. 68, Pl. LXXVIII; H. Wallis, *Egyptian Ceramic Art*, 1898, p. 6, Pl. II.
[10] F. W. von Bissing, *Fayencegefässe*, pp. xx f.   [11] G. A. Reisner, *Kerma*, IV–V, pp. 136–43.
[12] W. M. F. Petrie, *Prehistoric Egypt*, p. 42.   [13] See p. 167.
[14] This is friable and not the hard blue or green body material described later as Variant D: it has been noticed from the Eighteenth Dynasty.
[15] The colour suggests the use of powdered sand or sandstone.

Some small blue tiles of Third Dynasty date from the step pyramid at Saqqara [1] and from the adjoining large tomb have a very fine white core; specimens of Middle Kingdom date from Kerma described by Reisner vary in colour, the majority having a white or light grey core, though in some examples the core is dark yellowish drab, and in others dark grey or blackish; a number of pieces of inlay from the palace at El Amarna (Eighteenth Dynasty) have a coarse white core; the Nineteenth-to-Twentieth Dynasty specimens from Qantir [2] have a coarse brown core; of eighteen Graeco-Roman specimens from the Fayum twelve have a white, or practically white, core, five have a brown core and one a grey core, and four specimens of Islamic faience have a very white core.

The body material, whether fine or coarse, is seen when examined microscopically to consist of sharp, angular grains of quartz, without any visible admixture of other substance.

Only very few chemical analyses of this material can be traced, and of these many are unsatisfactory because no particulars of the kind or date of the specimens are given, while in some instances the material analysed was manifestly not ordinary faience but one of the variants. [2]

For the white body material only three origins seem possible, namely, powdered quartz rock, powdered rock crystal, or powdered white quartz pebbles, from all of which I have prepared by fine grinding a material practically identical with the ancient material. At least one of the modern forgers of faience uses both powdered quartz rock and powdered rock crystal.

For the brown, grey, and yellowish body material, powdered sand, sandstone, [3] or flint seem likely, the colour being due to natural impurities in the material employed.

Shaping

The next question to be considered is how such a material as powdered quartz was shaped. Burton's suggestion [4] that faience objects were carved out of sandstone cannot be accepted for many reasons, chiefly because the material has not the naturally rounded grains of sandstone, but sharp angular grains that prove it to be artificially prepared and because no such fine white sandstone is known, but also because the body material of faience is usually so friable that carving would have been impossible. The question, however, has been partly settled by the discovery of very large numbers of red pottery moulds, though none earlier than the Eighteenth Dynasty. Petrie 'brought nearly five thousand from Tell el Amarna after rejecting large quantities of the commonest'; [5] Winlock mentions 'hundreds of moulds for beads, pendants and finger rings' from the factories in the palace area of Amenhotpe III; [6] and Mahmud Hamza collected 'about ten thousand', of Nineteenth or Twentieth Dynasty date from Qantir, 'most of which still bear traces of the colour and the paste used in the process

---

[1] Cf. J.-P. Lauer, *Pyramide à degrés*, I, pp. 36–38.
[2] For analyses see pp. 474–5.   [3] Cf. G. A. Reisner, *Kerma*, IV–V, p. 136.
[4] W. Burton, *Journ. Royal Soc. of Arts*, LX (1912), pp. 594–9; cf. also W. Pukall, *Sprechsaal*, XLV (1912), No. 48, p. 729.
[5] W. M. F. Petrie, *Tell el Amarna*, p. 30.
[6] H. E. Winlock, *M.M.A. Bull.*, VII (1912), p. 187.

of manufacture';[1] similar moulds, also of New Kingdom date, were found at Tell el Yahudiyeh.[2] 'At Naukratis hundreds were found for making scarabs for the Greek trade':[3] 'Such moulds have been found in many other places, Memphis, Thebes, Gurob, etc.'[4] Writing of these moulds, Petrie says[3] 'They sometimes contain the remains of the siliceous paste with which they were choked when they were thrown away.' Most of the moulds referred to are for small objects, ornaments, pendants and scarabs, but there are also larger ones for shawabti and other figures. All the moulds found have been open, that is they are for one side (the front) of the object only. Petrie states[5] that the 'paste was roughly moulded into form and when dry it was graved with a point to give detail', and also that large objects were made in sections, which were joined together with some of the same paste before glazing. Hayes says of the faience from Qantir that 'The statues and all the larger tiles were modeled by hand, not cast in moulds. In the case of the tiles the front and back surfaces were wiped flat with a trowel or mason's float and the sides trimmed with an edge tool. Each of the statues was built up in several masses of the body material on a core of wooden rods.'[6] A certain proportion of the moulds have a narrow channel across the edges near the top of the mould in which a thick copper wire was placed. The mould was then filled with the plastic powdered quartz paste above the level of the wire. After firing, the wire was removed, leaving a hole in the object from one side to the other that could be used for suspension. One such wire, now very corroded, was found by Hamza at Qantir and is in the Cairo Museum.[7] The length is 8.1 centimetres and the diameter in its corroded state varies from one to two millimetres. The channels for the wire are apparently what Petrie calls 'ducts at the side for the outflow of the surplus material'.[8] The method of making the moulds for faience objects has been described by Roeder.[9]

Faience objects, however, were not always moulded, and von Bissing, who has described the technique of making faience vessels in some detail, concludes that although some were moulded, others were turned on a wheel like pottery, and others built up entirely by hand.[10] Reisner, too, states that the thin bowls, and probably the thicker bowls, the larger jars and some other jars from the Middle Kingdom Egyptian colony at Kerma in the Sudan had been turned on the wheel; that most of the smaller jars had been made on a core; that a few poor jars showed traces of gouging as if they had been formed solid and dug out while still moist; that the upper surfaces of tiles had been formed by hand and the edges trimmed with a knife; that figures and amulets had been modelled by hand and finished with a point or blade, and that none of the objects had been made in a mould.[11] I myself would venture to suggest that bowls and vases, especially such as the libation vases of 'teapot' form, could only

[1] M. Hamza, Ann. Serv., xxx (1930), pp. 42, 53–62.
[2] E. Naville and F. Ll. Griffith, Mound of the Jew and . . . Tell el Yahudiyeh, pp. 48–49.
[3] W. M. F. Petrie, Arts and Crafts, pp. 118–19.
[4] W. M. F. Petrie, Tell el Amarna, p. 30.
[5] W. M. F. Petrie, Arts and Crafts, pp. 115–16.
[6] W. C. Hayes, Glazed Tiles, pp. 8–9.
[7] No. J. 64523.   [8] W. M. F. Petrie, Naukratis, i, p. 37.
[9] G. Roeder, Ägyptische Bronzewerke, pp. 190–1.
[10] F. W. von Bissing, Fayencegefässe, pp. xxi f.   [11] G. A. Reisner, Kerma, iv–v, p. 137.

have been made by pottery methods and not by moulding, though the spouts and lids may have been moulded.

Glaze

The glaze, which is most frequently coloured blue, green, or greenish-blue, but is sometimes violet, white, yellow, or of two or more colours,[1] is what is termed an 'alkaline' glaze, and consists of glass; chemically it is essentially a sodium-calcium-silicate or a potassium-calcium-silicate without any lead compound.[2] Only two complete analyses of the glaze, of which sufficient details are given to make it certain that the specimen was from ordinary faience, can be traced.[3]

From the results of the analyses it is evident, first, that not only is the glaze glass but it is of similar composition to the ancient glass, except that the proportion of lime (calcium oxide) is lower and that of silica higher than is usual in the ancient glass; and second, that the colour, like that of much of the glass, is due to a copper compound. The large amount of potash and the small amount of soda present in one specimen show that the alkali employed for this particular glaze was plant ashes and not natron.

A partial analysis of the blue glaze on a predynastic chert bead made by Sir Herbert Jackson for Mr. Horace Beck showed that it consisted essentially of sodium silicate, with merely a trace of calcium, coloured with a copper compound.[4] In this instance, since the alkali was soda, the source of it must have been either natron or the ashes from special plants grown near salt water.[5]

Brongniart states [6] that the glaze of Egyptian faience was examined by Buisson, Laurent, Malaguti, and Salvétat, and that it consists of silica and soda coloured with a copper compound, and Franchet also says [7] that it consists of a compound of silica and soda. A blue glaze closely similar to specimens of Eighteenth Dynasty date was produced experimentally by Nicolini and Santini.[8]

Glazing kilns of Ptolemaic or Roman date were found by Petrie at Memphis.[9]

Decoration

After the glaze had been applied to the body material, and before an object received its final firing, decoration was frequently added, particularly in the case of vessels, tiles, and other larger pieces. Designs were painted in black upon the glaze, or incised into it and filled with glaze of a different colour and sometimes a thin layer of body material. The methods of decoration employed on the faience objects found at Kerma have been described in detail by Reisner,[10] while the technique of the tiles from Qantir and Medinet Habu, which also involved the building up of relief

---

[1] Black and red faience are described on pp. 162–3.

[2] For the reason for emphasizing this see pp. 165–6.

[3] For analyses see p. 475.

[4] H. C. Beck, *Ancient Egypt*, 1935, p. 23.   [5] See p. 171.

[6] A. Brongniart, *Traité des arts céramiques ou des poteries*, I, p. 506.

[7] L. Franchet, *Céramique primitive*, p. 92.

[8] L. Nicolini and M. Santini, *Bollettino del'Istituto centrale del restauro*, XXXIV–V (1958), pp. 59–70.

[9] W. M. F. Petrie, *Memphis*, I, pp. 14–15; *Historical Studies*, II, pp. 34–37.

[10] G. A. Reisner, *Kerma*, IV–V, pp. 138–42.

decoration in thick glaze and the inlaying of pieces of glass and faience on a gypsum base, has been discussed by Hayes [1] and Anthes.[2]

Faience with Extra Layer (Variant A)

Occasionally, instead of there being only two layers of material, namely an inner core coated with glaze, there is also an additional layer between the core and the glaze. This extra layer was first pointed out by Reisner,[3] whose description of it is the only one that I can trace. Any generalization with respect to the prevalence of this special layer would be dangerous without the examination of more specimens of faience of different kinds and dates than usually fall to the lot of any individual to handle, more especially as it is only with broken objects (which generally are not to be found on exhibition in museums) that its presence or absence can be detected; however, the writer's experience may be given. In addition to the occurrence of this layer in the Twelfth Dynasty faience from Kerma described by Reisner, it is also present in faience of the same period from Shalfak (Sarras), also in the Sudan, specimens of both of which I have examined. It was not present in forty-one specimens from the First and Second Dynasties; nor in the Third Dynasty blue tiles from Saqqara; nor in several specimens of the Twelfth Dynasty from Lisht; nor in one specimen of the same date from El Bersheh; and it was found only in one specimen (part of a blue-glazed tile from Deir el Bahari) out of several hundreds examined from the Eighteenth Dynasty, though it was present on several undated specimens probably from that Dynasty. It was rarely present in the late material, only comparatively few examples having been found out of many hundreds of specimens examined, these being (a) a few pieces of the coarse brown-body material found by Hamza at Qantir;[4] (b) one lot of shawabti figures of Twenty-sixth Dynasty date, and (c) two pieces of Graeco-Roman date out of many from the Fayum. It was not present on four specimens from the Arab period.

The extra layer, in those instances in which it has been measured (which, however, seem typical of the rest), varied in thickness from about 0.5 mm. to about 2.5 mm. In a Kerma specimen it was white on a light-grey body, and, as Reisner states, very like plaster of Paris in appearance; in a Shalfak specimen it was white on a light-blue body; on the Eighteenth Dynasty tile mentioned it was white on a faintly blue-tinted body; on the Qantir specimens it was white on a brown body; on the Twenty-sixth Dynasty shawabti figures it was white on a dark-grey body; on one of the Graeco-Roman specimens it was white on a reddish body and on the other it was white on a grey body, and in every instance in which it has been critically examined the extra layer has consisted of very finely powdered quartz, always more finely ground and more compact than the body substance. There can be little doubt that, as stated by Reisner, the special layer was employed for the purpose of enhancing or modifying the colour of the glaze. Thus, when a brown, grey, or yellowish body material would have lessened or spoilt the full brilliance of a blue glaze, a thin layer of a perfectly white material was interposed between the two; sometimes, when a

---

[1] W. C. Hayes, *Glazed Tiles*, pp. 8–10.
[2] R. Anthes, in U. Hölscher, *Excavation of Medinet Habu*, IV, pp. 42–44.
[3] G. A. Reisner, *Kerma*, IV–V, pp. 134–75.
[4] M. Hamza, *Ann. Serv.*, XXX (1930), pp. 31–68.

green glaze was required, a yellow layer was used underneath a blue glaze in order to give it a greenish tint; for a black glaze with violet tinge, a dark grey layer was employed, and occasionally a white layer was used under parts only of a dark-blue glaze in order to give to those parts a lighter colour, thus forming a light-blue pattern on a dark-blue ground.

With respect to the method of applying the 'special' layer, which consists of exceedingly finely ground quartz powder, it was found by experiment that a good, strongly adherent white layer of any thickness desired could be made by using a mixture of very fine quartz powder and natron solution, drying and firing. On account of the porosity of the body substance the mixture must not be too viscous (otherwise owing to abstraction of water by the quartz it becomes too thick to be laid on evenly) and if carefully poured on it forms a uniform layer with a flat surface, which when dried and fired becomes strongly adherent.

Black Faience (Variant B)

Black faience is not very common; it was used, however, for a small tile [1] and small pieces of inlay [2] of Third Dynasty date from Saqqara; for small beads of early dynastic date [3] (Sixth, Eighth, and Ninth Dynasties), though in some instances the glaze was possibly originally green that has changed to black; for beads of the Middle Kingdom and Second Intermediate period respectively;[4] for certain vessels found at Kerma (Middle Kingdom);[5] for inlay from El Amarna (Eighteenth Dynasty) and Qantir (Nineteenth to Twentieth Dynasty) and in plaques from the palace of Ramses III at Medinet Habu (Twentieth Dynasty). In the specimens examined (other than the beads, where the core was white) the core was either dark grey or dark brown, and consisted of the usual powdered quartz, coloured by means of oxide of iron, though the Kerma specimens were probably grey sandstone. It is most probable that the oxide of iron was added intentionally, and, therefore, that the material is a definite variant.

Red Faience (Variant C)

Very occasionally red faience is merely ordinary faience having a red glaze on a white, or almost white, body, for instance two small oblong tiles and several pieces of tiles of Third Dynasty date from Saqqara, now in the Cairo Museum,[6] and two specimens, both of Eighteenth Dynasty date, from El Amarna. Usually, however, red faience is a definite variant, the body material being red and the glaze sometimes red and sometimes having very little colour.

Petrie states that 'Red varying between red brick and maroon belongs to Akhenaten and is seldom, if ever, found in the Ramesside and later times.' [7] Since this was

---

[1] D. Valeriani and G. Segato, *Atlante del Basso ed Alto Egitto*, 1835, Pl. T37D.

[2] Cairo Museum, Nos. J. 69563 A, B, C; 69564 A, B, C, D, E, F, G; and 69565.

[3] Found by Mr. Guy Brunton (not yet all published), and examined by me. These are exclusive of the beads of black, glassy material described by H. C. Beck, in G. Brunton, *Qau and Badari*, II, pp. 23, 24.

[4] G. Brunton, *Mostagedda*, pp. 114, 125, 126, 134.

[5] G. A. Reisner, *Kerma*, IV–V, p. 136.

[6] Nos. J. 69565, 69566 A, 69566 B, 69566 C, 69567, 69568.

[7] W. M. F. Petrie, Burlington Fine Arts Club, *Exhibition of the Art of Ancient Egypt*, 1895, *Glass and Glazing*, p. xxviii.

written, however, much more red faience has been found, for example, the tiles already mentioned, as also a reference to similar red tiles, also of the Third Dynasty, from Saqqara; [1] a few red faience spheroid beads of the Second Intermediate period found by Brunton [2] and a very large amount of red faience from the Eighteenth, Nineteenth and Twentieth Dynasties respectively. From the Eighteenth Dynasty red faience occurs as beads, necklace-pendants, and inlay, such necklace-pendants and inlay being very common from El Amarna, and similar necklace-pendants having been found in the tomb of Tutankhamūn; from the Nineteenth Dynasty (reign of Ramses II) and Twentieth Dynasty (reign of Ramses III) red faience foundation deposits are known; during the Nineteenth and Twentieth Dynasties red faience was used for beads and also for inlay in the Ramessid palace at Qantir, and during the Twentieth Dynasty red faience inlay was employed in plaques in the palace of Ramses III at Medinet Habu. Specimens of all of the above-mentioned objects in the Cairo Museum have been examined.

Several pieces of early dynastic faience in the Cairo Museum seem at first sight to have a red core with a blue or green glaze, but on further examination it is found that although the surface of the core of an old break is red or reddish, this coloration is only superficial, being due apparently to a surface oxidation of the iron compounds present, and underneath the red the colour is brown, owing possibly to the use of a brown sand.

With regard to the composition of the red body material, Petrie says: '. . . for the red, a body mixed with haematite and covered with a transparent glaze.' [3] A number of specimens have been analysed, all of which consisted of a very fine, red, gritty powder, which proved to be powdered quartz, coloured by means of red oxide of iron, and from a comparison of specimens of red quartz sand powdered to the same degree of fineness and examined both microscopically and chemically side by side, it is practically certain that the red body material of the faience is not a natural red sand finely powdered (which would give a red quartz powder) but an artificial mixture of quartz and red ochre, or other form of iron oxide.

Red faience is quite distinct from the red glazed pottery of the Arab period.

Faience with Hard Blue or Green Body (Variant D)

This consists of a core of granular quartz, generally harder than that of ordinary faience and sometimes very hard, tinted blue or green and always coated with a definite and separate glaze of the same colour as the core, though usually of a lighter shade. At first sight the colour of the core might appear to have been caused by some of the glaze having accidentally penetrated the body material, but against this there are two objections: first, that the glaze would probably have been too viscous to have penetrated [4] and, second, that if there had been any such penetration, it would have been greatest near the surface and would have diminished progressively towards the centre, whereas there is no such gradation of tint, which is generally uniform

[1] D. Valeriani and G. Segato, *Atlante del Basso ed Alto Egitto*, 1835, Pl. T 37D; A. Lucas, *J.E.A.*, XXIV (1938), p. 245.
[2] G. Brunton, *Mostagedda*, p. 126; *Matmar*, p. 58.
[3] W. M. F. Petrie, *Arts and Crafts*, p. 118.
[4] See p. 173, where penetration of glaze certainly occurred.

throughout, though occasionally there are tiny particles of darker-coloured blue or green material, looking like glaze, scattered through the core. Franchet mentions this and says *que c'est, parfois, la glaçure bleue qui a été utilisée et on en distingue facilement les grains dans la masse de la pâte.* It seems likely, therefore, that a little finely powdered glaze, or a powdered mixture of the glaze materials, was deliberately mixed with the quartz, in order to make the fused object harder. Franchet makes a similar suggestion, and says that to overcome the fragility of ordinary faience glaze was mixed with the quartz of the body.[1] Although any admixed glaze would also act as a binder it could only function in this capacity after the firing, and in the case of non-moulded objects the usual adhesive would still be required in order to enable the material to be shaped and glazed. Another possibility is that specimens of faience, accidentally damaged during making, or imperfect from other causes, may have been ground up, body and glaze together, to make a new body material. This variant of faience it generally attributed to the Twenty-sixth Dynasty, but one piece of inlay of what apparently is this material is known from the Third Dynasty, having been found at Saqqara.[2] In addition to the examination of a large number of specimens with a lens, twelve examples have been examined miscroscopically.[3]

Glassy Faience (Variant E) [4]

A further step in the evolution of faience resulted in the production of a material which, although manifestly derived from the variant of faience just considered (Variant D), does not come within the definition of faience given and, therefore, strictly speaking, is not faience at all, since it does not consist of a body material coated with a separate glaze, but is entirely homogeneous in composition throughout, without any separate coating of glaze,[5] and with a compact surface quite unlike that of faience. The colour is invariably pale apple-green or pale turquoise blue, and the surface is generally matt, though occasionally glossy, and frequently marred by scattered areas of light brown stain. The hardness of the fabric is about 7 on the Mohs scale.[6] This material has often been called porcelain, though Burton [7] already pointed out that it was not, and referred to it as 'fritted siliceous ware'. Like Variant D, it is generally attributed to the Twenty-sixth Dynasty, for example by Petrie, who says that 'In the XXVIth dynasty there is a beautiful hard stoneware, apparently made by mixing some glaze with the body, enough to fuse it together into a solid mass throughout.' [8] Cooney, however, has published a statuette dating from the Twenty-second Dynasty, and shawabtis and other objects of the Twenty-fifth Dynasty are also known.[9] Undoubtedly, therefore, glassy faience was developed before the Saite

---

[1] L. Franchet, *Rapport sur une mission en Crète et en Égypte*, p. 116; *Céramique primitive*, pp. 42, 101.

[2] Cairo Museum, No. J. 69562.   [3] For chemical analyses see p. 475.

[4] Cf. J. D. Cooney, *Journ. Glass Studies*, II (1960), pp. 32–39.

[5] Sometimes it is very difficult to be certain whether there is a thin separate glaze or not and to know into which class, Variant D or Variant E, to place a particular specimen.

[6] For chemical analyses see p. 475.

[7] W. Burton, *Journ. Royal Soc. of Arts*, LX (1912), p. 599.

[8] W. M. F. Petrie, *Arts and Crafts*, p. 116.

[9] J. D. Cooney, *Journ. Glass Studies*, II (1960), pp. 33–36.

period, and its invention is probably to be attributed to the time of the Twenty-second Dynasty, coinciding to some extent with the decline in the use of glass. One specimen (part of a small bracelet) of what appears to be this material, of Third Dynasty date, was found at the step pyramid at Saqqara.[1] It is without separate glaze, homogeneous throughout, of a light-grey-blue colour, fairly hard and not glassy, and whether it should properly be classed as an example of glassy faience is doubtful. Several examples of sculpture in glassy faience from the Ptolemaic and Roman periods are described by Cooney.[2]

As may be seen by comparison of the analyses collected in the Appendix,[3] the composition of glassy faience stands somewhere between that of faience and glass. The proportion of silica present is less than that in ordinary faience or Variant D, but appreciably larger than that in glass, while the percentage of alkalies is greater than in faience but very much less than in glass. Oxide of copper, which is present in many specimens of glass and glaze, is also found in glassy faience and in Variant D, but has not been noted in the body material of ordinary faience.

A number of specimens of this material have been examined. Under the microscope it is seen to be very granular and to consist of what, for want of a better term, may be called imperfect glass, that is glass in which there is too small a proportion of alkali to combine with all the quartz, so that on firing there has been incomplete fusion, with the result that a considerable proportion of the quartz grains remain uncombined and embedded in a matrix of glass.[4]

Since this material is certainly not faience, and is equally certainly a kind of glass, though not normal glass, to call it 'glassy faience' or 'imperfect glass' seems to describe its nature and composition better than any other name that has been suggested.

Experiments to reproduce the material were made in the Brooklyn Museum by Mr. Anthony Giambalvo, who found that it had certain marked advantages over glass, particularly in the manufacture of sculptures. Whereas moulded glass can only be retouched after firing, the batch of glassy faience has something of the plasticity of clay and can be removed from the mould and finely worked over before being placed in the kiln, no retouching after firing being necessary.[5]

Faience (Variant F)

Egyptian faience consists, as already shown, of a powdered quartz base coated with an alkaline glaze, and this continued to be made certainly as late as the fourteenth or fifteenth century A.D. At a late period, the exact date of which is not certain, but is probably about the Twenty-second Dynasty, a new glaze was introduced, which contained a lead compound and which was occasionally applied to a powdered quartz base, and for a considerable period the two different glazes were used concurrently, both on a powdered quartz base, the older alkaline glaze, however being by far the commoner of the two. At a later date the alkaline glaze was also occasionally employed on a very siliceous pottery base, that is to say on a base of

---

[1] Cairo Museum, No. J. 69603.
[2] J. D. Cooney, *Journ. Glass Studies*, II (1960), pp. 37–39.
[3] See pp. 474–5.
[4] Cf. J. D. Cooney, *Journ. Glass Studies*, II (1960), p. 32.
[5] J. D. Cooney, *Journ. Glass Studies*, II (1960), pp. 32–33.

burnt clay ware containing a large proportion of quartz, and lead glaze was commonly used on ordinary pottery (ordinary burnt clay ware).

Thus there were three different bases, namely powdered quartz, highly siliceous clay, and ordinary clay, and two glazes, an alkaline glaze and a lead glaze. Five different combinations of these are possible and were made, namely (a) an alkaline glaze on powdered quartz, that is to say ordinary faience; (b) an alkaline glaze on highly siliceous burnt clay ware (glazed siliceous pottery), which does not come within the definition of faience and will be considered later; (c) a lead glaze on powdered quartz, which is a variant of faience (Variant F), and will now be described; (d) a lead glaze on highly siliceous burnt clay ware (glazed siliceous pottery) and (e) a lead glaze on ordinary burnt clay ware (glazed pottery). An alkaline glaze was not employed on ordinary burnt clay ware because, as explained by Burton,[1] 'Such glazes are very uncertain in use, and can only be applied to pottery unusually rich in silica (i.e. deficient in clay). Consequently these alkaline glazes cannot be used on ordinary clay wares, and when they have been used successfully, the clay has always been coated with a surface layer of highly siliceous substance (e.g. the so-called Persian, Rhodian, Syrian, and Egyptian pottery of the early Middle Ages).' A lead glaze, on the other hand, is very satisfactory on ordinary burnt clay ware (pottery).

As to the date of the first use of a lead glaze on any base there is a considerable difference of opinion. Thus Burton states that 'The fact that glazes containing lead oxide would adhere to ordinary pottery when alkaline glazes would not was discovered at a very early period, for lead glazes were extensively used in Egypt and the nearer East in Ptolemaic times, and it is significant that, though the Romans made singularly little use of glazes of any kind, the pottery that succeeded theirs, either in western Europe or in the Byzantine empire, was generally covered with glazes rich in lead.'[1] Petrie[2] says: '. . . lead is essential with iron for the Ptolemaic apple-green.' Hobson states[3] that 'Lead glaze has been freely used on late Roman pottery.' Dalton states that 'Pottery with a lead glaze is thought to have been first made in the first century B.C., when it appears on various sites at Alexandria, Tarsus in Asia Minor and in the Allier district of Gaul.'[4] Walters says: 'In the first century B.C. a new development may be observed in the introduction of a metallic, probably leaden, glaze used for coating clay objects in place of a slip or alkaline glaze.'[5] Harrison states that 'The first really satisfactory surface glass for use in pottery was what is called a lead glaze, known in Mesopotamia at any rate as early as 600 B.C.'[6] Sidney Smith illustrates 'Glazed ware of Babylonia and Assyria in the period 1000–600 B.C.',[7] but neither the nature of the body material, nor of the glaze, is given.

Unfortunately, owing to the confusion created by the use of 'pottery' for faience[8]

---

[1] *Ency. Brit.* 13th ed., v, article *Ceramics*, p. 706.

[2] W. M. F. Petrie, *Ancient Egypt*, 1923, p. 23 (Review).

[3] R. L. Hobson, *Guide to the Islamic Pottery of the Near East*, British Museum (1932), p. xv.

[4] O. M. Dalton, *Byzantine Art and Archaeology* (1911), p. 608.

[5] H. B. Walters, *Catalogue of Roman Pottery in the British Museum* (1908), p. xi.

[6] H. S. Harrison, *Pots and Pans*, pp. 52–53.

[7] Sidney Smith, *Early History of Assyria*, Pl. xv.

[8] The material described by Petrie as pottery ('The Pottery Kilns at Memphis', *Historical Studies*, II,; pp. 34–37, Pls. xiii–xx; *Memphis*, I, pp. 14–15, Pls. xlix–l) is probably largely, if not wholly, faience.

and also of 'faience' for pottery, it is sometimes impossible to know whether the material is really pottery or faience, as the case may be, especially for Islamic wares, since during the Arab period the two kinds of ware overlap one another. I have tested the glaze of a number of *faience* objects of different dates for lead, with the following results:

	Number tested	Alk. Glaze	Lead Glaze
IIIrd to XXIst Dynasties inclusive	8	8	0
XXIInd to XXXth Dynasties inclusive	4	1	3[a]
Ptolemaic and Roman periods	33	29	4[b]
Date unknown, but before Arab period	19	16	3[c]
Arab period	7[d]	4[e]	3[f]
	71	58	13

(*a*) One was a ram-headed bird amulet (Cairo Museum No. J. 56317) of XXIInd Dynasty date: another was a small statuette of Ptah-Seker-Osiris (Cairo Museum No. J. 54413) of the period XXIInd to XXVth Dynasties: a third was an inscribed vase (Cairo Museum No. J. 55621) of the Saite period. Two were green and one bluish-green.

(*b*) One was dated by Mr. O. Guéraud to the 3rd cent. B.C. (F. W. von Bissing *Fayencegefässe*, No. 18026). The proportion of lead was small. The exact dates of the others are unknown; all were green.

(*c*) The glaze was green in two cases and blue in one case.

(*d*) For three of these specimens I am indebted to Hussein Effendi Rashed, Curator of the Museum of Arab Art, Cairo, who was good enough to date all seven specimens.

(*e*) One 13th cent. A.D.; one 14th cent. A.D.; two 14th–15th cents. A.D.

(*f*) Two 11th–12th cents. A.D.; one 14th–15th cents. A.D.

The thirteen specimens with a lead glaze, therefore, were faience, Variant F, the rest being ordinary faience; the one of the Twenty-second Dynasty (950–730 B.C.) is the earliest example of faience with a lead glaze known to me.

The test for lead was the ordinary one with potassium iodide, with which soluble lead compounds give a canary-yellow precipitate of lead iodide, the glaze being first treated with a drop of hydrofluoric acid. The technique of the test was that suggested by E. S. Hawkins and described and used by MacAlister,[1] who says: 'The test is extremely sensitive and beautiful and can be used on specimens without damage being done.'

C. Glazed Solid Quartz

The objects of glazed solid quartz were mostly small, such as amulets, beads, and pendants,[2] though a few larger objects of this material are known, for example, part of a boat, which must have been about two feet long, but which was made in several sections, a sphinx, and part of a lion.[3] The quartz used was both quartz rock and rock

---

[1] D. A. MacAlister, 'The Material of the English Frit Porcelain: VI, Lead Oxide as a Factor in Classification', *The Burlington Magazine*, 54 (1929), pp. 192–9.

[2] H. C. Beck, *Ancient Egypt*, 1935, pp. 29–30.

[3] W. M. F. Petrie, *Prehistoric Egypt*, pp. 42–43.

crystal, and the glaze was an alkaline one. This material continued in use certainly as late as the Twelfth Dynasty.[1] Glazed quartz objects, some of them large, were found by Reisner in the Middle Kingdom Egyptian settlement at Kerma in the Sudan.[2] These the finder calls quartzite, but I have examined them in the Khartoum Museum and they are glazed quartz.

D. GLAZED POTTERY[3]

The glaze from a number of specimens of Islamic pottery of Egyptian origin [4] was tested with the following results:

	Number tested	Alk. Glaze	Lead Glaze
Red pottery	15	0	15
Buff and light-brown pottery[a]	18	0	18
Very siliceous pottery[b]	2	2[c]	0
	35	2	33

(a) Twelve are siliceous and several very siliceous.

(b) One reddish, one buff.

(c) In one of these specimens the glaze has almost entirely disappeared, and the adhesion, therefore, can never have been good. Both are 14th to 15th centuries A.D.

In connexion with glazed ware, glazed Greek pottery should be mentioned. Edgar says [5] of this pottery in the Cairo Museum that it includes objects acquired by purchase, as well as by excavation, and that 'most of the ordinary black-figured and red-figured vases are recent importations from Europe'. This type of pottery, however, was also 'manufactured in Egypt itself, many of the pieces . . . being products of a local fabric which flourished at Naukratis in the 6th century B.C.' [5] The black colour of the glaze of this pottery is attributed generally to ferrous silicate formed by the use of magnetic oxide of iron and an alkali.[6]

Slip

A slip [7] on glazed pottery is a thin layer of a light-coloured clay sometimes applied to the body material before glazing in order either to mask the colour of the body,

---

[1] W. M. F. Petrie, *Prehistoric Egypt*, pp. 42–43; H. C. Beck, *Ancient Egypt*, 1935, pp. 29–30.

[2] G. A. Reisner, *Kerma*, IV–V, pp. 49–55.

[3] Glazed pottery is only considered in connexion with the occasional late use on very siliceous pottery of an alkaline glaze similar to that employed for faience and the general use of a lead glaze. Lustre ware is intentionally omitted as being outside the scope of the present book.

[4] This pottery, which ranges in date from the 9th cent. A.D. to the 14th–15th cents. A.D., was kindly dated by Hussein Rashed, Curator of the Museum of Arab Art, Cairo, who supplied six of the specimens. For analyses of lead glaze see p. 497. Collie (J. N. Collie, *Trans. English Ceramic Soc.*, XV (1915–16), p. 161) reports lead glaze on pottery of Eleventh Dynasty date, also lead glaze on a bead (material not stated) of the same date.

[5] C. C. Edgar, *Greek Vases*, pp. iii, iv.

[6] W. Foster, 'The Composition of some Greek Vases', *Journ. American Chemical Soc.*, XXXII (1910), pp. 1259–64; 'Chemistry and Grecian Archaeology', *Journal of Chemical Education*, X (1933), pp. 270–7; L. Franchet, *Céramique primitive*, pp. 108–9; W. B. Pollard, *Cairo Sc. Journ.*, VI (1912), pp. 22–24.

[7] French *engobe*.

so that the glaze shall have its full colour effect, or to give a better adhesion to the glaze, in which latter case the slip is very siliceous. In part, and generally in large part, the function of the slip is analogous to that of the special layer applied to faience. A number of specimens of glazed pottery of the Arab period were examined for slip, with the following results:

	Number examined	Slip	No Slip
Red pottery	15	5	10
Buff and light-brown pottery	20	0	20
	35	5	30

ORIGIN OF GLAZING[1]

Wherever it may have been invented, there can be little doubt that glaze was first produced by accident, and a number of suggestions have been made to account for the discovery, three of which may be quoted. Petrie says [2] that it 'was invented from finding quartz pebbles fluxed by wood ashes in a hot fire', which evidently means that glaze was produced accidentally on quartz pebbles by means of the alkali from the ashes of a wood fire, and that this glaze was copied intentionally. Another suggestion, probably also Petrie's,[3] is that 'it seems likely that glazing was developed in the course of copper smelting. The wood ashes of fuel would give the alkali, and lime and silica would be in the copper ore. Such a coloured slag or a glass run from it on to the pebble floor of the furnace, would then be the starting point for artificial imitations.' Elliot Smith suggests [4] that 'smelters who were extracting copper discovered in the slag of their furnaces the secret of how to make glazes for pottery. . . .'

All trees and plants contain mineral matter, which is left in the form of ashes when the material is burned, and all such ashes contain alkali. In the case of trees and most land plants, this alkali consists largely of potassium carbonate, the ashes of herbs and grasses generally being richer in this constituent than the ashes of trees and bushes. In the case of certain plants growing on or near the seashore, or near salt lakes, the alkali, instead of being largely potassium carbonate, is principally sodium carbonate. The alkali, whether potassium or sodium carbonate, is never pure, but is always associated with potassium or sodium chloride and sulphate and calcium carbonate, together with small proportions of phosphates, silicates, magnesium carbonate, and oxide of iron.

A number of experiments were made by me with two lots of ashes from different sources, obtained by burning ordinary garden refuse. A little of the ash was placed

---

[1] Although the balance of evidence now appears to indicate that glazing did not, in fact, originate in Egypt (see pp. 464–5), there is still some room for discussion, and it has therefore seemed prudent to retain the present section with only minor modifications. It should, however, be noted that some of the arguments put forward may not apply if glaze is shown to be a Mesopotamian discovery.

[2] W. M. F. Petrie, Arts and Crafts, p. 107.

[3] Anonymous review, Ancient Egypt, 1914, p. 188.

[4] G. Elliot Smith, In the Beginning, p. 58.

on each of a number of large flat quartz pebbles, which were then strongly heated for about an hour in a small electric muffle furnace giving a nominal temperature of about 1,000° C. (1832° F.) and in some cases the pebbles were heated a second and even a third time, again for about an hour each time. Quartz sand was also covered with the ashes and strongly heated for about an hour. With one lot of ashes there was not any glaze whatever, either on the pebbles or on the sand, but with the other lot of ashes there were traces of a dark grey glaze on the pebbles, but none on the sand, the dark colour being due to particles of carbon from the ash having become entangled in the fused alkali. Although small variations in the results were obtained with plant ashes from two different sources, and therefore further slight variations might be expected with other ashes, it seems unlikely that any very marked glaze could be obtained in this manner, and still more unlikely that it could be obtained with ashes from wood fires, since these, as already stated, contain less alkali than plant ashes. Even if it be assumed that fires were made continuously on the same spot for weeks, or months, or even years together—not entirely an unreasonable supposition in certain cases—any glaze formed would have been dark-coloured and neither very noticeable nor very attractive. The first hypothesis, therefore, fails when tested experimentally, and it fails doubly because it also does not explain the production of the blue colour of the earliest glaze, which is due to a copper compound.

The second hypothesis is equally unsatisfactory; it assumes that the floor of a primitive copper-smelting-furnace was accidentally covered with, or intentionally composed of, quartz pebbles, for which there is neither evidence nor probability, and also, either that copper slag may be blue, which it is not, or that a blue-coloured glass might run from it, which I believe to be impossible, since the amount of alkali present from the ashes of the fuel would be quite inadequate, as is proved by the experiments already described. Also, as already shown, any glaze formed would have been a potash glaze and not a soda glaze, whereas the earliest glaze, so far as is known, is a soda glaze.

The third hypothesis is very vague, wholly inconvincing, and not supported by any evidence or experimental data.

Moreover, none of the hypotheses explains the production of glazed powdered quartz (faience), or of glazed steatite, both of which, on present evidence, were earlier than glazed solid quartz.

Since, so far as is known, the earliest glaze was not a colourless one that later developed into blue, but was blue from the first, the problem to be solved is the manner in which an accidental blue glaze that was easily noticeable and sufficiently desirable to be copied, could have been produced.

As Hocart says with reference to glass: 'It is impossible to profit by a lucky accident unless the mind has been prepared by a long course of thinking and experimenting.' [1] The state of mind, however, that could have led to the copying of an accidental blue glaze probably existed, namely the desire to possess blue beads, beads in themselves being highly desirable, as they were supposed to possess amuletic or magical properties, and blue beads being particularly desirable, as their colour had a special value. Since the only Egyptian stones that could have been made into blue

---

[1] A. M. Hocart, *The Progress of Man*, p. 49.

beads were turquoise, which was rare and expensive and often of a poor colour, and azurite, a blue ore of copper, which was also rare, not generally known, and not suited to carving, the only alternative was an artificial blue material, and hence any blue glaze produced accidentally on a stone would, sooner or later, have been noticed and copied.[1] The essential factors for the production of such a glaze were an alkali, copper or a copper compound, a stone to form a base for the glaze, and a fire. Since, as already shown, any glaze formed on quartz pebbles from the alkali in the ashes of a fire of wood or ordinary plants would have been negligible in amount, would not have been blue, and would have been a potash and not a soda glaze, this source of alkali may be ruled out. If so, then the alkali must have been either that from special plants growing on or near the sea-shore, or near a salt lake, or else natron.

The possibility of the use of plant ashes of a particular kind containing a high proportion of alkali in the form of sodium carbonate cannot be ignored, since an ash containing sodium carbonate obtained from special plants grown in certain localities bordering the Mediterranean, chiefly Spain, but also Sicily, Sardinia, and the Levant, was formerly in general use for glass-making, the material from Spain being called *Barilla* and that from the Levant *Roquetta*, and such plant ashes were at one time produced in Egypt for this purpose. Thus in 1610 G. Sandys, when passing through the desert between Alexandria and Rosetta, saw [2] 'here and there a few unhusbanded Palmes, Capers, and a weed called Kall [3] by the Arabs. This they use for feuel and then collect the ashes which crusht together they sell in great quantity to the Venetians; who equally mixing the same with the stones that are brought them from Pavia, by the river of Ticinum, make thereof their crystalline glasses.' Ray in 1693 [4] and Belon in 1553 [5] say much the same.

Natron is a naturally occurring compound of sodium carbonate and sodium bicarbonate, which in Egypt always contains sodium chloride (common salt) and sodium sulphate as impurities; it is found plentifully in the country, chiefly in three localities, namely, the Wadi Natrun, and the Beheira province in Lower Egypt, and El Kab in Upper Egypt, the first and third of these being known and worked anciently.

Since the earliest glaze in Egypt is of Badarian date on steatite, the next in chronological order being of early predynastic date (S.D. 31) on powdered quartz, and the third, of middle predynastic date (S.D. 48) on solid quartz, and since the alkali must have been either from special plant ashes or from natron, the problem can be narrowed down to (*a*) the manner in which a blue glaze was formed accidentally at a period when copper smelting and copper working were in their infancy, but when

---

[1] It seems, however, likely that blue glaze was valued primarily as a substitute for lapis lazuli, the blue stone *par excellence*, and the fact that the latter was not known in Egypt until some time *after* the earliest glaze would suggest that the possibilities of glaze were first realized elsewhere, in an area where lapis was already known and prized.

[2] *Sandys Travells* (1670), 6th ed., p. 90.

[3] Kali is probably meant.

[4] John Ray, *A Collection of Curious Travels and Voyages*, 1693.

[5] P. Belon, *Les Observations de plusiers singularitez et choses memorables, trouvées in Grèce, Asie, Indée, Égypte, Arabie et autres pays estranges, redigées en trois livres*, Mans, 1558 (original edition, 1553).

malachite was well known and largely used as an eye-paint,[1] and was therefore probably the source of the blue colour, and (b) to a district either on or near the sea-shore, or near a salt lake or natron deposit, or else to a place where special plant ashes or natron were being employed. Malachite, before being used as an eye-paint, was finely ground on hard stones, often quartz [2] or quartzite,[3] the grinding surface of which became coloured green in the process. In the presence of a little alkali, and if strongly heated, such grinding-stones would have become coated with a blue glaze. This has been proved by a number of experiments, a little malachite being rubbed on quartz pebbles, then a little powdered natron put on, and the pebbles strongly heated, when they became coated with a good blue glaze every time. But what was the source of the alkali? It seems possible that the fused ashes of special plants, or natron, might have been employed for some such purpose as washing clothes or the person, and that this alkali might have been broken up for use on the same stones that had been em-ployed for grinding malachite, and the stones afterwards strongly heated, for instance for putting into pots to boil water, or used to form a fireplace, or employed in some other manner in connexion with fire. In any case, whatever happened, it must have been something simple and something that occurred many times, since one occurrence would not have been enough for the glaze to be noticed and copied.

Method of Making Glaze

The essential ingredients of the ancient Egyptian blue glaze were an alkali, a very small proportion of a copper compound for colouring purposes a little calcium car-bonate (a trace of 'calcium' is given in a partial analysis of a predynastic glaze and 3.8 per cent of 'lime' in a glaze of Roman date; both of these being almost certainly present originally as calcium carbonate, which became converted into calcium silicate during heating), and a large proportion of silica. Since both powdered quartz and solid quartz are forms of silica, and since at a high temperature silica acts like an acid and attacks and combines with such substances as sodium carbonate, potassium carbonate, and calcium carbonate, it seemed likely that no further silica would be required. A little silica might also be present in the alkali, since plant ashes contain this ingredient, as do also the poorer qualities of natron; for example four specimens of natron analysed contained respectively 2.2 per cent, 6.7 per cent, 7.6 per cent,[4] and 9.6 per cent [5] of quartz sand. Also, since both plant ashes and natron contain a small proportion of calcium carbonate (the four specimens of natron already referred to containing 0.9 per cent, 1.3 per cent, 1.4 per cent, and 1.2 per cent respectively), and since even quartz contains a very small proportion (a white quartz pebble analysed containing 0.2 per cent), it was highly probable that no additional calcium carbonate would be needed. Experiments, therefore, were made with only alkali and malachite, and it was found that by strongly heating either potassium carbonate (the principal constituent of wood and ordinary plant ashes) or powdered natron, mixed with a small proportion of finely powdered malachite, on quartz pebbles, a beautiful

---

[1] See p. 169 n. 1.
[2] G. Brunton and G. Caton-Thompson, *Badarian Civilisation*, p. 112.
[3] G. Brunton, *Qau and Badari*, I, p. 62.
[4] Contained also a little clay.   [5] Largely, but possibly not entirely, quartz sand.

blue glaze was obtained every time. The reaction was not merely a fusing of the alkali and its colouration by means of the malachite, but the quartz was attacked by the alkali and, when the glaze was dissolved off, the surface of the pebbles was found to be much roughened underneath, the alkali having manifestly combined with some of the quartz, forming potassium or sodium silicate according to the nature of the alkali used. This has been noticed by Petrie, who says: [1] 'The fusion of the glaze on the stone partly dissolves the surface; and even after the glaze has been lost, its effect can be seen by the surface having the appearance of water-worn marble or sugar candy.'

In order to make quite sure that the addition of silica or calcium carbonate was not necessary, a number of experiments were made by adding various proportions of finely-powdered limestone to the alkali and malachite mixture, and other experiments were made with both finely-powdered limestone and finely-powdered quartz, but there did not appear to be any advantage, and there was a serious disadvantage in that the additions—as was only to be expected—made the fusion more difficult, with the result, either that no glaze whatever was formed, or that any glaze produced was poor.

Solid quartz having been successfully glazed, experiments were made with a view to glazing the powdered quartz base used for faience. This, however, was found to be more difficult, and when the alkali and malachite mixture was applied directly to the moulded material the glaze was never good and often very poor and sometimes there was none at all, the glazing mixture sinking into the quartz and colouring it blue. At first it was thought that the unsatisfactory result might be due to the heat employed having been too strong, or to the quartz not having been powdered finely enough, and so the experiments were repeated at a lower temperature and with a much finer and therefore denser quartz powder; but the results were only very slightly better. Eventually, however, a good glaze was obtained by first glazing solid quartz, then chipping off the glaze and powdering it finely, and finally covering the moulded powdered-quartz object with the fine powder and heating. It is not suggested that this was precisely the method employed anciently, but it seems probable that the glaze mixture was first fused in some manner and then powdered and used. Thus in describing an imperfectly glazed object Quibell says: 'a patch . . . is covered, not with smooth glaze like the rest of the figure, but with minute grains of blue frit, this must be due to imperfect firing and shows that the glaze was applied as a wash of ground frit. The same method is seen in the ushabtis of a far later period.' [2] Beck, as the result of his microscopical examination of Egyptian glazed objects, states that: 'All the specimens from Egypt, except a few which I believe to have been imported, appear to have had an already made glaze or else the ingredients to make a glaze powdered up and applied to the surface, and then to have been fused.' [3]

In the case of some larger objects the glaze may have been applied in a molten state. Thus Hayes says that the glaze of the faience statues from Qantir 'was applied

[1] W. M. F. Petrie, *Arts and Crafts*, p. 107.   [2] J. E. Quibell, *Ramesseum*, p. 3.
[3] H. C. Beck, *Ancient Egypt*, 1935, p. 21. Cf. also, H. C. Beck, *Ancient Egypt*, 1934, p. 69; H. C. Beck and J. F. S. Stone, *Archaeologia*, LXXXV (1936), pp. 207-11; J. F. S. Stone, *Proceedings of the Prehistoric Society*, XXII (1956), p. 38; D. B. Harden, in *History of Technology*, II, p. 311.

as a viscous fluid',[1] and Reisner supposes that some of the larger specimens of glazed quartz found at Kerma had a thick viscous glaze applied with a brush or rag.[2] Reisner also states that many of the faience vessels from Kerma had been glazed by dipping.[3]

The modern method of glazing is first to make the glaze, when it not only looks like lumps of glass, but really is glass, though called 'frit', next to powder it very finely and mix the powder with water to the consistency of thin mud, which is kept stirred to prevent the powder separating out, and then either to dip the objects in the 'mud' or to run the liquid 'mud' over the surface, the objects being afterwards dried and fired. A similar process on a small scale is used by several of the modern forgers of faience at Qurna. One particular forger seen by me buys small Venetian blue glass beads, powders them very finely, adds a little water, and to the 'mud' formed then adds rock salt, which is done by leaving lumps of rock salt to dissolve slowly. The object to be glazed is dipped in the 'mud', dried and fired, the crystallization of the salt on drying and before firing aiding the adhesion of the powdered glaze until it is fired.

A few experiments were made with a view to glazing steatite, using the alkali and malachite mixture. Although the results were not very satisfactory, a glaze was obtained in several instances, though it was always green and not blue; whether this was due to the presence of iron compounds in the steatite, or to too high a temperature, was not determined.

It may be pointed out that whatever the precise details of the ancient method of glazing were, there can be little doubt that the firing was carried out in a closed chamber of some sort, though probably only a small one, since it seems impossible that this should have been done in an open fire with the objects to be glazed in contact with the fuel. The modern forgers of faience at Qurna have evolved various ways of solving the difficulty: sometimes an earthenware pot is employed, sometimes a copper box, and sometimes a box of steatite, the objects in the latter case being stood on cubes of steatite.[4]

Recent experiments carried out by Nicolini and Santini [5] have shown that it is possible to produce a blue glaze of the colour and brilliance of typical Egyptian examples by first preparing a frit of the formula suggested for Egyptian blue ($CaO. CuO. 4 SiO_2$) and then converting it into glaze by the addition of gradually increasing proportions of the constituents necessary to produce vitrification at a given temperature. Analyses of the resulting glazes show them to be closely similar in composition to an actual specimen of Roman date.[6]

BINDING MEDIUM FOR BODY

An important matter in connexion with faience is the manner in which the body material, which when dry has no coherence whatever, was held together while being

---

[1] W. C. Hayes, *Glazed Tiles*, p. 9. [2] G. A. Reisner, *Kerma*, IV–V, p. 49.
[3] G. A. Reisner, *Kerma*, IV–V, pp. 138–42.
[4] Kindly communicated by Ahmed Fakhry, Chief Inspector, Department of Antiquities. The writer was shown only the copper box.
[5] L. Nicolini and M. Santini, *Bollettino del' Istituto centrale del restauro*, XXXIV–V (1958), pp. 59–70.
[6] See p. 475.

shaped and glazed. That some binding substance was used in small amount seems incontrovertible. This is frequently stated to have been clay, though lime, silicate of soda, and organic materials, such as oil, fat, gum, or glue have all been suggested. These will now be considered, and it will be shown that some of them are impossible and others unlikely, and that the binding material employed was almost certainly an alkali (probably natron), or salt.

Clay

The microscopic examination does not show the presence of any extraneous or added material of any kind, and although the chemical analysis gives 1.2 per cent of alumina as the mean of five specimens,[1] this, in the form of clay, would not be nearly sufficient to render the quartz powder plastic, and it is almost certainly merely an impurity present in the quartz, alkali or salt used, or picked up during the grinding or manipulation, as are also the oxide of iron, the lime, and the magnesia found on analysis. With respect to clay, Burton says:[2] 'After having tried many mixtures of the kind indicated by these analyses, I have been forced to the conclusion that the small amount of clay indicated by the percentage of alumina found would be entirely insufficient to give a material that could be shaped by pottery methods . . .' and of an Eighteenth Dynasty shawabti figure he examined he says[3] that there was 'no trace of any clay substance'.

Lime

The use of lime has been suggested by Beck, who says:[4] 'The core appears to be very nearly pure silica, has much the chemical composition of a silica brick, and is probably made in somewhat the same way. If powdered quartz crystals were mixed with about 2 per cent of lime and then heated in a furnace, a vitreous mixture would be formed which would cement the whole together, and it has been found in practice that this amount of lime, when added in the form of milk of lime, is sufficient to bind the dried material together before firing. . . . The analysis is practically the same as that given by Burton for Egyptian faience. I have examined some . . . sections of silica brick, and find that under certain conditions the quartz breaks and fuses in a manner extraordinarily similar to the faience. . . . One of the difficulties of this suggestion is that the lime and quartz would probably not fuse at a lower temperature than about 1,100° centigrade.' Beck also says: 'As the base of Egyptian faience consists of quartz grains fused together with a little lime . . .'[5]

In addition to the difficulty to which Beck draws attention, namely the very high temperature required to fuse a mixture of carbonate of lime and quartz, there are other difficulties; for example, in the case of sand-lime bricks it is slaked lime and not carbonate of lime that is used, and, as explained elsewhere,[6] there is little evidence that

[1] See p. 474. (Nos. 2, 4, 5, 6, 8)
[2] W. Burton, *Journ. Royal Soc. of Arts*, LX (1912), p. 595. Mr. Burton was closely connected with the ceramic industry.
[3] W. Burton, *Journ. Royal Soc. of Arts*, LX (1912), p. 596.
[4] H. C. Beck, in G. Brunton, *Qau and Badari*, II, pp. 22–25; also in G. Caton-Thompson, *Zimbabwe Culture*, Appendix I. Mr. Beck informed me that carbonate of lime and not quicklime or slaked lime was meant.
[5] H. C. Beck, *Ancient Egypt*, 1935, p. 23.   [6] See p. 74.

the Egyptians knew of lime before the Ptolemaic period; also when a sand-lime brick is examined it is seen that each grain of sand is surrounded by a thin film (probably consisting of silicate of lime), which is not the case with faience, the appearance of the two being totally different, and for the manufacture of sand-lime bricks a very considerable pressure (about 6 tons per square inch) is necessary for the moulding, after which a treatment with steam under pressure (120 to 200 pounds per square inch) in an autoclave is required, all of which would have been impossible in ancient Egypt.

A number of experiments were made by me, using both milk of lime (i.e. slaked lime and water) and powdered quicklime in varying proportions, ranging from 2 per cent to 50 per cent, the mixture being heated to the highest temperature available, about 1,000° C. In no case was there any cohesion or fusion, the mixture remaining in the original condition of a powder, though doubtless there would have been fusion at a still higher temperature.

Silicate of Soda

This is suggested by Sana Ullah of the Indian Archaeological Survey,[1] who says that 'possibly silicate of soda . . . was employed' for the flux. As will be shown, silicate of soda was the flux, but it was not used in that form, nor was it known to the ancients as a separate substance. The material employed was most probably natron or chloride of sodium (common salt), which produces silicate of sodium when heated with the quartz powder.

Organic Materials

With respect to the use of organic materials, such as oil, fat, gum, or glue, I thought at one time that there was possibly a small amount of evidence for their use, though this 'was too slight to be in any way conclusive'.[2] Thus in several instances, specimens of faience examined have shown a few small particles of black organic matter distributed throughout the mass that conceivably might have been the remains of some such adhesive, and in a large number of specimens from the Twenty-sixth Dynasty, constituting one lot of shawabti figures, the body material showed an inner grey-coloured core surrounded by a zone of white. Under the microscope the grey core was seen to contain numbers of black particles, which were probably charred organic matter, and, on being strongly heated, this core became definitely lighter-coloured, though not white. It was suggested, therefore, that some organic adhesive might have been used for binding the quartz together, and that the dark centre was due to this not having been completely burned away; but it is equally possible that the white outer layer was intentional and was the 'special' layer already described, put on in order to prevent the dark grey of the body from affecting the colour of the glaze, and that the grey may have been due to organic matter (accidentally present as an impurity, either in the quartz or in the natron) having been charred, but not burned out.

In order to test the value of organic materials as binders for quartz powder, a number of experiments were made with gum and oil, both of which formed with the quartz a paste that could be moulded and modelled. The objects made with gum

---

[1] In J. Marshall, *Mohenjo-daro and the Indus Civilization*, II, p. 687.
[2] See A. Lucas, *Ancient Egyptian Materials* (1926), pp. 34–35.

could not be removed from the moulds either when dry, when they were firmly cemented in, or after firing, as they were then too friable, and if modelled and fired, the gum burned out, leaving the objects so friable and fragile that it was impossible to handle them for glazing without breaking. The objects made with oil naturally did not dry, and therefore could not be removed from the moulds, and, whether moulded or modelled, after firing they were like those made with gum, so fragile that they could not be handled. Burton states:[1] 'I have with considerable difficulty succeeded in making a few small glazed figures by this method, they are softer and more rotten in body than any Egyptian glazed objects I have ever handled.'

Alkalies

The only alkalies known to the ancient Egyptians were (a) impure potassium or sodium carbonate in the form of plant ashes, and (b) sodium carbonate and bicarbonate in the form of natron; a simple addition of any of these would have been useless, as none of them is an adhesive. As, however, both potassium and sodium carbonate will combine chemically with quartz when strongly heated, forming potassium or sodium silicate, a large number of experiments were made with dry powdered natron and quartz powder, the latter obtained by grinding quartz pebbles very finely. The mixture was pressed with the fingers into small ancient faience moulds made of red pottery; these were heated in a small electric muffle furnace, the result being a coherent mass having varying degrees of hardness depending upon the proportion of natron present. With 2 per cent of natron the mass was so friable that it could not be removed from the mould without breaking; with 5 per cent of natron it approximated in friability to much of the ancient white faience body-substance;[2] with 10 per cent of natron it was slightly harder than ordinary faience, and with 20 per cent it was much harder. The experiments were repeated several times with substantially the same results. Natron, therefore, in the form of dry powder, added in the proportion of from about 5 per cent to about 10 per cent is a very effective binding agent, and may have been the one employed anciently.

But although dry natron might have been employed for objects that were moulded, it certainly could not have been used for objects that were shaped by hand. Experiments were, therefore, made with natron solution, and it was found that on account of the extreme fineness of the quartz powder any solution, even plain water, conferred on it a slight degree of plasticity, and that with a strong natron solution the plasticity was sufficient for the quartz to be made into a paste that with care might be fashioned into rough shapes, which, on partial drying, could be further shaped with a pointed instrument, and which when quite dry could be handled without damage and hence could be baked and glazed.

But it may be asked, if such a substantial proportion of natron as 5 or 10 per cent were used, why is it that it has hitherto escaped notice, and why it is not disclosed by chemical analysis? The reasons are briefly as follows: Natron consists essentially of sodium carbonate, sodium bicarbonate, and chemically combined water (water of crystallization), but it always contains both sodium chloride (common salt) and

---

[1] W. Burton, *Journ. Royal Soc. of Arts*, LX (1912), p. 599.
[2] C. G. Fink and A. H. Kopp, *Technical Studies*, VII (1939), pp. 116–17.

sodium sulphate and sometimes in considerable amount, the particular natron employed for many of the experiments containing 24 per cent of the former and 10 per
cent of the latter. When natron is strongly heated with quartz, the sodium chloride
largely disappears by volatilization; the sodium bicarbonate loses carbon dioxide
and water and becomes converted into carbonate; the sodium carbonate (both that
originally present and that formed from the bicarbonate) combines with some of the
quartz, forming sodium silicate and carbon dioxide, which latter escapes, together
with the water of crystallization and any moisture present. The total loss (sodium
chloride; carbon dioxide; combined water and moisture, the escape of which would
account for the air-holes in the finished product) would generally amount to more
than 70 per cent of the weight of natron used; thus for every 10 grams of natron
(supposing 10 per cent were used) not more than about 3 grams of material would
be left combined with every 100 grams of quartz. Considering the very minute
amount of the specimen taken for microscopical examination, it is no wonder that
such a small proportion of sodium silicate (which is without colour or other conspicuous characteristic) should escape notice. In the chemical analysis the silica part
of the sodium silicate, which is derived from and is identical with the quartz, cannot
be separated or distinguished from it; it is, therefore, necessarily reported with it,
and any small proportion of sodium found is reported as 'sodium oxide' or 'alkali'.

The experiments referred to were made by me probably some time during 1931
or 1932, the results being communicated to and shown to friends at the time, but
they were first published in 1933.[1] Subsequently I found that I had been forestalled
by some forty years, when analyses were made in the Museum of Practical Geology,
London, which showed that the white body of faience was 'composed of fine sand
cemented by silicate of soda. The soda was probably introduced in the form of
carbonate (derived, perhaps, from the Natron Lakes), and, having been mingled with
the sand, the mixture was moulded, fired and glazed.'[2]

Salt (Sodium Chloride)

This, like natron, will act as a binder for the quartz powder, and it is used for this
purpose by the modern forgers of faience at Qurna. That it is incorporated into the
glazing mixture has already been mentioned, but it is also used with the body-
material. As the result of a number of experiments, I have found that when salt is
mixed dry with powdered quartz, put into moulds and strongly heated, the greater
part of the salt disappears by volatilization, but sufficient combines with the quartz
(forming sodium silicate) to bind it together. Also, when a strong solution of salt is
mixed in the right proportion with powdered quartz, this can be shaped by hand or
by simple pottery methods, and when dried, the crystallization of the salt by holding
the quartz powder together imparts to it sufficient solidity to enable the mass to be
handled for glazing. After firing at a high temperature no evidence of salt can be
found on analysis.

---

[1] A. Lucas, *Analyst*, LVIII (1933), p. 657.

[2] Anon., *Handbook to the Collection of British Pottery in the Museum of Practical Geology*, London
(1893), pp. 37–38.

Chapter X

GLASS

Although the chemical composition of ancient Egyptian glass is essentially the same as that of the ancient glaze, there is the difference between them that has already been mentioned, namely, the manner in which they were used, glaze always being applied to the surface of an object, whereas glass was employed independently, and, although with glass there was sometimes a temporary core, it was one to which the material was not intended to adhere and which was removed when the object was finished. This distinction is a most convenient one that should be maintained, as the use of glass on a large scale, as distinct from glaze, marks a definite epoch.

ORIGIN AND DATE

In view of the very close connexion between glaze and glass, it seems highly probable that glass was not a separate discovery apart from glaze.

At what period glass objects were first made in Egypt is uncertain, but regular production on a large scale dates from about the beginning of the Eighteenth Dynasty and by the middle of the dynasty the technique had reached a very high standard of excellence. From the end of the Twentieth Dynasty the production of glass declined, and 'in the long period from c. 1050 B.C.–c. 400 B.C. glass is almost unknown in Egypt'. 'Indeed, it is probably only a slight exaggeration to say that glass was a discovery of the New Kingdom which achieved limited popularity during that period and was only occasionally used in the later periods of Egypt's history.' [1]

Cooney considers that 'The scattered examples of glass claimed for Egypt prior to Dynasty XVIII fall . . . into two classes, either they are misdated, actually belonging to a period much later than the New Kingdom or, if indeed of glass and of early date, they are invariably compositions intended as faience but ones which turned completely vitreous when they were overfired.' [2] As the production of glass in Egypt before the Eighteenth Dynasty, whether intentional or accidental, is of considerable importance in connexion with the history of the material, the evidence for this will be given.

The early glass objects are of two kinds, namely, (a) beads and tiny amulets, and (b) other objects, which will be considered separately.

Beads and Tiny Amulets

Predynastic Period. The examples known to me are (a) a glass bead found by Petrie

---

[1] J. D. Cooney, *Journ. Glass Studies*, II (1960), p. 29.
[2] J. D. Cooney, *Journ. Glass Studies*, II (1960), p. 11.

at Naqada,[1] of which Beck says [2] 'From a photograph of the beads associated with it, I doubt its being as early as Predynastic. One of the other beads is evidently VIth. dynasty, or First Intermediate . . . I think this bead is also VIth. dynasty'; (b) a necklace of green, blue and yellow glass beads found by MacIver and Mace at Abydos.[3] Beck says [4] 'I hestitate to date them as Predynastic until further evidence can be brought forward to prove it.' I, also, hesitate to accept the predynastic dating, as, in my opinion, the presence of the yellow beads makes it improbable, since yellow as a colour for either faience or glass is not otherwise known until later.

Although, therefore, the dating of the beads claimed to be of the predynastic period needs confirmation before it can be accepted, yet, in view of the fact that glaze, which is glass applied to another material, is admittedly as early as predynastic times, it is not impossible, nor should it be a matter of surprise, if a few small objects, such as beads, proved to be of glass, since, if a little glaze had been dropped by accident on the ground, it might have been more or less spherical in shape, and, if bored, it would have become a glass bead.

Fifth Dynasty. Examples are beads and tiny amulets found by Schiaparelli at Gebelein and now in the Cairo Museum.[5] There are two strings of beads (a) and (b) and one string of beads and tiny amulets. String (a) consists of about 320 small black and small blue beads of opaque glass arranged alternately. There cannot be any doubt that these beads must be either glass or faience, and as I have ascertained that they have no core, therefore they are glass. But, whether they were intended for glass is another matter, since, as Reisner says [6] with respect to some very tiny ring-beads of faience from Kerma, 'owing to their small size the cores may have been more highly affected by the heat than in the larger beads and may have been fused with the glaze during firing'. Brunton gives a similar explanation for some beads he found,[7] an explanation that is so highly probable as to be almost certainly correct. String (b) consists of several hundreds of small bead-like objects, which are so dirty that their nature cannot easily be determined, and which cannot readily be cleaned, but almost certainly they consist entirely of thread wound into tiny balls. There are also about twenty tiny green amulets, several of which are broken, and, as there is no core, the material must be glass, though it may originally have been intended for faience.

Sixth Dynasty. Examples are (a) a bead examined by Beck, who says [8] 'There is no reason to doubt either the material, or date, of this specimen'; (b) about twenty-seven small glass beads, some blue, others dark green and others greenish found by Brunton and examined by me, the blue and dark green specimens being from Matmar.

Old Kingdom. Myers found glass beads probably of Old Kingdom date at Armant.[9]

---

[1] A. Scharff, *Die Altertümer der Vor- und Frühzeit Ägyptens*, II, p. 108, No. 165, Tafel 25; F. Rathgen, *Über Ton und Glas in alter und uralter Zeit*, 1918, p. 18; *Sprechsaal*, XLVI (1913), p. 98; B. Neumann and G. Kotyga, *Zeitschr. f. angew. Chemie*, XXXVIII (1925), p. 776.

[2] H. C. Beck, *Ancient Egypt*, 1934, p. 9, No. 2.

[3] D. Randall MacIver and A. C. Mace, *El Amrah and Abydos*, p. 54.

[4] H. C. Beck, *Ancient Egypt*, 1934, pp. 9–10, No. 3.

[5] Cairo Museum, No. J. 64816.   [6] G. A. Reisner, *Kerma*, IV–V, pp. 91–92.

[7] G. Brunton, *Qau and Badari*, I, p. 33.

[8] H. C. Beck, *Ancient Egypt*, 1934, p. 14, No. 11.

[9] R. Mond and O. H. Myers, *Cemeteries of Armant*, I, pp. 21, 72, 83.

First Intermediate Period. (*a*) Beck describes six glass beads, two green, one turquoise, one bluish, one of which the colour is not given, and one transparent red.[1] The finder, Brunton, suggests that the red bead may be a late intrusion, and Beck is also uncertain as to its date; (*b*) more than seventy tiny blue amulets found by Brunton, who calls them 'openwork blue glaze with core dissolved in the glaze', which means that they are glass, although intended by the maker to be faience; (*c*) about 600 beads of various colours (blue, black, greenish) found by Brunton (some at Matmar) and examined by me. They have no core and, therefore, are glass.

Middle Kingdom. Examples are (*a*) the blue glass beads of Eleventh Dynasty date found by Winlock at Deir el Bahari; [2] (*b*) one blue and four red glass beads of Middle Kingdom date found at Armant; [3] (*c*) one blue glass bead of Twelfth Dynasty date identified by Beck; [4] (*d*) about six glass beads of Twelfth Dynasty date, of which the colour was not noted, and three others of the same date (opaque green with one end yellow) found by Brunton and examined by me.

Second Intermediate Period. About 550 glass beads of various colours (blue, black, red, green and yellow) found by Brunton and examined by me.

There is, therefore, no doubt whatever that glass beads and tiny glass amulets date from as early as about the Fifth Dynasty, and it is exceedingly probable that they were all of Egyptian manufacture and that they were the outcome of the use of glass as a glazing material for steatite and quartz (both solid and powdered). Some of these early beads, however, are not normal glass, but what elsewhere I have called 'imperfect glass',[5] and what Reisner and Brunton call having the core fused, or dissolved in the glaze. Though possibly intended as faience, which is glazed quartz frit, they are not, since the material is of similar composition throughout without any coating of glaze, and, therefore, they must be classed as glass. This imperfect glass consists of a glass matrix in which a considerable proportion of uncombined quartz is embedded.

The colours of the earliest glass beads are black, blue and green. Yellow and red beads appear later.

Objects other than Beads and Tiny Amulets

There are: (*a*) A Hathor head, which Petrie states [6] is predynastic and which he suggests is not Egyptian, but imported. Petrie, however, did not see this object in position as found, and, although he says that 'The grave is well dated by eight types of pottery', possibly the object may have been found elsewhere and temporarily deposited by the workman who found it, for safety or for ease of transport (without any thought of deception), in the small vase in which Petrie first saw it. (*b*) A number of small pieces of inlay of First Dynasty date on part of a wooden box found by Amélineau at Abydos,[7] and now in the Ashmolean Museum, Oxford. The finder

[1] H. C. Beck, *Ancient Egypt*, 1934, pp. 13–14, Nos. 10 and 12–16; G. Brunton *Qau and Badari*, II, p. 21.

[2] H. E. Winlock, *M.M.A. Bull., Egyptian Exped. 1921*, p. 52.

[3] R. Mond and O. H. Myers, *Cemeteries of Armant*, I, pp. 72, 113, 116.

[4] H. C. Beck, *Ancient Egypt*, 1934, p. 16, No. 22.

[5] See p. 165.   [6] W. M. F. Petrie, *Prehistoric Egypt*, p. 43.

[7] E. Amélineau, *Les nouvelles fouilles d'Abydos, 1895–1896*, pp. 128, 233-4, 306, Pl. xxxi.

describes the material as 'émail', which it is not. Beck states [1] that both 'Dr. Leeds and Mr. Harden have very carfully examined these specimens and are quite certain that they are faience and not glass'. Mr. Leeds kindly allowed me to examine this inlay, of which there are about ten pieces altogether, many black, or largely black with small green spots, one bluish-green and three green, one being very dark; all about one millimetre thick. In my opinion, the material is faience and not glass and it seems probable that the original colour was blue. Dr. Harden informed me that one piece that was taken out for further examination, the result of which had not then been received, had siliceous material at the back, which seems to prove that it is faience. In this connexion it may be pointed out that Petrie reports from the same place and of the same date 'A strange piece of inlay apparently green glass, partly decomposed with a dark strip let unto it.' [2] (c) Two udjat eyes of Tenth Dynasty date coloured black and white found by Brunton at Sedment, [3] of which there seems no reason to doubt either the material or the date. (d) A glass frog set in a silver ring of Twelfth Dynasty date. [4] (e) An 'eye' of transparent material and a fragment of yellow glass given to Parodi by Maspero, both from the tomb of Princess Khnumet at Dahshur. These were analysed by Parodi and stated by him to be glass. [5] The 'eye' is almost certainly the missing cornea from one of the eyes of the mask of Princess Khnumet. There are in the Cairo Museum three pairs of eyes of Twelfth Dynasty date from Dahshur, all of which are alike, and from one of which the cornea is missing. [6] The other five corneas are all rock crystal and not glass, my identification being based both on the appearance of the material when examined with a lens, and also upon the fact that one of these corneas, which is loose, has been tested by me and will scratch glass. Parodi's analytical result, however, is certainly that of glass. The other specimen from this same tomb analysed by Parodi is stated to have consisted of two kinds of glass, one yellowish and the other clair, apparently only the former of which he analysed. That this fragment was indeed of Twelfth Dynasty date seems doubtful, since there is nothing else like it known of that date. (f) The well-known mosaic of Amenemhet III in black and white glass, now in the Berlin Museum, of which Newberry says [7] 'That this is contemporary with the king whose name it bears appears to me certain.' Von Bissing, however, thinks it is of Roman age. [8] I have examined this and it is certainly glass, but of what date I am unable to say. It should not be forgotten, however, that Amenemhet III was deified in the Graeco-Roman period, if not earlier, and objects may have been then made bearing his name. Although the beginning of glass mosaic is often attributed to the Roman period, it is at least two to three hundred years earlier, as is proved by the bars of mosaic glass found at Nebesheh, [9] some of which date to the Ptolemaic period, the glass mosaic hieroglyphs on the coffin of

---

[1] H. C. Beck, Ancient Egypt, 1934, p. 10.

[2] W. M. F. Petrie, Royal Tombs, I, p. 38.

[3] W. M. F. Petrie and G. Brunton, Sedment, I, p. 6.

[4] E. R. Ayrton, C. T. Currelly and A. E. P. Weigall, Abydos, III, p. 50.

[5] H. D. Parodi, La Verrerie en Égypte, pp. 29–30.

[6] See pp. 103–4.

[7] P. E. Newberry, J.E.A., VI (1920), p. 159.

[8] F. W. von Bissing, Revue archéologique, XI (1908), p. 213.

[9] W. M. F. Petrie and F. Ll. Griffith, Tanis, II, Nebesheh and Defenneh, pp. 42–43.

Petosiris, which is dated to the early Ptolemaic period, and the glass mosaic figurines on a gilt mask of Ptolemaic date, both of which are in the Cairo Museum.[1] Also it should not be forgotten that the polychrome glass vases, some of which date back to the early part of the Eighteenth Dynasty, are really glass mosaics, and, in particular, that a single example from the reign of Thutmose III was made up of small pieces of glass of different colours, fused together and built up on a core.[2] (g) A lion mask of blue glass, bearing the name of Nubkheperrē Inyotef. This was originally dated to the Eleventh Dynasty,[3] but must, in fact, belong to the Seventeenth.[4] Beck considers that it is 'quite definitely a glass'. (h) A blue glass vase of Seventeenth Dynasty date found by Brunton at Qau.[5]

But, in addition to the mistakes just mentioned, other mistakes in connexion with early glass have been made, for example, the greenish-blue material in the First Dynasty bracelets found by Petrie at Abydos and thought by Vernier to be glass [6] is not glass, but turquoise, as described by the finder, as is also the similar material in the Twelfth Dynasty jewellery from Dahshur, also queried by Vernier.[7] The medallion from Dahshur, which is a small pendant with the figure of an ox on a light blue ground, often described as a glass mosaic, is now known to be painted on a background of small blue particles embedded in a white matrix.[8] The cover is rock crystal and neither Iceland spar (*spath*) as stated by the finder [9] nor fluorspar as suggested by Newberry.[10]

Most people are familiar with Pliny's story of the discovery of glass,[11] which is that a ship laden with natron (probably from Egypt) being moored at a certain spot on the shore of Phoenicia, 'the merchants, while preparing their repast upon the seashore, finding no stones at hand for supporting their cauldrons, employed for the purpose some lumps of natron which they had taken from the vessel', which the heat of the fire caused to combine with the sand and so produced glass. While this is certainly apocryphal, so far as the date and place are concerned, it is a perfectly feasible method of accidentally making a small quantity of glass and is by no means so fantastic as is often represented, those who criticize it adversely assuming wrongly that the sand must necessarily have been wholly siliceous and therefore that only sodium silicate, which is not glass, could possibly have been formed. But it is highly probable that the sand on the shore of Phoenicia was a quartz sand containing calcium carbonate, as is the case with much of the sand on the northern shore of Egypt, and such a sand, when fused with natron, will produce a soda–lime silicate, or true glass.

---

[1] A. Lucas, *Ann. Serv.*, XXXIX (1939), pp. 227–35; C. Picard, *B.I.F.A.O.*, XXX (1931), pp. 201–27; G. Roeder, *Ann. Serv.*, XXXIX (1939), pp. 739–43. See also W. Haberey, *Glastechnische Berichte*, XXX (1957), pp. 508–9.

[2] H. E. Winlock, *Treasure of Three Egyptian Princesses*, p. 61.

[3] H. C. Beck, *Ancient Egypt*, 1934, p. 15, No. 17.

[4] H. E. Winlock, *J.E.A.*, X (1924), p. 233 and *n.* 3.

[5] G. Brunton, *Qau and Badari*, III, p. 8.

[6] E. Vernier, *Bijoux et Orfèvreries*, pp. 10–11, 13–14.

[7] E. Vernier, *Bijoux et Orfèvreries*, pp. 88, 298, 299, 307, 336.

[8] A. Lucas and G. Brunton, *Ann. Serv.*, XXXVI (1936), pp. 197–200.

[9] J. de Morgan, *Dahchour, 1894–1895*, p. 67.

[10] P. E. Newberry, *J.E.A.*, VI (1920), p. 159.

[11] XXXVI: 65.

The remains of a number of glass works have been found in Egypt, the earliest being at Thebes and dating from the reign of Amenhotpe III [1] (late Eighteenth Dynasty); three or four are at El Amarna and belong to the reign of Akhenaten; [2] others of the Twentieth Dynasty are at Lisht [3,4] and Menshiyeh respectively; [3] others again, of which the dates are not known, occur in the Wadi Natrun; [5] to the south and south-west of Lake Mareotis [5] and at Gurob [6] and one of Ptolemaic date is at Nebesheh. [7]

Alexandria was one of the greatest glass-manufacturing centres of antiquity and Strabo (first century B.C. to first century A.D.) states [8] that he 'heard at Alexandria from the glass-workers that there is in Egypt a kind of vitrifiable earth without which multicoloured and sumptuous works in glass could not be executed . . .' In the literature of Roman times there are a number of references to Egyptian glass and under the Emperor Aurelian there was a tax on glass imported into Rome from Egypt. [9]

COMPOSITION

Ancient Egyptian glasses are generally of complex composition, and Geilmann has determined as many as twenty-one distinct constituents and four trace elements in a blue glass of the Eighteenth Dynasty. [10] Predominantly they are glasses of the alkali-lime-magnesia-alumina-silica type, the nature, though not the proportions, of the constituents being similar to those of a modern glass of ordinary quality, the latter, however, containing much more silica, a much smaller proportion of oxides of iron and aluminium, generally no oxide of manganese, much more lime, practically no magnesia, and much less alkali. [11] Certain glasses of late date are thicker, more opaque and less vitreous than glass of the New Kingdom, and may well be of different composition, though as yet no analytical confirmation is available.

The lower proportion of silica and lime, the greater proportion of oxide and iron and the considerably higher proportion of alkali in ancient Egyptian glass, as compared with modern glass, would all have acted in the way of materially lowering the temperature required for fusion, which was an important consideration and would have made the working of the glass easier, but at the same time the quality of the product would have been adversely affected, such glass being much less resistant to atmospheric influences that produce decay, especially damp. Another great difference between ancient and modern glass is that the latter, being largely employed to transmit

---

[1] P. E. Newberry, *J.E.A.*, VI (1920), p. 156; A. M. Lythgoe, *M.M.A. Bull., Egyptian Exped. 1916–1917*, p. 6; H. E. Winlock, *M.M.A. Bull.*, VII (1912), pp. 187–8.

[2] W. M. F. Petrie, *Tell el Amarna*, p. 25.   [3] P. E. Newberry, *J.E.A.*, VI (1920), p. 156.

[4] A. C. Mace, *The Murch Collection of Egyptian Antiquities* (Supplement to *M.M.A. Bull.*, Jan. 1911), p. 25.

[5] P. E. Newberry, *J.E.A.*, VI (1920), p. 160. One of these has been seen by me.

[6] G. Brunton and R. Engelbach, *Gurob*, p. 3.

[7] W. M. F. Petrie and F. Ll. Griffith, *Tanis*, II, *Nebesheh and Defenneh*, pp. 42–44.

[8] XVI: 11, 25.

[9] Glass of Roman date has been described in detail by D. B. Harden, *Roman Glass from Karanis*; R. Cottevielle-Giraudet, *Médamoud, 1930*, pp. 1–33; R. Mond and O. H. Myers, *Bucheum*, I, pp. 95–96.

[10] W. Geilmann, *Glastechnische Berichte*, XXVIII (1958), pp. 146–56.

[11] Cf. W. E. S. Turner, *Journ. Soc. Glass Technology*, XL (1956), pp. 162–86.

light, is generally transparent, whereas the former, not having been needed for that purpose, but being mainly ornamental, though sometimes translucent and even occasionally transparent, was more generally opaque. This opacity has been ascribed to a number of causes, including the presence of tin oxide, but is, in fact, due to the presence of countless minute bubbles uniformly dispersed through the mass, the bubbles being caused by incomplete and unsatisfactory fusion.

From the high proportion of oxides of iron and aluminium shown by the analyses and from the presence of oxide of manganese and of magnesia, it is clear that the glasses in question were not made from pure materials, and that the composition corresponds to what would be obtained by fusing together a mixture of sand and natron or sand and plant ash, none of which is chemically pure. The sands used, containing clay, felspar and other minerals as impurities, were probably the source of considerable alumina, varying amounts of iron oxide, lime (in some cases large quantities) and magnesia,[1] while manganese, too, would frequently be present in the sand and could also be derived from certain plant ashes.[2] Natural soda from the natron lakes would yield not only soda, but also much chloride and sulphate, while salt from evaporation of Nile water would account for sodium and potassium carbonates, with chloride and sulphate, as well as calcium and magnesium carbonates.[3] Plant ash would furnish sodium and potassium carbonates,[4] much chloride and sulphate, much calcium and magnesium carbonate, and phosphates.[3,5]

When yellow sand is used for glass making, the iron compounds present, to which the yellow colour is due, tend to produce a dirty green-yellow colour in the glass, but in most ancient Egyptian glasses, except the blue, this would not greatly have mattered, and it is probable that in some instances the effects of the iron were neutralized by the oxide of manganese naturally present,[6] which is a substance employed for this purpose in modern glass making.[7] On the other hand, quartz sand containing only a small amount of iron and having very little colour occurs plentifully in Egypt and may have been used for special work, and it seems likely that from experience the Egyptians came to recognize which sands produced a clean glass, i.e. those relatively free from iron or with sufficient manganese to counteract it.

It has been stated that at El Amarna glass was made from pure silica obtained by crushing quartz pebbles,[8] but the original account [9] is not explicit, and in view of the

---

[1] W. E. S. Turner, *Journ. Soc. Glass Technology*, XL (1956), pp. 277–300 (cf. pp. 162–86); F. R. Matson, *Journ. Chemical Education*, XXVIII (1951), pp. 82–87; *Glass Industry*, XXX (1949), pp. 548–52, 574. See also analyses of sand, p. 481.

[2] W. Geilmann and T. Brückbauer, *Glastechnische Berichte*, XXVII (1954), pp. 456–9; W. Geilmann, *Glastechnische Berichte*, XXVIII (1955), pp. 146–56.

[3] W. E. S. Turner, *Journ. Soc. Glass Technology*, XL (1956), pp. 277–300 (cf. pp. 162–86).

[4] Coastal or desert plants contain both sodium and potassium salts, but with a greater proportion of sodium salts in reactive form. Inland plants and trees contain more potassium salts than sodium salts. See W. E. S. Turner, *Journ. Soc. Glass Technology*, XXXVIII (1954), p. 441.

[5] Silica, alumina, iron oxide, lime, magnesia and alkali could also be derived from corrosion of the crucible. See W. E. S. Turner, *Journ. Soc. Glass Technology*, XXXVIII (1954), p. 441.

[6] It is possible, though unlikely, that oxide of manganese was added intentionally.

[7] The presence of phosphate might sometimes have resulted in the changing of an iron green to blue.

[8] W. M. F. Petrie, *Arts and Crafts*, p. 124.   [9] W. M. F. Petrie, *Tell el Amarna*, pp. 25–27.

evidence of the glass analyses,[1] which cannot be ignored and which point to the use of sand, it must be assumed either that the frit made at El Amarna was not intended for glass, or that the quartz pebbles were not, in fact, used to make the frit, but merely as flooring or as setters in the furnaces, as at Kerma.[2] If quartz pebbles, or any other form of pure silica, had been used, it would have been necessary to add calcium carbonate (carbonate of lime) also, since lime is an essential constituent of the ancient glass, but, with sand, the carbonate of lime would have been present as an impurity, and its presence would not even have been known to the glass maker, who would merely have realized that in order to produce a satisfactory product a particular kind of sand was required. Moreover, since the alkaline materials employed appear to have been free from alumina and iron oxide except in very small quantities, the resulting glass would also have been free from these constituents, unless they were derived from corrosion of the refractory material, which would also have yielded some silica and much smaller amounts of lime, magnesia and alkaline oxides.

The nature of the alkali used in Egyptian glass manufacture is a matter of some dispute, and the problem has recently been considered in detail by both Geilmann[3] and Turner,[4] the latter of whom notes four possible sources: (a) large-scale deposits such as the natron lakes; (b) evaporation of sea or river water; (c) leaching out of salts from the soil; (d) the ashes of vegetable matter. From the analyses[5] it will be seen that the alkali is largely in the form of soda and that although potash is sometimes also present it is generally only in very small proportion.[6] This would suggest that the alkali employed in the specimens analysed was natron, which consists of sodium carbonate and sodium bicarbonate, rather than plant ashes, in which there is a high percentage of potash. Browne, writing in 1799, says of glass making in Egypt in his day 'Glass for lamps and phials is made at Alexandria, both green and white. They use natron in the manufacture instead of barilla: and the low beaches of the Egyptian coast afford plenty of excellent sand.'[7] It has, however, been pointed out that the amount of potash present in some specimens, though small, is nevertheless more than could possibly be derived from natron or natural soda,[8] and the problem is further complicated by the presence in Egyptian glasses of a very small proportion of phosphate (phosphoric oxide) and of residues of sulphate and chloride.[9] While the traces of sulphate and chloride might suggest that natural soda was the alkali used, the

---

[1] See pp. 476, 478–80, in particular p. 479, No. 1. See also M. Farnsworth and P. D. Ritchie, *Technical Studies*, VI (1938), pp. 169–73.

[2] G. A. Reisner, *Kerma*, IV–V, pp. 140–1.

[3] W. Geilmann, *Glastechnische Berichte*, XXVIII (1955), pp. 146–56; cf. W. Geilmann and H. Jenemann, *Glastechnische Berichte*, XXVI (1953), pp. 259–63.

[4] W. E. S. Turner, *Journ. Soc. Glass Technology*, XL (1956), pp. 277–300.

[5] See pp. 476, 478–80. See also M. Farnsworth and P. D. Ritchie, *Technical Studies*, vl (1 :38), pp. 169–73.

[6] An exception is a specimen quoted by C. R. Lepsius, *Les métaux dans les inscriptions égyptiennes*, p. 27, but this analysis is queried by W. E. S. Turner, *Journ. Soc. Glass Technology*, XL (1956), p. 177.

[7] W. G. Browne, *Travels in Africa, Egypt and Syria*, 1799, p. 10.

[8] H. D. Parodi, *La Verrerie en Égypte*, p. 28; F. R. Matson, *Journ. Chemical Education*, XXVIII (1951), pp. 82–87; *Glass Industry*, XXX (1949), pp. 548–52, 574.

[9] W. Geilmann and H. Jenemann, *Glastechnische Berichte*, XXVI (1953), pp. 259–63; W. Geilmann, *Glastechnische Berichte*, XXVIII (1955), pp. 146–56.

invariable presence of the small proportions of potash and phosphate is against this, since neither has been found in analyses of Egyptian natron.[1] Geilmann suggests that the potash and phosphate may be explained as due to contamination of the raw materials with ash from the fuel during the process of fritting, and this seems likely in cases where the proportion of both is very low.[2] Alternatively, Geilmann admits the possibility of the use of the ashes of sea or salt-water plants, though the fact that the phosphate content of Egyptian glasses is so small, both absolutely and in relation to the potash content, makes the direct use of plant ashes somewhat unlikely. The constituents of plant ashes from various sources have been discussed by Geilmann and Turner.

The colour of ancient Egyptian glass may be amethyst, black, blue, green, red, white or yellow, and the nature of the various colouring matters may now be considered.

Amethyst Glass

Two specimens of dark amethyst-coloured glass, both of the Twentieth Dynasty, analysed by me, were found to owe their colour to a manganese compound; Neumann and Kotyga [3] found this same colouring matter in purple glasses of the Eighteenth Dynasty and Farnsworth and Ritchie found a manganese compound (0.5 to 0.7 per cent calculated as oxide) in two specimens of Eighteenth Dynasty amethyst-coloured glass.[4] In this connexion it may be mentioned that white glass of ordinary quality containing manganese compounds becomes coloured if exposed to strong sunlight for some time.[5] The colour so produced varies from a very light amethyst tint to a beautiful deep purple colour, and it is a matter of common observation in Egypt to find in the desert in the neighbourhood of towns, pieces of what have been white glass coloured in this manner. The colouration is due to manganese compounds in the glass having undergone some chemical change, which apparently is brought about by sunlight and is not caused either by heat or radio-activity, though the latter also produces a similar colouration. It is not, of course, suggested that the colour of ancient amethyst glass has been caused by exposure, or that it is other than original.

Black Glass

I have been unable to obtain any specimen of ancient Egyptian black glass for analysis, nor does Parodi give any analyses of this glass, but Neumann and Kotyga found that the colouring matter in two instances was due to copper and manganese compounds, and in a third case to a large proportion of an iron compound.[6]

Although black glass undoubtedly was made intentionally in Egypt at a late date, it is almost certain that the early black glass, such as that of the beads described

---

[1] See pp. 493–4. Cf., however, A. Lucas, *Ancient Egyptian Materials and Industries*, (3rd ed. 1948), p. 215, where it is stated that potash 'is usually present in very small amount'.

[2] Contamination due to corrosion of the refractory material is also possible.

[3] B. Neumann and G. Kotyga, *Zeitschr. f. angew. Chemie*, XXXVIII (1925), pp. 858, 863; XLII (1929), p. 835.

[4] M. Farnsworth and P. D. Ritchie, *Technical Studies*, VI (1938), pp. 167, 172.

[5] A. Lucas, *Cairo Sc. Journ.*, XI (1922–3), pp. 72–73; J. Hoffmann, 'Photochemical Changes of Manganese Glass', *Chemical Abstracts*, XXXI (1937), pp. 2293, 3649.

[6] B. Neumann and G. Kotyga, *Zeitschr. f. angew Chemie*, XXXVIII (1925), p. 864.

elsewhere,[1] was due to the use of impure materials, containing, for instance, a large proportion of iron compounds.[2]

Blue Glass

Ancient Egyptian blue glasses are of three principal shades: dark blues, imitating lapis lazuli (often with considerable success),[3] light blues imitating turquoise, and greenish blues imitating turquoise or felspar.

At the present day a cobalt compound is used for colouring blue glass, but as it only produces a dark blue colour, the turquoise blue and the greenish-blue of some of the Egyptian glass cannot ever be due to its use.[4]

Until comparatively recently the usual test for cobalt compounds, which is both sensitive and characteristic, was by means of a borax bead in the flame of a Bunsen lamp or blowpipe, cobalt compounds colouring the bead a transparent, bright blue, both in the inner (reducing) and outer (oxidizing) flame, but since copper compounds also give a blue bead in the outer (oxidizing) though not in the inner (reducing) flame, there is some slight possibility of a mistake between the two. In many of the cases mentioned in which cobalt compounds have been reported, the nature of the test applied is not given, though it was certainly not spectroscopic, but in three of them (that of Mr. Pollard, one of those quoted by Lepsius, and an earlier one by John[5]) the borax bead test was relied on. In one specimen analysed by Clemm and Jehn the cobalt was determined quantitatively and, in duplicate analyses, amounted to 2.86 and 2.82 per cent respectively expressed in terms of the oxide, and in a specimen analysed by Clemm, also quantitatively, there was 0.95 per cent of cobalt oxide. Even though the determination of cobalt about sixty years ago may not have been quite as accurate as would be the case today, it is unlikely that the analyses should be wholly wrong. The most reliable test for cobalt, though it has only been used comparatively recently for this purpose, is by means of the spectroscope.

Of the specimens analysed by me, three of the Eighteenth Dynasty and two of the Twentieth Dynasty all owed their colour to a copper compound; one specimen of dark blue glass from the tomb of Tutankhamūn analysed by W. B. Pollard for me was found to be coloured by a cobalt compound; [6] a sample of blue Arab glass analysed for me by J. Clifford was free from cobalt and copper compounds, its colour being due to an iron compound, as was also the case with two specimens of blue glass of the Ptolemaic period analysed for me by H. E. Cox; Parodi found a copper compound as the colouring matter in one specimen of Egyptian blue glass of Persian times [7] and a cobalt compound in seven specimens, four of the Eighteenth Dynasty, two of the Twentieth Dynasty and one of the Persian period; [7] a cobalt compound

---

[1] See p. 180.

[2] In this connexion see W. E. S. Turner, *Journ. Soc. Glass Technology*, XL (1956), pp. 162–86; S. F. Nadel and C. G. Seligman, *Man.*, XL (1940), pp. 85–86.

[3] Cf. E. Dillon, *Glass*, 1907, p. 32. Dillon states that in some cases even the white marbling and spots of the stone were reproduced, and quotes one instance where the characteristic pyrites was imitated by '*paillettes* of gold scattered in the paste'.

[4] Cf. M. Farnsworth and P. D. Ritchie, *Technical Studies*, VI (1938), p. 158.

[5] H. v. Minutoli, *Reise zum Tempel des Jupiter Ammon*, p. 352.

[6] A. Lucas, in H. Carter, *Tut-ankh-Amen*, II, p. 171 (Appendix II).

[7] H. D. Parodi, *La Verrerie en Égypte*, pp. 31, 33, 34, 38, 73.

was also found by Clemm and by Clemm and Jehn,[1] working in the laboratory of A. W. Hofmann (unfortunately the dates of the specimens are not given) and Lepsius, who quotes the analyses, mentions several other specimens in which a cobalt compound was present. Neumann and Kotyga did not find cobalt in any of the specimens of ancient Egyptian blue glass they examined and state that it was never used until Venetian times and that the colour is generally due to a copper compound, but occasionally to an iron compound.[2] Farnsworth and Ritchie [3] examined sixty specimens of ancient Egyptian blue and blue-green glass (fifty-eight from the Eighteenth Dynasty and two from the period eighth to sixth century B.C.) spectroscopically, with special reference to the presence or absence of cobalt, and found that cobalt was present in thirty-five instances (58.3 per cent). More recently, Geilmann [4] has detected traces of cobalt in three specimens of blue glass from the Eighteenth Dynasty, in which nickel and arsenic were also present. In the majority of cases, the colour of blue glasses, whether due to copper or cobalt, is modified by the presence of manganese.

The finding of cobalt in Egyptian glass, especially at so early a date as the Eighteenth Dynasty, is of considerable importance, since cobalt compounds do not occur in Egypt except as traces in other minerals,[5] and their presence in the glass, if confirmed, would seem to indicate that the Egyptian glass makers of that time were in contact with glass makers elsewhere, who were using this material. Even in countries where cobalt ore occurs (for example Persia and the Caucasus region) its use at an early period is of interest, as the ore is not blue and, therefore, its value as a colouring agent is not naturally suggested, but in Egypt, where the ore is not found naturally, its use is still more interesting.

Green Glass

A green colour in glass may be due either to compounds of copper or of iron, the colour of the modern green bottle-glass, for example, being produced by the latter. It is to a copper compound, however, that the green of the ancient Egyptian glass is due. One specimen of Eighteenth Dynasty date analysed by me was coloured by copper; also one of the Twentieth Dynasty examined by Parodi; [6] Neumann and Kotyga found copper compounds to be the colouring matter of specimens of Egyptian green glass examined by them [7] and Farnsworth and Ritchie found copper (and also lead) in a green glass of Eighteenth Dynasty date.[8]

Red Glass

The colour of the Egyptian red glass is due to red oxide of copper. This is evident from the green coating that forms on the surface when the glass decays and is confirmed by analysis. Two specimens of this glass, one from the Eighteenth Dynasty

---

[1] C. R. Lepsius, *Les métaux dans les inscriptions égyptiennes*, trans. W. Berend, 1877, pp. 26–27.
[2] B. Neumann and G. Kotyga, *Zeitschr. f. angew. Chemie*, XXXVIII (1925), pp. 862–3.
[3] M. Farnsworth and P. D. Ritchie, *Technical Studies*, VI (1938), pp. 155–73.
[4] W. Geilmann, *Glastechnische Berichte*, XXVIII (1955), p. 148.
[5] See pp. 259–60.
[6] H. D. Parodi, *La Verrerie en Égypte*, pp. 36, 69.
[7] B. Neumann and G. Kotyga, *Zeitschr. f. angew. Chemie*, XXXVIII (1925), p. 858.
[8] M. Farnsworth and P. D. Ritchie, *Technical Studies*, VI (1938), pp. 172–3.

and the other from the Nineteenth Dynasty, analysed by me were both found to owe their colour to a copper compound and the same result was found by Neumann and Kotyga,[1] and by Farnsworth and Ritchie.[2] Turner [3] has published partial analyses of eight specimens of sealing-wax-red glass (including those examined by Neumann and Kotyga and Farnsworth and Ritchie). Seven are of Eighteenth Dynasty date, six of them from El Amarna,[4] and one of the Nineteenth Dynasty, and in every case the colour was found to be due to cuprous oxide and not to haematite, as stated by Petrie. Another lump of red glass, probably from Memphis and of late date, is noted by Arkell,[5] who also refers to three other pieces mentioned by Petrie. A piece of orange-red glass inlay examined by Gettens owed its colour to cuprous oxide.[6]

White Glass

When glass is colourless and transparent or translucent it naturally does not contain any colouring matter, but when it is white and opaque this effect is generally produced by the addition of oxide of tin, which has been found in white opaque glass of the end of the Eighteenth Dynasty [7] and also of the Twentieth Dynasty and later.[7,8] A specimen of tin oxide, almost certainly artificially prepared, was found in the tomb of Tutankhamūn, which may possibly have been for use in making white opaque glass.

Yellow Glass

A specimen of Egyptian yellow glass of the Nineteenth Dynasty was found by me to be coloured by a compound of antimony and lead and these same ingredients were found by Parodi in Egyptian yellow glass of both Persian and Arab times.[9] The specimens analysed by Neumann and Kotyga owed their colour to an iron compound.[10] Farnsworth and Ritchie give five analyses of yellow glass of Eighteenth Dynasty date, but refrain from giving a definite opinion as to the origin of the colour, which they think may be due to the conditions of manufacture rather than the presence of lead, antimony or iron.[11] Lead occurs in all five of their specimens, but antimony in only four.

Colourless, Transparent Glass

When this was made first is uncertain, but from the Eighteenth Dynasty tomb of Tutankhamūn there are a number of examples, for instance, on the back of the throne, on a pair of earrings, on parts of four geese on the middle coffin, and on a gold heart-amulet with a *bennu*-bird, on all of which there are small painted designs covered with colourless, transparent glass. From the Nineteenth Dynasty there is

---

[1] B. Neumann and G. Kotyga, *Zeitschr. f. angew. Chemie*, XXXVIII (1925), p. 864.

[2] M. Farnsworth and P. D. Ritchie, *Technical Studies*, VI (1938), pp. 172–3.

[3] W. E. S. Turner, *J.E.A.*, XLIII (1957), pp. 110–12.

[4] Cf. W. M. F. Petrie, *Tell el Amarna*, p. 27.

[5] A. J. Arkell, *J.E.A.*, XLIII (1957), p. 110.

[6] E. Riefstahl, *Brooklyn Mus. Journ.*, 1943–4, p. 23.

[7] B. Neumann and G. Kotyga, *Zeitschr. f. angew. Chemie*, XXXVIII (1925), p. 863.

[8] H. D. Parodi, *La Verrerie en Égypte*, pp. 34, 39, 45, 73.

[9] H. D. Parodi, *La Verrerie en Égypte*, pp. 36, 39, 69. Cf. also R. J. Charleston, *Archaeometry*, III (1960), p. 3, *n.* 1.

[10] B. Neumann and G. Kotyga, *Zeitschr. f. angew. Chemie*, XXXVIII (1925), pp. 863–4.

[11] M. Farnsworth and P. D. Ritchie, *Technical Studies*, VI (1938), pp. 165, 166, 172.

part of a flail on the back of the figure of Anubis, and also the box or shrine on which the figure rests, which are painted and covered with colourless, transparent glass.[1] An apparently unique example is a royal head probably dating from very late in the Ptolemaic period. This is made from a transparent calcium glass of high alkali content, wine red in colour, in which circular sections of opaque white glass have been mixed, 'the effect being very like a bowl of jelly with segments of a white banana'. These white sections were mixed throughout the entire body of the glass, and the effect was probably intended to imitate imperial porphyry.[2]

MANUFACTURE

As already stated, the ingredients for glass making, until a late date, were quartz sand, calcium carbonate, natron, or plant ashes, and a small amount of the colouring material. It seems almost certain that at first the calcium carbonate was not added as such and that its presence was unknown, but that it was used unconsciously as an admixture with the sand, it being recognized that, in order to obtain the required results, sand from certain localities only must be employed, such sand being quartz sand containing a natural admixture of calcium carbonate, which is fairly common in Egypt.

The process of glass production involved two distinct stages, the first a comparatively low temperature operation, probably carried out at under 750° C., in which the sand and alkali were converted into a frit, the second the conversion of the frit to glass in crucibles in a melting furnace, the upper temperature limit probably not exceeding 1,100° C.[3] The preliminary fritting was done in saucer-shaped pans which were supported in the furnace on a group of cylindrical jars,[4] and the material was then put into clay crucibles and strongly heated in a special furnace until complete fusion and combination had taken place and the main body of the resulting glass had become homogeneous and clear. The knowledge of when this end-point was reached would soon become a matter of practice with a skilled workman, but in some cases it was determined by taking out small quantities of the fused mass by means of pincers for examination.[5] When finished, the glass was poured into moulds, or poured out a little at a time and roiled into thick round rods, which were then drawn out into thin 'cane' or flattened into strips, to be cut up into small pieces for inlay. Alternatively, the glass was allowed to cool in the crucible, which was then broken away, as also the frothy upper surface (caused by the escape of carbon dioxide gas and combined water), and the dirty lower surface (due to impurities and dirt sinking to the bottom), and the glass was re-melted and used as required.

Petrie found evidence of small crucibles at El Amarna,[5] which were two to three inches both in depth and in diameter, and Turner has shown that the larger cylindrical jars used to support the fritting pans, which he describes in detail, were also used as

---

[1] Cairo Museum, No. J. 31380. A. Lucas, *Ann. Serv.*, XXXIX (1939), p. 234.

[2] G. A. Wainwright and F. A. Bannister, *Ann. Serv.*, XXX (1930), pp. 95–101; J. D. Cooney, *Journ. Glass Studies*, II (1960), p. 31.

[3] W. E. S. Turner, *Journ. Soc. Glass Technology*, XXXVIII (1954), pp. 436–44.

[4] Specimens of both are in University College, London, and are described by W. E. S. Turner. *Journ. Soc. Glass Technology*, XXXVIII (1954), pp. 436–44.

[5] W. M. F. Petrie, *Tell el Amarna*, pp. 26–27; *Arts and Crafts*, pp. 120–5.

crucibles,[1] but judging by the size of the glass vessels made, even larger crucibles must sometimes have been used, and in New York there is a mass of glass [2] of such a size that it must have been melted in a crucible with a capacity of more than 5,000 cubic centimetres. In most of the so-called glass works in Cairo, which are very small and very primitive, and in which glass is not made, but old bottles melted up and the material re-used, there are not any separate crucibles, the receptacles in which the glass is melted being built in as part of the furnace, there being generally three to each furnace, each of three workers having one in front of him. May not this custom have come down from earlier times? If so, separate crucibles, if used at all, may always have been small and only for special purposes.

Until a late period, beads were made singly by hand by winding thin glass threads round a copper wire and breaking off the thread after each bead.[3] During the Coptic period, a different method was employed, namely by drawing out a glass tube to the required diameter and then cutting it into beads.[3]

Vases were made on a sandy clay core, enclosed in cloth tied on with string, to which a rod of copper or wood was attached as a handle. This core was dipped into the molten glass and turned round quickly a few times in order to distribute the glass fairly evenly,[4] though the vessels made are never very uniform in thickness. The core with the viscous glass on it cannot have been turned very much, since the air bubbles usually are spherical and not elongated, as they would have been with much turning. The irregular thickness of the vessels and the fact that the bubbles are spherical are also proof that the glass was applied to the core by dipping, and not by coiling heat-softened rods of glass spirally about the core as has often been stated.[5] If a pattern were required, this was made while the glass was still soft, by winding round the outside thin rods of differently coloured glass, the very common wavy effect being produced by dragging the applied rods up and down;[6] any other decoration was also applied to the outside and pressed into position. The whole was then rolled, probably on a stone slab, to produce a uniform and smooth surface, which was then ground and polished. The rim, foot, and handle, if any, were added separately, and finally the rod was withdrawn and the core scraped out. Glass vessels principally of this type, the earliest dating from the first half of the Eighteenth Dynasty, are listed and described by Fossing,[7] and to these must be added two glass goblets of the reign

---

[1] W. E. S. Turner, *Journ. Soc. Glass Technology*, XXXVIII (1954), pp. 436–44.

[2] Metropolitan Museum of Art, New York, *Glass* (1936), p. 2, n. 1.   [3] See p. 46.

[4] A. Kisa, *Das Glas im Altertume*, p. 52; W. M. F. Petrie, *Tell el Amarna*, p. 27; F. W. von Bissing, *Rec. Trav.*, XXVIII (1906), p. 21; H. E. Winlock, in Metropolitan Museum of Art, New York, *Glass* (1936), pp. 2–3; R. W. Smith, *Glass from the Ancient World*, p. 14; W. Haberey, *Glastechnische Berichte*, XXX (1957), p. 507; D. B. Harden, in *History of Technology*, II, pp. 319–20.

[5] W. M. F. Petrie, *Arts and Crafts*, pp. 124–5; P. E. Newberry, *J.E.A.*, VI (1920), pp. 157–8; D. B. Harden, *Antiquity*, VII (1933), p. 420; W. Wolf, *Das ägyptische Kunstgewerbe* (*Geschichte des Kunstgewerbes*, IV), p. 65; W. B. Honey, *Glass, A Handbook*, p. 16, n. 1; P. Fossing, *Glass Vessels before Glass-blowing*, p. 2; F. W. S. van Thienen, *Mededeelingen v. d. Dienst v. Kunsten en Wetenschappen*, V (1938), p. 30.

[6] P. E. Newberry, *J.E.A.*, VI (1920), p. 158, states that the rods were held in place by pins while this was done.

[7] P. Fossing, *Glass Vessels before Glass-blowing*, pp. 6–7, 8–23. Cf. also P. E. Newberry, *J.E.A.*, VI (1920), pp. 155–60. N.B. The vessels from the tomb of Maiherperi should be dated to the reign of Thutmose IV.

of Thutmose III, one of which was made up of bits of red, green, white, and yellow or brown glass, fused together in several fairly small areas and built up on a core.[1]

Small figures and certain other objects, such as the larger and more elaborate pieces of inlay,[2] can only have been made by moulding,[3] and it is extremely probable that a few open bowls of New Kingdom date and later were also made by pressing molten glass into a mould or spreading it over an inverted mould.[4]

Glass was also worked cold, and objects were either cut from a solid glass block, or first moulded to shape and subsequently finished by cutting, grinding, drilling and polishing.[5] Among specimens of this type of work may be mentioned the glass headrests of Tutankhamūn,[6] and a number of glass sculptures described by Cooney.[7] These include three shawabti figures, a few small statuettes, and several glass heads originally forming part of composite figures, the majority of New Kingdom date, and none earlier than the Eighteenth Dynasty.

Glass was not turned until the end of the first millenium B.C., and blown glass was not known until the Roman period, perhaps about the beginning of the Christian era,[8] the so-called glass blowers depicted in the tomb of Rekhmirē (Eighteenth Dynasty) being, in fact, metal workers.[9]

Glass inlay is often called enamel,[10] paste, or *pâte de verre*. It is certainly not enamel, which, although a vitreous material, is employed in the powdered state and fused into position by heat, whereas the ancient Egyptian material was always cut, or moulded, and cemented into position. The terms paste and *pâte de verre* are unsatisfactory, because meaningless, and they are often used very loosely and sometimes are even intended to be non-committal. The word paste, too, in connexion with glass has a very definite technical meaning and signifies the glass with a high refractive index and high lustre employed to imitate certain modern gems, particularly the diamond,

---

[1] H. E. Winlock, *Treasure of Three Egyptian Princesses*, p. 61.

[2] For glass inlay figures see A. Lucas, *Ann. Serv.*, XXXIX (1939), pp. 227–35; F. W. S. van Thienen, *Mededeelingen v. d. Dienst v. Kunsten en Wetenschappen*, V (1938), pp. 28–31; Burlington Fine Arts Club, *Catalogue of an Exhibition of Egyptian Art* (1922), p. 116, Pl. XLV.

[3] Griffith found both limestone moulds and clay moulds for glass of Ptolemaic date (W. M. F. Petrie and F. Ll. Griffith, *Tanis*, II, *Nebesheh and Defenneh*, p. 42). See also D. B. Harden, *Greece and Rome*, III, pp. 140–9.

[4] D. B. Harden, in *History of Technology*, II, p. 319; R. W. Smith, *Glass from the Ancient World*, p. 15. Cf. also F. Schuler, *Archaeology*, XII (1959), pp. 47–52.

[5] Cf. J. D. Cooney, *Journ. Glass Studies*, II (1960), pp. 13–14. The use of a cutting wheel for inscriptions and other decoration on glass has been suggested by R. W. Smith, *Glass from the Ancient World*, pp. 38–39, but Cooney, *loc. cit.* says 'There is not the slightest evidence that the wheel was known or used to finish details of these sculptures.'

[6] D. B. Harden, in *History of Technology*, II, p. 319; W. Haberey, *Glastechnische Berichte*, XXX (1957), p. 508.

[7] J. D. Cooney, *Journ. Glass Studies*, II (1960), pp. 11–31.

[8] D. B. Harden, *Greece and Rome*, III, pp. 140–9; *Antiquity*, VII (1933), p. 421; in *History of Technology*, II, p. 322; C. C. Edgar, *Graeco-Egyptian Glass*, pp. i–ii; G. Eisen, *American Journal of Archaeology*, XX (1916), pp. 134–43.

[9] Cf. F. W. von Bissing, *Rec. Trav.*, XXVIII (1906), pp. 20–22.

[10] Cf. G. Möller, *Metallkunst*, p. 26; E. Vernier, *B.I.F.A.O.*, VIII (1911), pp. 39–40; F. G. Hilton Price, *Proc. Soc. Antiquaries*, XIX (1901–3), pp. 290–2.

and it cannot correctly be used to describe the soft glass without brilliance, or sparkle, made by the ancient Egyptians in imitation of precious or semi-precious stones. It is suggested, therefore, that the terms paste and *pâte de verre* should be discarded and that the material used should always be called what it is, namely, glass.

Chapter XI
METALS AND ALLOYS: MINERALS

The principal metals employed in ancient Egypt were copper, gold, iron, lead, silver and tin, but one instance of the use of antimony and one of platinum are known.

Four principal alloys were also employed, namely, bronze, which is essentially an alloy of copper and tin; a copper-lead alloy; electrum, an alloy of gold and silver; and, at a very late date, brass, which is an alloy of copper and zinc. In addition to these metals and alloys, a number of ores and natural mineral substances were also used.

These metals, alloys, ores and minerals will now be described.

ANTIMONY

In view of the numerous erroneous statements that antimony was commonly employed in ancient Egypt, it becomes necessary to explain very clearly what antimony is. It is a bright, silver-white brittle metal, frequently having a crystalline structure, that is largely used at the present day for making certain alloys, such as type metals, Britannia metals and anti-friction metals. Although antimony occurs naturally in the free state as metal, this condition is extremely rare and it is generally found only in small amount, the antimony employed in industry being produced artificially from certain naturally-occurring compounds (ores). So far as is known, neither antimony nor antimony ores occur in Egypt, but probably traces of antimony compounds, though not recorded, are present in the local copper and lead ores, and a trace has been found in the nickel ore from St. John's island in the Red Sea.[1]

Antimony ores are found in many parts of the world that have no connexion with ancient Egypt, but they also occur in countries that were in contact with Egypt, for instance, they are plentiful in Asia Minor and occur also in Persia and, in small amount, in certain of the Greek islands (Mytilene and Chios).

Only one instance of the use of metallic antimony and very few instances of the use of antimony compounds in ancient Egypt can be traced. The former consists of some small beads from the Twenty-second Dynasty (950 to 730 B.C.) found by Petrie at El Lahun [2,3] and, as the production of the metal from its ore at that date is most improbable, since the process was not known in Europe until about the fifteenth or sixteenth century A.D., it is almost certain that the beads were made from native metal, but whether this was brought to Egypt as metal or already fashioned into beads cannot, of course, be stated.

The only other instances of the use of metallic antimony in antiquity of which any record can be found, are two mentioned by Dr. Gladstone, who says,[3] 'M.

---

[1] F. W. Moon, *Prel. Geol. Rept. on Saint John's Island*, p. 16.
[2] W. M. F. Petrie, *Illahun, Kahun and Gurob*, p. 25, Pl. XXIX (56).
[3] J. H. Gladstone, *P.S.B.A.*, XXIV (1891–2), pp. 223–7.

Oppert indeed found at Khorsabad a tablet of metallic antimony and M. Sarzec found at Tello part of a vase of pure antimony.' The vase from Tello mentioned is the same as the 'Chaldean vase' referred to by Berthelot.[1]

The instances of the use of antimony compounds in ancient Egypt that can be traced are (a) a Nineteenth Dynasty eye-paint consisting of antimony sulphide;[2] (b) an eye-paint (undated) which consisted of the sulphides of lead and antimony,[3] the relative proportions of the two not having been determined, though it is highly probable that the material was essentially galena (sulphide of lead) containing only a small proportion of sulphide of antimony as a natural impurity and (c) three other specimens of eye-paint, which contained traces of an antimony compound as an accidental impurity.[4] The general idea, therefore, that the ancient Egyptian eye-paint (other than the green malachite) consisted of, or contained antimony or an antimony compound is wrong, and there is no justification for calling it antimony, *stibium* (an early name for sulphide of antimony, transferred later to the metal), sulphide of antimony, or other name implying such composition. The misunderstanding has probably arisen from the fact that an antimony compound was employed as an eye medicine by the Greeks [5] and Romans.[6] The ancient Egyptian eye-paint, apart from the green malachite, consisted of galena (sulphide of lead) sometimes containing traces of sulphide of antimony as a natural impurity, with such occasional substitutes as black oxide of copper, black oxide of iron and black oxide of manganese.[7]

In addition to the very rare use of an antimony compound as an eye-paint (possibly only one and at the most two examples being known), a compound of antimony and lead has been found as the colouring matter of yellow glass of the Nineteenth Dynasty, Persian period and Arab period respectively,[8] and traces of antimony occur in sundry ancient Egyptian copper and bronze objects, having been derived from an impurity in the copper ore.

In order, if possible, to prevent the perpetuation of mistakes and also to avoid being taken to task for ignoring several recently published statements asserting that antimony was used in ancient Egypt, I feel obliged, though very reluctantly, to explain why these instances are not included with those enumerated. Three of the most recent of such statements will, therefore, be discussed, namely:

1. Howard Carter, referring to certain dockets on the lids of three boxes from the tomb of Tutankhamūn, says that these dockets, which give a list of the contents of the boxes (missing when the boxes were found), mention antimony among other objects and he adds, 'We found . . . antimony powder . . . dispersed on the floor of the chamber.' [9]

---

[1] *C.R.Ac.Sci.*, CIV (1887), p. 265, quoted by H. C. and L. Hoover, in their translation of Agricola's *De re metallica*, p. 429, *n*. 57; J. W. Mellor, *Inorganic and Theoretical Chemistry*, IX, p. 339.

[2] A. Wiedemann, in W. M. F. Petrie, *Medum*, p. 43.

[3] J. Barthoux, 'Les fards, pommades et couleurs dans l'antiquité', in *Congrès int. de géog.*, *Le Caire, 1925*, IV (1926), p. 254.

[4] See p. 82. [5] R. T. Gunther, *The Greek Herbal of Dioscorides*, V: 99.

[6] Pliny, XXXIII: 33, 34. [7] See p. 81. [8] See p. 190.

[9] H. Carter, *Tut-ankh-Amen*, III, p. 119.

The inscriptions are in hieratic characters and only in two instances were they legible when found, and one inscription is now masked by the paraffin wax used to coat the box.[1] Of the two inscriptions left, one mentions only incense and gum (probably odoriferous gum-resin being meant) and the other refers to various articles, among which were two objects 'to serve for the putting on of *msdmt*',[2] which is the word for eye-paint often translated as antimony. It does not, however, mean antimony, and it is highly improbable that the Egyptians of that date (if ever) had a special word for metallic antimony, which until comparatively recently was a very rare metal, since its natural occurrence is so limited that it cannot have been well known until it was produced artificially from its ores, which was not earlier than about the fifteenth century A.D. But even if it be assumed that when *msdmt* is translated antimony it means, not metallic antimony, but an antimony compound, in view of what has been proved respecting the composition of the Egyptian eye-paints, it is equally unlikely that it should have any such meaning.[3]

The 'antimony powder' stated to have been found in the tomb of Tutankhamūn, if the expression be taken literally, means metallic antimony in a finely divided condition. But, considering the scarcity of metallic antimony anciently, the occurrence of such a material is so very improbable that nothing less than a chemical analysis would be sufficient to establish its identity and the bright, light grey, gritty material obtained by powdering metallic antimony would have been very unsuitable for use as an eye-paint. Even if the word antimony is used loosely to mean an antimony compound, such as the sulphide or oxide, which are the only two antimony compounds at all likely to have been known at the time, the appearance of these is so little characteristic that again a chemical analysis would be necessary for identification. It is suggested that a confusion has arisen between sulphide of lead (galena), the principal use of which in ancient Egypt was as an eye-paint (and small lumps of which were found in the tomb and are now in the Cairo Museum) and sulphide of antimony.[4] I would like to mention, too, that I had the privilege of working with Mr. Carter at Luxor during eight seasons and that I saw and handled most of the objects from the tomb and that, as a chemist, I am perfectly familiar with the appearance of metallic antimony and with the tests for antimony and antimony compounds and that nothing that was either one or the other came under my notice.

2. Gauthier, in a recent history of Egypt, says with reference to a scene in a tomb of Middle Kingdom date at Beni Hasan 'en particulier la poudre d' antimonie très recherchée par les Égyptiens . . . comme fard pour les yeux'.[5] Here it is not a matter of a material whose identity could be fixed by chemical analysis, but a question of translation, and all that has just been said on this subject is equally applicable in this case.

3. Fink and Kopp state that antimony plating was known in Egypt in about the

---

[1] This inscription could probably be rendered legible either by the removal of the wax, or by photography, using ultra-violet or infra-red rays.

[2] Kindly translated by Prof. J. Černý.

[3] Cf. J. R. Harris, *Lexicographical Studies*, pp. 174 f.

[4] Garstang (J. Garstang, *Burial Customs*, p. 114) almost certainly makes a similar mistake when he says that 'fragments of antimony ore were found'.

[5] H. Gauthier, *L'Égypte pharaonique*, in *Précis de l'histoire d'Égypte*, I, p. 100.

Fifth or Sixth Dynasty.[1] The evidence adduced consists of a copper ewer and basin of that date on the former of which are smooth bright areas of 'considerable size' looking like silver and on the latter small scattered spots having the same silvery appearance, which when tested proved to be a thin layer of metallic antimony. The tests applied are given and there seems no doubt that the white metal is indeed antimony.

The possibility of the antimony having been derived from the copper is considered by Fink and Kopp and rejected, because (1) they were unable to find antimony in the copper; (2) they have never heard of a case of decuprification of the surface of a copper-antimony alloy and (3) a smooth bright deposit of antimony could never result from such a process. Hence they consider that the antimony plating was applied intentionally to simulate silver and two methods are suggested in which this might have been done, one using antimony sulphide and natron and the other oxide of antimony, 5 per cent acetic acid (equivalent to vinegar) and strips of iron, materials which it is stated 'are known to have been available in ancient Egypt'. These various arguments may now be considered.

1. That antimony was not found in the copper. Unfortunately neither the number of specimens of the copper tested, nor the method of testing are given. Naturally every possible care had to be taken to avoid disfiguring the objects and, therefore, large samples were impossible, but unless a number of samples were taken from different parts of the objects and unless these were tested by some very delicate method, such as the spectroscopic one, a small percentage of antimony might easily have been missed.

Antimony is not a very uncommon impurity in ancient Egyptian copper objects, and that it has not been found more frequently is probably largely owing to the fact that generally no search for it is made. However, it is recorded as present as a trace in a middle predynastic copper axe-head;[2] in three copper tools of the Fourth Dynasty;[3] in a copper axe from the Twelfth Dynasty in which there was a 0.2 per cent,[4] and in another copper axe, possibly from the same period, in which there was 0.7 per cent;[5] in a copper-lead statuette of Ptolemaic date, in which there was 0.7 per cent;[6] and in a further, undated but probably early, copper object in which there was a trace.[7]

2. That decuprification of the surface of a copper-antimony alloy is unlikely. If by this is meant the corroding away of the copper from the attacked surface of a copper object containing antimony, in such a manner as to leave the antimony, it is admitted that this is most improbable and that the antimony should be left as a thin, bright metallic layer is believed to be impossible.

That the ewer basin had not only been corroded, but probably corroded to a considerable extent, is proved by the fact that they had been cleaned and that chemical,

[1] C. G. Fink and A. H. Kopp, 'Ancient Egyptian Antimony Plating on Copper Objects', Metropolitan Museum Studies, IV (1933), pp. 163–7; C. G. Fink, Ind. and Eng. Chemistry, XXVI (1934), p. 236; Chemistry and Industry, LIII (1934), pp. 216–20.
[2] H. C. H. Carpenter, Nature, CXXX (1932), pp. 625–6.
[3] J. H. Gladstone, P.S.B.A., XIV (1892), pp. 223–7.
[4] J. H. Gladstone, P.S.B.A., XII (1890), pp. 227–34.
[5] G. B. Phillips, Ancient Egypt, 1924, p. 89.
[6] W. Flight, Journ. Chemical Soc., XLI (1882), p. 142, No. IX.
[7] M. Berthelot, in J. de Morgan, Recherches sur les origines de l'Égypte, I, pp. 223–9.

mechanical and electrolytic methods of cleaning had all been necessary. The effect of such corrosion must have been the destruction of all the original surface, with the formation of the usual products found on corroded copper objects from Egypt, namely, chiefly copper oxide and basic carbonate, with some basic chloride, and, if it be assumed that the copper contained a small proportion of antimony as an impurity, which is neither impossible nor unlikely, this latter would probably have been converted into oxide. Then came the cleaning. This is stated to have been done by means of alternating baths of dilute alkaline and acid solutions, the loosened material being removed with wooden instruments or brushes, an electrolytic treatment being also mentioned. But, if the corroded surface contained oxide of antimony, as suggested, and if the electrolytic treatment was that advocated by Fink and Eldridge,[1] as appears very probable, then iron anodes would have been employed and all the conditions necessary to produce a thin coating of metallic antimony on the copper would have been present, and this antimony layer would have been deposited in much the same manner as is suggested by Fink and Kopp was done anciently (except that it would have been in an alkaline and not in an acid solution), namely by means of iron. The improbability that the ancient Egyptians at any period, particularly at so early a date as that of the ewer and basin, knew antimony plating is so great that very much stronger evidence than that cited is necessary before it can be accepted as a proved fact, and I suggest that the patches and spots of plating found may have been the result of the process of cleaning employed, and that they were brought about by the reduction of oxide of antimony (or other antimony compound present in the corroded surface of the copper) to the metallic state.[2]

Fink and Kopp state that 'Antimony sulphide has been found in ancient specimens of Kohl . . . and antimony oxide is readily derived therefrom by roasting.' So far as is known, only one specimen of *kohl* (and that of a date from 1,100 to 1,500 years after that of the ewer and basin) has been found that consisted of sulphide of antimony; one other specimen may have contained a substantial proportion of sulphide of antimony, but it is more probable that it contained only a very small amount, and a few others contained traces. But, even if a few specimens of *kohl* of the necessary date did consist of sulphide of antimony (which is not probable and for which there is no proof), it would require considerable evidence to establish as a fact that some of this *kohl* was converted into oxide of antimony by roasting and that the oxide so obtained was then employed for plating a ewer and basin. It is most improbable, too, that strips of iron should have been employed in the Fifth or Sixth Dynasty. Even if iron were generally known, which was not the case, that it should have been used in the manner suggested is very unlikely.

COPPER, BRONZE AND BRASS
Copper [3]

Copper, which, unlike gold, is not usually found in nature in the metallic condition, but which generally must be produced artificially from unattractive-looking

---

[1] C. G. Fink and C. H. Eldridge, *The Restoration of Ancient Bronzes and other Alloys*, pp. 15–17.

[2] The usual form of plating known to the ancient Egyptians was that of hammering thin sheets of one metal on to another. See gold plating (pp. 232–3) and silver plating (pp. 251–2).

[3] Cf. J. R. Harris, *Lexicographical Studies*, pp. 50–62, 65–66.

ores, was yet one of the earliest metals known to man. In Egypt it was employed before gold as far back as Badarian and early predynastic times.

The earliest copper objects found are beads, borers and pins, which date from the Badarian period [1] and which continued in use during the early predynastic period, supplemented, however, by bracelets, small chisels, finger rings, harpoon heads, small implements, needles, tweezers, and other small articles.[2] 'All the objects previous to the middle predynastic are rare, small and flimsy,' [3,4] but, by the end of the predynastic period, the Egyptians 'were in possession of practical copper weapons' [3,5] and during the early dynastic period 'heavy practical axe-heads, adzes, chisels, knives, daggers, spears, implements and ornaments' [3] as well as household utensils, such as ewers and basins, were in use in considerable numbers.[6] The number of worked copper objects of First Dynasty date found by Petrie in the royal tombs or cenotaphs at Abydos was considerable, although these had been robbed and also excavated previously, and Emery also found a very large number of copper objects in the First Dynasty tomb of Djer at Saqqara, which included 121 knives, 7 saws, 68 vessels, 32 bodkins, 262 needles, 15 piercers, 79 chisels, 75 rectangular plates, 102 adzes and 75 hoes.[7]

It is sometimes stated that during the earlier periods when copper was used in comparatively small amount, it was obtained from native metal (i.e. copper found naturally in the metallic state),[8] but however this may be, which will be discussed later, there cannot be any doubt that in all subsequent periods it was derived entirely from the smelting of ores. A copper chisel of early dynastic date, analysed by Bannister and quoted by Desch, contained 2.51 per cent of silver and 4.14 per cent of gold, of which Desch says,[9] 'The composition of this specimen, with the high proportion of silver and gold, suggests that it is composed of native metal.' Coghlan also says [10] that a large percentage of gold and silver would indicate a native origin for the metal.

---

[1] G. Brunton and G. Caton-Thompson, *Badarian Civilisation*, pp. 7, 27, 33, 41; E. J. Baumgartel, *Cultures of Prehistoric Egypt*, II, pp. 2–3.

[2] G. Brunton and G. Caton-Thompson, *Badarian Civilisation*, pp. 56, 60, 71; E. R. Ayrton and W. L. S. Loat, *Predynastic Cemetery at El Mahasna*, pp. 18, 19, 21, 32, 33; D. Randall-MacIver and A. C. Mace, *El Amrah and Abydos*, pp. 16, 18, 20, 21, 23, 24; W. M. F. Petrie and J. E. Quibell, *Naqada and Ballas*, pp. 14, 20–24, 27–29, 45, 47, 48, 54; W. M. F. Petrie, *Diospolis Parva*, p. 24; *Prehistoric Egypt*, pp. 25, 26, 47; *Tools and Weapons*; E. J. Baumgartel, *Cultures of Prehistoric Egypt*, II, pp. 2–3.

[3] G. A. Reisner, *Nag-ed-Dêr*, I, pp. 127, 128, 134.

[4] Brunton found a large copper axe-head weighing three and a half pounds of the middle predynastic period (H. C. H. Carpenter, *Nature*, CXXX (1932), pp. 625–6).

[5] Cf. A. Scharff, *Die archaeologischen Ergebnisse des vorgeschichtlichen Gräberfeldes von Abusir-el-Meleq*, pp. 45–46; *Die Altertümer der Vor- und Frühzeit Ägyptens*, I, pp. 69–74; E. J. Baumgartel, *Cultures of Prehistoric Egypt*, II, pp. 10–23.

[6] Cf. A. Scharff, *Die Altertümer der Vor- und Frühzeit Ägyptens*, I, pp. 69–74; G. A. Reisner, *Naga-ed-Dêr*, I, pp. 114–16 (list).

[7] W. B. Emery, *Ann. Serv.*, XXXIX (1939), pp. 427–37; *Great Tombs*, I, pp. 20–57, Pls. VIII–X.

[8] Cf. H. H. Coghlan, *Prehistoric Metallurgy of Copper and Bronze*, pp. 12–14, 30; C. N. Bromehead, *Man*, XLVIII (1948), pp. 6–7; E. Voce, *Man*, XLVIII (1948), pp. 19–21; L. Aitchison, *History of Metals*, I, p. 25.

[9] C. H. Desch, 'Report on the Metallurgical Examination of Specimens for the Sumerian Committee of the British Ass.', *Report of the British Ass.*, 1928.

[10] H. H. Coghlan, *Antiquaries Journal*, XXII (1942), p. 24.

The chisel analysed by Bannister was supplied by me, and was received from the late Mr. C. M. Firth, who found it in Nubia. It is most unlikely that such a comparatively large object as the chisel in question and of the period to which it is dated should have been made out of native copper, and a very much more probable explanation is that the copper ore used had contained small proportions of gold and silver,[1] a phenomenon not unknown in the eastern desert, whence the copper ore was probably derived. Thus Ball states [2] that in the south-eastern desert 'Besides gold some of the quartz veins contain copper', and the Dungash gold mine (situated east of Edfu) also contains veins of copper ore.[3]

Rickard says [4] that 'native copper is far more abundantly distributed than is generally supposed' and that 'The use of native copper marks the beginning of very ancient metal culture.' That copper is found native in various parts of the world and that in certain localities, especially in North America, it occurs in abundance and that at one time this copper was used largely for making ornaments, weapons and tools, is well known, but the people who employed it never on their own initiative got beyond its use and never proceeded to the smelting of copper ores. That native copper was ever found and used in Egypt lacks proof, and though some few of the earliest copper objects, the Badarian beads for example, *may* have been made from native copper,[5] that they were so made is by no means certain, and such statements as the following go beyond the proved facts: 'The predynastic graves of Egypt . . . contain beads of native copper . . .';[6] 'in the Badarian graves of the Fayum there is native copper . . .';[7] 'Traces of copper, chiefly pins, needles and bodkins hammered out of native metal are found in the debris of the earliest agricultural settlements of the Nile Valley';[8] and 'It is now generally accepted that the first metal to be found on all prehistoric copper sites, at the earliest time, is native copper.' [9]

In any discussion of the question whether or not native copper was employed in Egypt there is one very important fact to be taken into account, namely, the use as eye-paint of considerable quantities of an ore of copper (malachite) that occurs in the country, that is easily converted into copper, that can be proved to have been employed later as a source of copper, and the use of which can be traced as far back as the use of copper and possibly even farther. The conditions in Egypt were therefore particularly favourable for the early discovery of copper by smelting the ore, and there is no need to postulate the occurrence and use of the native metal.

Copper ores occur within the geographical limits of modern Egypt in two widely separated localities, namely, in Sinai and in the eastern desert. The amount of ore, however, is not sufficiently large to warrant mining at the present day, since copper

[1] All Egyptian gold contains silver.
[2] J. Ball, *Geog. and Geol. of South-Eastern Egypt*, p. 353.
[3] See p. 205.
[4] T. A. Rickard, *Man and Metals*, I, pp. 105, 106, 108.
[5] Compare the analyses of two cutting implements of copper, of predynastic and protodynastic date respectively (E. Voce, *Man*, XLVIII (1948), pp. 19–21). Coghlan (*Prehistoric Metallurgy of Copper and Bronze*, pp. 116–18) regards these as too doubtful for comment.
[6] T. A. Rickard, *Man and Metals*, I, p. 96.
[7] T. A. Rickard, *Journ. Inst. Metals*, XLIII (1930), p. 305.
[8] E. A. Marples, *Ancient Egypt*, 1929, p. 97.
[9] H. H. Coghlan, *Antiquaries Journal*, XXII (1942), p. 22.

ores may be obtained in much greater quantity and in more easily accessible places elsewhere.

The evidence for ancient copper mining and smelting by the Egyptians is twofold, first, the existence of ancient mines with ruins of mining settlements and ancient slag heaps, and second, inscriptions in the neighbourhood of mines left by mining expeditions.[1]

Sinai [2]

Ancient workings, some of which are of considerable size, which admittedly were either for copper ore or for turquoise, exist at Magharah and at Serabit el Khadim, both of which are situated in the south-west of the peninsula of Sinai and about twelve miles apart.[3]

That many of these workings were not for copper ore, but for turquoise (which was employed for beads and jewellery in both the Old and Middle Kingdoms and even as early as the Badarian period),[4] there can be no doubt, since at both places turquoise is still found and at Magharah turquoise mining is carried on by the local bedouin at the present day, the main workings extending for about two kilometres on the west side of the valley.[5] At Serabit el Khadim, although turquoise occurs, it is only found at the present time in small quantity and is not now worked.[5,6]

In addition to turquoise, however, copper ore also may have been mined anciently at Magharah, since ruins of mining settlements exist, dating principally from the Old Kingdom, but also from the Middle Kingdom, in the former of which have been found 'a great amount of copper slag and waste scraps from smelting; also some chips of copper ore, many broken crucibles and part of a mould for an ingot',[7] and in the latter 'a great quantity of copper slag, scraps from smelting, pieces of crucibles, charcoal and, in one case, part of a crucible-charge of crushed ore not yet reduced',[8] also a mould (undated) for casting the blades of weapons.[9] Holland, however, denies that any traces of copper are to be found at Wadi Maghara,[10] and other authorities seem to be agreed that copper does not occur there in workable quantities.[11]

At Serabit el Khadim the proof of ancient copper mining is even less evident, as the workings have not been examined carefully from this point of view, but copper

---

[1] Cf. A. Lucas, *J.E.A.*, XIII (1927), pp. 162–70.

[2] Cf. J. Černý, *Inscriptions of Sinai*, II, pp. 5–7.

[3] J. de Morgan, *Recherches sur les origines de l'Égypte*, I, pp. 216–39; W. M. F. Petrie, *Researches in Sinai*, pp. 18, 19, 27, 46–53, 154–62; J. Ball, *Geog. and Geol. of West-Central Sinai*, pp. 11, 13, 163, 188, 190, 191; T. Barron, *Topog. and Geol. of the Peninsula of Sinai*, pp. 40–45, 166–9, 206–12; Mines and Quarries Dept., *Report on the Mineral Industry*, pp. 36, 38.

[4] See p. 208, *n.* 4, and also pp. 404–5.

[5] W. M. F. Petrie, *Researches in Sinai*, pp. 18, 19, 27, 46–53, 154–62; T. Barron, *Topog. and Geol. of the Peninsula of Sinai*, pp. 40–45, 166–9, 206–12; Mines and Quarries Dept., *Report on the Mineral Industry*, pp. 36, 38.

[6] J. Ball, *Geog. and Geol. of West-Central Sinai*, pp. 11, 13, 163, 188, 190, 191.

[7] W. M. F. Petrie, *Researches in Sinai*, p. 51.

[8] W. M. F. Petrie, *Researches in Sinai*, p. 52.

[9] J. de Morgan, *Recherches sur les origines de l'Égypte*, I, p. 229.

[10] F. W. Holland, *Quart. Journ. Geol. Soc.*, XXII (1866), p. 492.

[11] H. Bauerman, *Quart. Journ. Geol. Soc.*, XXV (1869), p. 34; M. Berthelot, in J. de Morgan, *Recherches sur les origines de l'Égypte*, I, p. 225.

ore occurs in the immediate neighbourhood and a crucible for melting copper was found in the temple.[1] Starr and Butin, however, state that 'The amount of mining carried out at Serabit in antiquity was immense' but that 'There is no evidence whatsoever that the Egyptians sought at Serabit anything other than turquoise',[2] and Holland says that the only copper there is a thin film of silicate too small to extract for any practical purpose.[3]

The copper ore, both at Magharah and at Serabit el Khadim, is largely the green carbonate (malachite), with a little blue carbonate (azurite) and a little silicate (chrysocolla), only small quantities of any of which now remain.[4]

The inscriptions left by the mining expeditions were [5] at Magharah; in the valley and mines near Serabit el Khadim; in the temple at Serabit el Khadim and the approach to it and in the Wadi Nasb.[6]

At Magharah there were [5] 45 records consisting of 36 inscriptions on the rocks, 8 graffiti and one stela. The inscriptions date principally to the Old and Middle Kingdoms, the earliest being of the Third Dynasty.

In the valley and mines near Serabit el Khadim there were [5] 15 records (10 from mines and one possibly from a mine) consisting of 13 inscriptions on the rocks and 2 stelae. Of these 10 date to the Twelfth Dynasty and 3 to the Eighteenth Dynasty.

In the temple and its approach there were [5] approximately 322 inscriptions, principally on loose blocks of stone, statuettes, free-standing stelae and other objects, but including a number of inscriptions on walls and pillars. These belong principally to the Middle Kingdom (roughly one-third) and to the Eighteenth, Nineteenth and Twentieth Dynasties.

In the Wadi Nasb there was one inscription on the rock, of the Twelfth Dynasty.

The inscriptions in those instances where there is any reference to the nature of the activities undertaken frequently make mention of turquoise,[7] but only once of copper, and they are very unsatisfactory for use as a history of Egyptian copper mining. Thus the earlier ones (Third, Fourth and beginning of Fifth Dynasties respectively) merely record the names and titles of the Pharaohs, then reference to the leaders and officers of the expeditions are included (Fifth Dynasty) and at later dates statements of the objects of the expeditions. Although there can be little doubt that all the expeditions were for the purpose of mining either turquoise or copper ore, there is no direct proof of this from the inscriptions themselves in the case of the earlier ones, which might have been merely punitive expeditions, though they are believed to have been more.

---

[1] W. M. F. Petrie, *Researches in Sinai*, p. 162.

[2] R. F. S. Starr and R. F. Butin, *Excavations and Protosinaitic Inscriptions at Serabit el Khadem*, 1936, p. 20.

[3] F. W. Holland, *Quart. Journ. Geol. Soc.*, XXII (1866), p. 492.

[4] J. de Morgan, *Recherches sur les origines de l'Égypte*, I, pp. 216–39; J. Ball, *Geog. and Geol. of West-Central Sinai*, pp. 188, 191; T. Barron, *Topog. and Geol. of the Peninsula of Sinai*, pp. 166, 208.

[5] The word is employed in the past tense as many of the inscriptions have either been destroyed or removed.

[6] *A.R.*, v (Index), pp. 95, 102; A. H. Gardiner, T. E. Peet and J. Černý, *Inscriptions of Sinai*, I (2nd ed.), pp. 9–19.

[7] The word used is *mfk3t*, which Breasted translates as malachite; see pp. 401, 405.

In addition to the doubtful workings at Magharah and at Serabit el Khadim, already mentioned, ancient workings for copper ore exist at the following-named places in the neighbourhood of Serabit el Khadim:[1]

1. Gebel (mount) Um Rinna, situated N.N.W. of Serabit el Khadim, where there is an excavation some 20 metres wide, one to two metres high and about 50 metres long. The ore extracted was malachite, traces of which still remain.[2]

2. Wadi (valley) Malha. These workings are close to Gebel Um Rinna, Wadi Malha draining the eastern flank of the mountain. The ore mined was malachite, small quantities of which still exist.[3]

3. Wadi (valley) Kharit, called Wadi Halliq by Barron. This is situated to the west of the northern portion of Wadi Nasb. Here there is an excavation about 100 metres long, 10 metres wide and two metres in average height. The ore extracted was malachite, which has been practically exhausted.[4]

In the south-east of the peninsula ancient workings for copper ore and ancient slag heaps exist in several places, namely:

1. Near the plain of Senned. The working here is in the nature of a dyke, which has been excavated for nearly two miles and is 'exceedingly rich' in the blue carbonate (azurite).[5]

2. In the hills west of the Nebk-Sherm plain. Some of the ore is malachite, and possibly this alone was worked anciently, but chrysocolla also exists, a deposit having been found by modern prospectors at Wadi Samra (sometimes called Wadi Samara).[5]

3. Near Wadi Ramthi, one of the feeders of Wadi Nasb, which enters the Gulf of Aqaba at Dahab.[6]

In addition to the slag heaps situated at some of the mines, which have already been mentioned, there are also a number of others where there are not any mines, the largest of which is in Wadi Nasb (called Wadi Nasib by Ball), which is situated north-west of Serabit el Khadim. In this wadi, as already stated, there is an inscription of the Twelfth Dynasty. In continuation of this heap there is much scattered slag all the way up the path to the stela of Amenemhet IV.[7]

Similar, but smaller, ancient slag heaps exist at the south side of Seh Baba (the lower part of Wadi Nasb), which is situated to the south-west of Serabit el Khadim.[8]

Another ancient slag heap is at Gebel (mount) Safariat south of Gebel Hebran.[9]

The position has been well summarized by Černý.[10] 'In the face of all this evidence

---

[1] Cf. J. Černý, *Inscriptions of Sinai*, II, pp. 5–7.

[2] J. Ball, *Geog. and Geol. of West-Central Sinai*, p. 188.

[3] T. Barron, *Topog. and Geol. of the Peninsula of Sinai*, p. 166.

[4] T. Barron, *Topog. and Geol. of the Peninsula of Sinai*, pp. 167, 206; J. Ball, *Geog. and Geol. of West-Central Sinai*, pp. 190, 191; J. Černý, *Inscriptions of Sinai*, II, pp. 30–31.

[5] W. F. Hume, *Topog. and Geol. of the Peninsula of Sinai*, pp. 118,119.

[6] Kindly communicated by Dr. Ball.

[7] W. M. F. Petrie, *Researches in Sinai*, p. 27; J. Ball, *Geog. and Geol. of West Central Sinai*, p. 13; T. Barron, *Topog. and Geol. of the Peninsula of Sinai*, pp. 44, 208; J. Černý, *Inscriptions of Sinai*, II, pp. 30–31; T. A. Rickard, *Man and Metals*, I, pp. 196–7.

[8] W. M. F. Petrie, *Researches in Sinai*, pp. 18–19.

[9] T. Barron *Topog. and Geol. of the Peninsula of Sinai*, p. 208.

[10] J. Černý, *Inscriptions of Sinai*, II, pp. 7, 5.

it would be idle to attempt to deny that copper was mined and smelted in the Sinai peninsula probably at an early period. At the same time there is not a scrap of evidence for believing that the miners were Egyptians' . . . 'Apart from the single inscription . . . which mentions copper . . . as one of the objects of an expedition, we have no proof that the Egyptians ever worked the copper deposits of Sinai on a large scale.'

Eastern Desert

Copper ore exists in a number of localities in the eastern desert, namely:

1. In Wadi (valley) Araba, which is situated almost due east of Beni Suef (about Lat. 29° N.), near the Gulf of Suez. A specimen of ore examined by me was chrysocolla: the amount of ore is only small,[1] but there is evidence that it was mined anciently, probably during the New Kingdom.[2]

2. At Gebel (mount) Atawi, which is situated a little south of the latitude of Luxor, but nearer the Red Sea than the Nile. There are ancient workings, but the nature of the ore is not stated.[1]

3. At Gebel (mount) Dara (approx. Lat. 28° N.; Long. 33° E.), where there are ancient workings. The ore is chrysocolla.[1,3]

4. In the Dungash gold mine, which is situated east of Edfu (approx. Lat. 24° 50′ N.; Long. 33° 45′ E.). The nature of the ore is not stated, nor whether it was worked anciently: the amount of ore is probably very small.[1]

5. Among the low hills south of Wadi (valley) Gemal (Lat. 24° 35′ N.; Long. 34° 50′ E.). The ore is malachite, but it is not stated whether there are ancient workings.[1,4]

6. At Hamish (Lat. 24° 32′ N.; Long. slightly E. of 34°). There are old workings with three main shafts. The ore is chalcopyrite (sulphides of copper and iron). The sides of one shaft are encrusted with blue copper compounds formed from the pyrites.[5]

7. At Abu Seyal (sometimes wrongly called Absciel) in Lat. 22° 47′ N. Wells reported that the ore occurred in the form of pyrrhotite (iron pyrites) associated with copper pyrites (copper sulphide),[6] but, although there may be copper pyrites at some distance below the surface, the ore exposed is chrysocolla. The mine was worked extensively in ancient times and some at least of the ore was smelted at the mine, as there are remains of ancient furnaces and slag.

8. At Um Semiuki at the foot of Gebel (mount) Abu Hamamid, about 50 kilometres from the coast north-west of Ras Benas, there are extensive ancient workings with several shafts. At the surface, the ore is malachite and azurite, of which there is a thickness of about seven metres and below this are copper and zinc sulphides and lead ore (the zinc sulphide containing silver). There are also ore crushers, pottery (possibly broken crucibles) and slag. These are the most important deposits of copper ore yet discovered in Egypt, some of the workings being 40 to 50 feet underground.[7]

---

[1] W. F. Hume, *Explan. Notes to the Geol. Map of Egypt*, p. 37.

[2] G. W. Murray, *Ann. Serv.*, LI (1951), pp. 217–18.

[3] T. Barron and W. F. Hume, *Topog. and Geol. of the Eastern Desert*, pp. 33, 259; J. Wells, *Report of the Dept. of Mines*, 1906, p. 34.

[4] W. F. Hume, *Prelim. Report on the Geol. of the Eastern Desert*, pp. 41, 56.

[5] Dr. J. Ball, private communication.

[6] J. Wells, *Report of the Dept. of Mines*, 1906, p. 34.

[7] W. F. Hume, *Geology of Egypt*, II, Part III, pp. 837–42.

In addition to the ancient slag heaps, already mentioned, situated at the various mines, there is also one where there are no mines, namely at Kubban on the east bank of the Nile opposite Dakka (Lat. 23° 10′ N.).[1] The origin of the ore smelted is not certain, though it is often assumed to have been that from the Abu Seyal mine, part of which at least, however, was smelted at the mine, as the remains of ancient furnaces and slag attest.

Quality of Ore

Very few analyses of Egyptian copper ore have been made or published and the only ones that can be traced are as follows:

Sinai. (*a*) South-western mines. This ore yields from 5 to 15 per cent of copper according to Rickard[2] and up to 18 per cent according to Rüppell.[3] (*b*) South-eastern mines. A specimen of ore analysed by Professor Desch gave 3 per cent of copper.[4]

Eastern Desert. (*a*) From Wadi Araba two specimens of ore analysed by the Chemical Department, Cairo, gave 36 and 49 per cent of copper respectively.[5] (*b*) It is stated that the Abu Seyal ore yields on an average well over 3 per cent of copper and that in places it is very rich and may give as much as 20 per cent.[6] (*c*) A specimen of ore from the Abu Hamamid mine gave 13 per cent of copper.[7]

Amount of Ore

Some evidence of the amount of ore dealt with anciently in certain districts may be obtained from the dimensions of the ancient slag heaps, though the data are very incomplete. Even if it be assumed that all the heaps exist and are known, which almost certainly is not the case, many of them have neither been measured nor examined. The various slag heaps that are known have been mentioned already, but the only ones of which any particulars are given are those of Wadi Nasb, Seh Baba and Kubban. These may now be considered, though it should be borne in mind that there is no certainty that the Sinai heaps are the result of Egyptian workings.

Slag Heap at Wadi Nasb. The dimensions of this given by Petrie in 1906 are 500 feet long, 300 feet wide and 6 or 8 feet high.[8] Petrie, however, quotes Bauerman (an English geologist who explored the district in 1868), for very different dimensions, namely 250 yards by 200 yards,[8] while another writer gives Bauerman's dimensions as being 350 yards by 250 yards by 8 or 10 feet.[9] Bauerman's own statement,[10] however, is that the slag forms a roughly elliptical heap, about 350 yards long and 200 yards in breadth, the depth being very variable and probably not more than 8 to 10 feet at the most, but that over the greater part of the area the slag forms only a

---

[1] J. Ball, *Geog. and Geol. of South-Eastern Desert*, p. 353; C. M. Firth, *Arch. Survey of Nubia, 1908–1909*, p. 24.

[2] T. A. Rickard, *Man and Metals*, I, p. 196.

[3] E. Rüppell, *Reisen in Nubien, Kordofan und dem petraischen Arabien*, p. 266.

[4] Result kindly supplied by Mr. G. A. Garfitt, Hon. Sec. Sumerian Committee, British Association.

[5] Figures kindly supplied by Dr. W. F. Hume.

[6] J. Wells, *Report of the Dept. of Mines*, 1906, p. 34.

[7] Kindly communicated by Mr. R. S. Jenkins, Insp. Dept. Mines and Quarries.

[8] W. M. F. Petrie, *Researches in Sinai*, p. 27.

[9] Anon., 'The Copper of Sinai', *Mining and Scientific Press*, Sept. 1919, pp. 429–30.

[10] H. Bauerman, *Quart. Journ. Geol. Soc.*, xxv (1869), p. 29.

thin coating on the rock. G. W. Murray of the Desert Surveys of Egypt, who measured the slag in 1929, found two heaps: '(1) An area roughly 230 × 110 metres,
with an average depth of 1 metre; (2) an area of 100 × 60 metres, very irregular, but
very thin.' [1]

Petrie's estimate for the amount of slag present is 100,000 tons, but Rickard, taking
Bauerman's measurements, makes the amount only 50,000 tons,[2] which seems much
too small for the dimensions given (which are in yards for the length and breadth
and not in feet, as in the case with Petrie's measurements) and if an average depth of
only two feet be allowed the result would be 118,000 tons.

In order to arrive at the weight of the slag it is necessary to know, not only the
measurements of the heap, but also the specific gravity of the material, and this does
not seem to have been determined, but only guessed. In the absence of specimens of
the Wadi Nasb slag, I determined the specific gravity of five specimens of similar
copper slag from Seh Baba, which were found to vary from 3.1 to 3.5, with a mean
of 3.36, and this will be assumed to be approximately correct also for the Wadi
Nasb slag. On this basis the calculated weight of the slag is as follows:

(a) From Petrie's dimensions, 98,000 tons, which is very close to Petrie's own
estimate of 100,000 tons.

(b) From Bauerman's dimensions, probably not less than 100,000 tons, since with
an average depth of only two feet the amount would be 118,000 tons.

(c) Murray's dimensions about 90,000 tons.

Rickard states the slag contains 2.75 per cent of copper,[3] which on 100,000 tons
of slag represents 2,750 tons of copper: he assumes this to be one-third the copper
content of the ore and therefore that two-thirds of the copper, or 5,500 tons, were
extracted.[4]

Slag Heap at Seh Baba. The dimensions of one heap as given by Petrie are 80 feet
by 60 feet,[5] but another estimate is 50 feet by 50 feet by 1 foot.[6] Greaves, however,
states that both these estimates are too high for the slag now present, but he also says
that the heap is gradually being washed away.[7] The specific gravity of the slag, as
already stated, is 3.36. The weight of the slag, therefore, from the dimensions given,
would be either 450 tons or 235 tons, according to which estimate is taken, and the
amount of copper extracted, represented by this slag, would be either 25 or 13 tons.

Slag Heap at Kubban. This heap is 105 feet long and 13 feet broad,[8] but the height

---

[1] G. W. Murray, private communication.

[2] T. A. Rickard, 'Copper and Gold Mines of the Ancient Egyptians', *Eng. and Mining Journal-Press,* June 20th, 1925, p. 1006.

[3] A specimen of slag, probably that from Wadi Nasb, analysed by Sebelien (*Ancient Egypt*
1924, p. 10) contained 21.65 per cent of copper. This slag, however, is not only not of uniform
composition, some being strongly fused and very hard, black and glassy-looking, and some being
very green and only partly fused, but it contains metallic copper, both in large pieces and in coarse
grains and, unless properly sampled by a competent person, an analysis of an isolated specimen is
likely to be misleading. Mr. G. W. Murray informed me that one specimen analysed gave 2.3
per cent of copper.

[4] T. A. Rickard, *Man and Metals,* I, pp. 196–7.   [5] W. M. F. Petrie, *Researches in Sinai,* p. 18.

[6] By Mr. R. S. Jenkins, Insp. Dept. Mines and Quarries. Private communication.

[7] Mr. R. H. Greaves, formerly Controller, Dept. of Mines and Quarries, private communication.

[8] Kindly measured for the author by Tewfiq Effendi Boulos, Chief Inspector, Dept. of
Antiquities, Upper Egypt, who also supplied specimens.

cannot easily be measured on account of the accumulated sand. Let it be assumed to be 2 feet. The specific gravity of the two specimens determined by the author was 2.8 and 3.0 respectively, or a mean of 2.9. The total amount of slag, therefore, is 220 tons and, if the amount of copper in the original ore and the proportion extracted be assumed to have been the same as for Sinai, this heap will represent about 12 tons of copper.

On the evidence of the slag heap at Wadi Nasb, the amount of metallic copper yielded anciently by the Sinai mines up to the date of this heap was at minimum 5,500 tons, though probably more. This must be supplemented by the amount smelted at Magharah, Seh Baba, Gebel Safariat, the plain of Senned and the hill region of the extreme south-east, which together was probably considerable, though except for a portion of that from Seh Baba, no estimate is possible. To the copper from Sinai (assuming that it was worked by the Egyptians) must be added that extracted from the mines of the eastern desert, for which the only basis for an estimate is the slag heap at Kubban, which certainly represents only a small fraction of the total ore smelted.

In any consideration of the total amount of copper yielded by the Egyptian mines and whether or not it could have been sufficient for the needs of the country until about the Eighteenth Dynasty, when admittedly copper was imported from Asia, it should not be forgotten that Egypt was then, as it still is, a comparatively small agricultural country where the greater proportion of the people did not use copper and more than 5,200 years after the first use of copper in Egypt, namely in the year A.D. 1800, or only 160 years ago, when copper was employed for many more purposes and very much more extensively than in ancient Egypt, the entire world's production only amounted to 10,000 tons.[1] In relation to the amount of copper used in ancient Egypt, the product of the Sinai and eastern desert mines must have been considerable and de Morgan's opinion that the quantity of ore from Sinai (he does not appear to have known of the eastern desert supply) was 'insignificant' [2] and that 'Egypt must be ruled out absolutely from among the copper-producing countries' [2] may be questioned. Although Lepsius did mistake the manganese ore capping some of the Sinai peaks for copper slag (he writes of 'great slag-hills' [3] and 'artificial mounds' 'covered with a massive crest of slag') [3] this in no way either destroys or lessens the value of the facts respecting the number and extent of the ancient workings for copper ore and the ancient slag heaps that have been enumerated.

Date of Earliest Mining

Owing to the fact that both turquoise and copper ore occur in the only two localities in Sinai where inscriptions have been found, namely at Magharah and Serabit el Khadim, and since both materials were used at an equally early date [4] (as

---

[1] R. Allen, *Copper Ores*, p. 1.

[2] J. de Morgan, *Prehistoric Man*, p. 114.

[3] R. Lepsius, *Discoveries in Egypt, Ethiopia and the Peninsula of Sinai*, p. 348.

[4] Copper ore (malachite), metallic copper and turquoise were all used in the Badarian period (G. Brunton and G. Caton-Thompson, *Badarian Civilisation*, pp. 27, 41, 56). Mr. Brunton has informed me that the material originally classed doubtfully as turquoise has now been definitely identified as turquoise.

also was metallic copper), there is nothing to show whether the earliest recorded expeditions were for turquoise or copper ore, or indeed for either. That during the Old Kingdom some at least of the mining was for copper ore is suggested by the finding of mining settlements of that date with copper ore, crucibles, copper slag, waste scraps from smelting and an ingot mould.[1] The fact, too, that a copper axe-head of middle predynastic date [2] and also the copper of which certain metal bands of First or Second Dynasty date [3] were composed contained manganese, is a very strong indication that the original copper ore had been obtained from the neighbourhood of the manganese ore deposits in Sinai, that is probably from Magharah, and, if so, then the Sinai ore was being smelted for copper as early as the middle predynastic period.

A stela has recently been found in the desert south-east of Aswan dating from the reign of Senwosret I (Twelfth Dynasty), on which it is stated that a certain official named Hor had been ordered by the king to collect 'copper of the Land of Nubia'.[4] This and the slag heap at Kubban are the sole evidence at present of any date in connexion with mining in the eastern desert, the fort at Kubban having certainly been occupied during the Empire, but not earlier than the Twelfth Dynasty.[5] It should be noted that in the enumeration of tribute taken by the Egyptians at various times from the peoples who dwelt to the south, there is no mention whatever of copper, thus suggesting that the copper mining in the eastern desert was always in the hands of the Egyptians and not of the Nubians. Strabo possibly refers to the eastern desert of Egypt when, in describing Ethiopia, he says that 'There are also mines of copper, iron and gold' [6] and Diodorus has practically the same statement, namely, 'It is said there are in it (i.e. in Ethiopia) mines of gold, silver, iron and brass . . .' [7] but the geography of this time was very vague, and southern Ethiopia, which was in the Sudan, or even the Sudan generally, where such mines exist, may have been meant, rather than the northern part of Ethiopia, which was in Egypt.

The earliest certain references to the importation of copper into Egypt from abroad are of the Eighteenth and Nineteenth Dynasties,[8] when copper was received from Retenu[9] and Djahi[10] in Syria; from Arrapachitis[11] in western Asia (which is thought to be the modern Kirkuk, situated between the two branches of the Zab river in Mesopotamia); from Asia;[12] from God's Land [13] (a name used to designate several different and widely separated places, including countries in western Asia, the eastern desert of Egypt and Punt); and from Isy [14] (which is often stated to mean Cyprus, but which Wainwright has shown not to be Cyprus, but a country situated on the coast of north Syria).[15]

---

[1] W. M. F. Petrie, *Researches in Sinai*, p. 51.

[2] See p. 200, *n.* 4.

[3] W. M. F. Petrie, *Royal Tombs*, II, p. 40.

[4] A. Rowe, *Ann. Serv.*, XXXIX (1939), pp. 188–91

[5] C. M. Firth, *Arch. Survey of Nubia, 1909–1910*. p. 5; A. E. P. Weigall, *Guide to the Antiquities of Upper Egypt*, pp. 525–7; W. B. Emery and L. P. Kirwan, *Excavations and Survey between Wadi Es-Sebua and Adindan, 1929–1931*, I, pp. 26–44.

[6] XVII: 2, 2.   [7] I: 3.   [8] Cf. J. R. Harris, *Lexicographical Studies*, pp. 56–57.

[9] *A.R.*, II, 447, 471, 491, 509, 790.   [10] *A.R.*, II, 459, 460, 462, 490.   [11] *A.R.*, II, 512.

[12] *A.R.*, II, 45, 104, 175, 614, 755; III, 217, 537, 910.   [13] *A.R.*, II, 274.

[14] *A.R.* II, 493, 511, 521.   [15] G. A. Wainwright, *Klio*, XIV (1915), pp. 1–36.

Presents of copper from Asia to Egypt in the Eighteenth Dynasty included 5 talents, 9 talents, 18 talents, 80 talents, 200 talents and 'much copper'.[1]

Copper Ores

The copper ores found in Egypt (including Sinai) are principally azurite, chrysocolla, malachite and sulphide, whose occurrence has already been dealt with in connexion with the ancient mines, but which may now be considered in greater detail.

Azurite is a beautiful deep-blue basic carbonate of copper that occurs in copper deposits and is found both in Sinai and in the eastern desert: being an oxidized product derived from the decomposition of copper sulphide, azurite always occurs at or near the surface and hence is found and worked easily: it does not occur in any great amount and is not nearly so plentiful as malachite, with which it is generally associated. Azurite was employed anciently in Egypt both as a source of metallic copper and as a pigment,[2] until for the latter purpose it was displaced by an artificial blue frit, and it is probable that it was used in the production of blue glaze.[3] A single instance of the use of azurite for beads has also been recorded.[4]

Chrysocolla is a blue or bluish-green ore of copper that chemically consists of the silicate: it occurs both in Sinai and in the eastern desert of Egypt, in both of which places it appears to have been worked anciently to a small extent as a source of metallic copper. Apart from this use of the ore, and its occasional employment as an eye-paint,[5] the only examples of chrysocolla from ancient Egypt that can be traced, are one fashioned into a small figure of a child that was found in a predynastic grave at Hierakonpolis,[6] and what may have been a preparation of chrysocolla for use, with a reducing agent, in soldering gold.[7]

Malachite is a green basic carbonate of copper that was the principal and earliest ore of copper used anciently, because, like azurite, it is an oxidized product derived from the decomposition of copper sulphide, and therefore is the ore found on the surface of most copper ore deposits: it occurs in Egypt both in Sinai and in the eastern desert, from one or both of which places the early supply was derived.

The use of malachite in Egypt goes back to the Badarian period, from which time onwards, until at least the Nineteenth Dynasty, it was employed as an eye-paint:[8] it was used, too, at an early date as a pigment for mural painting [9] and for other purposes, including the very important one of colouring glaze and glass,[10] and very occasionally also for making beads, amulets and other small objects;[11] but the principal value of malachite in Egypt was as a source of metallic copper, and it is the richest in copper of all the ores.

Copper Mining

Copper ores, principally malachite, almost certainly were obtained at first and for a long period entirely from surface deposits without any attempt at underground

---

[1] S. A. B. Mercer, *Tell-el-Amarna Tablets*, I, pp. 191, 199, 205.   [2] See p. 340.

[3] U. Hölscher, *Excavation of Medinet Habu*, II, p. 91.

[4] W. F. Hume, *Geology of Egypt*, II, Part III, p. 980.   [5] See p. 81.

[6] J. E. Quibell and F. W. Green, *Hierakonpolis*, II, p. 38; J. E. Quibell, *Hierakonpolis*, I, p. 7.

[7] R. Mond and O. H. Myers, *Temples of Armant*, I, p. 201.

[8] See p. 80.   [9] See pp. 344–5.   [10] See pp. 172–3.   [11] See p. 400.

mining. For extracting the ore nothing more elaborate than crude stone (flint) tools would have been required, but for cutting shafts at a later date, to follow the vein of ore underground, copper chisels undoubtedly were employed and suitable chisels existed from the late predynastic period onwards. In the Sinai mines Petrie found evidence of the use of copper chisels only, and not of stone tools for cutting the rock.[1]

Copper Smelting

After the ore had been mined it probably was crushed and hand picked and then smelted.

At the present day copper is obtained from its ores by means of an elaborate series of complicated metallurgical operations conducted in special furnaces, the exact nature of the operation and the type of furnace used depending upon the kind of ore dealt with. It is not proposed to describe these methods, but the treatment in its simplest form of the oxidized class of ores to which malachite belongs, may be mentioned. It consists in mixing the ore with coke and suitable fluxes and heating in a furnace provided with a blast. The ancient Egyptian substitute was to mix the broken ore with charcoal in a heap on the ground, or in a shallow pit, this sometimes being situated in a special position, such as the side of a hill, or in a valley, as in the case of the Wadi Nasb in Sinai, in order to take full advantage of the wind, the fact that a current of air caused the fire to burn more fiercely clearly having been noticed at a very early period. At a later date bellows were used.

Currelly found in Sinai the remains of an ancient furnace that had been used for smelting copper ore: it consisted of a hole in the ground about two and a half feet deep surrounded by a stone wall, through which there were two blast holes.[2]

Since copper melts at $1,083°$ C., this is not an impossible temperature to have been obtained with the primitive methods suggested, if only a small quantity of ore were operated upon at one time. Coghlan states [3] that to smelt copper from malachite or other carbonate ore a temperature of $700°$ C. to $800°$ C. is sufficient.

As a result of experiments in simple methods of smelting copper ores to produce metallic copper, Coghlan has suggested [4] that copper was first produced accidentally, not in a camp fire, hole in the ground, or other open fire, as has generally been supposed, but in a pottery kiln, that is in a closed chamber. This presupposes either that the discovery was made elsewhere than in Egypt (which is probably the case), or that as early as the Badarian period malachite was being used in connexion with the firing of pottery in a kiln, though Egyptian pottery was not glazed, and there is no reason why malachite should ever have been associated with the firing of pottery in Egypt.[5] It may be, however, that metallic copper was first discovered in connexion with the glazing of steatite or quartz, the latter either solid or powdered (faience core material), since it has been shown that a closed chamber must also have been used for making glazed steatite, glazed solid quartz and faience.[6] On the other

[1] W. M. F. Petrie, *Researches in Sinai*, pp. 48–49, 61, 161.

[2] C. T. Currelly, in W. M. F. Petrie, *Researches in Sinai*, pp. 242–3.

[3] H. H. Coghlan, *Antiquaries Journal*, XXII (1942), p. 27.

[4] H. H. Coghlan, *Man*, XXXIX (1939), pp. 106–8; *Trans. Newcomen Soc.*, XX (1939–40), pp. 49 f. Cf. also L. Aitchison, *History of Metals*, I, pp. 39–40.

[5] Cf. A. Lucas, *J.E.A.*, XXXI (1945), pp. 96–97.

[6] A. Lucas, *J.E.A.*, XXII (1936), p. 156. See also above, p. 174.

hand, it is possible, as Reed has suggested [1] and Coghlan now accepts,[2] that smelting was not a chance discovery, but a logical development from the melting of native copper. As Reed says, 'It seems unquestionable that the first source of supply consisted of lumps of native copper that were large enough to use, and that later they melted smaller particles to form a cake of workable size. They did not trouble to separate the copper particles from adhering minerals, depending on the melting to effect the separation. The melter would be astute enough to notice that the final cake appeared to contain more copper than appeared to be in the original material, and to observe also that the adhering mineral had suffered a change during the melting operation. He would then be led to try the effect of heat on the mineral, and be rewarded, in some cases, by obtaining metal from what was obviously not metal.'

When the smelting was finished, the unburnt and partly burned fuel probably would have been removed, so as to allow the metal to cool, which then would have been broken up into smaller pieces for use, this possibly having been done when it had just become solid, at which stage copper is peculiarly brittle and easily broken up by hammering.[3] Gowland states [4] that this method of treating copper still survived in Korea in 1884.

As pointed out by Rickard,[3] the primitive method of smelting practised must have resulted in 'a spongy mass of metal, incompletely fused and containing extraneous matter.'

Copper Working [5]

In order to shape the pieces of crude copper obtained by breaking up the mass (never very large) from the furnace and to fit them for use, necessarily they would have been hammered, since it would soon be discovered that copper was fairly soft and malleable, and this hammering would have consolidated the metal and would have freed it from some of the grosser impurities. At a later date the crude copper was probably re-melted in order to improve the quality. A crucible, probably for melting copper in order to re-melt it, or cast it, of Seventh to Eighth Dynasty date, was found by Brunton in the Qau-Badari district, of which he says [6] it 'is of rough grey clay or ash; the inside surface is vitrified in places and shows traces of copper slag. Outside it is coated with some kind of plaster. The opening is half-way down the side, and it has no spout. The height is about 5 inches.' Petrie also found crucibles that had been used for copper, of which, however, very few particulars are given.[7] As there were no such appliances at an early date as special tongs for holding hot metal, all hammering at first necessarily was done cold, which has been proved from the microscopical examination of ancient copper objects.

At a later period it was discovered that copper could be shaped more quickly and more easily by melting it and pouring it into moulds while liquid, the moulds being

---

[1] T. T. Reed, *American Journal of Archaeology*, xxxviii (1934), p. 383.

[2] H. H. Coghlan, *Prehistoric Metallurgy of Copper and Bronze*, pp. 22–23.

[3] T. A. Rickard, *Man and Metals*, I, p. 116.

[4] W. Gowland, *Journ. Royal Anthrop. Inst.*, xlii (1912), p. 241.

[5] Cf. in general, H. H. Coghlan, *Prehistoric Metallurgy of Copper and Bronze*, pp. 74–98; G. Möller, *Metallkunst*, pp. 15–35.

[6] G. Brunton, *Qau and Badari*, I, pp. 36, 67, Pl. xli (25).

[7] W. M. F. Petrie, *Researches in Sinai*, pp. 51, 162, Pl. 161; *Tools and Weapons*, p. 61.

open ones. Petrie states [1] that they were 'cut out of a thick piece of pottery and lined smooth with fine clay and ash', which seems unnecessarily complicated, since it would have been much simpler to have impressed the shape of a previously made object in wet clay and then dried and baked the clay, when it would have become a pottery mould. Stone moulds also were employed, a possible example being the one found in Sinai by de Morgan.[2] The earliest evidence of casting copper known to me is that of an axe-head of middle predynastic date found by Brunton and examined by Carpenter, who concludes 'that it was cast roughly to shape, and then either cold-hammered and annealed or hammered while hot.' [3]

The process of melting [4] the metal is frequently illustrated in tomb scenes. Blow-pipes were used for forcing the fire at least as early as the Fifth Dynasty,[5] whereas bellows are not shown before the Eighteenth Dynasty.[6] These are invariably bowl bellows, evidently known in Mesopotamia from the third millennium B.C.,[7] and their introduction into Egypt may perhaps be attributed to the Hyksos.[8]

When the cast object was a dagger, knife, or chisel, the cutting edge naturally would have been hammered to thin and shape it, and this hammering would have hardened the metal considerably, a fact that hardly could have escaped notice long. If hammered too much, however, copper becomes brittle, which also soon would have been observed and avoided, since it is not likely that the remedy for brittleness would have been discovered until much later. This remedy is to heat the copper to a temperature of from about 500° C. to 700° C. for a short time, the process being known as annealing or tempering, the tempering of copper being the softening and not hardening, as sometimes is wrongly stated. The only secret of hardening the ancient Egyptians knew was to hammer it, and the 'lost art' so often referred to is a myth. In an experiment made by Desch it was shown that copper with an initial hardness (Brinell scale) of 87 was raised to a hardness of 135 by hammering.[9] Modern steel tested in the same manner varies from 100 to 800.[10] The process of hammering 'produces an abnormal state of crystallization in which copper is harder than in the ordinary state. The abnormal state . . . would have relaxed after a certain time and the copper would have again assumed its ordinary soft state of crystallization.'[11]

Two axe-heads, one dating from the middle predynastic period and the other from about 1800 B.C., were examined by Carpenter. The Brinell hardness of the

[1] W. M. F. Petrie, *Arts and Crafts*, p. 100.

[2] J. de Morgan, *Recherches sur les origines de l'Égypte*, I, p. 229.

[3] H. C. H. Carpenter, *Nature*, CXXX (1932), pp. 625–6.

[4] Not smelting as is often stated. See G. A. Wainwright, *Man*, XLIV (1944), pp. 94–98; XLV (1945), p. 71.

[5] G. Steindorff, *Ti*, Pl. CXXXIV; P. Duell, *Mereruka*, I, Pls. XXX, XXXII; N. de G. Davies, *Deir el Gebrâwi*, I, Pl. XIV; II, Pls. X, XIX; P. E. Newberry, *Beni Hasan*, II, Pls. IV, VII, XIV. Cf. also J. H. Breasted (Jr.), *Servant Statues*, pp. 50–51.

[6] N. de G. Davies, *Rekh-mi-rē*, Pl. LII; *Puyemre*, Pls. XXIII, XXV; *Two Sculptors*, Pl. XI; *Menk-heperrasonb*, Pl. XII; H. H. Coghlan, *Prehistoric Metallurgy of Copper and Bronze*, p. 68, Fig. 10.

[7] G. A. Wainwright, *Man*, XLIV (1944), pp. 94–98; XLV (1945), p. 71; H. H. Coghlan, *Prehistoric Metallurgy of Copper and Bronze*, pp. 67–70.

[8] H. E. Winlock, *Rise and Fall of the Middle Kingdom*, pp. 166–7.

[9] C. H. Desch, 'The Tempering of Copper', *Discovery*, VIII (1927), pp. 361–2.

[10] R. A. Hadfield, *Metallurgy or Iron and Steel*, 1922, p. 44.

[11] T. W. Richards, in G. A. Reisner, *Mycerinus*, p. 232.

former was irregular, varying from 63 to 73 on the flat and increasing to a maximum of 85 near the edge, and examination of the microstructure showed that near the cutting edge the distortion of the metal was more pronounced than elsewhere, indicating that it had been more heavily worked. Carpenter concluded that the axe had been cast roughly to shape and then either cold hammered and annealed or hammered when hot, and that after this treatment it had been hardened by hammering it cold, the hammering being most severe near the edge.[1] The Brinell hardness of the latter specimen varied from about 90 on the flat to 112 at the edge, and Carpenter concluded that it had been cast to shape, worked to some extent, no doubt by cold hammering, and annealed at about 700° C., either during or after the mechanical working.[2]

The presence of arsenic in copper also adds significantly to its hardness, and Maréchal has shown experimentally that specimens containing 4.2, 5.94, and 7.92 per cent of arsenic respectively can be raised to a Vickers hardness of 195, 220, and 224 by hammering. After re-heating at 700° C. the hardness of the same specimens was only 55, 63, and 64, indicating that copper with even a high arsenic content can readily be softened to facilitate working and subsequently hardened by hammering.[3] Traces of arsenic have been found in many Egyptian copper objects, and in some the percentage present is sufficient to have produced a considerable hardening.[4]

The Egyptians at an early date became very expert in the art of working copper on a large scale, and a length of beaten copper piping has been found in the Fifth Dynasty pyramid complex of Sahurē.[5] Perhaps the most remarkable examples of copper working are the large statue of Pepi I (Sixth Dynasty) and the accompanying small statue,[6] which are the oldest Egyptian metal statues known,[7] one of them being also the largest. The metal of which these statues consist is often stated to be bronze, on the strength of an analysis quoted by Maspero [8] (who disregards it and calls the metal copper), which was made by Professor Mosso of Rome and shows 6.6 per cent of tin. There is, however, considerable probability that some confusion of samples occurred and that the specimen examined was not from the statues. The material was examined also by Dr. Gladstone,[9] who reports that the presence of tin was doubtful. I analysed a sample taken by myself from the larger statue and found the metal to be copper free from tin, and since then Professor Desch has published a detailed analysis showing 98.2 per cent of copper and no tin.[10] With respect to these statues it has never been established definitely whether they were hammered to shape, or cast, both opinions having been expressed. The finders thought that they

---

[1] H. C. H. Carpenter, *Nature*, cxxx (1932), pp. 625–6.

[2] H. C. H. Carpenter, *Nature*, cxxvii (1931), pp. 589–91.

[3] J. Maréchal, *Métaux, Corrosions, Industries*, xxxii (1957), pp. 132–3.

[4] See analyses, pp. 483–5.   [5] L. Borchardt, *Sahu-rē*, I, p. 78.

[6] J. E. Quibell and F. W. Green, *Hierakonpolis*, II, pp. 46–47.

[7] The Palermo stone, however, records that a copper statue of Khasekhemui was made during his reign (Second Dynasty), and also refers to two copper sun-boats made in the Fifth Dynasty. See K. Sethe, *Z.Ä.S.*, liii (1917), pp. 50–54; *J.E.A.*, I (1914), pp. 233–6.

[8] G. Maspero, *Guide to the Cairo Museum*, English trans., 1910, p. 73.

[9] J. H. Gladstone, in W. M. F. Petrie, *Dendereh*, pp. 61–62.

[10] C. H. Desch, 'Report on the Metallurgical Examination of Specimens for the Sumerian Committee of the British Ass.', *Report of the British Ass.*, 1928.

were hammered over a wooden core,[1] and this is also the view of Maryon and Plenderleith,[2] though Aitchison [3] has suggested that only the trunk and limbs were made of hammered sheets, while the face, feet and hands were castings, possibly made by the *cire perdue* process. In my opinion, casting on such a scale, which would have had to be done in closed moulds, would have been impossible at that period on account of the blistering that takes place due to the absorption of gases from the atmosphere when the copper is being melted and the giving off of these gases again when the copper cools. There is some evidence to suggest that certain small objects were cast in closed moulds, perhaps by the *cire perdue* process, as early as proto-dynastic times,[4] but what seem to be the earliest large castings of copper in closed moulds known in Egypt are the four copper boxes found by the French Archaeological Expedition at Tôd in Upper Egypt,[5] two of which measure approximately 30×19×13 cm., and two 45×29×19 cm., the metal being one millimetre thick. The lids slide in grooves, and on the bottom of each box there are two cross-pieces. Over large areas the metal is pitted with holes, which I believe to be 'blow' holes and not the result of corrosion, although the boxes were corroded superficially. On the larger of the two boxes in the Cairo Museum,[6] which I cleaned, there is a small patch on the under side of the lid and a very large patch (about half the area of the bottom) on the bottom. These I suggest are places where the casting failed. Although the contents of the boxes were non-Egyptian, it seems highly probable that the boxes were made in Egypt, since the inscriptions on them are in Egyptian hieroglyphs.

As excellent early examples of copper objects, the ewer and basin found by Reisner in the tomb of Hetepheres (Fourth Dynasty) [7] may be mentioned. The basin and body of the ewer have been hammered to shape, but the spout of the ewer has been cast and inserted, probably being fixed merely by cold hammering, since welding, brazing and the use of soft solder were not discovered until much later. Garland and Bannister state [8] that 'there is no positive evidence of welding or brazing of copper or bronze or of soft soldering before late Roman times'. Petrie,[9] and also Fink and Kopp,[10] mention other similar ewers and basins from royal tombs made in the same manner. At least one ewer of Old Kingdom date has the spout fastened on with copper rivets.[11]

Although soft solder was not known until late[12] there is an example of hard solder

---

[1] J. E. Quibell and F. W. Green, *Hierakonpolis*, II, pp. 46–47.

[2] H. Maryon and H. J. Plenderleith, in *History of Technology*, I, p. 641.

[3] L. Aitchison, *History of Metals*, I, p. 69.

[4] G. Möller, *Metallkunst*, p. 16; W. M. F. Petrie, *Tools and Weapons*, p. 61.

[5] F. Bisson de la Roque, *Tôd (1934 à 1936)*, Fouilles I.F.A.O., XVII (1937), pp. 114–15; F. Bisson de la Roque, G. Contenau and F. Chapouthier, *Trésor de Tôd*, Doc. de Fouilles I.F.A.O., XI, pp. 8–9; F. Bisson de la Roque, *Trésor de Tôd (Cat. Caire)*, pp. 1–2 and p. iii.

[6] Two of the boxes are now in the Louvre, Paris.

[7] G. A. Reisner, *Boston Bull.*, XXV (1927), p. 31; *History of the Giza Necropolis*, II.

[8] H. Garland and C. O. Bannister, *Ancient Egyptian Metallurgy*, p. 69.

[9] W. M. F. Petrie, *Arts and Crafts*, p. 99.

[10] C. G. Fink and A. H. Kopp, *Metropolitan Museum Studies*, IV (1933), pp. 164–5.

[11] Cairo Museum, No. J. 66924.

[12] Cf. H. H. Coghlan, *Prehistoric Metallurgy of Copper and Bronze*, pp. 97–98; H. Maryon, *Man*, XLI (1941), pp. 118–24; G. Möller, *Metallkunst*, pp. 17–19.

used for joining copper in the tomb of Hetepheres. When I was cleaning the cylindrical copper sockets in which the upright poles of the canopy rested (which are made of sheet copper formed into a cylinder with the two ends overlapping where they meet) a thin silver-white layer was noticed on both sides of the joints and between the two layers of copper. This on testing was found to consist largely, if not wholly, of silver, though the presence of a small proportion of copper cannot entirely be excluded, and it had manifestly been used as a solder. Silver solder was used to plug a hole in a bronze flower bowl of Eighteenth Dynasty date, and lead to plug holes in the model cow decorating the bowl.[1] The tubes of both the silver trumpet and the copper or bronze trumpet from the tomb of Tutankhamūn are soldered with a white solder that appears to be largely silver. The composition of a tin-lead solder from a bronze flute of late date agreed 'almost entirely with the best quality solder in present-day use',[2] and a bar of solder of unspecified date found at Gaza also consisted largely of tin and lead and was 'a true solder of quite modern type'.[3]

The plating of copper both with silver,[4] of which one example is known, and with gold,[5] of which there are numerous instances, was also practised, and copper was occasionally used to decorate gold objects.[6]

Thin sheet copper was used certainly as early as the First Dynasty for covering wood and was fastened on with copper nails, and narrow bands of thin copper were employed at an early date for binding joints in wood.

From the analyses of ancient copper objects,[7] it is evident that (as is only to be expected) the copper employed was never pure, but always contained small proportions of other ingredients, the most common of which were antimony, arsenic, bismuth, iron, manganese, nickel and tin, the total impurities generally amounting to less than one per cent, though occasionally they were more. All these impurities were derived accidentally from the ore employed, and, with the exception of the bismuth, which would be deleterious, they would harden the copper. Spectrographic analysis of several copper and bronze objets of Middle Kingdom date has also revealed the presence of magnesium,[8] which again was probably present as an accidental impurity rather than added intentionally to increase the hardness.

Statements are made sometimes with reference to the impurities in copper such as that 'Various small amounts of alloys were used to harden it, probably by mixing ores for reduction; bismuth, manganese, arsenic and tin are thus found used'[9] and 'Down to this age copper was used with only small amounts of hardening mixture'.[10] These statements, attributing to intention what was merely the result of natural conditions, are not only contrary to all probability, but are entirely unsupported by evidence. The only constituents which were certainly added intentionally to copper

[1] H. E. Winlock, *Metropolitan Museum Studies*, v (2) (1936), pp. 150, 152.
[2] R. Mond and O. H. Myers, *Bucheum*, I, p. 107 (61.49 per cent tin; 32.94 per cent lead)
[3] W. M. F. Petrie, *Ancient Gaza*, v, p. 16.
[4] See pp. 251–2.
[5] See pp. 232–3.
[6] J. D. Cooney, *Brooklyn Mus. Bull.*, XIX, No. 4 (1958), pp. 9–10.
[7] See pp. 483–5.
[8] D. Dunham, *J.E.A.,* XXIX (1943), p. 76.
[9] W. M. F. Petrie, *Social Life in Ancient Egypt*, pp. 149–50; *Egyptian Architecture*, p. 31.
[10] W. M. F. Petrie, *Arts and Crafts*, p. 100.

in Egypt were tin, which produced bronze, and lead, which was added both to copper, and, at a later period, to bronze, which it made easier to cast.

Bronze [1]

The word bronze as used today has a wide meaning, and includes a number of different alloys consisting wholly or largely of copper and tin, but in some cases containing also small proportions of other ingredients, among which zinc, phosphorus and aluminium may be mentioned. Early bronze, however, was much simpler and consisted only of copper and tin, with traces of such other ingredients as happened to be present in the raw materials employed. At a later date, as already mentioned, an addition of lead sometimes was made, but such an admixture, although of the bronze class, is not a typical or normal bronze. At the present day, ordinary bronze contains about 9 to 10 per cent of tin, but ancient bronze is more variable, the proportion of tin ranging from about 2 per cent to about 16 per cent. Tin in less proportion than about 2 per cent is due generally to the presence of a small amount of tin oxide in the copper ore, and it would be misleading to consider such a mixture to be bronze, since the production of the artificially-made alloy marks a definite stage in the history of early civilization that it is convenient and desirable to keep separate from the still earlier stage when the only metal employed was copper, although this copper was sometimes impure and might contain a trace of tin.

The advantages of bronze over copper are (a) that by the addition of small proportions of tin, up to about 4 per cent, the strength and hardness of copper is increased, particularly when hammered, though as much as 5 per cent of tin produces an alloy that becomes brittle when hammered, unless frequently annealed during the process [2] (at what date the danger of too much tin and the remedy of annealing for an overdose were discovered is not known); (b) that an addition of tin lowers the melting point of copper (copper, m.p., $1,083°$ C.: copper 95 per cent, tin 5 per cent, m.p. $1,050°$ C.: copper 90 per cent, tin 10 per cent, m.p. $1,005°$ C.: copper 85 per cent, tin 15 per cent, m.p. $960°$ C.); [3] (c) that tin 'notably increases the liquidity of the melt, thereby facilitating casting operations. Here we have the chief advantage of converting copper into bronze. Copper is a bad metal for casting, not only because it contracts on cooling . . . but on account of its tendency to absorb gases and to become porous thereby. The presence of tin checks the absorption of oxygen and other gases.' [4]

The early history of bronze is obscure, but one fact is certain, namely, that it was not discovered in Egypt, since, although it is now known that tin ore occurs in Egypt, there is no evidence and little probability that it was known or worked anciently, and more especially because bronze was used in western Asia a considerable time before it reached Egypt. Although claims have been made for both Europe

---

[1] Cf. J. R. Harris, *Lexicographical Studies*, pp. 57, 63–64, 65–66.

[2] T. A. Rickard, *Man and Metals*, I, pp. 131, 134; *Journ. Inst. Metals*, XLIII (1930), p. 316.

[3] J. W. Mellor, *Inorganic and Theoretical Chemistry*, VII, p. 355. Vickers (C. Vickers, *Metals and their Alloys*, 1923, p. 294), quoted by Rickard (T. A. Rickard, *Trans. Inst. Mining and Metallurgy*, 1934–5, p. 247) gives lower figures, namely $1,040°$ C., $994°$ C. and $944°$ C. respectively.

[4] T. A. Rickard, *Man and Metals*, I, p. 132; *Journ. Inst. Metals*, XLIII (1930), pp. 316–17.

and Africa, there is no doubt that bronze was an Asiatic discovery [1] and it has been found at Ur as early as about 3500 B.C. to 3200 B.C.,[2] and the knowledge of it must have spread from Asia to Egypt and later to Europe. Although used so early at Ur, bronze cannot have originated in southern Mesopotamia, since this country contains no metallic ores.

The simplest assumption to make with regard to the discovery of bronze is that it was an accident, and there are only four possible ways in which it could have happened, namely, first, by fusing together metallic copper and metallic tin; second, by smelting a mixture of copper ore and metallic tin; third, by smelting the naturally-occurring combined mineral of copper and tin (stannite); and fourth, by smelting either a naturally-occurring or artificially-made mixture of copper ore and tin ore. The first two methods are out of the question, unless tin were known before bronze, and all the evidence available points to a later knowledge. The third method is most improbable, not only because the combined copper-tin mineral, stannite, occurs only in small quantities and in a few localities and because, if ever it had been employed, it could never have led either to the use of the principal and only important ore (cassiterite), for the use of which at a later period there is ample proof, or to the production of metallic tin, but also because the resulting bronze would have contained a much larger proportion of tin and more sulphur than is found in early bronze. In one locality in China a lode of stannite is worked at the present day. 'The metal obtained on smelting . . . contains 42.57 per cent of tin, 49.7 of copper, 1.3 of sulphur and 1.8 of lead.' [3] Desch says,[4] too, that 'The analyses of the early bronzes offer no support for the suggestion that they were obtained accidentally by smelting minerals which contain both copper and tin. Such minerals are always of a complex character, and would not give rise to such pure alloys as the early bronzes are found to be. It would appear, therefore, that these bronzes have been made by mixing oxide ores of copper and tin, which must have been done deliberately.' Later, however, Desch says: [5] 'It seems natural to suppose that a mixed ore of copper and tin was used for the early alloys, so that the first bronzes were produced accidentally.'

Excluding, therefore, naturally-occurring minerals containing both copper and tin compounds, one is thrown back on an artifically-made mixture of the two ores, which, however, need not have been intentional in the first place, but which might have happened from the accident of the two ores having been found in close proximity, as until bronze was known there was no inducement to transport tin ore from one place to another.[6]

---

[1] This subject will be considered further in connexion with tin; see pp. 255–7.

[2] C. H. Desch, 'Report on the Metallurgical Examination of Specimens for the Sumerian Committee of the British Ass.', *Report of the British Ass.*, 1928, pp. 437–41; H. J. Plenderleith, in C. L. Woolley, *Ur Excavations, II, The Royal Cemetery*, p. 290.

[3] G. M. Davies, *Tin Ores*, p. 86.

[4] C. H. Desch, 'Third Report of the Sumerian Committee', *Report of the British Ass.*, 1930.

[5] C. H. Desch, *Trans. Newcomen Society*, XIV (1933–4), pp. 95–102.

[6] This subject has been discussed at length by me elsewhere (A. Lucas, *J.E.A.*, XIV (1928), pp. 106–7); cf. also T. A. Rickard, *Trans. Inst. Mining and Metallurgy*, 1934–5, p. 243; H. H. Coghlan, *Prehistoric Metallurgy of Copper and Bronze*, pp. 24–25.

Being of foreign origin, bronze naturally would have been scarce in Egypt for some time after it first became known and a considerable period would have elapsed before the new alloy was widely used, which is exactly what has been found. It is always assumed that, though at first imported, bronze was made eventually in Egypt, using imported copper and tin, but for this there is no direct proof. Since, however, other countries in the eastern Mediterranean (for example Greece) made bronze—otherwise there would have been no use for the tin from the west to the commerce in which Herodotus and other classical writers bear testimony—it is not unreasonable to suppose that Egypt was no exception.

Owing to the lack of a large series of chemical analyses of early Egyptian metal objects, there is still some uncertainty about the date when bronze was used first in the country. It is not unusual, too, to find in archaeological reports objects called copper or bronze without any discrimination and sometimes even called copper in one part of a report and bronze in another, as though the terms were synonymous. Disregarding these loose statements,[1] there are a few specimens of undoubted bronze that have been assigned to early periods, which may now be considered. The first in chronological order is a small piece of rod about $1\frac{1}{2}$ inches long with a square cross-section found by Petrie at Medum,[2] which, if contemporaneous with the material among which it was found, 'must be of the age of Seneferu'[2] (Fourth Dynasty, about 2700 B.C.). The finder calls it a 'freak'[3] and, although he believes it to be of the age stated, he admits that 'The only doubt can be whether it fell in from above during the work, as I did not find it myself.'[4] After this comes a ring dated by de Morgan to a little after the end of the Third Dynasty,[5] but stated by Berthelot to be of uncertain date.[6] The next in date order is a thin razor stated by Mond to be of the Fourth Dynasty, which on analysis by Desch proved to be bronze containing 8.5 per cent of tin.[7] Then comes a vase described as of the Sixth Dynasty, but about which no details are given,[6] and three 'bronze' tablets and a small 'bronze' bowl, also of the Sixth Dynasty, mentioned by Hayes,[8] From the Eleventh Dynasty there is a bowl[9] (but as this is merely stated to come from Luxor, without any further details, the dating may be wrong) and also a statuette (found at Meir and said to be the oldest bronze statuette known).[10] Not later than the Twelfth Dynasty are two bowls found by Garstang at Beni Hasan,[11] but as the analyst merely states that tin was present without giving the proportion, conceivably they might be of copper with a small natural admixture of tin, and not bronze. However, an axe or hatchet of similar date, also found by Garstang, contained a high percentage of tin and was therefore bronze.

---

[1] Cf. e.g. F. W. von Bissing, *Metallgefässe*, pp. 31, 32, 33, 42, 43, 46, 56.

[2] W. M. F. Petrie, *Medum*, p. 36; J. H. Gladstone, *P.S.B.A.*, xiv (1892), pp. 224–5.

[3] W. M. F. Petrie, *Arts and Crafts*, p. 104.

[4] W. M. F. Petrie, *Medum*, p. 36.

[5] J. de Morgan, *Recherches sur les origines de l'Égypte*, I, pp. 211–12.

[6] M. Berthelot, in J. de Morgan, *Dahchour, mars–juin 1894*, pp. 135, 139.

[7] C. H. Desch, *Report of the British Ass.*, 1933. No evidence for the date of this object is given.

[8] W. C. Hayes, *Scepter*, I, p. 128. No evidence for the identification is given.

[9] G. B. Phillips, *Ancient Egypt*, 1924, p. 89.

[10] J. de Morgan, *Recherches sur les origines de l'Égypte*, I, p. 204.

[11] J. Garstang, *Burial Customs*, pp. 43, 143, 144, 196.

From this same dynasty there are a number of other well-authenticated specimens of bronze including tools,[1] and the Middle Kingdom, therefore, may be considered as the beginning of the Bronze Age in Egypt. From the Eighteenth Dynasty [1] onwards bronze is well known and during the later periods it was employed extensively for casting small statuettes. The use of bronze, however, did not preclude a considerable use of copper; for instance in the tomb of Tutankhamūn there was more copper than bronze. Among the copper objects from this tomb there are a number of miniature implements belonging to the shawabti figures, which I analysed and found that generally they consisted of copper entirely free from tin or containing only a trace, though in a few instances there was a somewhat larger proportion, estimated to be not more than about 2 per cent.[2] One of the large metal tongues from the shrines that surrounded the sarcophagus, was also tested and proved to be of copper and probably, therefore, all the similar tongues are copper. Dr. A. Scott found the metal band round the base of the outermost shrine to be copper containing 2.5 per cent of tin.[3]

In this connexion it may be mentioned that although occasionally it may be possible to distinguish an ancient copper object from one of bronze by mere inspection, as, for instance, in the case of thin objects of beaten copper, it is never safe to trust to this for identification and certainty can come only from a chemical analysis.

The date of the earliest production of bronze by mixing and melting together the two metals has been discussed by Wainwright,[4] who describes two tomb scenes of Eighteenth Dynasty date and concludes that the innovation must have been introduced into Egypt between 1580 B.C. and 1450 B.C., probably about 1500 B.C. He suggests that the forward step was originally taken at Byblos some time between 2350 B.C. and 1600 B.C., and Schaeffer [5] also maintains that the mixing of the two metals was known at Byblos by the end of the third millenium B.C.

Bronze Working [6]

Bronze, like copper, was worked by being either hammered or cast. The value of hammering is shown by two experiments made by Desch,[7] in one of which bronze containing 9.31 per cent of tin, which had an initial hardness (Brinell scale) of 136, after hammering gave a hardness of 257, and, in the second of which, bronze containing 10.34 per cent of tin gave figures before and after hammering of 171 and 275 respectively, which, as Desch points out,[7] 'represent a very considerable hardness'.

Bronze was employed extensively in Egypt at a late date[8] for making statuettes,

---

[1] For references, see pp. 486–8. See also H. E. Winlock, *Treasure of El Lāhūn*, pp. 62, 63, 73, 74; W. C. Hayes, *Scepter*, I, pp. 241–2, 289, 296; G. A. Wainwright, *Antiquity*, XVII (1943), pp. 96–98; XVIII (1944), pp. 100–2; *Man*, XLIV (1944), pp. 94–98.

[2] A. Lucas, in H. Carter, *Tut-ankh-Amen*, III, p. 175 (Appendix II).

[3] A. Scott, in H. Carter, *Tut-ankh-Amen*, II, p. 205 (Appendix IV).

[4] G. A. Wainwright, *Antiquity*, XVII (1943), pp. 96–98; XVIII (1944), pp. 100–2.

[5] C. Schaeffer, *J.E.A.*, XXXI (1945), pp. 92–95.

[6] Cf. in general, H. H. Coghlan, *Prehistoric Metallurgy of Copper and Bronze*, pp. 74–98; G. Möller, *Metallkunst*, pp. 15–35.

[7] C. H. Desch, 'The Tempering of Copper', *Discovery*, VIII (1927), pp. 361–2.

[8] Some copper and bronze statuettes of earlier date, principally of the Middle Kingdom, are discussed by F. W. von Bissing, *Athenische Mitteilungen*, XXXVIII (1913), pp. 239–62; H. R. Hall, *Liverpool Annals*, XVI (1929), pp. 13–16.

which were cast either solid or hollow, the smaller ones usually being solid and the larger ones hollow, the limbs in human figures, especially the arms, often being cast separately and attached by means of mortise and tenon joints provided for in the casting. Not infrequently, several figures were combined into complicated groups by similar means.[1] The method of casting, which has been studied in great detail by Roeder,[2] was that known as the *cire perdue* (lost wax) process, the simplest form of which, as used for solid castings, was as follows, A model in beeswax, either formed by hand or moulded,[3] was made of the object to be cast: this was coated with a suitable material to form the mould, probably clay or a clay mixture, and embedded in sand or earth, which acted merely as a support: the whole was then heated, when the wax melted and either burnt away or ran out through the hole or holes provided to receive the molten metal and the mould became hard and rigid and ready for use: then the molten metal was poured in and allowed to cool, after which the mould was broken away and the object given the necessary finishing touches with a chisel.[4] A bronze statuette of Harpocrates, still in its original mould, has been described by Mrs. C. R. Williams.[5]

The casting of hollow objects was merely a modification of solid casting, manifestly introduced for the sake of economy, since the amount both of wax and of metal was reduced considerably. In this method, a core of quartz sand (probably mixed with a small proportion of organic material to give it sufficient plasticity to enable it to be roughly shaped) was covered with a thin coating of beeswax and the whole fashioned into the required form, which was then treated as described for solid casting, namely, by covering it with clay or clay mixture to form the mould, embedding it in sand or earth as a support and heating it, when the wax burnt off or escaped and the outer shell became hard and rigid. The molten metal was poured into the space occupied previously by the thin layer of wax between the inner core and the outer mould, and when the metal was cold the jacket was chipped away, the core as a rule being left.

Among the more interesting and spectacular examples of hollow casting may be mentioned a head, probably of Ramses III, in Hildesheim,[6] several large Osiris

---

[1] Cf. G. Roeder, *Z.Ä.S.*, LXXVI (1940), pp. 57–71; N. Bufidis and G. Roeder, *Z.Ä.S.*, LXXVII (1942), pp. 27–44.

[2] G. Roeder, *Z.Ä.S.*, LXIX (1933), pp. 45–67; *Jahrbuch Deutsch. Archäol. Inst.*, XLVIII (1933), pp. 226–63; *F.u.F.*, X (1934), pp. 401–3; *Ägyptische Bronzewerke*, pp. 187–220; *Ägyptische Bronzefiguren*, pp. 515–28. Cf. also H. H. Coghlan, *Prehistoric Metallurgy of Copper and Bronze*, pp. 58–59; P. Coremans, *Chronique d'Égypte*, XIII (1938), pp. 125–7; C. C. Edgar, *Greek Bronzes*, pp. ii–iii; *Greek Moulds*, pp. iii–xi; G. Möller, *Metallkunst*, p. 16; W. M. F. Petrie, *Tools and Weapons*, pp. 60–61; E. Vernier, *Bijouterie et Joaillerie*, pp. 100–11; L. Cayeux, *Ann. Serv.*, VIII (1907), pp. 117–8.

[3] For the production of the wax model see G. Roeder, *Z.Ä.S.*, LXIX (1933), pp. 45–67; *Jahrbuch Deutsch. Archäol. Inst.*, XLVIII (1933), pp. 228–34; *Ägyptische Bronzewerke*, pp. 192–9; *Ägyptische Bronzefiguren*, pp. 520–5.

[4] In some cases the carved effect may be due to casting from a carved wax original rather than to extensive tooling of the bronze itself. Cf. R. Raven-Hart, *Journal of Hellenic Studies*, LXXVIII (1958), pp. 87–91.

[5] C. R. Williams, *New York Historical Soc., Quarterly Bull.*, April 1919, pp. 3–7.

[6] G. Roeder, *Ägyptische Bronzewerke*, pp. 38–39, Pls. 23–26.

figures of Ramessid date,[1] a statuette of Osorkon I,[2] the statuette of Karomama in the Louvre,[3] a statuette of Horus[4] and two other Saite statuettes[5] also in the Louvre, a statuette of Horus published by Roeder,[6] and the well-known statuette of Takushet in Athens,[7] as well as a number of miscellaneous objects described by Pillet.[8]

Several specimens of core material from Egyptian bronze statuettes examined by me all consisted of blackened sand, that is, sand the particles of which were coloured black and not merely mixed with black material. The black was chiefly an iron compound together with occasionally a very small proportion of organic matter. Petrie also describes the core material as blackened sand,[9] but Edgar calls it 'a hard, gritty light-coloured composition like sand and plaster'.[10]

In what manner the core was fixed in the mould to prevent it moving about after the wax had melted and run out and before the metal was introduced is not known,[11] except that at a late date cross-supports of iron were employed.[12]

The process of casting metal (described in an accompanying inscription as from Syria) into the form of doors for the temple of Amūn at Karnak is shown in the tomb of Rekhmirē at Thebes (Eighteenth Dynasty).[13] The name of the metal being employed has been translated as copper or bronze, but it is almost certainly bronze, since the mould is certainly a closed one, for which copper would have been most unsatisfactory, especially for such a large object as a door, and bronze, besides being easier to manipulate, would have given much better results. Similar scenes of casting are depicted also in two other Eighteenth Dynasty tombs at Thebes.[14] Of what material the moulds were made it is impossible to determine from the illustrations. Half a closed stone mould for casting something in the nature of ornamental metal heads for poles or feet for furniture is in the Cairo Museum.[15] Garland and Bannister state that this 'was clearly used for making shell castings in the manner in which cheap statuettes are produced today, by filling the mould and, when a skin had solidified, pouring off the remaining liquid metal'.[16]

Alloys of different composition were sometimes used for separate parts of bronze

---

[1] R. Anthes, *Amtliche Berichte*, LIX (1938), pp. 72–76; G. Daressy, *Statues de divinités*, Nos. 38248, 38270, 38275, 38286, 38309.

[2] R. Lanzone, *Atti della Reale Accad. di Torino*, XI (1875–6), pp. 459–71.

[3] C. Boreux, *Antiquités égyptiennes, guide-catalogue sommaire* (Louvre), II, pp. 408–9, Pl. LV; Éditions 'Tel', *Les antiquités ég. du musée du Louvre*, Pl. CV.

[4] C. Boreux, *Antiquités égyptiennes, guide-catalogue sommaire*, II, pp. 565–6, Pl. LVI; Éditions 'Tel', *Les antiquités ég. du musée du Louvre*, Pls. CXX–CXXI.

[5] C. Boreux, *Antiquités égyptiennes, guide-catalogue sommaire*, II, pp. 333, 409–10, Pl. LVI; Éditions 'Tel', *Les antiquités ég. du musée du Louvre*, Pl. CVIII.

[6] G. Roeder, *Jaarbericht 'Ex Oriente Lux'*, VI (1943), pp. 265–78.

[7] G. Maspero, *Études de mythologie*, IV, pp. 259–66.

[8] M. Pillet, *Ann. Serv.*, XLIII (1943), pp. 45–65.

[9] W. M. F. Petrie, *Arts and Crafts*, p. 101.

[10] C. C. Edgar, *Greek Bronzes*, p. ii. See also C. G. Fink and A. H. Kopp, *Technical Studies*, VII (1939), pp. 116–17.

[11] W. M. F. Petrie, *Arts and Crafts*, p. 102.

[12] H. Garland and C. O. Bannister, *Ancient Egyptian Metallurgy*, pp. 39–40.

[13] N. de G. Davies, *Rekh-mi-rē*, Pl. LII.

[14] N. de G. Davies, *Puyemrê*, Pl. XXVI; *Menkheperrasonb*, Pl. XI.

[15] No. J. 37554.   [16] H. Garland and C. O. Bannister, *Ancient Egyptian Metallurgy*, p. 55.

objects, for example the bodies and handles of situlae,[1] and in some few instances composite castings involving the use of two different alloys were also attempted. A chisel, possibly of New Kingdom date, examined by Colson,[2] consisted of a blade of hard bronze[3] inserted in a 'sheath' of soft malleable bronze,[4] evidently applied to give the chisel some elasticity in resisting hammer blows. The exact method used in joining the two parts is uncertain, but it seems that either the hard core was cast in the softer sheath or the two were united by hammering at a high temperature. More recently, Young[5] has published details of a situla showing evidence of 'a technique in which a bronze casting was coated in some manner with a thin layer of a significantly different alloy of the same metal'. The core of the situla was bronze and the coating a copper-lead alloy, possibly used to simulate silver. Again the method by which the composite casting was produced is uncertain, but it is probable that the plating of copper-lead alloy was applied by dipping the bronze casting into a molten mass of the alloy after which the whole was re-chased and polished.

Copper-lead Alloys

It has already been noted that lead was added to copper and also to bronze, probably to facilitate casting, and many objects loosely described as copper or bronze are, in fact, copper-lead or copper-lead-tin alloys of this type. Among particular examples may be mentioned an Osiris figure of Ramessid date,[6] the famous tablet case of Shepenwepet,[7] an aegis of late date,[8] the outer layer of the situla referred to above,[9] and a figure of Ptolemaic date.[10]

Brass

Another alloy of copper is brass, which is a copper-zinc mixture, but this was not known until comparatively late in the history of metals, though it antedated by many hundreds of years the discovery of zinc as an individual substance and, therefore, brass, as at first produced, must have been made from copper or copper ore and zinc ore, but not from metallic zinc, and, like bronze, probably it was at first the result of an accident. Ores containing both copper and zinc compounds sometimes are found in nature, for example, in Egypt,[11] Georgia and Caucasia.

Petrie states that copper from the predynastic cemetery at Naqada contained 1.55 per cent of zinc and was therefore 'rather brass than bronze',[12] and this has recently been confirmed by the analysis of a pin from the same site, which revealed 2 per cent of zinc,[13] a proportion consistent with a natural mixture of the ores. A brass ring found in a tomb of Old Kingdom date at Armant, containing 31 per cent of zinc,

---

[1] R. Mond and O. H. Myers, *Bucheum*, I, pp. 105–6.

[2] M. A. Colson, *Ann. Serv.*, IV (1903), pp. 190–2.

[3] Copper 84.60 per cent; tin 13.30 per cent.

[4] Copper 92.60 per cent; tin 4.67 per cent.   [5] E. Young, *J.E.A.*, XLV (1959), pp. 104–6.

[6] R. Anthes, *Amtliche Berichte*, LIX (1938), p. 72. Copper 71; lead 25 per cent, approx.

[7] M. Berthelot, *Monuments Piot*, VII (1900), p. 125. Copper 49.3; lead 24.8; tin 4.5 per cent.

[8] D. Dunham, *Boston Bull.*, XXIX (1931), p. 109. Copper 69; lead 22 per cent, approx.

[9] E. Young, *J.E.A.*, XLV (1959), pp. 104–6. Copper and lead 'about equal'.

[10] W. Flight, *Journ. Chemical Soc.*, XLI (1882), p. 142, No. IX. Copper 68; lead 23 per cent, approx.

[11] See p. 205.   [12] W. M. F. Petrie and J. E. Quibell, *Naqada and Ballas*, p. 54.

[13] E. J. Baumgartel, *Cultures of Prehistoric Egypt*, II, p. 18.

was probably intrusive,[1] and a small vase of uncertain date in the Cairo Museum said to be brass[2] cannot be accepted without further analytical confirmation. 'Brass' was being shipped down the Red Sea from or through Egypt to Adulis (Massowa) in the first century A.D.,[3] and brass finger rings and earrings of late date have been found on Nubian sites.[4] A ring with 15 per cent of zinc was excavated at Gaza.[5]

GOLD AND ELECTRUM

Gold [6]

Gold is found very widely distributed in nature, chiefly in the metallic state, though practically never pure, but generally containing small proportions of silver,[7] sometimes copper and occasionally traces of iron and other metals. It occurs generally in one of two forms, either in alluvial sands and gravels, derived from the breaking down of gold-bearing rocks the debris from which has been washed into watercourses, now often dry, or in veins in quartz rock. In Egypt, gold is found in both these conditions. Owing to its local occurrence, its glittering yellow colour and to the simplicity of the treatment required to separate it for use, gold was one of the oldest metals known in Egypt, though not so old as copper, and it has been found in predynastic graves. Since the extraction of gold from sand and gravel is a simpler process than its extraction from hard rock, primitive races have usually begun gold mining with alluvial gold and the Egyptians probably were no exception to the rule.

The gold-bearing region of Egypt, which is 'immense',[8] lies between the Nile valley and the Red Sea, chiefly in that part of the eastern desert stretching south from the Qena-Quseir road to the Sudan frontier,[9] though several old workings have been found considerably north of the latitude of Qena, and many others lie beyond the confines of Egypt in the Sudan almost as far south as Dongola.[10] The greater part of this territory is in Nubia, the Ethiopia[11] of the classical writers, the modern Egyptian portion being Lower Nubia[12] (from Aswan to Wadi Halfa) and the Sudan portion Upper Nubia (from Wadi Halfa to Merowe). Referring to

---

[1] R. Mond and O. H. Myers, *Cemeteries of Armant*, I, pp. 117, 119.

[2] G. Bénédite, *Objets de toilette*, p. 56.

[3] W. H. Schoff, *The Periplus of the Erythraean Sea*, p. 24.

[4] M. F. L. Macadam, *Temples of Kawa*, II, p. 177 (probably the earliest example); C. L. Woolley and D. Randall MacIver, *Karanog*, pp. 62, 66; C. M. Firth, *Arch. Survey of Nubia, 1910–1911*, pp. 115, 157, 159, 165.

[5] W. M. F. Petrie, *Ancient Gaza*, V, p. 15.   [6] Cf. J. R. Harris, *Lexicographical Studies*, pp. 32–41.

[7] Sometimes gold objects have irregularly-distributed patches of silver, examples of which occur in the gold finger and toe stalls from the Twenty-second Dynasty tomb of Sheshonq found at Tanis in 1939 and from the tomb of another Sheshonq found at Mitrahineh.

[8] A. Llewellyn, *Bull. Inst. Mining and Metallurgy*, 352 (1934), p. 23.

[9] T. Barron and W. F. Hume, *Topog. and Geol. of the Eastern Desert*, pp. 259–62; E. S. Thomas, *Cairo Sc. Journ.*, III (1909), pp. 110–19.

[10] S. C. Dunn, *Notes on the Mineral Deposits of the Anglo-Egyptian Sudan*, p. 13; J. F. E. Moss, *Sudan Notes*, XX (1937), pp. 313–15.

[11] The term Ethiopia was employed very loosely and Abyssinia (the modern inhabitants of which call themselves Ethiopians) and the southern Sudan were sometimes included, though generally the ancient Ethiopia geographically was the equivalent of modern Nubia and did not include Abyssinia.

[12] Nubia did not become a part of Egypt until the Twelfth Dynasty.

Ethiopia, Herodotus says 'here is great plenty of gold'.[1] Dunn says 'Traces of ancient mining are found all over the Sudan north of the 18th parallel of latitude and there are at least eighty-five important old workings which can with certainty be imputed to the Egyptians or Medieval Arabs prior to the 10th century A.D.'[2] No occurrence of gold is known in Sinai, although the geological conditions are favourable and although some of the ancient texts might seem to imply that gold was obtained from that region.

The sources of Egyptian gold have been discussed in some detail by Vercoutter,[3] who divides the mines into three principal groups, (a) the northern group, in the eastern desert, round Wadi Hammamat and Wadi Abbad,[4] (b) the central group, also in the eastern desert, round Wadi Allaqi and Wadi Cabgaba, (c) the southern group, along the Nile valley itself, from Wadi Halfa to Kerma. Vercoutter shows that these three groups correspond to the ancient 'gold of Coptos', 'gold of Wawat', and 'gold of Kush' respectively, and discusses the textual evidence for the exploitation of different mines within each region, with particular reference to the exploitation and output of the mines of Kush. The gold production of Kush was initiated in the Middle Kingdom and reached its peak in the Eighteenth Dynasty, declining somewhat in the later New Kingdom, but increasing again during the Napatan period (c. 750–360 B.C.), and still continuing at an appreciable level into Meroitic times. Vercoutter examines the organization of the gold workers, and also notes that gold was probably received from regions even to the south of Kush.

Referring to alluvial (placer) gold, Rickard says[5] it is reported that in a particular district in the eastern desert there are alluvial workings of 'immense extent', the country having 'the appearance of having been ploughed' and that over an area of 100 square miles the ground has been worked to an average depth of seven feet, and Stewart states[6] that 'the whole of the small valleys in the schists are full of alluvial workings'. Some of these alluvial workings probably are comparatively modern, since gold was exploited in the eastern desert in Arab times. A few years ago Mr. A. H. Hooker, working on behalf of the Egyptian Government, found a very small amount of alluvial gold in the Wadi Korbiai in the south-eastern desert.

The total number of ancient workings in quartz has been estimated to be at least one hundred. Some of the mines were worked to a depth of about 300 feet. The ancient dumps are so poor in gold that the methods of extraction, primitive though they were, must have been very thorough.

But whether working alluvial (placer) deposits or veins in quart rock, the ancient Egyptians 'were very thorough prospectors and no workable deposits have been discovered that they overlooked'.[7]

---

[1] III: 114.   [2] S. C. Dunn, *Notes on the Mineral Deposits of the Anglo-Egyptian Sudan*, p. 13.

[3] J. Vercoutter, *Kush*, VII (1959), pp. 120–53. Cf. also T. Säve-Söderbergh, *Ägypten und Nubien*, pp. 210–14.

[4] Cf. also G. Goyon, *Nouvelles Inscriptions rupestres du Wadi Hammamat*, pp. 4–5; *Ann. Serv.*, XLIX (1949), pp. 337–92.

[5] T. A. Rickard, 'Copper and Gold Mines of the Ancient Egyptians', *Eng. and Mining Journal-Press*, 1925, p. 1008; cf. also *Man and Metals*, I, p. 206.

[6] P. C. Stewart, quoted by W. F. Hume in *Prelim. Rept. on the Geol. of the Eastern Desert*, p. 54.

[7] R. H. Greaves, and O. H. Little, 'Gold Resources of Egypt', *Report of the XV International Geol. Congress, South Africa*, 1929, pp. 123–7.

The gold industry in Egypt was revived some years ago [1] and, although it has now died down again, 84,074 ounces of fine gold of a value of over £357,914 sterling were extracted during the eighteen years from 1902 to 1919 inclusive, but during the following eight years, from 1920 to 1927 inclusive, only 2,867 ounces of a value of £13,106 were extracted.[2] Mining was discontinued, not because the gold was exhausted, but on account of the difficulty and cost of the work.

In view of the large amount of gold obtained in modern times and of that still remaining, there cannot be any doubt that the gold from the local mines provided most of the gold used in Egypt anciently, especially during the earlier periods, and that it was even sufficient to permit of export, as is proved by the El Amarna letters. Naturally, however, whenever possible additional gold was levied as tribute or taken as one of the fruits of victory after war, since it was a valuable and desirable metal to possess. The ten gold ingots weighing 6.5 kilograms of Twelfth Dynasty date found at Tôd in Upper Egypt were probably presents from abroad.[3]

Petrie's statements that 'The Asiatic gold was certainly used in the first dynasty, as it is marked by having a variable amount of silver alloy, about a sixth',[4] and that 'Gold from the Ist to the XIIth dynasty averages 16 per cent of silver, which marks it as Pactolan and not Nubian',[5] are based on a misconception of the nature of Egyptian gold, which always contains silver and often 16 per cent or more, as will be shown later. Petrie says also that in the Second Dynasty gold 'had antimony in it, which suggests a Transylvanian source, the telluride of gold and antimony'.[5] This has reference to the sard and gold sceptre of Khasekhemui, which was found by him at Abydos.[6] Peake and Fleure, elaborating Petrie's statement, say [7] '. . . a fragment of gold, found in the tomb of King Khasekhemui . . . has a red antimoniate crust.[8] Antimony combines with gold, so far as is known, only in the presence of tellurium, and the only region in the Old World in which gold and tellurium occur mixed is within the ring of the Carpathian mountains. The only rich gold-field within this ring is in Transylvania, where gold has been worked at least from Roman times onwards. . . . Meanwhile we note the possibility that gold from Transylvania found its way to Egypt about 3000 B.C.' Peake, writing later, is slightly more definite and says [9] that 'Gold from Transylvania seems to have reached Egypt before the close of the 2nd dynasty.' Heard repeats this statement in a still stronger form.[10] Myres, in

---

[1] R. H. Greaves and W. F. Hume, in W. F. Hume, *Geology of Egypt*, II, Part III, pp. 723–60. Cf. also T. A. Rickard, *Man and Metals*, I, pp. 224–8; G. Schweinfurth, *Ann. Serv.*, IV (1903), pp. 268–80.

[2] R. H. Greaves and O. H. Little, 'Gold Resources of Egypt', *Report of the XV International Geol. Congress, South Africa*, 1929, pp. 123–7; Mines and Quarries Dept., *Report on the Mineral Industry*, pp. 23, 50; *Report for 1928*, pp. 24–25, 44.

[3] F. Bisson de la Roque, *Tôd (1934 à 1936)*, Fouilles I.F.A.O., XVII (1937), pp. 116–18; F. Bisson de la Roque, G. Contenau and F. Chapouthier, *Trésor de Tôd*, Doc. de Fouilles I.F.A.O., XI, pp. 9–10; F. Bisson de la Roque, *Trésor de Tôd (Cat. Caire)*, p. 3.

[4] W. M. F. Petrie, *Arts and Crafts*, p. 83.

[5] W. M. F. Petrie, *Descriptive Sociology, Ancient Egyptians*, p. 57.

[6] W. M. F. Petrie, *Royal Tombs*, II, p. 27, Pl. IX.

[7] H. Peake and H. J. Fleure, *Priests and Kings*, 1927, pp. 14–15.

[8] This object is in the Cairo Museum, and no red colouration can be found on it.

[9] H. Peake, 'Gold', in *Ency. Brit.*, 14th ed. (1929), Vol. 2, p. 252.

[10] G. Heard, *Emergence of Man*, p. 161.

referring to this gold,[1] makes two slips, one in calling the ingredient that was found in the gold tellurium instead of antimony, there being no evidence that the gold contained tellurium, and the other in terming it a 'high percentage', whereas no statement of the proportion in which the antimony occurred has been made.[2] Since the origin of the early Egyptian gold is an important matter, these various statements about a possible Transylvanian source may be examined. Petrie says that the gold in question contained antimony, which is not doubted, as it is understood that the analysis was made by Dr. Gladstone. The proportion in which the antimony occurred, however, is not given,[2] which is to be regretted, since this information would have been valuable, but presumably it was present only in small amount, possibly as a trace. An ancient method of refining gold (how ancient is not known) was by means of sulphide of antimony, which was very liable to leave a little antimony in the gold, though, as this method was certainly not practised as early as the Second Dynasty, this does not explain the antimony in the particular gold under consideration, but it does show that the presence of antimony in gold is no proof that the gold was obtained from Transylvania.

The statement that, so far as is known, antimony combines with gold only in the presence of tellurium, is also misleading, since antimony alloys readily with gold in practically all proportions without the help of tellurium, and no evidence can be found that antimony ever forms a red antimoniate of gold.

That the gold in question was obtained from Transylvania and, therefore, that gold, especially in the form of such an ore as gold telluride, was being worked there and traded to Egypt (a country where gold occurred in abundance and as well known at the time) even in small amount, as early as the Second Dynasty (about 2800 B.C.) is so improbable that it may be disregarded. Moreover, gold telluride is grey in colour and therefore not like gold in appearance and hence probably was not known until a comparatively late date. Also it is a difficult ore from which to extract gold. And finally the gold telluride from Transylvania does not contain antimony.[3]

There are written records of gold being brought to Egypt from the South in the Twelfth Dynasty, but no record can be found of gold having been brought to Egypt from the North before the Nineteenth Dynasty. The places mentioned as sources of gold are as follows: [4]

South: Twelfth Dynasty [5] (Coptos; Nubia); Eighteenth Dynasty [6] (Highlands; Karoy; Coptos; Kush; South Countries); Nineteenth Dynasty [7] (Akita; God's Land; Karoy; Punt); Twentieth Dynasty [8] (Edfu; Emu; Coptos; Kush; Malachite Country; Negro Lands; Ombos).

North: Nineteenth Dynasty (Libya);[9] Twentieth Dynasty (Asia);[10] Twenty-second Dynasty (Khenthennofer).[11]

---

[1] J. L. Myres, 'Discovery and Early Use of Metals', *Early Man*, 1931, p. 143.

[2] Not published by Dr. Gladstone, but published by Petrie in 1940 as '$1\frac{1}{2}$% of antimony in the whole metal' (*Wisdom of the Egyptians*, pp. 91, 94).

[3] J. W. Mellor, *Inorganic and Theoretical Chemistry*, XI, p. 1.

[4] Cf. J. R. Harris, *Lexicographical Studies*, p. 33.　　[5] *A.R.*, I, 520, 521.

[6] *A.R.*, II, 262, 373, 502, 514, 522, 526, 652, 774, 889.

[7] *A.R.*, III, 37, 116, 274, 285, 286.　　[8] *A.R.*, IV, 30, 33, 34, 228, 409.

[9] *A.R.*, III, 584.　　[10] *A.R.*, IV, 26.　　[11] *A.R.*, IV, 770.

One of the oldest known maps in the world, now in the Turin Museum, is a papyrus showing a gold-bearing region in the eastern desert of Egypt. This dates from the reign of Seti I (Nineteenth Dynasty). The region has been variously identified but was probably in the Wadi Fawakhir.[1]

Gold Mining

The ancient method of treating gold ores to obtain the metal was very simple. In the case of alluvial gold, the sand or gravel was merely washed with running water, which carried away the lighter material, leaving the heavier gold particles behind, which were collected and fused into small ingots: occasionally small nuggets of gold were also found and two such nuggets were discovered at El Kab in a tomb of the archaic period.[2]

The Egyptian method of extracting gold from the veins in quartz rock is described by Agatharchides, a Greek writer of the second century B.C., who visited the mines and wrote a detailed account of what he had seen. Although the original work has been lost, the description of the gold mines has fortunately been preserved by Diodorus, who quotes it in full.[3] The rock was first cracked and broken by means of fire and then attacked by hammers and picks. The broken rock was then carried outside the mine, where it was crushed in large stone mortars to the size of peas and afterwards ground to fine powder in hand mills, this powder being washed with water on a sloping surface in order to separate the metal, which probably finally was fused into small ingots. Not all these processes were carried out at the mines themselves, and 'Only a few mines have permanent installations, huts, washing tables, furnaces, remains of melting pots and slag heaps',[4] probably belonging to a very late period. 'Usually the ancient gold mines show only a heap of broken stones and disused mills for crushing the ore. There are few traces of settlements, no washing tables, no furnaces, nor even wells.'[4] Indeed, Vercoutter[4] has found gold-washing basins, probably of Napatan or Meroitic date,[5] along the river bank, and it is evident that the washing of the ore and the subsequent treatment of the gold concentrates was done away from the mines.

The results of the analyses of various different specimens of gold from ancient Egyptian objects will be found in the Appendix,[6] from which it will be seen that the percentage of gold varies from 72.1 (17 carats) to 99.8 (23.5 carats). Mrs. Ransom Williams gives the fineness of the better quality of ancient Egyptian gold jewellery as ranging from 70.8 per cent (17 carats) to 91.7 per cent (22 carats), but mentions specimens as low as 13, 12 and 9 carats respectively.[7]

Thomas gives the results of the assay of five samples of gold from modern Egyptian mines as ranging from 84.0 per cent of gold (20 carats) to 90.3 per cent (21.5 carats),[8] assuming silver to have been the only impurity. A very considerable number of other

---

[1] See G. Goyon, *Ann. Serv.*, XLIX (1949), pp. 337–92, where previous identifications are discussed.

[2] J. E. Quibell, *El Kab*, p. 7.   [3] III: 1.

[4] J. Vercoutter, *Kush*, VII (1959), pp. 120–53 (p. 140).

[5] Cf. W. B. Emery and L. P. Kirwan, *Excavations and Survey between Wadi es-Sebua and Adindan, 1929–31*, pp. 108–11; M. F. L. Macadam, *Temples of Kawa*, II, pp. 220–1.

[6] See p. 490.   [7] C. R. Williams, *Gold and Silver Jewelry*, p. 25.

[8] E. S. Thomas, *Cairo Sc. Journ.*, III (1909), p. 112.

results taken from the actual working on a large scale of the six principal modern Egyptian mines varied from 76.0 per cent (18.2 carats) to 86.0 per cent (20.6 carats),[1] again assuming silver to be the only impurity.

Gold in the form of large rings, believed to have been alluvial gold from Abyssinia, received at the Egyptian Government Assay Office was about 91.7 per cent (22 carats) pure, and gold bars received for assay from a mine in the eastern desert were about 83.3 per cent (20 carats).

The principal impurity, and sometimes the only one of importance, in Egyptian gold is silver, with occasionally a little copper and a trace of iron.

Gold Refining

It is sometimes stated that the Egyptians knew how to refine gold before the New Kingdom, and even as early as the Eleventh or Sixth Dynasties,[2] though it is not clear on what evidence such statements are based. Judging from the results of the analyses of Egyptian gold objects,[3] gold was not purified or refined until about the Persian period (525 to 404 B.C.), and the various qualities of gold mentioned in the Harris papyrus and other texts of the Twentieth Dynasty and later almost certainly refer to different grades of native gold rather than to gold refined or purified in any way.[4] In the second century B.C. Agatharchides describes a method of refining gold practised in Egypt by heating it with lead, salt, tin and barley bran,[5] no provision, however, being made for the recovery of the silver, which must have been lost. Towards the close of the Eighteenth Dynasty and onwards gold was sometimes debased by the addition of copper, and Petrie states that many of the finger rings of the late Eighteenth Dynasty 'almost verge into copper'.[6] A ring of this nature, of late but uncertain date, analysed by me consisted of approximately 75 per cent of copper and 25 per cent of gold. A tube of what appears to be a gold-copper alloy is known from the predynastic period.[7]

Gold Working

That the Egyptian goldsmiths were craftsmen of a very high degree of skill is shown by many examples of gold work that have been preserved.[8] Among the most outstanding may be mentioned the four bracelets from Abydos [9] and that from Naga ed Der[10] (First Dynasty); the gold foil and the gold brads or rivets from Saqqara[11] (Third Dynasty); the gold bracelets and beads and the gold cosmetic receptacle from the pyramid of Sekhemkhet[12] (Third Dynasty); the gold work from the tomb

---

[1] Kindly communicated by Mr. R. H. Greaves, formerly Controller, Mines and Quarries Department, Egypt.

[2] Cf. H. Quiring, Geschichte des Goldes, pp. 6, 14–15, 38–39.   [3] See p. 490.

[4] Cf. J. R. Harris, Lexicographical Studies, pp. 34–38.

[5] Quoted by Diodorus, III: 1.   [6] W. M. F. Petrie, Arts and Crafts, p. 94.

[7] W. M. F. Petrie and J. E. Quibell, Naqada and Ballas, pp. 27–28; W. M. F. Petrie, Prehistoric Egypt, p. 27; E. J. Baumgartel, Cultures of Prehistoric Egypt, II, p. 4.

[8] Cf. C. R. Williams, Gold and Silver Jewelry, pp. 237–43; W. F. Hume, Geology of Egypt, II, Part III, pp. 700 f. For predynastic gold work see E. J. Baumgartel, Cultures of Prehistoric Egypt, II, pp. 3–6.

[9] W. M. F. Petrie, Royal Tombs, II, pp. 16–19, Pl. I.

[10] G. A. Reisner, Naga-ed-Dêr, I, pp. 30–31, 143–4.

[11] C. M. Firth, J. E. Quibell and J.-P. Lauer, Step Pyramid, I, pp. 140–1.

[12] Z. Goneim, Horus Sekhemkhet, I, pp. 13–14.

of Queen Hetepheres [1] (Fourth Dynasty); a gold belt of the Fifth or Sixth Dynasty; [2] the gold head of the hawk from Hierakonpolis [3] (Sixth Dynasty); the gold work found at Dahshur [4] and Lahun,[5] including diadems, pectorals, bracelets, anklets, etc. (Twelfth Dynasty); the jewellery of Queen Ahhotpe;[6] that of three princesses of the time of Thutmose III;[7] the treasure from the tomb of Tutankhamūn [8] (all Eighteenth Dynasty); the jewellery of Ramessid date from the Serapeum; [9] the Tell Basta hoard; [10] and the treasure of the kings of the Twenty-first and Twenty-second Dynasties from Tanis.[11] Some of the operations connected with gold working and the making of jewellery are illustrated on the walls of tombs,[12] for example in the tombs of Ti [13] and Mereruka [14] at Saqqara (Fifth Dynasty), in a tomb at Beni Hasan (Twelfth Dynasty) [15] and in the tomb of Rekhmirē at Thebes (Eighteenth Dynasty).[16]

Even as early as the Fourth Dynasty the ancient goldsmiths were manifestly able to manipulate comparatively large amounts of gold at one time, as shown by the gold work on the canopy of Hetepheres, and by the time of the Eighteenth Dynasty they were making solid gold coffins like that of Tutankhamūn, which is 6 feet 1¾ inch long, weighs approximately 296 pounds troy (110.4 kilograms) and is engraved inside as well as outside.

Gold was shaped both by hammering and casting (it melts at 1,063° C., or 20° C. lower than copper); it was engraved and embossed; it was used in the form of granules for decorative purposes; it was made into thin sheets for covering furniture, wooden coffins and other objects such as the rims of stone vessels, and for plating copper and silver; it was beaten into still thinner leaf for gilding; it was cast, beaten or cut into strips that were drawn into wire;[17] it was coloured, soldered[18] and burn-

---

[1] G. A. Reisner, *Boston Bull*, xxv (1927), Supplement; xxvi (1928), pp. 76–88; xxvii (1929), pp. 83–90; xxx (1932), pp. 56–60; *History of the Giza Necropolis*, II, pp. 23–47.

[2] E. Drioton, *Bull. Inst. d'Ég.*, xxvi (1944), pp. 77–90; A. Yousef, *Ann. Serv.*, LIV (1957), pp 149–51.

[3] J. E. Quibell, *Hierakonpolis*, I, p. 11; J. E. Quibell and F. W. Green, *Hierakonpolis*, II, p. 27.

[4] J. de Morgan, *Dahchour, mars-juin 1894; 1894–1895*; E. Vernier, *Bijoux et Orfèvreries*.

[5] G. Brunton, *Lahun*, I; H. E. Winlock, *Treasure of El Lāhūn*.

[6] F. W. von Bissing, *Ein Thebanischer Grabfund*.

[7] H. E. Winlock, *Treasure of Three Egyptian Princesses*.

[8] H. Carter, *Tut-ankh-Amen*, I–III.   [9] A. Mariette, *Le Sérapéum de Memphis*.

[10] C. C. Edgar, in G. Maspero, *Musée égyptien*, II, pp. 93–108, Pls. XLIII–LV; W. K. Simpson, *American Journal of Archaeology*, LXIII (1959), pp. 29–45.

[11] P. Montet, *Kêmi*, IX (1942), pp. 1–95; *Nécropole royale de Tanis*, I–III; *Monuments Piot*, XLI (1946), pp. 5–22.

[12] Cf. P. Montet, *Scènes de la vie privée*, pp. 275–87; L. Klebs, *Reliefs, A.R.*, pp. 84–86; *M.R.*, pp. 108–13; *N.R.*, pp. 107–21.

[13] G. Steindorff, *Ti*, Pl. CXXXIV.

[14] P. Duell, *Mereruka*, Pls. XXIX–XXX, XXXII–XXXIII.

[15] P. E. Newberry, *Beni Hasan*, I, Pl. XI.   [16] N. de G. Davies, *Rekh-mi-rē*, Pls. LIII, LV.

[17] G. Möller, *Metallkunst*, pp. 30–31; E. Vernier, *Bijouterie et Joaillerie*, pp. 58–62; *B.I.F.A.O.*, VIII (1911), pp. 28–31; XII (1916), pp. 40–42; C. R. Williams, *Gold and Silver Jewelry*, pp. 39–43. Petrie's statement (*Arts and Crafts*, p. 90) that drawn wire was not known is incorrect.

[18] Some of the gold 'sequins' from the tomb of Tutankhamūn have shanks at the back which are soldered on with gold of a slightly lower melting-point than that of the sequin, cf. A. Lucas, *Ann. Serv.*, XLI (1942), p. 146. For other examples of gold-soldering see, C. R. Williams, *Gold and Silver Jewelry*, pp. 37–39; E. Vernier, *Bijouterie et Joaillerie*, pp. 68–71; G. Möller, *Metallkunst*, pp. 17–19; H. Maryon, *Man*, XLI (1941), pp. 118–24.

ished, and, in fact, there are few of the modern practices of gold working that were not known and employed in ancient Egypt, many of them at a very early date. The details of the methods used in making jewellery and the construction of individual pieces have been studied and described by Moller,[1] Petrie,[2] Schäfer,[3] Vernier,[4] Mrs. Williams,[5] Winlock[6] and others.[7]

Gold Foil and Leaf

Specimens of sheet gold (foil) measured by me have varied from 0.17 mm. to 0.54 mm. in thickness, and the leaf has varied from 0.01 mm. to 0.09 mm. Petrie states that it 'was often about a 5,000th of an inch thick',[8] or 0.0051 mm., three specimens examined by Berthelot[9] were 0.001 mm. thick, and gold leaf from the Bucheum had an average, thickness of 0.0005 in.,[10] or approximately 0.013 mm. The ancient gold leaf, however, was not nearly as thin as the modern, which ranges from 0.00008 to 0.0002 mm. in thickness,[11] though it was as thin as any produced in Europe until as recently as the eighteenth century.[12] The size of the leaf probably varied, that on a coffin in the British Museum averaging 8.5 cm. square.

When thick sheet gold, which was generally embossed or engraved, was employed for decorating wooden objects,[13] it was put directly on to the wood, hammered into shape, and fastened in place with small gold rivets, as, for example, the gold foil on the plywood coffin of Third Dynasty date from Saqqara[14] and that on the first coffin of Queen Meryetamūn (Eighteenth Dynasty).[15] When thinner sheet gold was used, as in the case of the dummy vases from the mortuary temple of Neferirkarē (Fifth Dynasty),[16] the wood was generally first covered with a layer of special plaster (gesso) to which the gold was attached by means of an adhesive, probably glue, though occasionally, as on the first coffin of Queen Meryetamūn,[15] the thinner foil was glued directly to the wood. For gilding with the still thinner gold leaf, a similar layer of plaster was used, though the nature of the adhesive is not certain, and Laurie believes

---

[1] G. Möller, *Metallkunst*, pp. 15–57.

[2] W. M. F. Petrie, *Royal Tombs*, II, pp. 17–19; *Arts and Crafts*, pp. 83–96.

[3] H. Schäfer, *Ägyptische Goldschmiedearbeiten*.

[4] E. Vernier, *Bijoux et Orfèvreries; Bijouterie et Joaillerie*, pp. 52–141; *B.I.F.A.O.*, VI (1908), pp. 181–92; VIII (1911), pp. 18–41; XII (1916), pp. 38–40.

[5] C. R. Williams, *Gold and Silver Jewelry; M.M.A. Bull.*, X (1915), pp. 117–20.

[6] H. E. Winlock, *Treasure of El Lāhūn; Treasure of Three Egyptian Princesses; Ann. Serv.*, XXXIII (1933), pp. 135–9; *M.M.A. Bull.*, XXXII (1937), pp. 173–5.

[7] Cf. J. de Morgan, *Dahchour, mars–juin 1894; 1894–1895*; M. Berthelot, *Monuments Piot*, VII (1900), pp. 121–41; H. Maryon, *American Journal of Archaeology*, LIII (1949), pp. 93–125; H. Maryon and H. J. Plenderleith, in *History of Technology*, I, pp. 623–62; P. Montet, *Scènes de la vie privée*, pp. 275–87; N. de G. Davies, *Rekh-mi-rē*, pp. 52–54.

[8] W. M. F. Petrie, *Arts and Crafts*, p. 96.

[9] M. Berthelot, *Ann. Serv.*, II (1901), pp. 160–1.

[10] R. Mond and O. H. Myers, *Bucheum*, I, p. 109.

[11] Sir E. Thorpe, *Dict. of Applied Chemistry*, 1912, III, p. 781.

[12] L. Aitchison, *History of Metals*, I, p. 173.

[13] Cf. G. Möller, *Metallkunst*, p. 32.

[14] C. M. Firth, J. E. Quibell and J.-P. Lauer, *Step Pyramid*, I, p. 141.

[15] H. E. Winlock, *Meryet-Amūn*, p. 18.

[16] L. Borchardt, *Nefer-ir-ke-rē*, pp. 59–67; G. Möller, *Metallkunst*, p. 34.

that in one case he has found evidence of the use of white of egg for this purpose.[1] In the particular example investigated by Laurie there was a layer of yellow ochre between the plaster and the gold leaf, and on an object from the tomb of Tutankhamūn skin was embedded in the gesso to form a resilient backing for the leaf.[2]

Gold and other metals were also used for architectural decoration, and during the New Kingdom and later, obelisks, columns, doors, walls and reliefs were often overlaid with sheet metal.[3] In a tomb of the First Dynasty at Saqqara strips of gold foil were used to decorate the wooden facings of pilasters.[4]

Gold Plating [5]

Both copper and silver were plated with gold. The plating of copper was done in two different ways: one in which thin sheet gold was hammered on to the copper, and the other where thin gold leaf was fastened on with an adhesive, which, in the specimens that have been tested, is soluble in water and is, therefore, probably gum or glue. Examples of the former technique [6] are (*a*) two copper rods plated with gold from the First Dynasty; [7] (*b*) a small button seal of about the Sixth Dynasty kindly shown to me by Guy Brunton; (*c*) one ibis amulet (probably two),[8] and several objects, probably bracelets,[9] found by Brunton and dating from the period Seventh to Eighth Dynasty; and (*d*) a gold-plated copper collar from the Twelfth Dynasty. Examples of the latter technique are the large 'marguerites', probably of copper, that were sewn to the linen pall from the tomb of Tutankhamūn,[10] and possibly also the apparently identical 'marguerites' from the so-called tomb of Queen Tiy,[11] as well as perhaps the gilding of the toe-nails of the copper statue of Pepi I and the smaller statue found with it.[12] In the case of a copper diadem of Old Kingdom date, now in Boston,[13] and eight copper feathers of the Sixth Dynasty found by Petrie at Abydos,[14] the gold leaf was laid on a gesso base attached to the copper with a linen backing.

As instances of the gold plating of silver may be mentioned the Twenty-second Dynasty pectoral and the dagger blade both cleaned by me [15] and described by

---

[1] A. P. Laurie, *Analyst*, LVIII (1933), p. 468; *Technical Studies*, II (1933–4), pp. 213–16; in R. Mond and O. H. Myers, *Bucheum*, I, pp. 68–69.

[2] H. J. Plenderleith, *Conservation of Antiquities and Works of Art*, p. 21.

[3] Somers Clarke and R. Engelbach, *Ancient Egyptian Masonry*, p. 205; L. Borchardt, *Allerhand Kleinigkeiten*, pp. 1–11; P. Lacau, *Ann. Serv.*, LIII (1956), pp. 221–50; F. Daumas, *Revue de l'histoire des religions*, CXLIX (1956), p. 1, n. 1; *Les Mammisis des temples égyptiens*, pp. 152–8; H. W. Fairman, *Orientalia*, XXX (1961), p. 223; P. Gilbert, *Chronique d'Égypte*, XXIV (1949), pp. 223–34; J. Yoyotte, *Chronique d'Égypte*, XXVIII (1953), pp. 28–38; C. Desroches Noblecourt, *Rev. d'Ég.*, VIII (1951), pp. 47–61.

[4] W. B. Emery, *Great Tombs*, II, p. 11.

[5] Cf. G. Möller, *Metallkunst*, pp. 32–35; E. Vernier, *Bijouterie et Joaillerie*, pp. 132–5.

[6] G. Möller, *Metallkunst*, p. 32.

[7] W. M. F. Petrie, *Royal Tombs*, II, p. 36.

[8] G. Brunton, *Qau and Badari*, II, p. 12.

[9] G. Brunton, *Qau and Badari*, I, pp. 34, 66.

[10] H. Carter, *Tut-ankh-Amen*, II, p. 33, Pl. IV; A. Lucas, in H. Carter, *op. cit.*, p. 172 (Appendix II).

[11] T. M. Davis, *Tomb of Queen Tîyi*, p. 40.

[12] G. Möller, *Metallkunst*, p. 34.

[13] D. Dunham, *Boston Bull.*, XLIV (1946), pp. 23–29.

[14] W. M. F. Petrie, *Abydos*, II, p. 32, Pl. XXI.

[15] A. Lucas, *Ann. Serv.*, XXIV (1924), pp. 15–16.

Vernier,[1] and the ear-rings of New Kingdom date also described by Vernier,[2] which are plated with electrum.

Möller maintains that fire gilding was known as early as the Middle Kingdom and was common from the Eighteenth Dynasty onwards,[3] but these statements require confirmation.

Gold Colouring

One very noticeable feature of ancient gold is its varied colour, which comprises bright yellow, dull yellow, 'green', grey and various shades of red, including reddish-brown, light-brick colour, blood colour, dull purple (purple-plum colour) and a very remarkable rose-pink, all, except the last-named, probably being fortuitous. The bright yellow gold is fairly pure; the dull and tarnished yellow contains small proportions of other metals, such as silver and copper, which where exposed have undergone chemical change. The 'green' and grey gold contains a large proportion of silver, which on the surface has become converted into chloride of silver, that has darkened in the manner usual with this compound. The reddish-brown colour gives the tests for iron and copper and is evidently due to these metals having become oxidized. In some instances a red or purple colour has proved to be a staining of the gold by organic matter. The rose-pink colour occurs on a number of objects in the Cairo Museum, for example, on a gold 'marguerite' from the so-called 'Tomb of Queen Tiy' (Eighteenth Dynasty), on the diadem from the tomb of Queen Tewosret [4] (Nineteenth Dynasty) and on the earrings of Ramses XI (Twentieth Dynasty), but more particularly on a number of the gold objects from the tomb of Tutankhamūn, which latter was reported upon several years ago by me as follows:[5] 'The rose colour can be proved by chemical analysis not to be due to any colloidal modification of the gold, nor to any sort of organic lacquer or varnish, and the gold can be made red-hot without the colour being removed or diminished, but in some instances rather enhanced. The coloured film, however, is so extremely thin, being probably less than one hundred-thousandth of an inch in thickness, that without more material than it is desirable to use, chemical analysis becomes very difficult. A trace of iron is the only metal found so far, and since it is well known that native gold is sometimes reddened by being coated with a translucent film of oxide of iron, it is suggested that the colour in question is probably due to oxide of iron, but in what manner it was produced is not known, as it occurs on both sides of most objects on which it is present. This suggests that the object may have been dipped in a solution of an iron salt and then heated. That this colour is intentional is shown by its regular and systematic distribution on certain objects or on certain parts of objects.' The predictions that the rose-pink colour was due to a film of iron oxide and that it had been produced by heating have been confirmed by Professor R. W. Wood of the John Hopkins University, Baltimore, who has reproduced the colour so exactly that put side by side

---

[1] E. Vernier, *Bijoux et Orfèvreries*, pp. 240–1, 378–9, Pls. LXIII–LXIV, LXXVII; *B.I.F.A.O.*, XXV (1925), pp. 167–73.

[2] E. Vernier, *Bijoux et Orfèvreries*, pp. 130–1; *B.I.F.A.O.*, VIII (1911), pp. 38–39.

[3] G. Möller, *Metallkunst*, p. 34.

[4] T. M. Davis, *Tomb of Siphtah*, plate without number entitled 'Gold Bracelets and Ornaments of Queen Taousret' on which a rosette (possibly from the diadem) is coloured rose-pink.

[5] A. Lucas, in H. Carter, *Tut-ankh-Amen*, II, p. 174 (Appendix II).

with the original it cannot be distinguished from it. The colour was obtained by hammering and heating an alloy of pure gold with a small fraction of 1 per cent of iron, the purple film being formed at a little below dull red heat. The surface of the gold also showed traces of 'spitting', possibly due to the experimental fusing of the gold with orpiment, though Wood has suggested that both the purple colour and the 'spitting' might have resulted from the use of gold nuggets containing a trace of iron as an impurity and also some sulphates and arsenates.[1] More recently, however, an independent experiment carried out at the British Museum has shown that when gold containing silver and copper is fused with iron pyrites and soda, some of the silver and copper combines with the sulphur in the pyrites, rising to the surface as dross, and leaving the gold alloyed with iron. When this gold is hammered into sheets and given heat treatment, it develops a superficial colour like that of the Tutankhamūn objects. Iron pyrites has about the same melting-point as pure gold and often a similar yellow metallic appearance, so that the two may easily have been mixed accidentally.[2]

Electrum [3]

Electrum is an alloy of gold and silver, which may be either natural or artificial, but which originally was natural, that employed in ancient Egypt being probably nearly always natural. These alloys may contain almost any proportion of the two constituents, and when the amount of gold is high the appearance is that of ordinary gold, and when the content of silver is high the colour is silver-white and the metal would pass as silver. Such extremes, however, are not called electrum, the term being limited to an alloy of a pale yellow colour, and it was this that the Greeks termed *elektron* and the Romans *electrum*, usually stated to have been so-called from its resemblance in colour to amber, the name for which was also *elektron*, though, since the alloy was probably the earlier known, the reverse seems likely to have been the case.[4]

In the ancient records electrum is stated to have been brought to Egypt from Kush, Punt, Emu, the Highlands, the South Countries, from a mine east of Redesia and from the mountains,[5] all places south of Egypt, and there is no reference to its having been obtained from the north, and no evidence whatever that it ever reached Egypt from Pactolus, as stated by Petrie.[6] The division between gold and electrum is entirely arbitrary, and when the alloy contains less than 20 per cent of silver it is here called gold and when it contains 20 per cent or more of silver and is of a light yellow colour it is here called electrum, which accords with Pliny's definition.[7]

The various specimens of ancient Egyptian electrum of which analyses are recorded [8] show a silver content varying from 20.3 to 29.0 per cent, and some electrum

[1] R. W. Wood, *J.E.A.*, XX (1934), pp. 62–65. The specimen of gold coloured by Prof. Wood is now in the Cairo Museum.

[2] H. J. Plenderleith, *Conservation of Antiquities and Works of Art*, pp. 208–9.

[3] Cf. J. R. Harris, *Lexicographical Studies*, pp. 35, 44–50.

[4] Cf. Liddell and Scott s.v. ἤλεκτρον, p. 768.

[5] *A.R.*, I, 161; II, 272, 298, 374, 377, 387, 654; III, 403; IV, 28; J. R. Harris, *Lexicographical Studies*, p. 48.

[6] W. M. F. Petrie, *Social Life in Ancient Egypt*, p. 164.

[7] XXXIII: 23.   [8] See p. 491.

finger rings in the Cairo Museum, that it is not possible to analyse, have approximately the same shade of light yellow as a gold-silver alloy of 15 carats, which corresponds to 37.5 per cent of silver. Rose states[1] that 'nearly white electrum occurs native in a number of localities, and the proportion of silver, according to Phillips,[2] may exceed half the weight of the mixture and certainly reaches 39 per cent.'

From the results of the assay of modern Egyptian gold already quoted, there cannot be any doubt that electrum is found in the country and it seems highly probable that the supply sufficed to meet the local needs. The reason that electrum is not usually recognized as occurring in Egypt is that the modern gold prospector and gold miner consider it to be merely a poor quality of gold, since it has no value at the present day except as a source of gold and silver.

Electrum is harder than gold and, therefore, is the better fitted of the two for the wear and tear incidental to its use for jewellery, and this fact may have influenced its use in ancient Egypt.

Electrum was employed principally for jewellery and its use can be traced back to early dynastic times; it was used as late as the Twenty-first and Twenty-second Dynasties for jewellery and for finger and toe stalls, and in Nubian jewellery of the sixth century B.C. and later .[3]

Electrum was also used for overlaying obelisks, and there is some evidence to suggest that at least two obelisks were made entirely of electrum.[4]

IRON[5]

Though compounds of iron are exceedingly abundant in nature, metallic iron is rare and usually occurs in comparatively small amount. This native iron is of two different origins and two different kinds, (a) terrestrial, occurring generally as minute grains in certain volcanic rocks, but also, though very exceptionally, in large masses, probably only one such occurrence (in Greenland) being known; and (b) celestial, this being dust or fragments from meteorites consisting of, or containing, iron. Meteoric iron possesses one very useful distinguishing characteristic, namely, that it almost invariably contains the metal nickel, the proportion varying from about 5 to about 26 per cent,[6] but usually being about 7 or 8 per cent, whereas terrestrial iron and iron ores rarely contain nickel and, when present, it is only in very small amount.

Iron minerals are very plentiful in Egypt and at a very early date (predynastic times) an ore of iron (haematite) was fashioned into beads, amulets and small ornaments[7] and certain compounds of iron, namely, ochres, siennas and umbers, but more particularly red and yellow ochres, were used as pigments.[8] The ores are found chiefly

---

[1] T. K. Rose, *Metallurgy of Gold*, 1915, p. 84.

[2] *Gold and Silver*, 1867, p. 2.

[3] Cf. D. Dunham, *El Kurru; Nuri.*

[4] C. Desroches Noblecourt, *Rev. d'Ég.*, VIII (1951), pp. 47–61; J.-M. Aynard, *Le Prisme du Louvre AO 19.939*, pp. 23–25.

[5] Cf. J. R. Harris, *Lexicographical Studies*, pp. 58–60.

[6] T. A. Rickard, *Man and Metals*, II, p. 846.

[7] See p. 395.

[8] See pp. 346–8, 349–51.

in the eastern desert and in Sinai[1] and the ochres principally near Aswan[2] and in the oases of the western desert.[3]

There are few subjects that are more disputed than that of the date when iron first came into general use in Egypt.[4] Just as some wonderful and mysterious hardened copper or bronze (the composition and secret of the preparation of which have been lost) has been postulated to account for the early Egyptian work in hard stone, so it is often claimed that not only iron but steel must have been known and employed for this purpose.[5] The fact that a few specimens of iron of early date have been found has been used to support this argument, and it is stated that it is only on account of the easily oxidizable nature of iron that tools and other objects of this metal have not been discovered more frequently. Iron, however, although it does oxidize readily in damp soil, particularly if salt is present, is quite stable under the ordinary conditions that prevail in rock-cut and other tombs in Egypt into which water has not penetrated, and the fact that some few specimens of iron have survived is proof that had there been other examples under similar conditions these too would have lasted. It should not be forgotten also that iron when it oxidizes does not disappear, but is converted into a compound that it is not only permanent but which, on account of its reddish colour and of its greater volume than that of the original metal, should not escape observation.[6]

Those who believe that iron tools must have been employed for the early Egyptian work in hard stone attach considerable importance to a piece of iron found at the great pyramid of Giza,[7] and see in this a proof that iron tools were used in its construction, in support of which the reference in Herodotus to iron tools in connexion with the pyramid is quoted.[8] By far the greater part of the stone of the pyramid, however, is not hard and there would be no great difficulty in working it without iron tools, and the specimen of iron found is not a tool and does not appear to be part of a tool of any sort, and it is significant that the earliest iron objects are chiefly weapons and amulets and not tools. Herodotus was not discussing the tools employed in the construction of the pyramid, but the cost of the pyramid, and incidentally includes that of the tools, which he assumes to have been of iron because iron tools for stone working were familiar to him. Thus he says '. . . how much must needs have been expended on the iron with which they worked . . .' This same writer also says that

---

[1] W. F. Hume, *Distribution of Iron Ores in Egypt; Geology of Egypt*, II, Part III, pp. 848–52; *Explan. Notes to the Geol. Map of Egypt*, pp. 38–39; L. Nassim, *Minerals of Economical Interest*, p. 166; M. I. Attia, *Bull. Inst. d'Ég.*, XXXI (1949), pp. 49–68.

[2] W. F. Hume, *Geology of Egypt*, II, Part III, p. 851.

[3] L. Nassim, *Minerals of Economical Interest*, pp. 164–5.

[4] For a good general discussion see T. A. Rickard, *Journ. Iron and Steel Inst.*, CXX (1929), pp. 323–9. The textual evidence for the knowledge and use of iron in Egypt is discussed by G. A. Wainwright, *J.E.A.*, XVIII (1932), pp. 3–15, and J. R. Harris, *Lexicographical Studies*, pp. 50 f.

[5] R. Hadfield, *Journ. Iron and Steel Inst.*, 1912, pp. 134–86, 149, 150, 169, 182; J. de Morgan, *Recherches sur les origines de l'Égypte*, I, pp. 213, 214; H. Garland, *Cairo Sc. Journ.*, VII (1913), pp. 59, 186–93; H. Garland and C. O. Bannister, *Ancient Egyptian Metallurgy*, pp. 85–112; J. Capart, *Chronique d'Égypte*, XXII (1947), pp. 117–18; S. R. K. Glanville, *J.E.A.*, XIV (1928), pp. 190–1; etc.

[6] Cf. L. Aitchison, *History of Metals*, I, pp. 99–100.

[7] See p. 237.

[8] II: 125.

the Ethiopians marching in the army of Xerxes carried short arrows 'pointed not with iron but with a sharpened stone'.[1]

Iron was undoubtedly known in the Near East as early as the third millennium B.C.,[2] but the use of the metal was very limited, and the making of hard and useful iron on any scale was probably first achieved by the Hittites in the fifteenth century B.C.[3] Egypt was the last country in the Near East to enter the iron age, and although no doubt smelted iron gradually became known during the New Kingdom, the metal cannot have been well established until many centuries later.[4]

The specimens of early iron reported to have been found in Egypt may now be described.[5] The earliest are two lots of small tubular beads (one lot of seven and one lot of two) of predynastic date found by Wainwright at Gerzeh.[6] When found, the beads were entirely in the condition of oxide, but Professor Gowland, who analysed them, stated that originally they had been metallic iron and had been made by bending into tubular shape a thin strip of metal. These beads have since been analysed by Professor Desch and found to contain 7.5 per cent of nickel,[7] thus proving that the iron of which they were made was of meteoric origin. Also perhaps of predynastic date was a ring found at Armant [8] and subsequently lost in the post before any detailed examination could be made. The next specimen in date order is that already referred to from the pyramid of Giza which was found in the stonework on the outside.[9] Although the statements of the finder (Mr. J. R. Hill) and others, who examined the spot at the time, are very definite and precise and not lightly to be disregarded, it seems more probable, since the iron has been proved not to be meteoric,[10] that it is of recent date and that it had been lost down a crack in the stone facing of the pyramid when this was being removed for use as building material in modern times, long before Vyse's work.[11] The next specimen is iron oxide of Fourth

---

[1] VII: 69.

[2] Cf. H. H. Coghlan, *Prehistoric and Early Iron*, pp. 61–71; G. A. Wainwright, *Antiquity*, X (1936), pp. 5–24.

[3] Cf. H. H. Coghlan, *Prehistoric and Early Iron*, p. 71; L. Aitchison, *History of Metals*, I, p. 102; R. J. Forbes, *Metallurgy in Antiquity*, pp. 418, 425–6.

[4] H. H. Coghlan, *Prehistoric and Early Iron*, p. 66.

[5] Cf. H. H. Coghlan, *Prehistoric and Early Iron*, pp. 65–67.

[6] G. A. Wainwright, in W. M. F. Petrie, G. A. Wainwright and E. Mackay, *Labyrinth, Gerzeh and Mazguneh*, pp. 15–16; *Man*, XI (1911), pp. 177–8; *Report of the British Ass., Portsmouth*, 1911, pp. 515–16; *Revue archéologique*, 1912 (I), pp. 255–9; *Cairo Sc. Journ.*, VIII (1914), p. 178; *Bull. Soc. sult. de géog*, Cairo, IX (1919), p. 183; T. A. Rickard, *Journ. Inst. Metals*, XLIII (1930), p. 350; W. M. F. Petrie, *Prehistoric Egypt*, p. 27.

[7] C. H. Desch, 'Report on the Metallurgical Examination of Specimens for the Sumerian Committee of the British Ass.', *Report of the British Ass.*, 1928.

[8] R. Mond and O. H. Myers, *Cemeteries of Armant*, I, p. 117.

[9] H. Vyse, *Pyramids of Gizeh*, I, pp. 275–6. Cf. W. Flight, *Journ. Chemical Soc.*, XLI (1882), pp. 140–1, No. VII; H. R. Hall, *Man*, III (1903), pp. 147–9; O. Montelius, *Man*, V (1905), pp. 69–71; T. A. Rickard, *Man*, XXVII (1927), pp. 79–80; *Journ. Iron and Steel Inst.*, CXX (1929), pp. 323–4; C. F. C. Hawkes, *Antiquity*, X (1936), pp. 355–7.

[10] N. T. Belaiew, *Journ. Inst. Metals*, XLIII (1930), p. 353; C. F. C. Hawkes, *Antiquity*, X (1936), p. 356.

[11] At one time I thought that this iron must be contemporaneous with the pyramid, but on reconsidering the evidence in the light of the recently ascertained fact that the iron is not meteoric, I am now of opinion that the balance of evidence is against its being ancient. Cf. H. H. Coghlan, *Prehistoric and Early Iron*, p. 66.

Dynasty date found by Reisner in the Menkaurē Valley Temple at Giza, which originally had been a small piece of iron forming part of a 'magical set'.[1] This was examined spectrographically and no trace of nickel was found, proving that it was non-meteoric. After this there are several objects reported by Maspero, including pieces of chisels from Saqqara, stated to be of the Fifth Dynasty, pieces of a pickaxe found at Abusir, stated to be possibly of the Sixth Dynasty, and broken tools from Dahshur, said to be of similar date. The references to the finding of these objects are extremely vague and unsatisfactory, the finder himself being somewhat uncertain, and the correctness of the dating may therefore reasonably be questioned.[2] Next comes a mass of iron rust found by Petrie with copper adzes of Sixth Dynasty type,[3] of which the finder says 'this is absolutely certain and not open to any doubts'.[4] When tested chemically, this was found not to contain nickel and hence it is not meteoric.[5] There is no proof that it was a tool or implement of any kind and what it was and how it came to be placed in the foundations of a temple at Abydos will probably always remain a mystery; but it may have been a piece of iron produced accidentally that could not be used because the art of shaping it while red-hot had not then been discovered. Of the Old Kingdom or First Intermediate period were the remains of some beads found at Armant, though it is possible that these were not iron, but a copper-iron alloy.[6] Then comes a tiny *Pesesh-Kef* amulet having a silver head and an iron blade from the Eleventh Dynasty at Deir el Bahari, the blade of which has been analysed by Desch and found to contain 10 per cent of nickel and therefore to be of meteoric origin.[7]

After that comes an iron spear-head from Nubia, which is attributed to the Twelfth Dynasty,[8] but that iron should be known and employed in an out-of-the-way place in Nubia in the form of a large weapon for common use more than four hundred years before the time when the king of Egypt (Tutankhamūn) possessed only one small iron dagger, and more than 1,000 years before iron became common in Egypt, is so extraordinary that more evidence than that adduced is necessary before the date assigned to this object can be accepted, especially as it is practically identical with spear-heads used until not many years ago in the same locality. Wainwright points out that it is not tanged, as would be normal for the Twelfth Dynasty, but socketed.[9] Then come part of a chisel and part of the ferrule of a hoe handle, found in the pyramid of Mohammerieh near Esna and stated to be of the Seventeenth Dynasty,[10] but of which nothing precise is known. Of the Amarna period is an iron arrow-

---

[1] D. Dunham and W. J. Young, *J.E.A.*, xxviii (1942), pp. 57–58.

[2] Cf. O. Olshausen, *Zeitschrift für Ethnologie*, xxxvii (1907), pp. 373–4, Nos. 1–3; G.A.Wainwright, *Antiquity*, x (1936), pp. 8–9; H. H. Coghlan, *Prehistoric and Early Iron*, p. 66.

[3] W. M. F. Petrie, *Abydos*, ii, pp. 32–33.

[4] W. M. F. Petrie, *Arts and Crafts*, p. 104.

[5] C. F. C. Hawkes, *Antiquity*, x (1936), pp. 356–7.

[6] R. Mond and O. H. Myers, *Cemeteries of Armant*, i, p. 84.

[7] G. Brunton, *Ann. Serv.*, xxxv (1935), p. 214.

[8] D. Randall MacIver and C. L. Woolley, *Buhen*, pp. 193, 211, Pls. lxxxvi, lxxxviii; D. Randall MacIver, *Antiquity*, ix (1935), pp. 348–50; G. A. Wainwright, *Antiquity*, x (1936), pp. 9–11.

[9] G. A. Wainwright, *Antiquity*, x (1936), pp 9–11.

[10] G. Maspero, *Guide au Musée de Boulaq*, 1883, p. 296; O. Olshausen, *Zeitschrift für Ethnologie*, xxxvii (1907), p. 374, No. 4.

head or javelin-head with elongated triangular point and long slender tang, found in the middle palace of Amenhotpe III at Thebes, the residence of Akhenaten.[1] From the tomb of Tutankhamūn (late Eighteenth Dynasty) there are several iron objects,[2] namely, a dagger, a miniature head-rest, an amuletic eye set in a gold bracelet and sixteen implements having full-sized handles of some coniferous wood, but with blades so small and thin that they could not even have been used by the boy king to play with, the total weight of all the blades being only about four grams, and Wainwright has shown that these were probably magical implements for the ritual ceremony of 'Opening the Mouth' of the mummy of the dead pharaoh.[3] Whether these are of meteoric iron, as theoretically they should be, is not known, since an analysis has not yet been made. The head-rest, which is a typical Egyptian object, and therefore probably made in the country, has been badly welded and shows several imperfections due either to lack of experience in working iron or to the absence of a sufficiently high temperature: the metal, too, is of a different colour and quality from that of the dagger, eye and miniature implements, as it has a dark, smooth surface and has not rusted. It weighs approximately 47 grams (rather more than an ounce and a half). Of uncertain date, but probably of the late Eighteenth Dynasty, is a sickle found under a sphinx of Horemheb at Karnak.[4]

From the end of the Eighteenth Dynasty onwards there is a gradual increase in the number of iron objects found,[5] until the Twenty-fifth Dynasty, of which date there is a group of iron tools,[6] after which iron becomes much more common and at Naucratis and Defenneh in about the Twenty-sixth Dynasty (664 to 525 B.C.) it was as common as bronze or even commoner and was being smelted in the country.[7] In 255–254 B.C. iron tools were being supplied to quarrymen[8] and a papyrus of Ptolemaic date from the Fayum 'gives interesting details about tools and other objects made of iron'.[9]

It is evident, therefore, that on at least one occasion at a very early date a very small quantity of meteoric iron was found in Egypt and made into beads, but there was no knowledge of what iron was or how to extract it from its ores and possibly

---

[1] W. C. Hayes, *Scepter*, II, p. 255.

[2] H. Carter, *Tut-ankh-Amen*, II, pp. 109, 122, 135, Pls. LXXVII, LXXXII, LXXXVII; III, pp. 89–90, Pl. XXVII.

[3] G. A. Wainwright, *J.E.A.*, XVIII (1932), p. 7.

[4] G. Belzoni, *Travels*, I, pp. 235, 236, 252, 253; W. Flight, *Journ. Chemical Soc.*, XLI (1882), p. 140, No. VI.

[5] For some examples see G. A. Wainwright, *Cairo Sc. Journ.*, VIII (1914), pp. 177–8; in W. M. F. Petrie, G. A. Wainwright and E. Mackay, *Labyrinth, Gerzeh and Mazguneh*, p. 19; W. M. F. Petrie, *Ancient Egypt*, 1915, pp. 20–22; J. R. Partington, *Origins and Development of Applied Chemistry*, pp. 93–94; H. C. H. Carpenter and J. M. Robertson, *Journ. Iron and Steel Inst.*, CXXI (1930), pp. 417–54; *Nature*, CXXV (1930), pp. 859–62; W. L. Nash, *P.S.B.A.*, XXXIV (1912), p. 36; H. Junker, *Ermenne*, p. 68. *N.B.*—The sword of Seti II, often stated to be of iron, is in fact bronze, cf. M. Burchardt, *Z.Ä.S.*, L (1912), pp. 61–63.

[6] W. M. F. Petrie, *Six Temples at Thebes*, pp. 18–19.

[7] W. M. F. Petrie, *Naukratis*, I, p. 39; W. M. F. Petrie and F. Ll. Griffith, *Tanis*, II, *Nebesheh and Defenneh*, p. 77.

[8] J. P. Mahaffy, *Flinders Petrie Papyri*, II, p. 7; C. C. Edgar, *Studies Presented to F. Ll. Griffith*, pp. 211–12.

[9] C. C. Edgar, *Zenon Papyri*, IV, No. 59782.

not even the knowledge that this particular piece of material had fallen from the sky, though at a later date other finds of meteoric iron may have been recognized as such and may have been used for making small objects for ritual purposes, as suggested by Wainwright.[1] With several alleged exceptions (some of which are almost certainly of much later date than that assigned to them) this condition of things continued until the end of the Eighteenth Dynasty, when an iron dagger and sufficient iron to make sixteen tiny blades, a miniature head-rest and a small amulet came into the possession of Tutankhamūn, almost certainly having been presented to him by one of the kings of western Asia, the home of iron working. Iron must have been rare in Palestine and Syria also until at least the end of the Eighteenth Dynasty, since among the tribute levied by Egypt on the peoples she conquered only one mention of iron can be traced, namely, 'vessels of iron' received by Thutmose III from Tinay, an unknown country to the north of Egypt.[2] Also, Tusratta, king of Mitanni, presented to Amenhotpe III a 'dagger whose blade is of steel . . .'; 'one *mitten* of iron, overlaid with gold'; two 'hand-rings of iron, overlaid with gold'; 'one dagger, whose blade is of iron, whose shaft is trimmed with lapis lazuli . . .'; 'one dagger whose blade is of steel . . .',[3] and the same king presented to Amenhotpe IV 'Ten rings of iron, overlaid with gold . . .' [3]

In the tomb of Hekakheperrē Sheshonq (Twenty-second Dynasty) discovered at Tanis by Montet there was a sacred eye of iron mounted in a gold bracelet [4] and a very clumsily made miniature head-rest of badly prepared iron,[5] while another miniature head-rest was found in the tomb of Hornakht of similar date.[6] These finds seem to prove that as late as the Twenty-second Dynasty iron smelting and iron working were still in their infancy in Egypt.

Furnaces and substantial remains of iron working dating from the period of the Twentieth to Twenty-second Dynasties have been discovered at Gerar in Palestine.[7] However, the earliest date for which at present there is evidence of iron ores having been worked for metal in Egypt is the sixth century B.C., Petrie having found evidence of smelting at Naucratis [8] and Defenneh [9] in the Delta, though where the ore (specular iron ore) came from is not known. Iron ores, however, have been worked anciently in the eastern desert [10,11] and near Aswan,[11,12] in the former locality possibly by the Romans.

It is probable that iron was worked in Nubia somewhat earlier than in Egypt. Wainwright [13] was unable to quote any evidence for iron before the reign of Aspelta,

[1] G. A. Wainwright, *J.E.A.*, XVIII (1932), pp. 3–15.

[2] *A.R.*, II, 557; J. R. Harris, *Lexicographical Studies*, p. 59.

[3] S. A. B. Mercer, *Tell-El-Amarna Tablets*, I, pp. 81, 83, 85, 87, 137.

[4] G. Brunton, *Ann. Serv.*, XXXIX (1939), p. 546.

[5] P. Montet, *Kêmi*, IX (1942), p. 74; *Nécropole royale de Tanis*, II, p. 50.

[6] P. Montet, *Kêmi*, IX (1942), p. 49; *Nécropole royale de Tanis*, II, p. 70.

[7] W. M. F. Petrie, *Gerar*, pp. 14–16.

[8] W. M. F. Petrie, *Naukratis*, I, p. 39.

[9] W. M. F. Petrie and F. Ll. Griffith, *Tanis*, II, *Nebesheh and Defenneh*, p. 79.

[10] T. Barron and W. F. Hume, *Topog. and Geol. of the Eastern Desert*, pp. 44, 51, 86, 221, 222, 225, 239, 257; W. F. Hume, *Distribution of Iron Ores in Egypt*, p. 8.

[11] J. de Morgan, *Catalogue des monuments*, I, pp. 139–41.

[12] P. Bovier-Lapierre, *Ann. Serv.*, XVII (1917), pp. 272–3; R. Moss, *J.E.A.*, XXXVI (1950), p. 112.

[13] G. A. Wainwright, *Sudan Notes*, XXVI (1945), pp. 5–18.

and suggested that the knowledge of iron was first introduced into Nubia by Ionian and Carian mercenaries under Psammetichus II (595–589 B.C.). Arkell, however, favours an earlier date,[1] and states [2] that 'At Meroë . . . there was plenty of iron ore and wood fuel, and it is possible that Taharqa may have instituted iron working there soon after his contact with the Assyrians. Iron objects certainly do occur at Meroë in graves that date from this period,[3] but it is not until 600 B.C. or even later that iron objects become frequent in graves there. . . .' The later development of iron working in the Meroitic period,[4] and the subsequent spread of iron working southward from Meroe,[5] have been discussed in detail by Wainwright.

The principal reason that iron became known to man so much later than copper, although iron ores are far more abundant than copper ores and almost as easy to smelt, is probably that copper can be shaped by cold-hammering, whereas iron must be hammered hot, and doubtless impure metallic iron had been produced accidentally many times and rejected as useless long before someone tried hammering it while still hot and found that under such conditions it was almost as malleable as copper. Another difficulty was that hammering red-hot iron was impossible with hammers without handles, which apparently were the only kind known to the Egyptians until late.[6]

Iron ores can be reduced in the presence of carbon at a temperature not exceeding 500° C.,[7] and the iron becomes a pasty mass at from 800° C. to 900° C,[8] though it should not be assumed that ores could actually be smelted at these temperatures, or would then produce a metal that could be worked.[9] The reduction of oxides of iron between 700° C. and 800° C. yields a dark grey substance that is hardly metallic in any practical sense, being very porous and unsuitable for forging.[9] To obtain a reduction product that can be worked into usable iron by hammering, the reduction must take place at a temperature of about 1100° C. or 1150° C.,[9] but iron does not become liquid enough to be poured for casting until about 1530° C. This is much too high a temperature to have been obtained anciently, and furnace construction only advanced sufficiently for this to be done in the fourteenth century, only a few hundred years ago. Casting, therefore, was impossible and in this respect iron was inferior to copper and bronze and, since iron was also more difficult to work, because less malleable and, since it was little, if any, harder than copper and bronze, the new metal was at first not so satisfactory as the old ones.

The early wrought iron, on account of the way it was made, would contain little or no carbon (less than 0.2 per cent) and such iron is not hardened but softened if

---

[1] A. J. Arkell, *Antiquity*, XIX (1945), pp. 213–14.

[2] A. J. Arkell, *History of the Sudan*, p. 130.

[3] Cf. D. Dunham, *Nuri*, pp. 12, 19, 23.

[4] G. A. Wainwright, *Sudan Notes*, XXVI (1945), pp. 18–36. Cf. A. J. Arkell, *Antiquity*, XIX (1945), pp. 213–14; M. F. L. Macadam, *Temples of Kawa*, II, p. 246.

[5] G. A. Wainwright, *Uganda Journal*, XVIII (1954), pp. 113–36.

[6] Cf. L. Aitchison, *History of Metals*, I, pp. 100–1.

[7] H. Louis, *Nature*, CXXIII (1929), p. 762.

[8] T. A. Rickard, *Man and Metals*, I, p. 144. Cf. H. H. Coghlan, *Man*, XLI (1941), pp. 74–80, 88–89.

[9] L. Aitchison, *History of Metals*, I, p. 100; H. H. Coghlan, *Prehistoric and Early Iron*, p. 39.

heated and suddenly cooled; but with an increase in the proportion of carbon present, this property of being hardened is acquired, and it is this higher proportion of carbon (from 0.2 per cent to not more than 2.0 per cent), with the resultant virtue it imparts, that constitutes the difference between wrought iron and steel, steel being iron containing small proportions of added carbon (the carbon content of the ordinary modern product ranging from about 0.7 to 1.7 per cent) that imparts to it the property mentioned, and iron only became a thoroughly serviceable metal for weapons and tools after the discovery of the method (for a long time purely empirical and without any understanding of the underlying principle) of adding a little extra carbon (carburizing, as it is termed), so that when heated and suddenly cooled (quenched) it became hardened.[1] This result may be brought about by allowing the iron to remain in contact with carbon at a high temperature for some time, when a certain small proportion of the carbon is absorbed by the iron, the amount depending upon the length of time the two are kept in contact, being greatest at the surface and gradually lessening towards the centre. At one time a process (called the cementation process) employed for making steel, which is still used to some extent, was to pack the iron in charcoal and heat it strongly for several days. Such a considered method, however, is a comparatively late invention, but a similar result can be brought about by the frequent heating and reheating of iron in a charcoal fire, and this must have been the method practised anciently, probably an outcome of the hammering and reheating that were necessary to free the lumps of iron as at first produced, which would have contained air-holes and in consequence would have been spongy, from adherent slag and other impurities, to consolidate it and to shape it.

Nine iron objects from Egypt, the earliest dating from about 1200 B.C. according to Petrie, were examined microscopically and their Brinell hardness investigated.[2] Of the nine specimens, the two oldest (1200 B.C.) had been carburized but not quenched, three somewhat later (900–700 B.C.) had been both carburized and quenched, and one (A.D. 300) had been carburized, quenched and tempered. Four other specimens of Roman date have also been examined;[3] all were of wrought iron, and two had been carburized. These objects constitute the first definite evidence of carburizing, quenching and the use of heat treatment in general to increase hardness, though it must be admitted that the carburizing may have been accidental, and that the earlier specimens, even if correctly dated, may have been imported into Egypt.

Since the production of iron from its ores was not an Egyptian discovery,[4] it is most unlikely that the subsequent metallurgical treatment should have been Egyptian, and it seems highly probable, therefore, that blacksmiths from Asia were introduced into the country in order to teach the Egyptians how to smelt and treat the new metal. The theory that iron was first produced in Egypt from magnetite as a by-product of

---

[1] Steel may also be produced directly by smelting certain kinds of iron ore (H. Louis, *Nature*, CXXIII (1929), p. 762).

[2] H. C. H. Carpenter and J. M. Robertson, *Journ. Iron and Steel Inst.*, CXXI (1930), pp. 417–54; *Nature*, CXXV (1930), pp. 859–62; H. H. Coghlan, *Prehistoric and Early Iron*, pp. 134 f.

[3] H. H. Coghlan, *Prehistoric and Early Iron*, pp. 148–9, 187–9.

[4] On the discovery of iron in general, see H. H. Coghlan, *Prehistoric and Early Iron*, pp. 45–52, 71; *Man*, XLI (1941), pp. 74–80.

the refining of gold [1] is somewhat unlikely, and would require experimental verification before it could be accepted.[2]

A copper-iron alloy of early dynastic date was found at Abydos.[3]

LEAD [4]

Although never very extensively employed in ancient Egypt, lead was among the earliest metals known, since it dates from predynastic times.[5] The reason for this early knowledge of lead was doubtless owing to the facts, first, that lead ores occur in Egypt, one of them (galena) being very metallic-looking and, therefore, likely to attract attention, and second, that the metal is very easily obtained from the ore.

The principal locality in Egypt where lead ores are found is at Gebel Rosas,[6,7] which is situated about 70 miles south of Quseir and a few miles inland from the Red Sea, and where there is evidence from inscriptions of mining during the Saite period.[8] But there are deposits in other places, namely, at Ranga on the Red Sea coast;[6,7] in the Safaga district near the Red Sea,[6,7] where about two miles south of Safaga Bay there is an ancient working covering the whole side of a limestone hill;[9] associated with the Um Semiuki copper ore[10] and near Aswan.[6,7] Other deposits of lead ore have recently been found at Zug el Bahr and Um Reig on the coast south of Quseir. During the four years 1912 to 1915 inclusive when the Gebel Rosas mine was being worked it produced more than 18,000 tons of ore, in the form of mixed carbonate and sulphide of lead associated with carbonate of zinc.[6] The ore contains the equivalent of from 25 to 55 per cent of metallic lead, a very small proportion of silver and also a trace of gold.[11] Hall states that 'analyses show up to 58 per cent lead and 37 per cent zinc'.[12]

The principal ore of lead is the sulphide (galena), which was used in Egypt as an eye-paint from as early as Badarian times to as late as the Coptic period.[13]

The production of metallic lead from its ores is one of the simplest of all metallurgical operations and consists essentially in merely roasting the ore, which is now done in special furnaces, though doubtless in ancient times by simply heaping the ore on top of the fuel on the ground or in a shallow pit, the fused metal, which melts at 327° C. (or less than one-third the temperature required to melt gold) running out at the bottom of the heap.

---

[1] Cf. H. Quiring, *F.u.F.*, IX (1933), pp. 126–7; *Geschichte des Goldes*, pp. 8, 34; E. W. Hulme, *Antiquity*, XI (1937), pp. 222–3; R. J. Forbes, *Metallurgy in Antiquity*, pp. 403–4.

[2] H. H. Coghlan, *Prehistoric and Early Iron*, p. 51.

[3] E. Amélineau, *Fouilles d'Abydos, 1895–1896*, p. 275.

[4] Cf. J. R. Harris, *Lexicographical Studies*, pp. 67–68.

[5] W. M. F. Petrie, *Prehistoric Egypt*, p. 27.

[6] Mines and Quarries Dept., *Report on the Mineral Industry*, p. 24.

[7] W. F. Hume, *Explan. Notes to the Geol. Map of Egypt*, pp. 38–39; *Geology of Egypt*, II, Part III, p. 856.

[8] V. Vikentiev, *Ann. Serv.*, LIV (1957), pp. 179–89.

[9] C. J. Alford, *Trans. Inst. Mining and Metallurgy*, X (1901–2), p. 13.

[10] See p. 205.

[11] Kindly communicated by Mr. R. H. Greaves, formerly Controller, Mines and Quarries Dept.

[12] T. C. F. Hall, *Lead Ores*, p. 63.   [13] See p. 80.

Lead was used for many purposes, including small human and animal figures;[1,2] sinkers for fishing nets;[2] rings;[2] beads;[3] ornaments;[2] model dishes and trays;[2] plugs;[4] for adding to bronze (more than 20 per cent having sometimes been used, which must have lowered the melting-point of the bronze considerably, and thus made casting easier); occasionally for vessels;[5] for a tank;[6] for the head-dresses of gods, a group of twenty of which of unknown date and origin are in the Cairo Museum;[7] and sometimes for filling bronze weights and as a core for bronze statuettes. Sulphide of lead (galena), as already stated,[8] was extensively employed as an eye-paint; a compound of lead and antimony was used for producing a yellow colour in glass [9] and three examples are known of the use of oxides of lead as pigments, one being red oxide (red lead) in a mural painting of Graeco-Roman date,[10] the second being red lead on a scribe's palette (undated, but most probably of a late period)[11] and the third being yellow oxide (massicot) on a scribe's or artist's palette dating from about 400 B.C.[12]

There can be little doubt that most, if not all, the lead and galena used in Egypt until about the Eighteenth Dynasty was of local origin, and there is no evidence that it was 'probably brought from Syria' [13] until after the Egyptian conquests in Asia, when, according to historical texts, it was imported from Djahi,[14] Retenu[15] and Isy,[16] the latter probably not, as often stated, Cyprus, where lead ores do not occur, but, as suggested by Wainwright,[17] a country on the northern coast of Syria.

PLATINUM

Platinum is found only in the metallic state and never pure, but always associated with other metals, principally the closely related ones, iridium, palladium, osmium, rhodium and ruthenium, but also frequently with gold.

Only one occurrence of the intentional use of platinum in ancient Egypt is known, namely a narrow strip inlaid in a metal case of late date, which Berthelot examined and found to be 'd'un alliage complexe renfermant plusiers des métaux de la mine

---

[1] W. M. F. Petrie, *Prehistoric Egypt*, p. 27.

[2] W. M. F. Petrie, *Objects of Daily Use*, p. 49; including a hawk of sheet lead over a wooden core.

[3] J. E. Quibell and A. G. K. Hayter, *Saqqara, Teti Pyramid, North Side*, p. 7. Also one of the First Intermediate period found by Brunton.

[4] L. Borchardt, *Saḥu-rē*, I, pp. 76–77, Fig. 102.

[5] F. W. von Bissing, *Metallgefässe*, pp. 57, 64; E. A. Gardner, *Naukratis*, II, p. 29.

[6] W. M. F. Petrie, *Palace of Apries (Memphis, II)*, p. 2.

[7] Nos. J. 31589 to 31608. Cf. H. Garland and C. O. Bannister, *Ancient Egyptian Metallurgy*, p. 31, Fig. 4.

[8] See p. 80.   [9] See p. 190.   [10] See p. 348.

[11] J. Barthoux, 'Les fards, pommades et couleurs dans l'antiquité', *Congrés internat. de Géog.*, Le Caire, Avril, 1925, IV (1926), pp. 257–8.

[12] A. P. Laurie, *Archaeologia*, LXIV (1913), pp. 318–19.

[13] W. M. F. Petrie, *Arts and Crafts*, p. 103.

[14] *A.R.*, II, 460, 462.

[15] *A.R.*, II, 471, 491, 509.

[16] *A.R.*, II, 494, 521.

[17] G. A. Wainwright, *Klio*, XIV (1915), pp. 1–36.

de platine sans préjudice d'un peu d'or.' [1] Several gold objects of Twelfth Dynasty date in the Cairo Museum show numerous silver-white specks that I have tested, as far as was possible without injuring the objects, and found to be platinum. Petrie has reported in gold objects of this same dynasty similar hard, white specks, which he calls osmiridium [2] (a natural alloy of osmium and iridium), though no evidence is given for this and it is much more likely that they are largely platinum. Maspero states that certain Egyptian gold jewellery of the Eighteenth Dynasty contained platinum [3] and Mrs. C. R. Williams records similar particles in a number of instances in ancient Egyptian gold objects.[4]

Platinum has never been reported as occurring in modern Egyptian gold, so far as is known, but it does occur as a trace in the nickel ore from St. John's Island in the Red Sea [5] and has been found in gold from the Sennar province of the Sudan [6] and it occurs, and was being worked on a small scale a few years ago, in western Abyssinia.[7]

SILVER[8]

Silver is found in nature in two conditions, namely, as metal and in the non-metallic state.

Native silver, which is practically pure, occurs only in small quantity, generally in the crystalline form, as needles, filaments, network, or arborescent shapes, though also, but more rarely, massive in nuggets and thin plates. Silver also occurs in practically all gold, sometimes in considerable proportion.[9]

The principal ores of silver are silver sulphide, either alone or associated with sulphides of antimony or arsenic, and silver chloride. These, however, yield only about one-third of the world's supply of silver, the remaining two-thirds being obtained, not from silver ores proper, but from what are primarily lead, zinc and copper ores containing a very small proportion of silver (usually of the order of from 0.01 to 0.1 per cent), which may, therefore, be considered as low-grade silver ores.

So far as is known, neither native silver nor silver ores proper occur in Egypt, though all Egyptian gold contains silver, the proportion in that from the modern mines varying from 9.7 per cent to 24.0 per cent,[10] and in ancient Egyptian objects of

---

[1] M. Berthelot, *Monuments Piot*, VII (1900), pp. 132–3; *C.R. Ac. Sci.*, CXXXII (1901), pp. 729–32; *Ann. Chim. et Phys.*, XXIII (1901), pp. 20–22. Petrie mentions platinum also 'as an inlay in an unfinished bronze base of a statuette of Amenardas, XXVth dynasty, in the hands of a dealer in Cairo', but no evidence is given that this was identified by chemical analysis. (Petrie, *Wisdom of the Egyptians*, 1940, p. 91.)

[2] W. M. F. Petrie, *Ancient Egypt*, 1915, p. 23; W. M. F. Petrie and J. E. Quibell, *Naqada and Ballas*, p. 66.

[3] G. Maspero, *Dawn of Civilization*, 1901, p. 493.

[4] C. R. Williams, *Gold and Silver Jewelry*, p. 27.

[5] F. W. Moon, *Prel. Geol. Rept. on St. John's Island*, p. 16.

[6] F. Cailliaud, *Voyage à Méroé au Fleuve Blanc*, XII (1826), p. 19.

[7] Kindly communicated by Mr. A. D. Home, District Commissioner, Gallabat.

[8] Cf. J. R. Harris, *Lexicographical Studies*, pp. 41–44.

[9] See p. 224, n. 7. Sometimes irregularly-distributed patches of gold occur in ancient Egyptian silver objects, examples of which were found in the tomb of Tutankhamun (A. Lucas, in H. Carter, *Tut-ankh-Amen*, III, p. 175 (Appendix II)).

[10] See pp. 228–9.

gold and electrum that have been analysed the proportion of silver has varied from probably a trace (this particular specimen having almost certainly been refined) to as much as 29 per cent,[1] though there is no proof that the metal of all these was of Egyptian origin. Silver also occurs in very small amount in both the local lead ore [2] and in the nickel ore.[3] In an Egyptian lead net-sinker, dating from about 1400 B.C., probably made from local lead, there was 0.03 per cent of silver,[4] and 0.01 per cent in some galena from Gebel Jasus.[5]

Silver objects have been found in Egypt from as early as the predynastic period, the finds being rather more substantial than is generally realized,[6] but silver was comparatively rare until about the Eighteenth Dynasty, when it began to be a little more plentiful, and it was not until much later that it became fairly common. Occurrences of silver from the protodynastic period,[7] the Old Kingdom[8] and the First Intermediate period [9] are principally in the form of beads, amulets and other small objects, and the relative scarcity of silver is well illustrated by the tomb equipment of Queen Hetepheres (Fourth Dynasty).[10] In this gold was employed lavishly to ornament the furniture, as also in the form of small dishes, a drinking cup, and razors, whereas the only silver found consisted of twenty anklets (inlaid with turquoise,[11] lapis lazuli and carnelian), which, although having an appearance of solidity, because they are rounded on the outside, are only shells of very thin metal, and a small amount of silver leaf on a head-rest. Of Eleventh Dynasty date are several small pieces of silver jewellery,[12] including those from the tomb of Wah,[13] while during the Twelfth Dynasty the number and size of silver objects gradually increases,[14] notably in the jewellery from Dahshur [15] and Lahun,[16] from the tombs of Senebtisi [17] and Neferuptah,[18]

[1] See pp. 490–1.

[2] See p. 243.

[3] F. W. Moon, *Prel. Geol. Rept. on St. John's Island*. p. 16.

[4] J. Newton Friend, *Journ. Inst. Metals*, XLI (1929), p. 106.

[5] C. J. Alford, *Trans. Inst. Mining and Metallurgy*, X (1901-2), p. 13.

[6] E. J. Baumgartel, *Cultures of Prehistoric Egypt*, II, pp. 6–10; W. M. F. Petrie, *Prehistoric Egypt*, pp. 27, 43; *Diospolis Parva*, pp. 24–25, 29; W. M. F. Petrie and J. E. Quibell, *Naqada and Ballas*, pp. 45–46, 48; E. R. Ayrton and W. L. S. Loat, *Predynastic Cemetery at El Mahasna*, pp. 16, 30.

[7] R. Mond and O. H. Myers, *Cemeteries of Armant*, I, p. 91; A. C. Mace, *Naga-ed-Dêr*, II, pp. 26, 48; W. M. F. Petrie, *Royal Tombs*, I, p. 28.

[8] C. R. Williams, *Gold and Silver Jewelry*, p. 237; G. Brunton, *Qau and Badari*, II, p. 15.

[9] G. Brunton, *Qau and Badari*, II, p. 15; *Mostagedda*, pp. 110, 111.

[10] G. A. Reisner, *Boston Bull.*, XXV (1927); *History of the Giza Necropolis*, II.

[11] This was originally described as malachite by Dr. Reisner, who, however, later accepted my identification of turquoise. See G. A. Reisner, *History of the Giza Necropolis*, II, pp. 43–44.

[12] E. Naville, *XIth Dynasty Temple at Deir el Bahari*, I, p. 44; H. E. Winlock, *Excavations at Deir el Bahari, 1911–31*, p. 46; W. C. Hayes, *Scepter*, I, pp. 229–30, 236–9.

[13] H. E. Winlock, *Excavations at Deir el Bahari, 1911–31*, pp. 222–8; W. C. Hayes, *Scepter*, I, pp. 230–1.

[14] H. Frankfort, *J.E.A.*, XVI (1930), p. 219; E. R. Ayrton, C. T. Currelly and A. E. P. Weigall, *Abydos*, III, p. 8; R. Engelbach, *Harageh*, pp. 15–16; D. Randall MacIver and A. C. Mace, *El Amrah and Abydos*, p. 88; G. Bénédite, *Miroirs*, pp. 41–42.

[15] J. de Morgan, *Dahchour, mars–juin 1894; 1894–1895*; E. Vernier, *Bijoux et Orfèvreries*.

[16] G. Brunton, *Lahun*, I; H. E. Winlock, *Treasure of El Lāhūn*.

[17] A. C. Mace and H. E. Winlock, *Senebtisi*.

[18] *Illustrated London News*, May 12, 1956, p. 521.

and from the Egyptian settlement at Kerma in the Sudan.[1] The largest single hoard of silver from this period is the treasure found at Tôd, including no less than 153 silver cups.[2] In this particular instance the quantity of silver was far greater than that of gold, but this is quite exceptional. From the beginning of the Eighteenth Dynasty comes the silver boat found with the jewellery of Queen Ahhotpe,[3] while from the reign of Thutmose III are the various silver objects, including mirrors and vessels, found with the burial of three princesses of the court.[4] In the tomb of Tutankhamūn there were relatively few silver objects, though others may have been stolen, the two largest being a trumpet and a vase in the shape of a pomegranate. Of Ramessid date are the silver vessels from the Tell Basta hoard.[5] The burials of the Tanite kings included a considerable quantity of silver, notably a silver coffin and nine silver vessels, one very large, of the Twenty-first Dynasty, and a silver coffin and four small silver canopic coffins of the Twenty-second Dynasty, all of which are now in the Cairo Museum.[6]

Textual evidence suggests that until the end of the Middle Kingdom silver was considered to be more valuable than gold. During the New Kingdom the gold—silver ratio remained fairly constant at 2 : 1, as Černý has shown, and a silver unit came into use as the standard for assessing values.[7]

Petrie states that the silver employed in the predynastic period 'was obtained probably from Syria' [8] (to which cause he attributes its scarcity) and again that it 'could only be got by mining in North Syria,' [9] but there is no evidence for this,[10] and the principal source of supply may well have been local until after the Egyptian conquests in Asia during the Eighteenth Dynasty. The Twelfth Dynasty silver objects and ingots found at Tôd in Upper Egypt were probably presents from Asia. The ancient records are silent as to where silver came from until the Eighteenth Dynasty,[11] when it is stated to have been received from Assur,[12] Djahi,[13] Kheta,[14] Naharin,[15] Retenu [16] and Sengar,[17] all countries in Asia, and in the Nineteenth Dynasty it came from God's Land [18] (here manifestly from the context a country to the North of Egypt), Kheta [19] and Naharin,[20]

---

[1] G. Reisner, *Kerma*, IV–V, pp. 281–5.

[2] F. Bisson de la Roque, *Tôd (1934 à 1936)*, Fouilles I.F.A.O., XVII (1937), pp. 115–19; F. Bisson de la Roque, G. Contenau and F. Chapouthier, *Trésor de Tôd*, Doc. de Fouilles I.F.A.O., XI, pp. 9–10; F. Bisson de la Roque, *Trésor de Tôd (Cat. Caire)*, pp. 4–30 and p. iii.

[3] F. W. von Bissing, *Ein Thebanischer Grabfund*, p. 19, Pl. X.

[4] H. E. Winlock, *Treasure of Three Egyptian Princesses*, pp. 24, 49–50, 60–61, 63–64.

[5] C. C. Edgar, in G. Maspero, *Musée égyptien*, II, pp. 93–108, Pls. XLIII–LV; F. W. von Bissing, *Metallgefässe*, pp. 72–75; W. K. Simpson, *American Journal of Archaeology*, LXIII (1959), pp. 29–45.

[6] P. Montet, *Ann. Serv.*, XXXIX (1939), pp. 529–39; *Kêmi*, IX (1942), pp. 1–95; *Nécropole royale de Tanis*, I–III; G. Brunton, *Ann. Serv.*, XXXIX (1939), pp. 541–7; Z. Iskander, *Ann. Serv.*, XL (1940), pp. 581–8.

[7] J. Černý, *Cahiers d'histoire mondial*, I, No. 4 (1954), pp. 903–21; J. R. Harris, *Lexicographical Studies*, pp. 32–33, 41–42.

[8] W. M. F. Petrie, *Prehistoric Egypt*, p. 27; cf. *Social Life in Ancient Egypt*, p. 5.

[9] W. M. F. Petrie, *Ancient Egypt*, 1915, p. 16.

[10] See, however, p. 249.

[11] Cf. J. R. Harris, *Lexicographical Studies*, p. 42.

[12] *A.R.*, II, 446.   [13] *A.R.*, II, 459, 490.   [14] *A.R.*, II, 485.

[15] *A.R.*, II, 482.   [16] *A.R.*, II, 447, 491, 518, 820.   [17] *A.R.*, II, 584.

[18] *A.R.*, III, 116, 274.   [19] *A.R.*, III, 420.   [20] *A.R.*, III, 434.

again all Asiatic countries, but also from Libya,[1] a country to the north-west of Egypt.

As already stated, neither native silver nor silver ores proper occur in Egypt, though silver is found in very small proportion in both the local lead ore and the local nickel ore. Since, therefore, there was no native silver and no ores that could be treated to obtain the metal, and since there is no evidence and very little probability that the Egyptians of predynastic and early dynastic times had the necessary metal-lurgical knowledge to enable them to separate minute proportions of silver from lead ores[2] (though these were worked for galena to use as an eye-paint and also for smelting to obtain the metal), much less from nickel ores (which were not worked at all anci-ently), what then was the source of the ancient silver? It could not have been obtained from the local gold and electrum, though these contain considerable proportions, since the necessary knowledge of how to separate silver from gold was lacking, even as late as Greek times, as is proved by the method of refining gold (chiefly from silver) described by Agatharchides,[3] in which the silver was converted into chloride and rejected. In my opinion, there is no doubt that, both in Egypt and in western Asia, there were alloys of gold and silver, of the nature of electrum, so rich in silver that they were silver-white [4] and that it was these alloys that constituted the first ancient silver, that is to say they were 'white gold', which is what the Egyptians called silver. This seems to be proved by the fact that all the early silver from Egypt is in fact such an alloy and contains gold, sometimes in considerable proportion, the specimens of which analyses are available containing from 0.7 per cent to 38.1 per cent of gold.[5]

None of the Egyptian silver is of the nature or purity of that smelted from ore. Thus, some is not of a uniform white colour, as would be the case had it been ob-tained from ore, when necessarily it would have been melted and well mixed, but has yellowish patches manifestly due to the unequal distribution of the gold present. This occurs on the anklets of Hetepheres (Fourth Dynasty), on several of the objects from the tomb of Tutankhamūn (Eighteenth Dynasty), and on bracelets and on metal 'gloves', of late Nineteenth Dynasty date.[6]

That the ancient gold and electrum were natural products that still occur in Egypt will generally be admitted, and it is not unreasonable to suppose, therefore, that the silver was also a natural product, though the fact that an alloy of gold and silver, con-taining so large a proportion of the latter as to have a white colour, is still to be found is not usually recognized. Nowadays, however, such an alloy would generally be classed as a poor-quality gold and its true character might be masked by the manner in which it would be considered and reported. Anciently the case was different: silver was scarce and in consequence was several times the value of gold, and hence it would have been the object of diligent search and even the smallest deposits found would

---

[1] *A.R.*, III, 584.

[2] Both Hume (*Geology of Egypt*, II, Part III, p. 825) and Gowland (*Archaeologia*, XIX (1920), pp. 121–3) have suggested that the Egyptians may have worked very low-grade lead ores to obtain silver, and Aitchison (*History of Metals*, I, p. 47) is of the opinion that cupellation was practised as early as 2500 B.C. Cf. also Forbes (*Metallurgy in Antiquity*, p. 214).

[3] See p. 229.   [4] See pp. 234–5.

[5] See pp. 491–2. Cf. A. Lucas, *J.E.A.*, XIV (1928), pp. 313–19.

[6] Cairo Museum, Nos. C.G. 52577–8 and C.G. 52708–9.

have been highly prized and would have been worked until exhausted. That it still occurs, however, is proved by the results of the assay (by A. C. Claudet) of twenty-six specimens of modern Egyptian gold from quartz quoted by Alford.[1] When the ratio of silver to gold in these specimens is calculated it is seen that in fifteen instances this is one part or more of silver to one part of gold, the highest ratio being 3.3 parts of silver to one part of gold. All these specimens, therefore, would be silver-white, since a silver-gold alloy containing 50 per cent or more of silver has a white colour. Mellor mentions a specimen of natural silver-gold alloy from Norway that contained 28 per cent of gold and, therefore, by inference, 72 per cent of silver,[2] which also would be white. However, in no case is the percentage of gold as low as that recorded for some examples of Egyptian silver, and unless it is assumed that specimens with a very much lower gold content were found anciently it seems possible that silver may have been imported as early as the Old Kingdom at least.[3]

Eventually, silver was obtained, as it is largely today, from argentiferous lead ores, which is proved, by the exploitation of the mines of Mount Laurion in Attica (Greece), certainly as early as the fifth [4] and fourth centuries [5] B.C. and probably earlier. It is unlikely, however, that these, or indeed any Greek mines, were the first to be worked and probable that the earliest production of silver from an ore (which was certainly argentiferous lead ore) took place in western Asia, where such ores occur extensively. In Anatolia and Armenia there are many ancient silver mines, which unfortunately cannot be dated, the ores being chiefly argentiferous galena associated with sulphide of zinc.[6] In Georgia and Caucasia there are also similar ores, though whether they were worked anciently or not is uncertain.[7] In Persia, too, lead ores containing silver are widely distributed, but again it is not known whether they were exploited anciently or not.[8]

Copper is present in small proportion in many specimens of ancient Egyptian silver,[9] and in a few instances the quantity is such as to suggest an intentional alloy.[10] In one case the ratio of copper to silver was found to be approximately 2 : 1,[11] and a single example of an alloy of silver and tin has also been recorded.[12]

Niello

Pliny states [13] that 'The Egyptians stain silver', and goes on to say that 'strange to

---

[1] C. J. Alford, *Report on Ancient and Prospective Gold Mining in Egypt*, 1900, Appendix.

[2] J. W. Mellor, *Inorganic and Theoretical Chemistry*, III, p. 299.

[3] Cf. Z. Iskander, in F. Bisson de la Roque, *Trésor de Tôd (Cat. Caire)*, pp. 53–54; L. Aitchison, *History of Metals*, I, p. 180.

[4] Herodotus, VII: 144.   [5] Xenophon, *De Vectigalibus*, IV; Aristotle, *Ath. Pol.*, XLVII.

[6] H. A. Karajian, *Mineral Resources of Armenia and Anatolia*, pp. 140–60.

[7] D. Ghambashidze, *Mineral Resources of Georgia and Caucasia*, pp. 44–49.

[8] Moustafa Khan Fateh, *The Economic Position of Persia*, p. 32; Geog. Section, Naval Intell. Division, Admiralty, London, *Geology of Mesopotamia and its Borderlands*, p. 69.

[9] See analyses, pp. 491–2.

[10] Cf. A. H. Kopp, in H. E. Winlock, *Treasure of El Lāhūn*, pp. 73–74; W. B. Pollard, in J. E. Quibell, *Yuaa and Thuiu*, pp. 78–79; W. C. Hayes, *Scepter*, II, p. 61.

[11] A. H. Kopp, quoted by G. Brunton, *Ann. Serv.*, XXXV (1935), p. 215.

[12] C. R. Williams, *Gold and Silver Jewelry*, pp. 29, 92–93. Tin 15.2 per cent.

[13] XXXIII: 46, 131.

relate the value of the silver is enhanced when its splendour has been sullied. The preparation is as follows: one-third of a part of the finest Cyprian copper . . . is mixed with one part of silver and the same amount of live sulphur. The whole is heated in an earthen crucible luted with clay . . .' 'Silver can also be tarnished with the yolk of a hard-boiled egg'. The word 'stain' (*tinguit*) suggests some method of treating a silver object whereby it acquired a dark or black colour, particularly in view of the statement about tarnishing (*nigrescit*) silver by means of the sulphur compounds in egg-yolk, but the description given is not that of making a stain or varnish to be applied to silver, but of producing an alloy of silver and copper blackened by the sulphides of these metals, and apparently it was this black alloy that was employed in place of pure white silver, a strange taste, as Pliny remarks. This description strongly suggests a form of niello, a few examples of which have been reported from ancient Egypt.

The earliest alleged instances of the use of such an alloy date from the beginning of the Eighteenth Dynasty, on certain objects from the treasure of Queen Ahhotpe, though the statements of those who have examined the pieces do not agree, and there is some doubt about the identification in every case but one. Von Bissing, who first published the find, states that niello ('*Tula*') is present on four of the objects, the axe, the large dagger, a small dagger, and a pair of hawk-headed collar terminals,[1] and although he alone mentions the small dagger, both Möller[2] and Rosenberg[3] agree in describing the dark filling on the other three pieces as niello. Vernier, however, in discussing niello cites only the large dagger as an example,[4] and in his catalogue of the jewellery in the Cairo Museum, for which he examined the objects in detail, refers to niello on only two, namely the dagger[5] and the terminals.[6] Of the alleged niello on the smaller dagger he says nothing,[7] but in describing the axe-head[8] he states without reservation that the blackish substance with which it is inlaid is, in fact, lapis lazuli, now decomposed.[9] The lines of cleavage visible on the plate look more like the joins between pieces of inlay than cracks in a metallic composition,[10] and if the material is indeed lapis lazuli it seems likely that even Vernier may have been mistaken with regard to the terminals and that they, too, are inlaid with lapis as might be expected from comparison with other examples.[11] That the large dagger is decorated with a species of niello there can, however, be little doubt. The blade of the dagger is gold with a narrow band of black material down the centre of each side, this band being inlaid with inscriptions and designs in gold wire. The black material

---

[1] F. W. von Bissing, *Ein Thebanischer Grabfund*, pp. 1–4, 17, Pls. I, II, III (5), VIII (10), IX (1f–g).

[2] G. Möller, *Metallkunst*, pp. 26–27.

[3] M. Rosenberg, *Niello*, I, pp. 25–26.

[4] E. Vernier, *Bijouterie et Joaillerie*, pp. 28–31, Pl. XXIV (2); cf. also pp. 130–2. For the collar terminals cf. Pl. X (1).

[5] E. Vernier, *Bijoux et Orfèvreries*, pp. 209–10, Pl. XLV (No. 52658).

[6] E. Vernier, *Bijoux et Orfèvreries*, pp. 221–2, Pl. LII (No. 52672).

[7] E. Vernier, *Bijoux et Orfèvreries*, pp. 211–12, Pl. XLV (No. 52660).

[8] E. Vernier, *Bijoux et Orfèvreries*, pp. 205–7, Pls. XLII, XLIII (No. 52645).

[9] Cf. W. S. Smith, *Art and Architecture of Ancient Egypt*, p. 126.

[10] It has not been possible to check any of the actual pieces.

[11] It is surely significant that in previous editions of this book no mention was made of either the terminals or the axehead, since Lucas would have had ample opportunity to examine the objects. Cf. A. Lucas, *Ancient Egyptian Materials and Industries* (3rd ed. 1948), p. 283.

has the appearance of having been introduced into position while in a plastic condition, and while it was still in that state the gold ornamentation must have been inserted. The composition of the material has not been determined, though it is certainly not a metal. Traces of verdigris [1] suggest the presence of copper, and it may well be a copper sulphide or a mixture of metallic sulphides, in which case it is a form of niello.

Another example of what is almost certainly a kind of niello is on a small bronze tablet case of Twenty-fifth Dynasty date now in the Louvre. This case was examined carefully and the material analysed by Berthelot.[2] It consists of bronze containing a large proportion of lead, and is coated on both sides with a layer of black material about 0.5 mm. thick, which Berthelot considered to be niello. Inlaid in this material are inscriptions and designs, which can have been put in position only while it was plastic. The black material contains a large proportion of lead, together with copper and tin, but sulphide is also present and a trace of fatty matter. Berthelot concluded that the alloy had been an initial mixture of oxide of lead, clay and an oily substance, with traces of oxides of copper and tin, blackened by sulphides of lead and copper and possibly other metallic sulphides in small quantities, and thought that it had probably been applied cold.

No other supposed instances of niello have been described in any detail, but a bracelet of Twenty-second Dynasty date found at Tanis is said to be inlaid with niello,[3] and Roeder refers to possible cases of niello inlay on bronze figures of late date.[4]

How far any of the Egyptian examples may properly be classed as niello is perhaps open to question, since the term is more correctly used of a specific mixture of the sulphides of copper, silver and lead. This mixture, obtained either by mixing the sulphides and fusing them, or by mixing the metals and converting them to sulphides by the action of sulphur, is ground and applied to the engraved metal and then fused *in situ*.[5] There is little to suggest that such a precise mixture was ever used by the Egyptians, and the alloys that have been described were almost certainly not applied by fusion, but by a technique of controlled heating and rubbing, or possibly even cold.

Silver Plating [6]

The Egyptians early knew how to plate copper with silver, as is proved by a copper ewer of the Second Dynasty found by Brunton.[7] Professor Thompson, reporting upon this, says: 'The material of which the ewer is made contains tin. Whether this is present in sufficient quantity to constitute a bronze [8] cannot be determined without

---

[1] Cf. F. W. von Bissing, *Ein Thebanischer Grabfund*, p. 3, *n*. 7.

[2] M. Berthelot, *Monuments Piot*, VII (1900), pp. 121–41, Pls. XII, XIII; *Ann. Chim. et Phys.*, XXIII (1901), pp. 5–32.

[3] P. Montet, *Nécropole royale de Tanis*, I, p. 69.

[4] G. Roeder, *Ägyptische Bronzewerke*, p. 208; *Ägyptische Bronzefiguren*, p. 527.

[5] Cf. A. A. Moss, *Studies in Conservation*, I (1953), pp. 49–60.

[6] Cf. G. Möller, *Metallkunst*, pp. 32–35.

[7] G. Brunton, *Qau and Badari*, I, p. 69, Pl. XVIII (10).

[8] Bronze may almost certainly be excluded at so early a date as the Second Dynasty.

destroying the sample. The material is cold-worked and appears to have been hammered to shape from a sheet. There is a definite coating of either silver or tin on the outside of the ewer. The former is the more probable, though one cannot be sure without spoiling the vase. There are indications that this plating was done by hammering the other metal on the copper or bronze before the ewer was made. The spout appears to have been hammered on to the rest of the body.' This ewer was further examined by Professor H. B. Dixon, who stated that silver was certainly present on the surface of the copper as a very thin layer and tin absent, the silver having been put on either in the pure state or alloyed with copper. Neither the finder nor Thompson nor Dixon gives any details of the extent of the silver 'plating'. If it occurred only round where the spout was fastened in may it not have been solder, such as that already mentioned,[1] which had spread beyond the join? As an explanation of the method of plating employed, Brunton adopted a suggestion put forward by me, that the technique might have been analogous to that employed for making the 'gold' thread required in the manufacture of the 'Holy Carpet' formerly sent annually by the Egyptian Government to Mecca. This so-called 'gold' thread, which was really silver thread covered with a thin coating of gold, was made as follows:[2] A thick bar of silver was wrapped round with thin sheets of gold and heated in a small charcoal furnace, from which it was periodically removed and well rubbed with a thick agate rod, the gold eventually alloying with the silver, forming a thin, uniform, strongly and closely adherent coating. This was then passed through a series of draw-plates until thread of the required thinness was obtained, which had all the appearance of being gold though it was only silver plated with gold. Two small rectangular objects of copper (possibly knives or razors) of Old Kingdom date from Edfu have also been silvered,[3] and copper mirrors were often covered with silver,[4] apparently applied directly to the copper by means of an adhesive.[5]

The principal use of silver anciently was for beads, jewellery, bowls and vases, though, like gold, it was also beaten into foil and thin leaf and used for covering wood, examples of foil occurring for the garments of the king and queen on the throne of Tutankhamūn; for the 'slippers' on the bottom of the legs of a box; covering the sledge of a small shrine; covering the staples in the large shrines and the handles of the two sledges carrying the canopic box; and examples of leaf being on a writing board from this same tomb; on a head-rest from the tomb of Hetepheres (Fourth Dynasty); and on one of the coffins, a bed, and a shawabti from the tomb of Yuya and Tuyu (Eighteenth Dynasty). A specimen examined by Berthelot[6] varied in thickness from .001 to .0025 mm. Instances of the use of silver for soldering copper have already been given,[7] as also an instance of its use for plating copper.

---

[1] See pp. 215–6.
[2] A. Lucas and B. F. E. Keeling, 'The Manufacture of the Holy Carpet', Cairo Sc. Journ., VII (1913), pp. 129–30.
[3] Cairo Museum, Nos. 71827 A and B.
[4] Cf. G. Bénédite, Miroirs, Nos. 44035, 44049, 44074.
[5] G. Möller, Metallkunst, p. 34.
[6] M. Berthelot, Ann. Serv., II (1901), pp. 160–1.
[7] See pp. 215–6.

Pure silver melts at 960.5° C. (1,760.9° F.), this melting-point being raised by the presence of gold or copper.

TIN

The word 'tin' is often used loosely to designate both the metal and the ore, but in order to avoid ambiguity and misunderstanding, the term will here be restricted to its correct meaning of the metal.

In antiquity the principal use of tin was for making bronze, though occasionally it was employed alone. The early history of tin is very obscure and no evidence can be found to show when it was first discovered. The sequence of tin and bronze is also uncertain, though from the fact that the first recorded appearance of tin was in the form of its alloy bronze, as also from theoretical considerations, the probability is that bronze was made some considerable time before tin as an individual metal was isolated, just as brass (an alloy of copper and zinc) was known long before zinc itself was discovered. Either tin or tin ore, however, must have been used to produce bronze, in which tin is an indispensable constituent, though if the ore as distinguished from the metal, were employed, it need not necessarily have been recognized at first as being essentially different from copper, all the knowledge required being a realization that ore from a certain place when added to copper ore produced an improved form of copper.

Until recently it was thought that tin ore did not occur in Egypt, but a thin vein of tin oxide (cassiterite) was found in 1935 near Gebel Muelih, in the eastern desert, roughly half-way between Edfu and the Red Sea, and in 1940 further deposits were found in Gebel el Agala district in the neighbourhood of Quseir on the Red Sea coast, and in 1941 a small works was erected by the Egyptian Government, the ore being smelted on the spot. There is no evidence that this occurrence was known or worked anciently. The earliest use of tin, apart from bronze, and the earliest references to tin known to me are Egyptian. Thus the first objects of tin of which any records can be traced, namely a ring [1] (or rather the bezel of a ring, now in the museum of University College, London) and a pilgrim bottle,[2] are from Egyptian graves of the Eighteenth Dynasty (1580 B.C. to 1314 B.C.). A ring, consisting of an alloy of tin and silver, is also known from the same period,[3] and an ore of tin (the oxide) was employed in Egypt in small amount from the Eighteenth Dynasty onwards for imparting a white opaque colour to glass,[4] and such an oxide was found in the tomb of Tutankhamūn.[5] After this in chronological order comes an object of tin having the outlines of a winged scarab, which probably dates from about 600–700 B.C.[6] A tin solder was identified on an earring dating from the third century B.C. or later;[7] from the Roman

---

[1] W. M. F. Petrie, *Illahun, Kahun and Gurob*, p. 19; *Arts and Crafts*, p. 104; J. H. Gladstone *P.S.B.A.*, XIV (1892), p. 226.

[2] E. R. Ayrton, C. T. Currelly and A. E. P. Weigall, *Abydos*, III, p. 50.

[3] C. R. Williams, *Gold and Silver Jewelry*, pp. 29, 92.

[4] B. Neumann and G. Kotyga, *Zeitschr. f. angew. Chemie*, XXXVIII (1925), pp. 776–80, 857–64; H. D. Parodi, *La Verrerie en Égypte*, pp. 34, 45.

[5] A. Lucas, in H. Carter, *Tut-ankh-Amen*, III, pp. 176–7 (Appendix II).

[6] A. H. Church, *Chemical News*, 1877, p. 168.

[7] C. R. Williams, *Gold and Silver Jewelry*, p. 124.

period in Nubia there are two finger rings of tin,[1] two bronze bowls that have been tinned [1] and a bowl of pewter,[1] an alloy of lead and tin; in the third century A.D. tin plates inscribed with magical charms are mentioned,[2] and in A.D. 572 there is a recipe for making solder from lead (80 per cent) and tin (20 per cent) for soldering the pipes of a bath.[3]

Tin is mentioned in Breasted's translation of the Harris papyrus [4] of the reign of Ramses III (Twentieth Dynasty), and of another text of the Twenty-fifth Dynasty,[5] but the meaning of the word so translated is extremely doubtful.[6] Probably the earliest references to tin are in Homer (ninth century B.C.),[7] after which come four references in the Bible,[8] one in Numbers (about fifth century B.C.), a doubtful one in Isaiah (either eighth or fifth century B.C.) and two in Ezekiel (sixth century B.C.), then Herodotus [9] (fifth century B.C.), Diodorus Siculus [10] (first century B.C.), Julius Caesar [11] (first century B.C.), Strabo [12] (first century B.C. to first century A.D., in one instance quoting Posidonius of the second to first century B.C.), Pliny [13] (first century A.D.) and other classical writers.

In the first century A.D. tin was being shipped by way of Egypt to Somaliland and India,[14] but from where it was obtained is not stated.

Tin does not occur naturally in the metallic condition, the form in which it is found in nature being in the combined state as a mineral, the principal and only tin mineral of importance being the oxide (cassiterite or tinstone), though a sulphide combined with the sulphides of copper and iron (stannite, stannine or tin pyrites) is also found in small quantity in certain localities.

Metallic tin, which melts at 232° C., is one of the easiest metals to produce and it may be obtained by simply heating the oxide with charcoal, this being the fuel employed anciently and the fuel generally used for smelting until about the eighteenth century A.D. The metal, however, cannot be produced from the sulphide by any such simple means, which is proof that this ore was not employed anciently as a source of tin.

Tin oxide occurs in two forms, one in veins (lodes), frequently in granite or granitic rocks and occasionally associated with copper ore, and the other as pebbles, gravel or sand, derived from the disintegration of rocks bearing vein ore, the debris from which has been carried and deposited by water.

Tin ore (cassiterite) is heavy and usually dark brown or black in colour and, except the weight, there is nothing to suggest that it is a metallic compound. It is frequently

---

[1] C. L. Woolley and D. Randall MacIver, *Karanog*, III, p. 67.

[2] F. G. Kenyon, *Greek Papyri in the British Museum*, I, pp. 91, 93, 97, 99.

[3] B. P. Grenfell and A. S. Hunt, *Oxyrhynchus Papyri*, VI, pp. 268–9.

[4] *A.R.*, IV, 245, 302, 385.

[5] *A.R.*, IV, 929.

[6] Cf. J. R. Harris, *Lexicographical Studies*, pp. 66–67.

[7] *Iliad*, XI: 25, 34; XVIII: 474, 565; XX: 271; XXI: 592; XXIII: 503, 561.

[8] *Numbers*, 31: 22; *Isaiah*, I: 25 (the R.V. gives the alternative reading 'alloy'); *Ezekiel*, 22: 18, 20; 27: 12.

[9] III: 115.   [10] V: 2.

[11] *B.G.*, V: 12.   [12] III: 2, 9; 5, 11; XV: 2, 10.

[13] IV: 30, 34, 36; VII: 57; XXXIV: 47, 48.

[14] W. H. Schoff, *The Periplus of the Erythraean Sea*, pp. 33, 42, 45.

found in the same alluvial gravels as gold, and since both are obtained by the same method, namely by washing away the lighter material with running water, it is exceedingly probable that when gold was being searched for, the heavy tin oxide, which, however, is not nearly so heavy as gold, would be noticed, and it seems likely that the alluvial ore was discovered in this manner. On account of this association with gold, and also because the alluvial ore occurs in more accessible places and is more easily mined than the vein ore, it was probably alluvial ore that was worked first deliberately as a separate ore.

Claims have been made for Europe, Africa and Asia respectively as the place where tin was first discovered and the home therefore probably of bronze.

The claim for the European origin of tin [1] and bronze [2] has not found general support and, in my opinion, there is neither evidence nor probability that tin was being mined and bronze made in Central Europe as early as the Fourth Dynasty (about 2700 B.C. to 2550 B.C.), the possible date of two Egyptian bronze objects,[3] nor even at the time of the Middle Kingdom (about 2000 B.C. to 1800 B.C.), from which period a number of bronze objects have been found in Egypt.[4] That the still earlier Asiatic bronze should have come from Europe is even more unlikely.

With respect to Africa, although tin ores occur plentifully,[5] it is inconceivable that important materials, such as tin (or tin ore) and bronze, should have been traded in quantity for centuries to Egypt, and possibly through Egypt to Asia and Europe, without leaving some evidence of the traffic or some traces or knowledge of either tin or bronze on the way, and no such evidence or traces are known. Also, this would not explain the possession of bronze in Mesopotamia at a date considerably earlier than it was known in Egypt, unless the Mesopotamian bronze did not pass through Egypt, but reached that country by sea, and that any trade, much less a regular trade, should have been carried on between East Africa and the Persian Gulf as early as about 3500 B.C. to 3200 B.C., which is the approximate date of the earliest bronze found in Mesopotamia,[6] is most improbable.

From the evidence at present available there seems no doubt that the home of both tin and bronze was in western Asia, and it has been thought that the special locality was possibly in north-east Persia, where both tin and copper ores are known to occur.[7] Wainwright, however, has published an important article in which he shows that a likely early source of tin and bronze, particularly of the Egyptian supply, was the Kesrwan district of Syria,[8] which is situated a little to the north-east of the modern town of Beyrut, to the occurrence of tin in which I drew attention several years ago,[9] without, however, realizing its importance. Wainwright shows that both

---

[1] W. M. F. Petrie, *Medum*, p. 44.

[2] W. M. F. Petrie, *Arts and Crafts*, p. 101; H. C. Richardson, *American Journal of Archaeology*, xxxvIII (1934), p. 555; H. Quiring, *F.u.F.*, xvII (1941), pp. 172–4.

[3] See p. 219.   [4] See pp. 219–20.

[5] A. Lucas, *J.E.A.*, xiv (1928), pp. 100–1.   [6] See pp. 217–8.

[7] A. Lucas, *J.E.A.*, xiv (1928), pp. 100, 108. See also O. G. S. Crawford, *Antiquity*, xII (1938), pp. 79–81; H. Field and E. Prostov, *Antiquity*, xII (1938), pp. 341–5.

[8] G. A. Wainwright, *J.E.A.*, xx (1934), pp. 29–32. See also G. A. Wainwright, *Antiquity*, xvIII (1944), pp. 57–64; C. Schaeffer, *J.E.A.*, xxxI (1945), pp. 92–95.

[9] A. Lucas, *J.E.A.*, xiv (1928), p. 100.

tin ore and copper ore occur in the mountains of the Kesrwan district, through which flow two rivers, the Nahr Ibrahim and the Nahr Feidar (the ancient Adonis and Phaedrus) which enter the sea near the site of the ancient town of Byblos, which was *the* port for Egyptian trade from at least as early as the First Dynasty.

No evidence is known of either ancient or modern mining in the Kesrwan Mountains, but the country was prospected some years ago by two Australian mining engineers, who applied for the right to mine tin, copper and silver ores, which, therefore, they must have been satisfied existed in quantity, the work, however, being suspended on the outbreak of war and never resumed.[1] Wainwright suggests that fragments of tin ore or copper ore, or both, may have been brought down by the two rivers mentioned, the Adonis having a strong current all the year round and the Phaedrus a 'considerable flood after heavy rains', though it dries up during the summer. This dried river bed would have been a most likely place for discovering and collecting any fragments of ore there may have been, and it should not be forgotten that in the West, where alone there is early written evidence of tin working, the ore, which was alluvial, was derived from the dried beds of ancient water-courses. Thus, referring to Spain-Portugal, Strabo (first century B.C. to first century A.D.) quotes Posidonius [2] (second to first century B.C.) for the statement that the earth in which the tin ore occurred was 'brought down by the rivers: this the women scrape up with spades and wash in sieves . . .' and Pliny (first century A.D.) says [3] of the same Spanish-Portuguese tin ore that 'It is a sand found on the surface of the earth, and of a black colour, and it is only to be detected by its weight. It is mingled with small pebbles, particularly in the dried beds of rivers.' Manifestly, therefore, the ore described by both these writers was alluvial.

Diodorus, writing with reference to the inhabitants of Cornwall, states [4] that 'These are the people that make the tin, which with a great deal of care and labour they dig out of the ground; and that being rocky, the metal is mixed with some veins of earth, out of which they melt the metal and then refine it.' Although at first sight this description might suggest the mining of vein and not alluvial ore, it was almost certainly the latter that was meant, since in certain districts in Cornwall the alluvial gravels are not on the surface, but in one place, for example, they are beneath some 50 feet of sand and silt and in another place they are covered with peat, gravel and sand to a depth of 20 feet.[5] Also, all the available evidence points to 'tin streaming', as it was termed, having been a much older industry in Cornwall than the mining of vein ore.

In view of the probability, as shown by Wainwright, that some at least of the early tin ore found in the East was alluvial and was possibly accompanied by copper ore (almost certainly malachite, the usual ore of surface copper deposits, which would have been well known at the time and recognized as yielding copper when smelted), the explanation previously given by me to account for the discovery of tin and

---

[1] I. M. Toll, 'The Mineral Resources of Syria', *Eng. and Mining Journ.*, CXII (1921), p. 851.

[2] III: 2, 9.

[3] XXXIV: 47.

[4] V: 2.

[5] G. M. Davies, *Tin Ores*, pp. 28, 29.

bronze [1] may be much simplified. Although it was recognized that 'it was probably alluvial ore that was worked first deliberately as a separate ore',[2] it was assumed that bronze was first made accidentally by smelting associated ores of copper and tin, both derived from veins,[3] because no association of copper ore and alluvial tin ore was known, but it is now suggested that the sequence of events may have been much as follows.

First, the discovery of alluvial tin ore, possibly on the banks or in the bed of either the Adonis or Phaedrus, or both, and probably during a search for gold.[4]

Second, the realization that the comparatively heavy tin ore might be metalliferous, possibly even a kind of copper ore, and the consequent smelting of it, either alone, when tin would have been discovered, or more probably mixed with copper ore, when bronze would have been made.

Third, when the alluvial tin ore first found, which probably only occurred in comparatively small amount, was becoming exhausted, search was made for other supplies and the sources in Spain-Portugal, Cornwall, Brittany and elsewhere manifestly became known and eventually, at a very much later date and in some places only, the parent veins (lodes) from which some of the alluvial ore had originally been derived were tracked down and worked.

It should be pointed out that the hypothesis of the possible discovery of tin ore and bronze in a district in such close touch with Egypt, as was the neighbourhood of Byblos, leaves unexplained the fact of the knowledge of bronze in Mesopotamia at a much earlier date than in Egypt, unless other and earlier sources of tin ore were also known.

Hintze is quoted by von Bissing [5] for the statement 'that at Eskishehir [6] in Central Asia Minor, tin has been found quite recently, and that the mines were exploited under the old Turkish government'.

MINERALS

The dictionary definition of a mineral is 'a substance obtained by mining', but the word is here used, not in this wide sense, but with a very restricted meaning, since the most important minerals, namely, the metals and their ores, have already been dealt with, and certain other mineral substances, such as building stone, gypsum, ochres, orpiment, precious, semi-precious and other stones, either have been, or will be, separately described. The minerals to be discussed are alum, barytes, cobalt compounds, emery, graphite, manganese compounds, mica, natron, nitre, salt and sulphur.

ALUM[7]

So far as can be ascertained, alum has never been discovered in connexion with ancient Egypt,[8] and the evidence for its use is entirely circumstantial, namely, that

---

[1] A. Lucas, *J.E.A.*, XIV (1928), pp. 97–108, in particular pp. 106–8.
[2] A. Lucas, *J.E.A.*, XIV (1928), p. 98.   [3] A. Lucas, *J.E.A.*, XIV (1928), p. 107.
[4] See pp. 254–5.   [5] F. W. von Bissing, *Journ. Hellenic Studies*, LII (1932), p. 119.
[6] Called Eski Shehr by Wainwright (*J.E.A.*, XX (1934), p. 29).
[7] Cf. J. R. Harris, *Lexicographical Studies*, pp. 185 f.
[8] On the question of the use of alum in mummification, see p. 303.

alum occurs in Egypt; that it was mined anciently; that it was evidently used in tawing leather,[1] as a mordant in dyeing [2] and for medicinal purposes,[3] and that references to alum and other astringent materials occur in Egyptian texts.[4]

Alum is found in the Oases of Dakhla and Kharga,[5] which are situated in the desert west of the Nile valley; in Dakhla it is 'widely distributed in small quantities;[6] in Kharga there are 'ancient mines of the most extensive description;[7] 'hills . . . literally honeycombed with ancient workings';[7] 'Huge dump heaps'[7] and 'The extent and magnitude of the underground workings prove that whatever the mineral mined, it was a substance of considerable value in those days; and an examination of the blind termination of the tunnels occasionally reveals the presence of very thin seams of aluminium sulphate, which . . . we must conclude was the substance sought.'[7] Miss Caton-Thompson and Miss Gardner state that 'miles of outlying foothills and desert floor alike were seen to be riddled with shallow workings, giving the ground the appearance of having been shelled'.[8] 'Alum seems most likely to be the mineral sought.'[8] The deposits in Kharga were worked during 1918–19, when about 222 metric tons of alum were extracted.[9]

Some part at least of this mining is undoubtedly comparatively modern, thus Maqrizi states[10] that in Arab times 1,000 *kantars* (44 tons) of alum were sent annually from the Oases to Cairo; another Arab writer says[11] that the receipts from the alum mines formed part of the Government revenue; and in 1809 Hamilton wrote:[12] 'The trade of Goubanieh, which is a few miles below As Souan, consists in the fitting out annually a caravan of fifty camels for the purpose of procuring alum from a low spot in the Desert, ten or eleven days' journey South-West of the Cataracts. It is found in a single stratum from two to fifteen inches in depth covered with a layer of dry sand about half a foot thick and resting on a bed of moist sand. The alum when taken is broken in pieces, dried in the sun and at Goubanieh is sold at seven *pataques* the ardeb.'[13]

But this was not the earliest mining, since Egyptian alum is mentioned in Babylonian texts.[14] Herodotus (fifth century B.C.) says[15] that Amasis (569 to 526 B.C.) sent

---

[1] See pp. 34–35.   [2] See pp. 36, 153–4.

[3] Cf. H. v. Deines and H. Grapow, *Drogennamen*, pp. 22–23.

[4] Cf. J. R. Harris, *Lexicographical Studies*, pp. 185–9.

[5] Mines and Quarries Dept., *Report on the Mineral Industry*, p. 30.

[6] H. J. L. Beadnell, *Dakhla Oasis*, pp. 100–1.

[7] H. J. L. Beadnell, *Egyptian Oasis*, pp. 220–3; cf. J. Ball, *Kharga Oasis*, p. 84.

[8] G. Caton-Thompson and E. W. Gardner, *Geog. Journ.*, LXXX (1932), p. 372.

[9] For a chemical analysis see G. Hogan, 'Note on the Deposits of Aluminium Sulphate at Kharga Oasis, Egyptian Water Supplies', *Report and Notes of the Public Health Laboratories*, Cairo, 1920, pp. 11–12.

[10] Maqrizi, 'Description topographique et historique de l'Égypte', *Mém. Miss.*, XVII (1900), pp. 17, 691, 697, 698.

[11] S. Lane-Poole, *History of Egypt in the Middle Ages*, p. 304.

[12] W. Hamilton, *Remarks on Several Parts of Turkey*, Part I, Aegyptiaca, p. 428.

[13] This account apparently is taken from Girard (P. S. Girard, 'Mém. sur l'agriculture, l'industrie et le commerce de l'Égypte', *Description de l'Égypte, état moderne*, II, p. 623).

[14] Cf. M. Levey, *Chemistry . . . in Ancient Mesopotamia*, pp. 72, 110, 160; R. C. Thompson, *Dictionary of Assyrian Chemistry and Geology*, p. 33.

[15] II: 180.

from Egypt a thousand *talents'* worth of astringent earth (almost certainly alum) as a contribution towards the rebuilding of the temple at Delphi and that the Greek dwellers in Egypt sent a further twenty *minae* worth. Egyptian alum was also known to the Romans of Pliny's day (first century A.D.), since this writer, when enumerating the different sources of alum, includes Egypt and states that the Egyptian alum was 'the most esteemed'.[1] Miss Caton-Thompson and Miss Gardner state [2] that 'Sherds collected in field examination of mining areas . . . confirmed their Roman date.' Dioscorides states [3] that 'Almost every kind of alum is found in the same mines in Egypt.' Egyptian alum is also mentioned in one papyrus found in Egypt,[4] but unfortunately undated, and in two others dated A.D. 229 and A.D. 300 respectively.[5] During the Ptolemaic [6] and Roman [7] periods the alum deposits were controlled by the State.

At the present time alum is employed both as a mordant in dyeing and as a medicine, and Pliny refers to its use for both these purposes [1] and, therefore, when he also mentions the use in Egypt for dyeing cloth of what is certainly a mordant,[8] it is not unreasonable to suppose that he is referring to alum, more especially as alum occurs in Egypt, where it had been mined for several centuries at least before Pliny wrote.

BARYTES

Deposits of barytes occur in several localities in Egypt, as veins in granite at Wadi Dib,[9] and in sandstone at Baharia [10] and Dakhla.[11] Barytes workings apparently of Middle Kingdom date have been discovered at Wadi el Hudi,[12] but the purpose for which the mineral was sought is unknown. A heavy wedge-shaped pendant of this material, of protodynastic date, was found at Ma'adi.[13]

COBALT COMPOUNDS

The chief value of cobalt compounds is the deep permanent blue colour of some of them, on account of which they are highly esteemed as pigments by artists and are also employed to impart a blue colour to glass. So far as is known, cobalt blue was not employed as a pigment in ancient Egypt, although two instances of its alleged use have been reported. One of these is the statement by Toch [14] that he had found

---

[1] XXXV: 52.

[2] G. Caton-Thompson and E. W. Gardner, *Desert Fayum*, p. 372.

[3] V: 123.

[4] B. P. Grenfell and A. S. Hunt, *Oxyrhynchus Papyri*, II, pp. 134–6.

[5] A. S. Hunt, *Oxyrhynchus Papyri*, XVII, No. 2116; B. P. Grenfell and A. S. Hunt, *op. cit,*, XII, No. 1429.

[6] C. Préaux, *L'Économie royale des Lagides*, p. 253.

[7] A. C. Johnson, *Economic Survey . . . Roman Egypt*, p. 326.

[8] XXXV: 42.

[9] Mines and Quarries Dept., *Report on the Mineral Industry*, p. 39; T. Barron and W. F. Hume, *Topog. and Geol. of the Eastern Desert*, pp. 31, 239; cf. L. Nassim, *Minerals of Economical Interest*, p. 165.

[10] Mines and Quarries Dept., *Report on the Mineral Industry*, p. 39; J. Ball and H. J. L. Beadnell, *Baharia Oasis*, p. 49.

[11] H. J. L. Beadnell, *Dakhla Oasis*, pp. 103–4.

[12] A. Fakhry, *Inscriptions . . . at Wadi el Hudi*, pp. 7–8.

[13] O. Menghin and M. Amer, *Excavations of the Eg. University . . . at Ma'adi, First Prelim. Report*, p. 50.

[14] M. Toch, *Journ. Ind. and Eng. Chemistry*, X (1918), p. 118.

cobalt blue pigment on the walls of the Fifth Dynasty tomb of Per-nēb. This has since been shown to be a mistake, all the blue pigment in the tomb being the well-known blue frit coloured by means of a copper compound.[1] The other instance of the supposed use of cobalt blue is the statement by Wiedemann that Hofmann had found a blue pigment of the time of Ramses III (Twentieth Dynasty) to be a cobalt colour.[2] This, however, Mrs. Williams finds to be an error, Hofmann's reference being not to the use of cobalt blue as a pigment, but to the employment of smalt,[3] an artificial preparation of the nature of glass coloured by a cobalt compound, which, although it might be used as a pigment, might equally well have been for colouring glass.

The use of cobalt compounds for colouring blue glass has been dealt with in connexion with glass, the earliest date from which it is reported being the Eighteenth Dynasty.[4]

Cobalt ores, so far as is known, do not occur in Egypt, the only cobalt compounds yet found being traces in the alum minerals of both Kharga and Dakhla Oases [5] and in the nickel ore of St. John's Island in the Red Sea,[6] these occurrences being certainly unknown anciently and the compounds presenting almost insuperable difficulties of extraction. Any cobalt compound used, therefore, must have been imported, possibly from Persia or the Caucasus region, in both of which places cobalt ores occur. Traces of cobalt compounds have also occasionally been found in ancient Egyptian copper and bronze objects and in a specimen of ancient slag from Sinai,[7] which suggests that they may be present as traces in the Egyptian copper ore.

EMERY [8]

Emery is a greyish-black variety of corundum and consists essentially of oxide of aluminium, though it also contains an admixture of oxide of iron; its hardness is next to that of the diamond and when finely powdered it is largely used as an abrasive.

Beyond a statement that some of the sand at Aswan contains 15 per cent of emery [9] and Quatremère's assertion that emery is found in Nubia,[10] neither of which has been confirmed, there is no evidence of its occurrence in Egypt, but it is found plentifully in Asia Minor and in several of the Aegean islands.

A few objects, stated to be of emery (probably because the material scratches glass), mostly dating from predynastic and early dynastic times have been found in Egypt: these include a plummet,[11] a vase,[12] a tool,[13] three small blocks [11] (thought to have been

---

[1] C. R. Williams, Per-nēb, p. 27, n. 34.

[2] A. Wiedemann, P.S.B.A., xv (1892–3), pp. 113–14.

[3] C. R. Williams, Per-nēb, p. 27, n. 29.   [4] See pp. 188–9.

[5] H. J. L. Beadnell, Egyptian Oasis, p. 222; Dakhla Oasis, p. 103; W. F. Hume, Explan. Notes to the Geol. Map of Egypt, p. 40.

[6] F. W. Moon, Prel. Geol. Rept. on St. John's Island, p. 16.

[7] J. Sebelien, Ancient Egypt, 1924, p. 10.   [8] Cf. J. R. Harris, Lexicographical Studies, pp. 163 f.

[9] G. A. Wainwright, Balabish, p. 38, n. 3, quoting Schweinfurth.

[10] E. Quatremère, Mémoires géographiques et historiques sur l'Égypte, II, p. 11.

[11] W. M. F. Petrie and J. E. Quibell, Naqada and Ballas, pp. 29, 44, 45, 48; W. M. F. Petrie, Prehistoric Egypt, pp. 41–2.

[12] J. E. Quibell and F. W. Green, Hierakonpolis, II, p. 50; Ashmolean Museum, No. 1959.215.

[13] J. E. Quibell, Archaic Objects, p. 304.

used for polishing beads because of their grooved condition), a piece [1] and several hones,[2] the date of the latter being unknown, and a stick of 'what appears to be emery' found at Kerma.[3] The plummet, which was examined at the British Museum laboratory, was reported by Dr. Plenderleith to be ferruginous sandstone and not emery.[4] The double vase from Hierakonpolis has recently been checked in Oxford and is not emery. The tool [5] was kindly examined for me by Mr. O. H. Little, Director of the Geological Survey, Egypt, and it also was found to be ferruginous sandstone and not emery; the specific gravity is only 1.47. Two of the blocks [6] I was allowed to examine by Professor Glanville and the third [7] (which is at the Ashmolean Museum, Oxford) by Mr. Leeds. All three are ferruginous sandstone and not emery. Another object [8] called 'fragment of a corundum vase' is also ferruginous sandstone and probably is not part of a vase. In my opinion the blocks have not been used for grinding either beads or other objects, but may be moulds for tubular beads. It is often stated that emery was employed in ancient Egypt as an abrasive with drills and saws for working hard stones and, although some abrasive powder must have been used, it has never been proved that the material was emery, which in my opinion is most improbable. This alleged use of emery as an abrasive has already been dealt with fully in connexion with stone working.[9]

GRAPHITE

Graphite (often termed plumbago or blacklead) is a soft, black or dark grey substance consisting largely of carbon, the proportion of which usually varies from about 50 to 97 per cent, the admixture being clay and other impurities. It is widely distributed in nature and occurs in Egypt in certain schists in the eastern desert, especially in the gold-mining areas [10] and in the beryl-mica-schists at Wadi Um Deba'a [11] and in the quartz veins of the gold-bearing rocks.

A few specimens of graphite have been found in connexion with ancient Egypt, one of Sixth Dynasty date from Gebelein;[12] one of Eighteenth Dynasty date found by Petrie in a house at Gurob;[13] a graphite bead, a small lump and a little powder in one shell, and two other shells, each containing a little powder, found by Steindorff at Aniba in Nubia[14] and a number of small pieces found by Reisner at Kerma in the Sudan,[15] where it was used for blackening certain pottery. The Gurob specimen was

---

[1] D. Randall MacIver and A. C. Mace, *El Amrah and Abydos*, p. 49.

[2] British Museum, *Guide to the Third and Fourth Egyptian Rooms*, 1904, p. 43.

[3] G. A. Reisner, *Kerma*, IV–V, p. 93.

[4] University College, London, Museum, No. 4431 A. The analytical report was kindly shown to me by Professor S. R. K. Glanville.

[5] Cairo Museum, No. C.G. 14679.

[6] University College Museum, Nos. 4796 A and 5662.

[7] Ashmolean Museum, No. 1895.992, *Summary Guide*, 1931, p. 40.

[8] Ashmolean Museum, No. 1895.991, *Summary Guide*, 1931, p. 40.

[9] See pp. 72–74.

[10] W. F. Hume, *Prelim. Report on the Geol. of the Eastern Desert*, p. 40.

[11] W. F. Hume, *Geology of Egypt*, II, Part I, pp. 112, 114, 162, 165.

[12] Cairo Museum, No. J. 66842.

[13] W. M. F. Petrie, *Kahun, Gurob and Hawara*, p. 38.

[14] Examined by me. G. Steindorff, *Aniba*, I, p. 51. Cairo Museum, Nos. J. 65221 *a, b, c, d.*

[15] G. A. Reisner, *Kerma*, IV–V, p. 290.

analysed by Mitchell and proved to be very impure, containing much siliceous matter and only 39 per cent of carbon.[1]

MANGANESE COMPOUNDS

Manganese occurs in nature chiefly combined with oxygen as oxides, which are widely distributed in Egypt, the Nubian sandstone, for example, being permeated with veins of these compounds: they also occur at Gebel Ruzza north of the Fayum, at Gebel Alda in the northern part of the Red Sea hills, and plentifully in Sinai,[2] where from one area alone 1,084,699 metric tons were extracted during the years 1917 to 1928 inclusive.[3]

Petrie mentions three oxides of manganese, namely, wad (Twelfth Dynasty), pyrolusite (Eighteenth Dynasty), and psilomelane (undated) as having been found on ancient sites, but not known to have been used.[4]

Oxides of manganese were employed in ancient Egypt to impart a purple colour to glaze and glass, but their general use for any other purpose is unknown, though one instance of the use of pyrolusite as a black pigment for tomb-painting (Twelfth Dynasty) [5] is known and also two examples of a black oxide of manganese having been employed for decorating pottery (Eighteenth Dynasty)[6]. Oxide of manganese was also used as an eye-paint.[7] The earliest date recorded for the use of manganese compounds for colouring glass is the Eighteenth Dynasty,[8] but their use for colouring glaze was much earlier, though the precise date is uncertain. These oxides were required anciently in such small quantity and they occur so plentifully in the country that it is highly improbable there was any importation from abroad. Ancient workings have been reported from one locality in the eastern desert.

MICA

The micas are a group of minerals specially distinguished by their ready cleavage into thin plates: chemically they consist of silicates of aluminium combined with compounds of iron, magnesium, potassium or sodium; they occur as essential constituents of many rocks, such as granite and gneiss, and are very plentiful in Egypt. Mica, in the form of small glittering scales, is often present in Nile silt and in many Egyptian clays, from which sources it finds its way into some of the local pottery and may frequently be seen in both ancient and modern ware. A mica mine, almost certainly not of ancient date, has been found at Wadi el Hudi.[9]

Mica was used occasionally in Egypt in predynastic times,[10] though for what purpose is unknown; mica mirrors of archaic date have been found in Nubia [11] and in the

---

[1] C. A. Mitchell, *Analyst*, XLVII (1922), p. 380.

[2] Mines and Quarries Dept., *Report on the Mineral Industry*, p. 18; J. Couyat, *Bull. Soc. fr. de Minéralogie*, XXXV (1912), pp. 563–4; A. Fenine, *Bull. Inst. d'Ég.*, XIII (1931), pp. 15–26; A. H. Curtis, *Manganese Ore*, pp. 48–52; A. W. Groves, *Reports on the Mineral Industry of the British Empire*, etc. (2nd ed.), pp. 113–15.

[3] Mines and Quarries Dept., *Report for 1928*, p. 12.

[4] W. M. F. Petrie, *Descriptive Sociology, Ancient Egyptians*, p. 49.　　　[5] See p. 340.

[6] See p. 384.　　　[7] See p. 81, and cf. J. R. Harris, *Lexicographical Studies*, pp. 176 f., 183 f.

[8] See p. 187.　　　[9] A. Fakhry, *Inscriptions . . . at Wadi el Hudi*, p. 14.

[10] W. M. F. Petrie, *Prehistoric Egypt*, p. 44; W. M. F. Petrie and J. E. Quibell, *Naqada and Ballas*, p. 45.

[11] C. M. Firth, *Arch. Survey of Nubia, 1910–1911*, pp. 201, 209, 210.

Egyptian colony of Middle Kingdom date at Kerma in the Sudan small pieces of mica were employed for decorating caps.[1] Mica pendants of the Middle Kingdom from Lisht are in the Metropolitan Museum,[2] and a necklace of New Kingdom date includes elements of mica.[3] Mica was also found at Coptos, but no particulars are given.[4]

NATRON[5]

Natron is a naturally occurring compound of sodium carbonate and sodium bicarbonate. At the present time it is found in three localities in Egypt, two (the Wadi Natrun and the Beheira province) in Lower Egypt and one (El Kab) in Upper Egypt.

The Wadi Natrun is a depression in the Libyan desert, some 40 miles to the north-west of Cairo; it is about 21 miles long, and at the bottom there is a string of lakes, the water surface of which is about 76 feet (23 metres) below sea level and the number of which fluctuates with the season. During, and for several months after, the Nile flood (which usually begins at Cairo about the end of June and generally reaches its maximum in September, often in the latter half), when there is a considerable increase in the water supply entering the Wadi, and when, on account of the lower tempera-ture during the latter part of the period evaporation has decreased, there were a few years ago, when I stayed in the Wadi on several occasions, twelve lakes.[6] In summer there are always fewer than in winter, as some of the smaller and shallower ones dry up during the hot weather. Lakes varying in number from seven to sixteen are men-tioned by different writers about the end of last century,[7] though at the beginning of the century there were apparently only six.[8] At a still earlier date, however, there would seem to have been only either one or two lakes. Thus in 1780 Sonnini mentions two,[9] which he says became merged into one during the winter; in 1849 Gmelin describes one 'pit',[10] as he terms it, but at what time of the year is not stated.

The natron in the Wadi Natrun occurs dissolved in the lake water—from which a thick layer has gradually been deposited at the bottom of some of the lakes—and also as an incrustation on the ground adjoining many of the lakes. The amount present is very considerable, although the Wadi has been the source, not only of the principal Egyptian supply, but also of a small export trade, for several thousands of years.

About 30 miles due north of the Wadi Natrun, in the Beheira province, and some 14 miles to the west of the ruins of the ancient city of Naucratis, there is another, but much smaller, depression, slightly below sea-level, in which also are a number of shallow lakes containing natron, the largest having an area of between 200 and 300

[1] G. A. Reisner, *Kerma*, IV–V, pp. 272–80.   [2] W. C. Hayes, *Scepter*, I, p. 193.

[3] W. C. Hayes, *Scepter*, II, p. 20.   [4] W. M. F. Petrie, *Koptos*, p. 26.

[5] Cf. J. R. Harris, *Lexicographical Studies*, pp. 190 f.; A. Lucas, *J.E.A.*, XVIII (1932), pp. 62–66; R. O. Steuer, *Wohlriechende Natron*; *F.u.F.*, XIV (1938), pp. 54–55.

[6] One of these lakes was largely, if not wholly, caused by the waste water from the factory.

[7] A. Lucas, *Natural Soda Deposits in Egypt* (1912), p. 2; cf. G. Schweinfurth and L. Lewin, 'Beiträge z. Topographie u. Geochemie des ägyptischen Natron-Tals', *Zeitschrift der Gesellschaft f. Erdkunde zu Berlin*, XXXIII (1898), pp. 1–25.

[8] General Andréossy, 'Mémoire sur la vallée des lacs de natroun', in *Description de l'Égypte*, I (Paris, 1809), *État moderne*, p. 281.

[9] C. S. Sonnini, *Travels in Upper and Lower Egypt* (1780), trans. H. Hunter, II (1807), p. 139.

[10] L. Gmelin, *Handbook of Chemistry* (1849), trans. H. Watts, III, p. 78.

acres. In September each year the level of the subsoil water, owing to the general rise of the subsoil water of the Delta and the infiltration from neighbouring canals that run full during the Nile flood, begins to rise and manifests itself in such a manner that by December the permanent lakes have increased in size and other temporary shallower ones have been formed. During the summer the area partly dries up, leaving the natron in an easily accessible form. The amount of available material, though large, is very much less than that in the Wadi Natrun.[1] These deposits were known to Sonnini in 1780, who rightly places them near Damanhur;[2] at one time they were considered worked out, but during the past twelve years they have been exploited again to a small extent. This district is generally called either Barnugi or Harrara after two of the lakes, which are named from neighbouring villages. Browne describes the deposits as at Terane.[3]

The El Kab natron deposits have been described by Schweinfurth [4] and by Somers Clarke.[5] Schweinfurth, who gives a map of the neighbourhood of El Kab, shows five different localities where natron occurs, which he distinguishes as (a) the northern natron valley, (b) the northern natron plain, (c) the southern natron valley, (d) a natron efflorescence, and (e) the southern natron-salt plain. The natron is readily accessible, as the distance of the deposits from the river is only from about two kilometres to about seven kilometres.

El Kalkashandi, an Arab writer who died at the beginning of the fifteenth century A.D., describes two other natron deposits,[6] one of about 100 acres in extent at Tarabiya, near Behnesah, in Upper Egypt, which he states had been worked since the time of Ibn Tulun (A.D. 835–84) and which yielded an annual revenue of more than £50,000, and the other in the Fakus district in the Eastern Delta. These places are not now known as sources of natron.

In 1799 natron was imported in small quantity from Bir Natrun in the Sudan 125 miles west-south-west of Dongola. It was 'sold at a high price and . . . used principally in making snuff'.[7] Burckhardt, writing in 1819, says that 'Among the most important imports into Upper Egypt is natron from Darfour.' [8]

In ancient Egyptian texts the natron deposits both of the Wadi Natrun [9] and of El Kab [10] are referred to, but so far as can be ascertained the Barnugi deposit is not specific-

---

[1] This description was kindly communicated by Sir H. Sadek Pasha, formerly Controller, Mines and Quarries Department, Cairo.

[2] C. S. Sonnini, *Travels in Upper and Lower Egypt* (1780), I, p. 324.

[3] W. G. Browne, *Travels in Africa, Egypt and Syria* (1799), pp. 38–42.

[4] G. Schweinfurth, 'Die Umgegend von Schaghab u. El-Kab (Ober-Ägypten)', *Zeitschrift der Gesellschaft f. Erdkunde zu Berlin*, XXXIX (1904), pp. 574–93.

[5] Somers Clarke, *J.E.A.*, VIII (1922), p. 17.

[6] S. Lane-Poole, *History of Egypt in the Middle Ages* (1901), p. 304.

[7] W. G. Browne, *Travels in Africa, Egypt and Syria* (1799), pp. 187–8.

[8] J. L. Burckhardt, *Travels in Nubia*, n. p. 306. See also G. W. Murray, *Geog. Journ.*, XCIV (1939), p. 97.

[9] J. R. Harris, *Lexicographical Studies*, pp. 190 f.; H. Gauthier, *Dictionnaire des noms géographiques*, v, p. 56; H. Brugsch, *Dictionnaire géographique*, pp. 150, 496–7; A. Erman, *Literature of the Ancient Egyptians*, trans. A. M. Blackman, pp. 116, 117, 120.

[10] J. R. Harris, *Lexicographical Studies*, pp. 190 f.; H. Gauthier, *Dictionnaire des noms géographiques*, III, p. 99; H. Brugsch, *Dictionnaire géographique*, pp. 45, 355.

ally mentioned. In the reign of Ramses III (1198–1166 B.C.) natron gatherers of Elephantine are named.[1] This seems a most unlikely place for natron to occur in workable quantity and there is no evidence of any today. In Breasted's translation of an historical text from the reign of Thutmose III (1504–1450 B.C.) [2] natron is enumerated among items of tribute received from Retenu (Syria). This is a mistake due to the confusion of two similar Egyptians words, the material mentioned being, in fact, amethyst.

The classical writers, Strabo [3] (first century B.C. to first century A.D.) and Pliny [4] (first century A.D.), both mention natron deposits in Egypt. The former, in his description of a journey by boat from the coast to Memphis (apparently from Schedia by canal to the Canopic branch of the Nile and then by river) refers to two pits that furnished natron in large quantities, which he states were situated (as was also the Nitriote Nome) beyond (above, or south of) Momemphis and near to Menelaus. Then he goes on to say that on the left in the Delta was Naucratis and that at a distance of two *schoeni* from the river was Sais. The question that arises is whether the natron pits were those of the Wadi Natrun or those of Barnugi. This could be settled at once if the precise position of either Momemphis or of Menelaus were known, but unfortunately the positions of these places are doubtful. Parthey,[5] Perthes [6] and Dümichen [7] all show Momemphis well south of Naucratis, and Parthey shows Menelaus south of Momemphis. If these maps are correct the natron pits must have been those of the Wadi Natrun. The evidence for assigning the positions, however, is not given, but it may have been that the Barnugi deposit was not known to these cartographers and that they therefore fixed Momemphis and Menelaus with reference to the only natron deposit with which they were acquainted, namely that of the Wadi Natrun, and if so, then to appeal to these maps is to argue in a circle. Strabo's allusion to Naucratis and Sais immediately following his mention of Momemphis and Menelaus is ambiguous, but seems to be unconnected with his reference to the position of the natron pits, which, if near Naucratis, must have been those of Barnugi. This is confirmed by Butler's statement that Momemphis was close to Damanhur.[8]

With reference to Barnugi, Evelyn White wrote that 'There is strong evidence to show that Barnugi is the Coptic Pernoudj, and the latter is certainly Nitria. Barnugi then would be the modern representative of the famous Nitria (not the Wadi el Natrun). Ancient authors clearly show that natron was obtained in the N.W. Delta in the region of Naucratis—not far distant.' [9]

Pliny states [4] that in Egypt natron (*nitrum*) used to be found (*nitrariae . . . tantum solebant esse*) only near Naucratis and Memphis.[10] The position of the first-mentioned

---

[1] *A.R.*, IV, 148.

[2] *A.R.*, II, 518.

[3] XVII: 1, 22, 23.   [4] XXXI: 46.

[5] G. Parthey, *Zur Erdkunde des alten Aegyptens* (1859), Maps i, ii, viii, xv, xvi.

[6] J. Perthes, *Atlas Antiquus* (1879), Tab. 3.

[7] J. Dümichen, *Zur Geographie des alten Ägypten* (1894), Map viii.

[8] A. J. Butler, *Arab Conquest of Egypt*, 1902, p. 21.

[9] Private letter to Dr. W. F. Hume, who has kindly allowed me to make use of it. See also H. G. Evelyn White, *Monasteries of the Wadi 'n Natrun*, II (1932), pp. 17–42.

[10] White (*Monasteries of the Wadi 'n Natrun*, II, p. 22) suggests that Momemphis is meant.

deposit would fit that of Barnugi and, if so, then by exclusion the second would be that of the Wadi Natrun, since only two deposits are known in this locality. It is true that the Wadi Natrun is not very close to Memphis, but it is difficult to believe that this important source should be ignored in favour of some small and insignificant place nearer to Memphis, even if such existed, which is doubtful. Pliny's whole account of natron in Egypt, however, is very confused and often unintelligible. The natron from near Memphis is described as being inferior to that from near Naucratis, because the heaps petrify and are turned into rock, from which vessels are made; and it is further stated that the material is often melted and heated with sulphur—though for what purpose is not mentioned.

No analyses of the Barnugi natron can be traced, but it is almost certainly not so good as the best quality from the Wadi Natrun. Natron, from whatever source obtained, if stacked in heaps for a long period and exposed to occasional slight rain would become consolidated, but never very hard, and it is conceivable, though improbable, that a few small vessels might have been made as curiosities from such natron. That natron was ever heated with sulphur is highly improbable.

Pliny states, too,[1] that natron was prepared artificially in Egypt, in much the same manner as salt, the difference being that to make salt sea water was used, while to make natron the water employed was that of the Nile. From this account, which is largely wrong, and most misleading, especially in the analogy to sea water, it would seem that Pliny had some very confused idea of the manner in which natron occurs in Egypt, namely as a deposit in certain low-lying areas, which become flooded soon after the annual rise of the Nile, by reason of the infiltration water (either directly from the river or from canals or other sources fed by the river) that finds its way into them. The Nile water, however, does not, and never did, yield natron on evaporation.

It is suggested that the confusion may have originated in the following manner. When sea water evaporates, salt is left, and when the seepage water (either direct or indirect) from the Nile that finds its way into certain depressions evaporates, natron is left. Hence, at first sight, the two phenomena might appear to be similar, though they are fundamentally different. In the case of sea water, the salt is in solution in the water, and is left as a dry deposit when the water evaporates; whereas in the case of the Nile seepage, the natron exists not in the water, but in the low-lying ground into which the water penetrates, having slowly accumulated there as the result of chemical reactions that have taken place in the soil during the course of long ages; all that the water does is to dissolve the natron already present and to bring it to the surface, where it is left when the water evaporates. Pliny's reference to the hasty collection of the natron if rain falls, for fear it should be redissolved, is suggestive of the Barnugi deposit, rather than that of the Wadi Natrun, since in the latter the rainfall is insignificant and does not seriously effect the natron, while at Barnugi the amount of natron is less and the rainfall greater, and in the autumn, before the natron is gathered, there might be sufficient rain to flood the area that had dried during the summer and so spoilt the harvest.[2]

---

[1] XXXI: 46.

[2] Early rain at the Lake Mareotis salt works near Mex limits considerably the amount of available salt.

In ancient Egypt natron was used in purification ceremonies,[1] especially for purifying the mouth;[2] for making incense;[3] for the manufacture of glass,[4] glaze, and possibly the blue and green frits used as pigments, which may be made either with or without alkali, but which are more easily made if alkali is present; for cooking;[5] in medicine;[6] for bleaching linen [7] and in mummification.[8] Natron was still being used at Alexandria for glass making as late as 1799.[9]

During the Ptolemaic period natron was a royal monopoly;[10] in Arab times it was a considerable source of revenue to the Government [11] and at the present day a small royalty is paid on all that is extracted.

As found in Egypt, natron always contains sodium chloride (common salt) and sodium sulphate as impurities, these being present in very varying and often considerable proportions;[12] thus, in fourteen samples of natron from the Wadi Natrun analysed by me,[13] the proportion of common salt varied from 2 to 27 per cent and that of sodium sulphate from a trace to 39 per cent, while in three samples from El Kab the common salt varied from 12 to 57 per cent and the sodium sulphate from 11 to 70 per cent. In three samples of natron from El Kab analysed by Lewin the common salt varied from 25 to 54 per cent and the sodium sulphate from 12 to 54 per cent.[14] Natron has been found from as early as the Badarian period.[15]

NITRE

At the present time the word nitre means potassium nitrate (saltpetre) and only potassium nitrate, but the word is derived from the ancient Egypitan *nṯry*,[16] which meant what is now called natron, a natural soda consisting essentially of sodium carbonate and sodium bicarbonate. In consequence of this derivation there has always been considerable confusion between nitre and natron, and there is also confusion

---

[1] J. R. Harris, *Lexicographical Studies*, pp. 190 f.; A. M. Blackman, *J.E.A.*, v (1918), pp. 118–20.

[2] A. M. Blackman, *J.E.A.*, v (1918), pp. 156–7, 159, 161–3. At the present time natron mixed with tobacco is chewed in Egypt.

[3] British Museum, *Introductory Guide to the Egyptian Collections*, 1930, p. 5; cf. also R. O. Steuer, *Wohlriechende Natron*. Natron mixed with an odoriferous gum-resin, almost certainly incense, was found in the tomb of Tutankhamūn.

[4] The remains of ancient glass factories still exist in the Wadi Natrun.

[5] According to Pliny (XXXI: 46) the Egyptians used natron for cooking radishes, and at the present day it is used to a small extent in cooking vegetables.

[6] J. H. Breasted, *Edwin Smith Surgical Papyrus*, pp. 412, 491; B. Ebbell, *Papyrus Ebers*, passim; H. v. Deines and H. Grapow, *Drogennamen*, pp. 319, 369–72.

[7] C. C. Edgar, *Zenon Papyri*, III, No. 59304. Sonnini mentions the use of natron for the same purpose in his time (C. S. Sonnini, *Travels in Upper and Lower Egypt* (1807), trans. H. Hunter, I, pp. 321–2).

[8] See pp. 278 f.   [9] W. G. Browne, *Travels in Africa, Egypt and Syria* (1799), p. 10.

[10] E. Bevan, *History of Egypt under the Ptolemaic Dynasty* (1927), p. 148.

[11] S. Lane-Poole, *History of Egypt in the Middle Ages* (1901), p. 304.

[12] For detailed analyses, see pp. 493–4.

[13] A. Lucas, *Natural Soda Deposits in Egypt* (1912), pp. 15–16.

[14] G. Schweinfurth, 'Die Umgegend von Schaghab u. El-Kab (Ober-Ägypten)', *Zeitschrift der Gesellschaft f. Erdkunde zu Berlin*, XXXIX (1904), pp. 574–93.

[15] G. Brunton, *Mostagedda*, p. 33.

[16] J. R. Harris, *Lexicographical Studies*, p. 193; R. O. Steuer, *Wohlriechende Natron*, pp. 28 f.; J. H. Breasted, *Edwin Smith Surgical Papyrus*, p. 412.

between nitre and another natural product, sodium nitrate.[1] This confusion still persists and the *nitron* of Herodotus [2] and Dioscorides [3] and its Latin equivalent, the *nitrum* of Pliny,[4] are often wrongly translated as nitre, instead of natron, and sodium nitrate is frequently referred to as saltpetre. Thus the 'saltpetre' occurring in Sinai and used locally for making gun powder [5] and blasting powder [6] is almost certainly sodium nitrate and not potassium nitrate, the latter of which occurs, so far as is known, only in small quantity in one locality in Sinai,[7] whereas the former is much more common, being found over large areas in Upper Egypt, where it is exploited as a fertilizer for use on the crops, though whether it was employed anciently is not known. No evidence can be found that nitre (potassium nitrate) was either known or used anciently in Egypt, and where the word is employed in modern books in connexion with ancient Egypt, it is likely to be a mistranslation, as, for instance, with reference to mummification and glass making.[8]

The Hebrew word wrongly translated 'nitre' in the book of Proverbs [9] in the Bible certainly does not mean potassium nitrate, upon which vinegar has no action, but sodium carbonate (natron), which is dissolved by vinegar with effervescence, which fact was known to Robert Boyle in 1680.[10]

SALT[11]

Common salt (sodium chloride) occurs abundantly in Egypt. At the present time it is procured commercially in large amount from Lake Mareotis in the north-west of the Delta and from salines at Port Said, but small quantities are also obtained surreptitiously from local deposits in various places. Pliny mentions [12] a lake near Memphis from which salt, which he states was of a red colour, was extracted: he says,[12] too, that one of the Ptolemies found salt near Pelusium (Damietta) and that it occurred beneath the sand in the desert between Egypt and Arabia and also in the western desert and that on the coast of Egypt there were artificial salines for the extraction of salt from sea water. Salt is known in the Oases of the Western Desert,[13] and Forbes states [14] that at Siwa salt is found 'in the form of rock-salt in gypsum, with a salt content of some 10–20%'.

The flower of salt (*flos salis*) mentioned by Pliny [12] and Dioscorides [15] that occurred in Egypt and was supposed to float down the Nile, but was also found on the surface of the water of certain springs, has not been identified, but it was certainly not patches

---

[1] R. W. Sloley in reviewing a previous edition of this book (*J.E.A.*, xxxiv (1948), p. 125) further confuses natron and sodium nitrate.

[2] II: 86–88.   [3] v: 130, 131.   [4] xxxi: 46.

[5] G. W. Murray, *Sons of Ishmael*, p. 78.   [6] W. M. F. Petrie, *Researches in Sinai*, p. 257.

[7] F. W. Moon and H. Sadek, *Topog. and Geol. of Northern Sinai*, I, p. 75.

[8] Cf. M. Wagenaar, *Oud. Med. N.R.*, x (2) (1929), pp. 93 f.; *Chemisch Weekblad*, xxvii (1930), pp. 348 f.

[9] *Proverbs*, 25: 20.

[10] Robert Boyle, *Experiments and Notes about the Production of Chymical Principles* (1680), p. 30.

[11] Cf. J. R. Harris, *Lexicographical Studies*, pp. 189 f.   [12] xxxi: 39, 41, 42.

[13] J. Ball and H. J. L. Beadnell, *Baharia Oasis*, pp. 37, 41, 48, 65; H. J. L. Beadnell, *Dakhla Oasis*, p. 103; J. Ball, *Kharga Oasis* p. 84.

[14] R. J. Forbes, *Studies in Ancient Technology*, III, p. 167.

[15] v: 129.

of petroleum coming down from the White Nile, as suggested by Bailey,[1] though there may be petroleum beneath Lake Albert and in the bed of the Kafu (a tributary of the Victoria Nile). One has only to know the Nile in the Delta, and to realize that it has travelled nearly 4,000 miles before it reaches the Delta, to be quite sure that no petroleum comes down floating on the surface or that it ever did so come down.

Herodotus says[2] that in Egypt 'the ground is coated with salt (insomuch that the very pyramids are wasted thereby)' and he mentions [2] 'salting factories' at Pelusium and the use of salt for mixing with oil for lamps.[2]

A small aggregate of salt crystals, which I analysed and found to be very pure and free from natron and sodium sulphate, found at Gebelien in a box of Sixth Dynasty date,[3] and two bricks of salt ($20 \times 11 \times 3$ cm. and $19 \times 9 \times 4$ cm. respectively), unfortunately undated, from Deir el Medineh [4] are in the Cairo Museum. I have also examined two large lumps and several small lumps of salt of Eighteenth Dynasty date found by Bruyère at Deir el Medineh.

Salt, in addition to its use as a seasoning for food, was largely employed in ancient Egypt for preserving fish. The question of its use in mummification will be dealt with in connexion with that subject.[5] Salt was a royal monopoly in the Ptolemaic and Roman periods.[6]

SULPHUR

Sulphur occurs native in most volcanic districts and also, and usually in large quantities, associated with gypsum and it is in this latter connexion that it is found in Egypt: it occurs on Ras Jemsa (where it has been extensively worked in modern times); at Bir Ranga and at Ras Benas, all on the Red Sea coast.[7] Small fragments of sulphur are also found occasionally in the limestone near Cairo [7] and it is deposited from the warm 'sulphur' springs at Helwan.

Sulphur has been found on several occasions in connexion with ancient Egypt, for example, several small pieces evidently cast in a mould, weighing altogether about 6.5 grams and dating possibly from Roman times, were found by Brunton;[8] a small piece of about Twenty-sixth Dynasty date was discovered by Petrie at Defenneh,[9] and several pieces of native sulphur, probably of Graeco-Roman date, were found at Tanis.[10] Thirty-five small rosettes, nineteen bull-head amulets and four Bes-head amulets moulded from sulphur, of unknown, but probably late date, were purchased by the Cairo Museum,[11] and similar pieces were also purchased on behalf of the Louvre.[12] The Roman specimens showed signs of having been melted. The most likely source of the material is the Red Sea coast.

---

[1] K. C. Bailey, *The Elder Pliny's Chapters on Chemical Subjects*, I, p. 168.

[2] II: 12, 15, 62.   [3] No. J. 66842.   [4] No. J. 38646.   [5] See pp. 274–8.

[6] E. Bevan, *History of Egypt under the Ptolemaic Dynasty*, p. 149; C. Préaux, *l'Économie royale des Lagides*, pp. 249–52; A. C. Johnson, *Economic Survey . . . Roman Egypt*, pp. 325–6.

[7] W. F. Hume, *Explan. Notes to the Geol. Map of Egypt*, pp. 40–41; T. Barron and W. F. Hume, *Topog. and Geol. of the Eastern Desert*, pp. 194, 267.

[8] G. Brunton, *Qau and Badari*, III, p. 34.

[9] W. M. F. Petrie, *Tanis*, II, *Nebesheh and Defenneh*, p. 75.

[10] W. M. F. Petrie, *Tanis*, I, p. 39.

[11] Nos. J. 71593 A, B, C. L. Keimer, *Ann. Serv.*, XXXIX (1939), pp. 203–8.

[12] No. E 15659.

Chapter XII
MUMMIFICATION[1]

The earliest method of disposal of the dead in Egypt was burial in the ground, which goes back to the neolithic period, neither bodies, nor graves, if ever there were graves, from the still older paleolithic period having yet been found.

In a hot climate like that of Egypt, if a grave is a shallow one in porous sand, situated well above the maximum subsoil water level, the sand becomes intensely hot in the sun, and the body moisture slowly evaporates and escapes through the sand, and eventually the body is left dry, practically sterile, and in such a condition that it will last almost indefinitely if kept dry. Simple burial, therefore, in a shallow grave in the desert is an excellent method of preserving the body, though if the grave is too near the surface, or not protected in some manner, as, for instance, by stones the body may be dug up by wild animals, such as hyenas and jackals.[2]

During the neolithic and predynastic periods, the body was buried in a shallow grave, situated at the edge of the desert just beyond the cultivation, generally wrapped in an animal skin or loose folds of linen, but by the early dynastic period the graves of the kings and wealthier classes had become deeper, were lined with sun-dried mud bricks, or with wood, and often were covered with a superstructure; and the previous loose covering on the body had given place to close-fitting linen wrappings, which in some instances eventually became elaborated into the separate wrapping of each limb, with further wrappings for the whole body, examples of which are known from the First,[3] Second [4] and Third [5] Dynasties respectively, before mummification was introduced.

Concurrently with the covering of the body with a greater number and more elaborate wrappings and with its burial in a larger and deeper grave, what were thought to be additional means of protection were introduced, which included the enclosing of the body at first in a wooden coffin, and later also in a wooden or stone sarcophagus, until the culmination was reached, which is represented, in the case of kings, in the tomb of Tutankhamūn (mummification, sixteen layers of linen wrap-

---

[1] Cf. in general, T. J. Pettigrew, *History of Egyptian Mummies*; G. Elliot Smith and W. R. Dawson, *Egyptian Mummies*; R. Engelbach and D. E. Derry, *Ann. Serv.*, XLII (1942), pp. 233–65.

[2] Cf. A. Lucas, *Preservative Materials*, pp. 57–59.

[3] W. M. F. Petrie, *Royal Tombs*, II, p. 16.

[4] J. E. Quibell, *Saqqara, 1912–1914*, pp. 11, 19, 28, 32, Pl. XXIX (3); G. Elliot Smith, *Report of the British Ass.*, Dundee, 1912, pp. 612–13; *Journ. Manchester Egyptian and Oriental Soc.*, II (1913), pp. 77–78; *J.E.A.*, I (1914), p. 192; G. Elliot Smith and W. R. Dawson, *Egyptian Mummies*, pp. 73–74; A. Lucas, *J.E.A.*, XVIII (1932), p. 139.

[5] C. M. Firth, J. E. Quibell and J.-P. Lauer, *Step Pyramid*, I, pp. 100–1; D. E. Derry, *Ann. Serv.*, XXXV (1935), pp. 28–30; XLI (1942), pp. 241, 243. Cf. also J. Garstang, *Burial Customs*, pp. 29–30.

pings, three coffins, a stone sarcophagus and four shrines) by whose reign manifestly it had become conventional. But, long before this time, on account of the deepening and elaboration of the grave, and with each addition to the wrappings, coffins and other fancied means of protection, the desiccation of the body must have been more prolonged, and its preservation therefore less perfect, and, since the religious belief regarding a future life now demanded that the body should last for all time, a preservative method of treatment before burial became necessary, and therefore was employed, this process being what is known as embalming or mummification.

The word embalm is derived from the Latin *in balsamum*, meaning to preserve in balsam, or balm, which it actually was. The word mummy probably came from a Persian word *mummia*, signifying bitumen, and it was applied at a late date to the embalmed bodies of the dead in Egypt, owing to the mistaken idea that because the body so preserved was black and looked as though it had been soaked in bitumen, therefore, the preservative agent employed must always have been bitumen, which, however, was not so, though in one mummy of the Persian period bitumen has been found.[1] In many other mummies of this period which I have examined there has not been any evidence of bitumen.

Since the ancient Egyptians believed that the spirit, which had left the body at death, would return and be re-united to the body, it was of the utmost importance, not only that the body should be preserved, but also that it should be kept in as life-like a condition as possible, and these, therefore, were the main objects of mummification, the means adopted for carrying them out, and the success attained, varying at different periods.

At what date mummification was first practised is unknown, but the first definite evidence of any attempt is from the beginning of the Fourth Dynasty,[2] from which period there is the canopic box of Queen Hetepheres (mother of Khufu (Cheops), the builder of the greater pyramid at Giza), which contains packets wrapped in linen of what are almost certainly the viscera, immersed in what I have analysed and found to be a dilute (approximately three per cent) solution of natron, containing the usual impurities of sodium chloride and sodium sulphate.[3] This seems to be proof that the body also had been preserved, although the sarcophagus, which should have contained it, was empty, the mummy most probably having been taken out and destroyed by tomb robbers searching for the jewellery with which the queen had been buried. There was an Egyptian mummy in the Museum of the Royal College of Surgeons, London, of Fifth Dynasty date, which was destroyed during an air raid in 1941,[4] and mummies of similar date were found by Junker and Reisner at Giza.[5] The

---

[1] A. Zaki and Z. Iskander, *Ann. Serv.*, XLII (1943), pp. 223–50.

[2] Cf. D. Derry, *Ann. Serv.*, XLI (1942), pp. 241–6; G. Elliot Smith and W. R. Dawson, *Egyptian Mummies*, pp. 72–78.

[3] G. A. Reisner, *Boston Bull.*, XXVI (1928), pp. 80–81.

[4] W. M. F. Petrie, *Medum*, pp. 17–18; *Funeral Furniture*, pp. 16–17; G. Elliot Smith, *Cairo Sc. Journ.*, II (1908), pp. 339, 424; *Nature*, LXXVIII (1908), p. 342; *J.E.A.*, I (1914), pp. 191–3; *History of Mummification in Egypt*, pp. 6–7; G. Elliot Smith and W. R. Dawson, *Egyptian Mummies*, pp. 74–75.

[5] H. Junker, *Giza*, VI, p. 226; III, p. 224; G. A. Reisner, *Boston Bull.*, XI (1913), p. 58, Fig. 9; G. Elliot Smith and W. R. Dawson, *Egyptian Mummies*, p. 76; D. E. Derry, *Ann. Serv.*, XXXV (1935), pp. 29–30; XLII (1942), pp. 241–2.

remains of other mummies of the Fifth and Sixth Dynasties have also been discovered,[1] and from this time onwards mummification continued to be practised until the early Christian period, though for long after its introduction it was restricted to kings, the royal family, nobles, priests, high officials and the wealthy classes, and it was not until much later that mummification became general and that the poorer classes also were embalmed.

The only practical methods by means of which human bodies can be preserved indefinitely are:

1. By cold storage, which was unknown anciently in Egypt.

2. By the modern method of injecting into the blood vessels some fluid having germicidal and antiseptic properties, which diffuses slowly into the tissues and so preserves them. This also was unknown anciently.

3. By drying the body thoroughly and afterwards keeping it dry, which is what the ancient Egyptians did, desiccation being the essential preliminary treatment to mummification.

Since about 75 per cent of the human body by weight consists of water, to dry it thoroughly is not an easy matter, but there are two methods by which this may be done, one by heat, either the natural heat of the sun or the artificial heat of a fire, and the other by the use of a drying (dehydrating) agent, which will abstract and absorb the water. Drying such a bulky object, and one containing so much water as the human body, by exposure to the sun would be a very slow process, even in Upper Egypt, and still slower in Lower Egypt, where there are many sunless days and even some wet days, and to have buried the bodies and to have dug them up after several years when they were thoroughly dried, in order to put them into coffins and tombs, would have been very expensive and would have required such a detailed organization to ensure correct identification and to prevent confusion that it would have been impracticable on a large scale, and there is not the slightest evidence that any natural method of drying was ever employed deliberately, and the alternative, therefore, was an artificial method, which, as already stated, might theoretically have been either by means of the heat from a fire or by chemical desiccation.

It is sometimes suggested that the bodies of the dead were dried by artificial heat Thus Rouyer says [2] '*Il est certain que les embaumeurs . . . les plaçoient dans des étuves,*' and Dawson thinks [3] that it is 'probable that fire-heat was used, through the medium of some apparatus of which we at present have no information'. He also says [4] 'considerable heat must have been required to remove the moisture absorbed during their long immersion in salt water. We do not know, however, whether this was done by the heat of the sun, or by fire; probably both methods were employed . . .' During

---

[1] G. Elliot Smith and W. R. Dawson, *Egyptian Mummies*, pp. 77–78; D. E. Derry, *Ann. Serv.*, XXXV (1935), pp. 29–30; XLI (1942), pp. 241–6; XLVII (1947), p. 107; A. Batrawi, *Ann. Serv.*, XLVII (1947), pp. 97–109.

[2] P. C. Rouyer, 'Notice sur les embaumemens des anciens Égyptiens', *Description de l'Égypte, Antiquités, Mémoires*, I (1809), pp. 209, 212. Rouyer says that *natrum* was obtained from several lakes in Egypt, where it occurred abundantly as '*carbonate de soude*'.

[3] W. R. Dawson, *J.E.A.*, XIII (1927), p. 45.

[4] W. R. Dawson, 'Contributions to the History of Mummification', *Proc. Royal Soc. of Medicine*, XX (1927), p. 851.

the Mond excavations in the necropolis of Thebes a chamber was found in the tomb of a certain Hatiay, 'where a vast number of dried mummies were piled up almost to the ceiling',[1] and Yeivin, who was associated with the work, states [1] that 'the mummies, to judge from their appearance, seem to have been dried over a slow fire, which would explain the smoky appearance of all the chambers and passages above'. What there was about the mummies to suggest fire-drying is not mentioned. The mere fact of so many mummies being together in one tomb seems to be strong evidence against this having been the place where they had been prepared, for it is difficult to believe that a large number of people should have handed the bodies of their relatives to the embalmers and, in the absence of any general cataclysm, should never have reclaimed them.

The piling together of numbers of mummies in one tomb has often been reported, and Rouyer says [2] 'on trouve des milliers de momies entassées les unes sur les autres'; Pettigrew states [3] that Captain Light 'found thousands of dead bodies placed in horizontal layers side by side'; Rhind states [4] that 'bodies of the humbler classes were, at Thebes, deposited in large catacombs . . . and piled together to the number, it is said, of hundreds'; Belzoni states [5] that one place 'was choked with mummies' and again:[5] 'Thus I proceeded from one cave to another all full of mummies piled up in various ways', and Wilkinson explains [6] that 'mummies of the lower orders were buried together in a common repository'.

That the tomb described by Yeivin was smoke-blackened is no proof that the smoke was that from a fire used to dry human bodies, and there is ample evidence that such blackening of tombs, which is not uncommon, is generally due to one of several causes, namely, to the tomb having been occupied as a dwelling; to the use of smoky torches by robbers or sightseers, or to other reasons. Thus, on one occasion, in comparatively recent times, when certain tombs in the Theban necropolis were occupied by bands of robbers, the authorities killed the robbers by filling the mouths of the tombs with dry brushwood, which was then set on fire.[7] Jomard in 1809 mentions an accidental fire in a tomb, the walls of which were thereby blackened.[8] Davies suggests [9] that sometimes tombs were purified by fire. Not only in this case, but also in all others, there is a complete absence of evidence for the drying of human bodies in ancient Egypt by artificial heat. Such a method would have been very expensive on account of the great scarcity of fuel in the country, besides which it was not necessary, since perfect desiccation may be obtained by means of a dehydrating agent. The drying of the body is not mentioned either by Herodotus or by Diodorus in their accounts of the methods employed for embalming.

---

[1] S. Yeivin, *Liverpool Annals*, XIII (1926), p. 15.

[2] P. C. Rouyer, 'Notice sur les embaumemens des anciens Égyptiens', *Description de l'Égypte, Antiquités, Mémoires*, I (1809), p. 214.

[3] T. J. Pettigrew, *History of Egyptian Mummies*, p. 40.

[4] A. H. Rhind, *Thebes, its Tombs and their Tenants* (1862), p. 132.

[5] G. Belzoni, *Operations and Recent Discoveries in Egypt and Nubia* (1820), p. 157.

[6] J. G. Wilkinson, *The Ancient Egyptians*, 1878, III, p. 438.

[7] J. Bruce, *Travels to Discover the Source of the Nile*, II, 2nd ed., 1805, p. 33.

[8] E. Jomard, 'Description des hypogées de la ville de Thèbes', *Description de l'Égypte*, 1809, I, p. 317.

[9] N. de G. Davies, *Menkheperrasonb*, pp. 18–20, 24, 27, 28.

There are three common and cheap dehydrating agents, namely, quick lime, common salt and natron, which will now be considered.

LIME

The use of lime in mummification was suggested by Granville,[1] who thought it had been employed to remove the epidermis, which Pettigrew supposed [1] was done in order that the palm wine mentioned by Herodotus and Diodorus (which, however, according to these writers was only used for washing the viscera and not for the outside of the body) might act more readily upon the deeper layers of the skin, but the only evidence adduced in support of the use of lime is that in a certain mummy, from which the epidermis was missing, Granville found 'traces of lime'. Since, however, calcium carbonate (carbonate of lime) in small proportion is a common impurity of Egyptian natron, this might well have been the source of the 'lime' found.

Haas, having found a small proportion of calcium carbonate (8.6 per cent if calculated from the lime shown in the analysis) in a Twelfth Dynasty mummy, concluded that 'it would seem reasonable to suppose that the lime, which is at present combined in the form of carbonate, must have been originally added in the form of quicklime . . .' [2] Dr. Margaret Murray, summarizing Haas's chemical results, accepts this use of lime.[3] Since, however, the rock-cut tomb in which the mummy in question was buried was of limestone and was situated in a limestone district, and, since almost certainly the coffins (there were two, one inside the other) were first opened where they were found, contamination with limestone dust, either at the time of burial or when the coffins were opened, is not impossible, though it seems much more probable that such contamination took place during mummification before the body was wrapped up, or still more likely that the calcium carbonate may have been present in the natron used. Moreover, another mummy from the same tomb showed only 1.6 per cent of calcium carbonate, which, unless the reasonable explanation offered that one body, or one lot of natron, but not the other, was contaminated with limestone dust (the bodies were buried at an interval of several years) be accepted, must mean that two different methods of mummification, one with lime, and the other without lime, were employed, which is most improbable.[4]

Dr. F. Wood Jones seems to consider the use of lime possible, since he says [5] 'The epidermis, that was removed, either intentionally by the action of lime . . . or accidentally . . .'

There is not, however, the slightest evidence or probability that lime was ever used in mummification, and, so far as is at present known, lime was not employed for any purpose whatever in ancient Egypt until the Ptolemaic period.[6]

SALT[7]

Salt was used in ancient Egypt from a very early period for preserving fish, and, since it is very abundant, and very effective as a drying agent, it seems, from theoretical

---

[1] T. J. Pettigrew, *History of Egyptian Mummies*, p. 62.

[2] M. A. Murray, *Tomb of Two Brothers*, p. 46; P. Haas, *Chemical News*, c (1909), p. 296.

[3] M. A. Murray, *Tomb of Two Brothers*, p. 51.   [4] A. Lucas, *Chemical News*, ci (1910), p. 266.

[5] G. Elliot Smith and F. Wood Jones, *Arch. Survey of Nubia, 1907–1908*, ii, p. 200.

[6] See p. 74.   [7] Cf. A. Lucas, *J.E.A.*, xviii (1932), pp. 127–9, 136.

considerations, a likely material to have been used in mummification, but there is no evidence that it ever was so employed (except inadvertently as an impurity in natron) until early Christian times, and then not to the best advantage, but only in comparatively small amount often placed, not in contact with the body, but outside the clothes or wrappings, or between their different layers, where any drying effect must have been negligible, and its use may have been ritualistic, or conventional, rather than practical. However, in spite of considerable evidence to the contrary, it is still frequently stated that salt was employed for embalming. Thus Schmidt states [1] very emphatically that salt was used and not natron; Elliot Smith says [2] 'There can, however be no doubt that the body and viscera were primarily treated . . . by being immersed . . . in a bath of chloride of sodium'; Elliot Smith and Warren Dawson say [3] 'It can be confidently stated that at most periods common salt (mixed with certain natural impurities) was the essential preservative material employed by the Egyptians for embalming' and Dawson states [4] that 'In general terms it may be said that for the immersion-bath common salt (mixed with various impurities) and not natron was used.' [5] What the various natural impurities with which the salt was mixed consisted of is not stated, but if one of them was natron, then to call the material common salt is incorrect and misleading.

Egyptian natron always contains salt and often in considerable proportion, one specimen from El Kab analysed by me containing as much as 57 per cent, but this is exceptional and this particular specimen had no connexion with embalming and is not representative of the bulk of the natron from El Kab, another specimen of which contained only 12 per cent of salt, and much less is it representative of that from the Wadi Natrun, where the highest proportion of common salt in fourteen samples analysed by me was 27 per cent [6] and the lowest 2 per cent. To contend that the material employed in mummification, although nominally natron, was actually common salt would be fallacious, and if the mere presence of impurities, such as common salt and sodium sulphate, in Egyptian natron makes it reasonable to deny to it the name of natron, then there is no natron in Egypt, and it becomes absurd to speak of natron, or of the Wadi Natrun, or other natron deposits.

The facts respecting salt and mummies, so far as they have been placed on record, and so far as they can be traced, are as follows: In a Twelfth Dynasty mummy Haas found 1.89 per cent of chlorine [7] representing 4.8 per cent of common salt, whereas in a second mummy from the same tomb, and of nearly the same date, there was only 0.22 per cent of chlorine, which represents 0.6 per cent of salt. The difference in salt content of these two mummies may reasonably be accounted for by assuming

---

[1] W. A. Schmidt, 'Chemische u. biologische Untersuchungen v. ägyptischen Mumien-material, etc.', Zeitschr. f. allgem. Physiol., VII (1907), pp. 369–92.

[2] G. Elliot Smith, Mém. Inst. Ég., V (1906), p. 18.

[3] G. Elliot Smith and W. R. Dawson, Egyptian Mummies, p. 168.

[4] W. R. Dawson, J.E.A., XIII (1927), p. 49.

[5] Dawson, however, admits the use of crude natron as a dehydrating agent at a later stage (J.E.A., XIII (1927), p. 49).

[6] Natron bought locally, which probably was from the Wadi Natrun, though this is not certain, contained 29 per cent of salt.

[7] M. A. Murray, Tomb of Two Brothers, p. 47.

either the use of a different quality of natron in the two cases (there is a definite evidence of the use of natron in one case), one lot containing more salt than the other (there was an interval of several years between the two burials), or by the use in one instance of a more salty water for washing the body than in the other.

A few tiny crystals of salt were found on the skin on the top of the shoulders of the mummy of Tutankhamūn (Eighteenth Dynasty), and a very small aggregate of tiny salt crystals was also found inside the gold coffin at the head end.[1] The total amount of salt was so small that it cannot have been derived from the use of salt, and it is even unlikely that it came from the use of natron containing salt, and it seems much more probable that it originated in the water used for washing the body before it was wrapped up. Although the water from the Nile at Elephantine was esteemed the most efficacious for this purpose, it is improbable that it was always used, and, if not, then the alternative would have been water from the river locally, from a sacred pool,[2] or from the sacred lake of a temple, or well water, the last three of which might have contained a considerable proportion of salt.

Elliot Smith states [3] that the mummy of Meneptah (Nineteenth Dynasty) was 'thickly encrusted with salt'. This mummy, which is in the Cairo Museum, I have examined specially with the following results: The skin, which is mostly of a light brown colour, is very patchy and mottled, the patches consisting of a number of areas, some of considerable size, that are white, and the mottling taking the form of numerous small raised spots, practically the same colour as the skin, covering the chest and abdomen and occurring also on the forehead, and having the appearance of an eruption. Neither the white patches nor the mottling is salt. Salt, however, is present, but in very small amount, most of it being invisible to the naked eye, though there are a few very small areas where there are efflorescences of tiny salt crystals, so minute that they can only just be seen without a lens. The total amount of salt present is so small that it might have been derived from the use of natron containing salt, or from the use of salty water for washing, and probably was so derived.[4]

With respect to a Seventeenth Dynasty mummy, Elliot Smith writes [5] 'I submitted a piece of skin to Professor W. A. Schmidt . . . but he was unable to find any excessive quantity of salt in it, in fact no greater quantity of sodium chloride than the normal tissues of the body contain.' The skin was 'soft, moist, flexible'.

There was a small proportion of salt in the resin from the mummy of Neskhons (Twenty-first Dynasty) examined by me,[6] which, again, might have been derived from the water used in washing.

Salt was also found by me in a Coptic mummy (fifth century A.D.) from Naga el Deir;[6] on bodies of early Christian date from near Aswan, the wrappings of which were 'heavy and sticky with salt',[7] a number of specimens of which I analysed,[8] and

---

[1] D. E. Derry, in H. Carter, *Tut-ankh-Amen*, II, p. 152 (Appendix I).

[2] A. M. Blackman, *P.S.B.A.*, XL (1918), pp. 61–64.

[3] G. Elliot Smith, *Royal Mummies*, p. 67; *Ann. Serv.*, VIII (1907), p. 111.

[4] A. Lucas, *J.E.A.*, XVIII (1932), p. 128.

[5] G. Elliot Smith, *Royal Mummies*, pp. 1, 9.

[6] A. Lucas, *Preservative Materials*, pp. 19, 20.

[7] G. A. Reisner, *Arch. Survey of Nubia, 1907–1908*, I, p. 100.

[8] G. Elliot Smith and F. Wood Jones, *Arch. Survey of Nubia, 1907–1908*, II, p. 371.

on certain mummy tissues examined by Schmidt, who states [1] that the authentic embalmed material was largely impregnated with salt, in many cases the interiors of the mummies being entirely covered with salt crystals, the Coptic mummies containing the most salt, in one instance 8.5 per cent being present in the arm muscles. Ruffer, commenting on this, writes [2] 'These observations of Schmidt have not been confirmed so far, and are all the more remarkable because Coptic mummies (so-called) show no incision; salt has been placed on the integuments, and it is difficult, if not impossible, to understand how under such circumstances the quantity of salt mentioned by Schmidt can have penetrated into the muscles. I have seen the inner surface of the body cavities—the muscles, liver, and other organs—of Coptic mummies covered with white crystals, but these were crystals of fatty acids and not salt.[3] The mummies, which I have examined often, contained inside the wrappings lumps of common salt; and in one case a lump of sodium chloride about the size of a fist was lying on the anterior surface of the abdomen; but it appears to me very doubtful whether much salt had been used, as the wrappings had not been infiltrated with visible crystals of salt, and analysis did not reveal any abnormal quantity of salt in the skin or muscles.'

During early Christian times many of the bodies on which salt has been found, although called mummies, even by archaeologists, were not mummified,[4] and, therefore, may be left out of account in the present discussion, for example, the Coptic body from Naga el Deir mentioned, although called a mummy in the description that accompanied the specimen of salt received for analysis, almost certainly had not been mummified.

An embalmer's swab,[5] made of linen tied to the end of a small stick, of unknown but late date, found by Winlock at Thebes and examined by me contained a trace of salt, but no natron. A trace of salt, however, is of no significance in Egypt and might have come from the water used with the swab, or from the ground on which it was lying.

A wooden object,[6] possibly an embalmer's tool, of Twelfth Dynasty date, found by Lansing at Lisht, also examined by me, showed a trace of salt and also patches of oil, but no natron. Here again a trace of salt in no way proves the use of salt in embalming.

An ankh sign of Twelfth Dynasty date, made of thin vegetable fibre, found by Daressy in a sarcophagus at El Bersheh [7] is thickly encrusted with large salt crystals, an indication that at one time it was immersed in a strong salt solution, which slowly evaporated, for in that manner alone could the large crystals have been formed, but where it acquired the salt there is no evidence to show, and certainly no evidence that it was in connexion with embalming.

---

[1] W. A. Schmidt, 'Chemische u. biologische Untersuchungen v. ägyptischen Mumienmaterial, etc.', *Zeitschr. f. allgem. Physiol.*, VII (1907), pp. 369–92.

[2] M. A. Ruffer, *Cairo Sc. Journ.*, IX (1917), pp. 43–44.

[3] These were analysed by me. See A. Lucas, *Preservative Materials*, p. 55.

[4] G. Elliot Smith and F. Wood Jones, *Arch. Survey of Nubia, 1907–1908*, II, pp. 215–20.

[5] Cairo Museum, No. J. 56290.

[6] Cairo Museum, No. J. 63874.

[7] Cairo Museum, No. J. 32867. G. Daressy, *Ann. Serv.*, XI (1910), p. 40.

Salt, apart from that contained as an impurity in natron, has never been discovered among refuse embalming material (of which many deposits have been found), nor, if the ankh sign is excepted, in any manner suggestive of its use in embalming; the only instances where salt has been found from ancient Egypt are enumerated elsewhere.[1]

NATRON[2]

Solid natron has been found in connexion with ancient Egypt as follows:

1. In vases and jars in tombs. Examples: (a) in the tomb of Yuya and Tuyu (Eighteenth Dynasty).[3] This was refuse embalming material, since it was 'wrapped up in bits of cloth' contained in fifty-two large jars, and in one instance at least it was a mixture of natron and sawdust; (b) in ten large jars in the tomb of Maiherperi (Eighteenth Dynasty),[4] which also was refuse embalming material, as it was mixed with resin and sawdust; (c) in the tomb of Tutankhamūn (Eighteenth Dynasty).[5] In this tomb a vase containing natron was in the same 'kiosk' as another vase containing resin, and this probably had a direct connexion with embalming. Another specimen of natron was mixed with an aromatic gum-resin, almost certainly incense, while two other specimens were in a special form of alabaster stand placed in front of the canopy covering the canopic box; (d) in an Eighteenth Dynasty tomb at Thebes;[6] (e) in the Ramesseum (Nineteenth Dynasty) together with woven fabric;[7] (f) in a Twenty-first Dynasty tomb at Saqqara.

2. In packages in tombs. Describing the tomb of Meryetamūn at Thebes (Eighteenth Dynasty) Winlock says [8] 'Natron . . . seems to have been placed in the tomb as well. Small lumps of it, dumped out of their proper receptacles, had been swept up into basket B.' Wainwright found natron in a Twenty-fifth Dynasty tomb at Kafr Ammar.[9]

3. Buried in pits with refuse embalming material. At least ten lots, some of which were analysed by me, were found by Winlock at Deir el Bahari, ranging in date from the Eleventh to the Thirtieth Dynasty.[10] Four lots of similar material were found by Lansing, also at Deir el Bahari, three of which were not dated, the fourth probably being of the Saite period.[11]

The refuse embalming material, either from the embalming of Tutankhamūn, or

---

[1] See pp. 268–9.

[2] Cf. A. Lucas, *J.E.A.*, I (1914), pp. 119–23; XVIII (1932), pp. 125–40.

[3] J. E. Quibell, *Yuaa and Thuiu*, pp. 75–77. The analyses of some portions of this material submitted by Mr. Quibell were made by me.

[4] L.-C. Lortet and C. Gaillard, *La faune momifiée*, I–II, pp. 317–18; L.-C. Lortet and L. Hugounenc, *C.R.Ac.Sci.*, CXXXIX (1904), pp. 115–18.

[5] H. Carter, *Tut-ankh-Amen*, II, p. 32; III, pp. 39, 46; A. Lucas, in H. Carter, *Tut-ankh-Amen*, III, pp. 178–9 (Appendix II).

[6] Analysed by me. No details were given except the date and place where found.

[7] J. E. Quibell, *Ramesseum*, p. 4.

[8] H. E. Winlock, *Meryet-Amūn*, pp. 11, 46.

[9] G. A. Wainwright, in W. M. F. Petrie and E. Mackay, *Heliopolis, Kafr Ammar and Shurafa*, p. 35, Pl. XXIX.

[10] H. E. Winlock, *M.M.A. Bull., Egyptian Exped. 1921–1922*, p. 34; *1923–1924*, pp. 31–32; *1927–1928*, pp. 25–26.

[11] A. Lansing, *M.M.A. Bull., Egyptian Exped. 1916–1919*, p. 12.

from the embalming of the two children whose mummies were found in the tomb, was found about ten years before the tomb was discovered, and among it were 'small bags containing a powdered substance',[1] which later was found to be natron.[1] Lansing and Hayes found at Deir el Bahari 'jars, packed in sawdust, natron, and linen wadding', of Eighteenth Dynasty date,[2] and packages containing a mixture of natron, powdered limestone and organic matter, were found in a Theban tomb of the Eighteenth or Nineteenth Dynasty.[3] About one hundred bags of natron, almost certainly refuse embalming material, were discovered in a tomb chamber at Qurna,[4] and Naville found in the temple of Deir el Bahari 'pots containing nitre',[5] and also 'several large jars, some of which were filled with chopped straw for stuffing the mummies, while others contained numbers of little bags of nitre or some salt used in mummification'.[5] The so-called nitre was almost certainly natron. Jars containing natron were found in a cache of the Saite or Persian period discovered at Saqqara, other jars from the same cache containing a mixture of natron and a gum-resin. Bandages saturated with a natron-resin mixture were also found in this cache and in another of similar date.[6]

4. Encrusting a wooden embalming table and four wooden blocks belonging to it [7] that were doubtless used for supporting the body; also encrusting four wooden ankh signs and a wooden object connected with embalming.[8] These objects, which are all of Eleventh Dynasty date, were found by Winlock at Thebes and are now in the Cairo Museum, where I have examined them. The table and the wooden object have resin adhering to them in addition to natron. Other embalming tables of stone and wood, limestone blocks for supporting the body, and mats on which the body was laid have also been found, but no evidence of the presence of natron has been recorded.[9]

5. On certain mummies, examples being (a) a body of Middle Kingdom date found at Saqqara, where 'in the cavity of the chest were nodules of natron, about 10 of them . . .';[10] (b) impregnating the tissues of a Twelfth Dynasty mummy;[11] (c) in two packets attached to the mummy of an unknown woman found in the tomb of Amenhotpe II (Eighteenth Dynasty). In one of the packets there was a mass of epidermis and in the other were portions of the viscera, in both cases mixed with solid natron,[12] which was identified by me; (d) impregnating the brain of the mummy

[1] T. M. Davis, *Tomb of Harmhabi and Touatankhamanou*, p. 3; H. Carter, *Tut-ankh-Amen*, II, p. 98; III, pp. 88–89; H. E. Winlock, *Materials Used at the Embalming of King Tūt-ankh-Amūn*.
[2] A. Lansing and W. C. Hayes, *M.M.A. Bull., Egyptian Exped. 1935–1936*, p. 23.
[3] L. Habachi, *Ann. Serv.*, LV (1958), pp. 335–6.
[4] G. Schweinfurth and L. Lewin, *Z.Ä.S.*, XXXV (1897), pp. 142–3.
[5] E. Naville, *Temple of Deir el Bahari*, II, p. 6.
[6] J.-P. Lauer and Z. Iskander, *Ann. Serv.*, LIII (1956), pp. 169–94.
[7] H. E. Winlock, *M.M.A. Bull., Egyptian Exped. 1921–1922*, p. 34, Fig. 33.
[8] The ankh signs and the wooden object have unfortunately been cleaned since I tested them, probably under the mistaken idea that the encrusting material was extraneous dirt.
[9] H. E. Winlock, *Ann. Serv.*, XXX (1930), pp. 102–4; *M.M.A. Bull., Egyptian Exped. 1923–1924*, p. 32; *1927–1928*, pp. 25–26; *Materials used at the Embalming of King Tūt-ankh-Amūn*, p. 12.
[10] J. E. Quibell and A. G. K. Hayter, *Saqqara, Teti Pyramid, North Side*, p. 12.
[11] M. A. Murray, *Tomb of Two Brothers*, p. 47.
[12] G. Elliot Smith, *Royal Mummies*, p. 82.

of a boy from the tomb of Amenhotpe II;[1] (e) impregnating the resin from the cheeks, mouth, arm, and ribs of certain mummies of the Eighteenth and Twentieth Dynasties respectively;[1] (f) as small white crystals on a mummy probably of Twentieth Dynasty date in the Leeds Museum, which was analysed and found to consist 'almost entirely of carbonate of soda, with some muriate and sulphate,' [2] which is natron; also on the bandages from the same mummy; (g) covering an anonymous mummy from Deir el Bahari;[3] (h) as minute crystals on both the exterior and interior surfaces of a mummy examined by Granville, which were proved by analysis to consist of 'carbonate, sulphate, and muriate of soda', mixed with potassium nitrate and traces of lime,[4] that is to say natron containing the usual impurities.

6. Mixed with fatty matter in certain mummies. Examples: (a) on the body of Thutmose III (Eighteenth Dynasty);[5] (b) on the body of Meneptah (Nineteenth Dynasty),[6] and (c) in the mouth and body cavities of certain mummies of the Twenty-first and Twenty-second Dynasties.[6,7] The material was examined by Schmidt, who, in his original paper, attributed the fatty matter to butter that had been mixed with natron, and this is still quoted, although in a later paper [8] Schmidt stated very definitely that, as the result of further work, he had changed his opinion and that he believed the fatty matter to have been derived from the body; (d) from the pelvis of a female mummy called 'Mummy No. 1' found in the tomb of Amenhotpe II (Eighteenth Dynasty), the fatty matter having probably been derived from the body.[9]

Not only was natron employed in the solid state, but it was also sometimes used in the form of a solution, and such a solution has been found on two occasions, once by Brunton [10] in an alabaster canopic jar from a royal tomb of the Twelfth Dynasty at Lahun, in which, however, there were no viscera, and once by Reisner [11] in three compartments of the alabaster canopic box of Queen Hetepheres (Fourth Dynasty), the remaining compartment being dry, owing to leakage from a defect that exists in that particular corner of the box. This natron solution, which was analysed by me, is approximately of 3 per cent strength and contains the usual impurities of Egyptian natron, namely, common salt and sodium sulphate. In each compartment of the box is a flat package wrapped in woven fabric (presumably linen) that almost certainly contains viscera.

There is, therefore, a considerable amount of proof that natron was employed in mummification from certainly as early as the Fourth Dynasty to as late as the Persian

[1] A. Lucas, *Preservative Materials*, pp. 13–19; *Cairo Sc. Journ.*, II (1908), pp. 133–47, 273–8.

[2] W. Osburn, *Account of an Egyptian Mummy Presented to the Museum of the Leeds Philosophical and Literary Society*, pp. 8, 44.

[3] Mathey, *Bull. Inst. Ég.*, VII (1886), pp. 186–95.

[4] T. J. Pettigrew, *History of Egyptian Mummies*, p. 62.

[5] G. Elliot Smith, *Royal Mummies*, p. 32.

[6] G. Elliot Smith, *Royal Mummies*, p. 67; *Ann. Serv.*, VIII (1907), p. 111.

[7] W. A. Schmidt, 'Chemische u. biologische Untersuchungen v. ägyptischen Mumien-material, etc.', *Zeitschr. f. allgem. Physiol.*, VII (1907), pp. 369–92. Sec also G. Elliot Smith, *Royal Mummies*, pp. 99–103.

[8] W. A. Schmidt, 'Über Mumienfettsäuren', *Chemiker-Zeitung*, XXXII (1908), pp. 769–70.

[9] A. Lucas, *Preservative Materials*, p. 7; *Cairo Sc. Journ.*, II (1908), pp. 273–8.

[10] G. Brunton, *Lahun*, I, p. 20. Analysed by me.

[11] G. A. Reisner, *Boston Bull.*, XXVI (1928), p. 81.

period, and Herodotus, writing in the fifth century B.C., states that it was used in his day.

The reason for employing natron and not salt, which latter would have been equally good, if not better, as a dehydrating agent and which was more plentiful and, therefore, cheaper than natron, was undoubtedly because natron was regarded as the great purifying agent, probably because it cleanses by chemically destroying fat and grease and, therefore, purifies in a manner that salt cannot do, and hence it was natron and not salt that was employed in all purification ceremonies, for example in lustration and in the purification of the mouth, and it was also mixed with incense with the same idea,[1] and the embalmer's workshop, often a temporary structure, was called 'the pure place'.[2]

Manner in which Natron was Used

The next point for consideration is the manner in which the natron was used. Until I ventured to query the generally accepted explanation, it was always stated that the natron was employed in the form of a solution, that is as a bath, in which the body was soaked, apparently largely because certain translators of Herodotus incorrectly state or infer that a solution was used. At what date the idea of a bath originated it is unnecessary and profitless to inquire, but it certainly dates from Pettigrew's time (1834) and was accepted by him, since not only does he repeatedly refer to a bath, but he quotes [3] a translation of Herodotus's description of embalming, in which it is stated that in the first of the three methods described 'they steep the body in *natrum*', which can only mean in a solution, and that in the second method they 'lay the body in brine', again meaning a liquid, brine being a strong salt solution. In the third method the statement is merely that 'they salt the body', which is suggestive of the use of dry salt, rather than a solution. In a rendering by Elliot Smith and Warren Dawson of the passages in Herodotus relative to embalming it is stated [4] with respect to all three methods that they 'soak' the body 'in natron', which can only mean in a solution of natron. But the translations of Herodotus by Rouelle (1750), Rouyer (1809), Rawlinson (1862), Wilkinson (1878) and Godley (1926) respectively make no mention or suggestion of a bath or solution. According to Rouelle,[5] in the first method '*ils salent le corps en le couvrant de natrum*'; in the second method '*on sale le corps*', and in the third method '*on met le corps dans le nitre*'. Rouyer's translation [6] is identical with that of Rouelle, except that for the third method he uses the word *natrum* in place of nitre. Both Rouelle and Rouyer, however, not only translated

---

[1] A. M. Blackman, 'Purification (Egyptian)', *Hasting's Ency. of Religion and Ethics*, x, p. 476; *J.E.A.*, v (1918), pp. 118–20, 156–63; *Rec. Trav.*, xxxix (1921), p. 53; E. A. Wallis Budge, *Liturgy of Funerary Offerings*, 1909, pp. 155–7, 207–9.

[2] *Wb.* I. 284. 4–5; W. R. Dawson, *J.E.A.*, xiii (1927), p. 41.

[3] T. J. Pettigrew, *History of Egyptian Mummies*, p. 46.

[4] G. Elliot Smith and W. R. Dawson, *Egyptian Mummies*, pp. 57–58.

[5] G. F. Rouelle, 'Sur les embaumemens des Égyptiens', *Histoire de l'Académie Royale des Sciences* 1750 (Paris, 1754), p. 126. Rouelle states (p. 127) that the nitre of the ancients was not saltpetre, but *natrum*, '*un vrai sel alkali fixe*', that is to say natron.

[6] P. C. Rouyer, 'Notice sur les embaumemens des anciens Égyptiens', *Description de l'Égypte, Antiquités, Mémoires*, I (1809), p. 209. Rouyer says (p. 212) that *natrum* was obtained from several lakes in Egypt, where it occurred abundantly as '*carbonate de soude*'.

Herodotus correctly, but realized that the underlying principle of the process described was essentially one of desiccation. Thus Rouelle says *'les embaumeurs égyptiens ne saloient donc le corps avec le natrum que pour le dessécher'*; *'ces momies . . . ont été simplement desséchées en les salant avec le natrum'*; of a certain mummy he is describing he states *'le corps a été simplement desséché par le natrum'*; and *'ils enlevoient toutes les différentes liqueurs & les graisses aux cadavres par le moyen du sel alkali & . . . par ce moyen ils desséchoient si fort qu'il ne restoit que les parties fibreuses . . .'*; and Rouyer states *'et qu'ils soumettoient ensuite les corps . . . à l'action des substances qui devoient en opérer la dessiccation'*.

According to Rawlinson,[1] in the first method 'the body is placed in *natrum*'; in the second method the body is 'laid in *natrum*' and the third method is to 'let the body lie in *natrum*'.

According to Wilkinson,[2] in the first method 'they salt the body, keeping it in natron'; in the second method 'they keep it in salt' and in the third method 'they . . . salt it'.

According to Godley,[3] in the first method 'they conceal the body for seventy days,[4] embalmed in saltpetre',[5] which strongly suggests that it was hidden in, or covered with, solid material; in the second and third methods 'they embalm the body'.

Turning to the original Greek, the word used by Herodotus[6] to explain the operation of embalming in the three methods described is the same in each case, namely ταριχεύουσι, which is the third person plural, present indicative, active voice of the verb originally meaning to preserve fish with salt,[7] and hence the literal meaning is that they (the embalmers) preserve the body in a manner similar to that in which fish were treated. But, as the description is qualified in one place by the word λίτρῳ meaning 'with natron', to embalm, therefore, meant to preserve the body like fish, but using natron instead of salt. Both Herodotus[8] and Diodorus[9] employ other tenses and variants of the same verb and also related nouns in connexion with embalming. Variants of the verb are used, too, by Herodotus[10] with reference to preserved fish and preserved birds and by Diodorus[11] for preserved fish.

Athenaeus, a native of Naucratis in Egypt, who lived in Rome at the end of the

---

[1] G. Rawlinson, *Herodotus* (1862), II: 86–88.

[2] J. G. Wilkinson, *The Ancient Egyptians*, 1878, III, pp. 471–2.

[3] A. D. Godley, *Herodotus* (Loeb Classical Library, 1926), II: 86–88.

[4] Herodotus mistakenly attributes the time taken for the whole mummification process to the natron treatment alone.

[5] The word λίτρον, usually νίτρον in later Greek writings (e.g. Strabo, XVII: 1, 23), means natron (natural soda) and not saltpetre, as translated by Godley.

[6] II: 86–88.

[7] For the meaning and use of the word see H. Stephanus, *Thesaurus Graecae Linguae*, VII, 1843–47.

[8] II: 67, 69, 85–90; III: 10, 16; VI: 30.

[9] I: 7; II: 1.

[10] II: 77; IX: 120. Godley's translation 'preserved with brine' is misleading, since brine means a salt solution, whereas salt is not mentioned, but only inferred, and there is no indication that a solution was used and a strong probability that dry salt was employed.

[11] I: 3.

second century A.D., and the beginning of the third century, discourses at great length on the subject of preserved fish, mentioning it more than sixty times in the space of a few pages, and he always employs the same word, or one of its derivatives, that is used by Herodotus and Diodorus, not only for preserved fish, but also for mummies, and in one instance he calls attention to the use by Sophocles of the same word for mummy as for preserved fish.[1]

In a number of Greek papyri from Egypt, dating from about the first century A.D. to about the seventh century A.D.,[2] the same word, or a variant of it, that is used by Herodotus and Diodorus to describe both the making of mummies and the preserving of fish, is employed sometimes in connexion with mummies and sometimes in connexion with fish, and in one instance, where the context does not help, it has not been possible for the translators to decide whether a certain word means fish curers or embalmers.

There is nothing in the original Greek of Herodotus's description of embalming to warrant the idea that a bath or solution was employed in which the body was soaked. The phraseology of Herodotus, Diodorus, Athenaeus and other writers makes it perfectly clear that the ancient Egyptian process of embalming the human body was analogous to that for preserving fish, and Herodotus amplifies this by stating that the preservative agent was natron. The modern method of preserving fish, apart from smoking and tinning in oil, which were not known anciently, is usually by salting and drying, though a few kinds are preserved in brine, that is in a salt solution. In Egypt at the present day fish are generally preserved by means of dry salt. Anciently in Egypt fish were preserved by drying, with, or without, the use of salt.

Since the aim of mummification was not merely to preserve the body, but to preserve it in a dry condition, it would have been both unnecessary and irrational to have begun by soaking it in a solution for a lengthy period, especially when the material employed, if used in a dry state, would have given better results than when used as a solution, and without the very objectionable putrefaction and intensely disagreeable smell attendant upon the wet method. Another reason for thinking that the process was a dry and not a wet one is that human bodies were undoubtedly mummified in a manner analogous to that in which fish were preserved (fish curing antedating mummification), but with natron instead of salt, and both ancient and modern methods of preserving fish generally apply salt in the dry state and not as a solution. Sometimes, however, fish, especially certain kinds of fish, are preserved in a solution (brine), but in these instances the fish remain in the brine until sold to the consumer, since, if removed, they quickly putrefy, and this mode of preserving fish, therefore, has no bearing on the method of embalming, as it was in the dry condition that the mummy was returned by the embalmers to the relatives and in the dry condition that it was buried.

Although the viscera were usually placed in the tomb in a dry state, in at least one

---

[1] III: 116–21.

[2] B. P. Grenfell and A. S. Hunt, *Oxyrhynchus Papyri*, I, p. 84; III, p. 256; IV, p. 228; VI, p. 293; X, p. 254; *Amherst Papyri*, II, p. 150; B. P. Grenfell, A. S. Hunt and H. I. Bell, *Oxyrhynchus Papyri*, XVI, p. 202. B. P. Grenfell, A. S. Hunt and D. G. Hogarth, *Fayum Towns and their Papyri*, pp. 105, 107. The same rendering occurs also in the Zenon papyri and other papyri that need not be enumerated.

instance they were preserved and left in a solution of natron, namely, in the case of Queen Hetepheres, but the body had always to be dry, since it had to be bandaged, since amulets and jewellery had to be placed on it and since it was buried in a wooden or cartonnage coffin.

When the specimens of brain and resin impregnated with natron were examined and first described by me,[1] I thought that for the natron to have become so intimately incorporated with the material, it must have been used in the form of a solution, that is as a bath. I now realize, however, that there are other possible explanations; for instance, the body may have been washed with a natron solution, as was sometimes done,[2] or a little solid natron left on the body after treatment might have been dissolved by the water employed for the subsequent washing and so might have penetrated to the brain. The resin may have become contaminated by coming into contact with solid natron, either accidentally or intentionally, during the embalming process. In some such manner, too, the presence of natron on Granville's mummy, on the Leeds mummy, and on the mummy of Nekhtankh may reasonably be explained.

Turning now to the mummy itself to ascertain whether that ever shows evidence, such, for instance, as pathological changes, that would indicate the nature of the preservative agent used, the conclusions of Ruffer may be quoted, since, so far as is known to me, his are the only studies on the subject that have been made.

Ruffer at first accepted the current idea of a bath in which the body was soaked and, as the outcome of his earlier investigations, he stated [3] that 'It appears to me probable that the solution used was one of "natron", but that this "natron" consisted chiefly of sodium chloride with a small admixture of carbonate and sulphate of soda.' Later, however, as the result of further work, he evidently changed his opinion, since in an unfinished article published after his death he wrote as follows:[4]

'The histological study of the skin does not point to the regular use of a natron bath.' '. . . there is no evidence whatever for the supposition that the body was ever steeped in a natron solution.' 'The wound through which the organs were extracted is always clean, not encrusted with natron, and nothing in its state suggests exposure to the action of a caustic fluid.' 'Microscopical examination of the muscles of the abdominal wall does not suggest contact with natron. Even if, after immersion, the natron had been carefully washed out of the body—a very difficult and tedious operation—some chemical or histological evidence of use of the natron bath would have been expected. There is no such evidence.' 'The organs, which had first been removed from and then replaced in the body, also show no signs of having been steeped in natron, and it is very difficult to believe that any amount of washing could have removed the natron so thoroughly as to leave no trace of it behind.' 'Microscopically the parietal and visceral pleurae, the capsule of the liver, the kidneys and, above all, the intestines show no signs whatever of having been in contact with an alkaline fluid.' '. . . the contention of Schmidt, who asserts as a fact that the bath used was one of sodium chloride. The chemical evidence on which this theory is based is

---

[1] A. Lucas, *Preservative Materials*, pp. 13–18.
[2] A. M. Blackman, *Rec. Trav.*, xxxix, p. 53; *Hastings's Ency. of Religion and Ethics*, x, p. 476.
[3] M. A. Ruffer, *Mém. Inst. Ég.*, vii (1914), p. 31.
[4] M. A. Ruffer, *Cairo Sci. Journ.*, ix (1917), pp. 48–51.

of the thinnest and the biological evidence is practically nil.' 'My objection to the theory of the natron or salt bath is that, unless a saturated solution of either was used, it would have led to the most intense putrefaction . . . If, on the other hand, a saturated solution was used, then, in spite of all successive washings, some excess of salt or natron should be present either on the muscles, skin or elsewhere. This, however, is not the case.'

'Although, therefore, I agree that salt and natron were used by embalmers I can find no evidence that the bodies were placed either in a natron bath or in a salt bath.'

The evidence from the pathological examination of mummies, therefore, furnishes no justification for thinking that the bodies were soaked in a bath or solution, but all points in the opposite direction.

The various arguments advanced in favour of a bath are, first, that the epidermis of mummies is often missing; second, that the finger-nails and toe-nails are sometimes found tied on, manifestly to prevent them falling off during the mummification process; third, that the body-hair is frequently absent; fourth, that the packing of the limbs that was a special feature of mummification during the Twenth-first Dynasty could not have been carried out unless the skin and tissues had been softened by soaking, and fifth, that bodies evidently sometimes came apart, since they are occasionally wrongly assembled, or left with some of the limbs missing, and this dismemberment can only be accounted for by lengthy maceration in a bath.

Elliot Smith attributes the loss of the epidermis to the action of the bath and says 'the skin shows unmistakable signs of having been macerated until the cuticle . . . has peeled off';[1] 'the general epidermis, as it was shed (which occurred when the body was steeped . . . in the preservative brine bath)';[2] Elliot Smith and Warren Dawson say [3] 'in the steeping process the epidermis peeled off'; 'the epidermis is nearly always absent owing to maceration'.

Winlock states [4] 'After the removal of the viscera the body must have been given a more or less prolonged soaking in a saline bath. This we assume from the facts that all the finger and toe nails have been tied with thread to prevent their loss during the maceration in such a bath, and the skin presented an appearance difficult to explain in any other way', and again,[5] 'There was ample evidence for a bath in the mummies which dated from the XXI to the XXV Dynasties unwrapped by me. Packing of the legs and arms could only have been accomplished when the bodies were extraordinarily soft and pliable. The almost total disappearance of muscles and other soft tissues in the limbs can only be explained by prolonged maceration—not by drying. The soft, pulpy, and easily torn and abraded skin during manipulation would never have appeared on a dried body. It would never have been necessary to tie the finger and toe nails on with thread during drying but it would have been necessary during soaking. Epidermis fallen from dried bodies is paper thin—soles of feet from characteristic XXI–XXVI Dynasty mummies are fairly thick as though they had been pickled.

[1] G. Elliot Smith, *Mém. Inst. Ég.*, v (1906), p. 18.
[2] G. Elliot Smith, *Migration of Early Culture* (1929), p. 23.
[3] G. Elliot Smith and W. R. Dawson, *Egyptian Mummies*, pp. 88, 124.
[4] H. E. Winlock, *Meryet-Amūn*, p. 10.
[5] Private letter.

On the other hand XI Dynasty, Roman and Coptic mummies unwrapped by me appeared often to have been merely dried—either before or after burial—and showed none of the signs of soaking.'

Dawson states [1] 'During this long immersion the epidermis peeled off, taking with it the body-hair, and it was for this reason also that special care was taken to secure the nails so that they should not come away with the macerated skin and be lost. To accomplish this end, the embalmers cut the skin round the base of the nail of each finger and toe, so as to form a natural thimble. Around each such thimble they wound a thread or a twist of wire to hold the nail in place. In the case of kings and wealthy persons, the thimbles of skin with their nails were kept in position by means of metal stalls. The mummy of Tutankhamūn had a set of gold stalls in position. It is specially to be noted that the head was not immersed, for it always retains the epidermis and the hair (unless the scalp had previously been shaved) and does not present the same appearance of emaciation as the rest of the body.' Elliot Smith also notes the state of the skin and hair of the head, and suggests that the face may have been coated with a resin paste or that the body was so placed that the head was not submerged.[2]

Dawson again writes [3] 'I have examined a great number of mummies, and, with the exception of two cases, the epidermis was always entirely absent from the whole body, except from the head, fingers and toes where its cut edges are visible. I agree that simple maceration might not be sufficient to detach the whole of the cuticle, but it would certainly loosen it and make it easy to remove by scraping, a practice followed in other parts of the world. I have also both seen and read of packets of detached epidermis wrapped in linen and buried with the mummy. With the exception of the two cases afore-mentioned, I have never found any trace of pubic, axillary or other body-hair, nor even stumps that might indicate cutting or shaving. It always comes away with the epidermis.'

Professor Battiscombe Gunn writes:[4] 'One point, however, strikes me in this connection. The well-attested fact that mummies when unwrapped are often found either to have a limb or limbs missing, and replaced with sticks, etc., or else to be made up with other people's limbs, having three arms and one leg or vice versa—this fact is usually explained by the body having come apart in the pickling bath. If the bodies were merely dehydrated with dry natron, it is not easy to explain the loss of limbs. Have you any alternative explanation? I think that with many people such cases will constitute a strong objection to your theory.'

The various arguments quoted that have been put forward in favour of a soaking of the body will now be considered.

That the epidermis, except that on the head, fingers and toes, is often missing; that packets of shed epidermis occasionally have been found with mummies,[5] and that the body-hair generally is absent are not disputed. The suggestion that this condition was caused by prolonged soaking in a bath has been dealt with by Ruffer,

---

[1] W. R. Dawson, *J.E.A.*, XIII (1927), p. 43; *Magician and Leech*, pp. 39–40.

[2] G. Elliot Smith, *Ann. Serv.*, VII (1906), p. 161.

[3] Private letter, 1933.   [4] Private letter, 1933.

[5] G. Elliot Smith and F. Wood Jones, *Arch. Survey of Nubia, 1907–1908*, II, pp. 200–1.

who, therefore, may be quoted. He says of the mummy of a woman that 'the *rete mucosum* of the skin of chest and mammae is almost completely gone',[1] but he explains that at first he 'attributed this state of things to the effect of the salt bath, but that it cannot be wholly due to this is proved by the fact that the epidermis of bodies which had certainly never been placed in the bath had also fallen off'.[1] He states, too, that 'in many cases the epidermis, especially that of the toes and hands, is practically normal';[1] 'it has been taken for granted that the natron bath . . . would so soften the skin that the epidermis would either fall off in the bath or be easily stripped off afterwards, and because the epidermis has evidently been removed in some instances, this was assumed to have been the result of the natron bath';[2] 'very often . . . the epidermic layer is absent, but in mummies of the twenty-first Dynasty . . . the epidermic layer can often be demonstrated';[2] 'the skin of mummies of the Roman epoch is as a rule perfect, the epidermis shows no signs of having been shed';[2] 'it has been taken for granted that a solution of natron . . . would loosen the cuticle so much that this could easily be removed. As a matter of fact the evidence . . . is nil';[2] 'the fact that the skin, including the epidermis, of certain bodies was almost normal shows that the "natron" bath cannot always have had a very powerful macerating effect'.[1] Ruffer further explains that 'with the onset of putrefaction the epidermis is raised and ultimately falls off';[1] and quotes the instance of a body of a child where 'there was absolutely no sign that it had been touched by the embalmer',[1] and yet 'the whole of the epidermis of the soles of the feet and toes was almost completely detached'.[1] The fact that the epidermis of mummies is often absent, therefore, is not proof that the body had been soaked in a solution, since putrefaction alone may have been the responsible agent.

Further, that the epidermis may, at first sight, appear to be absent is no proof that it really is absent, since Elliot Smith says [3] of a particular mummy 'Unlike all other mummies examined by me (excepting only those of the Coptic period) the epidermis was not removed during the process of embalming. It is present, peeled off, it is true, but adhering to the bandages, wherever they came in contact with the body.' May it not be, therefore, that in other instances, for example where the bandages were in poor condition (the bandages next to the body are often blackened and friable and may even be in the condition of black powder) that the epidermis was present adhering to the bandages, but was not recognized?

With respect to the finger and toe-nails sometimes being tied on, may it not be that the drying and consequent shrinkage and emaciation, or incipient putrefaction, or both, would have so loosened the nails that these would have been in danger of falling off unless tied? The use of finger and toe stalls certainly was not to prevent the nails falling off, since the stalls were not put on until after the mummification was finished and after the fingers and toes had each been wrapped separately in linen, as is shown in the case of the mummy of Tutankhamūn. Thus Carter states [4] 'Each finger and thumb having been primarily wrapped in fine strips of linen, was enclosed in a gold sheath.'

---

[1] M. A. Ruffer, *Mém. Inst. Ég.*, VII (1914), pp. 14–17.
[2] M. A. Ruffer, *Cairo Sc. Journ.*, IX (1917), pp. 47, 48.
[3] G. Elliot Smith, *Royal Mummies*, p. 9.
[4] H. Carter, *Tut-ankh-Amen*, II, pp. 129–30.

The toes also had been treated in a similar manner and wrapped separately before the stalls were put on.

As for the body-hair being missing, this naturally would fall off with the epidermis, which Ruffer states was due to putrefaction and not to soaking. The caustic natron might also have a corrosive effect on the hair, which is easily destroyed by alkalies.

The packing of the legs and arms, as was done in the Twenty-first Dynasty, Winlock says [1] 'could only have been accomplished when the bodies were extraordinarily soft and pliable' and that the 'almost total disappearance of the muscles and other soft tissue in the limbs can only be explained by prolonged maceration—not by drying', but I do not agree, and the reasons will be given in due course. With respect to the action of a solution, Elliot Smith states [2] 'While the body is in the saline solution the skin and the lining of the body cavity become toughened by the action of the salt; but the soft tissues under the skin in the limbs, back and neck are not exposed to the action of the preservative agent and soon become reduced to a soft pulpy mass, which is of a fluid or semifluid consistency. It was the practice of the embalmers in the time of the 21st. dynasty to stuff into this pulpy mass large quantities of foreign materials so as to restore to the collapsed and shrunken members some semblance of the form and consistency they possessed during life.' But that any preservative or desiccating agent should pass through the skin and lining membranes of the body cavities, toughening them in the process, but softening and disintegrating the tissues underneath, seems most unlikely. There is also a contradiction in the statement itself, since 'a soft pulpy mass' is not quite the same as being of 'a fluid or semifluid consistency'.

Elliot Smith also writes [3] that 'The examination of mummies of the New Empire reveals the fact that during the process of mummification . . . the soft tissues of the body (excepting the skin which was exposed to the action of the preservative agent) became converted into a loose spongy material which was much too soft and too small in amount to keep the skin distended: as a result the limbs became reduced to little else than bones with an ill-fitting wrapping of deeply wrinkled skin . . . In the 21st. dynasty the embalmers endeavoured to remedy this effect by stuffing various materials . . . under the skin so as to distend it and mould it to the form of the body.' A 'loose spongy material', as now mentioned, is not the same as a 'soft pulpy mass' previously described, much less is it 'of a fluid or semifluid consistency'. These criticisms may at first sight appear trivial and unnecessary, but they are neither, since an important principle is involved, for if the tissues were reduced either to a soft pulpy mass, or to a fluid, or semifluid consistency, for which no evidence is given, this might prove that the bodies had been soaked in a solution for a lengthy period, whereas in my opinion a bath was never employed. In certain experiments I made with chickens and pigeons, I found that both the skin and the tissues became softened as the result of soaking, and that immediately after removal from the solution, although not reduced to a fluid or semifluid consistency, they were 'soft and pulpy to the touch',[4] and the skin had become so soft that 'it was difficult to handle the bodies without rubbing off portions of the skin'.[4] In such a condition I believe that it would not have been possible to have

---

[1] See p. 285.   [2] G. Elliot Smith, Mém. Inst. Ég., v (1906), p. 19.

[3] G. Elliot Smith, Mém. Inst. Ég., v (1906), p. 10.

[4] A. Lucas, Preservative Materials, pp. 9–10; J.E.A., xviii (1932), pp. 133–4.

packed any material under the skin, as was done by the embalmers of the Twenty-first Dynasty, without rupturing it considerably and partly destroying it; also, there would not have been any room for packing material, and it was only after the flesh had dried and shrunk that packing became either necessary or possible. The packing, therefore, instead of being evidence of soaking, is, in my opinion, proof of the contrary.

Ruffer states [1] that 'there is no proof that the tissues were changed into a soft pulpy mass. I have examined several mummies, the limbs of which had not been packed by the embalmers and I found the muscles, nerves and arteries etc. in a very good state of preservation.'

According to the experiments I made with pigeons and dry natron,[2] the body became much emaciated and the skin loose and wrinkled, in which condition it would have been an easy matter to have packed it in the manner that was customary during the Twenty-first Dynasty. Elliot Smith states [3] of a certain mummy that 'The skin is ... soft, moist and tough' and again 'the skin has become softened and flexible'. Elliot Smith and Warren Dawson state [4] that the skin of many of the bodies of early Christian date that had not been soaked, but on which salt was found, was 'entire, soft and pliable'. Soaking, therefore, was not necessary in order to make the skin soft and pliable. Also, it may be mentioned that the epidermis from the soles of the feet of the woman found in the coffin lid bearing the name of Setnakht,[5] which was examined by me, was very soft and pliable, and is still in the same condition, more than thirty years after its first examination, and it could be stretched and packed, and this skin certainly was preserved with solid natron, which was found with it. Also, if in any instance the skin were too dry and brittle to allow of packing, might not the anointing with oil or fat that followed the desiccation and was part of the mummification process have restored its pliability?

The facts mentioned by Gunn about the redundant limbs are well known.[6] Jomard in 1809 [7] refers to ancient false mummies and examples have been found in Nubia [8] and elsewhere. These defective and composite mummies are of two main classes, namely (a) those like the royal mummies found at Deir el Bahari and in the tomb of Amenhotpe II respectively, which had been maltreated by robbers in search of plunder and subsequently restored and re-wrapped and then hidden to protect them from further damage, the condition of which has no connexion with the manner of embalming, and (b) mummies not damaged by robbers and then re-wrapped. Some of these latter are deliberate frauds made in modern times and often put into genuine old coffins in order to sell to tourists. Jomard says [7] that not only were there ancient false mummies, but that in his day the Arabs and the Jews made modern ones,

---

[1] M. A. Ruffer, Mém. Inst. Ég., VII (1914), p. 10.

[2] A. Lucas, J.E.A., XVIII (1932), pp. 133–4.   [3] G. Elliot Smith, Royal Mummies, pp. 9–10.

[4] G. Elliot Smith and W. R. Dawson, Egyptian Mummies, p. 131.

[5] G. Elliot Smith and W. R. Dawson, Egyptian Mummies, p. 101; A. Lucas, Preservative Materials, pp. 6–7.

[6] Cf. also O. H. Myers, J.E.A., XXI (1935), pp. 126–8.

[7] E. Jomard, 'Description des hypogées de la ville de Thèbes,' Description de l'Égypte, 1809, I, pp. 345–6.

[8] G. Elliot Smith and F. Wood Jones, Arch. Survey of Nubia, 1907–1908, II, pp. 213–15.

and Pettigrew in 1834 states [1] that Mr. Madden saw 'a manufacture of mummies' at Qurna, opposite Luxor (where false mummies are still made), these being put into old coffins. Other defective mummies may be incomplete because the body had been allowed to undergo considerable decomposition before it was embalmed, as, for instance, according to Herodotus,[2] was customary in the case of women of the better class. With reference to this, Elliot Smith and Warren Dawson state [3] that 'It may be observed that there is abundant evidence that some of the bodies were in an advanced stage of decomposition when treated by the embalmers, and this condition in nearly every case applied to women.' Derry says [4] 'Some of these jumbled collections of bones are undoubtedly examples of bodies which have been disturbed either by robbers or otherwise, and subsequently re-wrapped by some person who discovered the remains and, while collecting them, included bones found in the vicinity from a neighbouring tomb.'

But, allowing for both of these categories mentioned, there still remain a large number of mummies the state of which requires accounting for. The usual explanation, either given or implied, is that their condition is due to the bodies having been soaked in an embalming solution in such a manner, or for such a period, that they became dismembered and that insufficient care was taken to keep the several parts of one body separate from those of others, in consequence of which mistakes were made in assembling the parts, whereby some bodies were left with limbs missing, or the limbs allotted to them did not belong. But no evidence is offered to show that soaking in a natron solution, even if prolonged, would cause the limbs to separate from the body, but that this might happen with certain strengths of natron is not denied, though it did not happen in some experiments made by me with chickens and pigeons that were soaked in natron solutions,[5] but it did occur in one instance when a solution of common salt was used in place of natron.[5] But, even though it be accepted that the use of a natron bath could cause dismemberment of the bodies, for which, however, there is no proof, this would solve only part of the problem. The defective and composite mummies that are not cases of re-wrapping are practically, if not entirely, limited to very late periods, Persian, Ptolemaic and Roman, and apparently most, if not all, are of persons of the poorer classes and, therefore, any explanaton, before it can be accepted, must show the reason for this limitation in both time and status, which the bath theory does not.

The condition of these late mummies is probably correlated to the fact that about the beginning of the period to which they belong 'less and less attention was paid to the body and more and more to the external wrappings',[6] and 'the processes were getting slipshod and the practitioners careless, when much of the care which in earlier times was devoted to the body itself was now being given mainly to the outward

---

[1] T. J. Pettigrew, *History of Egyptian Mummies*, p. 228.

[2] II: 89.

[3] G. Elliot Smith and W. R. Dawson, *Egyptian Mummies*, p. 125. Cf. also G. Elliot Smith and F. Wood Jones, *Arch. Survey of Nubia, 1907–1908*, II, pp. 212–13.

[4] D. E. Derry, *Ann. Serv.*, XLI (1942), p. 265.

[5] A. Lucas, *J.E.A.*, XVIII (1932), pp. 133–4.

[6] G. Elliot Smith and W. R. Dawson, *Egyptian Mummies*, p. 121.

appearance of the wrapped mummy',[1] and so long as this 'displayed a presentable exterior it seemed to matter little to the embalmer how careless and slipshod was the work upon the corpse concealed beneath the carefully wrought external coverings'.[2]

No wholly satisfactory solution of the difficulty can be suggested, but two facts are certain, namely, first, that the bodies must have been desiccated in some manner before they were wrapped up (which as shown elsewhere [3] was best attained by the use of dry natron), and second, that more than one body was dealt with at the same time and place, hence some 'wholesale' treatment seems indicated. Whatever it was there must have been some deviation from the old practice, since it is only at the late periods that the defective and composite mummies are found. Some method resulting in a considerable decomposition of the body seems certain, possibly a method dictated by the need of economy (since more expense was being incurred for the wrapping). One obvious economy would have been to reduce the amount of natron used (that the great purifying agent should have been entirely omitted is unlikely) and another might have taken the form of the repeated use and re-use of the same natron until it had little or no preservative property left.

One very strong argument against the use of a bath for soaking bodies on a wholesale scale is that even for two bodies a very large receptacle would have been required, and for a large number of bodies the receptacle would have been enormous. On the other hand, to place a number of bodies on the ground, or on mats, and to cover them with dry natron would have been an easy matter, and, if the bodies were those of poor people, who were paying the minimum price, it might well have happened that sometimes there was inadequate protection against pariah dogs, or even against jackals, and that occasionally bodies might have been disturbed by these animals, or even parts of a body might have been carried away.

As further evidence against the employment of a solution for embalming we have the fact that no vessel of the size or kind that must have been used for the bath has been found. Whether the body had been stretched at full length in the horizontal position in an oblong receptacle, or placed, as suggested by Dawson,[4] in a sharply flexed position in a large jar, the vessel would have been either pottery or stone; but no such vessel, either whole or broken, has ever been discovered, nor even any pieces of material suggesting such a vessel. Pottery jars of sufficiently large size to contain a human body are known, but they are often of a date anterior to mummification and they have never been found in such circumstances or in such a condition as to suggest their use in embalming. The pottery vessels employed by me for soaking the chickens and pigeons used in my mummification experiments were so impregnated with natron and salt respectively that there was no mistaking the nature of the solutions they had contained, and the condition of any pottery vessel used in mummifying the human body by soaking would have been equally unmistakable.

---

[1] G. Elliot Smith and F. Wood Jones, *Arch. Survey of Nubia, 1907–1908*, II, pp. 213–15.

[2] G. Elliot Smith and W. R. Dawson, *Egyptian Mummies*, p. 121.

[3] A. Lucas, *J.E.A.*, XVIII (1932), pp. 133–4.

[4] W. R. Dawson, *J.E.A.*, XIII (1927), pp. 44–45; *Magician and Leech*, p. 42; 'Contributions to the History of Mummification', *Proc. Royal Soc. of Medicine*, XX (1927), p. 850; cf. also W. R. Dawson, *J.E.A.*, XIV (1928), pp. 126–7. The significance of the figures adduced as evidence is extremely doubtful.

Although a pottery or stone vessel might have been used for the dry method of embalming, this would not have been essential, and a wooden box [1] would have been equally suitable; or the packing in natron might have been done on an embalming platform, such as that found by Winlock, or on a mat, such as was also found by Winlock, or even on the ground. The actual method of applying the natron is not known, but the repeated occurrence of a large number of small parcels of this material tied up in linen cloth found with refuse embalming material might be explained by supposing that each parcel was a unit of some kind, and that a number of them were packed into the body cavities (thorax and abdomen) [2] or placed on the body or only in special positions on the body, as for instance on the face,[3] the rest of the body being covered with the loose powdered material. That the natron was used in the form of dry powder is also suggested by the results of an examination of refuse embalming material recently undertaken by Iskander.[4] Specimens of natron from different jars in the same cache contained a varying percentage of fatty matter, evidently derived from the body, suggesting that the contents of one jar had been in close contact with the corpse, while those of the other had not. If a natron solution had been employed, the content of fatty matter in all specimens would have been similar. One frequent feature, too, of natron found with refuse embalming material is its admixture with sawdust, which may have been added as an additional absorbent.

In order to determine the action of salt and natron respectively I, then accepting the prevalent idea that the preservative material was employed in the form of a solution, soaked two chickens (plucked and eviscerated) for seventy days in an 8 per cent solution of natron and one chicken for the same length of time in an 8 per cent solution of common salt. There was much putrefaction with considerable smell in both cases. After the soaking, the chickens were immersed in water for about a minute and then exposed to the air for a fortnight to dry. As soon as the fowls were removed from the bath they were examined and it was found that all three, although plump, were soft and pulpy to the touch. It was very difficult to handle them without rubbing off portions of the skin, and of the two which had been in the natron, one was very much discoloured, with the bones of the lower part of one wing bare; the other also was discoloured in places, and some of the skin had disappeared, but there were no bare bones. The fowl which had been in the salt solution, however, was in a much worse condition than either of the other two; part of the neck, the ribs on one side of the body, the backbone, practically the whole of one wing and the lower part of one leg were entirely free from either flesh or skin, the bones being quite bare, and from the rest of the body the skin was in parts loose and hanging in strips. After the fowls had been exposed to the air for a fortnight they were again examined. They were all hard, dry and very much shrunken. Of the two which had been in the

---

[1] The wooden coffins that have been found containing refuse embalming material may have been used for this purpose.

[2] The value of this would have been the ease with which they could have been withdrawn when the operation was finished.

[3] In one case a small packet of white powder, probably natron, was found stuffed in the mouth of a mummy of Twenty-fifth Dynasty date (W. M. F. Petrie and E. Mackay, *Heliopolis, Kafr Ammar and Shurafa*, p. 35).

[4] J.-P. Lauer and Z. Iskander, *Ann. Serv.*, LIII (1956), pp. 180–94.

natron, one was practically all skin and bone, very much discoloured, with the bones of the lower part of one wing bare; the other retained a good deal of the flesh, which was pink; it was discoloured in places, and some of the skin had disappeared, but there were no bare bones. In the case of the fowl which had been in the salt solution, as already mentioned, practically the whole of one side consisted of bare bones, but the other side was white, dry and hard, and seemed to be nothing but skin and bones, and the skin which previously had been loose had adhered again.[1]

Under the conditions of the experiments and with the particular strength of solutions employed, all three chickens were preserved, but the two that had been in the natron solution were in a much better condition than the one that had been in the salt solution. These mummified chickens were kept for thirteen years before being destroyed, at the end of which time they were in as good a state of preservation as when they were first prepared. Unfortunately no determinations were made to ascertain whether or not the skin and flesh of the chickens had become impregnated with natron and salt respectively, and in order to remedy this omission, further experiments were carried out,[2] using pigeons in place of chickens and a 3 per cent solution of natron[3] and salt respectively instead of an 8 per cent solution, 3 per cent being the strength of the natron solution found in the canopic box of Queen Hetepheres.

Moreover, in order to determine the effects of dry natron and salt, experiments with both materials were also made as follows: a thick layer of natron[3] in one case and of salt in the other was put at the bottom of a glazed earthenware vessel, and on this in each vessel a pigeon (plucked and eviscerated) was placed, which was then thickly and completely covered with natron or salt, the body being concealed as described by Herodotus. The duration of all four experiments was reduced from seventy days, which was the period previously chosen, to forty days, the latter being probably more nearly the time taken anciently for this part of the embalming process.[4]

At the end of forty days the experiments were discontinued and the pigeons were taken out of the natron and salt and examined. The pigeon that had been in the natron solution was bleached white, but was whole, plump and in good condition with the skin intact. It was rinsed under the tap, immersed in water for fifteen minutes, drained and dried. While it was draining, putrescent blood-coloured fluid came away for several hours, and a slight smell of putrefaction remained for some weeks. The pigeon from the salt solution was no longer recognizable as such, having been reduced to a formless mass of skin, bones and fat (no flesh). The remains, which were bleached white, were rinsed, washed, drained and dried like the other pigeon. During the forty days the pigeons were soaking there was a very strong smell of putrefaction from both.

The pigeons that had been buried in solid natron and salt respectively were much alike, being hard, dry and much emaciated, with the skin intact; they were practically free from disagreeable smell, of which there had been very little during the forty

---

[1] A. Lucas, *Preservative Materials*, pp. 9–10; *Cairo Sc. Journ.*, II (1908), pp. 421–3.

[2] A. Lucas, *J.E.A.*, XVIII (1932), pp. 133–4.

[3] Containing 29.4 per cent of sodium chloride (common salt) and 9.8 per cent of sodium sulphate.

[4] See p. 299, *n*. 3.

days of burial. Neither pigeon was bleached. The natron from the one, where it had been in contact with the body, was discoloured and consolidated from the effects of the exuded body fluids and contained a large number of small dead insects (probably larvae). On dissolving this natron in water, the solution was much discoloured and a considerable number of additional insects became manifest. There were also a number of these insects adhering to the body. The salt from the other pigeon had become slightly consolidated from the exuded body fluids, but was not visibly discoloured, though on dissolving it in water a discoloured solution was produced, in which were a few dead insects similar to those from the first pigeon, but there were no insects on the body. After nine days' drying the pigeons were examined for the presence of natron and salt. There was no visible efflorescence or other perceptible indication of either, but on testing, salt was found in all four instances, in two of which it had manifestly been derived from that contained in the natron. There was no natron present on the two pigeons that had been treated with this material, the bodies being very slightly acid, as were also the two pigeons that had been treated with salt, though with these latter the acidity appeared to be slightly greater.

Birds (chickens and pigeons), therefore, may be preserved whole and in good condition by soaking them either in an 8 per cent solution of natron for seventy days, or in a 3 per cent solution of natron for forty days. Birds may be preserved, too, though not nearly in such good condition by soaking them for seventy days in an 8 per cent solution of common salt, but they are not preserved when the strength of the solution is reduced to 3 per cent. Birds are dried and excellently preserved by packing them for forty days either in dry natron, or dry salt. Birds that have been treated with natron do not contain natron, but are acid, the alkali of the natron having been more than neutralized by acid decomposition products of the body. These birds, too, contain salt, derived from that originally present as an impurity in the natron. Birds that have been treated with salt contain salt and also are acid from the acid decomposition products of the body.

The experiments prove very definitely the falsity of the argument often used against the employment of natron for desiccation, namely that mummies are generally acid and not alkaline, and that, therefore, an alkali cannot have been used. A body, however, may have been treated with natron and still be acid, as is proved by the two pigeons mummified by me, one of which had been immersed in a natron solution for forty days and the other buried in solid natron for the same period. The reason for this apparent anomaly is manifestly that in most cases the fatty acids and possibly other acid products of decomposition have more than neutralized the small amount of alkali (natron) left on the body after washing. The probability that this would prove to be the case was suggested by me many years ago.[1]

There cannot be any doubt whatever that the essential operation in all methods of mummification in ancient Egypt was the desiccation of the body, and although certain details of the mummification process varied from time to time, the deliberate drying of the body remained the principal feature and this, I believe, was brought about by the use of dry natron, and not by soaking in a solution.[2]

---

[1] A. Lucas, *Preservative Materials*, p. 11.

[2] Cf. A. Lucas, *J.E.A.*, XVIII (1932), pp. 137–8.

The Eleventh Dynasty royal bodies found by Winlock in the Mentuhotpe cemetery at Thebes [1] and examined by Derry would seem to have been an important
exception. These bodies had not been eviscerated and Derry states [2] 'Complete desiccation of the bodies before bandaging is ruled out because the skin is folded and bears
impressions of jewellery which shows that the bodies were still soft and pliable at the
time of bandaging and the mould-like form of the bandages shows that the emaciation
took place after wrapping', and 'liquids from decomposition had penetrated the
bandages even to the outside' and had made of them 'a more or less rigid mould of
the body. . . which held its shape after the body had shrunk to far smaller proportions'.
In some instances manifestly either the body had been treated only for a short time
with the desiccating agent (natron) and then wrapped up, or the body had been
wrapped up without any preliminary desiccation. From the condition of both the
body and the wrappings the second suggestion seems the more probable, although it
would have meant omitting, not only the drying properties of the usual natron,but
also its supposed purifying virtues. Special purification ceremonies, however, to
compensate for the absence of natron may have been used, or the washing of the
body may have been done with a natron solution. The desiccation in these instances
evidently took place wholly, or largely, in the tomb, but in the wrapped body it must
have been a very slow process, despite the tomb temperature, which may have been
as high as about 29° C. (84° F.).[3]

Other instances in which the body was not eviscerated are known. Thus Hayes
says [4] of five Eighteenth Dynasty burials found by him in the Theban necropolis
'Although the viscera, brains, etc. were not removed from the bodies and packing
inserted in their place, as in later periods of Egyptian history, the bodies themselves
had been "cured" by a long process involving the use of natron and other salts and
subsequently saturated with pitchy [5] preservatives, so that even after some 3,400 years
under the most adverse conditions much of the tissue, skin, and hair is still intact.'

Pettigrew noticed a similar fact and says [6] 'Mummies very richly furnished and
prepared in the most costly manner have been found without the ventral incision.'

Following the desiccation came the washing of the body, which must have been
necessary after the evisceration and natron treatment, but which is mentioned only
by Herodotus.[7] This was probably a simple washing with water, and is not to be
confused with the ceremonial purification by means of a solution of natron described
by Blackman,[8] which Grdseloff [9] has shown took place in a tent or other temporary
structure before the body was handed over to the embalmers. Stylized representations

---

[1] H. E. Winlock, *M.M.A. Bull., Egyptian Exped. 1920–1921*, pp. 37–52.

[2] From private notes kindly lent me by Dr. Derry. See also D. E. Derry, *Ann. Serv.*, XLI (1942),
pp. 246–57.

[3] A. Lucas, *Ann. Serv.*, XXIV (1924), pp. 12–14.

[4] W. C. Hayes, *M.M.A. Bull., Egyptian Exped. 1934–1935*, p. 20.

[5] Not, of course, pitch, but resin that had blackened and become pitchlike in appearance.

[6] T. J. Pettigrew, *History of Egyptian Mummies*, p. 60.

[7] II: 86.

[8] A. M. Blackman, *Hasting's Ency. of Religion and Ethics*, x, pp. 476–82; *J.E.A.*, v (1918), pp.
117–24, 148–65; *Rec. Trav.*, XXXIX (1921), pp. 44–78.

[9] B. Grdseloff, *Das Ägyptische Reinigungszelt.*

of this ritual purfication are found on the walls of several tombs.[1] The deceased, invariably depicted as though alive, is shown standing on a pedestal or in a pan or basin, or alternatively seated upon a large jar, while the purifying solution of natron in water is poured over him by two or more officiants. Somewhat similar scenes, apparently illustrating different stages in the process of lustration, also occur on two coffins published by Capart.[2] In these, the deceased, more realistically represented as a naked corpse, is shown standing in what appears to be a trough with steps on either side, and lying prone in a tank, while the purifying fluid is poured over him, and is finally pictured extended on a couch which is covered by a mat.

After the washing, an anointing with oil followed, which is referred to by Diodorus,[3] and as evidence of it may be mentioned the mats (one of a late period, Twenty-sixth to Thirtieth Dynasty, and the others of which the dates are not given) stained with oil found by Winlock in the Theban necropolis,[4] and the linen stained with oil found by Lansing in an embalmer's pit of Twenty-sixth Dynasty date, also at Thebes, part of which is in the Cairo Museum, where I have examined it. Some of this linen (originally five lots, of which the Museum took one) was wrapped into the shape of small mummies, the one I examined [5] being 33 cm. (13 inches) long, and containing a mixture of resin and sand, the linen being greasy in parts; other lots (originally twenty-nine, of which the Museum took nine,[6] called swabs in the Museum register, but probably embalmer's pads) were in various curious shapes. The linen was greasy and some of it was saturated with oil. With this linen there were two red pottery jars (one of which [7] I examined) with an embalmer's inscription on the neck, containing a compact mass of small bundles wrapped in greasy linen, all of which contained a mixture of resin and sand. Lansing and Hayes found 'oil-stained bandages' of Eighteenth Dynasty date, also at Deir el Bahari.[8]

No generalization can be made respecting the treatment of the body after lustration and before wrapping, since the procedure varied at different periods, at different places and with the social status of the dead person.

After about the beginning of the Eighteenth Dynasty [9] the brain was generally removed from the cranium, which sometimes was left empty and sometimes was filled with resin, or resin and linen, though occasionally during the Ptolemaic period it was filled with wood pitch (not bitumen).

The thorax and abdomen, from which the organs, except the heart, were removed, sometimes were left empty. Sometimes they were filled with a solid mass of resin, or more generally with linen soaked in resin (the resin manifestly having been employed in the molten state[10] and the linen probably having been used to economize resin), sawdust, or other materials. During the Twenty-first Dynasty and later the

---

[1] A. M. Blackman, Rec. Trav., XXXIX (1921), pp. 53–56; B. Grdseloff, Das Ägyptische Reinigungszelt, pp. 32–36.

[2] J. Capart, Chronique d'Égypte, XVIII (1942), pp. 191–8.

[3] I: 91.

[4] H. E. Winlock, M.M.A. Bull., Egyptian Exped. 1927–1928, pp. 25–26.

[5] No. J. 65385 B.   [6] No. J. 65385 A.   [7] No. J. 65385 C.

[8] A. Lansing and W. C. Hayes, M.M.A. Bull., Egyptian Exped. 1935–1936, p. 23.

[9] G. Elliot Smith, Cairo Sc. Journ., II (1908), p. 46.

[10] D. E. Derry, Ann. Serv., XXXIX (1939), pp. 411–16; XLI (1942), pp. 259, 263.

dried viscera were wrapped up in four 'canopic packets' (each with a figure of one of the four sons of Horus) and returned to the body.[1] Sometimes the whole body was covered with resin, and in the case of the earliest known mummy, which, until 1941 when it was destroyed by a bomb, was in the Museum of the Royal College of Surgeons, London, the whole body was encased in resin-soaked linen, which was carefully moulded into shape, and the body cavities were packed with linen and resin. With respect to the mummy of Queen Meryetamūn (Eighteenth Dynasty) Winlock states [2] that 'The body cavity was packed tightly with rags impregnated with resin and pure liquid resin was poured over the incision in the left flank until it formed a pool from 1 to 1.5 cm. deep.' 'The face was smeared with a black resinous paste.' 'After a few layers of cloth had been applied, the whole body was drenched in liquid resin.' 'Further wrappings and further drenchings were repeated.' With respect to one mummy he examined Derry writes [3] 'Two large fragments representing parts of the right and left sides of the thorax with the ribs in situ are filled with a mass which . . . proved to consist of linen combined with the same resinous material. This had evidently been introduced while hot . . .' In one instance of Eleventh Dynasty date the body was covered with beeswax.[4]

In many instances, especially with the later mummies, but also in the case of Tutankhamūn, the whole body is very black and in some cases, and again in that of Tutankhamūn, even the bones are black throughout, a condition that often is attributed to the body having been soaked in bitumen, for which there is neither evidence not probability, and, in my opinion, as a result of having examined many of these mummies, including that of Tutankhamūn, the blackening has been caused by a form of slow spontaneous combustion of the organic matter of that portion of the flesh remaining after the desiccation, and of the organic matter of the bones, whereby free carbon and carbonaceous matter have been formed.[5] It may be mentioned that there is so much organic matter (about 30 per cent) in fresh dry bones that when the mineral matter is dissolved out with acid the bones retain their shape and resemble in appearance a gelatine cast of the original. Why particular mummies, and those chiefly of late date, should exhibit this blackening is not known, but it seems possible that it commenced with a fungus growth (mould) caused by damp, which at a later stage became a chemical process. If so, then lack of complete drying after washing and before bandaging may have been the predisposing cause. When a body coated with resin is black, such blackening may be very different and may be due to the burning and consequent blackening of the resin while it was being heated in order to melt it for ease of application, though there is some slight evidence that certain resins may become black with age, especially when in contact with fatty matter.

As already stated, for a long period after the introduction of embalming, it was confined to the kings and wealthier classes, but eventually simpler and cheaper

---

[1] See G. Elliot Smith, *Ann. Serv.*, IV (1903), pp. 159–60; T. J. Pettigrew, *Archaeologia*, XXVII (1838), pp. 270–1; S. Birch, *Journ. Arch. Inst.*, VII (1850), pp. 277–9.

[2] H. E. Winlock, *Meryet-Amūn*, pp. 10–11.

[3] D. E. Derry, *Ann. Serv.*, XXXIX (1939), pp. 411–16.

[4] Mummy No. 23 found by Winlock in the Mentuhotpe cemetery at Thebes. From private notes kindly lent me by Dr. Derry. See also D. E. Derry, *Ann. Serv.*, XLI (1942), pp. 246–57.

[5] Cf. D. E. Derry, in H. Carter, *Tut-ankh-Amen*, II, p. 149 (Appendix I).

methods were introduced, so that even the poor were able to avail themselves of some preservative treatment, chiefly desiccation by means of natron, and so they, too, might hope to attain everlasting life.

So far, the only references made to any ancient description of the methods of mummification have been a few to Herodotus and Diodorus, who are the only early writers who have left actual accounts of the process, though allusions to embalming occur in the works of many other classical authors.[1] No extant Egyptian text contains any details of the methods of embalming, but Sethe has sought to connect certain passages in the Pyramid Texts with mummification,[2] and in a document dated to the First Intermediate period 'the secret art of the embalmers' is referred to.[3] The so-called 'Ritual of Embalming'[4] is essentially a religious text concerned with the application of unguents, the bandaging of the body and the placing of amulets, though details of embalming may once have been included, since the text is possibly incomplete. The Rhind papyri[5] are also largely concerned with the anointing and bandaging of the body and mention embalming only briefly. The earliest detailed description is that of Herodotus,[6] who travelled in Egypt about the middle of the fifth century B.C. (some time before 460 B.C.), the next earliest being that of Diodorus,[7] who visited the country about four hundred years later, during the first century B.C., each of whom wrote an account of what he had seen and heard, including a description of the process of mummification. From the Twenty-sixth Dynasty (664 B.C. to 525 B.C.), however, which is earlier than Herodotus, there is the Apis Papyrus,[8] which contains a description of the embalming of the sacred bull Apis, though the first part is lost, and only the sections dealing with bandaging and anointing are preserved. A convenient summary of the more important textual evidence, including the Egyptian papyri already mentioned, the accounts of Herodotus and Diodorus, and references to embalming in papyri of the Graeco-Roman period is given by Elliot Smith and Dawson.[9]

Apart from the representations of ritual purification mentioned above,[10] illustrations relating to mummification are extremely rare. Two similar scenes discussed by Dawson[11] may possibly show the mummy already wrapped with the final adjustments being made to the bandages, the application of resin to the bandages, the decoration of the mask, etc., but this interpretation is rendered doubtful by a third scene of

---

[1] W. R. Dawson, *Aegyptus*, IX (1928), pp. 106–12; M. M. Mercier and A. Séguin, *Thalès*, IV (1937–9), pp. 121–31.

[2] K. Sethe, *Zur Geschichte der Einbalsamierung* . . . (*Sitz. Berl. Ak.*, 1934, pp. 211–39). Cf. also A. Hermann, *Z.D.M.G.*, CV (1955), pp. 28–29; *Numen*, III (1956), pp. 81–96.

[3] A. H. Gardiner, *Admonitions of an Egyptian Sage*, p. 37.

[4] S. Sauneron, *Rituel de l'Embaumement*; G. Maspero, *Mémoire sur quelques papyrus du Louvre*; G. Roeder, *Urkunden zur Religion* . . ., pp. 297–305.

[5] G. Möller, *Die beiden Totenpapyrus Rhind*.

[6] II: 86–88.

[7] I: 7.

[8] W. Spiegelberg, *Z.Ä.S.*, LVI (1920), pp. 1–33. Parts are quoted in R. Mond and O. H. Myers, *Bucheum*, I, pp. 18–20, 60–64, 100–2.

[9] G. Elliot Smith and W. R. Dawson, *Egyptian Mummies*, pp. 45–56, 57–71.

[10] See p. 296.

[11] W. R. Dawson, *J.E.A.*, XIII (1927), pp. 46–47, Pls. XVII–XVIII.

the same type described by Davies,[1] from which it appears that the various operations are, in fact, the final stages in the preparation of the wooden coffin, and do not refer to the wrapped body. An actual part of the embalming process may, however, be illustrated by a unique vignette from the Book of the Dead, also published by Dawson,[2] which seems to represent an emaciated body lying on the embalmer's mat, perhaps immediately following the desiccation with natron.

References to the length of time taken for the mummification process are comparatively numerous, and it is clear that while seventy days was the most usual period for the whole process, extensions of one or two days were not uncommon, and even larger variations not unknown.[3]

According to Herodotus, three different methods of embalming were practised. In the first, which was the most expensive, the brain was removed, partly mechanically and partly by means of certain drugs (the nature of which is not given); the abdominal contents were removed (probably this was meant to include the thoracic contents also, except the heart, though this is not specifically stated) and the removed viscera were cleaned with palm wine and spices, the cavity being filled with myrrh, cassia and other aromatic substances (the kinds of which are not specified), frankincense, however, being excluded, and the body, after the embalming incision had been sewn up, was then treated with natron, after which it was washed and wrapped in linen bandages, which were fastened together with gum. In the second method, 'cedar oil' was injected into the body *per anum*, and the body was then treated with natron. The third method, which being the cheapest was adopted by the poorer classes, consisted in cleaning out the intestines by means of an injection *per anum*, and afterwards treating the body with natron.

The account given by Diodorus, though possibly based on that of Herodotus, supplies several particulars not given by him, though it is not so detailed. Although three grades of funerals are mentioned, only one method of embalming is given, namely, removal of the abdominal and thoracic viscera, except the heart and kidneys: cleaning the viscera with palm wine mixed with various spices (the kinds of which are not specified): anointing the body with 'cedar oil' and other precious ointments (the kinds not being stated) and finally rubbing it with myrrh, cinnamon and other materials in order to perfume and preserve it. In another connexion, when describing the bitumen of the Dead Sea, Diodorus states [4] that 'they transport this pitch into Egypt and there sell it for the use of the embalming of the dead; for if they do not mix this with other aromatic spices, the bodies cannot be preserved long from putrefaction'.

As the two accounts are so much alike, one writer merely supplying details omitted by the other, they will be summarized and considered together, various errors and omissions being pointed out and the materials used explained and commented

---

[1] N. de G. Davies, *Nefer-hotep*, I, pp. 45–47, Pl. XXVII.

[2] W. R. Dawson, *J.E.A.*, X (1924), p. 40, Pl. VIII.

[3] F. Ll. Griffith, *Stories of the High Priests of Memphis*, p. 29, n. 25; L. Habachi, *Ann. Serv.*, XLVII (1947), pp. 278–81; S. Sauneron, *Rituel de l'Embaumement*, pp. xv–xvii; G. Elliot Smith and W. R. Dawson, *Egyptian Mummies*, pp. 45–56; W. Spiegelberg, *O.L.Z.*, XXVI (1923), cols. 421–4; A. F. Shore and H. S. Smith, *Acta Orientalia*, XXV (1960), p. 290, n. 24.

[4] XIX: 6.

upon. It should not be forgotten, however, that these descriptions are of very late date and that during the interval between the first practice of mummification and the time they were written (about 3,000 years) the methods underwent considerable modifications, for instance during the Twenty-first Dynasty when the embalmers attempted to restore to the shrunken body the form it had lost, by packing under the skin linen, sawdust, earth, sand, or other materials, and that, therefore, it is not to be expected that the descriptions should be accurate in every detail for the whole period; but artificial desiccation with natron before burial, as described by Herodotus, was almost certainly the underlying principle of them all.[1]

In the most expensive method, though not in the less expensive ones, the brain and the abdominal and thoracic viscera, except the heart and kidneys were removed. This agrees in the main with the facts found from an examination of a very large number of mummies, the heart always having been left in position, and generally also the kidneys, but the brain and the rest of the viscera having been removed.[2]

The brain was usually removed through the nose by breaking the ethmoid bone, though other methods were also practised, including excerebration through the base of the skull or via a trepanned orbit.[3] The extracted brain was evidently not preserved, no doubt because it came away in too small fragments.

The position of the ventral incision for the removal of the viscera varies somewhat in different periods,[4] but except in very rare instances [5] it is on the left side. The extracted viscera were cleaned and dried and either preserved in separate canopic jars or returned to the body cavities in canopic parcels.

Bronze implements that may have been used in mummification have been described by Sudhoff,[6] who identifies the curved hook with which the brain was removed, the knife used in evisceration, and tongs employed in stuffing the body.

Sometimes, however, the mummies of those whose relatives would certainly have adopted the best and most expensive method of embalming in use at the time have been found that have not been eviscerated, for example that of Queen Aashayet, wife of Mentuhotpe II (Eleventh Dynasty), and that of Mayet (possibly a princess), who was buried with the wives of Mentuhotpe, both of whom were found by Winlock

---

[1] Cf. A. Zaki and Z. Iskander, *Ann. Serv.*, XLII (1943), pp. 245–7; Z. Iskander, *Ann. Serv.*, LIII (1956), pp. 193–4.

[2] G. Elliot Smith, *Mém. Inst. Ég.*, V (1906); *Royal Mummies*; W. R. Dawson, *J.E.A.*, XIII (1927), pp. 40–49; G. Elliot Smith and W. R. Dawson, *Egyptian Mummies*, pp. 146–7.

[3] F. Jonckheere, *Autour de l'autopsie d'une momie*, pp. 85–89; L. Nicolaeff, *l'Anthropologie*, XL (1930), pp. 77–92; B. Oetteking, *Archiv für Anthropologie*, VIII (1909), pp. 1–90; W. R. Dawson, 'Contributions to the History of Mummification', *Proc. Royal Soc. of Medicine*, XX (1927), pp. 844–5; D. A. MacAlister, *Journ. Royal Anthrop. Inst.*, XXIII (1894), p. 115; T. J. Pettigrew, *Archaeologia*, XXVII (1838), p. 269; *History of Egyptian Mummies*, pp. 262–73; K. Sudhoff, *Archiv für Geschichte der Medizin*, V (1911), pp. 161–71.

[4] W. R. Dawson, 'Contributions to the History of Mummification', *Proc. Royal Soc. of Medicine*, XX (1927), pp. 843–4; *J.E.A.*, XIII (1927), pp. 42–43; K. Sudhoff, *Archiv für Geschichte der Medizin*, V (1911), pp. 161–71.

[5] Cf. E. A. W. Budge, *Prefatory Remarks made on Egyptian Mummies*, p. 25; G. Elliot Smith and F. Wood Jones, *Arch. Survey of Nubia, 1907–1908*, II, p. 206.

[6] K. Sudhoff, *Archiv für Geschichte der Medizin*, V (1911), pp. 161–71. See also F. Jonckheere, *Autour de l'autopsie d'une momie*, pp. 90–93, 101–3.

at Deir el Bahari[1] and examined by Derry.[2] Pettigrew noticed a similar fact and states[3] that 'Mummies very richly furnished and prepared in the most costly manner have been found without the ventral incision'. A mummy of the Persian period examined by Granville had no embalming incision, but parts of the viscera had been cut away and extracted *per anum*,[4] and another mummy, probably of similar date and found in Nubia, also without ventral incision, had all the abdominal organs removed.[5] Inferior mummies of the New Kingdom from Deir el Medineh described by Bruyère lacked certain of the internal organs but had no embalming wound.[6]

The abdominal and thoracic cavities were cleaned with palm wine and spices, operations that naturally have not left any traces.

The body cavities were then filled with myrrh, cassia and other aromatic substances and the embalming incision sewn up. Herodotus specifically says that these operations took place before the natron treatment and, although Gannal,[7] Pettigrew,[8] Elliot Smith and Dawson[9] and others have doubted this statement, recent examination of refuse embalming materials by Iskander[10] strongly suggests that the body was, in fact, temporarily packed with dry natron, packets of a natron and resin mixture, and linen impregnated with resin, which were removed after the natron treatment. Such packing would speed the process of dehydration, prevent the collapse of the body wall, and combat the odour of putrefaction.

The final packing of the body cavities, and of the cranial cavity where this was done, undoubtedly took place after the natron treatment. The embalming incision, however, has rarely been found sewn up,[11] but is often covered with a plate of metal or beeswax, and neither myrrh nor cassia has been identified with certainty from the abdominal or thoracic cavities. The principal packing materials found have been linen, linen and resin, sawdust, sawdust and resin, earth and natron,[12] lichen, and occasionally one or more onions.

The body was treated with natron. This is mentioned only by Herodotus.

The body was washed. This also is mentioned only by Herodotus, but it seems most natural and likely, and certainly was generally carried out. I have suggested

---

[1] H. E. Winlock, *M.M.A. Bull., Egyptian Exped. 1920–1921*, pp. 36–42.

[2] D. E. Derry, in H. Carter, *Tut-ankh-Amen*, II, p. 146 (Appendix I); *Ann. Serv.*, XLI (1942), pp. 246–56.

[3] T. J. Pettigrew, *History of Egyptian Mummies*, p. 60.

[4] A. B. Granville, *Essay on Egyptian Mummies*; W. R. Dawson, *J.E.A.*, XI (1925), pp. 76–77.

[5] G. Elliot Smith and F. Wood Jones, *Arch. Survey of Nubia, 1907–1908*, II, p. 207; G. Elliot Smith and W. R. Dawson, *Egyptian Mummies*, pp. 123–7.

[6] B. Bruyère, *Deir el Médineh (1934–1935)*, p. 139.

[7] J.-N. Gannal, *Histoire des embaumements*, 1838, p. 81.

[8] T. J. Pettigrew, *History of Egyptian Mummies*, pp. 83–84.

[9] G. Elliot Smith and W. R. Dawson, *Egyptian Mummies*, p. 61; W. R. Dawson, *J.E.A.*, XIII (1927), p. 43.

[10] Z. Iskander, *Ann. Serv.*, LIII (1956), pp. 180–92.

[11] G. Elliot Smith and W. R. Dawson, *Egyptian Mummies*, pp. 61, 100, 103, 119.

[12] Specimen analysed by me from a body under examination by Dr. Derry, and probably about Twenty-second Dynasty date. (H. E. Winlock, *M.M.A. Bull., Egyptian Exped. 1920–1921*, pp. 35–36).

already that the greater deterioration that is often seen in the bandages nearest the body, as compared with those on the outside, may have been brought about in the first place by fungus, the growth of which would be due to the body's having been wrapped up while still damp.

The body was anointed with 'cedar oil' and other precious ointments, and then rubbed with myrrh, cinnamon and other fragrant material. This is mentioned only by Diodorus, but in view of the great part played by the use of oil and ointments for the living, some anointing of the dead seems practically certain, and the presence of an ointment among refuse embalming materials examined by Iskander [1] supports this. In some cases the body was then covered with resin before wrapping.

In the second method described by Herodotus, which was the middle and less costly way, cedar oil was injected into the body and prevented from escaping until the end of the natron treatment.

In the third method described by Herodotus, which was for the poorer classes, the nature of the injection employed for cleaning out the intestines is not stated, but almost any liquid, even plain water, if used in sufficient quantity, would have been effective.

It may be pointed out that in the description given by Herodotus natron and not salt is definitely stated to have been the drying agent used. Washing is mentioned by Herodotus, and anointing by Diodorus, but neither refers to the use of a bath, nor of artificial drying (other than that implied by the use of natron), which, if these were employed, is most astonishing.

The methods employed for mummifying animals were probably essentially similar to those used in the case of human beings, though in some instances the flesh may have been removed. Smaller animals, birds and fish were usually not eviscerated and were simply treated with natron and resin.[2] What was evidently an animal embalmer's workshop with stone embalming table, probably dating from the beginning of the Ptolemaic period, was found at Tuna el Gebel.[3]

The method of embalming the sacred bulls, as practised during the Twenty-sixth Dynasty, and given in the Apis Papyrus, was apparently similar to the second method of Herodotus, namely, injection *per anum*. There is not any mention of a bath, and solid natron was employed, though the manner of its use is not clear. The bodies of the bulls found by Myers at the Bucheum at Armant were so badly preserved that practically nothing was left except bones, though there was some evidence to confirm the anal treatment of the entrails, and an enema, a douche and two vaginal retractors of bronze were found.[4] Several embalming tables of late date for use in connexion

---

[1] Z. Iskander, *Ann. Serv.*, LIII (1956), pp. 180–92.

[2] Cf. L.-C. Lortet and C. Gaillard, *La faune momifiée*; C. Gaillard and G. Daressy, *La faune momifiée*; L.-C. Lortet, *Revue des deux mondes*, XXVII (1905), pp. 368 f.; L.-C. Lortet, L. Hugounenc and C. Gaillard, *Ann. Serv.*, III (1902), pp. 15–21; A. Batrawi, *Ann. Serv.*, XLVIII (1948), pp. 585–98; R. L. Moodie, *Roentgenologic Studies of Egyptian and Peruvian Mummies*, pp. 54–55; C. G. Fink and A. H. Kopp, *Technical Studies*, VII (1938–9), pp. 111–19.

[3] S. Gabra, *Chronique d'Égypte*, XIV (1939), pp. 93–94. The stone embalming table described by Winlock (H. E. Winlock, *Ann. Serv.*, XXX (1930), pp. 102–4) may also have been intended for animals.

[4] R. Mond and O. H. Myers, *Bucheum*, I, pp. 62–64, 100–2.

with the embalming of the sacred bull Apis have been found at Memphis, some of them being alabaster and others limestone.[1]

The materials mentioned by Herodotus and Diodorus as having been employed in the mummification process, as also certain materials stated by Pliny to have been used by the Egyptians for embalming, and those found in recent times in connexion with mummies, taking them in alphabetical order, are: alum, beeswax, bitumen, cassia, cedar oil, *cedri succus*, *cedrium*, cinnamon, gum, henna, honey, juniper berries, lime, natron, ointments, onions, palm wine, resins (including gum-resins and balsams), salt, sawdust, spices, and wood tar or wood pitch, all of which will now be considered, except lime, natron and salt, which have already been dealt with.

ALUM

So far as can be ascertained there is no evidence of the deliberate use of aluminium salts in mummification, though the finding of alum in a Twelfth Dynasty mummy has been taken as an indication of its employment.[2] It is, however, more likely that the presence of the alum was due either to its use as a mordant in dyeing the wrappings,[3] or to the existence of soluble aluminium compounds as impurities in the natron used in mummification.[4]

BEESWAX

Beeswax, which will be dealt with more fully in connexion with oils and fats, was often employed in mummification for covering the ears, eyes, nose, mouth and embalming incision [5] and eleven specimens of such material have been examined by me, the results of eight of which have been published:[6] beeswax was also employed on other parts of the body, thus in the case of a female mummy (No. 23) of the Eleventh Dynasty found by Winlock at Deir el Bahari, which Dr. Derry kindly allowed me to examine, there was a brown incrustation, about one to two millimetres thick, on the thighs and on the back, which on analysis proved to be beeswax.[7] The figures of the four sons of Horus that accompanied the canopic packages during the Twenty-first dynasty were also of beeswax.

BITUMEN

From a study of the literature of mummification there would seem at first thought to be no doubt whatever that natural bitumen (pitch) from the Dead Sea was employed extensively in Egypt in the preservation of the dead, thus both Diodorus [8] and Strabo,[9] when referring to the Dead Sea, state that the bitumen from it was used by

---

[1] J. Dimick, in R. Anthes, *Mitrahineh*, pp. 75–79; Mustafa el Amir, *J.E.A.*, XXXIV (1948), pp. 51–56.

[2] P. Haas, in M. A. Murray, *Tomb of Two Brothers*, pp. 48–49; E. Linder, in *op. cit.*, pp. 50–52; M. A. Murray, *op. cit.*, p. 53; P. Haas, *Chemical News*, C (1909), p. 296.

[3] J. Hübner, in M. A. Murray, *Tomb of Two Brothers*, p. 74.

[4] A. Lucas, *Cairo Sc. Journ.*, IV (1910), p. 67; *Chemical News*, CI (1910), p. 266; *Preservative Materials*, pp. 32–33.

[5] G. Elliot Smith, *Mém. Inst. Ég.*, V (1906), p. 28; G. Elliot Smith and W. R. Dawson, *Egyptian Mummies*, pp. 113, 117, 124.

[6] A. Lucas, *Preservative Materials*, p. 53.

[7] Cf. D. E. Derry, *Ann. Serv.*, XLI (1942), p. 248.

[8] XIX: 6.   [9] XVI: 11, 45.

the Egyptians for embalming, though the former makes no mention of it in his detailed description of the embalming process,[1] and all modern writers on mummification until comparatively recently also state that bitumen was used.[2] But I queried this some years ago, and my views on the subject [3] seem now generally to be accepted. Thus Ruffer, writing after he was aware of my opinion, says,[4] 'It is a peculiar fact that I have never yet found bitumen in any mummy, and my experience now extends from Prehistoric to Coptic times'; and Dawson writes [5] '. . . bitumen, although described in modern books as the staple embalming material, was never used until Graeco-Roman times, and, if then, by no means universally.' The mistake has been due to the facts that much of the material, especially from the later mummies, is black and looks very like bitumen and that no systematic examination by modern chemical methods was made. The only results that can be traced where such methods have been employed are by Reutter, by Spielmann, by Griffiths and by myself, and, more recently, by Zaki and Iskander.

Reutter analysed six specimens of Egyptian mummy material in all of which he states that bitumen was present.[6] Three of these specimens were from human mummies (one of the Thirtieth Dynasty and two undated); one was from a bird mummy (ibis) also undated; one consisted of a bundle of bandages from bird mummies (undated) and one was from a canopic box (undated). The first of these is very late and falls within the period when bitumen might have been used and the rest also may be late and within the same period. Also, if bitumen were used, it seems much more likely to have been for non-human mummies, such as those of birds, than for human mummies, since it was probably a cheaper material than resin. The specimen from the canopic box may not have been the material used for preserving the viscera, but an anointing substance poured over them after they had been put into the box, as was sometimes done [7] and, though the finding of bitumen in it would be of

---

[1] Herodotus, however, although he refers to bitumen on several occasions, and describes the methods and materials used by the Egyptians in embalming, does not mention bitumen as having been employed. Pliny, too, also frequently refers to bitumen, but says nothing about its use in mummification, though he mentions other materials that were so used, and Josephus and Tacitus both describe the Dead Sea and the occurrence of bitumen, but do not refer to any use of it for embalming.

[2] For a full discussion of earlier references to bitumen, see A. Lucas, *Preservative Materials*, pp. 34–50; *J.E.A.*, I (1914), pp. 241–5.

[3] A. Lucas, in G. Elliot Smith and F. Wood Jones, *Arch. Survey of Nubia, 1907–1908*, II, pp. 372–4; *Preservative Materials; J.E.A.*, I (1914), pp. 241–5; *Ancient Egyptian Materials* (1926), pp. 122–4. Lucas's conclusion that 'bitumen was certainly never employed for mummification until Ptolemaic times at the earliest, when possibly it may have been used' requires some modification in view of the results obtained by Zaki and Iskander (see pp. 306–7), though the general thesis that bitumen was not used until a comparatively late date holds good.

[4] M. A. Ruffer, *Mém. Inst. Ég.*, VII (1914), p. 6, footnote dated March 1911.

[5] W. R. Dawson, *J.E.A.*, XIII (1927), p. 46.

[6] L. Reutter, *De l'embaumement avant et après Jésus-Christ* (1912), pp. 45, 50, 56, 66, 67; 'De la Momie ou Mumia', *Bull. des sciences pharmacologiques*, Paris (no date), pp. 49–58; 'Analyse d'une masse résineuse égyptienne ayant servi à l'embaumement d'animaux sacrés conservés au Musée de Neuchâtel', *Sphinx*, XVII (1913), pp. 110–14; 'Analyse eines Harzes aus einem ägyptischen Sarkophage', *Chem. Zeitung*, XXXV (1911), p. 1277.

[7] See pp. 312–3.

interest, its classification as an embalming material may be incorrect. The tests relied upon by Reutter for the identification of bitumen were (a) that a blackish coloured residue that he separated from the material (in one instance by means of carbon disulphide) contained sulphur; (b) that in one instance this residue reduced sulphuric acid to sulphurous acid when heated and (c) that in one instance the residue had a bituminous smell. It is true that bitumen contains sulphur, but so do other materials: the production of sulphurous acid when the blackish residue was heated with sulphuric acid is in no way a test for bitumen, as the same reaction occurs when carbon or almost any carbonaceous matter is treated in this manner. To test for sulphur after having dissolved the material in carbon disulphide and evaporated off the solvent is unwise, as carbon disulphide often contains free sulphur, and to depend upon the smell for the recognition of bitumen is most unsatisfactory. By means of these same tests Reutter also identified bitumen in ancient Egyptian perfumes,[1] though it seems a most unlikely material to have been used for such a purpose.

Spielmann [2] relied upon the most modern methods for the detection of bitumen, namely, the behaviour of the specimens when exposed to ultra-violet rays and the spectroscopic analysis of the ash. The first of these methods had been tried previously by me with various resinous materials (two predynastic, three early dynastic, one Twentieth Dynasty and three of amber) with a view, if possible, to differentiating between them and so to separating them into groups according to their botanical origin; but unfortunately it has not yet been possible to continue the work, although the results were interesting and in some instances promising.

The specimens examined by Spielmann were all supplied by me and were as follows: namely, three of modern bitumen of Judea; one of modern wood pitch; one of probable wood pitch from a mummy (undated); four resins, manifestly without any admixture of bitumen; three from ancient graves and one from an ancient jar, but only one of them from a mummy (Ptolemaic) and five pitch-like materials all from mummies (one Twentieth Dynasty, one Twenty-first Dynasty and three Ptolemaic), all of which are late, three falling within the very late period when bitumen may have been used.

Spielmann states that the appearance of the specimens when exposed to the ultra-violet rays show that the black mummy materials 'occupy positions between the undoubted bitumens and the undoubted resins'. Although this is true, it has not necessarily any significance with respect to the presence or absence of bitumen, and Spielmann only suggests that it raises 'the expectation that the presence of bitumen would become substantiated by further work rather than disproved'.

The results of the spectographic analysis showed that the elements characteristic of bitumen were vanadium, nickel and molybdenum: the resins were free or almost free from these three elements and the black mummy materials contained vanadium varying from a very slight trace to a heavy trace and nickel and molybdenum from none to a heavy trace. A specimen of north European wood pitch did not contain any of the three elements in question.

If Dead Sea bitumen always contains vanadium, nickel and molybdenum (which

[1] See pp. 89–90.
[2] P. E. Spielmann, J.E.A., XVIII (1932), pp. 177–80.

is highly probable), then it follows that any mummy material without all three of these tell-tale elements cannot contain bitumen and, therefore, two of the specimens at least (one Twenty-first Dynasty and one Ptolemaic) are free from bitumen. With respect to the other three specimens, which contain all three of the tell-tale elements, Spielmann thinks there is 'strong evidence' for the presence of bitumen, and he suggests that the materials consist of wood pitch containing bitumen in 'a relatively low proportion . . . because the characteristic metals are not very pronounced' and also containing resin in 'a relatively low proportion . . . because the ochre fluorescence is not strong'. But it seems unreasonable to have added bitumen to wood pitch and likely, if bitumen had been employed, that it would either have been alone or in large proportion in any mixture. Also the results of my analyses of these same specimens [1] have not been taken into account. Thus, all the five black mummy materials were free from anything soluble in petroleum spirit, except fatty matter, derived from the bodies with which they had been in contact, whereas the specimens of genuine bitumen contained from 38.80 to 53.70 per cent of soluble matter. Again, three of the black mummy materials contained only 0.92, 1.45 and 1.93 per cent of sulphur respectively,[2] whereas two of the genuine bitumens contained 8.58 and 8.85 per cent respectively of sulphur,[2] and in the black mummy materials there was an absence of any smell suggestive of bitumen and an absence also of the fluorescence when the materials were dissolved in various solvents that is so characteristic of bitumen, and the colour and smell of the matter extracted by solvents were not those of bitumen.

Griffiths [3] states that in two of the four specimens of black material analysed by him mineral bitumen was absent; of a third he says that 'the low proportion of sulphur would seem to exclude the presence of mineral bitumen', while the fourth specimen was wood pitch 'with possibly a small addition of mineral bitumen'. As previously stated, it seems somewhat improbable that bitumen should have been added to wood pitch, and likely, if bitumen had been employed, that it would either have been alone or in large proportion in any mixture.

More recently, Zaki and Iskander [4] have published evidence of the use of bitumen in a mummy of the Persian period. Three samples of material (from the packing of the body, and from above and below the body) were examined chemically, spectrographically, and by ultra-violet light, and were each found to consist of a similar mixture of resin and bitumen in the approximate proportion of 3 : 2. The specimens were slightly soluble in ether, petroleum ether and acetone, more soluble in alcohol and turpentine oil, almost wholly soluble in benzine, and totally soluble in carbon disulphide. The alcohol soluble portions of the samples were wholly saponifiable, and were of a resinous nature, whereas the benzine soluble portions were wholly unsaponifiable, indicating the absence of resin, and gave a green fluorescence corresponding to that of bitumen of Judea. The percentages of sulphur determined in the three samples were 4.33, 3.07, and 3.18 respectively, the sulphur content of the ben-

[1] A. Lucas, *Preservative Materials*, pp. 39, 43.
[2] The other specimens were not examined for sulphur. A. Tschirch and E. Stock (*Die Harze*, II. Band, 2. Hälfte, 1. Teil, p. 997) give the amount of sulphur in Syrian bitumen as 6.1 per cent to 10.1 per cent.
[3] J. G. A. Griffiths, *Analyst*, LXII (1937), pp. 703–9.
[4] A. Zaki and Z. Iskander, *Ann. Serv.*, XLII (1943), pp. 223–50.

zine soluble portions being very much higher (almost double) than that of the original samples before separation. The presence of vanadium, nickel and molybdenum was revealed by spectrographic analysis.

The results obtained by Zaki and Iskander suggest that if a considerable number of specimens of material from mummies of late date were examined more definite proof of the use of bitumen might be found,[1] and the possibility of its occasional employment at least as early as the Persian period can no longer be discounted.

The name of a material mentioned in the Demotic text of one of the Rhind papyri (Ptolemaic period) as being employed for filling the cranial cavity has been translated by Möller as *syrischer Asphalt* (Syrian asphalt),[2] and by Brugsch as *syrisches Salz* (Syrian salt),[3] though both of these are guesses, the exact meaning of the Demotic word and its parallel in the hieroglyphic text being unknown. In my opinion they are more likely to refer to wood tar or wood pitch, or to resin, a much more important Syrian product to the Egyptians than either asphalt or salt, and one known and used in Egypt from a very early date. The lexicographical problem is complex,[4] but it may be observed that a similar word is also used to describe a certain material employed for covering or coating coffins, and this may have been either the varnish so common on coffins of a late date (from the Twentieth to about the Twenty-sixth Dynasties),[5] which consists of resin, possibly obtained from Syria or through Syria, or the black anointing material to be described later.[6]

In this connexion about twenty masses of black material, ranging in size from that of a fist to that of a child's head, found by Menghin and Amer at Ma'adi near Cairo,[7] may be mentioned, although there is no suggestion that it was used for mummification.[8] This material was reported by Dr. J. Gangl [9] of Vienna as asphalt 'very similar to that produced in Syro-Palestine'. Dr. Gangl's analysis was limited to the determination of the solubility in certain organic solvents, the determination of the ash and the determination of the fact that it neither softened nor melted at 150° C. I examined the material much in the same manner as Gangl, at first limiting the determination to its general characteristics and behaviour and its solubility in various organic solvents, from the results of which I concluded that it was an oleoresin from which the oil of turpentine had been lost, and I so reported it to Professor Menghin. As the result of further work, however, and additional experience of such materials, I now know that this method of examination, although necessary and useful as a preliminary measure, must be supplemented by further analysis, since by itself it yields results that lend themselves to a wrong interpretation. Before a final conclusion

[1] Cf. R. J. Forbes, *Studies in Ancient Technology*, I, p. 351.
[2] G. Möller, *Die beiden Totenpapyrus Rhind*, p. 3, l. 8.
[3] H. Brugsch, *A Henry Rhind's Zwei Bilingue Papyri*, I, p. 3, l. 4.
[4] Cf. J. R. Harris, *Lexicographical Studies*, pp. 173–4, 234; R. J. Forbes, *Ambix*, II (1938), pp. 68–74.
[5] See pp. 357–8.
[6] See pp. 312–6.
[7] O. Menghin and M. Amer, *Excavations of the Egyptian University ... at Ma'adi, Second Prelim. Report*, pp. 63–65.
[8] Cf. also M. Mercier, *Thalès* III (1936), pp. 68–69; P. Woog, *ib.*, pp. 70–82.
[9] In another report in *Journ. Royal Anthrop. Inst.*, LXVI (1936), pp. 65–69, the name is spelled Gange.

can be reached, the material must be saponified, acidified and extracted with solvents. Such an additional examination was made subsequently, with the result that the material was found to be wholly, or mainly, fatty matter, which had become oxidized and partly decomposed, a result that would, I am sure, be confirmed by Gangl. Since the material was practically insoluble in petroleum spirit it could not possibly be mineral bitumen (asphalt). Many years ago I pointed out that mummy tissue sometimes becomes so changed with age that it has the appearance of resin and behaves with solvents in the same manner as resin.[1]

CASSIA AND CINNAMON

Cassia and cinnamon will be considered together for reasons that will be apparent.

One difficulty encountered when dealing with ancient materials is that not infrequently the same name has been applied to different substances at different periods, cassia and cinnamon being cases in point, the cassia of the ancients sometimes having been the modern cinnamon.

Cassia and cinnamon are very similar to one another, both being the dried bark of certain varieties of laurel that grow in India, Ceylon and China (cassia being from *Cinnamomum cassia* and cinnamon from *Cinnamomum zeylanicum*), cassia, however, being more pungent, more astringent, less delicate in flavour and thicker than cinnamon. Anciently both cassia and cinnamon consisted not only of the bark, but included also flower-tops, twigs and wood; the leaves were called *malabathrum*.[2]

In Breasted's translations of Egyptian texts, notably in his version of the Harris papyrus, cassia or cassia wood,[3] and cinnamon or cinnamon wood [4] are frequently mentioned. While it is possible that these translations may, in fact, be correct,[5] they cannot be regarded as altogether certain, and are therefore of doubtful value as evidence for the use of these products by the Egyptians.

Both cassia and cinnamon were well known to the Greeks and Romans and are described by Herodotus,[6] Theophrastus,[7] Dioscorides,[8] Pliny [9] and other writers, Pliny stating that cinnamon 'grows in the country of the Ethiopians', which, however, is not so.

Assuming that cassia and cinnamon were known in Pharaonic times, they would naturally have been employed as flavouring and perfuming materials and also possibly as incense, and as already shown Herodotus mentions cassia and Diodorus mentions cinnamon (possibly the same material being meant in both cases) as having been used in mummification.

Two references to the finding of cassia or cinnamon in connexion with mummies can be traced, one by Osburn, who says of a mummy (probably of the Twentieth Dynasty) that 'a thick layer of spicery covering every part of it . . . this external covering, which is nowhere less than an inch in thickness and which is interposed everywhere between the bandages and the skin . . . still retains the faint smell of cinna-

---

[1] A. Lucas, *Preservative Materials*, pp. 50–52.

[2] E. H. Warmington, *Commerce between the Roman Empire and India*, 1928, pp. 186–8.

[3] *A.R.*, IV, 234, 344, 379.

[4] *A.R.*, II, 265; III, 116; IV, 234, 240, 287, 300, 344, 348, 378, 391, 394.

[5] Cf. V. Loret, *Flore Pharaonique*, 2nd ed., p. 51.

[6] III: 107–11.   [7] *Enquiry into Plants*, IX: 5, 1–3.   [8] I: 12, 13.   [9] XII: 41–43.

mon or cassia . . . but when mixed with alcohol or water and exposed to the action of heat the odour of myrrh becomes very powerfully predominant'.[1] This is quoted by Pettigrew,[2] who also says of a mummy he had examined, 'I have seen the cavity merely filled with dust of cedar, cassia, etc. and an earthy matter.'[3] Neither of these identifications can be considered satisfactory or final.

CEDAR OIL, CEDRI SUCCUS, CEDRIUM

These three materials have been dealt with by me elsewhere,[4] and it has been shown that the classical 'cedar', though a conifer, was almost certainly not the true cedar, but a juniper, and that the substance referred to by both Herodotus and Diodorus and translated 'oil of cedar' was probably therefore not a cedar product, but a juniper product, Moreover, these writers are at variance with respect to the method of its application, one stating that it was injected and the other that it was employed for anointing, and since each method would require a different material, it is impossible to be sure of its nature, and one must assume either that two distinct substances were meant, or that one or other was mistaken. If injected, it was probably either impure oil of turpentine or pyroligneous acid containing admixed oil of turpentine and wood tar, and if employed for anointing, it was probably some ordinary oil perfumed by volatile oil of juniper. In neither case could it have been a fixed oil of any coniferous tree, since no such oil was then known. The use of 'cedar' oil in connexion with burial was continued certainly as late as the end of the first century A.D.[5] The present-day 'cedar' oil is a product obtained by distillation (a process not known until a late date) from the American juniper (*Juniperus virginiana*).

The *cedri succus* (cedar juice) of Pliny [6] was the natural resinous exudation of some coniferous tree, probably never the cedar, but often the juniper, and for the extensive use of some such material by the Egyptians in embalming there is ample evidence.

Cedrium, as defined by Pliny,[7] was pyroligneous acid containing admixed oil of turpentine and wood tar, for the use of which no Egyptian evidence has been found. The term *cedrium*, however, might not unreasonably have been used to mean wood tar alone, which was sometimes employed by the Egyptians for embalming.[8]

HENNA [9]

Henna has been mentioned already in connexion with cosmetics and perfumes,[10] where it was suggested that the flowers, which are odoriferous, probably were employed in ancient Egypt for perfuming unguents and also that the leaves were used

---

[1] W. Osburn, *Account of an Egyptian Mummy presented to the Museum of the Leeds Philosophical and Literary Society*, p. 6.

[2] T. J. Pettigrew, *History of Egyptian Mummies*, p. 60.

[3] T. J. Pettigrew, *History of Egyptian Mummies*, pp. 62–63.

[4] A. Lucas, ' "Cedar"-Tree Products employed in Mummification', *J.E.A.*, XVII (1931), pp. 13–21.

[5] B. P. Grenfell and A. S. Hunt, *Amherst Papyri*, II, p. 150.

[6] XXIV: 11.

[7] XVI: 21.

[8] See pp. 325–6.

[9] Cf. L. Keimer, *Gartenpflanzen*, pp. 51–55.

[10] See p. 87.

as a cosmetic to colour the palms of the hands, the soles of the feet and the hair, as is done today.

The henna plant (*Lawsonia alba, Lawsonia inermis*) is a perennial shrub that is largely cultivated in Egypt; it is grown in gardens for its strong-smelling flowers and as a farm crop for its leaves, the chief use of which is as an article of toilet, a paste being prepared from them with which the hands, feet, nails and hair are coloured red: a decoction of the leaves is stated to be used occasionally for dyeing cloth.

That the finger- and toe-nails of mummies sometimes are stained has often been noticed. Thus Rouyer says [1] that certain mummies had the palms of the hands, the soles of the feet and the nails of the fingers and toes stained red with henna. This is quoted by Pettigrew, who says [2] that 'Mr. Davidson's mummy presented this stained appearance on the nails. Mr. Madden also says that the hands of many were dyed with the juice of the henna.' Naville states [3] that the finger-nails of an Eleventh Dynasty mummy were tinted with henna and Maspero thought that the hands of Ramses II were stained '*jaune-clair par les parfums*'.[4] Elliot Smith, suggests, however, that the discoloration had been caused by the embalming material, which may have also been the case with the mummy to which Naville refers, as it almost certainly was with the staining of the nails of a number of mummies examined by the author. Pettigrew well sums up the matter as follows:[2] 'The nails of the fingers and toes of some mummies have been observed to be stained, as if with henna . . . Whether this be really the case is not at all clear; the colour may probably be produced by the medicaments employed in the process of embalming.' Elliot Smith describes the hair of the mummy of Henttawi (Eighteenth Dynasty) as being dyed a brilliant reddish colour, which he suggests had been done with henna.[5] Brunton suggests [6] that a light brown-red colour of the hair of an old woman of Badarian date might be due to henna and he also says that an oldish woman of the pan-grave period 'had long henna-stained nails'.

Borchardt points out [7] that the finger- and toe-nails of statues are sometimes painted red.

HONEY
The alleged use of honey in mummification has already been discussed.[8]

JUNIPER BERRIES
Juniper berries, generally those of *Juniperus phoenicea*, but sometimes *J. drupacea*, have frequently been found in ancient Egyptian graves,[9] the earliest that can be

[1] P. C. Rouyer, 'Notice sur les embaumemens des anciens Égyptiens', *Description de l'Égypte, Antiquités, Mémoires*, I (1809), pp. 207–20.

[2] T. J. Pettigrew, *History of Egyptian Mummies*, p. 66.

[3] E. Naville, *XIth Dynasty Temple at Deir el Bahari*, I, p. 44.

[4] G. Elliot Smith, *Royal Mummies*, pp. 60–61.

[5] G. Elliot Smith, *Royal Mummies*, p. 19.

[6] G. Brunton, *Mostagedda*, pp. 45, 123.

[7] L. Borchardt, Z.Ä.S., xxxv (1897), p. 168.   [8] See p. 26.

[9] Cf. V. Loret and J. Poisson, *Rec. Trav.*, XVII (1895), p. 186; M. A. Beauverie, *B.I.F.A.O.*, XXX (1931), pp. 394–5, 401–2; XXXV (1935), p. 127; V. Täckholm and M. Drar, *Flora of Egypt*, I, pp. 75–78.

traced being one berry, of which the species was not determined, from the pre-dynastic period.[1] Juniper berries were found in the Djoser pyramid complex (Third Dynasty);[2] Schiaparelli found both species in a tomb of the Eighteenth Dynasty;[3] I have identified a large number from the tomb of Tutankhamūn, where four baskets were filled with them, in two baskets the berries being small and in two baskets larger; Macramallah found berries in a tomb of New Kingdom date;[4] Kunth found them among the Passalacqua collection;[5] Loret mentions specimens from two tombs at Thebes;[6] Newberry identified 'a quantity of twigs . . . to which in a few cases the berries were still attached' from crocodile mummies found by Petrie at Hawara;[7] in the description of the Christian bodies found in Nubia, Elliot Smith and Wood Jones mention 'little round berries',[8] which I saw at the time and believe to have been juniper berries, and in a report dealing with some of this material I stated [9] that 'In Nubia, in a cemetery thought to be about . . . the fifth century A.D., the bodies . . . were packed in large quantities of salt, mixed in some instances with the same kind of small globular fruit or berries already mentioned.' This reference is to another specimen of preservative material, submitted by Elliot Smith, from a Coptic 'mummy' of the fifth century A.D. from Naga el Deir, which 'consisted of a mixture of common salt and small globular fruit or berries about the size of a pea'.[9]

Writing of the Coptic monastery of Epiphanius at Thebes, Winlock says:[10] 'The body was then laid on the first grave sheet and handfuls of coarse rock salt and juniper berries were placed between the legs and over the trunk inside and outside the innermost wrappings', and again 'berries of *Juniperus phœnicea* were common enough to be used in large quantities as an embalming agent in the graves'.

In the Cairo Museum there are both juniper seeds and berries of Twentieth Dynasty date from the 'cache' at Deir el Bahari where the royal mummies were found and also berries of the Twenty-sixth Dynasty from Qurna.

It seems manifest that when juniper berries were placed on the body this must have been done either on account of some fancied preservative effect or because they had a ritual significance. But the former reason would not have led to the putting of the berries in baskets or other receptacles in the tomb as was done sometimes and, therefore, they probably always had some symbolical meaning. To me, these berries seem to be directly connected with the 'cedar' wood used for coffins and shrines and the 'cedar' oil employed for anointing the dead body, which played such important parts in the burial of royal and other prominent personages, since, as has been pointed out elsewhere,[11] the 'cedar' oil was probably not from the cedar, but often essential

---

[1] G. Brunton, *Mostagedda*, p. 91.

[2] V. Laurent Täckholm, *Bull. Inst. d'Ég.*, XXXII (1951), pp. 128–9.

[3] E. Schiaparelli, *La Tomba intatta dell' Architetto Cha*, p. 164, Fig. 148; p. 165, Fig. 150; O. Mattirolo, *Atti della Reale Accad. delle Scienze di Torino*, LXI (1926), pp. 545–68.

[4] R. Macramallah, *Un cimetière archaïque . . . à Saqqarah*, p. 76.

[5] C. Kunth, in J. Passalacqua, *Cat. des antiquités découvertes en Égypte*, p. 228.

[6] V. Loret, *Flore Pharaonique*, 2nd ed., p. 41.

[7] P. E. Newberry, in W. M. F. Petrie, *Hawara, Biahmu and Arsinoe*, pp. 48, 52.

[8] G. Elliot Smith and F. Wood Jones, *Arch. Survey of Nubia, 1907–1908*, II, p. 218.

[9] A. Lucas, *Preservative Materials*, p. 20.

[10] H. E. Winlock and W. E. Crum, *Monastery of Epiphanius*, pp. 48, 61.

[11] A. Lucas, *J.E.A.*, XVII (1931), pp. 14, 15, 21.

oil of juniper extracted from the berries by soaking them in some ordinary fixed oil, and juniper and other coniferous woods were substituted sometimes for cedar.

Although the juniper is distributed throughout the whole of the rest of the Mediterranean region, it does not grow in Egypt, but because the berries have been found so frequently in Egyptian tombs, it has been assumed that the tree must have flourished formerly in the country, for which there is no evidence, and the same line of reasoning would prove that it must have been common in Upper Egypt in early Christian times (since it was in Upper Egypt and at a very late period that the berries seem principally to have been used), though this is most unlikely and it is much more probable that the berries, like the wood, should have been imported from western Asia. I am informed that in 1943 about one hundred small juniper trees, species not stated, about eight metres high were growing on Jebel Telleg (north of Nekhl) in Sinai.

LICHEN

In the cases of the mummies of Siptah (Nineteenth Dynasty), Ramses IV (Twentieth Dynasty) and Djedptahefankh (Twenty-first Dynasty) respectively, the abdomen was packed with dried lichen (*Parmelia furfuracea*).[1]

OINTMENTS

The nature of the 'precious ointments' mentioned by Diodorus as having been employed for anointing the body after mummification is not stated, and there is no evidence from the mummies whereby the composition can be ascertained. Several late (Ptolemaic and Roman) papyri [2] give a description of the religious ceremony that took place after the body had been prepared by the embalmers, but before it had been wrapped and also during the wrapping, the former of which consisted in anointing the body with certain unguents composed of odoriferous gum-resins (frankincense and myrrh) and various oils and fats (including 'cedar' oil, boiled fat, ox fat and ointments) and another late papyrus (first century A.D.) [3] mentions among the funeral expenses the purchase of 'cedar' oil and olive oil.

But after the mummy had been prepared, anointed and wrapped there was apparently sometimes another ceremony which consisted in pouring a liquid or semi-liquid resinous material over the mummy and sometimes also over the coffin and over the viscera after they had been put into the canopic box. This also may not unreasonably be considered an anointing. This latter treatment has been recorded in a number of instances, thus Petrie describing two Fifth Dynasty burials at Deshasheh, says [4] of one '. . . coffin contained a woman fastened in place by some pitch poured over the body' and of another, 'The body wrapped up lay fixed by some pitch.' Mace and Winlock state [5] with regard to the Twelfth Dynasty mummy of Senebtisi that 'Immediately inside the coffin and overlying the mummy there was a layer of

---

[1] G. Elliot Smith, *Royal Mummies*, pp. 78, 83, 113; G. Elliot Smith and W. R. Dawson, *Egyptian Mummies*, pp. 100, 103, 122.

[2] A. Mariette, *Les papyrus égyptiens du Musée de Boulaq*; G. Maspero, *Mémoire sur quelques papyrus du Louvre*; G. Möller, *Die beiden Totenpapyrus Rhind*.

[3] B. P. Grenfell and A. S. Hunt, *Amherst Papyri*, II, p. 150.

[4] W. M. F. Petrie, *Deshasheh*, pp. 18, 31.

[5] A. C. Mace and H. E. Winlock, *Senebtisi*, pp. 17, 18.

some resinous material. . . . It is clear . . . that it was poured in semi-liquid state over the mummy. . . . The purpose of this resin treatment is not easy to explain, but from the evidence of the Dahshur burials and of other graves in the same cemetery at Lisht it was not an uncommon practice of the period.' They also say, 'From coffins now in the Metropolitan Museum it is clear that a similar treatment was in use at Meir, as resin was poured over the anthropoid coffin of Hapi Ankhtifi after placing it in the second coffin and before depositing the shawls and staves.' Among the Dahshur burials to which Mace and Winlock refer was that of King Hor (Twelfth Dynasty) and de Morgan, describing the *sceptres* in the coffin, says they were *demi pris dans le bitume*,[1] and in the Cairo Museum there is beadwork from outside this body that is embedded in a pitch-like mass. At Lahun, Brunton, in his description of a burial, also of Twelfth Dynasty date, states [2] that 'The coffin was probably placed in a stone sarcophagus, as we found a lump of pitch or bitumen giving the cast of the inside at one corner and also the cast of part of the head of an anthropoid coffin, with head-dress painted in stripes of blue and gold. The pitch had been poured over the sarcophagus after the burial in order to protect it.' Brunton also found in another tomb of the same dynasty (Twelfth) at Lahun certain canopic jars, the black material in which he describes as 'bundles of cedar pitch adulterated with mud'.[3] Elliot Smith, in his report on the mummy of Senebtisi, states [4] that two of the canopic jars contained a black resinous mass. Three of the canopic jars from the so-called 'Tomb of Queen Tiy' also contained a black, very pitch-like substance that had been poured over the packets of viscera. In the case of Tutankhamūn, a similar-looking material had been poured in large amount over the mummy (except the head) after it had been placed in the gold coffin; over the outside of this coffin after it had been put into the next coffin and also, but only in small quantity, over the foot end of the third (outermost) coffin.[5] A considerable amount of similar material had also been poured over the four miniature inlaid gold coffins containing the viscera after they had been placed in position in the canopic box.[6] The remains of what is apparently a similar black or dark brown material may be seen on the inside of the canopic box of Amenhotpe II, on the four canopic vases of Nofretiri and on other canopic vases in the Cairo Museum, and a number of large alabastar jars containing a similar-looking material were found many years ago by Howard Carter in the tomb of Meneptah, specimens of which he submitted to me for analysis.

The results of the examination of these materials, taking them in the order mentioned, may now be considered.

Petrie calls the Fifth Dynasty specimen 'pitch' (probably meaning mineral pitch), but no evidence is given that it was mineral pitch and it seems highly probable that it was not analysed, and that the only reason for thinking it to be mineral pitch was because it looked like it.

Mace and Winlock call the Twelfth Dynasty specimens from the tomb of Senebtisi

[1] J. de Morgan, *Dahchour, mars–juin 1894*, p. 98.
[2] W. M. F. Petrie, G. Brunton and M. A. Murray, *Lahun*, II, p. 29.
[3] G. Brunton, *Lahun*, I, pp. 19–20.
[4] G. Elliot Smith, in A. C. Mace and H. E. Winlock, *Senebtisi*, p. 120.
[5] H. Carter, *Tut-ankh-Amen*, II, pp. 79, 81, 83, 85, 87, 89, 90.
[6] H. Carter, *Tut-ankh-Amen*, III, p. 49–50.

'resinous material' and that from the coffin of Hapi Ankhtifi 'resin', but neither of these was analysed. In reply to an inquiry by me, Mr. Winlock says, 'My memory of the "resin" in Senebtisi is that it was a very dark-brown chocolate coloured material, approaching black, but not actually black.'[1] 'In the case of Hapi Ankhtifi the coffin was given a coating of the coal-black and shiny pitch-like material which you know on so much of the tomb furniture from the Eighteenth Dynasty; for example, the objects from the tomb of Horemheb. After the coffin had been laid in the outer coffin and the staves had been laid upon it, the liquid "resinous" material was poured over it. It had largely disfigured the coffin and was removed some time ago, but as far as my memory serves me it also was a very dark brown.'[1]

A specimen of the material from the beadwork belonging to King Hor now in the Cairo Museum examined by me was black, glossy and pitch-like and analysis showed it to be probably resin, since no evidence of wood pitch of other admixture was obtained: it had a slight fragrant smell when burned.

The Twelfth Dynasty specimen, called by Brunton 'pitch or bitumen', from the interior of a sarcophagus at Lahun, was examined at the time by me. I reported[2] that 'The sample has an aromatic odour with a slight pungency. The material is certainly not pitch (neither mineral pitch nor wood pitch), but is a resin, which at present has not been identified.'

The 'cedar pitch adulterated with mud' from Lahun was identified by Ruffer, apparently from the smell, since he says,[3] 'The wood pitch was certainly cedar, and my whole laboratory has smelt of it ever since the hot weather has set in. The pitch was adulterated with very fine mud, to the extent of 10 per cent, or perhaps more.' I made a preliminary analysis of this material at the time and found that it was almost certainly wood pitch, though more likely juniper wood pitch rather than cedar wood pitch.

In a preliminary report on the material from the canopic vases of 'Queen Tiy', I stated that it 'was probably wood pitch with a mixture of fatty matter, but whether resin was present could not be determined'.[4] This was analysed more fully by Griffiths,[5] who states that 'The data for this substance are consistent with wood pitch.' I found a little fatty matter in two vases, but none in a third. Griffiths did not find fatty matter.

The material from the tomb of Tutankhamūn has been analysed both by Plenderleith and by me. Plenderleith states[6] that the specimen submitted to him consisted of a mixture of odoriferous resins and pitch, but that he was unable to determine whether the pitch was mineral or vegetable. The specimen analysed, however, was possibly not a representative one. Thus, as shown below, the material varied from a thin, brittle substance to a thick viscous one and, although both had originally been part of the same mass, it is probable that the thin layer had not merely dried, but on account of its thinness had undergone more chemical change (especially in its content of fatty matter) than the thicker layer. Also, Plenderleith's sample was almost certainly taken from some of the material after it had been melted and that may even

---

[1] Private communication.   [2] W. M. F. Petrie, G. Brunton and M. A. Murray, *Lahun*, II, p. 15.
[3] G. Brunton, *Lahun*, I, pp. 19–20.   [4] A. Lucas, *Ann. Serv.*, XXXI (1931), pp. 120–2.
[5] J. G. A. Griffiths, *Analyst*, LXII (1937), pp. 703–7.
[6] H. J. Plenderleith, in H. Carter, *Tut-ankh-Amen*, II, pp. 215–16 (Appendix v).

have been partly burned, considerable heat having been applied in order to separate the gold mask from the gold coffin to which it was stuck fast by this black material, as also to separate the gold coffin from the middle coffin, which were also stuck together.[1]

My preliminary report on the Tutankhamūn samples, which were taken by myself before there had been any manipulation and which were thoroughly representative of the various portions (which differed among themselves in the proportion of the several constituents, especially fatty matter, present) was as follows:[2] 'The anointing material . . . which contained fatty matter, was black and lustrous and in appearance closely resembled bitumen or pitch; where the layer was thin, as on the lid of the gold coffin, the material was hard and brittle, but between the gold coffin and the next outer one and under the mummy, where a thicker layer had accumulated, the interior of the mass was still soft and plastic. When cold there was little or no smell, but when warmed, a strong, penetrating, not unpleasant, but rather fragrant smell was evident. A detailed chemical analysis has not yet been possible, but the material contains fatty matter and resin and is entirely free from bitumen or mineral pitch. One specimen examined contained 46 per cent of fatty matter (now largely or wholly fatty acids), 19 per cent of a brown resin and a black brittle organic residue that has not been identified.'

Since this report was made, additional specimens have been examined (altogether eleven different samples), most of which definitely contained fatty matter, and only in one instance was this not found. Two of the specimens were tested for phenols, as evidence of wood pitch, but the results were negative, though some of the features of the material are strongly suggestive of wood pitch. It is certain from the manner in which the material has 'run' and from the fact that it is still viscous in places that it was either liquid or semi-liquid when used: it is equally certain that it contains fatty matter and that this cannot have been derived from the body, as is sometimes the case with the fatty matter found in resinous materials that have been in direct contact with bodies. It is well known, too, that fat was used for anointing and hence its use in this particular anointing mixture is not surprising.

The black material from outside the canopic coffins of Tutankhamūn is probably of the same composition as that from the large coffins and appears to consist of a mixture of fatty matter and resin, with certainly no mineral pitch and no clear evidence of wood pitch. Griffiths[3] found that the material was largely resin, with about 9 per cent of natron and some vegetable debris, partly of coniferous origin. Mineral bitumen was absent.

The black material from the tomb of Meneptah examined in my laboratory was reported as being wood pitch in two instances and resin in a third. On reviewing the analytical results in the light of greater experience of these materials, aided by the re-examination of one of the specimens (the only one left) it is found that the material resembles very closely that from the tomb of Tutankhamūn; it has a similar fragrant smell and contains a considerable proportion of fatty matter. Griffiths[3] found that the material was probably a resin mixed with about 10 per cent of fatty matter.

---

[1] H. Carter, *Tut-ankh-Amen*, II, pp. 87–88.
[2] A. Lucas, in H. Carter, *Tut-ankh-Amen*, II, pp. 176–8 (Appendix II).
[3] J. G. A. Griffiths, *Analyst*, LXII (1937), pp. 703–7.

In a sandstone mummiform sarcophagus of the Eighteenth or Nineteenth Dynasty [1] there is a layer of black resinous-looking material about one centimetre thick, except at the head end, where it is thicker and in one place five centimetres. The material is essentially resin with a small proportion of fatty matter.

Before any final statement can be made regarding the composition of these black 'anointing' materials, a considerable amount of additional analytical work must be done, including the direct comparison of one specimen with another and with various mixtures made up for the purpose containing different proportions of resin and fatty matter, with and without wood pitch. If the material were originally black this may have been due either to the use of a resin that had been blackened (i.e. charred) during the process of heating it in order to make it sufficiently liquid for use, or to the presence of wood pitch, which is naturally black.

ONIONS [2]

Ruffer states [3] that 'Onions are not infrequently found among the bandages or in the coffins of mummies of the XXIst Dynasty and even as early as the XIIIth Dynasty and onion skins were sometimes placed over the eye of the dead.' Elliot Smith also found onions on mummies (often two, but sometimes only one), in the pelvis in seven cases; in the thorax in five cases; in the external ears in one case and in front of the eyes in one case,[4] and he states [5] that in the Twentieth, Twenty-first and Twenty-second Dynasties 'onions were used freely in the process of embalming'.

PALM WINE

Palm wine has been dealt with in connexion with alcoholic beverages,[6] but both Herodotus and Diodorus state that it was employed for cleaning the body cavities and viscera during the process of embalming. This must be accepted on trust, as it is not possible that any of this wine should have remained unaltered to the present time and, therefore, it cannot be found by testing. Dawson, however, says [7] that 'the presence of alcohol in some of the tissues lends support to Herodotus' statement that palm wine was used for cleaning', but no authority for the finding of alcohol is given and manifestly there is some mistake, as it is impossible that such a volatile substance should have remained. Reutter states [8] that probably there had been palm wine in certain of the mummy material he examined, because he found what he thought was a small amount of sugar, the presence of which, however, needs confirmation, as the test chiefly relied upon for its identification (the reduction of Fehling's solution) is not specific for sugar and is given by many other substances.[9]

RESINS

Resins are not now among the products of Egypt and whether they ever were

---

[1] Cairo Museum, No. J. 38167.   [2] Cf. V. Täckholm and M. Drar, *Flora of Egypt*, III, pp. 101–2.
[3] M. A. Ruffer, *Mém. Inst. d'Ég.*, I (1919), p. 76.
[4] G. Elliot Smith, *Mém. Inst. Ég.*, v (1906), pp. 28, 31.
[5] G. Elliot Smith, *Royal Mummies*, p. 64.   [6] See pp. 22–23.
[7] W. R. Dawson, *J.E.A.*, XIII (1927), p. 49.
[8] L. Reutter, *De l'embaumement avant et après Jésus-Christ*, pp. 38, 50.
[9] M. Wagenaar (*Oud. Med. N.R.*, x (2) (1929), pp. 93 f.; *Chemisch Weekblad*, XXVII (1930), pp. 348 f.) maintains that the concentrated juice of *Ficus sycomorus* was used in mummification, but this seems very doubtful, and would require further confirmation.

produced is doubtful: they occur to the north of Egypt in the countries bordering the east end of the Mediterranean; to the south in the Sudan, Abyssinia and Somaliland and to the east in Arabia, from most of which places they probably reached Egypt anciently.

As already shown in connexion with cosmetics, perfumes and incense,[1] resin was not infrequently buried in tombs long before mummification was practised, and it was suggested that this resin was such as was being used at the time for incense. After mummification (with its accompanying considerable use of resin) became general, resin was still put in the graves, some part probably still being incense, though judging from what was found in the tomb of Tutankhamūn, namely, resin associated in one instance with natron, some of it was probably connected with the mummification, and, in addition, in this particular tomb there were personal ornaments and other objects made of resin and resin was also used as a varnish and as a cementing material; in this tomb, too, which it should not be forgotten was a royal one, the incense no longer consisted of true resin from Asia, but of the more odoriferous and probably much more rare and costly gum-resin from the south.[2]

As it is the subject of mummification that is now being dealt with, only those resins that have been found directly associated with mummies will be considered, all resins of the Badarian, predynastic and early dynastic periods before the introduction of mummification being omitted.

In the literature of Egyptology there are many precise statements regarding the nature of the resins used in ancient Egypt, particularly for mummification, but many of these are merely guesswork, the nature of these resins having been very little investigated and very few of them having been identified with certainty. The only comparatively recent serious attempts to study the nature of these resinous materials, of which the results have been published and can be traced, are one analysis by Florence;[3] six analyses by Reutter;[4] several analyses by E. M. Holmes;[5] one by Coremans;[6] and my own work,[7] some of which has been confirmed by Griffiths.[8]

Florence, as the results of his analysis, concluded that the resin he examined, which was from the grave of a monkey (undated), was some kind of pine resin, though he was unable to give the particular species.

Reutter analysed six specimens of Egyptian mummy material,[4] three from human mummies (one of the Thirtieth Dynasty and two undated); one from an ibis mummy; one (consisting of a bundle of bandages) from bird mummies (undated) and one from a canopic box (undated). While recognizing the importance of this work and without in any way wishing to depreciate its value or to impugn the accuracy of the analyses, the author would like to suggest that some of the interpretations of the

---

[1] See p. 96.

[2] A. Lucas, in H. Carter, *Tut-ankh-Amen*, II, pp. 183–4; III, pp. 181–2.

[3] Quoted by L.-C. Lortet and C. Gaillard, *La faune momifiée*, I–II, pp. 319–21.

[4] For references, see p. 304, *n.* 6.

[5] E. M. Holmes, *Pharmaceutical Journal*, XIX (1888–9), pp. 387–9.

[6] P. Coremans, *Chronique d'Égypte*, XVI (1941), pp. 101–4.

[7] A. Lucas, *Preservative Materials*, pp. 22 f.; *Cairo Sc. Journ.*, II (1908), pp. 142 f.; in G. Elliot Smith and F. Wood Jones, *Arch. Survey of Nubia, 1907–1908*, II, pp. 372–3.

[8] J. G. A. Griffiths, *Analyst*, LXII (1937), pp. 703–7.

results may be erroneous. The first striking fact is the comparatively large number of different substances in each specimen of material examined, thus in one specimen he found storax; Aleppo resin; mastic; cedar resin; certain resins not identified; bitumen and sugar: in a second, certain resins not identified; gum or gum-resins; storax; wood pitch; bitumen; balsam of Illurin or Mecca balsam and sugar: in a third, bitumen; sugar; wood pitch; balsam of Gurjun and possibly balsam of Illurin or Mecca balsam: in a fourth, bitumen; myrrh; possibly aloes and probably balsam of Judea: in a fifth, bitumen; myrrh; aloes and probably Mecca balsam and in a sixth, bitumen; cedar resin; the resin from *Pistacia terebinthus* and sugar. This is quite contrary to my experience and of the very large number of different specimens of resinous materials I have examined from all periods, by far the greater number have been homogeneous resins or gum-resins of well defined character and only in a comparatively few instances were they mixtures and then with fatty matter.[1]

The rests relied upon by Reutter for the identification of bitumen [2] and sugar [3] respectively have already been discussed: the tests for storax and wood pitch are satisfactory ones. For the other materials Reutter in many cases made an 'ultimate analysis', determining the carbon and hydrogen by direct experiment and estimating the oxygen by difference (the usual method), and from the results obtained he calculated the percentage of the three elements present and from this he calculated a formula for the substance, which he then identified with the formula of a known substance. When, however, one considers the smallness of the portion of material operated upon (from 0.02 to 0.22 gram), which did not permit of a duplicate analysis as a check, the multiplication and division of the original figures necessitated by the calculations and the fact, to take one example, that 77.42 per cent of carbon and 10.43 per cent of hydrogen represent one substance (*gurjorésène*), and 77.3 per cent of carbon and 10.2 per cent of hydrogen represent a totally different substance (*masticorésène*), and the further facts that while 71.5 per cent of carbon and 8.6 per cent of hydrogen and 71.19 per cent of carbon and 8.64 per cent of hydrogen respectively represent the same substance (B-*heerabomyrrhol*), 71.0 per cent of carbon and 8.79 per cent of hydrogen represent a different substance (not identified), and 71.6 per cent of carbon and 8.05 per cent of hydrogen still another substance (not identified), one may be pardoned for thinking there is room for mistakes in identification. In several instances, too, Reutter bases a probable identification upon the smell of the material, or upon a process of exclusion, assuming that because negative results were obtained when certain specific resins were tested for and hence were presumably absent, therefore another resin, that it was thought might have been used, was probably present.

I have examined a very large number of resinous materials from mummies,[1] the results of which may now be considered. Reutter, in his criticism of this work, suggests that 'ultimate analyses' should have been made; but unfortunately, as explained at the time, this was not possible, partly because of the small size of the specimens and also because of the lack of the necessary time and facilities. In those cases, too, in which the material had become contaminated with natron or with fatty or other decom-

---

[1] A. Lucas, *Preservative Materials*, pp. 22 f.; *Cairo Sc. Journ.*, II (1908), pp. 142 f.
[2] See pp. 304–5.   [3] See p. 316.

position products of the body, or had intentionally been mixed with fatty matter, which were a large proportion of the total number, any 'ultimate analysis' would have been not only useless, but misleading. Since the original report was published, some of the same materials have been re-examined in greater detail and other specimens have been analysed. These resinous materials may be classified into two main groups, namely, true resins and gum-resins, which may separately be considered.

True Resins [1]

The botanical sources of the true resins, as distinguished from gum-resins, employed in mummification, as also of those found in predynastic and early dynastic graves before mummification was practised, are unknown and since the matter is of considerable importance, the present position may briefly be stated.

Both from practical considerations and also from references in the ancient Egyptian records, there cannot be any doubt that the resins now being considered were obtained from the eastern Mediterranean region. The principal resin-bearing trees of that region are the conifers (cone-bearing trees) and the principal coniferous trees are cedars, cypresses, firs, junipers, larches, pines, spruces and yews. Of these, the yews do not produce resin, and the cypresses and junipers [2] ordinarily do not produce resin, so all these may be excluded. Also, in view of the fact that many of the resins in question were reaching Egypt as early as predynastic times, the likely countries in the eastern Mediterranean region from which they were obtained may be limited to Syria, and the south of Asia Minor. If this limitation is accepted, then the possible principal resin-bearing conifers left for consideration are the cedar (*Cedrus Libani*) from the Lebanon mountains in Syria and from the Taurus mountains in Asia Minor; the Cilician fir (*Abies cilicica*) from north Syria and Asia Minor; the Aleppo pine (*Pinus halepensis*) from north Syria and Asia Minor; the Stone or Umbrella pine (*Pinus Pinea*) from Syria, and the Oriental spruce (*Picea orientalis*) from Asia Minor. The cedar, however, although it does produce resin when wounded, does not produce it readily or in great quantity, and, so for as is known to me, it has never been used as a source of resin, apart from its possible use in ancient Egypt now being considered, and, in my opinion, cedar resin may be excluded.

Since the nature of the coniferous woods from Syria and Asia Minor, but largely from Syria, that were used in ancient Egypt may throw some light upon the trees that were known, and, therefore, possibly upon the resins, it may be mentioned that these trees, which will be considered fully in connexion with wood, included cedar, cypress, fir, juniper, pine and yew. Excluding the cypress, juniper and yew, as non-resin-bearing trees, there remain, therefore, cedar, fir and pine. The cedar was the Lebanon cedar, the fir was probably the Cilician fir and the pine was probably the Aleppo pine.

In the ancient Egyptian records a highly valued wood (*'š (ash)* wood) is mentioned as having been obtained from Syria, and *ash* resin was employed for mummification.

Taking into account the colour of the *ash* wood (light yellow) as shown on the

[1] Cf. A. Lucas, *Preservative Materials*, pp. 22–26.
[2] A. Lucas, *J.E.A.*, XVII (1931), pp. 13–21. At the time this was written it was not realized that for all practical purposes the juniper was not a resin-producing tree.

monuments; the size, height and straightness of the tree necessitated by the uses to which the wood was put (for making temple doors; the sacred boat of Amūn; masts for boats, and for temple pylons); the place (the Lebanon mountains) from which the wood was obtained, and the fact that the tree yielded resin, Loret believes[1] that the true *ash* of ancient Egypt was the Cilician fir (*Abies cilicica*) and that the ordinary *ash* was a pine, probably usually *Pinus Pinea*, but he also suggests that the word may have been employed as a general term for a certain kind of timber from Syria. Jacquemin supports Loret [2] in his contention that *ash* was Cilician fir. Glanville agrees with Loret [3] that in certain instances the word 'is not so much the name of a tree as a type of timber derived from a number of different conifers—pines and firs —but especially *Pinus Pinea*'. If *ash* wood were Cilician fir, then *ash* resin must have been from the same tree. A representation of *ash* resin is shown and named in the Eighteenth Dynasty tomb of Rekhmirē at Thebes: it is in small rounded lumps coloured red.[4]

Adhering to the walls of a small, and otherwise empty, alabaster vase from the tomb of Tutankhamūn, which was marked *ash* resin, there was a very small amount of material, of which I examined a specimen and found it to be a true resin, as distinguished from a gum-resin, and, therefore, it was probably from a coniferous tree. The colour varied from light brown to dark brown; it was 90 per cent soluble in alcohol; completely insoluble in turpentine and in petroleum spirit, and left a considerable amount of ash, which, however, was calcium carbonate, probably derived from the vase itself; it did not give the colour test for colophony with acetic anhydride and sulphuric acid. Unfortunately the amount of material available was too small for further tests, and certain identification was impossible.

I also examined for Dr. Reisner a specimen of what he described as 'dried cedar oil' from Tomb No. b 2140 at Giza (reign of Khafrē). This was resinous-looking, very brittle, broke with a conchoidal fracture and was almost black in colour, though the edges when viewed with a lens were red and translucent, and it gave a reddish-brown powder. It burned with a smoky flame and had when burning a very fragrant smell, leaving 6 per cent of ash: it was 88 per cent soluble in hot alcohol; insoluble in petroleum spirit and 12 per cent soluble in turpentine. Manifestly, therefore, it was a true resin from a coniferous tree [5] and possibly *ash* resin.

Material from a vessel of unspecified date found at Memphis was examined by John, and identified as a coniferous resin, possibly from *Pinus halepensis*.[6]

Turning now to the resins used in connexion with mummification, the greater proportion of them resemble very much in appearance and general properties coniferous resins, except that most of them are insoluble in turpentine, whereas coniferous resins are largely soluble in this solvent. Of twenty predynastic and early dynastic

---

[1] V. Loret, *Ann. Serv.*, XVI (1916), pp. 33–51.

[2] M. Jacquemin, *Kêmi*, IV (1933), pp. 115–18.

[3] S. R. K. Glanville, *Z.Ä.S.*, LXVIII (1932), pp. 8–9.

[4] G. A. Hoskins, *Travels in Ethiopia* (1835). Plate between pp. 334 and 335.

[5] Possibly either *Abies cilicica* or *Pinus halepensis*; it may have been mixed with some other (volatile) substance to form a fragrant oil. Cf. G. A. Reisner, *History of the Giza Necropolis*, II, p. 75 (quoting A. Lucas).

[6] H. v. Minutoli, *Reise zum Tempel des Jupiter Ammon*, pp. 342–3.

resins specially tested, 90 per cent were insoluble, and 10 per cent partly soluble in turpentine, and of twenty-two later dynastic and Graeco-Roman specimens tested 86 per cent were insoluble and 14 per cent partly soluble in turpentine.

It is, of course, an easy matter to assume that the ancient resins have lost their solubility in turpentine on account of age and exposure, and there is evidence that colophony does become less soluble in petroleum spirit on keeping,[1] but the ancient Egyptian resins are still largely soluble in alcohol and certain other solvents. Also, one ancient resin, approximately two thousand years old, which I believe to be Chios turpentine,[2] is still practically as easily and as completely soluble in turpentine as the fresh material.

However, taking into consideration all the various factors in the case, and admitting that there is much that at present is not understood, it seems most probable that the greater proportion of the ancient Egyptian true resins, as distinguished from the gum-resins, were from coniferous trees (firs and pines) and probably from the Cilician fir, the Aleppo pine and the Stone or Umbrella pine.

There is one coniferous resin still to be mentioned, namely sandarac resin [3] from *Tetraclinis articulata* (*Callitris quadrivalis*), which grows in north-west Africa. There is, however, no evidence and little probability that any resin from this locality was imported into ancient Egypt, and, further, the appearance of the ancient resins does not agree with that of sandarac.

Two non-coniferous resins from the eastern Mediterranean that also may be mentioned are Chian (Chios) turpentine and mastic, both from species of Pistacia, the former from *Pistacia terebinthus* and the latter from *Pistacia lentiscus*. One specimen of the former has been identified from ancient Egypt,[2] but no specimens of the latter. A species of Pistacia, probably *P. terebinthus*, is rare but scattered in Sinai,[4] and *P. terebinthus* is common in the Palestine hills north of Beersheba.[4] Another species of Pistacia, *P. Khinjuk*, is found in the Galala district (Gulf of Suez) in Egypt.[5]

One of the most noticeable features of the true resins is the considerable difference in colour among them, some being reddish (almost orange-coloured and giving a yellow powder when finely ground); others black and pitch-like in appearance; others brown, and one a slate colour.

Of the reddish material, eleven specimens from mummies have been examined, seven of which were from the cranial cavity, three from the orbits and one from the nose, four being of the Twenty-first Dynasty and the others undated, but almost certainly late. The botanical sources of this resin has not been identified. A resin, almost identical in appearance with the eleven specimens mentioned and having a very similar solubility in various solvents, was found in the tomb of Tutankhamūn in a vase in the same 'kiosk' as another vase containing natron and this resin, therefore, may have had a direct connexion with the embalming.

Of the pitch-like material eleven specimens have been examined, five from human mummies (one Eighteenth Dynasty, one Twenty-first Dynasty, and three Ptolemaic);

---

[1] K. Dieterich, *The Analysis of Resins, Balsams and Gum Resins*, 1920, p. 161.
[2] See p. 324.   [3] Often wrongly called 'Gum Juniper'.
[4] Private letter from G. W. Murray.
[5] R. Muschler, *Manual Flora of Egypt*, I, p. 611.

one from a crocodile mummy (undated) and five from graves (all Ptolemaic), but it is not known whether these latter were taken from the mummy or not. Four of the specimens are reported by Spielmann to contain bitumen, but as two of them are without one or two of the tell-tale elements (vanadium, nickel and molybdenum) characteristic of bitumen this seems improbable, and I think that the presence of bitumen even in the other two has not been proved.[1] The botanical source of these black resins has not been identified.

It has not been found possible to determine the cause of the black colour, nor whether the material was originally black or has become black with age, but one of the specimens, though generally black and lustrous and very pitch-like, was in part a deep brown colour and in one corner almost ruby-red, and it would seem possible, therefore, for a resin, not originally black, to become black. Of the eleven specimens mentioned, nine contained fatty matter, and it has previously been suggested that possibly the presence of fatty acids from the body may have caused certain resins to become black.[2] Another possibility is that the black colour may have been caused by the material having been charred during the heating to which it was probably subjected in order to render it sufficiently liquid to enable it to be poured over the body or into the body cavities, as the case might be.

I have examined also two preserved crocodiles,[3] both of which were black and looked as though they had been treated with bitumen. On neither did I find anything but dried and blackened flesh, with a little fatty matter in one case.

Other black mummy materials are described in connexion with ointments and wood tar respectively.[4]

The brown specimens and the slate-coloured one were ordinary resinous-looking materials, of which it has not been possible to determine the botanical source.

Gum-Resins [5]

I have examined nine specimens of what proved on analysis to be gum-resins, all from mummies and five of them from royal mummies (two Eighteenth Dynasty, one Nineteenth Dynasty, two Twentieth Dynasty, three Twenty-first Dynasty and one Ptolemaic). These are believed to be either bdellium or myrrh (which are closely allied and very similar) and most probably myrrh.[6] A specimen of gum-resin from a tomb of Nineteenth or Twentieth Dynasty date at Abydos has been examined by Coremans, and identified as myrrh.[7]

Both Herodotus and Diodorus mention the employment of myrrh for mummi-

---

[1] See pp. 305–6.

[2] A. Lucas, Preservative Materials, p. 46.

[3] One Cairo Museum No. J. 29630; the other from the University of Michigan excavations in the Fayum.

[4] See pp. 312–6, 325–6.

[5] Cf. A. Lucas, Preservative Materials, pp. 26–29.

[6] With a portion of one of these specimens, which I supplied to M. R. Pfister, Professor Launoy obtained a reaction that he believes confirms the identification as myrrh. (R. Pfister, Nouveaux textiles de Palmyre, 1937, p. 10.)

[7] P. Coremans, Chronique d'Égypte, XVI (1941), pp. 101–4. Coremans points out that the Liebermann-Storch test may be useless, since it appears that certain ancient resins have lost most of their analytical characteristics.

fication: Pettigrew states [1] that 'Dr. Granville found . . . two or three small pieces of myrrh in their natural state', and that 'Dr. Verneuil says he has been able to recognize myrrh among the balsamic substances employed in embalming', both of which identifications appear to be largely of the nature of guesswork: Reutter reports myrrh as being present in two specimens of mummy material he analysed, one from human vertebrae and the other from a human hand, both undated.[2] Myrrh has already been described in connexion with incense.[3]

Miscellaneous Resins

Certain miscellaneous resins may now conveniently be dealt with. In one of the mummy materials examined by Reutter there were small fragments of a yellowish-brown somewhat transparent resin having an odour of turpentine, which was picked out, analysed separately and identified as probably Chios turpentine.[4] The slight solubility in alcohol, the high saponification value and the high melting-point, however, are all against this. Holmes also identified as Chios turpentine a specimen of resinous material found by Petrie in a jar at Naucratis, which was dated to about the sixth century B.C.[5] Chios turpentine is an oleo-resin obtained from *Pistacia terebinthus*, a shrub or small tree that grows in southern Europe, Asia Minor, Syria and North Africa and is often called the 'turpentine tree' from the large amount of oleo-resin (turpentine) [6] that is obtained from it; and it was possibly the product from this tree to which the name of turpentine was first applied and, since the greater proportion of this material at one time on the market was collected from the island of Chios in the Grecian archipelago, it was named Chios turpentine. Petrie states [7] that a layer of Chios turpentine had been poured over the nest of three wooden coffins of Horudja (Twenty-sixth Dynasty) after they had been placed in the stone sarcophagus. No evidence is given for the identification of the resinous material. Holmes also examined a specimen of resinous material from a sarcophagus found at Hawara, dating from the second century A.D.,[8] but on account of the very small amount of material available, only few tests were possible, as the result of which he suggested that it was either benzoin or storax and probably the former.[9] That it was one or the other seems certain, since benzoic acid was given off when it was heated and, although benzoin is obtained from the Far East (Siam, Sumatra, Borneo and Java) there would not have

---

[1] T. J. Pettigrew, *History of Egyptian Mummies*, p. 60 n.

[2] L. Reutter, 'De la Momie ou Mumia', *Bull. des Sciences Pharmacologiques*, Paris, no date, pp. 49, 58.

[3] See pp. 92–93.

[4] L. Reutter, *De l'embaumement avant et après Jésus-Christ*, pp. 35, 36, 48.

[5] E. M. Holmes, *Pharmaceutical Journal*, XIX (1888–9), pp. 387–9.

[6] The original name of the natural oleo-resinous exudation from the *Pistacia terebinthus*, as also from pines and certain other coniferous trees, was turpentine, and it is only comparatively recently that the name of the oil (spirit) prepared from it became shortened from oil of turpentine (spirits of turpentine) to turpentine and the natural product is still called turpentine scientifically, and certain kinds are still known as turpentine commercially, for example, Chios turpentine, Venice turpentine and Strassburg turpentine.

[7] W. M. F. Petrie, *Kahun, Gurob and Hawara*, pp. 10, 19.

[8] No record of such a sarcophagus can be traced in Petrie's reports on Hawara. It seems likely that a mistake has been made and that this is the sarcophagus of Horudja (Twenty-sixth Dynasty).

[9] E. M. Holmes, *Pharmaceutical Journal*, XIX (1888–9), pp. 387–9.

been any insuperable difficulty in its reaching Egypt at the late date mentioned, and benzoin is a well-known incense material in the East at the present day.

But resin was also employed where it served no useful purpose and where, there-fore, it probably had a ritual significance. Thus in a Twenty-sixth Dynasty tomb at Matarieh near Cairo [1] a large quantity (more than 50 kilograms) of resin was found between the sarcophagus (which is made of the light-coloured blue-grey 'schist' from the Wadi Hammamat, so much employed at this period) and the walls of the large hollowed-out monolithic 'case' of limestone into which the sarcophagus closely fitted. From the results of the analysis of the resin, which have been published else-where,[2] it is believed to be Chios turpentine. Four other examples of the similar use of resin have come under my notice,[2] namely, (a) small patches of an identical-looking resin on the sides of a sarcophagus similar to that just described and of the same period in the British Museum;[3] (b) a mixture of resin and limestone powder used to fill up the space between a sarcophagus and an inner coffin of Twenty-sixth Dynasty date from Saqqara;[4] (c) a mixture of resin and broken quartz pebbles used to fill up the space between a granite coffin and a wooden one of late date from Saqqara [5] and (d) a mixture of resin and powdered alabaster (both coarse fragments and fine powder) used as *colle de raccord* of a Third Dynasty alabaster sarcophagus from Saqqara.[6] The limestone powder, the quartz pebbles and the broken alabaster respectively were probably used in order to economize resin.

SAWDUST

Elliot Smith [7] and Elliot Smith and Dawson state [8] that sawdust, both alone and mixed with resin, has been found in the body cavities of mummies and that in one instance the skin was sprinkled with powdered aromatic wood or sawdust. In the chest cavity of the mummy of Senebtisi (Twelfth Dynasty) Elliot Smith found saw-dust,[9] and Verneuil found a canopic vase he examined filled with what he describes as cedar dust and natron.[10] Winlock found sawdust on several occasions among refuse embalming material from Deir el Bahari,[11] one specimen of which (from the Eleventh Dynasty tomb of Ipi) was examined by me, and in another case some material tied up in a piece of woven fabric from a Twelfth Dynasty tomb found by Winlock at Deir el Bahari consisted of a mixture of fine sawdust and quartz sand.[12] Among the refuse embalming material from the tomb of Yuya and Tuyu (Eighteenth Dynasty) there was at least one large jar containing a mixture of resin and sawdust,[13] and a jar

---

[1] Tomb No. 6 described by H. Gauthier, *Ann. Serv.*, XXXIII (1933), pp. 27–53, Pl. VI.

[2] A. Lucas, *Ann. Serv.*, XXXIII (1933), pp. 187–9.

[3] Called 'Grey basalt coffin of Wah-Ab-Ra' and stated to have come from Campbell's tomb, Giza, No. 1384.

[4] Submitted by C. M. Firth and examined by me.

[5] Found by J. E. Quibell at Saqqara.

[6] Submitted by J.-P. Lauer.

[7] G. Elliott Smith, *Royal Mummies*, Nos. 61052, 61085, 61087, 61088, 61089, 61095, 61097.

[8] G. Elliot Smith and W. R. Dawson, *Egyptian Mummies*, pp. 81, 84, 114, 115, 117, 118.

[9] G. Elliot Smith, in A. C. Mace and H. E. Winlock, *Senebtisi*, p. 119.

[10] de Verneuil, in J. Passalacqua, *Catalogue des antiquités découvertes en Égypte*, p. 286.

[11] H. E. Winlock, *M.M.A. Bull., Egyptian Exped. 1921–1922*, p. 34; *1927–1928*, p. 25.

[12] Submitted by Dr. Derry and examined by me.   [13] J. E. Quibell, *Yuaa and Thuiu*, pp. 75–77.

containing sawdust was found with refuse embalming material in a Theban tomb of Eighteenth or Nineteenth Dynasty date.[1] Some of the sawdust examined by me has been fragrant and possibly, therefore, juniper-wood sawdust. Elliot Smith also mentions fragrant (aromatic) sawdust,[2] and Wilkinson refers to the finding at Thebes of sawdust in linen bags enclosed in earthenware jars.[3] Bags of chaff and chopped straw have also been found among refuse embalming materials.[4]

SPICES

The use of spices in mummification is referred to by both Herodotus and Diodorus, but in neither instance is there any indication of the kind employed. Apart from the finding of what may have been cassia or cinnamon,[5] no reference can be traced to the presence of spices in mummies.

WOOD PITCH AND WOOD TAR

Wood pitch and wood tar may be classed together, as they are very closely connected both in composition and in method of production, wood tar being a thick, black liquid of complex constitution produced by the destructive distillation of resinous wood, and wood pitch being the solid residue left when the liquid tar is distilled for the recovery of certain volatile constituents contained in it (chiefly acetic acid, methyl alcohol, oils and creosote).

Wood tar was known to the Greeks of the time of Theophrastus[6] (fourth to third century B.C.) and Dioscorides [7] (first century A.D.) and to the Romans of Pliny's day [8] (first century A.D.), since these writers, who term the material 'pitch' (Pliny also calling it 'liquid pitch'), describe a primitive method of producing it. Hence, that wood tar or wood pitch should have been known to, and used by, the Egyptians, especially at a late date, is not surprising.

Reutter found wood tar (*goudron de bois*) in ancient Egyptian materials on two occasions, one on the mummy of an ibis (undated) and the other in the resinous material from a funerary vase (undated).[9]

Ruffer has already been quoted for the identification of 'cedar-wood pitch' of Twelfth Dynasty date from Lahun,[10] which I also examined and suggest that, although wood pitch, it was probably juniper-wood pitch and not cedar-wood pitch.

A number of specimens of ancient embalming material, chiefly from Ptolemaic mummies and often from inside the skull, which I have examined are believed to be wood pitch. Particulars of a few of these were published several years ago[11] and others

[1] L. Habachi, *Ann. Serv.*, LV (1958), pp. 335–6.

[2] G. Elliot Smith, *Royal Mummies*, No. 61052.

[3] J. G. Wilkinson, *Topography of Thebes and General View of Egypt* (1835), pp. 256–7.

[4] H. E. Winlock, *Materials used at the Embalming of King Tūt-ankh-Amūn*, pp. 10–11 and Pl. 3; E. Naville, *Temple of Deir el Bahari*, II, p. 6.

[5] See pp. 308–9.

[6] *Enquiry into Plants*, IX: 3, 1–3.

[7] I: 94.

[8] XVI: 21–22.

[9] L. Reutter, *De l'embaumement avant et après Jésus-Christ*, pp. 56, 59, 66, 68.

[10] See p. 314.

[11] A. Lucas, *Preservative Materials*, pp. 43, 46, 49; *J.E.A.*, I (1914), pp. 244–5.

have been examined since. The identification of two of these has been confirmed by Griffiths.[1]

Although wood tar is a secondary product obtained during the process of making charcoal, which was one of the important minor industries in ancient Egypt, there is no evidence that the tar produced was collected and utilized and, as the material found on, or in connexion with, mummies, is often fragrant and therefore almost certainly from coniferous woods (frequently probably juniper) which do not grow in Egypt, it seems highly probable that the wood tar or wood pitch used was imported and not produced locally.

---

[1] J. G. A. Griffiths, *Analyst*, LXII (1937), p. 707.

Chapter XIII

OILS, FATS AND WAXES

Fatty matter has frequently been found in Egyptian tombs and sometimes in considerable amount. Thus Petrie, referring to certain stone jars, says [1] 'The constant use of these jars was to contain ointment . . .' and again [2] 'Here the space was filled to three feet deep with sand saturated with ointment . . . hundredweights of it must have been poured out here . . .' It has, however, seldom been analysed, and of the few analyses of which any record can be traced none is conclusive. This inconclusiveness is inevitable, as all oils and fats, unless kept under special air-tight and sterile conditions, which is not the case when placed in jars in tombs, sooner or later decompose, and as some of the bodies formed escape, either by evaporation or by soaking into the material of the containing vessel, all that the analyst has for examination, although often still looking and feeling like a fat, is merely a portion of the products of decomposition, consisting generally of a mixture of certain bodies termed 'fatty acids', principally the solid acids, palmitic and stearic; and it is only by the separation, purification and identification of these and by a determination of the proportion in which each occurs in the mixture that the nature of the original oil or fat sometimes can be ascertained; and since what remains is generally only a part of that formed, and not necessarily a representative part, the problem may often be insoluble.

The only analyses of fatty material from Egyptian tombs that can be traced are those by Ure,[3] Friedel,[4] McArthur,[5] Chapman and Plenderleith,[6] Thomas,[7] Banks and Hilditch,[8] Hilditch,[9] Lijnst Zwikker,[10] Clarke,[11] Iskander,[12] and myself,[13] which may now be discussed.

---

[1] W. M. F. Petrie, *Diospolis Parva*, p. 15.

[2] W. M. F. Petrie, *Royal Tombs*, I, p. 14; W. M. F. Petrie and J. E. Quibell, *Naqada and Ballas*, pp. 39–40; G. A. Wainwright, *Balabish*, p. 14.

[3] Quoted by J. G. Wilkinson, *The Ancient Egyptians*, 1878, II, p. 401.

[4] Quoted by E. Amélineau, *Les nouvelles fouilles d'Abydos, 1895–1896*, pp. 275–80.

[5] Quoted by W. M. F. Petrie and J. E. Quibell, *Naqada and Ballas*, p. 39.

[6] A. C. Chapman and H. J. Plenderleith, *Journ. Chem. Soc.*, CXXIX (1926), pp. 2614–19; in H. Carter, *Tut-ankh-Amen*, II, pp. 206–10 (Appendix IV).

[7] Quoted by A. Lucas, in H. Carter, *Tut-ankh-Amen*, II, p. 177 (Appendix II).

[8] A. Banks and T. P. Hilditch, *Analyst*, LVIII (1933), pp. 265–9.

[9] T. P. Hilditch, *Analyst*, LXIV (1939), pp. 867–70.

[10] J. J. Lijnst Zwikker, *Oud. Med. N.R.*, XXIV (1943), pp. 97–105.

[11] H. T. Clarke, in H. E. Winlock, *Treasure of Three Egyptian Princesses*, p. 67.

[12] Z. Iskander, *Ann. Serv.*, LIII (1958), pp. 189–90. The specimen consisted mainly of fatty matter, wax, and limestone powder.

[13] A. Lucas, in H. Carter, *Tut-ankh-Amen*, II, pp. 176–7 (Appendix II); *J.E.A.*, XVI (1930), pp. 46–47; in J. E. Quibell, *Yuaa and Thuiu*, pp. 75–76.

Ure's analysis is wholly inconclusive, but in most of the other cases the material was found to consist largely of palmitic acid [1] or stearic acid [1] or of a mixture of the two, with, in some instances, small proportions of other fatty acids, of which oleic,[2] myristic, azelaic and nonoic acids have been identified.[3] These results indicate that the particular specimens examined probably had originally been animal fats, which is confirmed in at least one instance by the archaeological evidence, which proves that the material had been in a more or less solid condition and not a liquid oil.[4] In one instance, what was probably animal fat had been used as a lubricant.[5]

Banks and Hilditch point out that the results found make it most improbable that any of the specimens had been castor oil, which previous to their work had been suggested for four specimens (once by Friedel, once by Thomas and twice by me), since the principal constituent of castor oil is a variety of oleic acid (in the combined state) which like that contained in all the other specimens of fatty matter analysed (oleic acid being a constituent of most fixed oils and solid fats, particularly the former) would have wholly or largely disappeared.

Most of the specimens of ancient Egyptian fatty matter examined by me have consisted of solid fatty acids (essentially palmitic and stearic acids), and eleven specimens of Eighteenth Dynasty date found by Bruyère at Deir el Medineh and examined by me were of this nature, but thirteen other specimens of the same date and from the same place were different. They were all solid, some of a brown colour and others orange-red, and a common feature of them all was that they were elastic. There is no doubt whatever that they were some kind of altered oil or fat, probably oil, but unfortunately the amount of material available was much too small to allow of detailed analysis. I would suggest, however, that possibly they may have been originally some kind of drying oil, such as linseed oil, or safflower oil, which under the combined effects of heat and time has polymerized to a stiff elastic solid.

A very unusual find was a small painted pottery vase discovered by Pendlebury at El Amarna,[6] which was stated by the finder to be a Cypriot type of vase. The narrow neck of the vase was blocked by an accumulation of quartz sand, a small piece of red pottery and a resinous-looking material, which latter proved on analysis to be an altered product of the contents of the vase. A small hole was drilled in the bottom of the vase, which was found to be almost full of a dark brown viscous vegetable oil, entirely soluble in alcohol, but only partly soluble in petroleum spirit. Unfortunately the identity of the oil could not be determined, though it is hoped that this may be done at some future time.

A strong smell, reminiscent of rancid coconut oil, frequently noticed in the ancient

---

[1] Both palmitic and stearic acids are solid, white, tasteless and odourless bodies that are present in the combined state in most animal and vegetable oils and fats and form important constituents of the harder fats.

[2] Lijnst Zwikker identified decomposition products of oleic acid in three cases.

[3] In on instance succinic acid was present, but this was probably derived from some non-fatty material (almost certainly resin) mixed with the original fat.

[4] W. M. F. Petrie and J. E. Quibell, *Naqada and Ballas*, pp. 39–40.

[5] A. Lucas, in J. E. Quibell, *Yuaa and Thuiu*, p. 77.

[6] Museum No. J. 66743.

fatty materials, has led to the suggestion that the original fat had been coconut oil,[1] and the presence of palmitic acid has been taken to indicate an original palm oil,[1] but both these suppositions are demonstrably wrong, the smell being due to a very small proportion of nonoic acid, which had been formed as the result of decomposition, and palmitic acid being a constituent of most animal and vegetable oils and fats.

Although oils and fats are frequently mentioned in Egyptian texts, either their nature is often not stated or the meaning of the word used to describe them is unknown, and in consequence it has not yet been possible to translate many of the names.

The Greek papyri of the Graeco-Roman period found in the Fayum province also frequently refer to oils, the Greek names of most of which are well known. The oils mentioned are castor oil [2,3] (termed both *kiki* oil and *kroton* oil, though manifestly it cannot have been the modern croton oil); colocynth oil;[2] linseed oil;[2] olive oil;[4] radish oil (*rhaphanos* oil);[4,5] safflower oil [2] (termed *knekos* oil and *knekinon* and thought by Grenfell and Wright to be from the seeds of the thistle or artichoke) and sesame oil.[2]

The classical writers refer to the use in Egypt of almond oil;[6] *balanos* oil;[7] ben oil;[8] castor oil;[9,10] olive oil;[11] radish oil[10]; and several others of which the identification is uncertain.[12]

The various oils and fats mentioned will now separately be described, which may conveniently be done in alphabetical order.

Almond Oil

Pliny mentions the manufacture in Egypt of an unguent, the Mendesian unguent, containing oil of bitter almonds, which he says was expressed in Egypt.[13] If this were so, the almonds used almost certainly were imported, for although the almond tree grows in the country, it is comparatively rare, being only cultivated at the present day in gardens in the Delta. This statement of Pliny's is the only reference that can be traced respecting the use of almond oil in ancient Egypt. The almond fruit, however, was certainly known to at least some, though probably only a slight extent, since it has been discovered occasionally in tombs, the earliest known being of Eighteenth Dynasty date, about thirty almonds having been found in a small red pottery jar in the tomb of Tutankhamūn, and a number of stones from El Amarna

---

[1] W. M. F. Petrie and J. E. Quibell, *Naqada and Ballas*, pp. 39–40.
[2] B. P. Grenfell, *Revenue Laws of Ptolemy Philadelphus*, pp. xxxvi, 124, 126, 129, 135, 157.
[3] B. P. Grenfell and A. S. Hunt, *Hibeh Papyri*, I, pp. 320–3.
[4] B. P. Grenfell, A. S. Hunt and D. G. Hogarth, *Fayûm Towns and their Papyri*, pp. 234–7; B. P. Grenfell and A. S. Hunt, *Amherst Papyri*, II, p. 150.
[5] B. P. Grenfell and A. S. Hunt, *Oxyrhynchus Papyri*, VI, pp. 303–5; XVI, pp. 60–61.
[6] Pliny, XIII: 2.
[7] Pliny, XIII: 2; Theophrastus, *Concerning Odours*, IV: 15, 19.
[8] Pliny, XII: 46.
[9] Herodotus, II: 94; Diodorus, I: 3; Strabo, XVII: 2, 5.   [10] Pliny, XV: 7.
[11] Theophrastus, *Enquiry into Plants*, IV: 2, 9; Strabo, XVII: 1, 35; Pliny, XV: 4.
[12] Cf. in general T. Reil, *Beiträge zur Kenntnis des Gewerbes im hellenistischen Ägypten*, pp. 136–44.
[13] XIII: 2; XV: 7.

being in the Museum of the Royal Botanic Gardens, Kew.[1] Schiaparelli also found almonds of Eighteenth Dynasty date at Thebes.[2] Other examples that may be mentioned are four specimens identified by Newberry from the Ptolemaic cemetery at Hawara [3] and nine that have been in the Cairo Museum for many years, of which neither the place of origin nor date can be traced. The handle of a walking stick made of almond wood of Eighteenth Dynasty date is in the Museum of the Royal Botanic Gardens, Kew.

Animal Fats

Since the ancient Egyptians kept cows, sheep and goats, it is only natural that they should have been acquainted with the fat of these animals, including milk fat, and many different fats are mentioned in the texts,[4] notably ox fat,[5] goose fat,[6] and white fat,[7] and also, according to Breasted, 'butter'.[8]

The translation 'butter' is wrong, the word so translated meaning not butter, but butter fat,[9] the distinction between the two being a very real one. Butter is the material produced by churning milk or cream until the individual globules of fat previously in suspension coalesce; and though this fat is separated from the greater part of the liquid by straining and pressing, a certain amount of water and casein remain entangled with it, and the water naturally contains a proportion of the sugar and mineral constituents of the original milk. Butter fat, on the other hand, is made by melting butter by heat and allowing it to stand until the water and casein settle out, when the fat is poured off, and it is this that constitutes the modern Egyptian *samn* and the Indian *ghi*, which are used for eating with food and for cooking, but are never spread on bread in the manner of butter, which is entirely a custom of cold countries. The separation of butter fat from butter is a natural and unavoidable occurrence in a hot country like Egypt, especially in the summer, and the separated fat keeps much better than the original butter.

As already stated, a number of the specimens of the fatty matter from tombs that have been analysed probably originally had been solid animal fat, but so far there has been nothing characteristic left that would indicate from what particular kind of animal they were derived and it is impossible to say, for example, whether they were ox fat or sheep fat, but since it is known from the texts that ox fat was largely used, this is the more probable.

With fatty material of animal origin cheese may be included, since it has recently been shown that the contents of two alabaster jars of First Dynasty date found at Saqqara was cheese.[10]

An ointment for making the hair grow mentioned in the Hearst papyrus was made of gazelle fat, serpent fat, crocodile fat and hippopotamus fat,[11] and in the Ebers

---

[1] No. 47/1937.
[2] O. Mattirolo, *Atti della Reale Accad. delle Scienze di Torino*, LXI (1926), pp. 545–68.
[3] P. E. Newberry, in W. M. F. Petrie, *Kahun, Gurob and Hawara*, p. 47.
[4] Cf. H. v. Deines and H. Grapow, *Drogennamen*, pp. 112–21, 250–79.
[5] *A.R.*, II, 293. [6] *A.R.*, IV, 233, 376.
[7] *A.R.*, IV, 233, 239, 299, 300, 350, 376.
[8] *A.R.*, IV, 233, 301, 344, 350, 376. [9] *Wb.* IV.130.1–5.
[10] Ahmed Zaky and Zaky Iskander, *Ann. Serv.*, XLI (1942), pp. 295, 313.
[11] H. v. Deines, H. Grapow and W. Westendorf, *Grundriss der Medizin*, IV (i), p. 300.

papyrus, a remedy for the same purpose consisted of the mixed fats of the lion, hippopotamus, crocodile, cat, serpent and antelope.[1] Goose fat was an ingredient in many remedies, and the fat or oil of a variety of other animals is also prescribed.[2]

Balanos Oil

Balanos oil, which is not now known in Egypt, was the oil expressed from the kernels of *Balanites aegyptiaca* (the Heglig of the Sudan), a tree that at one time was abundant in Egypt, but which, though it still occurs in Upper Egypt and in Kharga Oasis, is rare, and still more so in the Delta, where only a few specimens grow in gardens, though it is plentiful in the Sudan and in Abyssinia.

Theophrastus states [3] that the *balanos* was an Egyptian tree, so named from the fruit because this was shaped like an acorn (*balanos*) and that the oil chiefly used in Greece for making perfumed ointments was that of the Egyptian or Syrian *balanos*,[4] the former being the more receptive and keeping the longer and, therefore, being the more suitable for choice perfumes. Pliny states [5] that oil of *balanus* was one of the ingredients of the Mendesian unguent.

The fruit, which in appearance somewhat resembles a date, consists of a thin, brittle shell enclosing a fleshy mass, inside which is a hard kernel; this kernel furnishes the oil, which is slightly yellow in colour and is highly prized in the Sudan.

The fruits and 'stones' have been found frequently in Egyptian tombs [6] and there are a number in the Cairo Museum stated to have been obtained from Gebelein, but unfortunately the date is not recorded. The earliest known specimens are some fruits found in the Djoser pyramid complex at Saqqara.[7] Newberry identified several hundred fruits and 'stones' of Twelfth Dynasty date found by Petrie at Kahun [8] and Quibell found stones of the same date in Upper Egypt.[9]

Ben Oil

Ben oil is the oil expressed from the nuts of *Moringa pterygosperma* (*M. oleifera*) and *Moringa aptera*, the oil from the two species being practically identical.[10] The *Moringa aptera* is a small tree with whip-like branches, scanty, minute leaves and pink flowers that grows in Egypt at the present time and is probably indigenous to the country. The refined oil has a yellowish colour, a sweet taste and is odourless and does not easily become rancid, for which reason it is much esteemed in the East for making cosmetics, for extracting perfumes from flowers and for cooking. The nuts, which are somewhat like three-sided hazel nuts (the sides being curved), consist of thin

---

[1] H. v. Deines, H. Grapow and W. Westendorf, *Grundriss der Medizin*, IV (i), p. 298.

[2] H. v. Deines and H. Grapow, *Drogennamen*, pp. 112–21, 250–79.

[3] *Enquiry into Plants*, IV: 1, 2, 6.

[4] *Concerning Odours*, IV: 15, 16, 19.

[5] XIII: 2.

[6] V. Loret and J. Poisson, *Rec. Trav.*, XVII (1895), pp. 196–7; E. Bonnet, *Nuovo Giornale Botanico Italiano*, N.S. II (1895), pp. 21–28; M. A. Beauverie, *B.I.F.A.O.*, XXXV (1935), pp. 143–4; E. Schiemann, *Mitt. Kairo*, X (1941), p. 128.

[7] V. Laurent Täckholm, *Bull. Inst. d'Ég.*, XXXII (1951), pp. 132–3.

[8] P. E. Newberry, in W. M. F. Petrie, *Kahun, Gurob and Hawara*, p. 49.

[9] J. E. Quibell, *Ramesseum*, p. 3.

[10] Anon., *Bulletin, Imperial Institute*, 28 (1930), pp. 276–9.

shells containing large, white, oily kernels, and are in a long pod. The nuts of *Moringa arabica* are imported into Egypt from Ceylon and southern India and are eaten by women who wish to grow fat.[1]

Ten nuts of *Moringa aptera* were identified by Newberry from the Graeco-Roman cemetery at Hawara.[2]

The moringa tree and ben oil are mentioned in Egyptian texts from as early as the Old and Middle Kingdoms respectively,[3] though the terms used have frequently been misinterpreted by translators as referring to the olive, and olive oil.[4]

Castor Oil [5]

The castor oil plant grows wild in Egypt at the present day and, since the seeds have been found in graves as early as the Badarian period,[6] the plant possibly is indigenous in the country.

Herodotus,[7] Diodorus,[8] Strabo[9] and Pliny[10] all mention the use in Egypt of castor oil for burning in lamps. Herodotus states that the seeds were either bruised and pressed, or roasted and boiled, in order to obtain the oil, which had a strong smell. Strabo states that the oil was used by the poorer people and labourers, both men and women, for anointing the body. Pliny says that in Egypt the oil was extracted without employing either fire or water, the seeds being first sprinkled with salt and then pressed. Dioscorides states[11] that castor oil was prepared in Egypt by grinding the seeds in a mill, putting the ground mass into baskets and pressing it.

The castor oil plant figured largely in the pharmacopoeia of ancient Egypt and the oil, berries and root are frequently mentioned in the medical papyri.[12] The oil is still largely used as a medicine at the present day and in Nubia it is used also for anointing the body and dressing the hair.

Sections of castor oil reed were employed as kohl tubes in the Eighteenth Dynasty.[13]

Colocynth Oil

The colocynth grows wild in Egypt, principally in the desert and largely in Sinai, but it is cultivated also to a slight extent for the fruit, which contains an active principle that has considerable medicinal use. The seeds when pressed yield an oil, which is not now used in Egypt.

Lettuce Oil [14]

The lettuce is cultivated largely in Egypt, and especially in Upper Egypt, for the

---

[1] A. H. Ducros, 'Essai sur le droguier populaire arabe de l'inspectorat des pharmacies du Caire', *Mém. Inst. d'Ég.*, xv (1930), pp. 39, 40.

[2] P. E. Newberry, in W. M. F. Petrie, *Kahun Gurob and Hawara*, p. 47.

[3] *Wb.* I. 423. 9–15; I. 424. 3–9; V. Loret, *Rec. Trav.*, vII (1886), pp. 101–6; *Flore Pharaonique*, 2nd ed., pp. 86–87; L. Keimer, *Kêmi*, II (1929), pp. 92–94; W. C. Hayes, *J.N.E.S.*, x (1951), p. 93; etc.

[4] Cf. A. Lucas, *Ancient Egyptian Materials and Industries*, 3rd ed., p. 386, n. 1–7.

[5] Cf. L. Keimer, *Gartenpflanzen*, pp. 70–73.

[6] G. Brunton and G. Caton-Thompson, *Badarian Civilisation*, pp. 38, 41.

[7] II: 94.   [8] I: 3.   [9] xvII: 2, 5.   [10] xv: 7.   [11] I: 38.

[12] H. v. Deines and H. Grapow, *Drogennamen*, pp. 526–7, 583–4.

[13] W. C. Hayes, *Scepter*, II, p. 191.

[14] Cf. L. Keimer, *Gartenpflazen*, pp. 1–6.

sake of the oil obtained from the seeds, which is used as a salad oil and in cooking.

Linseed Oil

Flax was extensively grown in Egypt from a very early date for the sake of the fibre for making linen and probably, therefore, linseed oil (which is the oil expressed from the seeds of the flax plant) was known also at an early date, though the first record if it that can be traced is of the Ptolemaic period.[1] It was used probably for cooking and for burning in lamps, for which purposes it is still employed by the poorer classes in Egypt. The principal present-day value of linseed oil is, however, as a paint oil, on account of its drying properties, but it was not employed for this purpose in Egypt, or elsewhere, so far as is known, even as late as the Roman period.

Malabathrum Oil

According to Warmington 'much malabathrum oil was produced in Egypt from raw stuff imported from India',[2] malabathrum being the leaves of cinnamon.[2]

Olive Oil

References to olive trees, olives, and olive oil in translations of Egyptian texts are to be treated with caution and cannot be regarded as valid evidence for the early cultivation of the tree in Egypt, since in many cases it is the Egyptian words for the moringa tree and ben oil [3] that have been incorrectly interpreted as olive.[4] In fact, the word for olive [5] does not occur before the Nineteenth Dynasty, though a fragment of a mural painting of the Eighteenth Dynasty shows part of a small olive tree with several olives growing on it.[6]

The classical writers, however, supply information respecting the olive tree in Egypt,[7] thus Theophrastus (fourth to third century B.C.) states [8] that the olive tree grew in the Thebaid, which statement is copied by Pliny,[9] and that 'The oil produced is not inferior to that of our country, except that it has a less pleasing smell . . .' Strabo (first century B.C. to first century A.D.) says[10] of the Arsinoite Nome (the Fayum) that 'It is the only nome planted with large, full-grown olive trees, which bear fine fruit. If the produce were carefully collected, good oil might be obtained, but this care is neglected, and although a large quantity of oil is obtained, yet it has a disagreeable smell. (The rest of Egypt is without the olive tree, except the gardens near Alexandria, which are planted with olive trees, but do not furnish any oil).' Pliny (first century A.D.) writes[11] that 'In Egypt, too, the berries, which are remarkably meaty, are found to produce very little oil.'

---

[1] See p. 329.

[2] E. H. Warmington, *Commerce between the Roman Empire and India*, pp. 186–90.

[3] *Wb.* I. 423. 9–15; I. 424. 3–9; V. Loret, *Rec. Trav.*, VII (1886), pp. 101–6; *Flore Pharaonique*, 2nd ed., pp. 86–87; L. Keimer, *Kêmi*, II (1929), pp. 92–94; W. C. Hayes, *J.N.E.S.*, X (1951), p. 93; etc.

[4] Cf. A. Lucas, *Ancient Egyptian Materials and Industries*, 3rd ed., p. 386, *n.* 1–7.

[5] *Wb.* V. 618. 4–5; V. Loret, *Rec. Trav.*, VII (1886), pp. 101–6; *Flore Pharaonique*, 2nd ed., pp. 58–59; L. Keimer, *Kêmi*, II (1929), pp. 92–94; *Gartenpflanzen*, p. 143.

[6] N. M. Davies, in *Mural Painting of El-Amarneh*, Pl. IX (c).

[7] Cf. C. Dubois, *Revue de Philologie*, 2e Sér., XLIX (1925), pp. 60–83; 3e Sér., I (1927), pp. 7–49.

[8] *Enquiry into Plants*, IV: 2, 7.

[9] XIII: 19.   [10] XVII: 1, 35.   [11] XV: 4.

Mahaffy [1] and Grenfell [2] both point out that in the legislation of Ptolemy Phila-delphus (285 to 246 B.C.) concerning oils and oil-pressing in Egypt there is not any reference to olive oil, commenting upon which Bevan says,[3] 'Olive trees grew in the Fayum, but olive oil does not seem to have been included in the monopoly.' The reason is not apparent, though it might possibly have been that the oil produced was too insignificant in quantity to be legislated for. Olives are mentioned in the Fayum about 257 B.C.[4] and young olive trees of the same date [5] in 256 B.C. One papyrus mentions the planting of olive shoots [6] and in another olive groves are referred to;[7] in 255 B.C. one papyrus [8] mentions the planting of olives and another [9] the planting of 3,000 shoots, and it is stated that 'the Egyptian olive is only suitable for parks and not for olive-groves'; in 251 B.C. olive shoots are mentioned;[10] olive oil is referred to in the second century A.D.[11] and olive-yards on several occasions ranging in date from A.D. 94 to A.D. 110.[12] The mere mention of olive oil, however, is not proof that it was of Egyptian origin, since, as already shown, this oil was imported into Egypt from Syria and particularly at a late date also from Greece. C. R. Scott, writing in 1837, that is during the reign of Mohammed Ali, states [13] that 'Vast tracts of land have been planted in various parts of the country with olive and mulberry trees.' In 1901, G. Bonaparte, of the School of Agriculture, Cairo, states [14] that the olive tree was only cultivated in Egypt to a very limited extent, chiefly in the Fayum and that the fruits were poor in oil. In 1927, Newberry writes [15] that the olive tree 'is only culti-vated in a very few gardens in Upper Egypt at the present day'.

Ruffer saw a few, but only very few, olive trees in the oases of Dakhla and Kharga in the western desert.[16] Beadnell says[17] that '. . . olives are grown in both Kharga and Dakhla, but only in comparatively small quantities.' Ball and Beadnell say [18] that '. . . olives . . . are grown in great numbers' in the oasis of Baharia. In 1923 Belgrave estimated that there were in Siwa oasis about 40,000 fruit-bearing olive trees.[19] According to the local Press, the Egyptian Government recently has planted a con-siderable number of olive trees in the country to the west of Alexandria.

The facts enumerated seem to show that, although the olive tree grows abundantly

---

[1] J. P. Mahaffy, in B. P. Grenfell, *Revenue Laws of Ptolemy Philadelphus*, p. xxxv.
[2] B. P. Grenfell, *Revenue Laws of Ptolemy Philadelphus*, p. 125.
[3] E. Bevan, *History of Egypt under the Ptolemaic Dynasty*, p. 149 n.
[4] B. P. Grenfell and A. S. Hunt, *Hibeh Papyri*, pp. 192–3.
[5] C. C. Edgar, *Zenon Papyri*, I, No. 59072.
[6] C. C. Edgar, *Zenon Papyri*, I, No. 59125.
[7] C. C. Edgar, *Zenon Papyri*, II, No. 59157.
[8] C. C. Edgar, *Zenon Papyri*, II, No. 59159.
[9] C. C. Edgar, *Zenon Papyri*, II, No. 59184.
[10] C. C. Edgar, *Zenon Papyri*, II, No. 59241.
[11] B. P. Grenfell, A. S. Hunt and D. G. Hogarth, *Fayum Towns and their Papyri*, pp. 234, 237.
[12] B. P. Grenfell, A. S. Hunt and D. G. Hogarth, *Fayum Towns and their Papyri*, pp. 261–74.
[13] C. R. Scott, *Rambles in Egypt and Candia*, II (1837), p. 166.
[14] G. Bonaparte, *Journ. Khedivial Agricultural Society*, III (1901), pp. 14–19.
[15] P. E. Newberry, in H. Carter, *Tut-ankh-Amen*, II, p. 195 (Appendix III).
[16] M. A. Ruffer, 'Food in Egypt', *Mém. Inst. d'Ég.*, I (1919), p. 81.
[17] H. J. L. Beadnell, *Egyptian Oasis*, p. 220.
[18] J. Ball and H. J. L. Beadnell, *Baharia Oasis*, p. 44.
[19] C. Dalrymple Belgrave, *Siwa*, p. 178.

in the countries on all sides of Egypt (across the Mediterranean to the north in Anatolia and Greece; on the north-east in Palestine and Syria; on the south in Abyssinia, where there are two kinds that grow wild, and on the west in Siwa and in Tunis and Algeria) it has never accommodated itself well to the conditions in Egypt, and that although the Greeks, who were accustomed to the cultivation of the olive tree in their own country, tried to grow it in the most likely localities in Egypt (the Fayum and the neighbourhood of Alexandria), it never really flourished and from an oil-producing point of view it has always been a failure.[1] Newberry has shown that the region adjoining the Nile Delta on the west was probably the original home of olive culture and the most ancient centre of commerce in olive oil.[2]

The evidence from the tombs for the cultivation of the olive tree in Egypt is very scanty and does not carry it farther back than the Eighteenth Dynasty, the period when Keimer states that probably it was introduced into the country.[3] The principal discoveries that can be traced are: in the tomb of Tutankhamūn, where there was a large funerary bouquet of persea, which contained a few very small olive twigs [4] and three wreaths partly composed of olive leaves;[5] part of a garland with three olive leaves from a tomb of the Eighteenth Dynasty at Thebes, and a leaf from a bouquet found in the tomb of Amenhotpe II;[6] olive twigs of the Twentieth Dynasty or later, identified by Schweinfurth;[7] a small twig with leaves in the Cairo Museum, marked as having been found by Schiaparelli at Thebes and dated to the period Twentieth to Twenty-sixth Dynasty; also in the same museum, a similar twig stated to have been found by Maspero at Gebelein and to be not earlier than the Ptolemaic period. Braun [8] refers to olive twigs and leaves (undated) in the Berlin Museum and to funeral wreaths of olive leaves (undated) in the Leyden Museum, Greiss [9] identified three bundles of olive twigs (undated) in the Cairo Museum, and Newberry[10] identified two olive stones from the Graeco-Roman cemetery at Hawara.

A general account of the olive in ancient Egypt, with particular reference to the Ptolemaic and Roman periods, is given by Dubois.[11]

Radish Oil

This oil, which has a disagreeable smell, was obtained from the seeds of the radish (*Raphanus sativus*) and Pliny states [12] that the radish was held in high esteem in Egypt

---

[1] The reason for this is probably primarily the scanty rainfall on the northern coast of Egypt as compared with that in the other countries named, even as compared with Tunis and Algeria, where there are mountains near the coast that precipitate the rain.

[2] P. E. Newberry, *Proc. Linnean Society of London, Session 150, 1937–8, Pt. 1, 31 Dec. 1937.*

[3] L. Keimer, *Gartenpflanzen*, p. 29; B.I.F.A.O., XXXI (1931), p. 133.

[4] H. Carter, *Tut-ankh-Amen*, II, p. 33.

[5] P. E. Newberry, in H. Carter, *Tut-ankh-Amen*, II, pp. 190–1 (Appendix III); H. E. Winlock, *Materials used at the Embalming of King Tūt-ankh-Amūn*, p. 17.

[6] L. Keimer, *Gartenpflanzen*, p. 29.

[7] G. Schweinfurth, *Pflanzenreste*, pp. 367–8.

[8] A. Braun, *Zeitschrift für Ethnologie*, IX (1877), p. 298; *Journal of Botany*, XVII (1879), pp. 52–53.

[9] E. A. M. Greiss, *Bull. Inst. d'Ég.*, XXXI (1949), p. 271; cf. also *Mém. Inst. d'Ég.*, LV (1957), pp. 154–5.

[10] P. E. Newberry, in W. M. F. Petrie, *Hawara, Biahmu and Arsinoe*, pp. 48, 52.

[11] C. Dubois, *Revue de Philologie*, 2ᵉ Sér., XLIX (1925), pp. 60–83; 3ᵉ Sér., I (1927), pp. 7–49.

[12] XV: 7; XIX: 26.

on account of the large amount of oil that was extracted from it. Dioscorides states [1] that the oil was used in Egypt medicinally. Although the radish is still grown plentifully in the country, the oil is no longer prepared.

Safflower Oil

Safflower oil is the oil expressed from the seeds of *Carthamus tinctorius* or false saffron, which is cultivated in Egypt at the present day chiefly for the sake of the oil, which is an agreeable, bland oil extensively used for salads and cooking.

Pliny mentions the safflower [2] which he calls by its Greek name of *cnecos*, and states that it was esteemed by the Egyptians on account of the oil it produced. Elsewhere, however, he seems to confuse the safflower with the nettle,[3] from which he says an oil (*cnidinum*, which apparently should be *cnecinum* and is *cnecinum* in another MS. reading) [4] was obtained.

The suggestion, already referred to,[5] that *cnecos* oil (*cnecinum*) was made from the seeds of the thistle or artichoke is without any support from the facts.

Sesame Oil

The sesame plant, which according to Muschler is probably of tropical African origin,[6] is grown plentifully in Egypt at the present day on account of the oil, which is expressed from the seeds. This oil is of a yellowish colour, clear and free from odour and has a bland agreeable taste. In 256 B.C. both sesame seed and sesame oil are mentioned,[7] and Pliny also refers to Egyptian sesame oil.[8] A type of oil frequently mentioned in Egyptian texts of the New Kingdom [9] and used as a food, for anointing, and for burning in lamps may well be sesame oil, though the identification is not certain.[10]

Uses of Oils and Fats

Oils and fats were employed in ancient Egypt for eating, cooking and illumination; for anointing both the living and the dead; for libations; as a base for perfumes; as medicines and vehicles for medicines and doubtless for many other purposes.

In addition to the large local supply, oil also was imported from abroad to some extent from an early period and to an increasing extent later, thus in the Eighteenth Dynasty there are records of oil having been brought from Naharin,[11] Retenu [12] and Djahi,[13] all in western Asia, and in the Twentieth Dynasty from Syria.[14]

Beeswax

The only wax used in ancient Egypt, so far as is known, was beeswax, which was employed as an adhesive;[15] for permanently fixing the curls and plaits in wigs;[16] in

---

[1] I: 45.   [2] XXI: 53.   [3] XV: 7; XXII: 15.
[4] B. P. Grenfell, *Revenue Laws of Ptolemy Philadelphus*, p. xxxvi.
[5] See p. 329.
[6] R. Muschler, *Manual Flora of Egypt*, II, pp. 884–5.
[7] A. S. Hunt, J. G. Smyly and C. C. Edgar, *Tebtunis Papyri*, III (Part II), No. 844.
[8] XV: 7.   [9] *Wb.* II. 302. 17–20.
[10] L. Keimer, *Gartenpflanzen*, pp. 18–20, 134–5; W. C. Hayes, *J.N.E.S.*, X (1951), p. 93, *n.* 142.
[11] *A.R.*, II, 482.   [12] *A.R.*, II, 473, 491, 509, 518.
[13] *A.R.*, II, 462, 510, 519.   [14] *A.R.*, IV, 233, 376.
[15] See pp. 2–3.   [16] See pp. 30–31.

mummification;[1] for coating painted surfaces;[2] as a paint vehicle in the encaustic process of painting;[3] at a very late date for covering the surface of writing tablets;[4] for shipbuilding [5] and for making figures of the four sons of Horus and the bennu bird,[6] and for other magical figures.[7] In several instances the melting temperature of the ancient Egyptian wax has proved to be considerably higher than that of modern beeswax, and it is therefore possible that for certain uses it was adulterated with a resinous substance, perhaps either a vegetable resin or propolis.[8]

It does not seem to have been the custom to place beeswax in tombs and no record of its having been so found can be traced, but at El Amarna a piece was found in a house.[9]

---

[1] See p. 303.

[2] See p. 352.

[3] See pp. 352-3.

[4] See p. 364.

[5] M. Rostovtzeff, *A Large Estate in the Third Century B.C.*, p. 123.

[6] G. Daressy, *Ann. Serv.*, VIII (1907), pp. 22 f.; C. R. Williams, *J.E.A.*, V (1918), pp. 273-4.

[7] L.-C. Lortet and C. Gaillard, *La faune momifiée*, III-IV, pp. 75-78, 209-13; C. R. Williams, *J.E.A.*, V (1918), p. 175.

[8] M. M. Mercier, *Mémoires de la Société nationale des Antiquaires de France*, 9ᵉ Sér., II (1951), pp. 127-60. See above, p. 3.

[9] T. E. Peet and C. L. Woolley, *City of Akhenaten*, I, p. 25.

Chapter XIV

PAINTING MATERIALS: WRITING MATERIALS

PAINTING MATERIALS[1]

Apart from the designs on the 'white cross-lined' and 'decorated' pottery, discussed below,[2] the earliest examples of painting from Egypt are a few of predynastic date. Fragments of gesso with simple daubs in black and red were found at Armant,[3] and Petrie mentions 'fragments of cloth painted with stucco in red, green, black and white' found at Naqada.[4] Pieces of painted leather with designs in red, green, black (or blue) and yellow are also recorded from Naqada,[5] and similar painted leather of First Dynasty date was found at Saqqara.[6] More advanced are the paintings on linen from Gebelein, now in the Turin Museum, with human figures and boats similar in style to those on the 'decorated' pottery,[7] and the famous wall painting from Hierakonpolis, now destroyed,[8] which evidently belongs to the late predynastic period. The walls and corridors of certain tombs of the First Dynasty at Saqqara were decorated with elaborate patterns in black, blue, red, white and yellow,[9] while in the Third Dynasty tomb of Hesirē, also at Saqqara, there were decorative panels and finely executed paintings of furniture, games, etc., the colours being predominantly browns, reds and yellows, though with some black, green and white.[10]

Pigments [11]

The freshness and brightness of the colours of the old Egyptian tomb paintings have often been commented upon, and it is sometimes assumed that the pigments employed were such as do not exist at the present day and even that their nature is

---

[1] Painting materials and methods are also discussed by C. R. Williams, *Per-nēb*; N. M. Davies and A. H. Gardiner, *Ancient Egyptian Paintings*, III, Introduction.

[2] See pp. 382–4.

[3] R. Mond and O. H. Myers, *Cemeteries of Armant*, I, pp. 121–2, 131.

[4] W. M. F. Petrie and J. E. Quibell, *Naqada and Ballas*, p. 21.

[5] W. M. F. Petrie and J. E. Quibell, *Naqada and Ballas*, pp. 48–49; W. M. F. Petrie, *Prehistoric Egypt*, p. 43.

[6] W. B. Emery, *Great Tombs*, II, p. 64.

[7] G. Galassi, *Rivista dell'Istituto nazionale d'archeologia e storia dell'arte*, n.s. IV (1955), pp. 5–17; H. W. Müller, *Alt-ägyptische Malerei*, p. 10, Fig. 2.

[8] J. E. Quibell and F. W. Green, *Hierakonpolis*, II, p. 21, Pls. LXXV–LXXIX.

[9] W. B. Emery, *Great Tombs*, I, p. 116, Pls. L–LII; III, p. 8, Pls. VI–VIII, XV–XVII. It is regrettable that the nature of these pigments was not determined.

[10] J. E. Quibell, *Saqqara, 1911–1912*, pp. 5–9, Pls. VIII–XIV.

[11] Cf. J. R. Harris, *Lexicographical Studies*, pp. 141–62; E. Iversen, *Some Ancient Egyptian Paints and Pigments*.

unknown. This, however, is not so, as they have been analysed frequently, and, with very few exceptions, they are either naturally occurring minerals, finely ground, or they have been made from mineral substances, to which fact is primarily due their excellent state of preservation.

The colours employed, taking them in alphabetical order, were black, blue, brown, green, grey, orange, pink, red, white and yellow, which may be separately considered. In the following discussion the analyses published by Barthoux [1] and Eibner [2] have been omitted, except in cases of particular interest. In neither instance are the specimens securely dated, and the exact nature of some of those examined by Barthoux is uncertain.[3]

Black

The black pigment was almost always carbon in some form, though possibly not always in the same form; generally it is in a very finely divided condition and consists of soot (probably scraped from cooking vessels), but occasionally it is fairly coarse. Soot, however, if carelessly collected, or if collected from masonry or plaster surfaces, might be contaminated with particles of mineral matter that would give it a coarse texture.

I examined twelve different specimens of black pigment, one of the Fifth Dynasty, three of the Sixth Dynasty, seven of the Eighteenth Dynasty and one of the Twenty-third Dynasty, all of which were carbon and eleven of which were fine soot, but one of which (Eighteenth Dynasty) was coarser than is usual with soot, and unfortunately in this particular case the amount of material available was too small for any detailed analysis.

Carbon black ('lamp black') has been identified on predynastic pottery by Ritchie,[4] and on the gesso-linen object of early predynastic date found by Myers at Armant.[5] Spurrell reports carbon black in paintings of Old, Middle and New Kingdom date,[6] soot was used in the Fifth Dynasty tomb of Per-neb,[7] Reisner mentions the use of lamp black at Kerma (Middle Kingdom),[8] and carbon black was identified in painting of the Amarna period by von Bissing and Reach.[9]

Borchardt notes the use of charcoal, with wax as a binding medium, on the head

---

[1] J. Barthoux, 'Les fards, pommades et couleurs dans l'antiquité', *Congrès Int. de Géog., Le Caire, Avril 1925*, IV (1926), pp. 251–67.

[2] A. Eibner, *Entwicklung und Werkstoffe der Wandmalerei*, pp. 580–9.

[3] An article by A. C. Fryer, *Proc. Clifton Antiquarian Club*, VI (1908), pp. 11–12, publishing identifications of pigments from an Eighteenth Dynasty tomb at Aswan, was brought to my notice too late to be incorporated in the text, but references to it have been included in the footnotes.

[4] P. D. Ritchie, in R. Mond and O. H. Myers, *Cemeteries of Armant*, I, pp. 181–5; *Technical Studies*, IV (1936), pp. 234–6.

[5] R. Mond and O. H. Myers, *Cemeteries of Armant*, I, pp. 121–2, 131.

[6] F. C. J. Spurrell, in W. M. F. Petrie, *Medum*, p. 28; *Arch. Journ.*, LII (1895), pp. 227, 229, 232. Cf. also A. C. Fryer, *Proc. Clifton Antiquarian Club*, VI (1908), pp. 11–12.

[7] C. R. Williams, *Per-nēb*, p. 25.

[8] G. A. Reisner, *Kerma*, IV–V, pp. 290–1.

[9] F. W. von Bissing and M. Reach, *Ann. Serv.*, VII (1906), p. 67; F. W. von Bissing, *Fussboden*, p. 15.

of Nefertiti,[1] Laurie found that a black pigment of the Nineteenth Dynasty was powdered charcoal,[2] and a specimen of late date examined by Wagenaar was also charcoal.[3] A black pigment from the tomb of Per-neb was identified by Toch as charcoal or bone black,[4] and bone black is said to have been employed on a wooden figure of the Amarna period.[5] The bone black reported by Beke[6] needs confirmation before it can be accepted, as Beke states that the recognition was made 'without the aid of chemical analysis'.

Spurrell identified a black pigment of the Twelfth Dynasty from Beni Hasan as pyrolusite,[7] a black ore of manganese that occurs plentifully in Sinai, and the pigment on a pottery vessel of Eighteenth Dynasty date was oxide of manganese.[8] Pyrolusite from the predynastic site at Maadi may also have been used as a pigment or eye-paint.[9] A blue-black pigment, not identified, but of which it is stated that it does 'not seem to be pounded charcoal', is known from the predynastic period.[10]

Blue [11]

The earliest blue pigment that can be traced is, as is only to be expected, a naturally occurring mineral, namely azurite (chessylite), a blue carbonate of copper that is found native both in Sinai and in the eastern desert. This was identified by Spurrell from a shell used as a palette found at Medum (Fourth Dynasty)[12] and, according to the same authority, the colour employed for painting the mouth and eyebrows on the cloth that covered the face of a mummy of the Fifth Dynasty was also azurite,[12] though he adds, 'It looks green from age and staining, which is an accident.' With respect to this same mummy, however, Petrie says,[13] 'The eyes and eyebrows were painted on the outer wrapping with green', and Elliot Smith states[14] that 'the eyes were represented by green paint' and also[14] that 'The pupils, edges of the eyelids and the eyebrows are painted with green malachite paste.' Azurite was also found by Spurrell in paintings of the Eighteenth Dynasty.[15]

The principal blue pigment of ancient Egypt was an artificial frit that consisted of a crystalline compound of silica, copper and calcium (calcium-copper silicate).[16] This was made by heating together silica, a copper compound (probably generally mala-

[1] L. Borchardt, *Porträts der Königin Nofret-ete*, p. 32.

[2] A. P. Laurie, *Materials of the Painter's Craft*, pp. 26–27.

[3] M. Wagenaar, *Pharm. Weekblad*, LXX (1933), pp. 894–902.

[4] M. Toch, *Journ. Ind. and Eng. Chemistry*, X (1918), pp. 118–19.

[5] H. Schäfer, *Z.Ä.S.*, LXX (1934), p. 3.

[6] C. T. Beke, 'Of the Colours of the Ancient Egyptians', *Trans. Royal Soc. of Literature* (1843), pp. 48–51.

[7] F. C. J. Spurrell, *Arch. Journ.*, LIII (1895), p. 229.

[8] See p. 384.

[9] O. Menghin and M. Amer, *Excavations of the Eg. University . . . at Ma'adi, Second Prelim Report*, p. 61.

[10] J. E. Quibell and F. W. Green, *Hierakonpolis*, II, p. 21.

[11] Cf. J. R. Harris, *Lexicographical Studies*, pp. 148–9.

[12] F. C. J. Spurrell, in W. M. F. Petrie, *Medum*, p. 29; *Arch. Journ.*, LIII (1895), p. 227.

[13] W. M. F. Petrie, *Medum*, p. 18.

[14] G. Elliot Smith, *J.E.A.*, I (1914), pp. 192–3.

[15] F. C. J. Spurrell, *Arch. Journ.*, LIII (1895), p. 232.

[16] Approximately $CaO. CuO. 4SiO_2$.

chite), calcium carbonate and natron. Petrie suggests that in at least one place the silica used was in the form of quartz pebbles,[1] that were employed on account of their practical freedom from iron compounds, which if present in more than traces would have produced a green instead of a blue colour. In the original description of this frit factory,[1] 'alkali' merely is referred to, without any statement whether it was potash or soda, there being no evidence on this point, but in a later account Petrie calls it potash,[2] though no proof is given that it was potash, and since soda occurs naturally in Egypt in the form of natron (which contains traces of potash as an impurity), whereas potash would have had to be made from plant ashes, it seems much more likely that soda was used and the few analyses of this frit that have been published in no case show more than a very small proportion, if any, of potash and in one instance a comparatively large proportion of soda. Vitruvius, too, states [3] that the Egyptian blue frit (which he calls *cæruleum* and which he says was invented at Alexandria, though it was known more than 2,000 years before Alexandria was built) was made by fusing together sand, copper filings and natron (*nitri flore*). It will be noticed that Vitruvius makes no mention of calcium carbonate, which was an essential ingredient in the manufacture of the frit, but, like the calcium carbonate required for making glass, this evidently was not recognized as such, and, although it must have been added separately when quartz pebbles were used, this need not have been the case when sand was employed, as much of the Egyptian sand is a mixture of quartz and calcium carbonate. Theophrastus refers to a material that he calls *kyanos*,[4] which he says was invented in Egypt, that was probably this blue frit, and Pliny mentions Egyptian *cæruleum*,[5] which he calls a kind of sand, which was possibly also this frit, though the references to it are somewhat obscure.

The composition of this frit has been investigated by many chemists,[6] the earliest researches, including those of Sir Humphry Davy,[7] dating from the beginning of the last century. Among the most significant of these earlier discussions may be mentioned those of Fouqué [8] and Russell,[9] both of whom succeeded in reproducing specimens of the blue, and that of Spurrell,[10] based on the evidence of frit production discovered at El Amarna. In 1914 Laurie, McLintock and Miles [11] confirmed Fouqué's work, and showed that Egyptian blue could be reproduced by heating together fine sand, copper carbonate, calcium carbonate and fusion mixture (sodium carbonate),

[1] W. M. F. Petrie, *Tell el Amarna*, p. 25.

[2] W. M. F. Petrie, *Arts and Crafts*, p. 117.

[3] VII: II, I.

[4] *On Stones*, XCVIII; cf. J. R. Harris, *Lexicographical Studies*, p. 148.

[5] XXXIII: 57–58; cf. J. R. Harris, *Lexicographical Studies*, p. 149.

[6] Cf. H. Rabaté, 'A propos du "bleu égyptien"', *Peintures, Pigments, Vernis*, XXXIV (1958), pp. 343–5.

[7] H. Davy, *Ann. de Chim.*, XCVI (1815), pp. 72, 193; *Phil. Trans.*, CV (1815), pp. 97–124.

[8] F. Fouqué, *C.R. Ac. Sci.*, CVIII (1889), pp. 325–7; *Bull. Soc. fr. de Minéralogie*, XII (1889), pp. 36–38.

[9] W. J. Russell, in W. M. F. Petrie, *Medum*, pp. 44–48; *Nature*, XLIX (1893–4), pp. 374–5; *Proc. Royal Institution*, XIV (1893–5), pp. 67–71.

[10] F. C. J. Spurrell, *Arch. Journ.*, LII (1895), pp. 232–5.

[11] A. P. Laurie, W. F. P. McLintock and F. D. Miles, *Proc. Royal Society*, LXXXIX (1914), pp. 418–29.

the blue crystals being formed at a temperature around 830° C.–850° C. Similar experiments were repeated by Miss Hodgson,[1] who also produced a frit with the marked pleochroism of the original by substituting salt (sodium chloride) for the fusion mixture and heating at 850° C. A single example of Egyptian blue examined by X-ray powder photography[2] was alleged to owe its colour to copper aluminate $(CuAl_2O_4)$, but more recent investigations have failed to support this. Schippa and Torraca[3] and Nicolini and Santini[4] have examined specimens chemically, microscopically and by X-ray powder photography, and have reproduced frit experimentally at 840° C., paying particular attention to the factors influencing the formation of the blue crystals. The results obtained have in each case tended to confirm the work of Fouqué and of Laurie and his collaborators, though it has not as yet been possible to determine the formula exactly.

The date at which this frit was first used is uncertain, but it has been recorded as early as the Fourth Dynasty by both Spurrell[5] and Laurie,[6] and Smith reports other alleged instances of similar date.[7] Soule identified frit in the Fifth Dynasty tomb of Per-neb,[8] which Mrs. C. R. Williams regards as the earliest certain occurrence,[9] and Laurie notes its use in the Eleventh Dynasty.[10] Spurrell examined frit of the Twelfth[11] and Eighteenth[12] Dynasties, and Russell found it from the Middle and New Kingdoms,[13] as well as from the Ptolemaic period.[14] The blue pigment on the head of Nefertiti is blue frit,[15] and frit is also reported on a wooden figure of Akhenaten[16] and in painting of the Amarna period.[17] Wagenaar identified two blue pigments of late date as frit.[18] I examined thirty specimens of blue colour that proved to be frit[19]

[1] L. Hodgson, *Occasional Papers, Society of Mural Decorators and Painters in Tempera*, III (1936), pp. 36–38.

[2] E. M. Jope and G. Huse, *Nature*, CXLVI (1940), p. 26; in R. Mond and O. H. Myers, *Temples of Armant*, I, p. 202.

[3] G. Schippa and G. Torraca, *Rassegna Chimica*, IX (1957), No. 6, pp. 3–9; *Bollettino del' Istituto centrale del restauro*, XXXI–II (1957), pp. 97–107.

[4] L. Nicolini and M. Santini, *Bollettino del' Istituto centrale del restauro*, XXXIV–V (1958), pp. 59–70.

[5] F. C. J. Spurrell, *Arch. Journ.*, LII (1895), p. 227.

[6] A. P. Laurie, *Archaeologia*, LXIV (1913), p. 317. No specific instance is quoted.

[7] W. S. Smith, *Sculpture and Painting*, p. 256.

[8] C. R. Williams, *Per-nēb*, p. 27, n. 34; cf. M. Toch, *Journ. Ind. and Eng. Chemistry*, X (1918), pp. 118–19.

[9] C. R. Williams, *Per-nēb*, p. 30.

[10] A. P. Laurie, *Materials of the Painter's Craft*, p. 24; *Archaeologia*, LXIV (1913), p. 317.

[11] F. C. J. Spurrell, *Arch. Journ.*, LII (1895), p. 228.

[12] F. C. J. Spurrell, *Arch. Journ.*, LII (1895), pp. 232 f.; in W. M. F. Petrie, *Tell el Amarna*, p. 14. Cf. also A. C. Fryer, *Proc. Clifton Antiquarian Club*, VI (1908), pp. 11–12.

[13] W. J. Russell, in W. M. F. Petrie, *Medum*, pp. 45–46.

[14] W. J. Russell, in W. M. F. Petrie, *Hawara, Biahmu and Arsinoe*, p. 11; in W. M. F. Petrie, *Medum*, p. 48; *Nature*, XLIX (1893–4), pp. 374–5; *Proc. Royal Institution*, XIV (1893–5), pp. 67–71.

[15] L. Borchardt, *Porträts der Königin Nofret-ete*, p. 32.

[16] H. Schäfer, *Z.Ä.S.*, LXX (1934), p. 3.

[17] F. W. von Bissing and M. Reach, *Ann. Serv.*, VII (1906), p. 67; F. W. von Bissing, *Fussboden*, p. 15.

[18] M. Wagenaar, *Pharm. Weekblad*, LXX (1933), pp. 894–902.

[19] A small proportion of colourless (uncombined) quartz was found in every case.

(Fifth Dynasty, four;[1] Sixth Dynasty, two; Thirteenth Dynasty, two; Eighteenth Dynasty, nineteen; Nineteenth Dynasty, two; Twentieth to Twenty-sixth Dynasty, two). What is described as 'a mass of powdered blue crystalline colouring matter' was found by Reisner in the Upper Temple of Menkaurē (Fourth Dynasty), but apparently it was not analysed; it is stated to be 'part of the original funerary equipment' and is described as 'the fine granular blue which is used in the wall paintings of the mastabas'.[2] It seems probable that this was the usual artificial blue frit.

In addition to its use as a pigment, the frit was made into beads, amulets and other small objects, and Miss Hodgson has shown that if powdered very finely and mixed with water it can be moulded, and that the objects when dried and fired retain their shape.[3] Matson points out that specimens have the appearance of devitrified glass, and suggests that they were produced by selecting the clearest pieces from a batch of frit intended for glass, powdering them, making the powder into a paste, perhaps with the addition of a binder, shaping the paste, drying, and firing at a relatively low temperature, thus causing the glassy particles to sinter together and form a solid mass.[4] Beads of blue frit are fairly common and are known from as early as the Fourth Dynasty, while cylinder seals are recorded from the Sixth Dynasty.[5] From the Eighteenth Dynasty onwards small objects of frit become more frequent, notable examples being two small sphinxes of the Eighteenth Dynasty in the Cairo Museum. Frit was used as a blue backing for glass inlay in a bronze figure examined by Gettens,[6] and at a late date it was added in powdered form to fine clay to produce blue or green pottery vessels.[7]

Laurie says of this frit that 'It was used not only in Egypt, but also in Rome in imperial times, as the universal blue for fresco-paintings',[8] and that it 'disappeared from the artist's palette somewhere between the second and the seventh century'.[9] Specimens of this frit found in Italy may be seen in the Naples Museum.

It is stated sometimes that powdered lapis lazuli and even that powdered turquoise were employed as pigments in ancient Egypt, but there is no evidence for the use of either and considerable probability that they were not employed. It is true that an excellent and permanent blue colour, ultramarine, may be obtained from lapis lazuli by a process of levigating the finely powdered material, but the yield is very low, being only about 2 per cent, and there is no proof that this was known until about the beginning of the eleventh century A.D.[10] Much of the ultramarine used at the present day is an artificial product first made in the early nineteenth century. I have proved experimentally that lapis lazuli merely powdered gives a very poor bluish-grey

---

[1] Including the blue colour in the inscriptions in the pyramid of Unis at Saqqara.
[2] G. A. Reisner, *Mycerinus*, pp. 18 (item 53), 237, 238.
[3] L. Hodgson, *Occasional Papers, Society of Mural Decorators and Painters in Tempera*, III (1936), pp. 36–38; H. C. Beck, *Ancient Egypt*, 1934, p. 8.
[4] F. R. Matson, in E. Schmidt, *Persepolis*, II, pp. 133–5.
[5] C. R. Williams, *Per-nēb*, p. 31; S. R. K. Glanville, *J.E.A.*, XIV (1928), p. 190.
[6] E. Riefstahl, *Brooklyn Mus. Journ.*, 1943–4, p. 22.
[7] D. B. Harden, in *History of Technology*, II, pp. 317–18.
[8] A. P. Laurie, *Materials of the Painter's Craft*, p. 24.
[9] A. P. Laurie, *Painter's Methods and Materials*, p. 95.
[10] Cf. R. J. Gettens, *Alumni*, XIX (1950), pp. 342–57.

colour. Turquoise, too, would also make a very poor pigment, and it would have been much too precious for use on the large scale required for tomb painting, even if it could have been obtained in sufficient quantity.

The use of a cobalt pigment was reported by Toch from the Fifth Dynasty tomb of Per-neb,[1] but the accuracy of this was questioned by me many years ago, and it has since been shown by Soule that the blue colour in this tomb is a calcium-copper silicate and not a cobalt blue.[2]

Sometimes Egyptian blue pigments, permanent as they usually are, have undergone a change of colour, thus the trefoil marks on the cow couch from the tomb of Tutankhamūn, although now of a very dark brown, almost black,[3] colour, manifestly were blue originally and still show a little blue underneath the black, and as the material is granular and gives the tests for copper, it may be a deteriorated blue frit. The background of the painting of the cylindrical alabaster 'cosmetic jar' with the recumbent figure of a lion on the lid, from the same tomb, also was blue originally and was still slightly blue in places when first examined.[3] It was not found possible to take any of this pigment for analysis without damaging the object and its nature was not determined. Also in some of the tombs, for example that of Amenhotpe II, the blue colour has darkened in places and has become black or almost black and this does not appear to be due to smoke, which is the usual cause of blackening in tombs.

Brown

The brown pigment used by the Egyptians was generally ochre or iron oxide, specimens of which have been identified from the Fourth Dynasty,[4] the Amarna period[5] and the late period.[6] However, certain brown pigments of Fourth Dynasty date examined by Spurrell were the result of painting a red colour over black,[7] and on the Eleventh Dynasty tomb models from the tomb of Meketrē brown was made by varnishing over a deep yellow ochre.[8] A specimen of brown pigment used for painting a box of Eighteenth Dynasty date examined by me consisted of oxide of iron and gypsum, but whether the mixture was natural or artificial it was impossible to determine, though natural mixtures of this nature are known. A good quality of brown ochre occurs in Dakhla Oasis.[9]

Green[10]

It is generally accepted that the green pigment of the ancient Egyptians owes its colour to copper and two different materials were mainly employed, one being powdered malachite (a natural ore of copper that occurs both in Sinai and in the

[1] M. Toch, *Journ. Ind. and Eng. Chemistry*, X (1918), p. 118.
[2] C. R. Williams, *Per-nēb*, p. 27, n. 34.
[3] Since covered with melted paraffin wax and further darkened.
[4] F. C. J. Spurrell, in W. M. F. Petrie, *Medum*, pp. 28–29.
[5] H. Schäfer, *Z.Ä.S.*, LXX (1934), p. 3; F. W. von Bissing and M. Reach, *Ann. Serv.*, VII (1906), p. 67; F. W. von Bissing, *Fussboden*, p. 15.
[6] M. Wagenaar, *Pharm. Weekblad*, LXX (1933), pp. 894–902.
[7] F. C. J. Spurrell, in W. M. F. Petrie, *Medum*, pp. 28–29.
[8] H. E. Winlock, *Models of Daily Life*, p. 74.
[9] H. J. L. Beadnell, *Dakhla Oasis*, p. 100.
[10] Cf. J. R. Harris, *Lexicographical Studies*, pp. 143–5, 152–3, also 117–18.

eastern desert), which was used for painting round the eyes as early as the Badarian and earliest predynastic periods [1] and the other an artificial frit analogous to the blue frit already considered. A green colour of predynastic date is described as being 'bright green, granular in structure, probably pounded malachite'.[2] Spurrell records the use of malachite, malachite and gypsum, and malachite over yellow in tomb paintings of the Fourth Dynasty,[3] and in paintings of the Middle [4] and New Kingdoms [5] he found both malachite and chrysocolla (another natural ore of copper), the former predominating. Soule identified the green colour from the Fifth Dynasty tomb of Per-neb as malachite,[6] Eibner notes the use of malachite over white in several instances,[7] and Wagenaar found both malachite and green frit among pigments of late date.[8] I found malachite in a Fifth Dynasty tomb painting at Giza and the green on two boats from the tomb of Tutankhamūn was not frit and may have been malachite, but the green colour in a Sixth Dynasty tomb was frit, as also were six specimens from the Eighteenth Dynasty, one from the Nineteenth Dynasty and one from the period Twentieth to the Twenty-sixth Dynasty. Russell identified frit from the Middle and New Kingdoms,[9] and Spurrell from the Amarna period.[10] Borchardt reports frit on the head of Nefertiti,[11] and Eibner mentions frit of Eighteenth Dynasty date.[12] A green coloured plaster from a stick of Eighteenth Dynasty date was found to owe its colour to a mixture of blue frit and a yellow colour that was not identified, but which was not yellow ochre and which was probably an organic material. Spurrell, who examined the pigments from certain Twelfth Dynasty tombs at El Bersheh for Newberry, stated that the green was chrysocolla in some instances and a mixture of blue frit and yellow ochre in others,[13] and von Bissing and Reach concluded that a green of the Amarna period might be a mixture of blue frit and ochre.[14] Layard states that the Egyptian green was 'a mixture of yellow ochre with the vitreous blue'.[15] A green examined by John was reported to consist of blue frit mixed with a vegetable yellow.[16]

---

[1] See p. 80.

[2] J. E. Quibell and F. W. Green, *Hierakonpolis*, II, p. 21.

[3] F. C. J. Spurrell, in W. M. F. Petrie, *Medum*, p. 29; *Arch. Journ.*, LII (1895), p. 227.

[4] F. C. J. Spurrell, *Arch. Journ.*, LII (1895), p. 227.

[5] F. C. J. Spurrell, *Arch. Journ.*, LII (1895), pp. 232–3. Cf. also A. C. Fryer, *Proc. Clifton Antiquarian Club*, VI (1908), pp. 11–12 (malachite).

[6] C. R. Williams, *Per-nēb*, p. 26, *n.* 24; cf. M. Toch, *Journ. Ind. and Eng. Chemistry*, X (1918), pp. 118–19.

[7] A. Eibner, *Entwicklung und Werkstoffe der Wandmalerei*, pp. 54, 55, 581, 586.

[8] M. Wagenaar, *Pharm. Weekblad*, LXX (1933), pp. 894–902.

[9] W. J. Russell, in W. M. F. Petrie, *Medum*, p. 46; *Nature*, XLIX (1893–4), pp. 374–5; *Proc. Royal Institution*, XIV (1893–5), pp. 67–71.

[10] F. C. J. Spurrell, *Arch. Journ.*, LII (1895), p. 234; in W. M. F. Petrie, *Tell el Amarna*, p. 14.

[11] L. Borchardt, *Porträts der Königin Nofret-ete*, p. 32.

[12] A. Eibner, *Entwicklung und Werkstoffe der Wandmalerei*, pp. 582–3.

[13] Letter dated March 26th, 1892, from Mr. Spurrell to Prof. Newberry, who kindly allowed me to make use of it.

[14] F. W. von Bissing and M. Reach, *Ann. Serv.*, VII (1906), p. 67; F. W. von Bissing, *Fussboden*, p. 15.

[15] A. H. Layard, *Niniveh*, II, p. 310.

[16] H. v. Minutoli, *Reise zum Tempel des Jupiter Ammon*, p. 332.

Grey

The ancient Egyptian grey pigment was generally a mixture of black and white, that in the Fifth Dynasty tomb of Per-neb being a mixture of gypsum and charcoal.[1] Spurrell found grey pigments from the Fourth Dynasty to consist of gypsum and lamp black and of a mixture of pale yellowish earth and lamp black.[2] Reisner notes that at Kerma a grey pottery pigment was produced from a sandy stone.[3]

Orange

Orange was generally produced by painting red over yellow, or by mixing red and yellow ochres.[4]

Pink

A pink colour was not uncommon in the New Kingdom, thus it is recorded from the tomb of Amenemhet (Eighteenth Dynasty) [5] and from the tomb of Menkheper-rasonb,[6] and I have noticed it in the tomb of Nofretiri (Nineteenth Dynasty) where it was used to a considerable extent. Glanville states [7] that 'in the New Kingdom pink colour was regularly obtained by simply mixing red and white', but no reference is given to any analysis. Spurrell, however, found pink of the Old [8] and New Kingdoms [9] to be a mixture of ochre and gypsum, and Borchardt reports that the flesh colour of the head of Nefertiti was also gypsum and ochre.[10] A pink colour from a tomb painting of the Graeco-Roman period was identified by Russell as consisting of madder (obtained from the roots of the madder plant, a native of Greece, often called Turkey red) on a base of gypsum [11] and a similar shade of colour, probably of the same composition, is sometimes present on coffins of this period. It seems likely that this madder colour was introduced into Egypt by either the Greeks or the Romans, as the former probably knew it and the latter certainly did, since there are specimens of it in the Naples Museum. A pink colour of late date examined by Wagenaar was identified as finely powdered shell of a natural red colour,[12] but this result requires confirmation.

Red [13]

The principal red pigments of ancient Egypt, and perhaps the only ones until a relatively late date, were the natural oxides of iron that occur plentifully in the

---

[1] C. R. Williams, *Per-nēb*, p. 25, n. 19; cf. M. Toch, *Journ. Ind. and Eng. Chemistry*, x (1918), pp. 118–19.

[2] F. C. J. Spurrell, in W. M. F. Petrie, *Medum*, pp. 28–29.

[3] G. A. Reisner, *Kerma*, iv–v, pp. 293–4.

[4] F. C. J. Spurrell, in W. M. F. Petrie, *Medum*, p. 28; W. J. Russell, *Nature*, xlix (1893–4), pp. 374–5; *Proc. Royal Institution*, xiv (1893–5), pp. 67–71.

[5] N. de G. Davies and A. H. Gardiner, *Amenemhet*, p. 98.

[6] N. de G. Davies, *Menkheperrasonb*, p. 25.

[7] S. R. K. Glanville, *J.E.A.*, xiv (1928), p. 190.

[8] F. C. J. Spurrell, in W. M. F. Petrie, *Medum*, p. 29.

[9] F. C. J. Spurrell, *Arch. Journ.*, lii (1895), p. 231.

[10] L. Borchardt, *Porträts der Königin Nofret-ete*, p. 32.

[11] W. J. Russell, in W. M. F. Petrie, *Hawara, Biahmu and Arsinoe*, p. 11; in W. M. F. Petrie, *Medum*, p. 47; *Nature*, xlix (1893–4), pp. 374–5; *Proc. Royal Institution*, xiv (1893–5), pp. 67–71.

[12] M. Wagenaar, *Pharm. Weekblad*, lxx (1933), pp. 894–902.

[13] Cf. J. R. Harris, *Lexicographical Studies*, pp. 141–2, 145–7, 150–2, 154–7.

country. These are of two main types, red iron oxides (anhydrous oxides of iron) and red ochres (hydrated oxides of iron),[1] which should be distinguished, though the terms are inexorably confused in archaeological literature, and are moreover loosely applied to certain clays and earths containing only a very small percentage of colouring matter. Red iron oxides and red ochres are also sometimes called haematite, and although this is strictly correct in that they are amorphous earthy varieties of the material, it would be better to restrict the term haematite in Egyptology to the black metallic-looking mineral employed for carving into beads, *kohl* sticks, scarabs and other small objects.

Several red pigments of predynastic date identified as red ochre are known,[2] and the reddish colours on the predynastic pottery have also been identified as red ochre.[3] Spurrell found red iron oxide (which he calls red haematite) and also red ochreous clays mixed with fibrous gypsum and some darkened by the presence of manganese from the Fourth Dynasty,[4] and red iron oxides, red ochre and burnt yellow ochre from both the Twelfth Dynasty [5] and the Eighteenth Dynasty.[6] Russell found red iron oxide from the Twelfth and also from the Eighteenth or Nineteenth Dynasty,[7] and red ochre like burnt sienna, which he thinks was probably burnt yellow ochre, from the Ptolemaic period.[8] Toch identified red iron oxide from the tomb of Per-neb (Fifth Dynasty)[9], iron oxide mixed with an earthy substance has been reported on an Eleventh Dynasty stela in Cracow,[10] and red iron oxide was also identified on a wooden figure of Akhenaten [11] and in painting of the Amarna period.[12] Two red pigments of late date examined by Wagenaar were found to be red ochre.[13] I identified both red ochre and red ochre mixed with gypsum from the Sixth Dynasty; ten specimens of red ochre and one of red ochre mixed with gypsum from the Eighteenth Dynasty; one specimen of red ochre from the Nineteenth Dynasty and two from the period Twentieth to Twenty-sixth Dynasty. The Egyptian earths, *sinopis* and *rubrica*, referred to by Pliny as being employed by the Romans for pigment purposes,[14] were almost certainly red ochre.[15] Vitruvius mentions red ochre

---

[1] Mines and Quarries Dept., *Report on the Mineral Industry*, p. 32; N. Heaton, *Outlines of Paint Technology* (3rd ed. 1947), pp. 109–10. Red ochres vary widely in composition, the iron oxide content ranging from 15 to 50 per cent.

[2] J. E. Quibell and F. W. Green, *Hierakonpolis*, II, p. 21; R. Mond and O. H. Myers, *Cemeteries of Armant*, I, p. 131; G. Brunton, *Mostagedda*, p. 57.

[3] P. D. Ritchie, in R. Mond and O. H. Myers, *Cemeteries of Armant*, I, pp. 181–5; *Technical Studies*, IV (1936), pp. 234–6.

[4] F. C. J. Spurrell, in W. M. F. Petrie, *Medum*, pp. 28–29; *Arch. Journ.*, LII (1895), p. 226.

[5] F. C. J. Spurrell, *Arch. Journ.*, LII (1895), p. 227.

[6] F. C. J. Spurrell, *Arch. Journ.*, LII (1895), p. 231; in W. M. F. Petrie, *Tell el Amarna*, p. 14. Cf. also A. C. Fryer, *Proc. Clifton Antiquarian Club*, VI (1908), pp. 11–12 (haematite).

[7] W. J. Russell, in W. M. F. Petrie, *Medum*, p. 44.

[8] W. J. Russell, in W. M. F. Petrie, *Hawara, Biahmu and Arsinoe*, p. 11; in W. M. F. Petrie, *Medum*, p. 47; *Nature*, XLIX (1893–4), pp. 374–5; *Proc. Royal Institution*, XIV (1893–5), pp. 67–71.

[9] M. Toch, *Journ. Ind. and Eng. Chemistry*, X (1918), pp. 118–19.   [11] H. Schäfer, *Z.Ä.S.*, LXX (1934), p. 3.

[10] J. Černý, *J.E.A.*, XLVII (1961), p. 9.

[12] F. W. von Bissing and M. Reach, *Ann. Serv.*, VII (1906), p. 67; F. W. von Bissing, *Fussboden*, p. 15.

[13] M. Wagenaar, *Pharm. Weekblad*, LXX (1933), pp. 894–902.

[14] XXXV: 13–15.   [15] Cf. J. R. Harris, *Lexicographical Studies*, pp. 161–2.

from Egypt,[1] and Dioscorides says that the best red ochre was the Egyptian.[2]

The usual manner of making red ochre in Europe before the modern methods of manufacture from various by-products were introduced was by calcining yellow ochre,[3] and though in any locality in Egypt in which yellow, but not red, ochre occurred the latter might have been made from the former by heating it, this was certainly not usual, the red ochre used being generally the material as found naturally. There is no justification whatsoever for Toch's statement [4] that all Egyptian red ochre was produced from yellow ochre, and what evidence Spurrell and Russell had for calling some of the red ochre they examined burnt yellow ochre is not clear. It is impossible as a rule to distinguish one from the other, especially when dealing with a very small quantity of pigment scraped from an ancient object. A good quality ochre of a deep-red shade is found in several localities in Egypt, of which two may be mentioned, one near Aswan,[5] where it was worked anciently, and the other in the oases of the western desert.[6] A number of instances are recorded in Egypt in which yellow ochre on a tomb wall has been changed to red by the heat produced from a fire in the tomb.

A red pigment used for painting and on pottery at Kerma is stated by Reisner to have been obtained from sandstone,[7] and a red pigment of Graeco-Roman date from Hawara was identified by Russell as red lead [8] (a red oxide of lead that occurs naturally), one of the few instances which has been reported from Egypt, though it was well known to the Romans of Pliny's day and probably was introduced by them into Egypt.

Recently, Iversen [9] has pointed out that certain Egyptian pigment lists provide evidence of the use of realgar, the red sulphide of arsenic, during the New Kingdom, though as yet this has not been directly confirmed by analysis. Spurrell, however, mentions the use of realgar ground together with orpiment,[10] and among the 'fards' examined by Barthoux was one composed of orpiment and realgar.[11] A piece of orpiment streaked with realgar was found by Petrie at Tanis,[12] and realgar is reputed to occur on St. John's Island in the Red Sea.[13]

White

The use of white pigment for mural painting is known from the predynastic

---

[1] VII: 7, 2.   [2] V: 112.

[3] The change of colour on heating is due to the conversion of iron oxide to the anhydrous condition.

[4] M. Toch, *Journ. Ind. and Eng. Chemistry*, X (1918), pp. 118–19.

[5] L. Nassim, *Minerals of Economical Interest*, p. 164.

[6] W. F. Hume, *Explan. Notes to the Geol. Map of Egypt*, p. 38; *Geology of Egypt*, I, p. 209; H. J. L. Beadnell, *Dakhla Oasis*, pp. 99–100.

[7] G. A. Reisner, *Kerma*, IV–V, pp. 291–2.

[8] W. J. Russell, in W. M. F. Petrie, *Hawara, Biahmu and Arsinoe*, p. 11; in W. M. F. Petrie, *Medum*, pp. 44–48.

[9] E. Iversen, *Some Ancient Egyptian Paints and Pigments*, pp. 39–42. Cf. also J. R. Harris, *Lexicographical Studies*, pp. 141–2.

[10] F. C. J. Spurrell, *Arch. Journ.*, LII (1895), p. 232.

[11] J. Barthoux, 'Les fards, pommades et couleurs dans l'antiquité', *Congres Int. de Géog., Le Caire, Avril 1925*, IV (1926), pp. 251–67.

[12] W. M. F. Petrie, *Tanis*, I, p. 39.   [13] J. Barthoux, *loc. cit.*; Pliny, XXXV: 22.

period,[1] but the nature of the material then employed has not been determined, though it must have been either calcium carbonate (whiting, chalk), or calcium sulphate (gypsum), as these were the only two white pigments known. Ritchie describes the pigment used on predynastic pottery as a white calciferous clay,[2] and pure calcium carbonate was identified on an Eleventh Dynasty stela in Cracow.[3] Spurrell found gypsum from the Fourth Dynasty [4] and from the Eighteenth Dynasty,[5] and calcium carbonate from the Twelfth Dynasty at El Bersheh.[6] Borchardt reports calcium carbonate on the head of Nefertiti,[7] and both chalk and gypsum are said to have been used on a wooden figure of Akhenaten.[8] Russell found gypsum from the Graeco-Roman period at Hawara.[9] I identified calcium carbonate from the Fifth Dynasty; calcium sulphate from the Sixth Dynasty; twelve specimens of calcium carbonate and two of calcium sulphate from the Eighteenth Dynasty and calcium carbonate from the Twenty-third Dynasty. Both calcium carbonate and calcium sulphate occur plentifully in the country. A white pigment of late date examined by Wagenaar was identified as powdered shell or cuttle-fish bone,[10] but this result requires confirmation.

Yellow [11]

Two different yellow pigments were employed by the ancient Egyptians, one being yellow ochre, which occurs plentifully in the country and the colouring matter of which is due to hydrated oxide of iron, and the other being orpiment, a natural sulphide of arsenic. Yellow ochre was used in predynastic times [12] and has been identified by Ritchie on pottery of that date.[13] Spurrell found yellow ochre from the Fourth,[14] Twelfth [15] and Eighteenth [16] Dynasties respectively, Toch identified it from the Fifth Dynasty,[17] and von Bissing and Reach from the Amarna period.[18] Russell

---

[1] J. E. Quibell and F. W. Green, *Hierakonpolis*, II, p. 21.

[2] P. D. Ritchie, in R. Mond and O. H. Myers, *Cemeteries of Armant*, I, pp. 181–5; *Technical Studies*, IV (1936), pp. 234–6.

[3] J. Černý, *J.E.A.*, XLVII (1961), p. 9.

[4] F. C. J. Spurrell, in W. M. F. Petrie, *Medum*, pp. 28–29; *Arch. Journ.*, LII (1895), p. 226.

[5] F. C. J. Spurrell, *Arch. Journ.*, LII (1895), p. 232. Cf. also A. C. Fryer, *Proc. Clifton Antiquarian Club*, VI (1908), pp. 11–12.

[6] Letter dated March 26th, 1892, from Mr. Spurrell to Prof. Newberry, who kindly allowed me to make use of it.

[7] L. Borchardt, *Porträts der Königin Nofret-ete*, p. 32.   [8] H. Schäfer, *Z.Ä.S.*, LXX (1934), p. 3.

[9] W. J. Russell, in W. M. F. Petrie, *Hawara, Biahmu and Arsinoe*, p. 11; in W. M. F. Petrie, *Medum*, pp. 44–48.

[10] M. Wagenaar, *Pharm. Weekblad*, LXX (1933), pp. 894–902.

[11] Cf. J. R. Harris, *Lexicographical Studies*, pp. 150–2, 153–4.

[12] J. E. Quibell and F. W. Green, *Hierakonpolis*, II, p. 21.

[13] P. D. Ritchie, in R. Mond and O. H. Myers, *Cemeteries of Armant*, I, pp. 181–5; *Technical Studies*, IV (1936), pp. 234–6.

[14] F. C. J. Spurrell, in W. M. F. Petrie, *Medum*, pp. 28–29; *Arch. Journ.*, LII (1895), p. 226.

[15] F. C. J. Spurrell, *Arch. Journ.*, LII (1895), p. 227.

[16] F. C. J. Spurrell, *Arch. Journ.*, LII (1895), p. 231; in W. M. F. Petrie, *Tell el Amarna*, p. 14. Cf. also A. C. Fryer, *Proc. Clifton Antiquarian Club*, VI (1908), pp. 11–12.

[17] M. Toch, *Journ. Ind. and Eng. Chemistry*, X (1918), pp. 118–19.

[18] F. W. von Bissing and M. Reach, *Ann. Serv.*, VII (1906), p. 67; F. W. von Bissing, *Fussboden*, p. 15.

reports ochre from the New Kingdom [1] and Ptolemaic period,[2] and I found that three specimens of yellow pigment from the Eighteenth Dynasty, one from the Nineteenth, and two from the period Twentieth to Twenty-sixth Dynasty were ochre. Certain tombs of the New Kingdom at Deir el Medineh have monochrome decoration in yellow ochre,[3] and Bruyère notes the use of yellow ochre varnished to simulate gold.[4] Yellow ochre occurs near Cairo [5] and in the oases of the western desert.[6]

So far as can be ascertained, orpiment was not used until the latter half of the Eighteenth Dynasty. It was found by Spurrell in painting of the Amarna period,[7] and is reported by Borchardt on the head of Nefertiti,[8] and by Schäfer on a wooden figure of Akhenaten.[9] Mackay refers to the use of orpiment in certain tombs in the Theban necropolis,[10] eight specimens of yellow pigment from the Eighteenth Dynasty examined by me were found to be orpiment, and its use is also recorded by Russell.[11]

At one time orpiment, originally the naturally occurring mineral and afterwards an artificial product, was largely employed as a pigment in Europe, but its use was discontinued on account of the very poisonous nature of the artificial substance. The natural mineral, however, is not poisonous and it was this that was used in ancient Egypt. In addition to its identification as a pigment on various objects and mural paintings a small quantity of the mineral in its natural state was found in a linen bag in the tomb of Tutankhamūn and was examined by me.[12] Petrie found a little orpiment on the town site of Gurob, probably of late Eighteenth or Nineteenth Dynasty date,[13] and a large piece of laminated orpiment of Ptolemaic or Roman date was found at Tanis.[14] So far as is known, orpiment does not occur in Egypt, though Couyat refers to a specimen of orpiment reputedly from Kharga oasis,[15] and elsewhere suggests that orpiment may have come from St. John's Island in the Red Sea.[16] It is more probable, however, that orpiment was imported from Persia, though it also occurs in Armenia and Asia Minor.

Other yellow pigments apart from ochre and orpiment have also been recorded. Thus Reisner mentions a yellow derived from sandstone used at Kerma (Middle Kingdom),[17] massicot, a yellow oxide of lead, was found on a palette of about 400

---

[1] W. J. Russell, in W. M. F. Petrie, *Medum*, p. 44.

[2] W. J. Russell, in W. M. F. Petrie, *Hawara, Biahmu and Arsinoe*, p. 11; in W. M. F. Petrie, *Medum*, p. 47; *Nature*, XLIX (1893–4), pp. 374–5; *Proc. Royal Institution*, XIV (1893–5), pp. 67–71.

[3] B. Bruyère, *Tombes à décor monochrome*, pp. 9–10.

[4] B. Bruyère, *op. cit.*, p. 9.

[5] L. Nassim, *Minerals of Economical Interest*, p. 165.

[6] W. F. Hume, *Explan. Notes to the Geol. Map of Egypt*, p. 38; *Geology of Egypt*, I, p. 209.

[7] F. C. J. Spurrell, *Arch. Journ.*, LII (1895), pp. 231–2.

[8] L. Borchardt, *Porträts der Königin Nofret-ete*, p. 32.

[9] H. Schäfer, *Z.Ä.S.*, LXX (1934), p. 3.   [10] E. Mackay, *Ancient Egypt*, 1920, p. 37.

[11] W. J. Russell, *Nature*, XLIX (1893–4), pp. 374–5; *Proc. Royal Institution*, XIV (1893–5), pp. 67–71.

[12] A. Lucas, in H. Carter, *Tut-ankh-Amen*, III, p. 177 (Appendix II).

[13] W. M. F. Petrie, *Kahun, Gurob and Hawara*, p. 38.

[14] W. M. F. Petrie, *Tanis*, I, p. 39.

[15] J. Couyat, *Bull. Soc. fr. de Minéralogie*, XXXI (1908), p. 348.

[16] J. Barthoux, Les fards pommades et couleurs dans l'antiquité, *Congrès Int. de Géog., Le Caire, Avril 1925*, IV (1926), pp. 251–67.

[17] G. A. Reisner, *Kerma*, IV–V, pp. 292–3.

B.C.,[1] and vegetal yellows were identified by John.[2] The yellow pigment on an Eleventh Dynasty stela in Cracow was found to be powdered calcium carbonate coloured yellow with an organic substance,[3] and an intense yellow of late date examined by Wagenaar was determined as ochre with traces of some organic material.[4]

Paint Brushes

These have already been described in connexion with Fibres.[5]

Palettes

These are described below in connexion with Writing Materials.[6]

Paint Vehicles

Much discussion has taken place respecting the nature of the paint vehicles employed in ancient Egypt. The colours used, which have just been described, were ordinary well-known materials, but in what state were they applied?

In modern painting practice there are two principal vehicles, one being a mixture of a fixed oil that dries (i.e. oxidizes) on exposure to the air (usually linseed oil, though formerly sometimes poppy seed oil or walnut oil) and a volatile oil (generally oil of turpentine, though recently sometimes a light petroleum spirit) and the other being a mixture of water and some adhesive, often size (gelatine or glue) or gum. Paints of the first kind are oil paints and those of the second kind are tempera paints (distempers).

It is clear on examination that the ancient Egyptian paintings are not oil paintings, but tempera paintings.[7] Although linseed oil was probably known in Egypt from a very early date it was not used for painting until late, probably not until about the sixth century A.D. or after. Oil of turpentine, too, although certainly known in Pliny's day, since he describes a method of making the crude product,[8] and also probably to the Greeks at an earlier period,[9] was not employed for painting at that time, and petroleum spirit is entirely a modern product.

The ancient Egyptian painting being tempera painting, it follows that some adhesive was used in its production, in the same manner as size and gum are employed today, since although pigments, such as soot and red and yellow ochres, will adhere to plaster and stone to some extent if applied dry, and although the ochres will adhere still better if wetted, others of the ancient pigments, such as azurite, malachite and the blue and green frits, will not normally adhere without some binding material.[10]

---

[1] A. P. Laurie, *Archaeologia*, LXIV (1913), pp. 318–19.

[2] H. v. Minutoli, *Reise zum Tempel des Jupiter Ammon*, pp. 335–6.

[3] J. Černý, *J.E.A.*, XLVII (1961), p. 9.

[4] M. Wagenaar, *Pharm. Weekblad*, LXX (1933), pp. 894–902.

[5] See pp. 133–4.

[6] See p. 366.

[7] Excluding painting executed with a wax medium which will be described separately; see pp. 352–3.

[8] XV: 7.

[9] A. Lucas, *J.E.A.*, XVII (1931), p. 16.

[10] Mrs. C. R. Williams states that in the tomb of Per-neb malachite and frit were simply embedded in a thick layer of plaster (C. R. Williams, *Per-nēb*, p. 33).

The possible and likely materials to have been used seem to be limited to size (gelatine, glue), gum, and albumin (white of egg), which have already been discussed.[1]

One material used in Egypt for painting and for coating paintings, about which there is no uncertainty, is beeswax. Its use for mural paintings seems first to have been pointed out by Mackay,[2] who mentions eight Eighteenth Dynasty tombs in the Theban necropolis in which there is evidence of wax, these ranging in date from the time of Amenhotpe I to that of Amenhotpe II. Although in some instances the wax is intimately mixed with the pigment, as though used as a binder, in other instances apparently it has been applied to the surface of the finished painting as a protective coating. Eibner[3] refers to the use of wax varnish in the tomb of Seti I, stating that the colour was mixed in a little, and Petrie mentions the use of wax[4] 'as a filling of the hieroglyphs on the red granite coffin of Ramessu III in the Louvre; also in incised figures on the wooden coffins'. He also states[4] that 'The use of wax over colours was noted on the late sarcophagus of Ankhrui at Hawara.' The use of wax in the Eighteenth Dynasty was noticed by Spurrell, who found it on a pavement from El Amarna,[5] and by Davies, who says with respect to the mural paintings in the tomb of Puyemrē, 'A film of wax seems present on many figures, but whether this was a medium used with the colours or was applied afterwards is not clear.'[6] Wax was used as a binder for the charcoal black pigment on the head of Nefertiti,[7] and I found one instance of the use of wax in the tomb of Tutankhamūn, where there was a wooden box having an incised inscription filled with yellow pigment (orpiment) that was coated with beeswax, which had deteriorated, causing the pigment to appear almost white.[8] A similar use of beeswax, which had become 'whitish' on a wooden coffin of late date has been pointed out by Carter.[9] Spurrell states that frit and powdered malachite were mixed with wax on pottery and woodwork,[10] and the occurrence of wax as a binder for malachite is also mentioned by Eibner.[11]

The use of wax as a medium for painting was well known to the Romans and is described by Pliny,[12] whose account of the method of 'encaustic' painting has been studied in detail by Laurie[13] and others.[14] Many portraits in this technique, dating

---

[1] See pp. 3–5, 5–6, 1–2. For a single reported instance of the use of resin as a binding material, see p. 8.

[2] E. Mackay, *Ancient Egypt*, 1920, pp. 35–38.

[3] A. Eibner, *Entwicklung und Werkstoffe der Wandmalerei*, pp. 583–5.

[4] W. M. F. Petrie, *Ancient Egypt*, 1920, p. 38.

[5] F. C. J. Spurrell, *Arch. Journ.*, LII (1895), p. 239.

[6] N. de G. Davies, *Puyemrê*, I, p. 11.

[7] L. Borchardt, *Porträts der Königin Nofret-ete*, p. 32.

[8] A. Lucas, in H. Carter, *Tut-ankh-Amen*, II, p. 180 (Appendix II).

[9] H. Carter, *Ann. Serv.*, II (1901), p. 144.

[10] F. C. J. Spurrell, *Arch. Journ.*, LII (1895), p. 239.

[11] A. Eibner, *Entwicklung und Werkstoffe der Wandmalerei*, pp. 54–55.

[12] XXXV: 31, 39, 41.

[13] A. P. Laurie, *Greek and Roman Methods of Painting*, pp. 54–68.

[14] H. Cros and C. Henry, *l'Encaustique*, pp. 1–6; O. Donner von Richter, *Über Technisches in der Malerei der Alten, inbesonders in deren Enkaustik*, passim; E. Berger, *Die Maltechnik des Altertums*, pp. 185–96; H. Schmid, *Enkaustik und Fresko auf antiker Grundlage*, pp. 82–90; A. Eibner, *Entwicklung und Werkstoffe der Wandmalerei*, pp. 77–102; C. Lüdecke, *Fette, Seifen, Anstrichmittel*, LXIII (1961), pp. 38–41.

from the Roman period (principally second and third centuries A.D.), mostly on wood, but a few on canvas, used to place over the faces of mummies, have been found in the Fayum province of Egypt.[1] That the medium of these portraits is basically beeswax can scarcely be doubted,[2] though the fact that the melting temperature of most specimens examined is considerably higher than that of crude beeswax has given rise to some discussion. Experiments have shown that the melting temperature of beeswax can be raised slightly by a process of purification akin to that described by Pliny for the making of 'Punic wax', and that it can be further raised by the addition of pigment, though even then it is not as high as that recorded for some of the ancient specimens. Whether this discrepancy is due to the addition of some other substance such as resin, or to the oxidation of some of the low-melting-point constituents of the beeswax has not yet been determined, though the latter seems somewhat improbable.[3] The methods employed in the actual execution of the Fayum portraits have been outlined by Petrie [4] and others.[5] A bowl of late date, probably Coptic, with polychrome designs in the encaustic technique is described by Edgar, who states that 'The colours have been mixed with wax and put on with the brush'.[6]

Painting Grounds

The principal materials used in ancient Egypt for painting upon, taking them in alphabetical order, were canvas, papyrus, plaster, pottery, stone and wood. Of these, the earliest to be used was pottery, and this painted pottery will be dealt with separately.[7]

The next material in chronological order was plaster, of which several kinds were employed, namely, clay, gypsum and whiting (chalk). The earliest mural painting known in Egypt, which is of predynastic date, is executed directly on clay plaster [8]

[1] Cf. P. Buberl, *Die Griechisch-Ägyptischen Mumienbildnisse der Sammlung Th. Graf.;* E. Coche de la Ferté, *Les Portraits Romano-Égyptiens du Louvre*; G. Ebers, *Antike Portraits: Die Hellenistischen Bildnisse aus dem Fajjûm*; C. C. Edgar, *Graeco-Egyptian Coffins, Masks and Portraits*; Th. Graf, *Katalog zu Th. Graf's Galerie antiker Porträts aus Hellenistischer Zeit*; W. M. F. Petrie, *Roman Portraits and Memphis*, IV; *The Hawara Portfolio: Paintings of the Roman Age*; A. Strelkov, *Fajjumskij Portret*; H. Zaloscer, *Porträts aus dem Wüstensand.*

[2] Cf. H. Kühn, *Studies in Conservation*, V (1960), pp. 71–81; E. Coche de la Ferté, *Les Portraits Romano-Égyptiens du Louvre*, p. 23.

[3] Cf. G. L. Stout, *Technical Studies*, I (1932), pp. 82–93; E. Dow, *Technical Studies*, V (1936), pp. 3–17; A. P. Laurie, *Technical Studies*, VI (1937), pp. 17–18; C. L. Burdick, *Technical Studies*, VI (1937), pp. 183–5.

[4] W. M. F. Petrie, *Hawara, Biahmu and Arsinoe*, pp. 18–19; *Man*, XI (1911), pp. 145–7; *Roman Portraits and Memphis*, IV, pp. 9–11.

[5] E. Coche de la Ferté, *Les Portraits Romano-Égyptiens du Louvre*, pp. 11–12; *Bull. Soc. fr. d'Égyptologie*, XIII (June 1953), pp. 69–78; C. C. Edgar, *Graeco-Egyptian Coffins, Masks and Portraits*, pp. xii–xiii; A. P. Laurie, *Technical Studies*, VI (1937), pp. 17–18; A. M. Lythgoe, *M.M.A. Bull.*, V (1910), pp. 67–72; G. L. Stout, *Technical Studies*, I (1932), pp. 82–93; A. Strelkov, *Fajjumskij Portret*, pp. 77–92; M. H. Swindler, *Ancient Painting*, pp. 320–4; H. Zaloscer, *Porträts aus dem Wüstensand*, pp. 19–23.

[6] C. C. Edgar, *Greek Vases*, No. 26347, p. 81.

[7] See pp. 382–4.

[8] J. E. Quibell and F. W. Green, *Hierakonpolis*, II, p. 21.

and this was also used as a painting ground at later periods, particularly in the Eighteenth Dynasty at El Amarna, where, both in the palaces of the king and also in private houses, the most beautiful painting was done directly on the clay plaster with which the walls of the sun-dried bricks were faced. The usual Egyptian plaster for painting upon, however, was either gypsum or whiting, the former being employed largely for mural paintings and the latter being used chiefly as a covering for wooden objects, such as coffins, boxes and stelae, which subsequently were to be painted.

Gypsum plaster has already been considered:[1] a comparatively coarse quality was used for covering up faults and irregularities in the stone wall that was to be sculptured or painted or both and on this was laid a finer quality of similar plaster in order to obtain a smooth surface, this latter often being coated with whitewash to fill up the pores before painting.

Whiting plaster also has been briefly mentioned,[2] but may further be considered. This plaster, which is a mixture of whiting and glue, is generally called 'gesso' by Egyptologists, but the term is ambiguous and is used sometimes for gypsum plaster or for gypsum and glue plaster. In medieval Italy and Spain, gypsum mixed with glue water (size) was employed by artists to produce a ground for painting upon, which was termed *gesso*, an Italianized form of the Latin word *gypsum*, which is derived from the Greek γύψος. The term *gesso* in Italian, however, may mean any kind of gypsum or gypsum plaster. According to Cennino Cennini (fifteenth century)[3] gesso was of two kinds, *gesso grosso*, which was unslaked gypsum, and *gesso sottile*, which was slaked gypsum, both being used with glue. Theophilus, writing about the eleventh or twelfth century,[4] refers to the use of both slaked lime and glue and whiting and glue for coating skins as a ground for painting upon and Church states [5] that 'The ordinary ground for Italian and Spanish tempera-paintings consisted either of whitening and size or of burnt gypsum . . . mixed with size.' This use of two different materials for the same purpose and the application of the same name to both is very confusing. Even *The New English Dictionary* gives the meaning of the Greek word γύψος as 'chalk, gypsum' as though these were synonymous, whereas they are two entirely different materials, and Church writes,[6] 'Gesso, made of plaster of Paris and size, or of whitening and size . . .' Laurie [7] mentions instances of painting on gesso, and an outstanding example is the casket found in the tomb of Tutankhamūn, which is a very ordinary wooden box coated on the outside with whiting plaster, on the surface of which, exquisitely painted in colours, are miniature battle and hunting scenes.[8]

Stone was often painted or colour-washed, not only the stone walls of tombs and temples, but also stone statues, statuettes, sarcophagi and other objects, especially, though not exclusively, those of limestone and sandstone, other stones, however, in-

---

[1] See pp. 76–79.
[2] See p. 76.
[3] A. P. Laurie, *Materials of the Painter's Craft*, pp. 189–92.
[4] A. P. Laurie, *Materials of the Painter's Craft*, pp. 157, 159–60.
[5] A. H. Church, *Chemistry of Paints and Painting*, 1915, pp. 22–23.
[6] A. H. Church, *Chemistry of Paints and Painting*, p. 32.
[7] A. P. Laurie, *Materials of the Painter's Craft*, pp. 26–28.
[8] H. Carter, *Tut-ankh-Amen*, I, pp. 110, 111, Pls. XXI, L–LIV.

cluding granite, alabaster, quartzite and schist [1] also sometimes being painted. Before painting the scenes on the walls of tombs and temples a thin coat of whitewash was often, though not always, applied to the stone,[2] thus with respect to the painting of the walls of the temple of Medinet Habu, Nelson says, 'As the sandstone was too rough to take paint satisfactorily, a thin wash was applied to the stone before the colour was laid on.' [3]

The use of papyrus for painting upon is so well known that no description is necessary.

Canvas as a painting ground has been referred to already in connexion with the portraits of Roman date found by Petrie in the Fayum,[4] some few of which are on this material. Other examples of painted canvas are the so-called 'painted handker-chief' from Deir el Medineh,[5] a number of small painted cloths of Eighteenth Dynasty date that were found at Deir el Bahari [6] and the painted linen shrouds so well known from the Greek and Roman periods. The earliest known instance of painting on linen, which dates from the predynastic period, is that found at Gebelein and now in the Turin Museum.[7]

Wood usually was covered with plaster before being used as a painting-ground, though this was not always so, the paint sometimes being put directly on the wood, especially in the case of furniture and boxes, which often were painted in one colour only, usually red, white or brownish-yellow. Painting was also executed on wooden panels,[8] and there is evidence for easel painting from the Old Kingdom.[9]

Since the greater number of the ancient Egyptian paintings are on the walls of tombs and temples and since fresco painting is a common form of mural decoration (as, for example, the palace paintings at Knossos in Crete and those at Tiryns on the mainland opposite, the paintings at Herculaneum and Pompeii respectively and many of the medieval wall paintings in Italy) the Egyptian mural paintings are often called frescoes, which are paintings executed on a damp surface made caustic with lime and without any other medium than water, which the Egyptian paintings never are.[10] With respect to the painted pavement found by Petrie at El Amarna, the discoverer states [11] that 'the colours were laid on while the plaster was wet and even while it could still be moved by the brush', which suggests a true fresco and which has been interpreted in that sense,[12] but fortunately I have been able to analyse a specimen of this plaster kindly supplied by Glanville, which proved to be gypsum containing a

[1] G. A. Reisner, *Mycerinus*, p. 127.

[2] See p. 77.

[3] H. H. Nelson and Others, *Medinet Habu*, I, p. 7.

[4] See pp. 352–3.

[5] Cairo Museum, No. J. 54885.

[6] E. Naville, *XIth Dyn. Temple at Deir el Bahari*, III, pp. 15, 16, Pls. xxx, xxxi.

[7] G. Galassi, *Rivista dell' Istituto nazionale d'archeologia e storia dell'arte*, n.s. IV (1955), pp. 5–17; H. W. Müller, *Alt-ägyptische Malerei*, p. 10, Fig. 2.

[8] W. M. F. Petrie, *Deshasheh*, pp. 20, 46, Pl. xxvi.

[9] W. P. Duell, *Mereruka*, I, Pls. vi–vii; *Technical Studies*, viii (1939–40), pp. 175–91; T. G. H. James, *Mastaba of Khentika*, Pl. x.

[10] Cf. N. M. Davies and A. H. Gardiner, *Ancient Egyptian Paintings*, III, p. xxxi.

[11] W. M. F. Petrie, *Tell el Amarna*, p. 12.

[12] S. R. K. Glanville, *J.E.A.*, xiv (1928), pp. 189–90 (review).

large proportion of calcium carbonate (a very common impurity in Egyptian gypsum) and particles of unburnt fuel. Professor Laurie informed me that he found by practical experience that gypsum plaster, if painted upon before it was thoroughly dry, would show brush marks. A similar painted pavement from Hawata, also of the Amarna period, was examined by von Bissing and Reach, who concluded that it was not a true fresco.[1]

One interesting fact that may be mentioned in connexion with painting is that in some instances pigments have corroded the ground on which they were painted, thus Mr. and Mrs. Davies state that some of the colours 'eat away' the plaster, leaving depressions,[2] and Mace and Winlock describe a painted canopic box where the pigment, probably blue, had corroded the wood in such a manner that what were originally painted inscriptions are now merely a series of holes in the wood, looking almost as though they had been burned.[3] This is attributed to the chemical composition of the pigment; but it seems much more likely that in all such cases the fault lies not with the pigment but with the vehicle which was either acid when used, or became acid subsequently, owing to chemical decomposition having taken place.

Varnish

The ancient Egyptian varnish is of two kinds, one originally colourless or practically colourless, though now brown, yellow or red and the other originally black and still black, both of which may now be described.

The colourless varnish was employed for covering mural paintings, wooden coffins, wooden canopic boxes, wooden stelae, occasionally painted pottery, and other objects.

The use of varnish in certain tombs in the Theban necropolis is mentioned by Mackay,[4] Davies,[5] and Davies and Gardiner,[6] Mackay giving a list of ten late Eighteenth Dynasty tombs in which it has been used. In addition to its employment in the usual manner as a coating over the paintings, Mackay suggests that in some instances the pigment and varnish may have been mixed and applied together. Sometimes the varnish covers the whole surface of a wall, as for example in the tomb of Kenamun,[7] but more usually only certain colours, generally red and yellow, are varnished. This selective treatment also may be seen in the temple of Hatshepsut at Deir el Bahari.

As examples of the use of varnish other than for mural paintings may be mentioned (a) the wooden box with the painted miniature hunting and battle scenes from the tomb of Tutankhamūn, which is covered with a thin uniform coat of varnish, originally colourless, but now yellow;[8] (b) various painted dummy wooden vases of

---

[1] F. W. von Bissing and M. Reach, *Ann. Serv.*, VII (1906), pp. 64–70; F. W. von Bissing, *Fussboden*, pp. 11–15.

[2] Communicated verbally. See also N. M. Davies and A. H. Gardiner, *Ancient Egyptian Paintings*, III, p. xlvi.

[3] A. C. Mace and H. E. Winlock, *Senebtisi*, p. 32, Pl. VIII; and verbal statement by Mr. Mace.

[4] E. Mackay, *Ancient Egypt*, 1920, pp. 36–37.

[5] N. de G. Davies, *Nefer-hotep*, I, pp. 12, 59, 63; *Puyemrê*, I, p. 11.

[6] N. de G. Davies and A. H. Gardiner, *Huy*, pp. 2, 7, 22.

[7] N. de G. Davies, *Nakht*, p. 57, n. 4; *Ken-Amūn*, I, p. 60.

[8] This box has now been treated with melted paraffin wax in order to preserve it.

the Eighteenth Dynasty, including two from the tomb of Yuya and Tuyu [1] and two painted red pottery vases of the same dynasty;[2] (c) especially the highly decorated wooden coffins and canopic boxes of the Twentieth Dynasty to about the Twenty-sixth Dynasty, which are usually varnished, the varnish often having been badly applied and put on thickly in some places and thinly in others; (d) a cylindrical 'kohlbox' found in the Roman-Nubian cemetery at Karanog, which is coated 'with a kind of gummy varnish, light brown in colour, which gave it a red lustrous appearance' [3] (apparently the coating was not tested, but 'gummy varnish' is a contradiction in terms and it seems probable that it was a resin varnish); (e) a small oval painted box of Roman date from the Fayum described by Wainwright,[4] who states that 'The whole has been given a coat of varnish, which has now turned black with age.' This is in the Cairo Museum and the coating was examined by me and was found to be soluble in alcohol and to exhibit all the characteristics of a resin varnish. A similar box of about the same date found by Petrie at Hawara is stated by him to be 'coated with glue'.[5] As the coating was scaling off Petrie treated it with paraffin wax in order to preserve it, which unfortunately prevents any simple chemical examination.

No certain use of a transparent varnish can be traced before the late Eighteenth Dynasty and only two instances of its use after the Twenty-sixth Dynasty, and it appears to have been almost unknown in both Ptolemaic and Roman times. Daressy, writing of certain painted wooden coffins, states [6] that the custom of varnishing them began in the Twentieth Dynasty and that it diminished and was lost a short time after the Twenty-second Dynasty.

There cannot be any doubt that this varnish, which is sometimes brown, though generally yellow where the coating is thin and orange-red where the coating is thick, was originally colourless, or practically so, since there are a number of instances where a white painted surface, which is partly varnished and partly unvarnished, is now yellow or red in the former case, but remains white in the latter case, and the edges of the varnished portions are so very irregular and unsightly that this cannot have been the original appearance and it can only be explained on the assumption that when the varnish was applied it was colourless and transparent and therefore it did not show, or, as aptly expressed by Davies,[7] 'The original transparency of the varnish is proved by the carelessness with which it was applied.'

Laurie states [8] that 'The reddish colour is very likely due to the introduction of a red like dragon's-blood', but there is no evidence whatever that the red is original and a practical certainty that it is adventitious.

Only very few analyses of this varnish can be traced, namely, one by Laurie,[9] who

---

[1] J. E. Quibell, *Yuaa and Thuiu*, pp. 45–46, Nos. 51075 and 51083.

[2] Cairo Museum, Nos. J. 72517–72518.

[3] C. L. Woolley and D. Randall MacIver, *Karanog*, III, 1910, pp. 71–72.

[4] G. A. Wainwright, *Ann. Serv.*, XXV (1925), p. 97.

[5] W. M. F. Petrie, *Hawara, Biahmu and Arsinoe*, p. 12, Pl. XIX (25).

[6] G. Daressy, *Cercueils des cachettes royales*, p. iii.

[7] N. de G. Davies, *Nakht*, p. 57, n. 4.

[8] A. P. Laurie, *Materials of the Painter's Craft*, p. 31.

[9] A. P. Laurie, *Materials of the Painter's Craft*, pp. 27–31; *Greek and Roman Methods of Painting*, pp. 113–14.

states that his specimen (Nineteenth Dynasty) was soluble in alcohol and that it did not agree in its properties with pine resin, mastic or sandarac, though it was most like pine resin, which might have become altered through time; one (undated) by Crow,[1] which was soluble in alcohol, and ether, but insoluble in turpentine and petroleum spirit, and a number by me (six Eighteenth Dynasty; one Twenty-first Dynasty; one of the period Twentieth Dynasty to Twenty-sixth Dynasty and several undated), which were all very similar in character and soluble in alcohol (both ethylic and amylic); slightly soluble in acetone and chloroform; insoluble or slightly soluble in ether and insoluble in turpentine, petroleum spirit and benzol. The ash in all cases was alkaline to phenolphthalein. The varnish is manifestly some kind of resin, but too little work has been done on the subject for any definite statement to be made respecting the nature of the resin, though as stated elsewhere,[2] the solubility and non-solubility in the various solvents, especially the insolubility in turpentine (in which most resins are soluble) are suggestive of shellac, which is a product of the lac insect, parasitic on certain trees that grow in Ceylon and farther India. That it is shellac, however, seems improbable, partly because it is more aromatic than shellac, but chiefly on account of the colour, natural shellac being dark, whereas the Egyptian varnish was originally practically colourless and even now is never so dark as the shellac obtainable anciently, the modern methods of bleaching shellac being then unknown. It should not be forgotten, however, that the solubility of a material often decreases with age and exposure, for example that of colophony in petroleum spirit [3] and, therefore, insolubility in a particular solvent may be not an original, but an acquired characteristic.

Black Varnish

The black varnish was used on wood, possibly sometimes to simulate ebony or sometimes because a black colour was required for certain funerary objects. It is found, for example, on the wooden sarcophagi, the wooden canopic boxes and the food boxes of Yuya and Tuyu, on a number of objects from the tomb of Tutankhamūn (two large wooden statues, numerous shrine-shaped boxes, the bases of three large couches, steering paddles for boats, certain human and animal figures and other objects), on a number of broken objects from the tomb of Horemheb (large statues, human and animal figures and parts of couches) and on certain late (probably Persian or Ptolemaic) coffins of cats and possibly of other animals. The varnish on one cat's (and cat-shaped) coffin in the Cairo Museum that has been examined by me is very glossy and similar in composition to the black varnish from the Eighteenth Dynasty.

So far as can be ascertained this black varnish was not employed before the late Eighteenth Dynasty, any black coating on wooden funerary objects of earlier date, for example, that on three sarcophagi from Qurna in the Cairo Museum dated to the Thirteenth or Fourteenth Dynasty (which has not been analysed, but which is mat and not glossy) is probably black paint and not varnish, and a black varnish-like coating on some copper funerary vases of Middle Kingdom date examined by me

[1] J. K. Crow, *Ann. Serv.*, IV (1903), pp. 242–3.
[2] A. Lucas, *Ann. Serv.*, IX (1908), p. 7.
[3] K. Dieterich, *Analysis of Resins* (1920), pp. 161, 166.

proved to be a nitrogenous adhesive, probably either glue or albumin (white of egg) coloured with carbon. As already mentioned, this black varnish was in use as late as about Ptolemaic times.

Though often called bitumen or pitch, this varnish is neither, nor does it contain bitumen or pitch, but it consists of a comparatively low-melting-point resin, largely soluble in alcohol (from 51.6 to 90.5 per cent in the specimens tested) and acetone; insoluble or practically insoluble in turpentine, petroleum spirit, carbon disulphide, ether and benzol; soluble in pyridine and saponifiable with caustic soda. The specimens tested all gave off ammoniacal vapours when heated with quick lime, which indicates nitrogenous organic matter, but this may have been glue used as a sizing material on the wood before varnishing.

Since the varnished objects were originally and intentionally black, the varnish cannot have blackened with age, as resins sometimes do, but must have been a naturally black resin. A few such resins are known, thus there is a black dammar resin from *Canarium strictum*, which grows in western and southern India and which would be a suitable material for making black varnish. Natural black varnishes that require no preparation are also known, such as the resin from *Rhus vernicifera* (Japan and China); the resin from *Melanorrhœa usitata* (Cochin-China and Cambodia); the resin from a species of *Melanorrhœa* (China) and the resin from *Melanorrhœa laccifera* (Indo-China), all of which are greyish-white viscous liquids when fresh and on exposure in thin films they dry to a hard black lustrous surface and are used as lacquers, and it seems probable that something of the kind may have been employed in Egypt.

Mode of Use

Before leaving the subject of varnish it becomes necessary to say something about the manner in which it was applied. The base of the old Egyptian varnishes, as of modern varnishes (excepting the very recent cellulose varnishes), is resin, but before resin can be applied as a thin coating it must be in a more or less liquid condition and the present-day varnishes consist of a particular kind of resin dissolved in a 'drying' oil (generally linseed oil), turpentine or alcohol. Had a drying oil been employed anciently there would be abundant evidence, but there is no such evidence, and neither turpentine nor alcohol was known until a very late date; moreover the ancient varnish is insoluble in turpentine. Petrie suggests [1] that strong wine may have been used as a solvent, but I have tried to make a varnish from old Egyptian resins and also from modern varnish resins (mastic, sandarac and shellac) using sherry, the strongest white wine obtainable, [2] but without success, and the ancient varnish was found to be insoluble in sherry. The alternatives, therefore, seem to be, either a resin that did not require an extraneous solvent, or a resin soluble in a solvent such as the Egyptians might have possessed. The former means a naturally occurring resin already liquid. Such resins, which are termed oleo-resins, are plentiful (pine and larch resins are of this class), the solvent being a volatile oil (oil of turpentine) that gradually evaporates

---

[1] W. M. F. Petrie, *Medum*, p. 29.

[2] Sherry being what is termed a 'fortified' wine (i.e. one to which alcohol in addition to that naturally present has been added) is the strongest in alcohol of any wine, except port (which was too highly coloured for the experiments), and almost certainly stronger than any of the old Egyptian wines.

on exposure. The only solvent that can be suggested that the ancient Egyptians might have used is a solution of natron in water and the only resin soluble in alkaline water solutions that is known to me is shellac, from which an excellent varnish may be made by dissolving it in a solution of borax or ammonia in water, both of which materials, however, were probably unknown in ancient Egypt, though natron was well known and its possible use will be discussed later.

The oleo-resins, though nominally liquid, are at best of a thick syrupy consistency, which, however, may be reduced by warming. A natural oleo-resin applied warm, therefore, seems a possible explanation, and Laurie accepts this as being likely and states that 'As such volatile mediums as alcohol, turpentine and petroleum spirit were almost certainly unknown in ancient Egypt, we are driven to conclude that this varnish was a natural semi-liquid resin as obtained from the tree . . . probably laid on after warming.' [1] According to Davies a scene in an Eighteenth Dynasty tomb at Thebes representing coffin-making shows 'resinous varnish being heated and stirred in a great pan set on a fire'.[2] Another suggestion that has been made is that the resin was applied in a finely powdered condition and was then liquefied and spread by means of heat,[3] but this does not appear feasible, and, in the case of a vertical surface, like a tomb wall, the resin would have had to be made to adhere first before it could have been spread. Laurie explains, too, that 'A solid resin, if fused by heat, cannot be spread on a surface properly and at once cracks on cooling',[1] and for this reason Mackay thinks [4] that the varnish on some tomb walls must have been applied after being liquefied by heat, because certain of the varnished surfaces are cracked, though he suggests the use of a solvent in other instances.

I have made a large number of experiments with a typical oleo-resin as obtained from the tree, namely Venice turpentine [5] (larch turpentine; the oleo-resinous exudation of *Larix Europœa* or *Larix decidua*), which at 20° C. (68° F.) was a viscous liquid, like thick syrup. Even in this condition it was found possible to apply it to wood (previously well sized with glue size) by means of a stiff bristle brush. The layer, however, though fairly thin, was not at first of uniform thickness and was covered with brush marks, but on standing a very short time the brush marks disappeared entirely and the layer became uniform. At temperatures of 30° C. (86° F.) and 35° C. (95° F.) the material, though less viscous, was still syrupy, but at 60° C. (140° F.) it became much thinner and could be taken up readily on a brush and applied to the wood, but the material cooled so quickly that, before it could be brushed on as a thin uniform coating, it became syrupy and much in the same state as at 20° C. (68° F.) and similarly was covered with brush marks and, except for the ease of filling the brush, there was practically no advantage in using it at the higher temperature. One great disadvantage of the particular oleo-resin tried, and therefore presumably of all oleo-resins, is the very slow drying. In the experiments made (the temperature of the room being

---

[1] A. P. Laurie, *Materials of the Painter's Craft*, pp. 30–31.
[2] N. de G. Davies, *Nefer-hotep*, I, pp. 45–46, Pl. XXVII.
[3] R. S. Morrell, *Varnishes and their Compounds*, p. 2.
[4] E. Mackay, *Ancient Egypt*, 1920, p. 37.
[5] A specimen guaranteed pure was kindly supplied by Messrs. The British Drug Houses Limited, London.

about 15° C. to 20° C. (59° F. to 68° F.) during the day and lower at night) the 'varnish' took about five days before it was anything like dry, and even then it was a little tacky and remained so for about seven weeks, when it was completely dry.

Experiments also were made with shellac (both button lac and garnet lac of the best qualities obtainable) and a solution of natron, using various proportions of shellac and various strengths of natron. The solution that appeared to give the best results, so far as the experiments were carried, was 16 per cent of natron (containing 7 per cent of sodium chloride and 3 per cent of sodium sulphate) and 20 per cent of shellac, which were boiled together for about ten minutes. This, while hot, could be brushed on to the wood (previously well sized with glue size), but, owing to the shellac becoming quickly insoluble (or largely insoluble) on cooling, the coating was not continuous, but patchy and fairly thick. This coating soon became hard, but it did not possess the glossy appearance of varnish, and both the solution and the applied coating were of a dark reddish-violet colour, totally unlike the colour of the ancient varnish. It seems quite probable that as a result of further experiments with other strengths of natron and shellac, and possibly also different ways of affecting the solution, a fairly thin coating might be obtained, but the experiments were discontinued, since any coating obtainable would still have had the dark colour of the shellac that makes it impossible that this could have been the ancient varnish. Any artificial bleaching of the shellac at the early date when the varnish was used appears highly improbable.

The summary of the matter is that a coniferous oleo-resin although it gives a fairly satisfactory varnish-like coating of a light brownish-yellow colour that resembles the ancient varnish in being soluble in alcohol, seems excluded, because all these oleo-resins are soluble in spirits of turpentine, whereas the ancient varnish is insoluble, and shellac also seems to be excluded, because, although readily soluble in alcohol and insoluble in turpentine, and so resembling the ancient varnish in these respects, the colour is much too dark. No other resins having the characteristics of the ancient varnish that could be dissolved in any solvent known to the ancient Egyptians can be suggested, though possibly some resin (not a coniferous one) may ultimately be found that is sufficiently liquid to be applied with a stiff brush and that is insoluble in turpentine. As any such resin is likely to have been a product of western Asia and to have been used there for varnish before it became known in Egypt, the early history of the use of varnish in Persia might throw some light on the problem.

That such a useful material as varnish should have practically disappeared without leaving any substitute, as the Egyptian varnish did during the Ptolemaic and Roman periods,[1] is unusual, a possible explanation being that the source of supply of the resin was cut off, for example by wars in Asia.

WRITING MATERIALS[2]

For the purposes of description the ancient Egyptian writing materials may be

---

[1] One instance only of the late use of varnish is known; see p. 357.

[2] Cf. J. Černý, *Paper and Books in Ancient Egypt*, pp. 11–13; R. Pietschmann, 'Leder und Holz als Schreib materialien bei den Aegyptern', *Beiträge zur Kenntnis des Schrift-, Buch- und Bibliothekswesens*, Heft 2 (1895), pp. 105–15; Heft 4 (1897), pp. 51–82; V. Wessetsky, 'Az óegyiptomi könyv', *Antik Tanulmanyok*, v (1958), pp. 1–24.

divided into two main classes, namely, those that were essential and those that were accessory. The primary materials comprised the ink, the ground on which the ink was placed in the act of writing and the implements (pens) used to transfer the ink to the ground destined to receive it. The secondary materials included the grinders used by the scribes to prepare the ink and the receptacles on, or in, which the ink and pens were kept when not in use. All these objects may now be described.

Pigments

The ink was in the form of small cakes of solid material, resembling, except in shape, modern water-colours, and was generally of two kinds, black and red, the latter being used for the rubrication of headings, notes, etc.[1] Occasionally additional colours occur on a palette, these, however, being employed by the artist for illustrated scenes and not by the scribe in writing. One such palette, bearing the name of Meritaten, was found in the tomb of Tutankhamūn[2] on which there had been originally six colours, only five, however, (black, green, red, white and yellow), now remaining, one (almost certainly blue) being missing. Another, cited by Davies and Gardiner, had six oval pans containing red, dark yellow, light yellow, green, blue, and white.[3]

In the Graeco-Roman period, faience palettes with as many as nine or ten cup-shaped receptacles were common.

The cakes of colours probably were made by mixing finely ground pigment with gum and water and drying, and they were used in the same manner as modern water-colours, namely, by dipping the pen in water and rubbing it on the ink.

Garstang reports carbon and red ochre respectively for the black and red colours on a palette of Middle Kingdom date.[4]

Laurie found the colours on an Egyptian palette dating from about 400 B.C. to consist respectively of charcoal, red ochre, gypsum, blue frit and yellow oxide of lead.[5]

Hayes found 'sections of thick reed containing carbon used in the manufacture of ink' of Eighteenth Dynasty date at Thebes.[6]

Barthoux examined the pigments from certain Egyptian palettes, which unfortunately were undated,[7] though judging from the results, some were of a very late period. The white was calcium carbonate in some instances and magnesium carbonate in others; some of the red was red ochre and some red lead (minium); the brown was limonite (one form of oxide of iron); the yellow was yellow ochre containing in some instances calcium sulphate; the green is reported as powdered glass and the blue was a frit. As the use of minium in Egypt is very unlikely before Roman times, this specimen was probably of very late date. The calcium sulphate found with

---

[1] The use and technique of rubrication have been studied by G. Posener, *J.E.A.*, xxxvii (1951), pp. 75–80.

[2] H. Carter, *Tut-ankh-Amen*, iii, Pl. xxiii (A).

[3] N. M. Davies and A. H. Gardiner, *Ancient Egyptian Paintings*, p. xxxii.

[4] J. Garstang, *Burial Customs*, p. 77.

[5] A. P. Laurie, *Archaeologia*, lxiv (1913), pp. 318–19.

[6] W, C. Hayes, *M.M.A. Bull., Egyptian Exped. 1934–1935*, p. 34.

[7] J. Barthoux, 'Les fards, pommades et couleurs dans l'antiquité', *Congrès internat. de géog., Le Caire, Avril, 1925*, iv (1926), pp. 257–8.

the yellow ochre was probably a naturally occurring impurity and the green described as glass was probably the well-known artificial green frit. The black was carbon.

I have examined nine specimens of pigments from palettes, one white, of Old Kingdom date, which proved to be calcium carbonate and eight of the Eighteenth Dynasty; one white, which was calcium sulphate; one bright yellow, which was orpiment (sulphide of arsenic); three red, all of which were red ochre; and three black, which were carbon.

Of the ink on documents, only one published analysis can be traced, which is by Wiesner, given in his account of the Rainer papyri from the Fayum,[1] which date from the ninth to the thirteenth century A.D. Wiesner states that the papyri are written with two different kinds of ink, one a carbon ink and the other an iron ink. Schubart also mentions two kinds of ink on papyrus,[2] one black and one brown, the latter dating from the fourth century A.D., but the nature of this ink, the brown colour of which suggests an iron ink, apparently was not determined.

Specimens of black ink on Coptic ostraca were found by Crum to consist essentially of carbon.[3]

Various specimens of black ink on documents have been examined by me.[4] These included a number on ostraca (undated), a number on papyri, ranging in date from Roman times to the ninth century A.D., all of which were carbon, and a number on parchment documents dating from the seventh to the twelfth century A.D., in all of which cases the ink was an iron compound.

The carbon used for making ink was soot in most cases, probably generally scraped from cooking vessels, though occasionally specially prepared, the charcoal found by Laurie being exceptional. One method of making carbon for ink to be used for writing religious books, which was kindly supplied to me by a priest of the Coptic Church, is as follows: Put a quantity of incense on the ground and round it place three stones or bricks, and, resting on these, an earthenware dish bottom upwards, covered with a damp cloth; ignite the incense. The carbon formed is deposited on the dish, from which it is removed and made into ink by mixing with gum arabic and water. An old Arabic book in the Royal Library at Cairo (unfortunately anonymous and undated) contains a receipe for making what is called Persian ink. The method is to take date stones, put them in an earthenware vessel stoppered with clay and put the vessel over a fire until the next day, then remove the vessel, allow it to cool, grind and sift the contents and make into ink with gum arabic and water. An ink such as this last, however, would be of poor quality and would contain very little free carbon.

Carbon is the oldest ink material known and in Egypt its use for writing can be dated back to a period before the beginning of the First Dynasty, that is before about 3400 B.C., Petrie having found 'dozens of pottery jars with ink inscriptions' of a date 'probably half-way back in the dynasty before Mena'.[5] From the First Dynasty there

---

[1] J. Wiesner, *Mittheilungen aus der Sammlung der Papyrus Erzherzog Rainer*, 1887, pp. ii–iii, 239, 240.

[2] W. Schubart, *Einführung in die Papyruskunde*, 1918, p. 44.

[3] W. E. Crum, *Coptic Ostraca*, p. x, n.

[4] A. Lucas, *Analyst*, XLVII (1922), pp. 9–14.

[5] W. M. F. Petrie, *Abydos*, I, p. 3.

are also examples of black ink writing, some on pieces of broken stone bowls;[1] one on a jar-sealing [1] and two on wooden tablets.[2] It is true that in none of these instances has the ink been analysed, but that it should be anything other than carbon is most unlikely.

Writing Grounds

The materials on which the ancient Egyptian writing was executed were very varied, and, taking them in alphabetical order, included bone (the shoulder blade of a camel with a Coptic inscription in ink is in the Cairo Museum); clay (several tablets of dried clay of Eleventh Dynasty date, some with incised inscriptions and some with ink inscriptions are in the Cairo Museum and, as the El Amarna letters show, baked clay tablets were used for official correspondence between Egypt and western Asia in the Eighteenth Dynasty, the writing on these latter being in incised cuneiform characters in the Babylonian language); ivory; leather (some Egyptian manuscripts on leather are in the British Museum [3] and one of Sixth Dynasty date unrolled by Dr. Ibscher is in the Cairo Museum);[4] linen; metal (one specimen of 'bronze' and one of lead, both bearing writing in incised characters and both of Roman age are in the Cairo Museum); papyrus; parchment and vellum (the former being made from the skins of sheep and goats and the latter from the more delicate skins of calves and kids and neither having been employed before a very late period); pottery; reed (a large split reed with a Coptic inscription written in ink on the inside is in the Cairo Museum); stone (chiefly small flat pieces of limestone); wax (beeswax in the form of a thin uniform coating, usually coloured black, spread on wooden tablets, the writing being incised in the wax by means of a pointed implement called a stilus which was not used before Graeco-Roman times) and wood (both plain and coated with a thin coating of plaster).[5] The most important writing material, however, was papyrus, which has already been dealt with in connexion with Fibres,[6] but cheaper substitutes were used for unimportant and ephemeral purposes, the principal of which were fragments of broken pottery and fragments of limestone, to both of which the name of ostraca has been given.

Pens [7]

From a very early period until about the third century B.C., an interval of several thousand years, the ancient Egyptian writing implement, as proved by numerous specimens that have been preserved, was a particular kind of rush [8] (not reed, as

---

[1] W. M. F. Petrie, *Royal Tombs*, I, pp. 15, 21.

[2] W. M. F. Petrie, *Royal Tombs*, II, p. 38; J. E. Quibell, *Saqqara, 1912–1914*, p. 6.

[3] S. R. K. Glanville, *J.E.A.*, XIII (1927), p. 232; *B.M. Quarterly*, VIII (1933), pp. 52–53.

[4] Cf. R. Pietschmann, 'Leder und Holz als Schreibmaterialien bei den Aegyptern', *Beiträge zur Kenntnis des Schrift-, Buch- und Bibliothekswesens*, Heft 2 (1895), pp. 105–15.

[5] Cf. R. Pietschmann, 'Leder und Holz als Schreibmaterialien bei den Aegyptern', *Beiträge zur Kenntnis des Schrift-, Buch- und Bibliothekswesens*, Heft 4 (1897), pp. 51–82. For examples of writing boards, cf. *ibid.*, pp. 54–56; W. C. Hayes, *Scepter*, I, p. 294; B. Van de Walle, *Bull Musées royaux d'art et d'histoire, Bruxelles*, 1935, pp. 106–11.

[6] See pp. 137–40.

[7] Cf. J. Černý, *Paper and Books in Ancient Egypt*, p. 12.

[8] For examples see V. Täckholm and M. Drar, *Flora of Egypt*, II, pp. 477–81.

generally stated), *Juncus maritimus*, that grows plentifully in Egypt at the present day (generally in salt marshes). Portions of this of the required length were taken, and, as shown experimentally by Dr. H. Ibscher, who kindly demonstrated it to me, one end was cut to a flat chisel-shape and the fibres split by chewing so as to produce a fine brush. With the flat side the thicker lines were made and, with the fine edge, the thinner lines. Eleven specimens from the Eighteenth Dynasty measured by me varied from 6.3 inches (16 cm.) to 9 inches (23 cm.) in length and were all approximately one-sixteenth of an inch (1.5 mm.) in diameter. A bunch from the Twelfth Dynasty measured by Quibell were all 16 inches long and one-tenth of an inch in diameter.[1] From the Graeco-Roman period onwards the rush pen was superseded by a piece of reed, *Phragmites communis*, cut to a point and split in the same manner as the quill pen formerly employed in Europe. This reed, which was used by both the Greeks and Romans 'from the 3rd century B.C. onwards'[2] was doubtless the Egyptian reed mentioned by Pliny (first century A.D.) as being employed for writing.[3] Petrie illustrates a number of these pens of Roman date found by him in Egypt.[4] Winlock says[2] that 'The complete adoption of the split pen by the Egyptians may be safely related to the adoption of the Greek alphabet for writing the Egyptian language during the 4th century A.D.' The monks of the Christian Monastery of Epiphanius at Thebes in the sixth or seventh century A.D. were using split pens. 'The pens were made of reeds, which averaged about 1 cm. in diameter. An unused new pen . . . was 26.5 cm. long. The old pens had been resharpened so often that finally they were mere stumps less than 6 cm. long . . . and one of them had been lengthened by sticking a bit of wood into the end.'[2] Pens of this kind are still being employed in Egypt at the present day, though their use is gradually dying out.

Erasers

Writing was normally erased with the tongue or with a wet rag,[5] but small sticks of sandstone also appear to have been used to rub out signs.[6] One such eraser has been described in detail by Drioton,[7] and others were found wrapped in linen in a tomb of Twelfth Dynasty date.[8] Two similar sticks are in the Ashmolean Museum, Oxford.

Grinders

The grinders employed by the scribes to prepare their 'ink' were usually small rectangular pieces of stone, having a slight depression in the middle of the top and a raised edge all round[9] with a small pestle or muller (often cone-shaped) of similar stone,[9] or occasionally instead of the pestle, a small stone spatula.

---

[1] J. E. Quibell, *Ramesseum*, p. 3.

[2] H. E. Winlock and W. E. Crum, *Monastery of Epiphanius*, pp. 93–94.

[3] XVI: 64.

[4] W. M. F. Petrie, *Objects of Daily Use*, Pl. LVIII (54, 55, 56, 58).

[5] J. Černý, *Paper and Books in Ancient Egypt*, p. 24.

[6] H. Grapow (*Z.Ä.S.*, LXXI (1935), p. 161) refers to some signs in the Ebers papyrus as 'ausgekratzt'.

[7] E. Drioton, *Ann. Serv.*, XLI (1942), pp. 91–95.

[8] W. C. Hayes, *Scepter*, I, p. 296.

[9] W. M. F. Petrie, *Objects of Daily Use*, Pl. LVI; W. C. Hayes, *Scepter*, I, p. 296.

Palettes [1]

The palettes, which were made of various materials, were rectangular in shape and provided with depressions (usually circular, but sometimes rectangular) for the cakes of ink, and a recess for holding the 'pens'.[2] The materials included ivory (two examples of which were found in the tomb of Tutankhamūn);[3] wood; wood covered with gold (an example was in the tomb of Tutankhamūn) [3] and stone, often alabaster, sandstone, 'schist', or serpentine. The long narrow palettes probably also served as rulers.

In the tomb of Tutankhamūn, in addition to the normal palettes there were twelve others that were purely funerary,[4] having imitation cakes of pigment, some of stone and some of glass, and imitation pens of glass.

The 'pens' were sometimes provided with special pen-cases, examples of which were found by Carter at Thebes.[5] One very ornate specimen from the tomb of Tutankhamūn is in the Cairo Museum.[3] The ink, too, was sometimes kept in a separate receptacle,[6] shells occasionally being used for this purpose, and the water with which the ink was mixed was carried in a small vessel. The hieroglyph for 'scribe' represents a pen-case, water pot, and palette with cakes of ink.

Marking Ink

In connexion with ink, it may be mentioned that the Egyptians frequently had their linen garments marked with their names in 'ink', one specimen of which was analysed by Mitchell and proved to be an organic material, free from carbon, that was not identified.[7] Other specimens, also examined by Mitchell, were from a Second Dynasty tomb at Saqqara and proved to be iron oxide.[8] The use of such marking ink is fairly common, and examples have been noted from the Eleventh [9] and Eighteenth [10] Dynasties.

---

[1] Cf. J. Černý, *Paper and Books in Ancient Egypt*, pp. 12–13.

[2] W. M. F. Petrie, *Objects of Daily Use*, Pl. LVII.

[3] H. Carter, *Tut-ankh-Amen*, III, Pl. XXII.

[4] H. Carter, *Tut-ankh-Amen*, III, p. 79.

[5] Carnarvon and H. Carter, *Five Years' Explorations*, pp. 70, 75, Pl. LXVI.

[6] W. M. F. Petrie, *Objects of Daily Use*, Pl. LVI; W. C. Hayes, *Scepter*, I, p. 296.

[7] C. A. Mitchell, *Analyst*, LII (1927), p. 27; *Ancient Egypt*, 1927, p. 18.

[8] C. A. Mitchell, *Analyst*, LXV (1940), pp. 100–1.

[9] H. E. Winlock, *Slain Soldiers*, pp. 25 f.; *Excavations at Deir el Bahari, 1911–1931*, p. 227.

[10] E. Schiaparelli, *La Tomba intatta dell' Architetto Cha*, pp. 93, 98, 99; H. E. Winlock, *Meryet-Amūn*, pp. 11, 57, 70 87–89; *Materials used at the Embalming of King Tūt-ankh-Amūn*, pp. 8–9.

Chapter XV

POTTERY

By pottery is meant ware made from clay, moulded into shape while wet and then hardened by being baked, faience, which has already been dealt with, not being pottery.

The principal use of pottery in Egypt was for making vessels, though it was also employed to a considerable extent for modelling. Figures of human beings and animals, usually small, are known from as early as the predynastic period,[1] and larger pieces have occasionally been found, such as the lion from Hierakonpolis,[2] of early dynastic date, and a pottery bust now in the British Museum.[3] Pottery shawabtis are quite common, particularly during the New Kingdom, and shawabti boxes, canopic jars and coffins of pottery are also known. Pottery (terracotta) was employed extensively in the Ptolemaic and Roman periods for making votive figures of deities, lamps and other small objects, the majority of which were cast in moulds.[4]

The production of pottery may now be described.

Clay

Clay is a colloidal, plastic material of secondary origin, derived from the disintegration and decomposition of certain kinds of primary rocks. The essential constituent of all clays is hydrated aluminium silicate, but with this are mixed variable, though usually small, proportions of natural impurities, chiefly alkalies (combined, not free), iron compounds (to which the colour is largely due), calcium carbonate, organic matter (humus), quartz sand and water, and it is the kind and amount of impurities present that condition the nature of the clay.

The water contained in clay is in two forms, one mechanically mixed, and it is on this that the plasticity depends, and the other chemically combined, and when clay is dried, the former, or interstitial water, is driven off and the material temporarily loses its softness and plasticity and becomes hard and friable, but if wetted it will take up water and become plastic again; when clay is more strongly heated or baked, the chemically combined water is also driven off and the material then becomes very hard and entirely loses its capacity for being acted upon by water and if wetted it does not revert to its former plastic condition.

---

[1] W. M. F. Petrie, *Prehistoric Egypt*, pp. 7–10, Pls. III–VII; A. Scharff, *Die Altertümer der Vor- und Frühzeit Ägyptens*, II, pp. 31–47, Pls. X–XV; E. J. Baumgartel, *Cultures of Prehistoric Egypt*, II, pp. 66–69, Pl. V.

[2] J. E. Quibell, *Hierakonpolis*, I, pp. 11–12, Pls. XLIV–XLV.

[3] H. R. Hall, *J.E.A.*, XIV (1928), pp. 209–10.

[4] Cf. P. Perdrizet, *Terres Cuites grecques d'Égypte*; W. Weber, *Die Ägyptisch-Griechischen Terrakotten*; E. Breccia, *Terrecotte greche e greco-egizie del Museo di Alessandria*; K. M. Kaufmann, *Ägyptische Terrakotten*; C. C. Edgar, *Greek Moulds*, pp. xiii–xvi.

The Egyptian clay employed for pottery making is essentially of two kinds one of a brown or blackish colour when wet, but a brownish-grey when dry, which contains a comparatively large proportion of organic matter and iron compounds, together with varying amounts of sand, and this kind becomes brown or red when heated, and the other of a brownish-grey colour when wet, but grey when dry, which contains very little organic matter, but a comparatively large proportion of calcium carbonate, and this, which is a calcareous clay or marl, burns to a grey colour. The former occurs throughout the Delta and the Nile valley, whereas the latter is found only in a few localities, of which Qena and Ballas in Upper Egypt are the most important.[1]

Pottery making is one of the oldest of the arts and in Egypt dates back to neolithic times. At first the pots were of coarse material, crude workmanship, devoid of finish and badly baked, but by the Badarian and the succeeding predynastic periods the Egyptian potter was producing wares that for beauty of form and finish were extraordinarily good.

In the making of a pottery vessel there are four main stages, namely, kneading the clay, shaping the clay into a pot, drying the pot and finally baking it. All these processes are represented in the scenes of pottery making shown on tomb walls,[2] and in wooden models of potters' workshops,[3] and may now be considered.

Kneading

Before clay is fashioned into pots any small stones or other foreign material are usually first picked out and the clay then brought to a uniform and right consistency, which is done in Egypt at the present day, and, therefore, doubtless also anciently,[4] by thoroughly kneading it with water by means of the feet, with sometimes the addition, when the clay is too 'rich' or too 'fat', of organic matter in the form of finely chopped straw, fine chaff or powdered animal dung. These are used in order to reduce the stickiness (which makes it difficult to manipulate), to assist the escape of water during drying and to prevent undue shrinkage with its accompanying cracking and distortion during drying, also to strengthen 'poor', 'lean' or sandy clay. This 'tempering' of the clay is not merely a modern device, but was employed anciently, as is proved by the fact that it is not unusual to find in predynastic and early dynastic pottery either chopped straw or evidence that this had been used and had burned out during baking.[5] Grit, shell, flint chips, etc., were occasionally employed instead of chaff.[6]

Shaping

In the early days of pottery making in Egypt, that is during neolithic, Badarian and predynastic times, pots were made by hand, though it is possible that in shaping some predynastic pottery the clay was placed on a mat which could be rotated on the

---

[1] Analyses of specimens of this type of clay will be found on p. 496.

[2] P. Montet, Scènes de la vie privée, pp. 254–6; H. Balcz, Mitt. Kairo, III (1932), pp. 82–84.

[3] J. H. Breasted (Jr.), Servant Statues, pp. 49–51.

[4] This is almost certainly shown in a Twelfth Dynasty tomb at Beni Hasan (P. E. Newberry, Beni Hasan, I, Pl. XI).

[5] J. E. Quibell, Archaic Objects, pp. 137–77.

[6] R. Mond and O. H. Myers, Cemeteries of Armant, I, pp. 50, 177–81.

ground.[1] Such a technique was still in use during the Middle Kingdom at Kerma, where pots were also built up inside a basket or bag.[2]

The date of the introduction of the wheel is a matter of some controversy. Miss D. Billington suggests that the necks of some predynastic pots may have been turned on a slow wheel,[3] and Petrie states that 'The first use of the wheel regularly is for the great jars of the royal factory in the Ist Dynasty.' [4] Reisner, however, says that the beginning of wheel-made pottery dates from the period between the reign of Khase-khemui and the accession of Snofru,[5] and Frankfort states that the potter's wheel was only generally used in Egypt 'about the Fourth Dynasty, though sporadically appearing since the First'.[6] Junker maintains that all prehistoric and early dynastic pottery was made by hand, and that the wheel was only introduced during the Old Kingdom.[7]

Deductions based on the appearance of early pottery are apt to be misleading, for pots built up by hand on a table turned on the ground may well have traces of 'wheel-marks'.[8] The earliest form of wheel (the so-called 'slow wheel') was merely a development of this technique, a small circular turntable rotated by hand on a vertical pivot or shaft, the turntable having only a very limited momentum. The use of such a wheel is illustrated in a Fifth Dynasty tomb at Saqqara,[9] and in tombs of the Twelfth Dynasty at Beni Hasan [10] and El Bersheh,[11] as well as by small figures of potters at work found in tombs of the Old and Middle Kingdoms.[12] From the Eighteenth Dynasty there is evidence of a wheel moved with the foot or by an assistant,[13] but this, too, appears to be a form of turntable rather than a swiftly spinning wheel of the modern type, and Frankfort maintains that the pivoted turntable was the only wheel known in Egypt until the Ptolemaic period.[14] Wheel-made pottery, however, has never entirely displaced the hand-made variety in Egypt, the latter being still made to some extent at the present day.[15]

The final stage in the shaping of a pot is usually to smooth the surface with the wet hand, which not only improves the appearance but also makes the pot less permeable to liquids by filling up the pores with fine particles of clay. This, as pointed out by

---

[1] Cf. R. Mond and O. H. Myers, *Cemeteries of Armant*, I, p. 69.

[2] G. A. Reisner, *Kerma*, IV–V, p. 323.

[3] D. Billington, in R. Mond and O. H. Myers, *Cemeteries of Armant*, I, pp. 177–81.

[4] W. M. F. Petrie, *Descriptive Sociology, Ancient Egyptians*, p. 57.

[5] G. A. Reisner, *Naga-ed-Dêr*, III, p. 185; cf. also *Mycerinus*, p. 174.

[6] H. Frankfort, *Studies in Early Pottery of the Near East*, I, p. 107, *n*. 5.

[7] H. Junker, *Giza*, I, p. 125.

[8] Conversely, wheel-made pottery may not show clear traces of 'wheel-marks', since pots were frequently wheel finished for about two-thirds, of their height and then roughly cut away, from the mass of clay on the wheel. See H. Frankfort, *Studies in Early Pottery of the Near East*, I, p. 8, *n*. 1; P. E. Newberry, *Beni Hasan*, I, Pl. XI.

[9] G. Steindorff, *Ti*, Pls. LXXXIII, LXXXIV. Cf. also a determinative in the Pyramid Texts, *Pyr.* 1184a, 1185a.

[10] P. E. Newberry, *Beni Hasan*, I, Pl. XI; II, Pl. VII.

[11] P. E. Newberry, *El Bersheh*, I, Pl. XXV.

[12] J. H. Breasted (Jr.), *Servant Statues*, pp. 49–51.

[13] N. de G. Davies, *Ken-Amūn*, Pl. LIX; W. Wreszinski, *Atlas*, I, p. 301.

[14] H. Frankfort, *Studies in Early Pottery of the Near East*, I, p. 8.

[15] W. S. Blackman, *Fellāhīn of Upper Egypt*, pp. 136–7.

Peet, 'often gives the impression that a separate slip of finer clay has been applied when this is not really the case'.[1]

Wash and Slip [2]

Both wash and slip are applied to pottery in the leather hard condition, the former consisting of more or less pure pigment mixed with water, whereas the latter is a thicker paste of clay and water with or without the addition of pigment. In practice it is not always easy to distinguish between the two, and a thick wash may often appear like a slip. The slip most commonly used on Egyptian pottery consists of finely levigated, light-coloured, non-red-burning clay mixed to the consistency of cream and applied before the pot is completely dried.[3] It has four functions: primarily, if applied to a red-burning clay, it changes the colour of the pot to drab or buff, a colour that at certain periods was more fashionable, or that may have been thought to be more agreeable than red, but it also makes the pot less permeable to liquids, lends additional smoothness to the surface and makes an admirable ground for painting. A wash of red ochre was frequently applied to the surface of red ware in order to improve the colour.[4]

Drying

After the pot is made it is wet, sticky and useless until it has been dried, which must be done before baking, otherwise the rapid vaporization and escape of the mechanically-held water that would take place in the fire or kiln would rupture the pot.

Polishing

The only period during which a clay pot can be polished by simple rubbing with a pebble or other hard smooth object is when the clay is almost but not quite dry. This is a phenomenon depending upon the physical nature of clay, which is a material that it is impossible to polish by simple rubbing when wet or when quite dry (as just before baking) or after being hardened by baking, and it is only by the use of certain materials such as oil, wax or graphite (blacklead) that it is possible to polish dry or baked clay. The polish produced by rubbing varies with the nature of the clay, being more brilliant on a 'rich', 'fat', or well-levigated clay than on a poor, calcareous or coarse one.

When an unbaked clay vessel, either with or without a wash of red ochre, is pebble-polished and then baked, the colour is so altered, first by the polishing and then by the baking, that often it seems hardly to be the same vessel, which facts need to be taken into account before deciding whether or not a vessel has been treated with a slip or wash. Peet says [5] 'In a polished vase the fact that the surface is darker than the fracture does not prove the presence of a slip, for the very process of polishing almost always darkens the surface colour.'

---

[1] T. E. Peet, *Cemeteries of Abydos*, II, p. 12.

[2] See P. D. Ritchie, in R. Mond and O. H. Myers, *Cemeteries of Armant*, I, pp. 181–5; *Technical Studies*, IV (1936), pp. 234–6.

[3] See p. 496.

[4] Cf. H. Junker, *Giza*, I, p. 114.

[5] T. E. Peet, *Cemeteries of Abydos*, II, p. 11, *n*. 2.

The polish applied to clays before baking not only persists after baking and blackening, but often is more brilliant on the final black than it was on the original red, probably purely an optical effect due to the different manner in which the two colours reflect the light. Petrie states [1] that 'The reason of the polish being smoother on the black than on the red parts is that carbonyl gas—which is the result of imperfect combustion—is a solvent of magnetic oxide of iron and so dissolves and re-composes the surface facing.' In another place[2] Petrie says 'This is probably due to the formation of carbonyl gas in the smothered fire; this gas acts as a solvent of magnetic oxide, and hence allows it to assume a new surface, like the glossy surface of some marbles subjected to solution in water.' There is, however, no evidence for any such reaction, which is most improbable. Forsdyke says [3] 'The difference between the reflecting powers of black and red surfaces need hardly be remarked; but it is well illustrated in the well-known predynastic Egyptian vases which are bright red with a black band at the lip. The polish is certainly stronger on the black part, but it extends all over the surface and is hardly visible on the red colour.'

With certain ancient red-polished sherds that were blackened by making them red-hot and then burying them in sawdust, the polish not only became more brilliant, but acquired the metallic sheen seen on much of the black of the Badarian and predynastic black-topped ware, which is very like a graphite polish in appearance, which of course it cannot have been on the treated sherds and which it probably is not on the Badarian and predynastic pottery. A graphite polish, however, was found by Reisner [4] on some of the ware from the Middle Kingdom Egyptian colony at Kerma in the Sudan, and graphite is used to-day in certain districts of the Sudan for giving a polish to a surface already black,[5] but there is not any evidence for its use in Egypt. Polishing makes pottery impermeable to liquids.

Baking

Finally, the pot is baked in order to drive off the chemically-combined water, the loss of which is necessary to convert the clay from its original weak, friable state, in which it is softened by water, into a hard, durable, stone-like mass, unacted upon by water. This reaction takes place between 500° C. (937° F.) and 600° C. (1,112° F.), the combined water (13–14 per cent) being rapidly given off at ordinary atmospheric pressure as the temperature rises beyond 500° C.[6]

As for the manner of baking, there can be little doubt that at first the dried pots were baked on the ground as a mixed heap of pots and fuel, probably covered over with animal dung to conserve the heat, as is done today in the Sudan and by primitive people elsewhere. The fuel available was principally straw, chaff, animal dung, reeds, rushes and sedges. At a later date, the heap might have been surrounded by a low wall of clay and the dung covering replaced by clay and finally a simple kiln with a separation between the pots and the fuel would be evolved. As a pottery kiln is shown in a

[1] W. M. F. Petrie, *Arts and Crafts*, p. 130.
[2] W. M. F. Petrie, *Diospolis Parva*, p. 13.
[3] E. J. Forsdyke, *Journ. Hellenic Studies*, XXXIV (1914), p. 141.
[4] G. A. Reisner, *Kerma*, IV–V, p. 329.
[5] J. W. Crowfoot, *Sudan Notes*, VIII (1925), pp. 133–4.
[6] J. W. Mellor, *Inorganic and Theoretical Chemistry*, VI, p. 482.

Fifth Dynasty tomb at Saqqara,[1] its use must have been well established at that date: pottery kilns are also depicted in Twelfth Dynasty tombs at Beni Hasan [2] and in an Eighteenth Dynasty tomb at Thebes.[3] A battery of four double-tier ovens, of uncertain but late date found at Tanis, have been described by Fougerousse.[4] The purpose of these ovens is uncertain, but it is probable that they were used to fire pottery, and perhaps also faience. The so-called pottery kilns found at Memphis [5] seem, however, to have been employed exclusively for faience.

Colour [6]

An important feature of pottery is its colour, which may now be considered.

The colour of pottery, apart from any slip, wash or paint, depends upon several factors, the principal of which are the kind of clay used and the nature of the firing.

Even a mere enumeration of the different colours of pottery is not without difficulty, partly on account of the large variety of shades or gradations of colour that occur and partly because some of the colours are usually described by terms such as 'drab' and 'buff' that lack precision of meaning and, therefore, are not always employed in the same sense. The colours of the plain, unpainted and undecorated pottery that will specially be discussed are brown, black, red, partly black and partly red, and grey, and the nature and cause of these colours will now be considered.

Brown Ware

A brown colour in pottery is generally that of the clay used, which has not been modified, or only slightly modified (apart from any lightening of the colour due to drying), by the very imperfect baking, the black patches often present being smoke stains and manifestly, therefore, the fire must have been a poor and smoky one. This colour, although usually confined to the most primitive pottery, may occur at almost any period. The Egyptian neolithic pottery and some of the Badarian pottery are of this kind.

Black Ware [7]

Black pots probably were first produced occasionally by accident, but accident cannot account for a continuous production of black ware, which arose doubtless from a deliberate attempt to cover up the inevitable and disfiguring smoke stains of the earliest pottery by utilizing a smoky fire, such as caused them, to make the pots wholly black, or as so well expressed by Myres,[8] 'what had begun as an accidental disfigurement had been seized and utilized . . . and developed into an intentional

---

[1] G. Steindorff, *Ti*, Pl. LXXXIV. In plates Nos. LXXXV and LXXXVI the two scenes described as 'Brennen von Töpfen' depict the heating of pots in connexion with bread baking and not the burning of pottery.

[2] P. E. Newberry, *Beni Hasan*, I, Pl. XI; II, Pl. VII.

[3] N. de G. Davies, *Ken-Amūn*, p. 51, Pl. LIX.

[4] J. F. Fougerousse, *Kêmi*, VIII (1946), pp. 1–28.

[5] W. M. F. Petrie, *Memphis*, I, pp. 14–15; *Historical Studies*, II, pp. 34–37.

[6] Cf. A. Lucas, 'The Nature of the Colour of Pottery, with Special Reference to that of Ancient Egypt', *Journ. Royal Anthrop. Inst.*, LIX (1929), pp. 113–29.

[7] A. Lucas, *Journ. Royal Anthrop. Inst.*, LIX (1929), pp. 116–21, 121–9.

[8] J. L. Myres, 'The Early Pot Fabrics of Asia Minor', *Journ. Royal Anthrop. Inst.*, XXXIII (1903), p. 368.

technique'. It would soon be realized, however, that a fire continuously smoky was not satisfactory for the production of well-baked pottery and that the best way of obtaining pots that were both hard and black was to bake them first in a fire as hot as could be obtained and to blacken them after the baking by exposing them to dense smoke.

Black pottery is not at all uncommon in Egypt at the present day and it is made in a very simple manner. Ordinary red or reddish pottery is first made in the usual way and at the end of the baking, when the flames of the fuel have died down, but while the pots are still red-hot, the furnace door is opened and some smoke-producing combustible (in one factory it was pitch and another a mixture of coal and pitch) is thrown on to the hot ashes. This, which does not come into contact with the pottery, produces dense smoke, which blackens the pots. The resulting ware, although generally described as black, is really not black, but a very dark grey, not only on both surfaces, but through to the centre, with, however, sometimes a suspicion of brown just below the surface.

Crowfoot [1] and other writers [2] describe primitive modern processes of making black pottery in which the pots direct from the fire and still red-hot are buried in and covered with organic material, such as chaff, dung and leaves, which in contact with the hot pots smoulders and gives off dense smoke that in a very short time blackens the pots, not merely on the surface, but throughout if the vessels are thin, or well into the substance of the ware when the vessels are thick.

I have produced black pottery on a small scale in the laboratory [3] in the same manner by heating ancient red ware (fragments), modern red ware (miniature pots) and modern grey ware (fragments and miniature pots) in an electric furnace until red-hot and then immediately burying them in sawdust, chopped straw or chaff and allowing them to remain for various periods of time varying from a few minutes to about half an hour. The sawdust, chopped straw or chaff, becoming carbonized, produced dense smoke, which not only blackened the surface of the pottery, but definitely penetrated below the surface, and when the pottery was broken it was seen to be black at both sides with a grey zone in the centre. In other experiments pieces of modern grey ware (cold) were suspended by wire inside and near the top of a metal cylinder, which was closed except for the two small holes in the top through which the wire passed. At the bottom of the cylinder a deep layer of sawdust, chopped straw or chaff was placed and heat was applied to the outside of the bottom of the cylinder until smoke ceased to issue from the top. In every instance the pottery was blackened and in every instance, too, the black penetrated below the surface, in some cases the ware becoming grey through to the centre. There is not any layer of soot on the surface of this blackened pottery and it may be handled freely without soiling the hands and even when rubbed with a clean white fabric this is only slightly discoloured.

In this connexion it may be mentioned that, although smoke consists of solid particles, these are very minute, being of the order of from about one-thousandth of a millimetre to about one-hundred-thousandth of a millimetre in diameter [4] and they are so small that they cannot separately be seen by the naked eye, the 'blacks' or

[1] J. W. Crowfoot, *Sudan Notes*, VIII (1925), p. 131. [2] Several quoted by Crowfoot.
[3] A. Lucas, *Ann. Serv.*, XXXII (1932), pp. 93–96. [4] W. E. Gibbs, *Clouds and Smoke*, p. 130.

'smuts' observed when a chimney or lamp smokes not being what is scientifically meant by smoke, but immensely larger particles. It may be pointed out, too, that the ancient pottery is often of a very porous nature and that in any application of smoke, such as described, the penetration of the smoke would be aided by the contraction of the air in the pores of the pottery as cooling progressed. The carbonization during baking of any organic matter present in the clay would intensify any black colour due to smoke, especially in the centre of the ware.

Although, as shown, pottery undoubtedly does become, not only blackened, but blackened throughout in the presence of dense smoke, it has been stated by several writers [1] that the smoke is not an essential factor; that smoke cannot penetrate pottery and that the phenomenon is not due to the smoke but is caused by reducing gases accompanying the smoke that convert the red oxide of iron present into a black modification. Whether such a change can or does take place may now be discussed.

That the colour of black pottery may be due to the presence of black oxide of iron produced from red oxide by the action of reducing gases in the fire is theoretically possible and from a chemical point of view is very attractive, but that any such reduction actually occurred during the baking of Egyptian black and black-topped ware has not been proved. The available facts may now be considered.

Frankfort states [2] that a black colour due to black oxide of iron produced from red oxide by reduction 'can clearly be distinguished' from a black colour due to carbonaceous matter because the former is changed back to the original red on heating (from which the black may be regenerated by further reduction), whereas the latter is burned out and disappears. This argument, however, contains several omissions and fallacies. Thus the nature of the clay is not taken into account and, although it is true that if black pottery when heated becomes 'pale or yellow-red' the black must have been due to the presence of carbonaceous matter (including smoke), which has been burned out by the heat, there is more than this, namely, that the clay must either have been free from iron compounds or contained them in only very small proportion, or that these must have been of such a kind, or were associated with calcium carbonate in such a manner, that they did not produce red oxide when heated. And the fact that certain black pottery became red when heated is not proof that the black was due to black oxide of iron, unless it could be shown that the clay was not of the red-burning type, since pottery blackened by carbonaceous matter (including smoke) would behave exactly in the same manner if the clay were a red-burning one. The difference in the behaviour of the two kinds of black pottery referred to by Frankfort almost certainly was due to the fact that the one was made from a red-burning clay and the other was not.

As there appears to be a certain amount of confusion respecting the oxides of iron (the black colour of ancient pottery having been attributed by different writers to different oxides, for example, by Frankfort [3] and Forsdyke [4] to ferrous oxide; by

---

[1] W. M. F. Petrie, *Arts and Crafts*, pp. 130–1; E. J. Forsdyke, 'The Pottery called Minyan Ware', *Journ. Hellenic Studies*, XXXIV (1914), p. 139.

[2] H. Frankfort, *Studies in Early Pottery of the Near East*, I, p 10.

[3] H. Frankfort, *Studies in Early Pottery of the Near East*, I, p. 10; II, p. 65, *n*. 2; p. 141, *n*. 2.

[4] E. J. Forsdyke, *Journ. Hellenic Studies*, XXXIV (1914), pp. 137–9.

Petrie [1] to magnetic oxide and by Franchet [2] partly to ferrous oxide and partly to magnetic oxide) these oxides may be considered.

There are three oxides of iron: ferrous oxide, which is black; ferrous-ferric oxide or magnetic oxide, which is also black, and ferric oxide, which is red. Manifestly, therefore, any black oxide must be either ferrous oxide or magnetic oxide.

Ferrous oxide may be produced in the laboratory by heating ferric oxide either in a current of hydrogen to about 300° C.[3] or in an atmosphere of hydrogen and steam to a much higher temperature (700° C. to 1000° C.).[4] Neither of these temperatures, however, is that at which primitive pottery was baked, 300° C. being too low and 700° C.–1000° C. too high, the dehydration temperature of clay being from about 500° C. to about 600° C. Also the atmosphere surrounding pots fired in a primitive manner is neither an atmosphere of hydrogen, nor of hydrogen and steam at any time and, although a very small amount of hydrogen might have been produced by the combustion of the fuel, this could not possibly have continued to exist in the free state in an open fire, but would at once have been burned up with the formation of water vapour. Another and insuperable objection to the black of ancient pottery being due to ferrous oxide is that this oxide is an extremely unstable substance, which cannot exist in the free state, but which is oxidized immediately it is formed. But possibly those who mention ferrous oxide, not being chemists, do not mean the free oxide, but a ferrous compound that for the sake of convenience may be regarded as consisting of this oxide combined with some other substance, such for instance as silica, but in which the oxide has lost its separate identity, the real body present in the example given being ferrous silicate. This would seem to be indicated in at least one instance [5] by a reference to the Staffordshire blue brick (the colour of which is probably due to ferrous silicate) as an example of the reduction of ferric oxide to ferrous oxide. As, however, the brick is *blue* and not black, its colour cannot be any proof that the colouring agent of *black* pottery (which is very black and not blue-black) is either ferrous oxide or ferrous silicate. Moreover, the Staffordshire blue brick is produced in a modern kiln, where the air conditions may be regulated to a nicety and where a reducing atmosphere may readily be obtained and maintained, whereas the early ancient black pottery was fired in a primitive manner in an open fire with an atmosphere that cannot have been a reducing one. The absence of a highly oxidizing atmosphere, as proved by the presence of smoke, is sometimes taken to mean that, therefore, the atmosphere must be a reducing one, but this is not so. The presence of smoke indicates a comparatively low temperature and the partial exclusion of air, but not necessarily the presence of a reducing atmosphere, this being not merely the absence of the usual complement of oxygen, or even the momentary presence of small proportions of reducing gases, but the presence of a considerable proportion of such gases operating over a somewhat lengthy period of time.

---

[1] W. M. F. Petrie, *Arts and Crafts*, p. 130; *Cairo Sc. Journ.*, VI (1912), p. 67; *Diospolis Parva*, p. 13; W. M. F. Petrie and J. E. Quibell, *Naqada and Ballas*, pp. 12, 37.
[2] L. Franchet, *Céramique primitive*, pp. 21, 34, 84, 136, 137.
[3] T. Turner, in Sir Ed. Thorpe, *Dict. of Applied Chemistry*, III (1928), p. 677.
[4] Roscoe and Schorlemmer, *Treatise on Chemistry*, II (1913), p. 1218.
[5] E. J. Forsdyke, *Journ. Hellenic Studies*, XXXIV (1914), p. 140.

Magnetic oxide, which Petrie states is the colouring matter of the ancient black pottery, may be produced in the laboratory by reducing the red oxide by means of hydrogen or carbon monoxide at a temperature of 500° C.[1] or by a mixture of hydrogen and steam at 400° C.,[2] but the primitive method of baking did not provide an atmosphere of hydrogen, carbon monoxide, hydrogen and steam, or a reducing atmosphere of any kind. Ferric oxide also may be converted into magnetic oxide by heating it to a very high temperature (above 1350° C.),[3] a temperature that it is improbable could have been attained under the conditions of the firing of primitive pottery. Usually, too, when ferric oxide is heated in a reducing atmosphere it is metallic iron that is formed. Also if the black is magnetic oxide, it should be magnetic, which is not so. When powdered and tested with a magnet a few tiny particles are found that are magnetic, but these are not nearly sufficient in quantity to account for the black colour and, as magnetic oxide of iron is a common constituent of Egyptian clays, the very small amount of this material present in the black pottery is almost certainly original to the clay, and has not been produced by any chemical reduction of red oxide during baking.[4]

Many of the proofs given that the black of the ancient Egyptian black pottery is not due to black oxide of iron are negative ones, but there are two good positive proofs, namely, first, that a large number of specimens of both ancient and modern Egyptian black ware have been analysed by me and the presence of carbon (smoke) proved chemically in every instance,[5] and second, that pottery made from grey-burning clay without any wash of red ochre, where there is not any red oxide to be reduced, may be blackened by smoke in the manner described.

The presence of carbon was proved by strongly heating finely powdered specimens of the black ware with lead chromate and passing the evolved gas into lime water, which was turned milky every time, thus showing that the gas produced was carbon dioxide, and hence that carbon had been present in the pottery.

Red Ware [6]

Among the brown smoke-stained pots at first produced, there probably would have been an occasional one that was red, because it happened to have been better baked than usual and, as a hotter and brighter fire became more common, so the colour of the pots would improve, until eventually a good red would be quite ordinary. But meanwhile it was discovered that a red colour could be obtained by coating the pots with red ochre.

The various shades of red (including brown) of pottery are always caused by the presence of red oxide of iron, which is due generally to the use of clay containing a relatively large proportion of iron compounds of such a nature that they become

---

[1] H. Abraham and R. Planiol, *Journ. Chemical Society*, Abs. CXXVIII (1925), II, pp. 587–8.

[2] Roscoe and Schorlemmer, *Treatise on Chemistry*, II (1913), p. 1220.

[3] Roscoe and Schorlemmer, *Treatise on Chemistry*, II (1913), p. 1222; T. Turner, in Sir Ed. Thorpe, *Dict. of Applied Chemistry*, III (1928), pp. 677–8.

[4] A. Hopwood, 'Magnetic Materials in Claywares', *Proc. Royal Society*, LXXXIX (1914), pp. 21–30.

[5] Cf. also W. B. Pollard, *Cairo Sc. Journ.*, VI (1912), pp. 72–75.

[6] A. Lucas, *Journ. Royal Anthrop. Inst.*, LIX (1929), pp. 113–15.

converted into red oxide when strongly heated, but, as already mentioned, the red may be caused by the application of red ochre to the surface.

Red pottery may be either uniformly red throughout or, more generally (especially in the case of the thicker and coarser kinds), it is red on both surfaces, but grey or black in the centre, this central zone varying from a thin line to a broad band. The grey or black is due to the carbonization of organic matter, either contained as a natural impurity in the clay in the form of decayed material of vegetable origin (humus), an occurrence by no means infrequent, or else artificially added in order to temper the clay. When clay containing organic matter is heated with free access of air this organic matter at first carbonizes and becomes black, the action beginning from the surface and slowly extending inwards, and, if the walls of the vessel are thin, or the heat considerable or long continued, this blackened matter then gradually burns away, with the simultaneous conversion of the iron compounds into red oxide; but if the vessel is thick, or the heat not great or not of long duration, the organic matter in the thickness of the ware is merely charred and remains, giving a grey or black colour to the zone in the centre. In order to produce a good red surface, not only must the clay be of the right kind, but the fire must be hot and free from smoke at the end of the baking and, with such a fire, any smoke stains produced in the earlier stages of the baking are burned off.

When a red colour other than paint is applied to the surface of a vessel, it is always in the form of a red ferruginous earth made into a wash with water. As this red is a natural earthy form of haematite, it is often termed haematite, but it will save confusion and will serve to distinguish it from the black opaque mineral with a metallic lustre employed for beads, amulets and other small objects, if it be given the better and more correct name of red ochre.

In a review of the second edition of this book,[1] I was accused of lack of precision and of confusing slip and wash, because I called the coating of red ochre a wash, whereas the reviewer considered it to be a slip, since red ochre usually contains a small proportion of clay. The matter is entirely one of definition, and if wash is defined as a mixture of pigment and water, and slip as a mixture of clay and water, with or without pigment, then red ochre, which is primarily a pigment, with a small amount of clay naturally associated, is a wash and not a slip.[2]

I believe that the use of a red wash on ancient Egyptian pottery is less common than is supposed. Polishing so modifies the surface of clay that the light is reflected differently, which naturally affects the colour and may suggest the use of a wash when there is none.[2]

Black and Red Ware [3]

In addition to black pottery and red pottery, a pot partly black and partly red became fashionable at an early date, perhaps simply as the result of the accidental production of a few such pots, though more probably in deliberate imitation of a

---

[1] O. H. Myers, *J.E.A.*, XXI (1935), pp. 126–8.

[2] See P. D. Ritchie, in R. Mond and O. H. Myers, *Cemeteries of Armant*, I, pp. 181–5; *Technical Studies*, IV (1936), pp. 234–6.

[3] A. Lucas, *Journ. Royal Anthrop. Inst.*, LIX (1929), pp. 121–9, 116–21.

gourd bowl with its rim fired black.[1] The Badarian and predynastic black-and-red wares take the form of a black top, with often also a black interior, to an otherwise red vessel.

The black of this black-topped ware, like that of the entirely black ware already dealt with, is a carbon black, that is to say it is a smoke black and not an oxide of iron black, as often stated. The proofs of this are the same as those already given for the entirely black ware and may briefly be recapitulated.

The black cannot be ferrous oxide, as the formation of this compound in pottery is impossible; nor can it be ferrous silicate, since this is not black, but bluish-grey; although the black may contain a few magnetic particles derived from the clay used, it is not magnetic and, therefore, it cannot be magnetic oxide; the atmosphere of the open fire employed for baking the early pottery, although it may have contained a very small proportion of reducing gases (chiefly carbon monoxide), could not have been a reducing one of the kind or to the extent required to reduce red oxide of iron to black oxide, the presence of smoke not being evidence (as it is sometimes thought to be) of a reducing atmosphere, but merely a sign of the absence of a highly oxidizing one, which is only a negative condition, whereas a reducing atmosphere means the positive presence of a large proportion of reducing gases; also, when ferric oxide is heated in a reducing atmosphere it is usually metallic iron that is produced; the black, too, always gives the reactions for carbon (smoke) when tested.[2] Moreover, the black top and black interior may be duplicated under conditions that make it impossible that it should be the product of the reduction of red oxide to black oxide, these conditions being the very short time (a few minutes only) necessary to produce the blackening, the rapidly falling temperature of the pottery during the operation and particularly that the black may be produced in the absence of red oxide with clay (without any wash of red ochre) that is not red-burning but grey-burning. Finally, it may readily be proved that the black is not due to any compound (whether ferrous oxide, ferrous silicate or magnetic oxide) formed by the reduction of red ferric oxide by taking two sherds, if possible from the same pot, one from the red body and the other from the black rim, reducing the red of the former in the laboratory by means of hydrogen and comparing the result with the black sherd. The difference is very marked. The colour of the treated sherd is a dark bluish-grey and not black, and on powdering it and adding hydrochloric acid an immediate and vigorous reaction is produced, and on continued treatment practically all the colour disappears, leaving a very light-grey (almost white) coloured residue from which carbon and carbonaceous matter are manifestly absent. If the experiment has been carried out with due precautions against oxidation, the solution on testing is found to contain iron compounds in the ferrous condition. In the case of the sherd originally black, this, under identical conditions, shows no immediate or pronounced action with the acid and, even after prolonged treatment, the residue remains black; there are no ferrous compounds in the solution and the black gives the tests for carbon.

Before being in a position to explain the mode of production of this black-topped ware, it is necessary to know something more about it than the mere fact that one

[1] A. J. Arkell, *Shaheinab*, p. 75; *J.E.A.*, XLVI (1960), pp. 105–6.
[2] Cf. W. B. Pollard, *Cairo Sc. Journ.*, VI (1912), pp. 72–75.

part of a pot is red and another black, and the detailed description of this pottery may, therefore, be given.

The outside of the body of the pot is red, this red being generally thicker than can be accounted for by a red wash and, therefore, the ware itself must have been baked red; the red does not penetrate through the ware, nor even as a rule to the centre, but there is always a thick black stratum below it; a little red occasionally may be seen on the rim (generally inside) amid the black,[1] showing that the surface originally had been red and subsequently was covered with black, some of the red, however, having escaped the action, and, what is most significant, when the black is scraped off carefully there is red below, which can only mean that the red has not been changed into black but that it has been covered with black. The top (mouth) of the pot and often also the interior are black.

There are only two ways in which such pottery could have been made, namely, (a) by the simultaneous production of the red of the body (apart from any wash of red ochre) and the black of the interior and rim, or (b) by producing ware wholly red first and then by a secondary operation blackening the interior and rim.

The first method was adopted by H. L. Mercer, a pottery manufacturer of Pennsylvania, who in one continuous operation made excellent imitations of the red-bodied black-topped ware, which are now in the Pitt-Rivers Museum at Oxford. His description of the process is as follows:[2] 'Having made a pot of ferruginous clay which in a clear kiln fire would burn red, I rubbed red ochre diluted in water upon it with the hand when half dry. Immediately polishing the surface by rubbing with the circumference of a blown glass bottle in lieu of a pebble, I next thoroughly dried the pot and then stood it upside down with the rim buried an inch deep in a layer of rather fine white pine sawdust in the centre of which immediately under the vessel I placed a piece of resin of the size of a chestnut. Over the bowl thus arranged I so bent a piece of common wire netting (meshed at about two inches) as to entirely surround and overarch the pot at a distance from it of about two inches. Both wire and sawdust stood within a circle of about three feet in diameter of loosely piled stones about one foot high. Upon this I threw about a bushel of finely chipped dry rye straw so as to fill the stone circle and entirely cover the bowl and wire. The straw when ignited burnt about three-quarters of an hour, leaving the pot when cool a duplicate (even to the waving buff-grey zone below the black) of the original specimen.'

At one time I thought and stated [3] that some such process as that of Mercer (without, of course, the wire netting, but with some other method of keeping the fuel from close contact with the pot) had been practised anciently and, although this may have been so (as manifestly it is not impossible) I am unable to conjecture how it could have been done, and Petrie, who first suggested this method,[4] gives no explanation beyond that the pots were baked mouth downwards with the rims in the ashes. It

[1] As examples of this may be mentioned pots Nos. 2002, 2007, 2012, 2015 and 18812 (and probably others) of those described by von Bissing (F. W. von Bissing, *Tongefässe*, 1).
[2] H. L. Mercer, in D. Randall MacIver and C. L. Woolley, *Areika*, p. 17; cf. also W. B. Pollard, *Cairo Sc. Journ.*, VI (1912), pp. 72–75.
[3] A. Lucas, *Journ. Royal Anthrop. Inst.*, LIX (1929), pp. 127–9.
[4] W. M. F. Petrie, *Arts and Crafts*, p. 130.

may be pointed out, too, that in order to bake a large number of pots together with all the rims in the ashes, a considerable area of ground would have been required. Ashes, too, are produced only towards the end of the baking, when the smoke is over. I now think it more likely that the method employed consisted of two distinct operations (as in the making of modern black pottery in Egypt), the first being the making of a red pot (the red of the clay being enhanced in some instances by a wash of red ochre) and the second being the subjecting of the rim and interior of the pot to the action of dense smoke in order to blacken them, this second operation (first suggested as being likely by J. W. Crowfoot) [1] being analagous to that practised in the Sudan and elsewhere at the present day and already described,[2] but instead of the whole pot being covered with chaff or other material, which produces a pot entirely black, the rim only would have been covered, as only this and the interior had to be blackened.

The obvious way of carrying out the operation seemed to be to stand the pots red-hot from the fire mouth downwards on the fuel and this method, therefore, was tried.[3] Miniature pots of two different kinds of clay were procured from a local potter, who supplied them wet; these were partially dried, coated with a thin wash of red ochre by smearing it on with the fingers, polished with a quartz pebble, thoroughly dried, baked in a small electric muffle furnace, and when red-hot placed mouth downwards on a layer of sawdust [4] (which was the fuel chosen) in which the rim was buried. The result was a red pot with a black rim and generally, though not always, a black interior, but the red body at first was almost always badly smoke-stained. In order to avoid this staining, various modifications of the method were tried and eventually it became clear that the exact temperature of the pots was of little importance, provided that they were hot enough to char the fuel and not sufficiently hot to enflame it, and that the principal precaution necessary was to prevent the sawdust giving off smoke from the top, which could be done by manipulating it in such a manner that the smouldering took place entirely beneath the surface so that practically no smoke escaped, which was effected by pressing down the sawdust and covering it up with fresh material whenever any signs of burning manifested themselves, or better, by covering the sawdust, after the pot had been placed in position, with a thin layer of dry earth or sand.[5] There is not any thick layer of soot on the black rim or black interior, which may be handled without soiling the hands and, even when it is rubbed with a clean white fabric, this is only slightly blackened.

Another way of avoiding smoke stains on the bodies of the pots is by burying them, direct from the furnace, mouth upwards in sand, leaving only the rims exposed, covering the rims, while still hot, with sawdust and placing a little sawdust inside the pots. Although this method is very satisfactory in the laboratory, it might not be practicable on a large scale; to bury a number of red-hot pots upright and very

---

[1] A. Lucas, *Journ. Royal Anthrop. Inst.*, LIX (1929), p. 129, *n.* 2.

[2] See pp. 372–6.

[3] A. Lucas, *Ann. Serv.*, XXXII (1932), pp. 93–96.

[4] Anciently, chopped straw or chaff may have been used.

[5] It occasionally happened that a pot accidentally fell over on to its side in the sawdust, which charred in contact with the hot clay and stained the pot, and the black stains on the ancient pottery may have been caused in this manner.

quickly, before they have time to cool, in sand or earth is not easy and in winter the rims of the pots would probably cool so rapidly that they would not be hot enough to char the sawdust and, if the ground were wet, it would be impossible without cracking the pots.

Professor Gordon Childe, in collaboration with Professor Barger, carried out a few experiments, which were 'undertaken primarily to determine whether the highly burnished, light grey ware characteristic of "neolithic" sites on Malta should be assigned to the "reduced" or to the "carboniferous" group'.[1] Since any discussion of the whole subject would be not only too long but also out of place here, the results of only one of the experiments, that with Egyptian pottery, will be considered. The specimen used for the experiment was part of the black rim of a red-bodied, black-topped predynastic pot. This was heated for ten minutes to a dull red heat in a current of oxygen, when the black colour disappeared entirely, giving place to a deep red colour similar to that of the body of the pot. Carbon dioxide was given off, and, therefore, free carbon (due to smoke) was present. When subsequently heated in a reducing atmosphere the red colour disappeared and the sherd became deep black, though a slightly poorer black than it was originally.

Gordon Childe, while admitting that the Egyptian black-topped ware 'may contain free carbon', suggests that the attribution of a grey or black colour in pottery, including Egyptian ware, exclusively to carbon is not justified. With respect to the Egyptian black and black-topped pottery, however, Childe refers to an article written by me in 1929,[2] but he does not seem to have noticed the results of later work published in 1932 [3] and 1934 [4] respectively, which have been summarized above, and which, in my opinion, prove definitely that the black of the Egyptian black and black-topped ware is due to carbon, since the presence of carbon has been determined by analysis and since, too, pottery made from grey-burning clay, without any coating of red ochre, where there is not any red oxide of iron to be reduced, may be blackened by carbon in a manner similar to that of the Egyptian ware.

Grey, Drab and Buff [5] Ware [6]

The various shades of grey (generally ash-grey or greenish-grey), drab and buff of some of the ancient Egyptian pottery are due to the use of a special kind of clay [7] (brownish-grey colour) practically free from organic matter (which is dark coloured and which darkens further on heating, unless it is entirely burned away) which, although it contained iron compounds, also contained a considerable proportion of calcium carbonate, since it is only such clays that become greenish-grey when strongly heated, although when only lightly baked they are often of a slight reddish tint, which is the opposite of what might be expected, and the opposite of what

---

[1] V. Gordon Childe, 'On the Causes of Grey and Black Coloration in Prehistoric Pottery', *Man*, XXXVII (1937), pp. 43–44.

[2] A. Lucas, *Journ. Royal Anthrop. Inst.*, LIX (1929), pp. 113–29.

[3] A. Lucas, *Ann. Serv.*, XXXII (1932), pp. 93–96.

[4] A. Lucas, *Ancient Egyptian Materials and Industries*, 2nd ed., 1934, pp. 316–33.

[5] Buff means having a yellowish tint.

[6] A. Lucas, *Journ. Royal Anthrop. Inst.*, LIX (1929), pp. 115–16.

[7] Cf. J. R. Harris, *Lexicographical Studies*, pp. 202–4.

occurs with many clays; usually the greater the heat the redder the ware. The Qena and Ballas clays of which the modern *qulleh* and *ballas* are made are of this type.[1] Grey, drab or buff pottery occasionally shows a dark zone in the centre of the ware, which is due to the same cause as in the case of red pottery, namely the carbonization of organic matter present in the clay.

Decoration

Apart from any ornamentation of pottery by such means as a light-coloured clay slip, a red wash, smoke-blackening (either of the whole pot or of the top only) or burnishing, the ancient Egyptian pottery sometimes was decorated with incised or painted designs, or with painted figures or scenes, which may now be described.

Incised Designs. As examples of incised designs the brown or black 'Tasian' ware, the Egyptian and Nubian black predynastic ware, and the Nubian brown or black C-group ware may be mentioned, all of which have geometrical patterns incised on them before firing, these incisions being filled in subsequently with white pigment, which, in the case of the Egyptian ware, Quibell states[2] was 'probably gypsum', though he does not give any evidence in support of this. Arkell[3] maintains that pottery of this type is of Sudanese origin. Another example of incised design is the 'rippling' of the finer kinds of Badarian pottery, probably executed with a comb.[4]

Painted Designs, Figures and Scenes. The early Egyptian painted pottery has been classified by Petrie as 'white cross-lined' and 'decorated' respectively.[5]

The former is a red ware with a wash of dark reddish-brown (almost chocolate-coloured) oxide of iron, which was then polished and afterwards painted, before firing, with geometrical designs or with figures of plants, men and animals in a white, or yellowish-white, pigment. Petrie calls it 'polished red pottery with white cross-lines'[6] and says[6] that it 'is painted with a white slip clay upon the base of the polished red pottery'. In another place, however, he states[7] that 'This white paint was put over a bright red[8] facing of haematite'; Frankfort says[9] that it is made 'of ferruginous clay and bears rectilinear designs in chalky white paint on a red haematite wash' and Childe calls it[10] 'essentially red-polished ware ornamented with patterns in dull white paint'. After a comparatively short life this 'white cross-lined' pottery disappeared, giving place to the 'decorated' ware about to be described. Petrie's statement that the white pigment used was a white clay has been confirmed by Ritchie,[11] who analysed

---

[1] Cf. G. A. Reisner, *Kerma*, IV–V, pp. 320 f. An analysis of a present-day typical pottery clay from Ballas shows it to contain a comparatively large proportion of iron compounds (6 per cent) and more than 20 per cent of calcium carbonate. For details of analyses, see p. 496.

[2] W. M. F. Petrie and J. E. Quibell, *Naqada and Ballas*, p. 13.

[3] A. J. Arkell, *J.E.A.*, XXXIX (1953), pp. 76–79; *Bibliotheca Orientalis*, XIII (1956), pp. 123–4.

[4] G. Brunton and G. Caton-Thompson, *Badarian Civilisation*, pp. 20–26.

[5] W. M. F. Petrie, *Prehistoric Egypt*, pp. 14, 16; *Diospolis Parva*, pp. 13–17. See p. 385.

[6] W. M. F. Petrie and J. E. Quibell, *Naqada and Ballas*, p. 37.

[7] W. M. F. Petrie, *Arts and Crafts*, p. 129.

[8] On the pots in the Cairo Museum examined by me this colour is dark reddish-brown and not bright red, as described by Petrie.

[9] H. Frankfort, *Studies in Early Pottery of the Near East*, I, p. 94.

[10] V. Gordon Childe, *New Light on the Most Ancient East*, p. 77.

[11] P. D. Ritchie, in R. Mond and O. H. Myers, *Cemeteries of Armant*, I, pp. 182, 184, 185; *Technical Studies*, IV (1936), pp. 234–6.

specimens from Armant. In this connexion it may be mentioned that a mass of white clay was found in the predynastic cemetery at Mahasna.[1]

The 'decorated' ware, which, though still predynastic, is later than the 'white cross-lined' ware, is sometimes of a drab colour and sometimes of a pale red colour with the painting (principally ships and wading birds, with occasionally men and animals), which was done before the firing, in dark reddish-brown oxide of iron, which often has a slight purple tint. Sometimes patches of a pot are drab and other patches pinkish. The drab ware was apparently so much esteemed that occasionally it was imitated by putting a thin slip of a drab colour on a pale red-coloured pot before painting. The pale red ware is probably the same as the drab ware, but baked at a much lower temperature, since specimens that were strongly heated by me (to about 1000° C.), in an electric muffle furnace became greenish-grey.

Peet, describing the 'decorated' ware, says [2] it is 'unpolished with or without slip', and that 'The clay is pink or buff'; Frankfort says [3] 'the paint is (except in a few cases) applied directly to the pinkish buff body of the pots without interposed slip'; Childe says[4] that the pottery is a 'light-coloured buff clay painted with patterns in brownish-red', and Petrie says [5] 'The later prehistoric painting was in dull red on a buff body.'

I have examined sixty-nine specimens of this predynastic 'decorated' ware in the Cairo Museum and found that thirty-five (51 per cent) were drab, twenty-two (32 per cent) pinkish-drab, four (6 per cent) partly drab and partly pink, three (4 per cent) pale red with drab slip, and five (7 per cent) clear, bright pale red, which seems unlikely to have been the original colour, but which may be due to the unintentional removal of a drab coating by washing. Brunton says [6] 'The entire surface of most Predynastic decorated pots was covered with a thin whitish coat presumably so that the paint should show up better than it would on the plain red pottery. This coat being easily soluble in water has generally disappeared, especially when the pots have been washed to clean them, or soaked for the removal of salt.' The paint is a similar dark reddish-brown in all cases.

Up to the time of this 'decorated' ware, the only clay employed for all Egyptian pottery was that brought down and deposited by the Nile, either in the Delta or in the Nile Valley, at the sides of the river, that from one locality differing from that from another locality principally in the degree of fineness of the particles and in the proportion of sand present, or in some places in Upper Egypt by the presence of numerous tiny flakes of mica. The clay of the drab ware,[7] on the other hand, is not a Nile deposit, but is a desert product composed of an intimate mixture of very fine clay and very fine calcium carbonate (carbonate of lime), which has been washed out of the limestone hills that border the Nile Valley and deposited at, or near, the mouths of certain smaller valleys that enter the main river valley, two well-known localities

[1] E. R. Ayrton and W. L. S. Loat, *Predynastic Cemetery at El Mahasna*, p. 12.
[2] T. E. Peet, *Cemeteries of Abydos*, II, p. 12.
[3] H. Frankfort, *Studies in Early Pottery of the Near East*, I, p. 96.
[4] V. Gordon Childe, *New Light on the Most Ancient East*, p. 90.
[5] W. M. F. Petrie, *Arts and Crafts*, p. 129.
[6] G. Brunton, *Ann. Serv.*, XXXIV (1934), p. 153.
[7] Also used for other objects, including crucibles and magical bricks, see analyses, p. 496. Cf. J. R. Harris, *Lexicographical Studies*, pp. 202–4.

for this clay being Qena and Ballas, both in Upper Egypt, where the deposits have been exploited from an early period. Other, but less important, deposits occur in Middle Egypt, as for instance at Sohag.[1] Geologically this material is a calcareous clay or marl.

The Nile Valley clay always burns to a brown or red colour, whereas the calcareous clay becomes of a pale red or pinkish colour when lightly burned, and drab, buff, or greenish-grey when strongly burned, the stronger the heat the greener the resulting colour, which accounts not only for the varied colours of the ware but also for the fact that sometimes a pot meant to be drab may be partly or wholly pink, owing to the heat not having been very strong, or not uniform. But the high temperature necessary to produce drab-coloured ware may also produce a purple tint in the red oxide of iron used as a pigment, certain kinds of red oxide of iron becoming purplish when strongly heated.[2] With reference to this purple colour Mackay writes [3] 'A warm purplish black was used on much of the predynastic pottery of Egypt. It has a manganese base and was especially suited to withstand the heat of the furnace when the jar was baked.' The colour of the pigment of the Egyptian predynastic 'decorated' ware, however, is never quite black and, therefore, it cannot be black oxide of manganese, nor does black oxide of manganese become purple when strongly heated. It is true that a purplish colour in glaze and glass is often due to the use of oxide of manganese, which forms a purple compound with other ingredients present, but when oxide of manganese is merely painted on a pot and heated, such purple compounds are not formed, whereas certain oxides of iron become purple when heated, and the purple colour, therefore, is an indication that the pigment consists of oxide of iron and not of oxide of manganese. That this actually is so I have proved by the analysis of specimens of this purple colour from predynastic 'decorated' pots, and I have found that in every instance it consisted of oxide of iron and was free from manganese compounds. Since the painting was done before firing, a carbon-black pigment could not be employed, as the carbon would have burned off during firing, and, so far as is known to me, a black pigment, although in early and common use for tomb painting, was not used for pottery before the Eighteenth Dynasty, when it was applied after firing.

The Eighteenth Dynasty pottery may now briefly be considered. The nature and colour of certain pottery wine jars from the end of the Eighteenth Dynasty (tomb of Tutankhamūn) have already been dealt with.[4] Other pottery of this same dynasty from El Amarna and Giza respectively examined by me was a drab-coloured ware painted with light blue, red and black pigments after firing. The blue was the usual Egyptian blue frit; the red was red ochre and the black was carbon. In one instance of drab ware, however, a black pigment consisted of oxide of manganese, and in one of red ware with a yellowish-white slip, the black pigment, although possibly intended to be oxide of manganese, was actually black oxide of iron containing a very small proportion of oxide of manganese, these two oxides frequently occurring naturally together. Pottery of the New Kingdom is frequently covered with an engobe of

[1] G. A. Reisner, Kerma, IV–V, p. 321.

[2] J. W. Mellor, Inorganic and Theoretical Chemistry, XIII, pp. 782–3.

[3] E. Mackay, Report on Excavations at Jemdet Nasr, Iraq, p. 232.

[4] See pp. 19–20.

gypsum,[1] and a few specimens of painted pottery of Eighteenth Dynasty date are varnished.[2]

The use of the terms 'white cross-lined' and 'decorated' in the foregoing discussion does not imply approval of Petrie's original system of pottery classification, which is based on inconsistent principles and is altogether unsatisfactory.[3] The primary consideration in any sound system must be the nature of the body material, other factors such as surface colour, decoration, and form being then used for secondary subdivision. Several attempts have been made to establish a more scientific classification,[4] the most adequate being that formulated by O. H. Myers.[5]

---

[1] Cf. B. H. Stricker, *Oud. Med. N.R.*, XXIV (1943), pp. 92–93.

[2] Cairo Museum, Nos. J. 72517, 72518.

[3] Cf. T. E. Peet, *J.E.A.*, XIX (1933), pp. 62–64. Peet rightly calls the classification 'faulty' and 'the paraphernalia of the Dark Ages'.

[4] E.g. T. E. Peet and J. P. Droop, in T. E. Peet, *Cemeteries of Abydos*, II, pp. 10–13; G. A. Reisner, *Naga-ed-Dêr*, I, pp. 90–91.

[5] R. Mond and O. H. Myers, *Cemeteries of Armant*, I, pp. 49–58.

Chapter XVI

PRECIOUS AND
SEMI-PRECIOUS STONES

The stones used in ancient Egypt for amulets, beads, jewellery,[1] scarabs and other personal ornaments, although doubtless all costly and highly prized at the time, include many that nowadays would not be called precious, but at the most semi-precious, and in some instances not even that. Many of these stones were also employed as inlay for the decoration of boxes, coffins, furniture and other objects.

The principal stones used were agate, amethyst, beryl, calcite, carnelian, chalcedony, coral, felspar, garnet, haematite, jade, jadeite, jasper, lapis lazuli, malachite, olivine, onyx, pearl, peridot, rock crystal, sard, sardonyx and turquoise. With these it will be convenient to include amber and other resins, which, although not stones, were regarded as semi-precious materials and sometimes were used for many of the purposes of gem stones. The diamond, opal, ruby and sapphire were not known to the ancient Egyptians.

Precious stones are mentioned frequently in Egyptian texts as having been employed for particular purposes and received as tribute or taken among the spoils of war and, although many of these stones are referred to individually by name, the translation of some of these names is still uncertain.[2] Pliny mentions about thirty different kinds of precious stones obtained from Egypt and Ethiopia,[3] but relatively few of these can be identified.

Many of the stones enumerated were employed as early as Badarian and predynastic times, while others only came into use at a very late period and, with a few exceptions, they were all local products.

Agate, Onyx, Sardonyx

Agate, onyx and sardonyx are all banded forms of chalcedony and, being very closely related, they are often classed together as agate; they all consist of silica,[4] the principal difference between them being in the colour of the bands: in agate, the bands, which are frequently irregular and ill-defined, but usually more or less concentric, are generally white and brown, with sometimes a little blue; in onyx and

---

[1] For the so-called Egyptian cloisonné work see G. Möller, *Metallkunst*, pp. 24–26; M. Rosenberg, *Ägyptische Einlage in Gold und Silber*; E. Vernier, *Bijouterie et Joaillerie*, pp. 96–100; *B.I.F.A.O.*, VI (1908), pp. 190–2; C. R. Williams, *Gold and Silver Jewelry*, pp. 31–33.

[2] Cf. J. R. Harris, *Lexicographical Studies*, pp. 95–140.

[3] XXXVII.

[4] Where silica is mentioned as distinct from quartz, this means that the material, although of the same composition as quartz, is not crystalline.

sardonyx the bands are generally straight and comparatively regular, in onyx being milk-white alternating with black and in sardonyx white alternating with reddish-brown or red, this stone, as its name indicates, consisting of onyx stratified with bands of sard. The greater part of the agate, onyx and sardonyx, especially the onyx, used for jewellery at the present day is artificially stained.

Agate occurs plentifully in Egypt, chiefly in the form of pebbles, but it has been found also in small quantity associated with jasper and chalcedony in a dyke rock at the head of Wadi Abu Gerida in the eastern desert.[1] Onxy and sardonyx probably also occur in Egypt, though no mention of them can be found in the geological reports. Pliny refers to Egyptian agate from Thebes and states that it is destitute of red and white veins and is an antidote to scorpion poison.[2]

Agate pebbles have been found in predynastic graves [3] and both agate beads [4,5] and onyx beads [5] of this date are known, Beads, amulets and other small objects of agate are known from all periods, and the stone was also used to a limited extent in jewellery. The earliest use of sardonyx that can be traced is from the Twenty-second Dynasty,[6] and the discs from the Nineteenth Dynasty temple of Meneptah at Memphis, but certainly of later date,[7] called onyx by the finder, appear from the description (white, red and brown) to be sardonyx. The principal use of these three stones, was, however, at a late period, from about the Twenty-second Dynasty onwards, but more especially during the Greek and Roman epochs. A very fine set of agate vessels, of unknown but probably Roman date, was found at Qift in Upper Egypt, of which six were acquired by the Cairo Museum [8] and two (the largest) by a dealer. These probably came from India and may be 'murrhine' vessels, such as Pliny describes.[9] At a late date agate and onyx beads were imitated in glass.

Amber and other Resins

Although amber and other resins are neither precious nor semi-precious stones, they may conveniently be included here as they were used for amulets and in jewellery in the same manner as these stones.

Petrie mentions two inscribed scarabs that he terms amber,[10] and the large scarab in the pectoral of Hatiay of the Twenty-first Dynasty [11] and a scarab of uncertain date in the British Museum [12] are both called amber. That amber may have been used by

---

[1] T. Barron and W. F. Hume, *Topog. and Geol. of the Eastern Desert*, p. 266; W. F. Hume, *Geology of Egypt*, II, Part III, p. 862.

[2] XXXVII: 54.

[3] W. M. F. Petrie, *Prehistoric Egypt*, p. 44; *Diospolis Parva*, p. 27.

[4] W. M. F. Petrie and J. E. Quibell, *Naqada and Ballas*, pp. 10, 44.

[5] W. M. F. Petrie, G. A. Wainwright and E. Mackay, *Labyrinth, Gerzeh and Mazghuneh*, p. 22.

[6] Examples in the Cairo Museum.

[7] W. M. F. Petrie, *Memphis*, I, p. 12, Pl. XXVIII (12).

[8] R. Engelbach, *Ann. Serv.*, XXXI (1931), pp. 126–7, Pl. I.

[9] S. H. Ball, *A Roman Book on Precious Stones*, pp. 217–21. Cf., however, A. I. Lowenthal and D. B. Harden, *Journ. Roman Studies*, XXXIX (1949), pp. 31–37; D. B. Harden, *Journ. Roman Studies*, XLIV (1954), p. 53.

[10] W. M. F. Petrie, *Scarabs and Cylinders*, p. 9; cf. H. R. Hall, *Catalogue of the Eg. Scarabs . . . in the Brit. Mus.*, p. xxix.

[11] E. Vernier, *Bijoux et Orfèvreries*, p. 397.

[12] H. R. Hall, *Catalogue of the Eg. Scarabs . . . in the Brit. Mus.*, p. xxix.

the ancient Egyptians, especially at a late date, is not denied, but that all the objects termed amber are indeed amber has not been proved, and some at least are almost certainly other kinds of resin, lumps of which are very common in ancient Egyptian graves of all periods, particularly in those of Badarian, predynastic and early dynastic date. Worked resin that is not amber is also known, for example, in the tomb of Tutankhamūn [1] there was a double finger ring of resin engraved with the royal cartouches; two large resin scarabs, one having a bird carved in relief on the surface; a necklace of about fifty-five resin beads graduated from comparatively small ones to very large ones; a necklace of alternate resin and lapis lazuli beads; a pair of earrings made up of alternate resin and gold beads; a broken object (gold mounted) of resin, probably one of a pair of earrings; a hair-ring of resin; two knuckle bones of resin and a resin knob of a box. The resin of all these objects is very brittle, dark red by transmitted light and almost black by reflected light; I believe it is not amber, principally on account of its ready solubility in many of the ordinary organic solvents, for example, alcohol and acetone in which amber is only slightly soluble. Small resin beads from periods other than the Eighteenth Dynasty are also known and these, too, whenever I have tested them have been found to be easily soluble in alcohol and many other organic solvents and, therefore, it is improbable that they are amber, a characteristic feature of which is its very slight solubility in such solvents.

Doran analysed several predynastic resin beads found by Myers at Armant and he says 'The evidence, so far as it goes, supports the assumption that specimens Ar. 1403 and Ar. 1424a are natural amber. . . . They show differences from the characteristics ordinarily assigned to amber, but these differences are of the same order and of a kind which is consistent with age-long maturing of the resin.' [2] Is it justifiable, however, to assume that amber, which had already undergone 'age-long maturing' before it was found and used by man, undergoes further alteration when kept for a few thousand years more?

Pliny quotes Nicias for the statement that amber was produced in Egypt,[3] which, however, is not so.

Amethyst [4]

Amethyst consists of transparent quartz coloured by a trace of some compound of manganese. It was used largely in ancient Egypt in the form of beads, chiefly for necklaces, but also for bracelets, amulets and scarabs, the majority of specimens being pale in colour. From the First Dynasty there are bracelets containing amethyst beads, it was much employed during the Middle Kingdom, occasionally during the Empire (for example two amethyst scarabs were found in the tomb of Tutankhamūn) and its use continued until Roman times. The predynastic bead from Naqada, now in the Museum of University College, London, where I have examined it, which Petrie calls amethyst,[5] although it looks somewhat like very pale amethyst is certainly not amethyst, as it can be scratched with a knife.

---

[1] A. Lucas, in H. Carter, *Tut-ankh-Amen*, II, p. 184 (Appendix II).

[2] W. Doran, in R. Mond and O. H. Myers, *Cemeteries of Armant*, I, pp. 96–100. Cf. also Hallimond's observations, *ib.*, p. 94.

[3] XXXVII: II.   [4] Cf. J. R. Harris, *Lexicographical Studies*, pp. 121–2.

[5] W. M. F. Petrie, *Prehistoric Egypt*, p. 44.

Amethyst workings, apparently dating from the Old Kingdom, have been found in the western desert, about forty miles north-west of Abu Simbel,[1] and these were probably also known during the Middle Kingdom, though the chief source of amethyst at that period was evidently at Wadi el Hudi, about twenty miles south-east of Aswan, where extensive workings and numerous inscriptions have been discovered.[2] Other ancient workings, exploited during the Roman period in particular, exist near Gebel Abu Diyeiba in the Safaga district of the eastern desert,[3] the stones occurring in cavities in a red granite. Pliny refers to Egyptian amethyst.[4]

Beryl

Beryl may be green, pale blue (aquamarine), yellow or white, but so far as is known, only the green variety occurs in Egypt or was used by the ancient Egyptians.

Beryl occurs in the Sikait-Zubara region of the Red Sea hills, where there are extensive old workings,[5] probably of Graeco-Roman age, and there is no evidence that the mines were worked in the reign of Amenhotpe III as stated by Wilkinson.[6] These mines are mentioned by Strabo [7] and Pliny [8] and by many Arab historians,[9] and were probably the original and only source of beryl in classical times. The stones are found in mica-talc schists in the form of hexagonal prisms having characteristic vertical striations. Several attempts have been made in modern times to reopen the mines, all of which have proved commercial failures, largely because the stones are not of sufficiently good quality for modern requirements. Beryls are always transparent or translucent and never opaque, and though stones of a good enough quality to rank as true emeralds (the emerald being only a particularly good quality beryl) [10] may well have been found in the past, none such has been found in modern times. 'Most of the crystals are pale whitish-green, full of flaws and unfit for jewellery, but

---

[1] R. Engelbach, *Ann. Serv.*, XXXIII (1933), p. 69; O. H. Little, *Ann. Serv.*, XXXIII (1933), p. 80; R. Engelbach, *Ann. Serv.*, XXXVIII (1938), p. 370; G. W. Murray, *Geog. Journ.*, XCIV (1939), p. 105.

[2] L. Nassim, *Minerals of Economical Interest*, p. 167; A. Fakhry, *Ann. Serv.*, XLVI (1947), pp. 51–54; *Inscriptions . . . at Wadi el Hudi*.

[3] Mines and Quarries Dept., *Report on the Mineral Industry*, pp. 37–39; G. W. Murray, *Cairo Sc. Journ.*, VIII (1914), p. 179; D. Meredith, *Eos*, XLVIII (2) (1957), pp. 117–20.

[4] XXXVII: 40.

[5] Mines and Quarries Dept., *Report on the Mineral Industry*, pp. 37–39; W. F. Hume, *Geology of Egypt*, II, Part I, pp. 107–25; O. Schneider, *Zeitschrift für Ethnologie*, XXIV (1892), pp. 41–100; K. Fitzler, *Steinbrüche und Bergwerke*, pp. 99–101; D. A. MacAlister, *Geog. Journ.*, XVI (1900), pp. 537–49; G. W. Murray, *J.E.A.*, XI (1925), pp. 144–5; H. W. Seton Karr, *Eastern Desert of Egypt. Expedition to the Emerald Mines of Sikait and Zabara*; A. Stella, *Boll. Soc. Geol. Ital.*, LIII (1935), pp. 329–32; E. S. Thomas, *Cairo Sc. Journ.*, III (1909), pp. 267–72; E. Vernier, *Bijouterie et Joaillerie*, pp. 16–19. For further bibliography see W. F. Hume, *loc. cit.*; O. Schneider, *loc. cit.*; A. H. Keldani, *Bibliography of Geology and Related Sciences Concerning Egypt*; C. D. Sherborn, *Bibliography of Scientific and Technical Literature Relating to Egypt*.

[6] J. G. Wilkinson, *The Ancient Egyptians*, 1878, I, p. 154.

[7] XVII: 1, 45.

[8] XXXVII: 16–18.

[9] See O. Schneider, *Zeitschrift für Ethnologie*, XXIV (1892), pp. 41–100.

[10] Beryl and emerald have the same composition, both being double silicates of beryllium and aluminium, the only difference between them being one of quality, the deeper coloured and more transparent variety being called emerald and the lighter coloured and less transparent stones being beryl.

occasionally the colour is darker and the stones may be classed as inferior emeralds.'[1] Beryl was used in Egypt at first in the form of the natural hexagonal crystals in which it occurs, since being slightly harder than quartz the Egyptians were unable to cut it satisfactorily until a later date, although it was sometimes bored.

Beryl is frequently cited as the material for beads and other small objects, but many of these identifications are incorrect, and none can be accepted that has not been verified by a mineralogist. In fact, so far as can be ascertained, beryl was never used in ancient Egypt until a late period and chiefly from Ptolemaic times and all the stones of earlier date called beryl that have been examined by me have been found not to be beryl. Thus the stones in the Dahshur jewellery called emerald and Egyptian emerald when first described [2] are green felspar; the stone of Twentieth Dynasty date called an uncut emerald [3] is also green felspar; the beads of Twelfth Dynasty date from Naqada [4] are most unlikely to be beryl at that period; the green stone of the three Twelfth Dynasty [5] scarabs and of one of the two Eighteenth Dynasty scarabs [5] described as beryl has been examined by me and is not beryl (the other Eighteenth Dynasty scarab also described as beryl could not be found, but it is very improbable that it is beryl). Petrie states [6] that 'Beryl or emerald is unknown in scarabs and was only worked after the cessation of scarab making.' The amulets, beads and pendants (predynastic, early dynastic and New Kingdom) found in Nubia and called beryl [7] are almost certainly none of them beryl, as some of the beads that were later submitted to me for verification were olivine and some green felspar. Beryl objects were found at Coptos,[8] but no particulars are given, and beryl amulets stated to be of about the end of the Twenty-sixth Dynasty [9] and of the Thirtieth Dynasty [10] respectively are recorded. Many small objects found at Nuri and other sites in the Sudan have been loosely described as beryl [11] in the excavation reports, though the correctness of these identifications must be doubted, since of two specimens submitted for verification one proved to be nephrite jade and the other a species of microline felspar.[12] There are, however, large beryls in the silver jewellery discovered at Qustul,[13] and a single uncut 'emerald' was identified in a necklace from a predynastic grave at Kubanieh.[14]

---

[1] Mines and Quarries Dept., *Report on the Mineral Industry*, pp. 37–38. Cf. W. F. Hume, *Geology of Egypt*, II, Part III, p. 859.

[2] J. de Morgan, *Dahchour, mars–juin 1894*, pp. 60, 63, 64, 66–70, 112–14; *Dahchour, 1894–1895*, pp. 51, 53, 58–65; In several instances Vernier repeats de Morgan's mistake, for example, J. de Morgan, *Dahchour, mars–juin 1894*, p. 66, Pl. XX (15, 16), and E. Vernier, *Bijoux et Orfèvreries*, p. 21, Nos. 52026–7.

[3] G. Maspero, *Guide to the Cairo Museum*, English trans., 1903, p. 519.

[4] W. M. F. Petrie and J. E. Quibell, *Naqada and Ballas*, p. 45.

[5] P. E. Newberry, *Scarab-shaped Seals*, Nos. 37410, 37413, 37419, 36236, 37487.

[6] W. M. F. Petrie, *Scarabs and Cylinders*, p. 8.

[7] G. A. Reisner, *Arch. Survey of Nubia, 1907–1908*, I, pp. 33, 35, 123, 132; C. M. Firth, *Arch. Survey of Nubia, 1908–1909*, pp. 62, 78; *1909–1910*, pp. 53, 74, 97; *1910–1911*, p. 221.

[8] W. M. F. Petrie, *Koptos*, p. 26.

[9] W. M. F. Petrie, *Kahun, Gurob and Hawara*, pp. 18–19.   [10] W. M. F. Petrie, *Abydos*, I, p. 38.

[11] Also as turquoise, amazon stone and emerald matrix.   [12] D. Dunham, *Nuri*, p. 5.

[13] W. B. Emery, *Royal Tombs of Ballana and Qustul*, pp. 110, 183, 185, 187, 189, 191, 197, 198, 258.

[14] H. Junker, *Bericht über die Grabungen . . . auf den Friedhöfen von El-Kubanieh—Sud*, p. 102. Identified by Prof. Doelter.

Calcite, Iceland Spar

Calcite is simply the geological name for what is termed alabaster in Egypt; in thin plates it is translucent and in this form it was employed as inlay for jewellery and furniture, for example on some of the objects from the tomb of Tutankhamūn.

A very pure and transparent variety of calcite termed 'Iceland spar' was used occasionally for small objects, a cylinder seal of this material from the Sixth Dynasty being known [1] (though Iceland spar is neither glass-hard nor natural glass as stated in the description), as also beads of the Eighteenth, Twenty-second and Twenty-third Dynasties respectively. Brunton reports a green calcite bead of Badarian date.[2] The transparent cover of the small 'ox' pendant from Dahshur is neither Iceland spar (*spath*) as stated by the finder,[3] nor fluorspar as suggested by Newberry,[4] but rock crystal.[5]

All varieties of calcite occur abundantly in the eastern desert of Egypt, Iceland spar being found west of Asiut (from which place there is a fine specimen in the Geological Museum) and also at El Amarna.

Carnelian, Sard [6]

Carnelian is a translucent red chalcedony, the colour being due to the presence of a small amount of oxide of iron; in the form of pebbles it occurs abundantly in the eastern desert of Egypt and certainly in one locality at least in the western desert.[7] It was much used from predynastic times onwards,[8] at first for beads and amulets and later also for inlay for jewellery,[9] furniture and coffins, and occasionally for finger rings and small vessels.[10] In the Cairo Museum there is a decorated (etched) carnelian scaraboid of the Eighteenth Dynasty (possibly of Amenhotpe III).[11] This is the only example of decorated carnelian known to me from Egypt, though this technique is very common from India and Mesopotamia. Myers found a few glazed carnelian beads of predynastic date at Armant.[12]

During the Eighteenth Dynasty an imitation carnelian consisting of translucent quartz set in a red cement was often employed to supplement the genuine article as inlay, for instance, on two of the coffins of Yuya, on the coffin formerly supposed to be that of Akhenaten, but now thought to be that of Smenkhkarē, and on several of

---

[1] H. R. Hall, *Catalogue of Eg. Scarabs . . . in the Brit. Mus.*, p. xxvi.

[2] G. Brunton, *Mostagedda*, p. 36.

[3] J. de Morgan, *Dahchour, 1894–1895*, p. 67.

[4] P. E. Newberry, *J.E.A.*, VI (1920), p. 159.

[5] A. Lucas and G. Brunton, *Ann. Serv.*, XXXVI (1936), pp. 197–200.

[6] Cf. J. R. Harris, *Lexicographical Studies*, pp. 120–1.

[7] R. Engelbach, *Ann. Serv.*, XXXVIII (1938), p. 370; G. W. Murray, *Geog. Journ.*, XCIV (1939), p. 105.

[8] W. M. F. Petrie, *Prehistoric Egypt*, p. 44; G. Brunton and G. Caton-Thompson, *Badarian Civilisation*, p. 56.

[9] E.g. in the anklets of Queen Hetepheres (G. A. Reisner, *History of the Giza Necropolis*, II, p. 44).

[10] J. de Morgan, *Dahchour, mars–juin 1894*, p. 70, Pls. XIX, XXV; W. M. F. Petrie, *Royal Tombs*, II, p. 12.

[11] W. M. F. Petrie, *Historical Scarabs*, 1889, No. 819. Museum No. $\frac{14}{26}\frac{5}{4}$; H. C. Beck, *Antiquaries Journ.*, XIII (1933), p. 395.

[12] R. Mond and O. H. Myers, *Cemeteries of Armant*, I, p. 72.

the objects from the tomb of Tutankhamūn, including the mask, the four miniature canopic coffins and the large gold coffin.

Sard is the name applied to the darker varieties of carnelian, some of which are almost black: it was used to a small extent from predynastic times onwards,[1] for example in the sard and gold sceptre of Khasekhemui (Second Dynasty),[2] and for a decorative plaque of Amenhotpe III.[3] Pliny states [4] that sard occurs in Egypt, which is probably so.

A yellow variety of carnelian was used occasionally for beads in the Twelfth Dynasty,[5] and in the jewellery from the tomb of Tutankhamūn.

Chalcedony

Chalcedony is a form of silica, translucent and somewhat waxy in appearance and, when pure, white or greyish-white in colour with often a slight bluish tint: it may, however, be of almost any colour owing to the presence of a small proportion of impurity, many of the coloured varieties having special names.

Chalcedony occurs in Egypt near Wadi Saga [6] and in Wadi Abu Gerida [6] in the eastern desert; in the Baharia Oasis of the western desert;[7] about forty miles north-west of Abu Simbel;[8] in the Fayum province [7] and in Sinai.[7] It was employed occa-sionally in ancient Egypt for beads, pendants, and scarabs,[9] its use dating as early as predynastic times,[10] and as late as the Roman period.

Chrysoprase

Chrysoprase is an apple-green coloured variety of chalcedony. A pendant of pre-dynastic date found at El Amrah is stated to be chrysoprase,[11] as also a fish and an amulet of unknown date.[12] Predynastic beads from Matmar were tentatively identified as chrysoprase,[13] and chrysoprase has been reported in several pieces of jewellery in the Berlin Museum.[14]

Coral

Coral consists of the hard skeletons of various marine organisms and it may be white, various shades of red, or black in colour. Only the white and red kinds need be considered, as there is not any record of the black variety having been used anciently, although it occurs in the Mediterranean.

Two instances of the ordinary white coral having been used in ancient Egypt

---

[1] W. M. F. Petrie, G. A. Wainwright and E. Mackay, *Labyrinth, Gerzeh and Mazghuneh*, p. 22.

[2] W. M. F. Petrie, *Royal Tombs*, II, p. 27.

[3] *J.E.A.*, III (1916), p. 74, Pl. XI.   [4] XXXVII: 31.

[5] W. M. F. Petrie, G. Brunton and M. A. Murray, *Lahun*, II, p. 13.

[6] T. Barron and W. F. Hume, *Topog. and Geol. of the Eastern Desert*, p. 266; W. F. Hume, *Geology of Egypt*, II, Part III, p. 862.

[7] Specimens from these sources may be seen in the Geological Museum, Cairo.

[8] O. H. Little, *Ann. Serv.*, XXXIII (1933), p. 80.

[9] W. M. F. Petrie, *Scarabs and Cylinders*, p. 8; H. R. Hall, *Catalogue of the Eg. Scarabs . . . in the Brit. Mus.*, p. xxvii; H. Carter, *Tut-ankh-Amen*, II, p. 127.

[10] W. M. F. Petrie, G. A. Wainwright and E. Mackay, *Labyrinth, Gerzeh and Mazghuneh*, p. 22.

[11] D. Randall MacIver and A. C. Mace, *El Amrah and Abydos*, p. 49.

[12] A. Brongniart, in J. Passalacqua, *Catalogue des antiquités découvertes en Égypte*, p. 223.

[13] G. Brunton, *Matmar*, p. 23.

[14] H. Schäfer, *Ägyptische Goldschmiedearbeiten*, Nos. 13, 34, 35, 37.

which can be traced were respectively at Gurob (Nineteenth Dynasty) [1] and at Defenneh (seventh to sixth century B.C.), at which latter place there was a large quantity in the form of natural branches.[2]

There are two varieties of red coral, one the well known, solid, branching kind (*Corallium nobile; Corallium rubrum*) used at the present day for jewellery, especially for necklaces, an d the other the lesser known 'pipe' or 'organ' coral (*Tubipora musica*), which, as the name indicates, occurs in the form of hollow tubes, the appearance of which is somewhat suggestive of miniature organ pipes.

The former, or precious coral, is obtained mainly from the western Mediterranean and was an important article of commerce in Roman times. All the examples known from ancient Egypt are of late date, ranging chiefly from the Ptolemaic to the Coptic period and they consist either of amulets, or more generally, of beads or small branched pieces bored for suspension round the neck. Beads of this coral are common in the graves of late date discovered by Emery at Qustul, near Abu Simbel in Nubia.[3]

Pipe coral occurs on the shores of the Red Sea; Pococke saw it at Tor (Sinai) [4] and in the Geological Museum at Cairo there is a specimen from Dahab (East Sinai), but it is found also farther south.[5] This coral was known and used anciently, and beads of it, both of Badarian and early predynastic date, have been found [6] and also pieces broken up ready for threading;[7] it has been found, too, in a Nubian grave of about Old Kingdom date [8] and also in an Eighteenth Dynasty house at El Amarna.[9]

In addition to the specimens enumerated, other examples of coral are known, of which neither the kind nor colour are mentioned, for instance a pierced branched piece of Badarian age;[10] a specimen of predynastic date;[11] a lump of 'fossil coral';[12] a 'large piece',[13] and one or two bits.[14] At Coptos both red and white coral were found.[15]

Green Felspar [16]

Green felspar (microcline) or amazon stone, as it is sometimes called, is an opaque pale green stone, not very uniform in colour, consisting of a double silicate of

---

[1] W. M. F. Petrie, *Kahun, Gurob and Hawara*, p. 38.

[2] W. M. F. Petrie and F. Ll. Griffith, *Tanis*, II, *Nebesheh and Defenneh*, p. 75.

[3] W. B. Emery, *Royal Tombs of Ballana and Qustul*, pp. 47, 53, 109, 111 ,196, 202, 203, 205.

[4] R. Pococke, *Description of the East and some other Countries*, p. 141.

[5] T. Barron and W. F. Hume, *Topog. and Geol. of the Eastern Desert*, p. 137.

[6] G. Brunton and G. Caton-Thompson, *Badarian Civilisation*, pp. 38, 56. This material, which is now in the Cairo Museum, is organ coral and not dentalium as reported by the specialist to whom it was submitted by the finder: G. Brunton, *Mostagedda*, pp. 43, 51, 52, 71.

[7] W. M. F. Petrie and J. E. Quibell, *Naqada and Ballas*, p. 21.

[8] G. A. Reisner, *Arch. Survey of Nubia, 1907–1908*, I, p. 42. These beads are described as 'shell or coral' and the colour is not stated, but the late Mr. C. M. Firth informed the author that the material was pale red pipe coral.

[9] T. E. Peet and C. L. Woolley, *City of Akhenaten*, I, p. 21.

[10] G. Brunton and G. Caton-Thompson, *Badarian Civilisation*, p. 35

[11] G. Brunton and G. Caton-Thompson, *Badarian Civilisation*, pp. 56, 63.

[12] G. Brunton, *Qau and Badari*, I, p. 26.

[13] A. C. Mace, *M.M.A. Bull., Egyptian Exped. 1920–1921*, p. 12.

[14] E. Naville, *XIth Dyn. Temple at Deir el Bahari*, III, p. 18.

[15] W. M. F. Petrie, *Koptos*, p. 26.   [16] Cf. J. R. Harris, *Lexicographical Studies*, pp. 115–16.

aluminium and potassium. Ball found small crystals at Gebel Migif in the eastern desert;[1] Robinson found 'a large perfect crystal in Wadi Abu Rusheid, a tributary of Wadi Nugrus';[2] Ahmed Ibrahim Awad[3] found a broad seam of the blue-green variety with ancient workings in Wadi Higelig about seven miles west of Gebel Migif, and numerous large lumps have been found on the lower slopes of the Hafafit range. Some years ago it was suggested that the Libyan massifs might yield sources of felspar,[4] and extensive workings, some of ancient date, have since been discovered at Zumma in the Eghei mountains north of Tibesti.[5] It is possible that some of the felspar used in Egypt may have come from this source, but as yet proof is lacking.

Green felspar was employed on a small scale for beads from as early as the neo-lithic period[6] and was much used in the Twelfth Dynasty, for example, in the jewellery from Dahshur and Lahun respectively, in the description of the former of which it is wrongly termed emerald. It was used also during the New Kingdom, for instance, for amulets and inlay in the tomb of Tutankhamūn, and, exceptionally, for a small *kohl* pot.[7]

Green felspar is frequently confused with other green stones and is sometimes called 'mother of emerald', though it has no connexion whatever with emerald or beryl. Not infrequently this stone has a bluish tint and sometimes is definitely blue.

Fluorspar

One bead of green fluorspar and five beads of yellow fluorspar, of predynastic date, were found by Myers at Armant,[8] and another bead also of predynastic date and thought to be fluorspar was found at Matmar.[9] Petrie refers to a fragment from the base of a statue of Ramses II which he describes as purple fluor,[10] and a purple and green fluorspar cup of Roman date said to have been found in Egypt is in the Ashmolean Museum, Oxford.[11]

Garnet [12]

Garnet is the name applied to a group of minerals, consisting of double silicates of certain metals, that are distributed widely in nature, but generally are too dull for use as gem stones. The garnet employed by the ancient Egyptians was a dark red or reddish-brown translucent stone that occurs plentifully in the country, namely at Aswan, in the eastern desert,[13] at Kharga Oasis[14] and in Sinai,[15] the stones, however,

---

[1] J. Ball, *Geog. and Geol. of South-Eastern Egypt*, p. 272.

[2] G. Robinson, in W. F. Hume, *Geology of Egypt*, II, Part III, p. 863.

[3] Geological Survey of Egypt.

[4] G. Caton-Thompson and E. W. Gardner, *Desert Fayum*, p. 87.

[5] M. Dalloni and T. Monod, *Mission scientifique du Fezzan*, VI (1948), pp. 133, 153–4; A. J. Arkell, *Kush*, VII (1959), pp. 15–16, 24–25.

[6] G. Caton-Thompson and E. W. Gardner, *Desert Fayum*, pp. 32, 40, 56, 87, 90.

[7] H. E. Winlock, *Treasure of Three Egyptian Princesses*, p. 51.

[8] R. Mond and O. H. Myers, *Cemeteries of Armant*, I, pp. 72, 84, 103, 104.

[9] G. Brunton, *Matmar*, pp. 19, 23, Pl. LXX.   [10] W. M. F. Petrie, *Wisdom of Egypt*, p. 97.

[11] D. B. Harden, *Journ. Roman Studies*, XLIV (1954), p. 53.

[12] Cf. J. R. Harris, *Lexicographical Studies*, pp. 118–20.

[13] T. Barron and W. F. Hume, *Topog. and Geol. of the Eastern Desert*, pp. 170, 218; W. F. Hume, *Geology of Egypt*, II, Part III, pp. 863–4; J. Couyat, *Bull. Soc. fr. de Minéralogie*, XXXV (1912), p. 561.

[14] J. Couyat, *Bull. Soc. fr. de Minéralogie*, XXXI (1908), p. 348.

[15] T. Barron, *Topog. and Geol. of the Peninsula of Sinai*, p. 203.

usually being too small for use, especially those from Aswan, the largest being those from western Sinai.[1] Garnet was used for beads as early as predynastic times,[2] and was employed to some extent during the Middle Kingdom, both for beads [3] and inlay.[4] It was also used occasionally in the Second Intermediate period,[5] and during the New Kingdom.[6] Cailliaud, in 1821, says that at Aswan and at Elephantine he saw in the hands of 'the Arabs' perfectly crystallized garnets, one of which was an inch in diameter. He was unable to ascertain from where they had been obtained, but thought it could not be far away.[7]

Haematite [8]

Haematite is an oxide of iron much used as an ore for the production of the metal: it occurs in different forms and colours and may be black, red, brown or foliated and micaceous. An earthy variety also occurs, but it will save confusion if this latter is called red iron oxide or red ochre. The particular haematite used by the ancient Egyptians for beads, amulets, *kohl* sticks and small ornaments was a black opaque kind with a metallic lustre, which was employed as early as the predynastic period.[9]

Although haematite occurs plentifully in Egypt and although it was worked in the eastern desert at a late period (probably Roman) for the production of metallic iron,[10] it is not known from where the small amount was obtained that was used earlier. Dioscorides says [11] that it was dug out of mines in Egypt. Several pieces of typical kidney-ore haematite were found by the Oriental Institute of Chicago in rubbish heaps in the temple of Medinet Habu.

Occasional instances of the use of magnetite (magnetic iron ore) for small amulets have also been recorded,[12] and a statuette of limonite is in the Metropolitan Museum, New York.[13]

---

[1] W. F. Hume, *Geology of Egypt*, II, Part III, pp. 863–4.

[2] W. M. F. Petrie, *Prehistoric Egypt*, p. 44; W. M. F. Petrie and J. E. Quibell, *Naqada and Ballas*, pp. 10, 24, 44, 45, 67; G. Brunton and G. Caton-Thompson, *Badarian Civilisation*, p. 56; E. R. Ayrton and W. L. S. Loat, *Predynastic Cemetery at El Mahasna*, p. 30; D. Randall MacIver and A. C. Mace, *El Amrah and Abydos*, p. 48; H. Junker, *Bericht über die Grabungen . . . auf den Friedhöfen von El-Kubanieh—Sud*, p. 101.

[3] W. M. F. Petrie, *Diospolis Parva*, p. 44; *Gizeh and Rifeh*, p. 13; J. Garstang, *El Arabah*, p. 29; R. Engelbach, *Harageh*, p. 13; H. Junker, *Bericht über die Grabungen . . . auf die Friedhofen von El-Kubanieh—Nord*, p. 147.

[4] H. E. Winlock, *Treasure of El Lāhūn*, pp. 24, 31. See also above, p. 126.

[5] D. Randall MacIver and A. C. Mace, *El Amrah and Abydos*, pp. 69, 87; W. M. F. Petrie and G. Brunton, *Sedment*, I, p. 19.

[6] W. M. F. Petrie and G. Brunton, *Sedment*, II, p. 23.

[7] F. Cailliaud, *Voyage à l'oasis de Thèbes et dans les deserts*, pp. 12, 80, Pl. IX (7); J. Couyat, *Bull. Soc. fr. de Minéralogie*, XXXV (1912), pp. 561–2.

[8] Cf. J. R. Harris, *Lexicographical Studies*, pp. 168–70, 233–4.

[9] W. M. F. Petrie, *Prehistoric Egypt*, p. 43: E. R. Ayrton and W. L. S. Loat, *Predynastic Cemetery at El Mahasna*, p. 11.

[10] See p. 240.

[11] V: 144.

[12] H. Brugsch, *Z.Ä.S.*, XXX (1892), pp. 110–12; H. v. Minutoli, *Reise zum Tempel des Jupiter Ammon*, pp. 345–6.

[13] W. C. Hayes, *Scepter*, I, p. 214.

Jade

The term jade includes two distinct minerals, nephrite or true jade and jadeite, which are so much alike that unless examined chemically or microscopically they cannot be distinguished with certainty from one another. Both may be coloured white, grey or various shades of green and both are translucent with a somewhat waxy or greasy lustre. The specific gravity and hardness also are much alike and may overlap, jadeite, however, being slightly the harder and heavier of the two. Chemically, the composition of the two materials is very different, nephrite being essentially a double silicate of calcium and magnesium and jadeite a double silicate of aluminium and sodium.

In the Old World nephrite occurs in the valley of the Kara Kash river in the Kwen Luen mountains north of Kashmir and other localities in the neighbourhood, where there are ancient workings that are now almost exhausted; in Siberia, west of Lake Baikal and in small quantity in Silesia,[1] in Liguria,[1] in the Harz mountains [1] and possibly in other localities in Europe. Jadeite is found principally in Upper Burma, but also in China, Tibet and Brittany.[2]

Several specimens of what may be nephrite or jadeite have been found in Egypt, for example, a neolithic celt from the Fayum, now in the Peabody Museum of Harvard University, and described as nephrite;[3] a small axe-head discovered by Junker at the neolithic settlement of Merimda-Benisalame and now in the Cairo Museum, which the finder calls 'Nephrit (Chloromelanit)';[4] two axe-heads of predynastic date, one of which is in the Cairo Museum [5] and the other in University College, London, where there is also a heart scarab dated to the period Eighteenth to Twenty-second Dynasty and another of Eighteenth or Nineteenth Dynasty date;[6] several objects in the Berlin Museum, including an ointment pot [7] and a heart scarab [8] said to be jadeite, and a ring [9] and another heart scarab (in the Kennard amulet board) [10] said to be nephrite; a double signet ring found in the tomb of Tutankhamūn,[11] and several other objects in the Cairo Museum stated to be possibly jade,[12] which latter in my opinion are neither nephrite nor jadeite. As it would be impossible to examine any of these objects either chemically or microscopically without destroying them, the only determination that could be made is that of specific gravity. This was done for three of the objects in the Cairo Museum with the following results, namely,

---

[1] L. J. Spencer, *A Key to Precious Stones*, p. 211.

[2] C. Daryll Forde, *Journ. Royal Anthrop. Inst.*, LX (1930), pp. 221–4.

[3] O. Bates and J. E. Wolff, *Man*, XV (1915), pp. 132–4.

[4] H. Junker, *Merimde-Benisalâme von 7.Februar bis 8.April 1930*, p. 80, Pl. VII. Cairo Museum, No. J. 57954.

[5] J. E. Quibell, *Archaic Objects*, No. 14259.

[6] W. M. F. Petrie, *Scarabs and Cylinders*, pp. 8, 29, Pl. XLVIII, Nos. 20, 21.

[7] H. Schäfer, *Ägyptische Goldschmiedearbeiten*, No. 19.

[8] H. Schäfer, *Ägyptische Goldschmiedearbeiten*, No. 35.

[9] H. Schäfer, *Ägyptische Goldschmiedearbeiten*, No. 226.

[10] G. Möller, *Amtliche Berichte*, XXXIV, No. 2 (1912), col. 24; G. Roeder, *Ägyptische Inschriften aus den Königlichen Museen zu Berlin*, II, p. 312.

[11] A. Lucas, in H. Carter, *Tut-ankh-Amen*, III, p. 182 (Appendix II).

[12] J. E. Quibell, *Archaic Objects*, Nos. 14251, 14256–14258.

neolithic axe-head, 3.35; predynastic axe-head, 2.98; Tutankhamūn ring, 3.04,[1] from which it seems possible that the neolithic axe-head may be jadeite, though it does not look like it, and the predynastic axe-head and the ring may be nephrite. In my opinion, however, the identity of the majority of these objects is by no means yet certain, and some of them may be amphiboles of the tremolite-actinolite group, which are found in the eastern desert of Egypt, for instance in Wadi Hafafit,[2] while others may prove to be green jasper or green serpentine, both of which can easily be mistaken for nephrite.[3] But the ring is almost certainly nephrite, as also an unspecified object from Nuri, originally described as beryl,[4] and that from the end of the Eighteenth Dynasty small pieces of this material should have reached Egypt from Asia would not be surprising.

Jasper [5]

Jasper is an impure, opaque, compact variety of silica, that may be coloured red, green, brown, black or yellow by compounds of iron, the red being the kind principally used in ancient Egypt, though the other colours were occasionally employed.

The recognition of red and yellow jaspers presents no difficulty, but in the case of green, brown and black jaspers mistakes of identification are not uncommon, and statements about their use need verification before they can be accepted.

Red jasper, the use of which dates back to predynastic times,[6] was employed chiefly for beads and amulets, though sometimes as inlay for jewellery, and occasionally for scarabs and other purposes. Parts of two shallow bowls of red jasper are known from the First Dynasty,[7] a foot from a composite statue was discovered at El Amarna,[8] a large carved hand found at Medinet Habu is now in the Cairo Museum,[9] and fragments of the nose and toe of a statue formerly in the Carnarvon collection are now in the Metropolitan Museum.[10] Unworked samples of red jasper were included among foundation deposits of Ramses IV,[11] and a large rough block of red jasper of late date was found at Memphis.[12]

Green jasper is known from as early as the Badarian period for an amulet and for

---

[1] A. Lucas, in H. Carter, *Tut-ankh-Amen*, III, p. 182 (Appendix II), where the specific gravity is stated to be 3.4 instead of 3.04, which caused it to be classed as jadeite instead of nephrite, which it probably is.

[2] Kindly communicated by Mr. J. Dudler.

[3] The heart scarab in the Kennard board was originally described as jasper, which it probably is. See *Catalogue of the Kennard Collection*, 1912, p. 54, No. 530.

[4] D. Dunham, *Nuri*, p. 5.

[5] Cf. J. R. Harris, *Lexicographical Studies*, pp. 111–13, 123–4, and 113–15, 130–1.

[6] R. Engelbach, *Harageh*, p. 14.

[7] J. E. Quibell, *Saqqara, 1912–1914*, pp. 16, 17, Pl. XII. Mr. Quibell kindly showed me part of a second similar bowl. Hume, *Geology of Egypt*, II, Part III, p. 701, refers to a jasper pot from the tomb of Khasekhemui.

[8] J. D. S. Pendlebury, *City of Akhenaten*, III, Pl. CVI (5).

[9] No. J. 59740.

[10] Burlington Fine Arts Club, *Catalogue of an Exhibition of Egyptian Art* (1922), p. 80, No. 39.

[11] Carnarvon and H. Carter, *Five Years' Explorations*, p. 48, Pl. XL; W. C. Hayes, *Scepter*, II, p. 32.

[12] W. M. F. Petrie, *Meydum and Memphis*, III, p. 40.

a bead,[1] for beads also from the Fourth Dynasty,[2] and from the Middle Kingdom for scarabs [3] and beads.[4]

Brown and black jasper date back to the Middle Kingdom, from which period there are several scarabs of these stones.[3]

Yellow jasper, so far as is known, was not used before the Eighteenth Dynasty, the best example being the well-known broken head of Nefertiti or Tiy formerly in the Carnarvon collection and now in the Metropolitan Museum;[5] part of a hand in yellow jasper found at Medinet Habu is now in the Cairo Museum.[6]

A weight said to be of opal jasper is in the Metropolitan Museum.[7]

The jaspers of Egypt are well known and specimens of a brown jasper (sometimes banded) are exhibited in mineral collections in London, Vienna and Prague and possibly elsewhere. Red jasper occurs as bands in certain rocks in several localities in the eastern desert, for example in the neighbourhood of the Hadrabia hills;[8] near Wadi Saga [8] and in Wadi Abu Gerida,[8] in some of which places there is evidence of ancient mining: brown jasper is found plentifully in the form of pebbles: a large vein of green jasper spotted with red, which had been worked anciently, was seen by Bruce on his journey from Qena to Quseir:[9] whether black jasper is found naturally in Egypt cannot be stated, but it probably is, though no record of its occurrence can be traced. A piece of worked jasper, evidently a fragment of a statue, partly red and partly yellow, was found by Myers at Armant,[10] which proves that both colours occur naturally together, and since the red variety is Egyptian the yellow probably also is Egyptian. The red jasper hand already mentioned has also a small vein of yellow on the under side, and in the Cairo Museum there is also a beautiful small plaque of green and yellow jasper carved with a Hathor head in relief, probably of Saite date.

Lapis Lazuli [11]

Lapis lazuli is an opaque stone of a dark blue colour with often spots, patches or veins of white (calcite) and sometimes minute, yellow spangles of iron pyrites, looking like specks of gold. Chemically, lapis lazuli consists of silicates of aluminium and sodium together with sodium sulphide. It is certainly the σάπφειρος of Theophrastus [12] and the *sapphirus* of Pliny.[13]

---

[1] G. Brunton, *Mostagedda*, pp. 38, 41, 51.

[2] G. Brunton, *Qau and Badari*, II, p. 20.

[3] W. M. F. Petrie, *Scarabs and Cylinders*, p. 8; H. R. Hall, *Catalogue of the Eg. Scarabs . . . in the Brit. Mus.*, pp. xxvi–xxvii.

[4] W. M. F. Petrie, G. Brunton and M. A. Murray, *Lahun*, II, p. 13.

[5] Burlington Fine Arts Club, *Catalogue of an Exhibition of Egyptian Art* (1922), p. 80, No. 40, Pl. VI.

[6] No. J. 59793.

[7] W. C. Hayes, *Scepter*, I, p. 71.

[8] T. Barron and W. F. Hume, *Topog. and Geol. of the Eastern Desert*, pp. 52, 221, 228, 266; W. F. Hume, *Geology of Egypt*, II, Part III, p. 862.

[9] J. Bruce, *Travels to Discover the Source of the Nile*, II, 2nd ed., 1805, p. 89.

[10] R. Mond and O. H. Myers, *Temples of Armant*, p. 62.

[11] Cf. J. R. Harris, *Lexicographical Studies*, pp. 124–9, 134–5.

[12] *On Stones*, XLIII; cf. E. R. Caley and J. F. C. Richards, *Theophrastus on Stones*, pp. 136–7.

[13] XXXVII: 39.

So far as is known, lapis lazuli does not occur in Egypt, though, 'Its abundant use at a very early date does suggest the possibility that it may be found in Egypt or its immediate neighbourhood.' [1] Several statements that it does so occur have been made. Thus MacIver says [2] that 'lapis lazuli is known to be native of Egypt', but no evidence for this is given and the value of the statement is much discounted by the further statement that garnets are not found in Egypt, whereas they occur plentifully. Idrisi mentions [3] a mine of lapis lazuli near Kharga Oasis, but no confirmation can be obtained for any such occurrence and von Bissing states that lapis lazuli occurs in Abyssinia.[4]

The chief Old World source of lapis lazuli is Badakshan in the north-east corner of Afghanistan, but it also occurs near Lake Baikal in Siberia. The Badakshan mines are referred to by Marco Polo in the thirteenth century [5] and probably were the original source of the material. Although it is stated frequently that lapis lazuli was mined anciently in Persia,[6] no confirmation of this can be obtained and the statement may be due to a confusion between lapis lazuli and turquoise, the latter of which does occur in that country, or to the fact that the lapis lazuli trade passed through Persia or was in the hands of Persian merchants.

Lapis lazuli was used in ancient Egypt from predynastic times [7] onwards for beads, amulets, scarabs and other small objects as well as for inlay in jewellery, for which purpose it was employed extensively during both the Middle Kingdom and the Empire. Two small tubes of lapis lazuli mounted in gold, of predynastic date and unknown use, are in the Cairo Museum [8] and the Ashmolean Museum [9] respectively, beads of dark purple lapis were found in a protodynastic tomb at Abydos,[10] and two small statuettes, also of protodynastic date, are in Cairo [11] and Oxford.[12] The silver bracelets of Queen Hetepheres (Fourth Dynasty) were inlaid with lapis lazuli, turquoise and carnelian,[13] and lapis inlay occurs in the jewellery from Dahshur [14] and Lahun [15] (Twelfth Dynasty). The Tôd treasure, also of the Twelfth Dynasty, included a large number of lapis lazuli objects, among them many cylinder seals with cuneiform inscriptions and obviously of foreign origin.[16] Lapis was much used in the jewellery from the tomb of Tutankhamūn, and in the jewellery of the Twenty-first

---

[1] W. F. Hume, *Geology of Egypt*, II, Part III, p. 864.

[2] D. Randall MacIver and A. C. Mace, *El Amrah and Abydos*, pp. 48–49.

[3] *Geography*, French trans. by P. Amédée, I, Paris, 1836, p. 122.

[4] F. W. von Bissing, *Archiv für Orientforschung*, V (1928–9), p. 75 (*n.* 2 from p. 73).

[5] *The Travels of Marco Polo the Venetian*, p. 84 (Everyman's Library).

[6] The Geological Museum, South Kensington, has a piece of lapis lazuli (No. 24105) said to come from Persia, though the exact source is not known.

[7] W. M. F. Petrie, *Prehistoric Egypt*, p. 44; *Diospolis Parva*, p. 27.

[8] No. J. 31340. J. E. Quibell, *Archaic Objects*, p. 279, No. 14517, Pl. LIX.

[9] No. 1895. 987. W. M. F. Petrie and J. E. Quibell, *Naqada and Ballas*, p. 28.

[10] W. M. F. Petrie, *Royal Tombs*, II, p. 18.

[11] See A. Lucas, *Ancient Egyptian Materials and Industries* (3rd ed., 1948), p. 456, *n.* 1.

[12] No. E 1057. J. E. Quibell and F. W. Green, *Hierakonpolis*, II, p. 7, Pl. XVIII; J. Garstang, *Ann. Serv.*, VIII (1907), p. 135, Pl. II.

[13] G. Reisner, *History of the Giza Necropolis*, II, p. 18.

[14] J. de Morgan, *Dahchour, mars–juin 1894; 1894–1895.* [15] H. E. Winlock, *Treasure of El Lāhūn.*

[16] F. Bisson de la Roque, *Trésor de Tôd* (*Cat. Caire*), pp. 30 f., Nos. 70640–70754; see also p. iii for other objects in the Louvre, Nos. E 15214–15273 and 15278–15318.

and Twenty-second Dynasty kings found at Tanis.[1] At least two small vessels of lapis lazuli are known.[2]

Lapis lazuli is mentioned frequently in Egyptian texts from the Old Kingdom onwards,[3] and is stated to have been obtained from various localities in western Asia, including Assur, Babylon, Djahi, Khatti, Naharin, Retenu, Sengar and Syria, as well as from Meroe and Punt to the south of Egypt, and particularly from a region called Tefrer, the location of which is unknown. Since lapis lazuli is not known to occur in western Asia or in the countries to the south, the stones from these sources must originally have been traded from elsewhere, and it seems likely that Tefrer was also a trading station, probably on the route from Badakhshan.[4]

Malachite [5]

Malachite is a copper ore of a fine green colour, a fractured surface of which often displays a beautiful and characteristic zonary structure, the successive layers showing strata of alternating light and dark tints; chemically it consists of hydrated (basic) carbonate of copper.

Although malachite is very common in ancient Egyptian graves of all periods from the Badarian and predynastic to certainly as late as the Nineteenth Dynasty, the principal and almost the only forms in which it is found are that of powder (either loose or slightly cohering together) for use as an eye-paint, as lumps of the raw material from which the powder was made, or as stains on palettes and stones on which the powder was ground, and it is only very rarely indeed that malachite has been discovered either as worked objects or as inlay in jewellery. The few instances of this use of malachite that can be traced are as follows: a few large roughly made beads of predynastic date from Girga;[6] some beads from Ballas of the same period;[7] one or two small scorpions of the archaic period;[8] two pieces cut for ornament of the First Dynasty;[9] a miniature mace head of early dynastic date;[10] a few beads[11] and a tiny broken worked fragment from the Eighteenth Dynasty (the tomb of Tutankhamūn); a small animal-shaped amulet of archaic form from the Nineteenth Dynasty;[12] a scarab[13] and two oval plaques[14] of unknown date.

---

[1] P. Montet, *Nécropole royale de Tanis*, I–III; *Monuments Piot*, XLI (1946), pp. 5–22; E. Dhorme, *Monuments Piot*, XLI (1946), pp. 23–28.

[2] W. M. F. Petrie, *Gizeh and Rifeh*, p. 4, Pls. III, V; J. de Morgan, *Dahchour, mars–juin 1894*, p. 71, Pls. XIX, XXV.

[3] *Wb.* III. 334.1–13; *A.R.*, I, 534, 667, 668; II, 446, 447, 448, 459, 462, 484, 493, 509, 518, 536; III, 116, 434; IV, 30; J. R. Harris, *Lexicographical Studies*, pp. 124–9, 134–5.

[4] J. R. Harris, *Lexicographical Studies*, pp. 126, 134–5.

[5] Cf. J. R. Harris, *Lexicographical Studies*, pp. 102–4, 132.   [6] In the Cairo Museum, No. J. 44488.

[7] W. M. F. Petrie and J. E. Quibell, *Naqada and Ballas*, p. 10.

[8] J. E. Quibell and F. W. Green, *Hierakonpolis*, II, p. 38. In *Hierakonpolis*, I, Petrie says (p. 8) that one of the scorpions is of black haematite.

[9] W. M. F. Petrie, *Royal Tombs*, II, p. 37, Pl. XXXV.

[10] A. Scharff, *Die Altertümer der Vor- und Frühzeit Ägyptens*, I, p. 82, No. 156.

[11] A. Lucas, in H. Carter, *Tut-ankh-Amen*, II, p. 185 (Appendix II).

[12] The Egyptian Exploration Society, *Catalogue of Exhibits*, 1926, p. 12. Examined by me.

[13] W. M. F. Petrie, *Scarabs and Cylinders*, p. 8; but cf. H. R. Hall, *Catalogue of Eg. Scarabs . . . in the Brit. Mus.*, p. xxvii.

[14] Cairo Museum No. $\frac{17}{62}\frac{12}{89}$.

Malachite has frequently been confused with other green stones, such as green turquoise, green felspar and even beryl. Thus, although the necklace of Twelfth Dynasty date from Dahshur in the Cairo Museum, stated [1] to have lozenge-shaped plaques of malachite, cannot be identified with certainty, no necklace of any date with malachite on it can be found in the Museum. There are, however, two belts from Dahshur that answer to the general description of the necklace referred to, both of which have lozenge-shaped plaques, but in one case the green stone is green felspar and in the other it is turquoise. The beads in the collar and the stones in the bracelet, both of Graeco-Roman age, stated by Maspero [2] to be malachite, and in the case of the bracelet, also thought by Vernier [3] possibly to be malachite, are beryl, the bizarre shape of the stones commented upon by Vernier being simply the natural hexagonal form of the beryl crystal as found, the Egyptians apparently not having any means of cutting this stone, which is slightly harder than quartz, until a very late date, though they were able to bore it.

Malachite occurs in Sinai and in the eastern desert of Egypt, from both of which places it was obtained anciently, at first probably merely from surface outcrops for use as an eye-paint and later by mining for the production of copper.

From two of the same localities in Sinai where copper ore occurs, namely Magharah and Serabit el Khadim, turquoise was also obtained anciently [4] and this occurrence in the same place of two different materials, one (malachite) green and the other (turquoise), though often blue, frequently greenish-blue or even definitely green, has given rise to considerable confusion, so much so that malachite has been termed turquoise matrix, though the two materials are totally different in composition and have no connexion with one another. It has also resulted in the ancient Egyptian name for turquoise (mfk3t) being translated sometimes as malachite,[5] which if accepted, would mean that malachite was associated with silver, gold and costly stones, particularly lapis lazuli, and was used plentifully for finger rings, collars, inlay and scarabs and that there is no mention in ancient Egyptian texts of turquoise, whereas the Egyptian objects in the various museums prove the contrary, namely, that it was turquoise that was largely used in jewellery (particularly with lapis lazuli), for inlay and for scarabs and not malachite, which was very rarely employed as a gem stone.[6]

Pearl

Pearls are calcareous concretions of peculiar and characteristic lustre produced by various molluscs, chiefly, however, by the pearl-oyster and the pearl-mussel, the former of which is found on the Red Sea coast of Egypt, as well as in the Persian Gulf, off the coast of Ceylon and in other localities.

Although mother-of-pearl was used in Egypt from predynastic times, the pearl was not employed until the Ptolemaic period. To this only one exception is known

---

[1] G. Maspero, *Guide to the Cairo Museum*, English trans., 1903, p. 511.

[2] G. Maspero, *Guide to the Cairo Museum*, English trans., 1903, p. 527.

[3] E. Vernier, *Bijoux et Orfèvreries*, p. 64, No. 52151, Pl. xvi.

[4] See pp. 202–3.

[5] *A.R.*, v (Index), p. 143; C. R. Lepsius, *Les Métaux dans les inscriptions égyptiennes*, pp. 35 f.

[6] For the Egyptian names for malachite see J. R. Harris, *Lexicographical Studies*, pp. 102–4, 132, 143–5.

to me and that not of true pearls, namely the button pearls in the necklace of Queen Ahhotpe, mother of King Ahmose, of the beginning of the Eighteenth Dynasty.[1]

Olivine, Peridot

Olivine is a compound silicate of magnesium and iron widely distributed in Egypt; it is transparent or translucent and usually of a pale green colour. It was employed as early as predynastic times for beads,[2] and, as already stated,[3] some and probably most of the beads and other objects found in Nubia and termed beryl are olivine.

Peridot, a transparent pale green stone, is merely the gem form of olivine; it is found on St. John's Island in the Red Sea [4] and is probably the stone that Strabo [5] and Pliny [6] call *topazos*, as both writers state that this was obtained from such a locality. Strabo refers to the golden lustre of the stone, but Pliny states that it was leek-green and mentions its softness compared to other gem stones.

The only example of the use of peridot in ancient Egypt of which any record can be found is that of a scarab of the Eighteenth Dynasty.[7]

Quartz, Rock Crystal [8]

Quartz is a crystalline form of silica which when pure is colourless, but which may be translucent or opaque, like that found near the 'Chephren' diorite quarry about forty miles north-west of Abu Simbel.[9] The former is termed rock crystal and the latter milky or cloudy quartz, the milkiness being due to multitudes of small air cavities. Sometimes quartz is coloured from light brown to almost black and is then termed smoky quartz, which particular kind has been found in an ancient gold mine at Romit in the eastern desert,[10] or it may be amethyst-coloured in patches, when it is termed amethystine quartz, one occurrence of which is near the 'Chephren' diorite quarry already mentioned.[11] Also in the same locality were found 'large quantities of strange multi-coloured quartz'.[12] Petrie notes the use of a green quartz for a scarab,[13] and the same colour was also employed for some beads of Eighteenth Dynasty date.[14]

Quartz occurs abundantly as veins in igneous rocks in the eastern desert [15] and at

---

[1] A. Lucas, *Ann. Serv.*, XXVII (1927), pp. 69–71.

[2] W. M. F. Petrie and J. E. Quibell, *Naqada and Ballas*, p. 44; G. Brunton and G. Caton-Thompson, *Badarian Civilisation*, p. 56; G. Brunton, *Mostagedda*, p. 86; *Matmar*, p. 23, Pl. LXX. In describing certain objects from Abydos, Petrie says (*Royal Tombs*, II, p. 37) 'a piece of the clear green serpentine which is frequent in prehistoric work'.

[3] See p. 390.

[4] Mines and Quarries Dept., *Report on the Mineral Industry*, p. 25; J. Couyat, *Bull. Soc. fr. de Minéralogie*, XXXI (1908), pp. 344–8.

[5] XVI: 4, 6.   [6] VI: 34; XXXVII: 32.

[7] W. M. F. Petrie, *Scarabs and Cylinders*, p. 8.

[8] Cf. J. R. Harris, *Lexicographical Studies*, pp. 110–11.

[9] R. Engelbach, *Ann. Serv.*, XXXIII (1933), p. 67; O. H. Little, *Ann. Serv.*, XXXIII (1933), p. 77.

[10] J. Ball, *Geog. and Geol. of South-Eastern Egypt*, p. 353.

[11] R. Engelbach, *Ann. Serv.*, XXXIII (1933), p. 69; O. H. Little, *Ann. Serv.*, XXXIII (1933), p. 80.

[12] R. Engelbach, *Ann. Serv.*, XXXIII (1933), p. 69; XXXVIII (1938), p. 372; O. H. Little, *Ann. Serv.*, XXXIII (1933), p. 79.

[13] W. M. F. Petrie, *Scarabs and Cylinders*, p. 8.

[14] H. E. Winlock, *Treasure of Three Egyptian Princesses*, p. 24.

[15] T. Barron and W. F. Hume, *Topog. and Geol. of the Eastern Desert*, pp. 218, 221; W. F. Hume, *Geology of Egypt*, II, Part II, pp. 584–7.

Aswan,[1] at which latter place an outcrop of quartz is shown to tourists as alabaster. This has been worked anciently to some extent and a few blocks of it may be seen at the north end of the island of Philae.[1] Quartz crystals (rock crystal) are found in geodes in limestone in the district stretching from the Fayum to Baharia Oasis and as pebbles derived from such geodes, and also in Sinai.

Rock crystal was employed in ancient Egypt in small amount from predynastic times onwards,[2] being fashioned into beads and other objects including small vases,[3] particularly those in magical sets for the 'Opening of the Mouth' ritual, and the cornea of eyes in statues and on coffins. In the Eighteenth Dynasty, as already mentioned,[4] it was employed as inlay, being set in red cement to imitate carnelian and in this same dynasty the handle of the iron dagger from the tomb of Tutankhamūn is ornamented with a finely-worked knob of rock crystal,[5] which, however, is probably not of Egyptian origin. A large rough block of rock crystal, of late date, was found at Memphis.[6] Amethystine quartz was employed occasionally in the early dynastic period for making small vases. In the Cairo Museum there are a number of large implements of opaque quartz (possibly of paleolithic date) from Aswan and fifteen smaller implements;[7] also a number of small triangular-shaped implements [8] and a broken implement with serrated edges [9] of clear rock crystal, all of early date.

All varieties of quartz are much harder than glass, which they scratch easily, and they are also harder than steel, and, therefore, they cannot be marked with a file.

Silica Glass [10]

In 1932 an occurrence of silica glass (fused quartz) [11] in lumps of up to 10 lb. in weight was found over an area of some 80 by 25 km. to the south-west of the sand sea in the Libyan desert. No well-worked tools were recognized, though a few flakes had certainly been made by man, probably in late neolithic or predynastic times, and there were signs that large lumps had been broken up. The stone has a specific gravity of 2.21 and a hardness of 6 on the Mohs scale. The typical colour is pale greenish yellow and the material is in part quite clear and transparent, though some pieces are cloudy owing to the presence of minute bubbles and when these are particularly abundant the colour is milky white; clear specimens when cut and polished make quite effective gemstones. The origin of the occurrence is not known, and no crater has been found in the district.

---

[1] J. Ball, *First or Aswan Cataract*, p. 84.

[2] W. M. F. Petrie, *Prehistoric Egypt*, p. 44.

[3] W. M. F. Petrie, *Royal Tombs*, I, Pls. IV–VII; II, Pls. V, XLVI, XLVII; *Gizeh and Rifeh*, p. 5; A. Scharff, *Die Altertümer der Vor- und Frühzeit Ägyptens*, I, pp. 240–1, Nos. 729–34; P. Montet, *Kêmi*, VIII (1946), pp. 157 f., Pls. II, III.

[4] See pp. 391–2.

[5] H. Carter, *Tut-ankh-Amen*, II, p. 135.

[6] W. M. F. Petrie, *Meydum and Memphis*, III, p. 40.

[7] Nos. J. 67414–67428.

[8] Nos. J. 56607–56623.

[9] No. J. 57176.

[10] Anon. *Nature*, CXXXII (1933), p. 22; L. J. Spencer, *Gemmologist*, III (1933), pp. 111–13; P. A. Clayton and L. J. Spencer, *Geog. Journ.*, LXXXII (1933), pp. 375–7; *Mineralogical Magazine*, XXIII (1934), pp. 501–8; P. A. Clayton, *Bulletin de l'Institut Fouad I du désert*, I (2) (1951), pp. 34–38.

[11] Analysis shows 97.6 per cent of silica.

Turquoise [1]

Turquoise consists of hydrated phosphate of aluminium coloured by means of a trace of a copper compound; it is never crystalline, but occurs in opaque amorphous masses filling veins in the mother rock. The typical colour is a delicate sky-blue, though many stones are greenish-blue and others definitely green, since turquoise has a tendency to deteriorate in colour, a fact which was recognized by the Egyptians themselves.

The chief source of the turquoise employed in ancient Egypt was undoubtedly Sinai, at Wadi Magharah and Serabit el Khadim, where the stone occurs in seams in a sandstone rock. In both these places there are ancient workings, the former of which are still exploited unsystematically and intermittently by the local bedouin.[2] Whether the turquoise used in the neolithic period came from Sinai has, however, been doubted, and it is suggested that exploration of the Libyan massifs might yield alternative sources,[3] though this has yet to be proved. Another ancient and well-known source of turquoise was Persia.

There is no truth whatever in the suggestion of Peet [4] and Weill [5] that turquoise was chiefly used by the Egyptians as a colouring matter for glazes and paints and that it was only rarely employed in jewellery.

Turquoise has been known and used in Egypt from as early as the neolithic,[6] Badarian [7] and predynastic [8] periods respectively. Its authenticity has been doubted in the case of several bracelets of First Dynasty date from Abydos [9] in which it is present and it has been thought to be glass,[10] though it is undoubtedly turquoise as originally described by the finder, much of it, however, being green and not blue. It was employed as inlay in a number of anklets found by Reisner in the Fourth Dynasty tomb of Hetepheres at Giza,[11] where it was at first described as malachite,[12] and it occurs plentifully in the Twelfth Dynasty jewellery from Lahun,[13] and Dahshur,[14] where some examples have been thought to be artificial on account of their

---

[1] Cf. J. R. Harris, *Lexicographical Studies*, pp. 106–10.

[2] Mines and Quarries Dept., *Report on the Mineral Industry*, p. 38; J. Ball, *Geog. and Geol. of West-Central Sinai*, pp. 11, 163; T. Barron, *Topog. and Geol. of the Peninsula of Sinai*, pp. 209–12; G. W. Murray, *Cairo Sc. Journ.*, VI (1912), pp. 264–73; E. S. Thomas, *Cairo Sc. Journ.*, VI (1912), pp. 56–60; J. C. Davey, *Transactions of the Royal Geological Soc. of Cornwall*, XVI (1928–36), pp. 43–65; J. Černý, *Inscriptions of Sinai*, II, pp. 3 f.; R. Weill, *Recueil des inscriptions égyptiennes du Sinai; La presqu'ile du Sinai*; W. M. F. Petrie, *Researches in Sinai*; H. Brugsch, *Wanderung nach den Türkis-Minen und der Sinai-Halbinsel*. See also H. A. Ducros, *Ann. Serv.*, VII (1906), pp. 30–32.

[3] G. Caton-Thompson and E. W. Gardner, *Desert Fayum*, p. 87.

[4] T. E. Peet, *Journ. Manchester Egyptian and Oriental Soc.*, VIII (1919), p. 21.

[5] R. Weill, *Recueil des inscriptions égyptiennes du Sinai*, p. 25.

[6] G. Caton-Thompson and E. W. Gardner, *Desert Fayum*, pp. 53, 56, 87, 90.

[7] G. Brunton and G. Caton-Thompson, *Badarian Civilisation*, pp. 27, 41, 56. See p. 208, *n.* 4.

[8] W. M. F. Petrie, *Prehistoric Egypt*, p. 44; W. M. F. Petrie and J. E. Quibell, *Naqada and Ballas*, p. 44; G. Brunton, *Mostagedda*, pp. 71, 86.

[9] W. M. F. Petrie, *Royal Tombs*, II, pp. 17–19.

[10] E. Vernier, *Bijoux et Orfèvreries*, pp. 10–11, 13–14.

[11] G. A. Reisner, *History of the Giza Necropolis*, II, p. 44.

[12] See p. 246, *n.* 11.

[13] H. E. Winlock, *Treasure of El Lāhūn*.

[14] J. de Morgan, *Dahchour, mars–juin 1894; 1894–1895*.

excellent colour.[1] Inlay of early Eighteenth Dynasty date, called enamel or glass paste by von Bissing,[2] and amazonite by Vernier,[3] has been identified as turquoise,[4] and turquoise is present as beads and in inlay in jewellery of the time of Thutmose III.[5] It also occurs in small amount in the jewellery from the tomb of Tutankhamūn, namely as a scarab of a good blue colour and as greenish-blue inlay on two pectorals. The use of turquoise for scarabs is relatively rare.[6]

As already pointed out,[7] Breasted's translation of the ancient Egyptian records makes no mention whatever of turquoise, which, considering the extensive and early use of this material, is remarkable and is due to the ancient Egyptian word for tur-quoise having been wrongly translated malachite. That the word, in fact, refers to turquoise has been definitely established by Loret [8] and others.[9]

---

[1] E. Vernier, *Bijoux et Orfèvreries*, pp. 88, 298, 299, 307, 336.

[2] F. W. von Bissing, *Ein Thebanischer Grabfund*, p. 17.

[3] E. Vernier, *Bijoux et Orfèvreries*, p. 222.

[4] A. Lucas, *Ann. Serv.*, xxvii (1927), p. 70.

[5] H. E. Winlock, *Treasure of Three Egyptian Princesses*.

[6] W. M. F. Petrie, *Scarabs and Cylinders*, p. 8; H. R. Hall, *Catalogue of the Eg. Scarabs . . . in the Brit. Mus.*, p. xxvii.

[7] See p. 401.

[8] V. Loret, *Kêmi*, I (1928), pp. 99–114.

[9] J. Černý, *Inscriptions of Sinai*, II, pp. 7 f.; J. R. Harris, *Lexicographical Studies*, pp. 106–10.

Chapter XVII

STONES OTHER THAN BUILDING STONES AND PRECIOUS STONES: STONE VESSELS

Certain stones have already been discussed in connexion with building materials, but stone was employed in ancient Egypt, not only for building, but also for obelisks, sarcophagi, statues and other monuments, as well as for smaller objects, such as statuettes, bowls, vases, tools and weapons and the earliest objects that have survived to the present day in Egypt, as in many other countries, are of stone (chiefly flint). The stones employed, excluding precious and semi-precious stones, which have been dealt with separately, comprise alabaster, anhydrite, basalt, breccia, chert, diorite, dolerite, dolomite, flint, granite, gypsum, limestone, marble, obsidian, porphyry and porphyritic rocks, quartz, quartzite, rock crystal, sandstone, 'schist' (greywacke, tuff and volcanic ash), serpentine, slate and steatite, and few countries possess such a variety of stones as Egypt, many of them being very handsome when cut and polished.

There are few subjects in Egyptology that are so full of confusion, and even of contradiction, as that of the nomenclature of the various kinds of stone employed by the ancient Egyptians and I propose to try and unravel the tangle to at least some extent. It is realized that in any scheme of classification there must be difficulties and anomalies and that it is practically impossible to frame definitions that will be satisfactory from every point of view, and the final court of appeal must, of course, be the petrologist, but it is thought that guided by a few broad principles, with which it is hoped every one will be in agreement, the matter may be much simplified. The principles are, first, that for the purposes of Egyptology any highly technical description of the various rocks is unnecessary and that general features and broad characteristics alone need be taken into account, and hence that many of the finer distinctions of the geologist may be disregarded, and second, that old names that are well rooted in the literature of Egyptology should be retained whenever possible, unless seriously wrong, though the better and more scientific name should also be given.

Alabaster [1]

The nature and occurrence of alabaster have already been dealt with in connexion with its use as a building material [2] and, therefore, need not again be discussed. This stone was always a favourite with the ancient Egyptians, doubtless partly owing to

---

[1] Cf. J. R. Harris, *Lexicographical Studies*, pp. 77–78; K. Sethe, *Bau- und Denkmalsteine*, pp. 882–9 (21–28).

[2] See pp. 59–61.

the fact that it not only looked well and took a good polish, but also because, being a soft stone, it was easy to work.

In addition to its employment as a building material, alabaster was used for many other purposes, and objects of this stone are known that range in date from predynastic times to a very late period, one of its commonest and earliest uses being for making vases and another early, but occasional, use being for mace-heads; it was also employed, though somewhat rarely, for sarcophagi (for example those of Hetepheres and Seti I respectively), and for canopic boxes, canopic jars, statues, statuettes, offering-tables, bowls, dishes and other objects.

Basalt

Basalt and its occurrence in Egypt have been treated in relation to its use as a building material [1] and, therefore, need not further be described; but long before it was employed for building and despite its hardness and the consequent difficulty of working it, this stone was used for making vases, some of which date back to neolithic times [2] and others to the Badarian [3] and predynastic [3,4] periods respectively. Axe-heads of basalt of neolithic date are also known.[5]

One occasional use of basalt in the early dynastic period was for sarcophagi (though not every sarcophagus called basalt is basalt), for example the sarcophagus found by Vyse in the pyramid of Menkaurē (Mycerinus) (which was lost at sea on its way to England, but of which a small piece was sent to the British Museum) [6] is stated to have been of basalt,[6] though 'the brittle quality of the stone' [7] referred to by Vyse is not easy to understand. A small piece of stone exhibited at the British Museum with the wooden coffin from the pyramid of Menkaurē, as seen through the glass of the case appears to be basalt, and this may be the piece referred to, though pieces of two different sarcophagi, both called basalt, were sent by Vyse to the British Museum.[8] Of the sarcophagi stated by Vyse to be basalt, one, at least, is certainly not basalt, but light blue-grey, 'schist'. Thus he found a number of sarcophagi in Campbell's tomb at Giza, three of which he calls basalt,[9] and in the British Museum (No. 1384) there is a blue-grey 'schist' sarcophagus labelled 'Grey basalt coffin of Wah-Ab-Ra' and stated to be of the Twenty-sixth Dynasty from Campbell's tomb, which is almost certainly one of these.

In addition to the use of basalt for sarcophagi it was also occasionally employed for statues, though on account of the frequent confusion of basalt with dark-grey granite, black granite and 'schist', objects have frequently been called basalt that are not basalt.

Breccia

Breccia is composed of angular fragments of one or more kinds of rock embedded in a matrix of another material, the characteristic feature being that the

---

[1] See pp. 61–62.   [2] G. Caton-Thompson and E. W. Gardner, *Desert Fayum*, pp. 72, 138.
[3] G. Brunton and G. Caton-Thompson, *Badarian Civilisation*, pp. 5, 7, 28, 41, 57.   [4] See p. 421.
[5] G. Caton-Thompson and E. W. Gardner, *Desert Fayum*, pp. 26, 38, 81, 84–87, 138.
[6] H. Vyse, *Pyramids of Gizeh*, II, p. 84, and *n*. 4.
[7] H. Vyse, *Pyramids of Gizeh*, II, p. xviii.
[8] H. Vyse, *Pyramids of Gizeh*, I, pp. 214–15, *n*. 3.
[9] One found under the red granite sarcophagus Y; one marked X and one marked B. (H. Vyse, *Pyramids of Gizeh*, II, pp. 131, 132, Figs. 2 and 3.)

included fragments are sharp-edged and unworn, as distingushed from the worn and rounded fragments of a conglomerate. The name breccia, therefore, denotes the structure of the rock and not its composition. A number of different breccias occur in Egypt and were used anciently, of which two may be mentioned specially, namely, a red and white variety and a green variety.

The red and white breccia is calcareous and consists of white fragments embedded in a red matrix; it is found abundantly on the west bank of the Nile in several localities, for instance, north of Minia,[1] near Asiut,[1] at Thebes [1] and near Esna [1] and it also occurs in the eastern desert.[2] This stone was used in predynastic and early dynastic times chiefly for vases and apparently not again until the Romans worked it for exportation to Italy.

The green breccia consists of fragments of rocks of the most varied description embedded in a matrix, which is variable in colour with green predominating; it is, however, not a typical breccia, as while some of the fragments are angular, others are rounded, and it is sometimes called a brecciated conglomerate; but since in the past it has always been termed breccia and was the *breccia verde antico* of the Romans, it is much better to retain the old name.

This green breccia is found in several localities, the best known of which is the Wadi Hammamat in the eastern desert on the Qena-Quseir road,[3] where it occurs extensively and where it was worked anciently, though so far as is known, not until a very late period; it is not, however, the typical rock of the Wadi, as is often stated, this being schist. Green breccia occurs too at the mouth of the Wadi Dib;[3] in the region to the west of Gebel Dara and Gebel Mongul in the El Urf chain [3] and at Gebel Hamata,[4] all of which are situated in the eastern desert, and also in Sinai.[5]

The green breccia of the Wadi Hammamat was used occasionally in Egypt at a late period, but it was quarried chiefly by the Romans for export to Italy. The principal and probably the only objects of this breccia in the Cairo Museum are parts of a broken sarcophagus of Nekhthorheb (Nectanebo II) (Thirtieth Dynasty) and in the British Museum there is a similar sarcophagus of Nekhtnebef (Nectanebo I). Legrain described [6] a number of statues from Karnak as being of green breccia, but those that the author has been able to examine are not green breccia.

Fragments of breccia of foreign origin, probably from Greece, have been found in excavations at Alexandria.

Diorite, Gabbro

Diorites and gabbros are crystalline, granular rocks consisting essentially of plagioclase felspar (white) and hornblende or augite (black or dark green), and may be either fine grained or coarse grained. They occur extensively in Egypt in several localities, namely, near Aswan, in the eastern and western deserts and in Sinai.

---

[1] W. F. Hume, *Explan. Notes to the Geol. Map of Egypt*, p. 46.

[2] T. Barron and W. F. Hume, *Topog. and Geol. of the Eastern Desert*, p. 171.

[3] T. Barron and W. F. Hume, *Topog. and Geol. of the Eastern Desert*, p. 263; W. F. Hume, *Geology of Egypt*, II, Part I, pp. 256–60.

[4] J. Ball, *Geog. and Geol. of South-Eastern Egypt*, p. 351.

[5] W. F. Hume, *Explan. Notes to the Geol. Map of Egypt*, p. 49.

[6] G. Legrain, *Statues et Statuettes*, I, pp. 1, 41; II, pp. 3, 36, 89, 98.

The use of diorite in Egypt goes back to neolithic times, from which period there are several worked fragments including axes, palettes, a (?) bowl and a mace-head.[1]

The dioritic rock employed anciently was of several different kinds, one of the most characteristic being a coarse-grained black and white speckled variety in which the component minerals (white felspar and black hornblende) are fairly evenly distributed. This was used in predynastic and early dynastic times for mace-heads, bowls and vases and occasionally for palettes, and is loosely termed diorite, spotted diorite and gabbro by archaeologists. This particular variety was probably obtained from Aswan, where an identical rock is known to occur [2] and where another rock, granite, was being worked at an early date, and, although a similar diorite is largely developed in the eastern desert in the hills north of the Qena-Quseir road and was worked in Wadi Semna (north-west of Quseir) by the Romans,[3] there is no evidence of earlier working.

Another kind of rock that is called diorite by archaeologists (the name being well rooted in the literature) is that of which the well-known statues of Khafrē (Chephren) in the Cairo Museum are made,[4] the use of which is not known before the early dynastic period [5] and is principally confined to the Old Kingdom.[6] This rock, which is banded, or mottled, dark green and white or black and white, varies considerably in appearance, even in different parts of the same block, and the general effect may be dark green, dark grey, light grey or white slightly flecked with black, the last-named variant having been much employed for making bowls and vases, the other varieties having been used for statues, especially during the Fourth Dynasty.

Some years ago, I suggested [7] that, since this rock has a gneissic structure, a suitable name for it would be diorite-gneiss, which would indicate both its composition and structure, and Mr. O. H. Little, Director of the Geological Survey of Egypt, in a recent description of it states,[8] 'If diorite-gneiss were substituted for diorite, it would be more correct, though the term is not applicable to all varieties.' Anorthosite-gneiss would be still better.[9]

In the past there has been much speculation respecting the locality from which this particular diorite-gneiss was obtained, which was unknown until comparatively recently, when the source was discovered in the western desert about forty miles north-west of Abu Simbel in Nubia.[10] It is only a special variety, possibly, however,

---

[1] G. Caton-Thompson and E. W. Gardner, *Desert Fayum*, pp. 32, 33, 40, 87.

[2] J. Ball, *First or Aswan Cataract*, Pl. v (2); W. F. Hume, *Geology of Egypt*, II, Part III, p. 867.

[3] T. Barron and W. F. Hume, *Topog. and Geol. of the Eastern Desert*, pp. 221, 265.

[4] L. Borchardt, *Statuen und Statuetten*, I, pp. 9–16, Nos. 9–14.

[5] E.g. an anorthosite bowl of Second Dynasty date from Wardan (H. Larsen, *Orientalia Suecana*, v (1956), pp. 7–10). Some of the neolithic fragments are similar in appearance (G. Caton-Thompson and E. W. Gardner, *Desert Fayum*, p. 87).

[6] Cf. J. Couyat, *Bull. Soc. fr. de Minéralogie*, XXXI (1908), pp. 338–41; B.I.F.A.O., VI (1908), p. 54; B.I.F.A.O., VII (1910), pp. 35–39; G. Andrew, *Bull. Inst. d'Ég.*, XVI (1934), pp. 105–9.

[7] A. Lucas, *Ancient Egyptian Materials*, 1st ed., 1926, p. 181.

[8] O. H. Little, *Ann. Serv.*, XXXIII (1933), pp. 75–80.

[9] W. F. Hume, *Geology of Egypt*, II, Part III, p. 867, Pl. CXCIVa. This term is also used by Andrew, Sudan Government geologist.

[10] R. Engelbach, *Ann. Serv.*, XXXIII (1933), pp. 65–74; *Ann. Serv.*, XXXVIII (1938), pp. 369–90; O. H. Little, *Ann. Serv.*, XXXIII (1933), pp. 75–80; W. F. Hume, *Geology of Egypt*, II, Part I, pp. 299–300; G. W. Murray, *Geog. Journ.*, XCIV (1939), pp. 97–111.

unique, of a diorite-gneiss that occurs in other localities.[1] Another variety of diorite (porphyritic-diorite), composed of a compact black matrix in which are embedded conspicuous white fragments, will be considered when dealing with porphyry.

The ancient Egyptian name for the 'Chephren' diorite was *mntt*, though whether this term also included other varieties is uncertain.[2]

Dolerite, Diabase

As already explained,[3] dolerite is merely a coarse-grained basalt and there is no fundamental difference and no hard and fast line of demarcation between the two. Diabase is properly an altered dolerite, but the term is often loosely used by archaeologists as synonymous with dolerite.

Dolerite occurs in several localities in the eastern desert of Egypt, namely, in the neighbourhood of Wadi Esh near Quseir;[4] in Wadi Atolla, a little south of Wadi Esh, where in one place the rock is marked with a cartouche of Ramses III (Twentieth Dynasty)[5] and near Gebel Dokhan, where there are ancient quarries probably of Roman date.[6] It is also found in Sinai, and dolerite workings, probably of Old Kingdom date, have been found in the Fayum.[7]

One important use of dolerite in ancient Egypt was for pounders for working hard stone, and roughly spherical specimens of this rock may still be seen in large numbers in the ancient granite quarries at Aswan and in the quartzite quarry at Gebel Ahmar near Cairo, where they have remained since they were employed by the ancient quarrymen. Spherical masses of dolerite, resembling these pounders, occur naturally in certain places in the cataract regions of the Nile and in the eastern desert.[8]

Dolomite [9]

Dolomite is a definite compound (and not merely a mixture) of calcium carbonate and magnesium carbonate in the proportion of 54.4 per cent of the former and 45.6 per cent of the latter. Magnesium carbonate is a very common constituent of limestone, but is usually present in very small proportions, thus out of 132 specimens of limestone from the neighbourhood of Cairo analysed by me all contained magnesium carbonate, but only fifteen contained more than 5 per cent and only two contained more than 20 per cent, the proportion of magnesium carbonate in these being 30 per cent and 37 per cent respectively. When the proportion of magnesium carbonate is substantial, as in the two cases mentioned, but not sufficient to form dolomite, the rock is termed dolomitic limestone (or magnesian limestone) and, since dolomite and

---

[1] G. Andrew, *Bull. Inst. d'Ég.*, XVI (1934), pp. 105–9. The source of the diorite used in neolithic times is uncertain (G. Caton-Thompson and E. W. Gardner, *Desert Fayum*, p. 87).

[2] Cf. J. R. Harris, *Lexicographical Studies*, pp. 87–88, 231; K. Sethe, *Bau- und Denkmalsteine*, pp. 910–11 (49–50); R. Engelbach, *Ann. Serv.*, XXXIII (1933), p. 66.

[3] See p. 61.

[4] T. Barron and W. F. Hume, *Topog. and Geol. of the Eastern Desert*, pp. 52, 236, 263.

[5] T. Barron and W. F. Hume, *Topog. and Geol. of the Eastern Desert*, pp. 217, 263.

[6] T. Barron and W. F. Hume, *Topog. and Geol. of the Eastern Desert*, pp. 26, 236.

[7] G. Caton-Thompson and E. W. Gardner, *Desert Fayum*, pp. 136–8; cf. p. 87. See above, pp. 61–62.

[8] W. F. Hume, *Prelim. Report on the Geol. of the Eastern Desert*, p. 49.

[9] Cf. J. R. Harris, *Lexicographical Studies*, pp. 100–101.

dolomitic limestone are so much alike that they cannot be distinguished except by chemical analysis, they are usually classed together.

Both dolomite and dolomitic limestone were employed in ancient Egypt in early dynastic times for bowls and vases and occasionally at later periods for other objects.[1] Petrie reports forty-four vases of what he terms 'dolomite marble' from the First Dynasty [2] and I have analysed the material of a number of broken vases of Third Dynasty date from Saqqara, some of which were dolomite or practically dolomite and others dolomitic limestone.[3]

Petrie, describing the 'dolomite marble', says:[4] 'This material varies much, but cannot be confounded with any other class. It is hard, opaque, white with veins; sometimes the veining is of clearer white, but usually of grey and sometimes of quartz, almost black. The magnesia of the dolomite is left on the surface as a powdery white incrustation, if it has been exposed to solution by weathering.'

The specimens examined by me have all been white with veins or patches of dark grey; the surface has always been dull, though probably it was polished originally; the white has been chalky in appearance and a fine white powder has rubbed off when the specimens have been handled. The characteristic appearance of this stone, together with the fact that cold dilute hydrochloric acid causes little or no effervescence, makes it easy to identify. Dolomite occurs in the eastern desert in several localities.[5]

Flint, Chert [6]

The stone first used in Egypt, as in many other countries, was flint, and from it, before metal was known, Stone Age man fashioned his weapons and tools [7] and even long after copper was generally employed, the use of flint, although it naturally decreased considerably, did not entirely cease, but continued for certain purposes, some of which were purely ceremonial. The manufacture and use of flint knives is shown in tomb paintings of Twelfth Dynasty date at Beni Hasan,[8] when manifestly it was still a living industry. A very large number of flint implements (knives and scrapers) and also sickle flints were found by Emery in a First Dynasty tomb at Saqqara.[9]

Flint was also used at an early date for personal ornaments, chiefly bracelets, and occasionally even for bowls, one such of Second Dynasty date having been found in the Fourth Dynasty temple of Menkaurē.[10]

Flint consists of a very compact form of silica; it is dark grey or black in colour; breaks with a conchoidal fracture and affords sharp cutting edges; it occurs plentifully

---

[1] E.g. shawabti figures of Taharqa (D. Dunham, *Nuri*, p. 5).
[2] W. M. F. Petrie, *Royal Tombs*, II, p. 41, Pls. IX (2–10), II (c, d, e); *Abydos*, I, p. 7, Pl. IX (5, 6, 7, 10).
[3] Cf. also A. J. Arkell, *J.E.A.*, XLII (1956), p. 116.
[4] W. M. F. Petrie, *Royal Tombs*, II, p. 44.
[5] W. F. Hume, *Geology of Egypt*, II, Part I, pp. 89, 144, 160.
[6] Cf. J. R. Harris, *Lexicographical Studies*, pp. 138–9.
[7] Cf. E. J. Baumgartel, *Cultures of Prehistoric Egypt*, II, pp. 24–43.
[8] P. E. Newberry, *Beni Hasan*, I, p. 31, Pl. XI; II, p. 47, Pl. IV; F. Ll. Griffith, *Beni Hasan*, III, pp. 33–38, Pls. VII, VIII, IX, X.
[9] W. B. Emery, *Hemaka*, pp. 18–27, 33.
[10] G. A. Reisner, *Mycerinus*, p. 102.

in certain districts in Egypt in the form of nodules and layers in the limestone rock and in such localities it is also found scattered about the surface of the desert, having been freed by the weathering of the limestone. Ancient flint mines have been found in the eastern desert.[1]

Chert is an impure kind of flint of a light grey or light brown colour and, although it is largely composed of silica, it breaks with a more or less flat fracture instead of the conchoidal fracture of flint; it occurs like flint in limestone and was sometimes used in place of flint.

Granite [2]

Granite and its occurrence have already been described in connexion with building materials,[3] where it was stated to be the name of a large class of crystalline rocks of igneous origin, the individual minerals of which, chiefly felspar, quartz and mica, are sufficiently large to be visible to the naked eye. The typical granite of ancient Egypt is the coarse-grained red variety that forms the greater part of the hills between Aswan and Shellal. This is a true granite and its recognition presents no difficulty and leaves no room for doubt or confusion. Granite, however, being a natural material, is not uniform in structure, composition or even colour, but varies considerably in all three respects, thus the grain of the rock may be coarse or fine, the relative proportion or distribution of the contained minerals may vary and the felspar may be red, white or occasionally green, the rock in the first case being coloured red, in the second case, black and white or light grey, or when the darker minerals (mica and hornblende) preponderate, dark grey or even practically black and in the third case green. Granite, too, merges into rocks of other types without any hard and fast line of demarcation.

The geologist divides granite into a number of sub-classes in accordance with their composition, but with these divisions Egyptology is not concerned, all that is required being a broad classification, subtle distinctions being quite unnecessary. Thus the geologist's hornblende-biotite-granite may reasonably be called dark grey or black granite, as the case may be, by the archaeologist. There will probably be some difference of opinion as to the degree of elasticity that may be allowed in calling stone granite, or in other stone nomenclature, but for the purposes of Egyptology the boundaries should be as wide as possible. It may, however, be noted that certain objects have been described as granite which are definitely not, for example a number of shawabti figures of Taharqa, which on examination proved to be (*a*) dolomite or ankerite, (*b*) serpentinized peridotite.[4]

Granite was employed in predynastic times, though only sparingly and chiefly for bowls and vases, but in the early dynastic period it was worked to a much greater extent on account of the increased use of copper tools and, in addition to its use as a building material, it was also employed for sarcophagi, and at later periods for statues, obelisks, stelæ and other objects.

---

[1] H. W. Seton Karr, *Journ. Royal Anthrop. Inst.*, xxvii (1898), pp. 90–92; E. J. Baumgartel, *Ancient Egypt*, 1930, pp. 103–8.

[2] Cf. J. R. Harris, *Lexicographical Studies*, pp. 72–74; K. Sethe, *Bau- und Denkmalsteine*, pp. 876–82 (15–21).

[3] See pp. 57–59.   [4] D. Dunham, *Nuri*, p. 5.

The occurrence of granite in Egypt has already been described [1] in connexion with its use for building purposes.

Gypsum, Anhydrite [2]

Gypsum, as already explained when dealing with plaster,[3] although often occurring in scattered masses of loosely aggregated crystals, quite useless for carving, is also found in compact rock-like formation, for example in the Mariout region to the west of Alexandria; between Ismailia and Suez; in the Fayum and very plentifully near the Red Sea coast.

Gypsum consists of hydrated calcium sulphate and in appearance it much resembles alabaster (calcite), which is calcium carbonate, and it is often called alabaster and even claims, probably wrongly, priority for the name.

Apart from its use for mortar and plaster, gypsum was employed only to a comparatively small extent in ancient Egypt. Miss Caton-Thompson has shown that a very large number of gypsum vases and dishes were made in the Fayum during the Third Dynasty [4] and Petrie found at Giza [5] several intact and many broken gypsum vases of Second or Third Dynasty date that probably came from the Fayum factory. Among the objects from the tomb of Tutankhamūn two of the knobs on the saddles of the chariot harness are gypsum, the others that have been tested by me being alabaster (calcite).[6] Petrie found a gypsum dish [7] of protodynastic date and a few gypsum boxes of Roman date.[8] Myers found a gypsum vase of predynastic date at Armant.[9]

Until recently a pale blue material used chiefly in the Middle Kingdom for small vases was assumed to be marble on account of its appearance and has always been called 'blue marble',[10] but a doubt about the identity of the material having been raised Mr. O. H. Little, Director of the Geological Survey of Egypt, determined the specific gravity of a fragment and found that it was not marble, but anhydrous calcium sulphate (anhydrite), and I made a chemical analysis with the same result. The source of this material is not known, but it is most probably local. Petrie suggests, without any evidence whatever, that it 'seems to have been brought from the north of the Mediterranean',[11] and again 'The bluish marble of the Aegean is found in many examples there' (at Kahun).

Gypsum is softer than alabaster (calcite) and may be scratched with the fingernail, whereas alabaster cannot be scratched with anything softer than steel. The anhydrous form of calcium sulphate (anhydrite) is about the same hardness as calcite.

---

[1] See pp. 58–59.
[2] Cf. J. R. Harris, *Lexicographical Studies*, pp. 90–91, 101, 190–1.
[3] See p. 78.
[4] G. Caton-Thompson and E. W. Gardner, *Desert Fayum*, pp. 105–7.
[5] W. M. F. Petrie, *Gizeh and Rifeh*, p. 7.
[6] A. Lucas, in H. Carter, *Tut-ankh-Amen*, II, p. 168 (Appendix II).
[7] W. M. F. Petrie, *Prehistoric Egypt*, p. 36.
[8] W. M. F. Petrie, *Hyksos and Israelite Cities*, p. 58, Pl. XLIII (24–31).
[9] R. Mond and O. H. Myers, *Cemeteries of Armant*, I, p. 36.
[10] Cf. J. Garstang, *El Arabah*, pp. 28–29.
[11] W. M. F. Petrie, *Kahun, Gurob and Hawara*, pp. 30, 42.

Limestone [1]

Limestone has already been dealt with in connexion with building materials.[2] In addition to this use, however, it was largely employed for other purposes, including vases, and it was one of the first stones used, except for weapons and tools, because it was soft and easily worked and also because it lent itself admirably to carving on account of its fine texture; its use dates back to neolithic times. The wide distribution of limestone in Egypt has already been mentioned.

Black crystalline limestone was used occasionally during the predynastic period for vessels, such a limestone occurring in the eastern desert [3] and in the Cairo-Suez district.[4] A hard fine-grained yellow limestone also was sometimes used and a similar stone occurs behind Gebel el Geir east of Qift [5] and also between Kharga Oasis and the Nile.[6] A pink limestone occurs plentifully in Egypt, particularly in the western desert on the Edfu-Dush road and on the Asiut-Kharga road and also between Ismailia and Suez, and was used occasionally.

Marble [7]

Marble is a crystalline form of limestone having a compact structure that enables it to take a high polish; it is usually white or grey, but may be of almost any colour and is often veined in different colours.

The known occurrences of marble in Egypt are chiefly confined to the eastern desert, where it is recorded from several localities,[8] namely, a grey saccharine-looking variety from Wadi Dib (west of Gebel Zeit and fairly close to the Red Sea coast) and both a white and a colourless kind from Gebel Rokham (near the upper part of Wadi Miah, east of Esna and roughly two-thirds of the way between the Nile and the Red Sea), the latter of which was exploited to a small extent in Arab times [9] and possibly earlier; a third occurrence is in the far south-eastern desert.[10] A hard crystalline limestone, practically marble, occurs at Beni Sha'ran opposite Manfalut, and recently a yellowish-grey, very nummulitic marble with brown patches has been discovered at Geran el Ful on the northern edge of the plateau to the west of the Giza pyramids; this, however, was not used and was probably not known anciently. Good quality marble of different colours has been reported over a large area near Wadi Haimur.[11] From where the comparatively small amount of marble employed anciently was obtained is not known.

---

[1] Cf. J. R. Harris, *Lexicographical Studies*, pp. 69–71; K. Sethe, *Bau- und Denkmalsteine*, pp. 866–73 (5–12).

[2] See pp. 52–55.

[3] W. F. Hume, *Geology of Egypt*, II, Part I, pp. 201, 203.

[4] T. Barron, *Topog. and Geol. of the District between Cairo and Suez*, pp. 27, 99, 100, 101.

[5] Information kindly supplied by Mr. J. Dudler.

[6] W. F. Hume, *Geology of Egypt*, I, p. 134.

[7] Cf. J. R. Harris, *Lexicographical Studies*, pp. 96–97, 100–101.

[8] W. F. Hume, *Explan. Notes to the Geol. Map of Egypt*, p. 47; T. Barron and W. F. Hume, *Topog. and Geol. of the Eastern Desert*, pp. 32, 119, 240, 266–7; W. F. Hume, *Geology of Egypt*, II, Part I, pp. 101, 171, 172.

[9] J. Barthoux, *Mém. Inst. d'Ég.*, V (1922), p. 33.

[10] J. Ball, *Geog. and Geol. of South-Eastern Egypt*, pp. 348–9.

[11] L. Nassim, *Minerals of Economical Interest*, p. 168.

Marble was used to a small extent for vases in predynastic and early dynastic times; it was used for statues during the Eighteenth and Nineteenth Dynasties (examples: a beautiful small statue of Thutmose III in white marble slightly veined in grey, now in the Cairo Museum,[1] and a number of large statues in the temples at Luxor and Karnak respectively and several in the Cairo Museum) and it was employed for statues and portrait heads in Roman times, numerous examples of which are in the Museums at Cairo and Alexandria. Fragments of foreign marble from Greece have been found in excavations at Alexandria.

Pliny mentions [2] 'marbles of Alexandria', the Augustan and Tiberian, which were discovered in Egypt in the reigns of the emperors Augustus and Tiberius respectively. The stones, he explains, differ. 'in the arrangement of their spots', one having them 'undulated and curling to a point', whereas in the other 'the streaks are white, not involved, but lying wide asunder'.

This same writer also mentions [2] a third kind of marble called '*memphites*' after Memphis, where it was found, which he says was 'of a nature somewhat analagous to the precious stones'. Whether all, or any, of these stones were marble in the modern sense is uncertain, though if *memphites* were indeed obtained from near Memphis, it was probably some sort of limestone, since no other kind of stone is known to occur in that locality. A 'very hard marbly white limestone' was used for sculptures in the Labyrinth.[3]

The so-called 'blue marble', used principally in the Middle Kingdom for making small vases, as already stated,[4] is not marble but anhydrite.

Obsidian [5]

Obsidian is a glassy-looking material that breaks with the conchoidal fracture of glass and is a natural glass of volcanic origin. The colour is usually black or green, but obsidians may range 'from clear to gray to black with all variations of reddish-browns to reddish-blacks and with all degrees of banding or mottling'.[6] These variations are due to differences of chemical composition or to physical properties relative to cooling. The majority of samples from Egypt appear to be of rhyolitic obsidian, though a trachytic variety, quite brown in thin section, has also been identified.[6]

So far as is known obsidian is not found naturally in Egypt, but it occurs in Abyssinia,[7] in the Sudan, in Arabia in the Aden Protectorate, in the Hadramaut and elsewhere, in Armenia, in Asia Minor and in various Mediterranean islands.

Obsidian was used in ancient Egypt in small amount from predynastic times,[8] at first in the form of flakes for use as implements, and as weapons, such as lance-heads, and later as amulets, beads, scarabs, eyes and pupils of eyes in statues and statuettes,

---

[1] No. J. 43507 A.

[2] XXXVI: 11.

[3] W. M. F. Petrie, G. A. Wainwright and E. Mackay, *Labyrinth, Gerzeh and Mazguneh*, p. 31.

[4] See p. 413.

[5] Cf. J. R. Harris, *Lexicographical Studies*, pp. 110–11, 228–9.

[6] I. Friedman and R. L. Smith, *American Antiquity*, xxv, No. 4 (1960), pp. 476–522 (pp. 484–5).

[7] H. Salt, *A Voyage into Abyssinia*, pp. 190–4; W. H. Schoff, *The Periplus of the Erythraean Sea*, pp. 23, 66; Pliny, xxxvi: 67.

[8] W. M. F. Petrie, *Prehistoric Egypt*, p. 43; E. Massoulard, *Rev. d'Ég.*, ii (1936), pp. 158–9.

small vases (particularly during the Middle Kingdom),[1] and other purposes,[2] notable examples of its use being the head of Senwosret III or Amenemhet III (Twelfth Dynasty),[3] another fragmentary head of Twelfth Dynasty date,[4] a broken mask, foot and small piece of neck and the head of a life-size statue (Eighteenth Dynasty), the latter four from Karnak.[5] Pliny states that 'Tiberius Caesar returned to the people of Heliopolis an obsidian image of Menelaus that had been found among the property left by one of the prefects of Egypt'.[6]

The subject of the use of obsidian in ancient Egypt, with particular reference to its place of origin, has been discussed at length by Wainwright [7] and shortly by Frankfort,[8] the latter of whom gives some physical constants of obsidian from various sources. Wainwright concludes that the obsidian used in Egypt was obtained from Armenia. In a former edition of this book I suggested that as there was a coasting trade down the Red Sea from very early times, and as obsidian occurred on the coast of Abyssinia, some at least of that employed in Egypt and the Sudan, especially that from the Sudan and from Nubia, may have been obtained from Abyssinia, which is also the view of von Bissing.[9] Since then I have examined most of the obsidian objects in the Cairo Museum and many belonging to friends, and a large number of specimens from Abyssinia, Armenia, and the Mediterranean Islands, the results of which have been published.[10] An important feature of Abyssinian obsidian is its comparatively high density, which is paralleled by that of the Egyptian objects examined, my conclusion being that 'There is ample evidence, therefore, that some of the material of the obsidian objects found in Egypt, and probably the greater part, was obtained from Abyssinia.'

Porphyritic Rock

The name porphyry (derived from the Greek word meaning purple) was originally applied to a certain kind of purple-tinted rock (imperial porphyry) but in geology this primary significance has given place to one in which structure, and not colour, is the guiding characteristic, a porphyritic rock being any kind of igneous rock in which there are conspicuous crystals scattered throughout a differently coloured ground-mass or matrix of apparently homogeneous material.

Porphyritic rocks varying considerably both in the nature and size of the conspicuous crystals and also in colour are widely distributed in Egypt and occur near Aswan, in the eastern desert and in Sinai.

---

[1] J. E. Quibell, *Archaic Objects*, pp. 193–4; J. de Morgan, *Dahchour, mars-juin 1894*, p. 71; H. E. Winlock, *Treasure of El Lāhūn*, p. 67; P. Montet, *Byblos et l'Égypte*, p. 155 (cf. p. 157, an obsidian box); D. Randall MacIver and C. L. Woolley, *Buhen*, p. 194.

[2] See G. A. Wainwright, *Ancient Egypt*, 1927, pp. 88, 91.

[3] C. Ricketts, *J.E.A.*, IV (1917), pp. 71–73.

[4] A. C. Mace, *The Murch Collection of Egyptian Antiquities* (Supplement to *M.M.A. Bull*, Jan. 1911), p. 26, Fig. 17.

[5] G. Legrain, *Statues et Statuettes*, I, pp. 58–59, Nos. 42101–2.

[6] XXXVI: 67.

[7] G. A. Wainwright, *Ancient Egypt*, 1927, pp. 77–93.

[8] H. Frankfort, *Studies in Early Pottery of the Near East*, II, pp. 190–3.

[9] F. W. von Bissing, *Archiv für Orientforschung*, V (1928–9), p. 75, *n.* 2 from p. 73.

[10] A. Lucas, *Ann. Serv.*, XLI (1942), pp. 271–5; XLVII (1947), pp. 113–23.

Porphyritic rock was used largely in the predynastic and early dynastic periods for making vessels,[1] the particular variety generally chosen being black and white (white crystals in a black matrix). This stone occurs in the Esh-Mellaha range near the Red Sea (south of Jemsa Bay).[2]

The best known of the porphyritic rocks quarried anciently is without doubt the beautiful fine-grained purple-coloured rock (*porfido rosso antico*), often termed imperial porphyry, that was obtained from Egypt by the Romans from the first to the fourth century A.D. and employed extensively in Italy as an ornamental stone.[3] This is found in three localities in the eastern desert, namely at Gebel Dokhan,[4] which is situated in about the same latitude as Asiut, but nearer the Red Sea than the Nile; at Gebel Esh,[4] some distance north-east of Dokhan and nearer the coast and at El Urf near Wadi Dib.[4] It was from the first-named locality, however, that the Romans obtained their supply.

Probably the Egyptian stone referred to by Pliny,[5] which he describes as being of a red colour and which he calls *porphyrites*, was imperial porphyry. The quarries, Pliny says, were able to furnish blocks of any dimensions however large. He also states that certain columns in the Egyptian Labyrinth were of *porphyrites*;[6] he further says that the steward in Egypt for the emperor Claudius brought to Rome from Egypt statues made of this stone, 'a novelty which was not very highly approved of, as no one has since followed his example'.[5]

Only four examples of the use of imperial porphyry in Egypt before Roman times are known to me, one being a small amuletic claw of 'prehistoric' date,[7] another, part of a small fluted bowl, probably of protodynastic date,[8] found at Ballas in Upper Egypt,[9] the third, part of the lid of a small vase from the Third Dynasty step pyramid at Saqqara,[10] and the fourth, a fluted bowl 'like some pieces found at Naqada, which were probably of the same age.' [11] This was from 'B' cemetery at Abydos, S.D. 79. This, however, does not mean that imperial porphyry was being quarried at such early periods, as a piece sufficiently large to make the objects in question might well have been found lying loose on the surface of the desert near where the porphyry occurs.

---

[1] For a particularly elaborate example see E. M. Burgess and A. J. Arkell, *J.E.A.*, XLIV (1958), pp. 6–11.

[2] Information kindly supplied by Mr. J. Dudler.

[3] A. Delesse, *Bulletin de la société géologique française*, VII (1850), pp. 524–40; *Ann. Chim. et Phys.*, 3ᵉ Sér., XXX (1850), pp. 81–87; O. Schneider, *Naturw. Beitr. Georgr. u. Kultur*, 1885, pp. 75–176; F. Rutley, *Quart. Journ. Geol. Soc.*, XLI (1885), pp. 157–61; J. C. Barthoux, *C.R.Ac. Sci.*, CXLVII (1908), pp. 988–90; J. Couyat, *B.I.F.A.O.*, VII (1910), pp. 25–33; G. Andrew, *Bull. Inst. d'Ég.*, XX (1938), pp. 63–81.

[4] T. Barron and W. F. Hume, *Topog. and Geol. of the Eastern Desert*, pp. 118, 238, 241, 262; W. F. Hume, *Geology of Egypt*, II, Part I, pp. 273–82; G. Andrew, *Bull. Inst.d' Ég.*, XX (1938), pp. 63–81; K. Fitzler, *Steinbrüche und Bergwerke*, pp. 94–99.

[5] XXXVI: 11.   [6] XXXVI: 19.   [7] W. M. F. Petrie, *Amulets*, p. 13, Pl. II (24a).

[8] Called Old Kingdom by Petrie, but Mr. Guy Brunton tells me that it is probably proto-dynastic.

[9] W. M. F. Petrie and J. E. Quibell, *Naqada and Ballas*, pp. 10, 36. Figured in W. M. F. Petrie, *Funeral Furniture of Egypt*, Pl. XVI (209).

[10] Cairo Museum, No. J. 69493.

[11] W. M. F. Petrie, *Royal Tombs*, II, p. 43, Pl. XLVIII (88).

Even at a late period date, imperial porphyry seems rarely to have been employed in Egypt, as only very few objects made from it can be traced, namely, a bust of a Roman emperor in the Cairo Museum; a carved lid of a sarcophagus of late date in the Alexandria Museum; [1] a large mutilated statue of a male figure seated on a throne, possibly dating from the fourth century A.D., also in the Alexandria Museum; [2] a torso of a Byzantine emperor from Alexandria in the Berlin Museum; some re-used pieces of Roman date built into the *Madrassa* of the Sultan Barquq mosque at Cairo, [3] and a thin polished slab (probably from a building) in the Museum of Arab art. [4]

Small pieces of broken worked objects of porphyritic rock, very dark green, or almost black in colour (black matrix with well-defined crystals of felspar of a light green colour) have been found on several occasions in Egypt, for example, there are four specimens in the Geological Museum, Cairo, presented by Père Bovier-Lapierre, which are labelled 'Labradorite-porphyry from Babylon and Fostat'; and in the Cairo Museum there are six small specimens, one (No. 65537) described in the register as 'End of 3rd cent. A.D. From Kom Auchim, University of Michigan (Petersen) 1930–35'; another (No. 66317) described as 'Roman, Mond-Myers Exped. Armant, 1936'; a third marked 'Minia Mag.' (meaning from the store of the Inspector of Antiquities at Minia), and three not marked.

Mr. O. H. Little, Director of the Geological Survey, Egypt, tells me that he does not know of any occurrence of this rock in Egypt.

Professor Alan Wace informs me that quarries of this stone occur at the ancient Croceae in Greece, midway between Sparta and Gytheion, near the modern Levetsova, and were worked in Mycenean times and also in later Roman times and that vessels of this stone have been found at Mycenae and other Mycenean sites, and he showed me a small piece of such a vessel, which I compared with the specimens above in the Cairo Museums, and there is no doubt that the stone is identical, and, therefore, it is practically certain that the Egyptian objects, or the stone for them, were imported from Greece. This stone should not be confused with green breccia.

Quartzite [5]

Quartzite and its occurrence in Egypt have already been dealt with in connexion with building materials, [6] but in addition to its use for building this stone was employed extensively for other purposes, principally for sarcophagi and statues. Examples of the former are the sarcophagus in the Hawara pyramid (Twelfth Dynasty), and the series of royal sarcophagi of the Eighteenth Dynasty, [7] including those of Thutmose I (?), Thutmose II, Hatshepsut, Thutmose III, Amenhotpe II, Thutmose IV and Tutankhamūn, all of brownish yellow quartzite. Examples of the latter include a head of Djedefrē (Fourth Dynasty), and statues of Senwosret III (Twelfth Dynasty),

---

[1] E. Breccia, *Alexandrea ad Aegyptum*, 1922, p. 103.

[2] E. Breccia, *Alexandrea ad Aegyptum*, 1922, p. 235.

[3] Kindly communicated by Professor K. A. C. Creswell.

[4] See R. Delbrueck, *Antike Porphyrwerke*, 1932.

[5] Cf. J. R. Harris, *Lexicographical Studies*, pp. 75–76; K. Sethe, *Bau- und Denkmalsteine*, pp. 889–94 (28–33).

[6] See pp. 62–63.

[7] W. C. Hayes, *Royal Sarcophagi of the XVIII Dynasty*, pp. 31–32.

Thutmose IV and Senmut (Eighteenth Dynasty), Ptah (Nineteenth Dynasty), and the emperor Caracalla (Roman).

With respect to the nature of the stone of which the Colossi of Memnon are made, which sometimes has been called quartzite and sometimes Nubian sandstone, Varille states [1] that *'Malgré l'avis des géologues aucun doute ne peut donc subsister sur la localisation de "la Montagne de grès" où furent taillés les colosses de Memnon'*, which he believes to be Gebel Ahmar near Cairo. The 'pebbly' nature of part of the stone, which seems to be a difficulty with some archaeologists in assigning the stone to Gebel Ahmar, may be closely matched in the very coarse material from that quarry.

Sandstone [2]

Sandstone has already been dealt with as a building material,[3] but it was also employed for many other purposes, such as statues, stelæ and other objects. Notable examples of its use are the statues of Akhenaten (Eighteenth Dynasty) from Karnak, discovered a few years ago, and the colossal statues at Abu Simbel (Nineteenth Dynasty).

'Schist' (Greywacke), Tuff, Mudstone, Slate

After limestone, sandstone and granite, one of the most largely used rocks in ancient Egypt was what is generally called 'schist', though, since it is a sedimentary and not a metamorphic rock, it cannot be schist. It is greywacke,[4] a fine-grained, compact, hard, crystalline, quartzose rock, very like slate in appearance and generally of various shades of grey, ranging from light to dark, with sometimes a greenish tint. With this may be grouped other allied rocks, namely, tuff (volcanic ash), mudstone and slate, since they are frequently so much alike that they cannot be distinguished except by a microscopical examination of thin sections, and they all occur in the same locality.[5]

Artifacts of volcanic ash are known from the neolithic period,[6] and greywacke and sometimes tuff and mudstone were employed during the predynastic and early dynastic periods for bracelets, bowls and vases, and greywacke later for sarcophagi, naoi and statues, slate being sometimes used for palettes.[7]

Greywacke,[8] tuff [9] and slate [10] all occur in several localities in the eastern desert,

---

[1] A. Varille, *Ann. Serv.*, XXXIII (1933), pp. 85–94.

[2] Cf. J. R. Harris, *Lexicographical Studies*, pp. 71–72; K. Sethe, *Bau- und Denkmalsteine*, pp. 873–6 (12–15).

[3] See pp. 55–57.

[4] E. Fraas, *Zeitschr. der deutsch. geol. Gesellsch.*, Berlin, Bd. III, Heft 4 (1900); W. F. Hume, *Geology of Egypt*, II, Part I, pp. 263–6; G. Andrew, *Bull. Inst. d'Ég.*, XXI (1939), pp. 153–90.

[5] Cf. N. Shiah, *Ann. Serv.*, XLI (1942), pp. 199–205.

[6] G. Caton-Thompson and E. W. Gardner, *Desert Fayum*, p. 87.

[7] W. F. Hume, *Geology of Egypt*, II, Part III, p. 865.

[8] T. Barron and W. F. Hume, *Topog. and Geol. of the Eastern Desert*, pp. 217–21, 224, 226, 236, 238–9, 249, 264; J. Ball, *Geog. and Geol. of South-Eastern Egypt*, pp. 337–50; W. F. Hume, *Geology of Egypt*, II, Part I, pp. 263–6.

[9] T. Barron and W. F. Hume, *Topog. and Geol. of the Eastern Desert*, pp. 221, 236, 239, 249; W. F. Hume, *Geology of Egypt*, II, Part I, pp. 249–50.

[10] T. Barron and W. F. Hume, *Topog. and Geol. of the Eastern Desert*, pp. 217–18, 221, 226, 238, 264; W. F. Hume, *Geology of Egypt*, II, Part I, pp. 194, 203, 227–8, 230, 256.

though the principal and possibly the only ancient source of the two former was the neighbourhood of the Wadi Hammamat on the main road from Qena to Quseir, where there are extensive ancient quarries [1] with more than 250 inscriptions ranging in date from the protodynastic period to the Thirtieth Dynasty.[2] These quarries and the stone from them are frequently mentioned in ancient texts.[3]

There can be little doubt that the greywacke of Wadi Hammamat was the stone called *bḥn* (*bekhen*) by the Egyptians,[4] since at least nine inscriptions referring to *bḥn* are directly connected with the Wadi, where greywacke was the stone principally sought. Moreover, of six objects bearing inscriptions indicating that they are of *bḥn*, two [5] are certainly the Hammamat greywacke, while three others,[6] loosely described as black basalt, have not been competently examined and are in all probability greywacke. The sixth [7] is certainly not greywacke, but a fine-grained grey granite (psammite gneiss) with a fair proportion of red felspar, though the general appearance of the stone is grey, and from a distance it is not unlike greywacke.

Serpentine, Steatite

Serpentine and steatite are very similar in composition, though not identical, both being hydrated silicates of magnesium, but in different states of hydration.

Serpentine is a non-crystalline rock of a dull serpent-like mottled appearance, usually dark green to almost black in colour; it is fairly soft, though harder than steatite, and may readily be cut or scratched; it is widely distributed in the eastern desert, the principal centres being the Baramia-Dungash area,[8] in Wadi Shait,[8] near Gebel Derrera,[8] in the hills north of Sikait [8] and at Gebel Sikait,[8] in the Muqsim area [8] and in the far eastern desert where it covers an area of about 400 square miles from Ras Benas southwards to Cape Elba.[9] A green variety occurs in Wadi Umm Disi

---

[1] J. Couyat and P. Montet, *Les Inscriptions hiéroglyphiques et hiératiques du Ouâdi Hammâmât* (*Mém. Inst.* XXXIV), pp. 18–30; G. Goyon, *Nouvelles Inscriptions rupestres du Wadi Hammamat*, pp. 1–9; K. Fitzler, *Steinbrüche und Bergwerke*, pp. 99–101.

[2] *A.R.*, I, 7, 10, 295–301, 386–9, 427–56, 466–8, 674–5, 707–9; IV, 457–68; W. M. F. Petrie, *History of Egypt*, I (1924), pp. 102, 110, 144, 146, 153, 161, 175, 184, 193, 233; II (1924), pp. 97, 206; III (1928), pp. 119, 166, 280–1, 288, 294, 335, 340, 348, 360, 364, 369–70; A. E. P. Weigall, *Travels in the Upper Egyptian Deserts*, p. 39; J. Couyat and P. Montet, *Les Inscriptions . . . du Ouâdi Hammâmât*; G. Goyon, *Nouvelles Inscriptions rupestres du Wadi Hammamat*.

[3] J. R. Harris, *Lexicographical Studies*, pp. 78–82; K. Sethe, *Bau- und Denkmalsteine*, pp. 894–909 (33–48); A. Varille, *B.I.F.A.O.*, XXXIV (1934), pp. 93–102; A. Lucas and A. Rowe, *Ann. Serv.*, XXXVIII (1938), pp. 127–56, 677; G. Brunton, *Ann. Serv.*, XL (1941), pp. 617–18; N. Shiah, *Ann. Serv.*, XLI (1942), pp. 189–205; A. Lucas and A. Rowe, *Ann. Serv.*, XLI (1942), p. 347.

[4] Cf. J. R. Harris, *Lexicographical Studies*, pp. 78–82; K. Sethe, *Bau- und Denkmalsteine*, pp. 894–909 (33–48).

[5] A naos of Nectanebo I (Cairo 70019) and a pair of obelisks of Nectanebo II (Brit. Mus. 523, 524+a fragment, Cairo 17030).

[6] An obelisk in Marseilles, a statue of Horudja in University College, London, and part of a frieze in Bologna.

[7] A naos of Amasis (Cairo 70011), stated by G. Roeder, *Naos*, pp. 38–42, to be 'grau gesprenkelter feinkörniger Granit'.

[8] W. F. Hume, *Prelim. Report on the Geol. of the Eastern Desert*, p. 34; *Geology of Egypt*, II, Part I, pp. 111, 204; L. Nassim, *Minerals of Economical Interest*, p. 168.

[9] J Ball, *Geog. and Geol. of South-Eastern Egypt*, pp. 320–30; W. F. Hume, *Geology of Egypt*, II, Part I, pp. 144–59.

(which is situated between Wadi Qena and the Red Sea)[1] and at the foot of Gebel el Rebshi,[1] and a black variety in Wadi Sodmen,[1] both these latter places being north-west of Quseir. Serpentine was employed for vases and other objects [2] as early as pre-dynastic times. A head of Amenemhet III (Twelfth Dynasty) is of this material.[3]

Steatite is a form of talc and is usually white or grey in colour, though occasionally it is smoke-black, this latter colour being natural and not artificial, as has been stated; it has a greasy or soapy feel and was used from Badarian times onwards for beads, vases and other small objects, which sometimes were glazed, the greater proportion of the scarabs known being of steatite, many glazed, but a large proportion not now glazed, though probably glazed originally, the glaze having perished.

Steatite is found at Gebel Amr near Aswan,[4] near Bir Muelih, north-east of Aswan,[5] at Gebel Fatira [6] (about the latitude of Tahta, but much nearer the coast than the Nile) and in Wadi Gulan (opposite Gulan Island, which is north of Ras Benas), where it is now being exploited.[7] In the former locality there are ancient mines, which were reopened temporarily in 1918 when 137 tons of material were extracted;[6] it has been worked on a very small scale for many years by the local 'Arabs', who fashion it into bowls and pipes.[8]

STONE VESSELS[9]

The earliest stone vessels made in Egypt that have been found are a few basalt vases of neolithic date from the Fayum and Merimda-Benisalame respectively; then in chronological order come a few more basalt vases from the Badarian civilisation, followed by a large number of vessels of different kinds of stone from various pre-dynastic sites, the stones that can be identified from the archaeological reports being alabaster, basalt, breccia, granite, limestone, marble and porphyritic rock from the early predynastic period, and the same stones, with the exception of granite, but with the addition of diorite (speckled, not the 'Chephren-statue' kind), greywacke (schist,) gypsum, mudstone, serpentine, steatite and volcanic ash from the middle and late predynastic periods. About 73.5 per cent of the stone used was of three kinds only, namely, in order of the numerical frequency of their occurrence, limestone, 36.0 per cent; basalt, 21.5 per cent; alabaster, 16.0 per cent and about 17.5 per cent breccia, marble and serpentine together, leaving only about 9.0 per cent for the other kinds of stones mentioned.

The stone vessel industry reached its zenith during the early dynastic period, and nowhere has there been found such a wealth of beautifully made, handsome stone vessels as in Egypt, the stones employed being of the kinds already mentioned, together with the 'Chephren-statue' variety of diorite, flint, red jasper, obsidian, amethystine

---

[1] T. Barron and W. F. Hume, *Topog. and Geol. of the Eastern Desert*, p. 265.

[2] W. M. F. Petrie, *Prehistoric Egypt*, p. 44.

[3] C. Ricketts, *J.E.A.*, IV (1917), pp. 211–12.

[4] W. F. Hume, *Geology of Egypt*, II, Part I, pp. 131–2, 164–5.

[5] L. Nassim, *Minerals of Economical Interest*, p. 167.

[6] Mines and Quarries Dept., *Report on the Mineral Industry*, p. 37.

[7] Information kindly supplied by Mr. O. H. Little, Director, Geological Survey of Egypt.

[8] P. S. Girard, *Description de l'Égypte, état moderne*, II, 1812, pp. 590–1.

[9] Cf. A. Lucas, *J.E.A.*, XVI (1930), pp. 200–12; E. J. Baumgartel, *Cultures of Prehistoric Egypt*, I, pp. 102–19.

quartz, opaque quartz and rock crystal, all these stones, except obsidian, which was imported, occurring naturally in Egypt. Petrie states [1] that 'From the point of view of magnificence and skill in using hard and beautiful stones we must say that the Egyptians gradually rose to their highest level in the later prehistoric and early dynastic times', and, since this was written many thousands of additional vessels of early dynastic date have been found at Saqqara.

With reference to the royal tombs of the early dynastic period Petrie says [1] that 'hundreds of stone bowls were buried with each king of the Ist. Dynasty, and many are found in tombs of the IIIrd. and IVth. Dynasties' and again,[2] 'Roughly speaking, between 10,000 and 20,000 pieces of vases of the more valuable stones were found, and a much larger quantity of slate and alabaster.' In the First Dynasty tomb of Aha found by Emery at Saqqara there were 653 stone vessels of which 93.3 per cent were alabaster and 3.8 per cent basalt, but no greywacke (schist), the other stones used being breccia (two); limestone (fourteen); porphyritic rock (two); and serpentine (two).[3] In the First Dynasty tomb of 'Hemaka' at Saqqara (later than that of Aha) there were 384 stone vessels, of which 50 per cent were alabaster; 34.4 per cent greywacke (schist), with a few of mudstone and volcanic ash, and the rest (11.7 per cent) of eight other different kinds of stones, but no basalt.[4] In the Third Dynasty step pyramid at Saqqara there were literally tens of thousands of stone vessels, more than 400 having been found in a shaft in the south wall, and about 30,000 in one of the galleries, the weight of these latter being estimated at about ninety tons.[5]

Towards the end of the Old Kingdom the number of stone vessels decreased considerably, most of the harder stones going entirely out of use for this purpose, thus in the Fourth Dynasty tomb of Queen Hetepheres there were only thirty-eight stone vessels, all of which were of alabaster.[6] This, however, was a reburial and not the original tomb, which had been robbed, but whether any stone vessels had been taken by the robbers, which seems unlikely, or left behind in the original tomb, when the transfer to the new tomb was made, it is, of course, impossible to determine.

From the Middle Kingdom a few vases of alabaster, two very small ones of lapis lazuli, another of carnelian and a few of obsidian have been found, and a fresh, though not very hard, stone came into use, chiefly for small toilet vases, this being what until recently was called 'blue marble', but which is now known to be anhydrite, almost certainly an Egyptian stone, though where it is found is not known.[7] Petrie says [1] 'But in the XIIth. Dynasty the softer serpentine and alabaster supplanted the fine diorites and porphyries and in the XVIIth. Dynasty the art of working hard stone was forgotten for anything but statuary.'

In the Eighteenth Dynasty tomb of Tutankhamūn there were altogether seventy-

---

[1] W. M. F. Petrie, *Diospolis Parva*, p. 18.

[2] W. M. F. Petrie, *Royal Tombs*, I, p. 18.

[3] W. B. Emery, *Hor-Aha*.

[4] W. B. Emery, *Hemaka*, pp. 55–56.

[5] C. M. Firth, J. E. Quibell and J.-P. Lauer, *Step Pyramid*, I, p. 130.

[6] Now in the Cairo Museum. The proportionate increase in the use of alabaster is tabulated by Reisner (*Mycerinus*, pp. 139–40, 180).

[7] See p. 413.

nine stone vessels, all but three being alabaster, these three exceptions being serpentine, a fairly soft and easily worked stone.

The method of making stone vessels has been described at length by several authorities including von Bissing,[1] Bonnet,[2] Petrie, Quibell[3] and Reisner,[4] some of whose conclusions may now be reviewed.

Bonnet[2] has examined the technique of several different types of stone vessel in great detail, with particular reference to the marks of work left on the vessels themselves. These marks fall into three groups, corresponding to the three principal stages in the manufacture: (a) traces of the tool used to rough out the vessel from the block; (b) traces of the smoothing of the exterior of the vessel, showing that this was normally done vertically and from the top downwards; (c) traces of the boring tool on the interior, the differing shapes of the holes bored suggesting the use of correspondingly different borer heads.

Quibell[3] states that 'The outside of the vase was finished before the hollowing out of the block was commenced. On the shoulder of two vases we have noticed two horizontal grooves, opposite to one another, which as Mr. Lacau observed, were probably intended to give a good hold to the tool by which the block was rotated. An amethyst vase spoilt in the making . . . was finished externally, but the inside, only begun, showed a rough surface obtained by careful picking with a point grain by grain. . . . It seems that for dressing the outer surface the vase itself was rotated, for hollowing the inside the vase was fixed, embedded in pitch[5] or clay.'[6] With reference to the use of tubular drills Quibell says[7] 'nothing is more certain than that such drills were in current use' and 'Cylindrical drills were used and used in vase-making; we have found cores of diorite and granite, also the ends of drill holes in alabaster and dolomite (?). But by what device the first cylindrical hole in a narrow necked vase was enlarged into the shoulder is still far from clear.'

Reisner[8] states that 'The large jars appear to have been bored by successively larger stones for which room was first made by hand at the top of the previous hole', but Bonnet,[9] while mentioning Reisner's theory, is rather of the opinion that the first hole was enlarged by holding the borer at an oblique angle, and Petrie[10] also speaks of 'enlarging the inside by drills of stone . . . skew across the hole. . . .' It is, however, doubtful whether the heavy crank borer could have been successfully operated in any but a vertical position, and Reisner's reconstruction, though not entirely convincing, must be regarded as the most plausible.[11]

Reisner has also detected certain differences in the techniques used for predynastic

---

[1] F. W. von Bissing, *Steingefässe*, pp. i–vi.
[2] H. Bonnet, *Ein frühgeschichtliches Gräberfeld bei Abusir*, pp. 7–34 (in particular pp. 10–13).
[3] J. E. Quibell, *Ann. Serv.*, xxxv (1935), pp. 76–80.
[4] G. A. Reisner, *Naga-ed-Dêr*, I, p. 105; *Mycerinus*, pp. 130, 138, 179–80.
[5] Certainly not pitch.
[6] Cf. J. E. Quibell and F. W. Green, *Hierakonpolis*, II, p. 49.
[7] J. E. Quibell, *Ann. Serv.*, xxxv (1935), pp. 77–78.
[8] G. A. Reisner, *Naga-ed-Dêr*, I, p. 105.
[9] H. Bonnet, *Ein frühgeschichtliches Gräberfeld bei Abusir*, pp. 16–17.
[10] W. M. F. Petrie, *Social Life in Ancient Egypt*, pp. 153–4.
[11] Cf. also E. Vernier, *Bijouterie et Joaillerie*, pp. 137–9.

vessels and those of the Old Kingdom. Of the former he says that 'The boring marks are coarser and less regular than in the later stone vessels and appear to have been produced by a different method of boring, perhaps not by using the crank-borer represented in the reliefs of the Old Kingdom. The hole bored by the predynastic borer is of two forms: (1) straight sided with fine striation marks due to a continuous boring from top to bottom with one stone; and (2) concave sided with broad concave grooves finely striated due to boring with stones of different sizes or rubbing with a stone held in the hand. The interior has seldom been dressed smooth except in bowls. The exterior surface has usually been beautifully dressed by rubbing, not turning.[1] He ascribes the invention of the weighted stone borer turned with a crank to the early dynastic period,[2] and says of the vessels of the Old Kingdom that 'The methods of boring stone vessels with a boring stone fixed in a forked shaft weighted at the top and turned by a crank continued to be used for all sorts of vessels. The cylindrical hole was enlarged by rubbing with a stone held in the hand. The outside seems to have been finished by rubbing, but some of the unfinished hard stone vessels showed bruising marks as if they had been roughly formed before boring by hammering. No evidence was found of turning, such as concentric scratches on the outside of the vessel. In addition to the stone borer, a cylindrical tube borer was also used, especially for limestone and alabaster. . . . The tube may have been weighted with stones and worked by a crank handle or turned back and forth between the palms of the hands. The grooves on the cores and on the unsmoothed sides appear to be spiral, as if the turning were continuous in one direction. The outside surface was finished by rubbing, as in the case of the stone-bored vessels.'[3]

Petrie says[4] of the predynastic stone vases 'All these stone vases were shaped by hand without any lathe or turning instrument, the lines of scraping and polishing running diagonally; the insides were ground out by blocks of sandstone, or emery.'[5]

Petrie also says[6] of the stone vessels from the Fourth Dynasty 'Not only was a rotating tool employed, but the further idea of rotating the work and fixing the tool was also familiar to the earliest Egyptians. The fragments of bowls turned in diorite, which are here, will show this. One piece of the bottom of a bowl shows the characteristic mark of turning . . . Other specimens of turning in black granite, basalt and alabaster, all of the pyramid period, are also here. The finest examples of turning in hard stone are in the British Museum.' Also[6] 'A very favourite plan for narrow-necked vessels was to turn them in two or three parts, and join them together, sometimes finishing off the inside on a fresh centering on the lathe. For this finishing and also for the hollowing out vessels in one piece a hook tool must have been used.'

Petrie further says[7] 'The interior of stone vases was cleared by a tube-drill of the size of the mouth, and then enlarging the inside by drills of stone, fed with emery,[5] skew across the hole . . . The outside was worked diagonally by blocks of emery.[5]

---

[1] G. A. Reisner, *Mycerinus*, p. 130.

[2] G. A. Reisner, *Mycerinus*, p. 138.

[3] G. A. Reisner, *Mycerinus*, pp. 179–80.

[4] W. M. F. Petrie, *Diospolis Parva*, p. 19.

[5] Not emery, see pp. 72–74.

[6] W. M. F. Petrie, *Journ. Royal Anthrop. Inst.*, XIII (1884), pp. 88–106.

[7] W. M. F. Petrie, *Social Life in Ancient Egypt*, pp. 153–4.

There was no lathe cutting, even in Roman times; . . . All kinds of short cuts were made in decadent times, as forming stone vases in two halves joined round the greatest diameter (in IInd. dynasty); drilling a vase right through and plugging the bottom; making a lip in a separate piece; and using a paste of blackened mud, with chips of white limestone in it to imitate porphyry.' Again,[1] 'Tube drills were also in constant use for beginning the hollowing out of the great diorite bowls . . .' and 'The tube drills were also used in hollowing more upright vessels.' [2]

Scenes illustrating the manufacture of stone vases occur in a number of tombs, where both the smoothing of the exterior of the vessel and the process of boring with different drills are shown.[3] The use of the weighted crank drill is frequently depicted, for example on a limestone relief from a tomb of Fifth Dynasty date from Saqqara, which is now in the Cairo Museum;[4] in a Fifth Dynasty tomb at Saqqara;[5] in the Sixth Dynasty tomb of Mereruka at Saqqara;[6] in a Sixth Dynasty tomb at Deir el Gebrawi;[7] in a Twelfth Dynasty tomb at Meir;[8] in three Eighteenth Dynasty tombs [9] and in a Twenty-sixth Dynasty tomb in the Theban necropolis.[10] Also a similar drill is shown in use in a wooden model of Middle Kingdom date (or earlier) from Saqqara, which is now in the Cairo Museum.[11] This weighted drill has been described by Borchardt [12] and Bonnet,[13] and both stone weights [14] and stone heads from such borers have been found, the latter of chert, diorite, flint, limestone, quartzite and sandstone.[15] Certain lunate flints of unknown use are perhaps also to be regarded as drill heads.[16]

In the thickness of the walls (not penetrating) of several alabaster vessels from the First Dynasty tomb of 'Hemaka' at Saqqara there are holes made by a tubular drill. Also a shallow oval dish of dolomite has shallow tubular-drill holes that do not penetrate the vessel, but are similarly placed one near each end. In this connexion, though it is not a vessel, a hollow wand of alabaster of Fourth Dynasty date from Giza may

---

[1] W. M. F. Petrie, *Journ. Royal Anthrop. Inst.*, XIII (1884), pp. 88–106.

[2] Cf. G. A. Reisner, *Naga-ed-Dêr*, I, p. 134.

[3] P. Montet, *Scènes de la vie privée*, pp. 295–8; H. Balcz, *Mitt. Kairo*, III (1932), pp. 84–86.

[4] No. J. 39866. J. E. Quibell, in G. Maspero, *Musée égyptien*, III, pp. 25–27, Pl. XXII.

[5] G. Steindorff, *Ti*, p. 134, Pl. CXXXIV.

[6] J. de Morgan, *Recherches sur les origines de l'Égypte*, I, p. 165; P. Duell, *Mereruka*, I, Pls. XXX, XXXI.

[7] N. de G. Davies, *Deir el Gebrâwi*, I, Pl. XIII.

[8] A. M. Blackman, *Meir*, I, Pl. V.

[9] N. de G. Davies, *Rekh-mi-rē*, Pl. LIV; *Two Sculptors*, Pl. XI; *Puyemrê*, Pls. XXIII, XXVII.

[10] N. de G. Davies, *Deir el Gebrâwi*, I, Pls. XIII, XXIV.

[11] No. J. 45319. J. E. Quibell and A. G. K. Hayter, *Excavations at Saqqara, Teti Pyramid, North Side*, p. 40, Pl. XXIV.

[12] L. Borchardt, *Ne-user-rē*, p. 143. Cf. also *Z.Ä.S.*, XXXV (1897), p. 107.

[13] H. Bonnet, *Ein frühgeschichtliches Gräberfeld bei Abusir*, p. 12.

[14] A. Rowe, 'Excavations at Medum', *The Mus. Journ.*, Philadelphia, XXII (1931), p. 41, Pl. 15.

[15] J.-P. Lauer, *Pyramide à degrés*, I, pp. 234–5; II, Pl. XCVI; III, pp. 74–75, Pl. XIX; J. E. Quibell and F. W. Green, *Hierakonpolis*, II, pp. 17, 49, Pls. XXXII (3), LXII, LXVIII; W. M. F. Petrie, *Abydos*, I, pp. 25–26, Pl. LIII; *Meydum and Memphis*, III, p. 44, Pl. XXXIX; W. M. F. Petrie and J. E. Quibell, *Naqada and Ballas*, Pl. LXXV; A. Scharff, *Die Altertümer der Vor- und Frühzeit Ägyptens*, I, pp. 65–66.

[16] J.-P. Lauer, *Pyramide à degrés*, I, p. 234; J.-P. Lauer and F. Debono, *Ann. Serv.*, L (1950), pp. 1–18.

be mentioned.[1] It is broken in several pieces so that the interior may be seen. One end is closed and one end is open and in the inside of the closed end is part of the narrow core, proving that the drilling was done by means of a tubular drill.

Certain statements in the literature of archaeology having reference to the origin of the stone-vase industry in Egypt may now be quoted, which are as follows:

'But as early as S.D. 38 a fresh influence came in . . . Its origin has been provisionally assigned to the Red Sea district as it introduced hard stone vases . . .'[2]

'The home of this second civilization must have been mountainous by the supply of stone instead of clay for vases . . .'[3]

'Petrie has rightly insisted that the home of the stone vase industry can ultimately only be sought in the mountains between Egypt and the Red Sea where all the stones used for the purpose do actually occur . . .'[4]

'The only definite indication as to their home is the fact that their most characteristic contributions to the prehistoric civilization are the stone vases and their pottery imitations: and the region which is most likely to have bred people knowing how to work stone and which is near enough to Egypt to allow permanent intercourse with the Nile Valley. . . is the Arabian desert along the western shore of the Red Sea.'[5]

Peake and Fleure say 'and stone bowls and vases seem first to have been made in the Arabian desert, which lies between the Nile and the Red Sea . . .';[6] 'stone pots, which were introduced into the valley about this time . . .'[6] 'The inhabitants of the Arabian desert may have learned of themselves how to make stone bowls . . .'[6] 'At the same time appeared higher up the Nile, possibly from the Arabian desert on the east, a fresh people who were skilled in the art of making stone bowls';[6] 'the stone bowl people who had perhaps come from the Arabian desert. . . .'[7] 'The use of stone bowls, first introduced from the Arabian desert at the beginning of the predynastic period . . .'[7]

Often no reasons are given for the statements made, but when reasons are advanced they are, first, that the stones used for the predynastic stone vessels occur in the eastern desert, and, second, that 'Even now the inhabitants . . . still use stone for the objects that are made of pottery in the Nile Valley, as for instance, vessels and pipes.'[8] At first thought these facts, which are not disputed, might appear to provide a reasonable foundation for the statements, but on reflection this will be found to be an illusion, as will now be shown.

It is possible to determine from the archaeological reports only the approximate and not the exact number of predynastic stone vessels made from each of the different kinds of stone used. These approximate figures were put together and published by me some time ago,[9] since when I have recalculated them in a different manner and find

---

[1] Now in the Cairo Museum, No. J. 60545.
[2] W. M. F. Petrie, Ancient Egypt, 1917, p. 33.
[3] W. M. F. Petrie, Prehistoric Egypt, p. 48.
[4] A. Scharff, J.E.A., XIV (1928), p. 273.
[5] H. Frankfort, Studies in Early Pottery of the Near East, I, p. 100.
[6] H. Peake and H. J. Fleure, Peasants and Potters, pp. 71, 76, 80, 142.
[7] H. Peake and H. J. Fleure, Priests and Kings, pp. 63, 88.
[8] H. Frankfort, Studies in Early Pottery of the Near East, I, pp. 100, 101.
[9] A. Lucas, J.E.A., XVI (1930), pp. 200–12.

that the fresh results differ from the previous ones only by $2\frac{1}{2}$ per cent. Although it is in no way claimed that the results are anything more than a rough approximation, they are sufficiently accurate to establish the arguments based on them.[1] The figures are as follows:

Nature of Stone	No. of Vessels	Fayum, Nile Valley, Aswan	E. Desert
		%	%
Alabaster [2]	48	16.0	—
Basalt...	65	21.5	—
Breccia	25	8.0	—
Diorite [3]	2	1.0	—
Granite	7	2.0	—
Gypsum	1	0.5	—
Limestone	108	36.0	—
Marble	17	—	5.5
Porphyritic rock ...	6	—	2.0
Schist [4]	4	—	1.5
Serpentine	12	—	4.0
Steatite	7	—	2.0
	302	85.0	15.0

If these results are accepted as approximately correct, which I believe them to be, then a comparatively small proportion only (about 15 per cent) of the stones used for making the predynastic vessels were obtained from the far eastern desert, and by far the larger proportion (about 85 per cent) came from the Fayum, Aswan and the Nile Valley, which involves the further proposition that the home of the stone-vessel industry was not in the eastern desert, but in the Nile Valley (in which Aswan may reasonably be included). The Nile Valley, in the sense in which it is used here, comprises the low hills and plateaux bordering the valley, and the side valleys that enter the river valley to within a distance that could readily be worked by the valley people from their homes (which during the predynastic period must have been further from the river and nearer the cliffs than they are today on account of the marshes then bordering the river), in the same manner as rock salt, gypsum for plaster, limestone for building, and nitrous earth for the crops are now worked. Even the stones that occur at a considerable distance from the Nile were also available near the Coptos-Quseir road, along which there was constant traffic at an early period, as is proved, for instance, by the Red Sea shells which are such a marked feature of the earliest graves. The Nile Valley, therefore, and not the eastern desert, was the home of the early stone-vase industry.

The facts that the Beja tribe of Arabs in the eastern desert use stone at the present day for making cooking vessels and tobacco pipes,[5] and that the Sinai Arabs also

---

[1] Vessels published since the date of my article (1930) have not been included.

[2] Calcite.

[3] Not the 'Chephren-statue' variety, but a speckled variety, probably from Aswan.

[4] Includes greywacke, mudstone and volcanic ash.

[5] P. S. Girard, *Description de l'Égypte, état moderne*, II, 1812, pp. 590–1; G. W. Murray, *Sons of Ishmael*, p. 84.

make stone pipes,[1] have no bearing whatever on the problem, since the stone employed by these people is steatite, which is so soft that it may be cut readily with a knife, and since the vessels made are very crude. There is no evidence at all for postulating a desert stone-vessel-making people, and also no need, since there is no proof of any break in the continuity of the stone-vessel industry, but only evolution and progress, the beginning being with basalt (one of the hardest stones used) during the neolithic period, and, as time passed, more kinds of stone were employed and more vessels made, until the culmination in numbers, material and workmanship was reached in the early dynastic period.

---

[1] G. W. Murray, *Sons of Ishmael*, p. 84.

Chapter XVIII
WOOD[1]

Egypt is, and during the historical period always has been, poorly provided naturally with large trees and it has been necessary from very early times to import a portion of the wood required (though probably not so much as is sometimes thought), a practice that continues to the present day, and on the Palermo Stone it is stated [2] that as early as the reign of Snofru (Fourth Dynasty) forty ships laden with timber were brought to Egypt.

FOREIGN TIMBER

Among the places from which the foreign timber (excluding ebony) was obtained were Arrapachitis,[3] Assur,[4] God's Land,[5] the Hittite country,[6] Lebanon,[7] Naharin,[8] Punt,[9] Retenu [10] and Djahi,[11] all except Punt (the wood from which consisted of ebony and certain sweet and fragrant woods, the latter manifestly not being for use as timber but probably for making incense and perfumes) being situated in western Asia.

Although a large number of different kinds of imported wood are mentioned by name in Egyptian texts, only comparatively few of these names have been translated.[12] Even then, the translations are often only tentative and based on insufficient evidence, and the identity of much of the imported timber still remains in doubt.

The only certain method of identifying wood is by an expert examination of its structure with a microscope, and the following list gives all such identifications of foreign woods (except ebony) found in Egypt that can be traced:[13]

Wood	Date	Object
Ash	XVIIIth Dyn.	Compound bow[1]
	XVIIIth Dyn.	Axle, felloes and frame of floor of chariot [2]
Beech	3rd–4th cent. A.D.	Mummy label [3]
Box	XVIIIth Dyn.	Chair and razor handle [4]
	XVIIIth Dyn.	Inlay [5]
	3rd–4th cent. A.D.	Mummy labels [3]

---

[1] Cf. in general, W. Boerhave Beekman, *Hout in Alle Tijden*, pp. 399–578.
[2] A.R., I, 146.
[3] A.R., II, 509, 512.   [4] A.R., II, 449.   [5] A.R., II, 321, 888.   [6] A.R., II, 485.
[7] A.R., III, 94; IV, 577.   [8] A.R., II, 434.   [9] A.R., II, 265; III, 527.
[10] A.R., II, 447, 471, 491, 509, 525, 838.
[11] A.R., II, 490.
[12] In Breasted's translations in addition to such indefinite names as aromatic wood, fire wood, fragrant wood and sweet wood, the names of twelve woods, out of a total of twenty-four, are left untranslated.
[13] For references see end of table.

Wood	Date	Object
Cedar	Predynastic	Small pieces [6]
	Xth–XIth Dyn.	Coffins [3]
	XIIth Dyn.	Sarcophagus [7,7a]
	XIIth Dyn.	Boxes [8]
	Middle Kingdom	Coffin [9]
	XVIIIth Dyn.	Shrines (panels) [10]
	XVIIIth Dyn.	Dowels [10]
	XXth–XXVIth Dyn.	Coffin [9]
	XXVIth Dyn.	Coffin [7]
	XXVIth Dyn.	Coffin [11]
	Ptolemaic	Coffin or coffins (two pieces) [12]
	c. 2nd cent. A.D.	Tree trunk (small) [13]
	Late	Small piece [14]
Cypress	Predynastic	Small pieces [6]
	IIIrd Dyn.	Coffin [15]
	Middle Kingdom	Coffin lid [16]
	XVIIIth Dyn.	Small box [5]
	XXVIth Dyn.	Coffin [7]
	Late 4th cent. B.C.	Coffin [17,18]
	Late 5th cent. A.D.	Base of nilometer [19]
Elm	XVIIIth Dyn.	Yoke, handrail and other parts of chariot [2]
	XVIIIth Dyn.	Body and wheel of chariot [15,20]
	XVIIIth Dyn.	Pieces of pole or axle of chariot [15,20]
Fir	Vth Dyn.	Dummy vase and piece [17,21]
	Late 7th cent. B.C.	Coffin [7]
	Roman	Mummy label [12]
Juniper	IIIrd Dyn.	Coffin [15]
	c. IIIrd Dyn.	Lid (small) [12]
	Roman	Mummy label [12]
	Late 5th cent. A.D.	Base of nilometer [19]
Lime	Late 4th cent. B.C.	Coffin [17,18]
	2nd cent. A.D.	Mummy portrait [22]
	3rd–4th cent. A.D.	Mummy label [3]
Liquidambar	XVIIIth Dyn.	Piece (shaped) [23]
Maple	XVIIIth Dyn.	Frame of floor of chariot [2]
Oak	XVIIIth Dyn.	Dowel [24]
Pine	Predynastic	Piece (trimmed) [6]
	IIIrd Dyn.	Coffin [15]
	XVIIIth Dyn.	Model brick mould [25]
	Late 5th cent. A.D.	Base of nilometer [19]
Plum	XVIIIth Dyn.	Spokes of chariot [2]
Yew	VIth–XIIth Dyn.	Coffins (seven pieces) [26]
	VIth–XIIth Dyn.	Coffin peg [26]
	XVIIIth Dyn.	Head of Queen Tiy [27]

---

[1] Identified for me by Dr. L. Chalk. Cf. A. Lucas, *Ann. Serv.*, XLI (1942), p. 144.

[2] U. Fasolo, in G. Botti, *Aegyptus*, XXXI (1951), pp. 192–8.

[3] K. P. Oakley, *Analyst*, LVII (1932), pp. 158–9.

[4] A. Lansing and W. C. Hayes, *M.M.A. Bull., Egyptian Exped. 1935–1936*, pp. 13, 28.

[5] W. C. Hayes, *M.M.A. Bull., Egyptian Exped, 1934–1935*, p. 29.

[6] G. Brunton and G. Caton-Thompson, *Badarian Civilisation*, pp. 62–63.

[7] R. Engelbach, *Ann. Serv.*, XXXI (1931), p. 144.

[7a] The coffin and canopic box belonging to this burial are also cedar.

[8] T. G. B. Osborn, *Mem. and Proc. Manchester Lit. and Phil. Soc.*, LIII (1909), No. 9.

[9] Identified by Dr. L. Chalk (Imperial Forestry Institute, Oxford, *Eighth Annual Report*, 1931–2, p. 11).

[10] Several specimens identified by Dr. L. Chalk (Imperial Forestry Institute, Oxford, *Eighth Annual Report*, 1931–2, p. 11); a number of other specimens identified by me; three specimens identified for me at the Royal Botanic Gardens, Kew.

[11] G. Ebers, *Der geschnitzte Holzsarg des Hatbastru*, p. 5. Identified by Prof. Kunze.

[12] W. Ribstein, *Botanisches Archiv*, IX (1925), pp. 194–209. Ribstein also identified fragments of furniture (IIIrd Dyn.) as a species of cork wood (*Aeschynomene sp.*).

[13] G. W. Murray, *J.E.A.*, XVII (1931), p. 82.

[14] R. Mond and O. H. Myers, *Bucheum*, I, p. 59.

[15] Identified by Dr. L. Chalk (Imperial Forestry Institute, Oxford, *Ninth Annual Report*, 1932–3, p. 12). Cf. A. Lucas, *Ann. Serv.*, XXXVI (1936), pp. 1–4. (coffin only).

[16] Found by Petrie at Lahun and examined by Prof. Irving Bailey, Harvard. Communicated by G. Brunton.

[17] L. Wittmack, *Sitzungsberichte der Gesellschaft Naturforschender Freunde zu Berlin*, IV (1910), pp. 181–92.

[18] C. Watzinger, *Griechische Holzsarkophager*, p. 81.

[19] V. Täckholm and M. Drar, *Flora of Egypt*, I, p. 75.

[20] Cf. A. Lucas, *Ann. Serv.*, XLI (1942), p. 144.

[21] L. Borchardt, *Nefer-ir-ke-rē*, pp. 61, 63.

[22] E. Coche de la Ferté, *Les Portraits Romano-Égyptiens du Louvre*, p. 11.

[23] Identified at the Royal Botanic Gardens, Kew. Cf. A Lucas, *Ann. Serv.*, XLI (1942), p. 144.

[24] H. Carter, *Tut-ankh-Amen*, II, p. 39; III, p. 153.

[25] Z. Iskander, *Ann. Serv.*, XLVII (1937), p. 157. Identified by M. El-Gindi.

[26] G. Beauvisage, *Rec. Trav.*, XVIII (1896), pp. 78–91.

[27] L. Wittmack, *Berichte der Deutschen botanischen Gesellschaft*, XXX (1912), pp. 275–8; L. Borchardt, *Der Porträtkopf der Königin Teje*, p. 10.

The various woods enumerated may now be considered.

Ash (Beekman, p. 432)

The ordinary ash (*Fraxinus excelsior*) is common in Europe, in Asia, including Asia Minor, and in North Africa. One species (*Fraxinus ornus*) grows on the Lebanon mountains in Syria. The wood is hard, tough and elastic. The only specimens of ash from ancient Egypt that are known to me are the wood of a compound bow from the tomb of Tutankhamūn and that used for the axle, the felloes and part of the frame of the floor of the Eighteenth Dynasty Egyptian chariot in the Museum at Florence.[1]

Beech (Beekman, p. 424)

The beech tree (*Fagus sylvatica*) is found both in Europe and in western Asia and the occurrence, therefore, of a small specimen of the wood in Egypt at a late date is not surprising.

Birch (Beekman, pp. 423–4)

This wood is not known with certainty from ancient Egypt, but only the bark,[2] though Mackay suggests that certain staves of Old Kingdom date from Kafr Ammar may be from a species of birch.[3]

Box (Beekman, pp. 438–9)

The box tree (*Buxus sempervirens*) grows in Europe, western Asia and north Africa

---

[1] G. Botti, *Aegyptus*, XXXI (1951), pp. 192–8.   [2] See Bark, pp. 454–5.
[3] W. M. F. Petrie and E. Mackay, *Heliopolis, Kafr Ammar and Shurafa*, p. 10.

and, since the wood was used by both the Greeks [1] and Romans,[2] it is in no way strange that a small piece should have been found in Egypt at a late period. But it has also been found much earlier. A seal and some inlay panels of Middle Kingdom date are said to be boxwood,[3] parts of a carved chair, a carved handle for a bronze razor, and applied strips framing inlays of faience on a jewel box, all of Eighteenth Dynasty date, have been found at Thebes, and several other objects in the Metropolitan Museum [4] and elsewhere [5] are stated to be wholly or partly of boxwood. The oriental box tree (*Buxus longifolia*) grows in Palestine and Syria. The kings of Mitanni and Alasia respectively sent boxwood objects and boxwood to Egypt.[6]

Cedar (Beekman, pp. 424–8) [7]

There is only one family of true cedars, which comprises three members, namely, the cedar of Lebanon (*Cedrus Libani*), the Atlas cedar (*Cedrus atlantica*) and the Indian cedar (*Cedrus deodara*). Although it is not impossible that the wood of the Atlas cedar (which grows on the Atlas mountains in Morocco) might have found its way occasionally into Egypt, there is no evidence and little probability of this, the ancient imports of timber into Egypt (excepting ebony) being chiefly from Syria. Although the woods of the Lebanon and Atlas cedars cannot be distinguished from one another microscopically, it may be accepted that any cedar wood found in Egypt is *Cedrus Libani* and, since its use goes back to the predynastic period, it was evidently being imported into Egypt at that early date. It is found also plentifully on the Taurus mountains in Asia Minor.[8]

At the present day a large number of different trees that are not cedar are called cedars,[9] among them being one (an American juniper, *Juniperus virginiana*) that yields the fragrant red wood employed for making pencils, cigar boxes and other objects. The modern 'oil of cedar', too, is generally a product of this same tree. This confusion of nomenclature, however, is not new, as the classical writers, both Greek and Latin, applied the term 'cedar' to many trees that were not cedars, but often junipers.[10] It seems, therefore, not only possible, but probable, that the word 'cedar' has always been used in a loose manner and that, even when there is no longer any difference of opinion about the ancient Egyptian name for the true cedar, there will still remain a doubt whether a particular wood so designated was indeed cedar. Many of the objects loosely described as 'cedar' in museum catalogues and excavation reports are almost certainly not, though it is quite clear from the identifications listed above that the wood of the true cedar was in fact, employed in Egypt for making sarcophagi, coffins and other appurtenances of burial, such as shrines, from at least as early as the Tenth or Eleventh Dynasty to as late as the Ptolemaic period.

---

[1] Theophrastus, *Enquiry into Plants*, v: 3,7; 7, 7–8.
[2] Pliny, xvi: 28.
[3] W. C. Hayes, *Scepter*, i, pp. 223, 247.
[4] W. C. Hayes, *Scepter*, ii, pp. 146, 189, 196, 201, 202, 227.
[5] B. Bothmer, *Boston Bull.*, xlix (1951), pp. 9–11.
[6] S. A. B. Mercer, *Tell-el-Amarna Tablets*, i, pp. 145, 147, 205.
[7] See also V. Täckholm and M. Drar, *Flora of Egypt*, i, pp. 46–50, 66–68.
[8] H. B. Tristram, *Natural History of the Bible*, 1911, p. 344.
[9] H. Stone, *Timbers of Commerce*, p. 297.
[10] A. Lucas, *J.E.A.*, xvii (1931), p. 14.

The Eighteenth Dynasty shrines of which specimens of the wood have been examined are those that enclosed the stone sarcophagus (containing the nest of three coffins with the mummy) of Tutankhamūn.[1] These shrines are large, oblong, roofed wooden structures with a double door at one end and are covered, both inside and outside, with a thin coating of plaster (made of whiting and glue), which is decorated with funerary scenes and inscriptions and then thickly gilt, exceptions being the roofs of the two larger shrines, which are mostly coated with black varnish, and the outside of the largest shrine, which in addition to gold, is ornamented with blue faience. In the tomb, the shrines were placed one outside the other, the outermost, which practically filled the burial chamber, being about $16\frac{1}{2}$ feet (5 metres) long, 11 feet (3.3 metres) wide and 9 feet (2.8 metres) high. Each shrine consists of a number of sections, which had been assembled in the tomb, and which had to be taken apart to remove them from the tomb, the larger sections or panels being made of separate planks fastened together with wooden pegs, the sections being joined by means of mortise and tenon joints or flat dowels.[2] The wood is about $2\frac{1}{4}$ inches (57 mm.) thick. It was not possible to see any part of the bare wood until the shrines had been taken to pieces and then only some of the edges and parts of the tenons and dowels and, before any critical examination could be made, it became necessary to treat both surfaces of all the sections with melted paraffin wax in order to consolidate and preserve the gilt plaster, in doing which the wood of the edges of the sections and of the exposed parts of the tenons and dowls also became covered with wax, thus concealing its appearance. However, when the surplus wax was being removed (which was done by me at the Cairo Museum by means of electrical heaters) a certain amount of examination was found possible and was made. This consisted of (a) a careful examination of all the exposed parts with the naked eye and with a lens [3] and the comparison of the wood with small specimens previously taken from the shrines, sections of which had been examined microscopically by Dr. L. Chalk of the Imperial Forestry Institute, Oxford, and identified as cedar and sidder respectively, and (b) a microscopical examination of additional sections (prepared for me in Germany), using Chalk's photomicrographs as standards, the sections having been taken from broken edges of the planks and from a large number of the dowels (many of these having been sawn off, either in the tomb to enable the sections to be taken apart, or to facilitate packing, or in the Museum to allow the sections to be fitted together when the shrines were being re-erected.) [4]

---

[1] H. Carter, *Tut-ankh-Amen*, I, pp. 180–3, Pl. XLV; II, pp. 31–33, 39–47, Pls. XII, XIII, XIV, XV, LIV, LVI, LVII, LVIII, LIX.

[2] In most cases the dowels were wood, but in some instances they were of copper (analysed by me and found to be free from tin and therefore not bronze). In many cases, too, the dowels, although of wood, were not of the same kind of wood as the planks. Altogether 177 dowels were examined by me, of which 107 (60 per cent) were probably cedar and 70 (40 per cent) were probably sidder (*nabk*). In the largest (outermost) shrine, out of 93 tongues examined, 47 were probably cedar and 46 probably sidder (*nabk*).

[3] After scraping off the wax.

[4] In the case of the largest shrine, there were so many dowels broken and missing that these had to be replaced before the shrine could be erected, which was done with new dowels of beech wood.

The main wood of the shrines, so far as it has been examined, is cedar, but as much of it cannot be seen and never has been seen since the shrines were made more than 3,200 years ago, the nature of the part concealed naturally cannot be proved, though, judging both by analogy and probability, this, too, is cedar.

The wooden dowels, so far as they have been examined, are essentially of two very distinct kinds, which differ considerably in appearance and thickness, one being light-brown with characteristic darker reddish-brown markings, which varies in thickness from about 0.67 inch (17 mm.) to about 0.79 inch (20 mm.), and the other being of a uniform and different shade of brown without conspicuous markings and much thinner, being only from about 0.24 inch (6 mm.) to about 0.43 inch (11 mm.). The former is cedar and the latter is sidder (*nabk*). One dowel, however, was oak and one acacia, and the matter will be discussed further in connexion with these woods.

Cypress (Beekman, p. 428)

Although a few specimens of the cypress tree (*Cupressus sempervirens*) are grown in gardens in the Delta at the present day, the cypress is not an Egyptian tree and probably was not introduced into the country until modern times; it grows, however, plentifully in both southern Europe and western Asia. Since the wood of predynastic date identified as probably cypress was found at the same place as some cedar, which is a typically Syrian tree, that particular piece of cypress had probably been imported from Syria, and therefore, possibly also the later specimens. The Third Dynasty specimen was from a six-ply wooden coffin found in the step pyramid at Saqqara.[1] The Eighteenth Dynasty specimen was a small jewel box having a lid of tamarisk and inlays of boxwood and faience. Several objects in the Metropolitan Museum are stated to be wholly or partly of cypress.[2]

Ebony (Beekman, pp. 429–31, 434–8) [3]

Whatever difficulties there may be in the recognition of most of the kinds of wood imported into Egypt, there is none with respect to ebony, the ancient Egyptian name (*hbny*) being well known and the wood, on account of its characteristic colour and appearance, being recognized readily without microscopical examination. The ancient Egyptian (Sudan) ebony is not always black, but may be partly or wholly dark brown.

In ancient Egyptian texts ebony is stated to have been obtained from Genebteyew,[4] Kush,[5] Negro Lands,[6] Nubia,[7] Punt [8] and the South Countries,[9] all of which are situated to the south of Egypt. This does not necessarily mean that ebony grew in all these places, but merely that it reached Egypt from the south. Even at the beginning of last century, small logs of ebony, about a foot in length, were articles of trade at Shendi,[10] which is situated a little north of Khartum. In the Punt scenes in the mortuary

---

[1] J.-P. Lauer, *Ann. Serv.*, XXXIII (1933), pp. 163–5, Fig. 5, Pl. II; A. Lucas, *Ann. Serv.*, XXXVI (1936), pp. 1–4.

[2] W. C. Hayes, *Scepter*, I, pp. 162, 210; II, pp. 196, 202, 227.

[3] See also V. Loret, *Rec. Trav.*, VI (1885), pp. 125–30.

[4] *A.R.*, II, 474.   [5] *A.R.*, II, 494, 502, 514.   [6] *A.R.*, I, 336.

[7] *A.R.*, II, 375.   [8] *A.R.*, II, 265, 272, 486.   [9] *A.R.*, II, 652.

[10] J. L. Burckhardt, *Travels in Nubia*, 1819, p. 313.

temple of Hatshepsut at Deir el Bahari, Egyptians are shown cutting branches from ebony trees.[1]

Herodotus states [2] that ebony was an article of tribute from Ethiopia; Diodorus [3] and Strabo [4] both say that ebony trees grew in Ethiopia; but Pliny, commenting upon the statement of Herodotus, throws doubt upon its accuracy [5] and in a later book states [6] that the ebony tree did not grow in Egypt, in which term apparently he included Ethiopia. Dioscorides says [7] that Ethiopian ebony is the best.

What is ordinarily called ebony is the black heart wood of a number of different kinds of tropical trees, up to about forty years ago the true ebony of commerce being the wood of *Diospyros ebenum*, which grows in southern India and Ceylon, but at the present time it is largely *Diospyros Dendo* from West Africa. As, however, the word ebony is derived from the ancient Egyptian *hbny*, the original ebony was that known in ancient Egypt, which has been identified as the wood of *Dalbergia melanoxylon*,[8] a tree that grows in tropical Africa. A specimen of ebony of Fifth Dynasty date examined by Wittmack is stated to be *Diospyros ebenum*,[9] but as it seems most improbable that ebony should have been obtained from India or Ceylon at such an early period, and as it is difficult to be sure of the species from an examination of the dead wood, this identification needs confirmation before it can be accepted.

Mention is made in the texts [10] of the employment of ebony in Egypt for making chests, coffins, a harp and shrines; a shrine, statues, staves and whips of ebony, though whether made in the country or not is not stated; and ebony chairs and ebony statues as spoils of war. Most of these kinds of ebony objects, except coffins and harps, have been found in graves, the statues, however, being very small. In the tomb of Tutankhamūn the ebony objects included a bed, bolts for shrine doors, a chair and the legs of a second one, the framework of boxes, a stand for a gaming board, a stool and veneer and inlay.[11]

Amenhotpe III sent four ebony beds, an ebony head-rest, ten ebony footstools and six ebony chairs to the king of Babylonia and thirteen ebony chairs and one hundred pieces of ebony to the king of Arzawa.[12]

One great use of ebony in Egypt was as veneer and inlay (generally in conjunction with ivory) for the ornamentation of furniture, boxes and other objects.[13]

Small ebony objects (tablets and part of a cylinder seal) are known from the First Dynasty,[14] and the wood is mentioned in inscriptions as early as the Third Dynasty.[15] Ebony arrow-heads of Eleventh Dynasty date have been found,[16] and the Lahun treasure (Twelfth Dynasty) included caskets of ebony.[17] Among ebony objects of the

---

[1] E. Naville, *Temple of Deir el Bahari*, III, p. 15.

[2] III: 97.   [3] I: 3.   [4] XVII: 2, 2.   [5] XII: 8.   [6] XXIV: 52.   [7] I: 129.

[8] G. Beauvisage, *Rec. Trav.*, XIX (1897), pp. 77–83.

[9] L. Borchardt, *Nefer-ir-ke-rē*, p. 68.

[10] *A.R.*, V (Index), p. 121; V. Loret, *Rec. Trav.*, VI (1885), pp. 125–30.

[11] H. Carter, *Tut-ankh-Amen*, I, pp. 113, 114, 115, 119, 203; II, pp. 31, 33; III, pp. 130, 232.

[12] S. A. B. Mercer, *Tell-el-Amarna Tablets*, I, pp. 17, 185.   [13] See p. 454.

[14] W. M. F. Petrie, *Royal Tombs*, I, pp. 11, 22, 40; II, p. 22.

[15] M. A. Murray, *Saqqara Mastabas*, I, p. 35.

[16] H. E. Winlock, *Slain Soldiers*, pp. 11–13.

[17] A. C. Mace, *Ancient Egypt*, 1921, pp. 4–6; H. E. Winlock, *Treasure of El Lāhūn*, pp. 12 f.

Eighteenth Dynasty may be mentioned shawabti figures of Amenhotpe III, various small statuettes,[1] and a panel and door from part of a shrine.[2] The well-known head of Queen Tiy in Berlin is not ebony as so frequently stated, but yew, though the inlaid eye-lashes are ebony.[3] Cramps of ebony 30–40 cms. in length, identified as *Dalbergia melanoxylon*, were used to fasten blocks in the mortuary temple of Ramses III at Medinet Habu (Twentieth Dynasty).[4] A specimen of ebony also identified as *Dalbergia melanoxylon* was found at Karanis in the Fayum, dating from the period third to fifth century A.D.[5]

Elm (Beekman, p. 432)

The specimens of elm referred to were two pieces from one of the chariots of Tutankhamūn (one from a wheel and one from the body) and also two other pieces (found on the floor) from another chariot from the same tomb, which were either from the axle or from the pole, and probably from the pole. The species of elm could not be identified. Elm is also known from another Egyptian chariot of the same dynasty now at Florence, where it is used for the yoke and its appendages, the curved handrail of the body, the spindles of the wheels and other parts.[6] Neither the pole nor the axle of this chariot is elm, as has been stated, the one being willow, the other ash.[6]

Elm is still employed by the modern wheelwright. The common elm (*Ulmus campestris*) is widely distributed in Europe and Asia, including western Asia, Asia Minor and northern Palestine, from one of which places it doubtless reached Egypt, since there is no doubt that, although chariots in Egypt were originally importations from Asia, they were being made in the country during the Eighteenth Dynasty, this industry being pictured on the walls of several tombs of that period,[7] and, during the reign of Solomon, chariots were imported into Palestine from Egypt.[8]

Fir (Beekman, p. 429)

Two of the specimens of fir examined are stated to be probably the Cilician fir (*Abies cilicica*), which grows in Asia Minor and Syria.[9] The species of the third specimen could not be determined. A papyrus dated 256 B.C. refers to the planting of 300 fir trees in Egypt.[10]

Hornbeam (Beekman, p. 432)

This tree (*Carpinus Betulus*) is a native of Europe and western Asia; the wood is whitish, very hard, close-grained and heavy. That it was ever used in Egypt must be regarded as extremely unlikely. The yoke of the Eighteenth Dynasty chariot in the

---

[1] L. Borchardt, *Porträtkopf der Königin Teje*, p. 14.
[2] E. Naville, *Temple of Deir el Bahari*, II, pp. 1–4, Pls. xxv–xxix; G. Roeder, *Naos*, pp. 1–11, Pls. I–III.
[3] L. Borchardt, *Porträtkopf der Königin Teje*, p. 10.
[4] U. Hölscher, *Excavation of Medinet Habu*, IV, p. 31.
[5] Kindly communicated by Mr. S. Yeivin.
[6] G. Botti, *Aegyptus*, XXXI (1951), pp. 192–8.
[7] J. G. Wilkinson, *The Ancient Egyptians*, 1878, I, pp. 227, 232, Figs. 60, 64, 65.
[8] 1 *Kings*, 10: 29; 2 *Chron.*, I: 17.
[9] See p. 319.
[10] C. C. Edgar, *Zenon Papyri*, II, No. 59157.

Museo Archeologico, Florence, is not hornbeam as formerly stated, but elm,[1] and no other reported instance of the use of hornbeam is known to me.

Juniper (Beekman, pp. 433–4) [2]

The juniper, of which there are a number of different species, is a tree with a fragrant red wood, which is, and apparently always has been, confused with the cedar and was so confused by the Greeks [3] and Romans.[3] The particular species of juniper represented by the specimens could not be determined with certainty, though in the case of that from the Third Dynasty, which was from the plywood coffin found at Saqqara,[4] it is suggested that it may be *Juniperus phoenicea*.[5] Twigs of *J. phoenicea* found in the Graeco-Roman cemetery at Hawara are in the Museum of the Royal Botanic Gardens, Kew.[6]

The juniper is very plentiful on the Syrian mountains, but it is found also in Asia Minor. From inquiries made there would seem to be in Syria at the present time only one kind of juniper (*J. excelsa*) that grows to the dimensions of a tree, which it is stated may reach a height of between 60 and 70 feet (about 20 metres), the other kinds of juniper being only bushes.[7]

Lime (Beekman, p. 434)

The lime tree is a native of middle and southern Europe, from where the wood might easily have reached Egypt. In view, however, of the identification by Newberry [8] of two flowers of *Tilia europaea* (fragile and short-lived objects that are most unlikely to have been imported) among the vegetable remains from the Graeco-Roman cemetery at Hawara, it seems probable that one or more specimens of the tree may have been cultivated in the Fayum province of Egypt at a late period and, therefore, that the pieces of wood examined (a mummy portrait and a mummy label) may have been of local origin. Wilcken states [9] that lime was used for mummy portraits, but no evidence of identification is given.

Liquidambar

This tree (*Liquidambar orientalis*), which grows in Asia Minor, has long been familiar in connexion with ancient Egypt on account of its producing a balsam (storax),[10] which was used in perfumery and in embalming, but, so far as is known, only one specimen of the wood has been found, namely a piece from the tomb of Tutankhamūn (Eighteenth Dynasty). The specimen, which was identified at the Royal Botanic Gardens, Kew, as *Liquidambar sp.*, probably *orientalis*, was about seven

---

[1] G. Botti, *Aegyptus*, XXXI (1951), pp. 192–8.

[2] See also pp. 310–12.

[3] See A. Lucas, *J.E.A.*, XVII (1931), pp. 13–21.

[4] J.-P. Lauer, *Ann. Serv.*, XXXIII (1933), pp. 163–5, Fig. 5, Pl. II.

[5] A. Lucas, *Ann. Serv.*, XXXVI (1936), pp. 1–4.

[6] No number visible; marked 1888 from W. M. F. Petrie.

[7] See also Royal Botanic Gardens, Kew, *Official Guide No. 4* (1919), p. 47.

[8] P. E. Newberry, in W. M. F. Petrie, *Kahun, Gurob and Hawara*, p. 46; L. Keimer, *Gartenpflanzen*, pp. 61–62.

[9] U. Wilcken, *Archäologischer Anzeiger*, IV (1889), p. 2. Cf. also T. Reil, *Beiträge zur Kenntnis des Gewerbes im hellenistischen Ägypten*, p. 73.

[10] See p. 95.

inches (18 cm.) long with an almost square section (0.3×0.4 inch—8×10 mm.). One end is shaped like the cutting end of a chisel and the other end is square. In the tomb records there is no reference to this, from which it is probable that it was found on the floor, its connexions and purpose being unknown.

Maple

Part of the frame of the floor of the Eighteenth Dynasty chariot in the Museo Archeologico, Florence, has been identified as *Acer sp.* by Fasolo,[1] and is probably from either the common maple (*Acer campestre*) or the great maple (*Acer pseudoplatanus*). The former is native to Europe, the Caucasus and western Asia, while the latter is found principally in central Europe.

Oak (Beekman, p. 431)

L. A. Boodle, formerly of the Jodrell Laboratory, Royal Botanic Gardens, Kew, identified a specimen of wood from one of the dowels of the large gilt shrines that enclosed the sarcophagus of Tutankhamūn as oak, possibly *Quercus Cerris*.[2] This identification has since been confirmed at Kew and, as was only to be expected, is undoubtedly correct. Other specimens of dowels from the shrines were also kindly examined for me at Kew, and with one exception, which was acacia, they were cedar and sidder respectively. Parts of some Middle Kingdom tomb models [3] and the lid of a coffin of New Kingdom date [4] are stated to be oak, but in neither case can the identification be regarded as certain. The pole, axle and spokes of the Eighteenth Dynasty chariot now in Florence, formerly said to be oak, have been identified as willow, ash and plum respectively.[1] Oak bark was found among the remains of the predynastic tannery at Gebelein,[5] and a pair of cork soles, stated to be from *Quercus suber*, were found in the Graeco-Roman cemetery at Hawara.[6] Theophrastus states that the oak grew in the vicinity of Thebes,[7] and Pliny, probably copying him, makes the same statement.[8]

Pine (Beekman, p. 439)

The specimens of pine wood from ancient Egypt that have been found up to the present are three only, a trimmed piece of predynastic date, a piece from the Third Dynasty plywood coffin found in the step pyramid at Saqqara,[9] and a model brick mould of the Eighteenth Dynasty.[10] The species of two of the specimens could not be determined, but that from the Third Dynasty is probably *Pinus halepensis*.[11] As the predynastic specimen was found at the same place as some pieces of cedar, a typically Syrian tree, probably it, too, had been brought from Syria, though the pine also grows in Asia Minor and *Pinus halepensis* (the Aleppo or Jerusalem pine) is the

---

[1] G. Botti, *Aegyptus*, XXXI (1951), pp. 192–8.

[2] H. Carter, *Tut-ankh-Amen*, II, p. 39; III, p. 153.

[3] H. E. Winlock, *Models of Daily Life*, p. 73.

[4] L. Borchardt, *Nefer-ir-ke-rē*, p. 75.

[5] G. A. Bravo, *Lavorazione delle pelli*, p. 87.

[6] P. E. Newberry, in W. M. F. Petrie, *Hawara, Biahmu and Arsinoe*, p. 52.

[7] *Enquiry into Plants*, IV: 2, 8.   [8] XIII: 19.

[9] J.-P. Lauer, *Ann. Serv.*, XXXIII (1933), pp. 163–5, Fig. 5, Pl. II.

[10] Z. Iskander, *Ann. Serv.*, XLVII (1947), p. 157.

[11] A. Lucas, *Ann. Serv.*, XXXVI (1936), pp. 1–4.

commonest pine in the Mediterranean region. Several varieties of pine (*P. Pinea and P. halepensis*) are found in gardens in Egypt, but the pine has never been plentiful.

Plane

It has been suggested that some of the coffins of the Third to Eleventh Dynasties found at Tarkhan were made of plane (*Platanus orientalis*),[1] but this is almost certainly incorrect. Although Theophrastus [2] states that the tree grew in the Nile valley in his day, it is not native to Egypt, and it is extremely unlikely that timbers should have been brought from western Asia at an early date.

Plum

The plum proper (*Prunus domesticus*) is native to Europe and western Asia, but not to Egypt, the 'Egyptian plum' mentioned by Theophrastus [3] being the Myxa (*Cordia Myxa*) and that referred to by Pliny [4] probably another species of *Prunus*. The axles of the Eighteenth Dynasty chariot now in Florence have been identified as *Prunus domesticus*.[5]

Yew (Beekman, p. 439) [6]

The common yew (*Taxus baccata*) grows both in western Asia and in southern Europe, but it was probably from Asia and possibly from the Taurus mountains that the specimens of this wood found in Egypt were brought, all of which were of fairly early date, eight being from the Sixth to Twelfth Dynasties and the ninth from the Eighteenth Dynasty. A notable example of the use of yew is the well-known head ascribed to Queen Tiy and now in the Berlin Museum.[7]

The yew is one of the few conifers that do not produce resin and, therefore, it cannot possibly be the ancient *ash*, as suggested by Ducros,[8] the resin from which was as important as the wood.

EGYPTIAN TIMBER

Trees are often depicted on the walls of tombs and temples, but they are usually drawn in so conventional a manner that only very few can be recognized with certainty, namely, the acacia,[9] the date palm, the dom palm and the sycamore fig. The principal trees that grew in Egypt in dynastic times of which the timber was employed by the carpenter and joiner were acacia, sycamore fig and tamarisk, though the wood of other trees was also sometimes used, especially that of the date palm, the dom palm, the sidder (*nabk*), the persea and the willow. In Egyptological literature, wooden objects are very often stated to be of acacia, sycamore and tamarisk, and although many of these identifications may well be correct, only those based on adequate scientific examination can be accepted. The following list gives all the recent identifications by modern methods of Egyptian woods that can be traced: [10]

---

[1] W. M. F. Petrie and E. Mackay, *Heliopolis, Kafr Ammar and Shurafa*, p. 23.

[2] *Enquiry into Plants*, IV: 8, 2.   [3] *Enquiry into Plants*, IV: 2, 10.   [4] XIII: 19.

[5] G. Botti, *Aegyptus*, XXXI (1951), pp. 192–8.

[6] See also G. Beauvisage, *Rec. Trav.*, XVIII (1896), pp. 78–91.

[7] L. Borchardt, *Der Porträtkopf der Königin Teje*; H. Schäfer, *Z.Ä.S.*, LXVIII (1932), pp. 81–86.

[8] H. A. Ducros, *Ann. Serv.*, XIV (1914), pp. 1–12.

[9] Excellent representations of acacia trees occur in a Twelfth Dynasty tomb at Beni Hasan (F. Ll. Griffith, *Beni Hasan*, IV, Frontispiece, Pls. VI, VII).

[10] Branches and twigs have generally been omitted unless of early date.

Wood	*Date*	*Object*
Acacia [1]	Predynastic	Log [2]
	Predynastic	Roots [3]
	Ist Dyn.	Charcoal [4]
	Ist–IIIrd Dyn.	Piece and charcoal [3]
	c. IIIrd Dyn.	Beam [5]
	IIIrd, IVth and Vth Dyn.	Trunks and branches [6]
	VIth–XIIth Dyn.	Coffin peg [7]
	XIIth Dyn.	Sarcophagus dowels [8]
	XIIth Dyn.	Coffin dowels [8]
	XIIth Dyn.	Box dowels [8]
	XIIth Dyn.	Knobs [8]
	XVIIIth Dyn.	Part of body of chariot [9]
	XVIIIth Dyn.	Two pegs [10]
	XVIIIth Dyn.	Dowel [11]
	New Kingdom (?)	Bolt [12]
	Ist cent. B.C. (?)	Boning rod [13]
	Late	Pegs from box [5]
	Roman	Mummy label [5]
	Late 5th cent. A.D.	Base of nilometer [14]
Almond	XVIIIth Dyn.	Walking-stick handle [15]
Carob	Middle Kingdom	Bow [15]
Fig	3rd cent A.D.	Mummy portrait [16]
Palm (date)	New Kingdom	Piece of box [17]
Persea [18]	New Kingdom	Head-rest [5]
Sidder (*Nabk*)	IIIrd Dyn.	Coffin [19]
	IXth Dyn.	Piece [20]
	XVIIIth Dyn.	Bow [21]
	XVIIIth Dyn.	Stick [22]
	XVIIIth Dyn.	Dowels [23]
	XVIIIth Dyn.	Dowels [24]
	Roman	Mummy label [5]
	Undated	Peg [5]
Sycamore fig [25]	Predynastic	Roots [3]
	Vth Dyn.	Dummy vases [26,27]
	Vth Dyn.	Column base [26,27]
	XIth Dyn.	Roots [28]
	XIIth Dyn.	Sarcophagi [8]
	XIIth Dyn.	Coffin and tenons [8]
	XIIth Dyn.	Box [8]
	XIIth Dyn.	Coffin [13]
	XIIth Dyn.	Statuette [13]
	XIIth Dyn. (?)	Coffin [29]
	XVIIIth Dyn.	Model building cradles [13]
	New Kingdom (?)	Miniature coffins [30]
	XXth–XXVIth Dyn.	Coffin [23]
	Late (?)	Piece from coffin [31]
	Ptolemaic (?)	Waggon [32]
	Ptolemaic-Roman (?)	Coffin [5]
	Coptic and very late	Seven specimens [5]
	Late 5th cent. A.D.	Base of nilometer [14]
Tamarisk [33]	Late Quaternary	Stems and branches [34]
	Neolithic	Twigs [35]
	Neolithic	Worked sticks [36]
	Badarian	Pieces [37]

Wood	Date	Object
	Predynastic	Root and twigs [38]
	Predynastic	Pieces [39]
	Ist–IIIrd Dyn.	Charcoal [38]
	XIth Dyn.	Roots [28]
	Middle Kingdom	Walking stick and throw stick [15]
	XVIIIth Dyn.	Lid of box [40]
	XVIIIth Dyn.	Foot of pall support [41] and throw stick [24]
	New Kingdom	Twig [35]
	XXth–XXVIth Dyn.	Coffin [23]
	XXth–XXVIth Dyn.	Coffin pegs [23]
	Roman	Five specimens [5]
	4th cent. A.D.	Pieces [42]
	Undated	Piece [35]
Willow	Protodynastic	Knife handle [26,43]
	IIIrd Dyn.	Parts of box [5]
	XVIIIth Dyn.	Pole of chariot [9]
	Roman	Mummy label [5]

[1] For other doubtful identifications of acacia see, G. Brunton, *Mostagedda*, pp. 58, 111; W. Ribstein, *Botanisches Archiv*, IX (1925), pp. 194–209 (several specimens).

[2] G. Brunton and G. Caton-Thompson, *Badarian Civilisation*, p. 95.

[3] R. Mond and O. H. Myers, *Cemeteries of Armant*, I, pp. 7, 138.

[4] W. B. Emery, *Hor-Aha*, p. 70.

[5] W. Ribstein, *Botanisches Archiv*, IX (1925), pp. 194–209.

[6] V. Täckholm, *Bull. Inst. d'Ég.*, XXXII (1951), pp. 133–4; W. Ribstein, *op. cit.*; L. Borchardt, *Nefer-ir-ke-rē*, p. 43.

[7] G. Beauvisage, *Rec. Trav.*, XVIII (1896), p. 85.

[8] T. G. B. Osborn, *Mem. and Proc. Manchester Lit. and Phil. Soc.*, LIII (1909), No. 9. Cf. M. A. Murray, *Tomb of the Two Brothers*, p. 11.

[9] U. Fasolo, in G. Botti, *Aegyptus*, XXXI (1951), pp. 192–8.

[10] L. Borchardt, *Der Porträtkopf der Königin Teje*, p. 11.

[11] Identified at the Royal Botanic Gardens, Kew.

[12] L. Borchardt, *Sahu-rē*, I, p. 56.

[13] K. P. Oakley, *Analyst*, LVII (1932), pp. 158–9.

[14] V. Täckholm and M. Drar, *Flora of Egypt*, I, p. 75.

[15] In the Museum, Royal Botanic Gardens, Kew (No. 61/1923).

[16] E. Coche de la Ferté, *Les Portraits Romano-Égyptiens du Louvre*, p. 11.

[17] E. Schiemann, *Mitt. Kairo*, X (1941), p. 128; R. Anthes, *Mitt. Kairo*, XII (1943), p. 62.

[18] For another doubtful identification of persea see W. Ribstein, *Botanisches Archiv*, IX (1925), pp. 194–209 (a Roman mummy label).

[19] Identified by Dr. L. Chalk, Cf. A. Lucas, *Ann. Serv.*, XXXVI (1936), pp. 1–4.

[20] G. Brunton, *Matmar*, p. 53.

[21] L. Wittmack, in H. Schäfer, *Armenisches Holz in altägyptischen Wagnereien* (*Sitz. Preuss. Ak.*, 1931, pp. 730–42).

[22] O. Mattirolo, *Atti della Reale Accad. delle Scienze di Torino*, LXI (1926), pp. 545–68.

[23] Several specimens identified by Dr. L. Chalk (Imperial Forestry Institute, Oxford, *Eighth Annual Report*, 1931–2, p. 11); a number of other specimens identified by me.

[24] Identified by Dr. L. Chalk; three other specimens identified at a later date at the Royal Botanic Gardens, Kew.

[25] For other doubtful identifications of sycamore see, G. Brunton, *Mostagedda*, p. 111.

[26] L. Wittmack, *Sitzungsberichte der Gesellschaft Naturforschender Freunde zu Berlin*, IV (1910), pp. 181–92.

[27] L. Borchardt, *Nefer-ir-ke-rē*, pp. 21, 60–62.

[28] H. E. Winlock, *M.M.A. Bull., Egyptian Exped. 1921–1922*, pp. 26–28.

[29] G. Beauvisage, *Annales de la Société botanique de Lyon*, xx (1895), p. 2.

[30] L. Borchardt, *Sahu-rē*, I, pp. 102–3.

[31] M. Wagenaar, *Oud. Med. N.R.*, x (2) (1929), pp. 93 f.; *Chemisch Weekblad*, xxvII (1930), pp. 348 f.

[32] K. H. Dittmann, *Mitt. Kairo*, x (1941), pp. 60–64.

[33] For other doubtful identifications of tamarisk see, G. Brunton, *Mostagedda*, pp. 33, 58, 59, 91, 111.

[34] K. S. Sandford, *Quart. Journ. Geol. Soc.*, LXXXV (1929), p. 503.

[35] E. A. M. Greiss, *Bull. Inst. d'Ég.*, xxxI (1949), pp. 262–73.

[36] G. Caton-Thompson and E. W. Gardner, *Desert Fayum*, pp. 45–46.

[37] G. Brunton and G. Caton-Thompson, *Badarian Civilisation*, p. 38.

[38] R. Mond and O. H. Myers, *Cemeteries of Armant*, I, pp. 137–8.

[39] G. Brunton and G. Caton-Thompson, *Badarian Civilisation*, p. 62.

[40] W. C. Hayes, *M.M.A. Bull., Egyptian Exped. 1934–1935*, p. 29.

[41] Identified by Dr. L. Chalk (Imperial Forestry Institute, Oxford, *Ninth Annual Report*, 1932–3, p. 12). Cf. A. Lucas, *Ann. Serv.*, xLI (1942), p. 144.

[42] R. Mond and O. H. Myers, *Temples of Armant*, I, p. 204.

[43] G. Möller and A. Scharff, *Das vorgeschichtliche Gräberfeld von Abusir El-Meleq*, p. 47.

The various woods mentioned may now be considered.

Acacia (Beekman, pp. 414–15) [1]

A number of different varieties of acacia grow in Egypt and the wood has been identified as having been used as early as the predynastic period.

Acacia is mentioned in ancient texts as having been obtained in the Sixth Dynasty from Hatnub in Middle Egypt and from Wawat in Nubia [2] and used for making boats and warships.[2,3] Herodotus states [4] that acacia wood was employed in Egypt, not only for boat building, but also for the masts; Theophrastus says [5] that the acacia was an Egyptian tree used for roofing and for the ribs of ships; Strabo refers [6] to the Thebaic acacia; Pliny, apparently quoting Theophrastus, mentions [7] an Egyptian thorn, evidently the acacia from the description, that was used for making the sides of ships, which tree he states grew in the vicinity of Thebes, and Dioscorides says that the acacia grew in Egypt.[8] Acacia is still used in Egypt for boat building as well as for other purposes. Acacia blossoms have been identified in garlands and floral collars.[9]

Almond (Beekman, pp. 443–4)

The almond tree has been discussed already in connexion with almond oil.[10] The one specimen of this wood known from ancient Egypt was found in a tomb at Thebes dating from about 1500 B.C.[10]

---

[1] See also G. Jéquier, *B.I.F.A.O.*, xIx (1922), pp. 31–37.

[2] *A.R.*, I, 323, 324.   [3] *A.R.*, IV, 229, 283, 387, 916, 1023.

[4] II: 96.   [5] *Enquiry into Plants*, IV: 2, 1, 8.

[6] xVII: 1, 35.   [7] xIII: 19.   [8] I: 133.

[9] M. A. Beauverie, *B.I.F.A.O.*, xxxV (1935), p. 138; H. E. Winlock, *Meryet-Amūn*, p. 51; G. Schweinfurth, *Pflanzenreste*, p. 363. Cf. also V. Loret and J. Poisson, *Rec. Trav.*, xVII (1895), pp. 191–2.

[10] See pp. 329–30.

Carob (Beekman, pp. 432–3) [1]

The carob, or locust-bean tree (*Ceratonia Siliqua*), is a native of south Europe and the Mediterranean region. Theophrastus states [2] that 'some call it the Egyptian fig —erroneously; for it does not occur at all in Egypt, but in Syria and Ionia and also in Cnidos and Rhodes.' Pliny copies Theophrastus.[3] Strabo says [4] that carob trees are found in abundance in Ethiopia.

In Breasted's translations of Egyptian texts objects of carob wood are frequently mentioned,[5] and while it is possible that the words so translated [6] may, in fact, refer to carob, the identification, proposed by Loret,[7] cannot be regarded as altogether certain.

Loret states [8] that the fruit of the carob tree is known from Egypt from the Twelfth Dynasty; Bruyère found it from the Eighteenth Dynasty [9] and Newberry identified one pod and six seeds of Twelfth Dynasty date from Kahun and two pods and several seeds from the Graeco-Roman cemetery at Hawara.[10] A simple bow of carob wood from Thebes, dating from about 1700 B.C., presented by Newberry is in the Museum of the Royal Botanic Gardens at Kew.[11]

The Egyptian name for the carob fruit has been identified with some degree of certainty [12] and occurs on two pottery jars from the First Dynasty tomb of 'Hemaka' at Saqqara.[13]

At the present time the only carob trees that can be traced in Egypt are a number of scattered ones growing along the north coast all the way from Alexandria to Sollum.[14]

Fig (Beekman, p. 442) [15]

The fig (*Ficus carica*) was cultivated in Egypt from an early date and is frequently mentioned in offering lists and other texts from the Old Kingdom onwards. The only recorded instance of the use of fig wood is for a mummy portrait of the third century A.D.[16]

Date Palm (Beekman, pp. 416–17) [17]

The date palm (*Phœnix dactylifera*) has been cultivated in Egypt from very remote

---

[1] See also V. Loret, *Rec. Trav.*, xv (1893), pp. 111–30.
[2] *Enquiry into Plants*, IV: 2, 4.   [3] XIII: 16.   [4] XVII: 2, 2.
[5] *A.R.*, I, 372; II, 436, 447, 449, 490, 491, 509, 512, 525; IV, 391.
[6] *Wb.* II. 378.2–7; IV. 279. 7–9.
[7] V. Loret, *Rec. Trav.*, xv (1893), pp. 111–19; *Flore Pharaonique*, 2nd ed., pp. 87–89.
[8] V. Loret, *Rec. Trav.*, xv (1893), p. 111.
[9] B. Bruyère, *Deir el Médineh (1934–1935)*, p. 108.
[10] P. E. Newberry, in W. M. F. Petrie, *Kahun, Gurob and Hawara*, pp. 47, 48, 50.
[11] No. 61/1923.
[12] V. Loret, *Rec. Trav.*, xv (1893), pp. 122–4; *Flore Pharaonique*, 2nd ed., pp. 87–89; L. Keimer, *Ann. Serv.*, XLII (1943), pp. 279–81.
[13] Z. Y. Saad, in W. B. Emery, *Hemaka*, p. 51; L. Keimer, *Ann. Serv.*, XLII (1943), pp. 279–81.
[14] Communicated by Mr. G. W. Murray.
[15] See also R. Muschler, *Manual Flora of Egypt*, I, pp. 246–7.
[16] E. Coche de la Ferté, *Les Portraits Romano-Égyptiens du Louvre*, p. 11.
[17] See also E. A. M. Greiss, *Mém. Inst. d'Ég.*, LV (1957), pp. 31–40, 146–7; M. A. Beauverie, *B.I.F.A.O.*, XXXV (1935), pp. 123–4; V. Täckholm and M. Drar, *Flora of Egypt*, II, pp. 203 f.

times and is often represented on tomb walls, for example, in a number of Eighteenth Dynasty tombs in the Theban necropolis.

The wood of the date palm, on account of its loose fibrous texture, is quite unsuitable for joiners' work, but the split trunk of the tree was employed anciently for roofing, as it still is occasionally at the present day. A tomb of the Second or Third Dynasty at Saqqara was roofed with palm logs,[1] and in a tomb of early date at Qau[2] near Asiut, in a Fourth Dynasty tomb adjoining the pyramid of Khafrē and in the Fifth Dynasty tomb of Ptahhotpe at Saqqara a roof of this kind has been copied in stone. In the Graeco-Roman city of Karanis in the Fayum palm wood was employed in the houses,[3] in the form of trunks sawn longitudinally into long or short beams (of semicircular cross-section) used mainly for roofing.[4] The cultivation and use of both date and dom palm in Graeco-Roman Egypt have been discussed by Hohlwein, with reference to the classical sources.[5]

Miss Caton-Thompson and Miss Gardner found fruit stones of a wild date (*Phœnix sylvestris*) of early Upper Paleolithic times in a deposit of late Pleistocene age in the Kharga Oasis.[6]

Dom Palm (Beekman, pp. 417–18) [7]

The dom palm (*Hyphœne thebaica*) is represented in an unmistakable manner in several Eighteenth Dynasty tombs in the Theban necropolis. Theophrastus, who states that the dom palm was an Egyptian tree,[8] comments upon the characteristic bifurcation of the trunk, which in the palm family is exceptional, and he contrasts it with the undivided trunk of the date palm; he describes the wood as being very compact and hard and, therefore, very different from that of the date palm, and states that it was employed by the Persians for making the feet of couches. Delile states [9] that the wood was used in Egypt at the time he wrote (1809) for making doors and, probably, therefore, it was sometimes employed anciently by the carpenter and joiner.

The dom palm does not grow in Lower Egypt, and probably never did: it still grows, however, in Upper Egypt from about Abydos southwards and the fruit is a very common object in graves and has been found from as early as the predynastic period.[10]

The fruit of the Argun palm (*Medemia Argun*) has also been found from as early as the Old Kingdom,[11] but no instance of the use of the wood of this species has been recorded.

---

[1] J. E. Quibell, *Saqqara, 1912–1914*, p. 21.

[2] Villiers Stuart, *Funeral Tent of an Egyptian Queen*, p. 83.

[3] A. E. R. Boak and E. E. Peterson, *Karanis*, p. 52.

[4] Kindly communicated by Mr. S. Yeivin.

[5] N. Hohlwein, *Études de Papyrologie*, v (1939), pp. 1–74.

[6] G. Caton-Thompson and E. W. Gardner, *Geog. Journ.*, LXXX (1932), p. 384.

[7] See also E. A. M. Greiss, *Mém. Inst. d'Ég.*, LV (1957), pp. 40–48, 147–8; M. A. Beauverie, *B.I.F.A.O.*, XXXV (1935), pp. 121–2; V. Täckholm and M. Drar, *Flora of Egypt*, II, pp. 280 f.

[8] IV: 2, 7.   [9] M. Delile, in *Description de l'Égypte, Histoire naturelle*, I (1809), p. 54.

[10] G. Brunton and G. Caton-Thompson, *Badarian Civilisation*, p. 63.

[11] V. Täckholm and M. Drar, *Flora of Egypt*, II, pp. 298–300; M. A. Beauverie, *B.I.F.A.O.*, XXXV (1935), pp. 122–3; V. Loret and J. Poisson, *Rec. Trav.*, XVII (1895), p. 182.

Persea (Beekman, p. 418) [1]

The persea tree (*Mimusops Schimperi*) is referred to in Egyptian texts from the Eighteenth Dynasty onwards.[2] and is mentioned by several of the classical writers Thus Theophrastus [3] describes it as an Egyptian tree that grew in abundance in the Thebaid; he states that it was evergreen (which it is) and that the wood, which was strong and black, like that of the nettle tree, was used for making images, beds, tables and other objects. Dioscorides states[4] that the persea was an Egyptian tree, bearing an edible fruit that was good for the stomach. I fortunately had an opportunity of examining this wood when a persea tree, planted by Schweinfurth in the garden of the Cairo Museum, was being trimmed, and found that it was very light brown, almost white, in colour with a very slight yellowish tint and that, although it darkened a little on exposure, it did not become more than brown. Pliny [5] states that the persea was an Egyptian tree and he mentions a confusion existing in his day between the persea and the *persica* (peach).

Twigs and leaves of persea have been found in tombs of various dates from the Twelfth Dynasty [6] to Graeco-Roman times and in the tomb of Tutankhamūn (Eighteenth Dynasty) there were bouquets (several very large) made of twigs with leaves,[7] together with dried fruit and two glass models of the fruit. Twigs were also found in the Eighteenth Dynasty tombs of Kha [8] and Meryetamūn,[9] though the latter examples may have been deposited at a later date (Twenty-first Dynasty). Persea fruits have been found in many tombs,[10] the earliest specimens being of the Third Dynasty, from the Djoser pyramid complex at Saqqara.[11] The head-rest identified by Ribstein as being made of persea wood was of New Kingdom date.

Poplar

Theophrastus[12] states that the poplar grew in the Nile valley in his day, and it is still found in the little oasis at the present time.[13] Leaves of *Populus euphratica* have been identified in a garland of uncertain date in the Louvre,[14] but no definite instance of the use of the wood has been recorded. The protodynastic knife handle examined by Ribstein may have been either willow or poplar.[15]

---

[1] See also L. Keimer, *Gartenpflanzen*, pp. 31–37.

[2] *Wb.* IV. 435. 10–14; L. Keimer, *Gartenpflanzen*, p. 144.

[3] *Enquiry into Plants*, IV: 2, 1, 5, 8.

[4] I: 187.

[5] XIII: 17; XV: 13.

[6] P. E. Newberry, *P.S.B.A.*, XXI (1899), p. 304; in W. M. F. Petrie, *Kahun, Gurob and Hawara*, p. 49; in W. M. F. Petrie, *Hawara, Biahmu and Arsinoe*, pp. 48, 53.

[7] H. Carter, *Tut-ankh-Amen*, I, Pl. XXVII; II, p. 33.

[8] E. Schiaparelli, *La Tomba intatta dell' Architetto Cha*, p. 166.

[9] H. E. Winlock, *Meryet-Amūn*, p. 52.

[10] Cf. V. Loret and J. Poisson, *Rec. Trav.*, XVII (1895), pp. 188–9; M. A. Beauverie, *B.I.F.A.O.*, XXXV (1935), pp. 133–4; E. Schiemann, *Mitt. Kairo*, X (1941), p. 128.

[11] V. Laurent Täckholm, *Bull. Inst. d'Ég.*, XXXII (1951), pp. 129–30.

[12] *Enquiry into Plants*, IV: 8, 2.

[13] R. Muschler, *Manual Flora of Egypt*, I, pp. 243–4.

[14] V. Loret and J. Poisson, *Rec. Trav.*, XVII (1895), pp. 187–8; M. A. Beauverie, *B.I.F.A.O.*, XXXV (1935), p. 129.

[15] W. Ribstein, *Botanisches Archiv*, IX (1925), pp. 194–209.

Sidder (Beekman, pp. 418–19) [1]

As there are various species of sidder, and as it is difficult or even impossible to identify closely related species from the anatomical features seen in a microscopical section of the wood, the specimens found to be sidder may be one of several kinds, though from collateral evidence they are practically certainly either *Zizyphus mucronata* or *Zizyphus spina Christi* and probably the latter.

The first of the two sidders mentioned (*Z. mucronata*) is very widespread in Africa, being common all over the drier parts of tropical and south Africa, including the Sudan, and, therefore, it might have been used in ancient Egypt, though this seems improbable, unless it then grew in the country, for which there is no evidence, since the only woods that were brought into Egypt from the south, of which there are records, were ebony and certain sweet and fragrant woods, probably for use as incense or for making perfumed ointments. The second species of sidder mentioned (*Z. spina Christi*) grows in the Mediterranean region generally, including Egypt, where it is indigenous, and possibly also in tropical Africa.[2] In Egypt it is called the *nabk*, although strictly this is the name of the fruit and not of the tree. The fruit is about the size of a small cherry and not unlike a yellowish-coloured cherry in appearance and it has one stone, not unlike a cherry stone in size and shape. The dried fruit is known in Egypt from predynastic times [3] and has often been found in tombs,[4] for instance in a First Dynasty tomb at Saqqara,[5] in the Djoser pyramid complex at Saqqara,[6] and in the Eighteenth Dynasty tomb of Tutankhamūn. This tree, although not large enough to have provided the planks that formed the main parts of the shrines mentioned (those of Tutankhamūn and Queen Tiy respectively) is sufficiently large to have been used for dowels and, as it grows in the country and is a good hard durable wood, it is not to be wondered at, if the amount of cedar available were not sufficient for all the dowels, that local woods should have been used for most of the remainder. One of the woods used in a Third Dynasty plywood coffin was sidder.[7]

Hamilton states [8] that the timber of the *nabk* 'is one of the most serviceable in Egypt, the greater part of the Persian water wheel being made of it', and as the wood has been found so useful in modern times, it is only reasonable to suppose that it was also employed anciently.

Sycamore Fig (Beekman, pp. 419–21)

The sycamore [9] fig (*Ficus sycomorus*) which is often called the sycamore and is the sycamore of the Bible, has no connexion with the sycamore of colder climates, which latter is a species of maple (*Acer pseudoplatanus*).

---

[1] See also L. Keimer, *Gartenpflanzen*, pp. 64–70.

[2] W. G. Browne (*Travels in Africa, Egypt and Syria*, 1799, p. 270) states that he found two species of sidder in Darfur, one of which appeared to be the same that he had seen in Alexandria.

[3] W. M. F. Petrie, *Prehistoric Egypt*, p. 44.

[4] Cf. V. Loret and J. Poisson, *Rec. Trav.*, XVII (1895), pp. 193–4; M. A. Beauverie, *B.I.F.A.O.*, XXXV (1935), pp. 140–1.

[5] Z. Y. Saad, in W. B. Emery, *Hemaka*, p. 52; L. Keimer, *Ann. Serv.*, XLII (1943), pp. 279–81.

[6] V. Laurent Täckholm, *Bull. Inst. d'Ég.*, XXXII (1951), pp. 131–2.

[7] A. Lucas, *Ann. Serv.*, XXXVI (1936), pp. 1–4.

[8] W. Hamilton, *Remarks on Several Parts of Turkey, I, Ægyptiaca*, 1809, pp. 71, 424.

[9] The New Oxford Dictionary states that the spelling sycamore is more usual than sycomore.

The sycamore fig is referred to frequently in ancient Egyptian texts, thus in the Eighteenth Dynasty [1] and in 251 B.C. [2] sycamore wood to be used for building a boat is mentioned, and in the Twentieth Dynasty statues of the wood [3] and sycamore gardens [4] are also mentioned. The tree is represented frequently on tomb walls of the Eighteenth Dynasty at Thebes.

Diodorus [5] refers to the sycamore, which he calls the Egyptian fig tree, as growing in Egypt; Theophrastus [6] also describes the sycamore as an Egyptian tree and says that the wood was useful for many purposes; Strabo [7] states that it grew in Ethiopia and Pliny, [8] who quotes Theophrastus, also calls the sycamore the Egyptian fig and states that the wood was among the most useful known.

Either the wood or the fruit of the sycamore fig (which of the two is not stated) has been found in graves as early as the predynastic period, [9] roots from the predynastic period and the fruit from both the predynastic period [10] and the First Dynasty. [11] In the Cairo Museum there are six readily recognized models of the sycamore fig tree in a miniature garden of the Eleventh Dynasty, found by Winlock at Thebes, and Winlock also discovered roots of this same tree in the courtyard of the Eleventh Dynasty temple of Mentuhotpe at Deir el Bahari. [12] In the Museum of the Royal Botanic Gardens at Kew there are small branches of Twentieth Dynasty date [13] and, as will be seen from the list given, the wood has been identified in objects varying in date from the Fifth Dynasty to a very late period. The tree still grows plentifully in the country.

Tamarisk (Beekman, p. 421) [14]

The tamarisk tree, of which there are many species in Egypt, is manifestly indigenous to the country, since semi-carbonized stems and branches of considerable size have been found by Sandford in the Wadi Qena, [15] which he attributes to late Quaternary times, and tamarisk wood has been identified from as early as the neolithic, [16] the Badarian [17] and the predynastic [17] periods respectively, to as late as Graeco-Roman times, two species, *T. nilotica* and *T. articulata*, having been used at Karanis in the Fayum. [18]

The tamarisk is occasionally mentioned in the ancient texts from the Old Kingdom onwards [19] and bundles of tamarisk wood are referred to in the Twentieth Dynasty. [20] Herodotus states [21] that certain rafts used in connexion with boats were of tamarisk.

---

[1] *A.R.*, II, 326   [2] C. C. Edgar, *Zenon Papyri*, II, No. 59270.   [3] *A.R.*, IV, 303, 349, 395.

[4] *A.R.*, IV, 380.   [5] I: 3.   [6] *Enquiry into Plants* IV: 2, 1, 2.   [7] XVII: 2, 4.   [8] XIII: 14.

[9] W. M. F. Petrie and J. E. Quibell, *Naqada and Ballas*, p. 54.

[10] G. Brunton, *Mostagedda*, p. 91.

[11] W. M. F. Petrie, *Royal Tombs*, II, pp. 36, 38.

[12] H. E. Winlock, *M.M.A. Bull., Egyptian Exped. 1921–1922*, pp. 26, 28.

[13] No. 85/1885.   [14] See also L. Keimer, *Gartenpflanzen*, pp. 55–57.

[15] K. S. Sandford, *Quart. Journ. Geol. Soc.*, LXXXV (1929), p. 503.

[16] G. Caton-Thompson and E. W. Gardner, *Desert Fayum*, pp. 45, 46, 88, 89.

[17] G. Brunton, *Mostagedda*, pp. 33, 59, 67; G. Brunton and G. Caton-Thompson, *Badarian Civilisation*, pp. 38, 62.

[18] Kindly communicated by Mr. S. Yeivin.

[19] *Wb.* I. 130. 1–6; A. Erman, *Literature of the Ancient Egyptians*, trans. A. M. Blackman, pp. 3, 18; L. Keimer, *Gartenpflanzen*, pp. 155–6.

[20] *A.R.*, IV, 241, 379, 392.   [21] II: 96.

Winlock found evidence to show that a grove of tamarisk trees once existed in front of the Eleventh Dynasty temple of Mentuhotpe at Deir el Bahari;[1] the tree still grows plentifully in the country.

Willow (Beekman, pp. 422–3) [2]

The Egyptian willow tree (*Salix safsaf*), whether indigenous or not in the country, is manifestly of considerable antiquity, as the handle of a flint knife of protodynastic date has been identified as probably willow, another example of its early use being for a box of the Third Dynasty. It was also employed during Graeco-Roman times and is still utilized for making camel saddles, the screw of the Archimedian water elevator and for vine supports.[3] Leaves of the willow tree were used for making funerary garlands;[4] examples of Eighteenth and Twenty-first Dynasty date, some from the tomb of Tutankhamūn,[5] are in the Cairo Museum, and others were also found in the tomb of Queen Meryetamūn.[6] In a papyrus dating from 243 B.C. there is a request for willow for making tent poles.[7]

WOOD WORKING[8]

The art of wood carving and the crafts of the carpenter and joiner cannot have been known in Egypt before the late predynastic period, since it was not until then that metal (copper) tools were available, and the few specimens of worked wood of earlier date that have been found must have been fashioned in the very rough manner that alone was possible without metal tools.

Because of the early and constant importation of timber into Egypt it has been stated that wood working cannot have originated in the country, but must have been introduced from abroad. This, however, does not necessarily follow, since there have always been, as there are today, plenty of comparatively small indigenous trees, such as acacia, sidder (*nabk*), sycamore fig, tamarisk and willow that could have been used for making boats, boxes, coffins, furniture and other objects, and unless there had been some previous knowledge of wood working, it is difficult to understand why there should have been any demand for wood from abroad. The need was not for timber of any kind, but for timber of better quality and larger size than that obtainable locally.

The tools employed in ancient Egypt by the carpenter and joiner are well known from illustrations on tomb walls and on coffins of the Middle Kingdom,[9] and also from actual specimens, either full size, or miniature, that have been found in tombs.[10] They were adzes, axes, chisels, reamers and saws, all, except some of the chisels, hav-

---

[1] H. E. Winlock, *M.M.A. Bull., Egyptian Exped. 1921–1922*, pp. 26, 27.

[2] See also L. Keimer, *B.I.F.A.O.*, XXXI (1931), pp. 177–227.

[3] Kindly communicated by Professor F. W. Oliver, F.R.S.

[4] L. Keimer, *B.I.F.A.O.*, XXXI (1931), pp. 196–206.

[5] P. E. Newberry, in H. Carter, *Tut-ankh-Amen*, II, pp. 191–2 (Appendix III).

[6] H. E. Winlock, *Meryet-Amūn*, p. 51.

[7] C. C. Edgar, *Zenon Papyri*, III, No. 59353.

[8] Cf. A. Lucas, 'Wood Working in Ancient Egypt', *Empire Forestry Journal*, XIII, No. 2 (1934), pp. 213 f.

[9] G. Jéquier, *Frises d'Objets*, pp. 269–79.

[10] E.g. W. C. Hayes, *Scepter*, I, pp. 287–9; H. E. Winlock, *Models of Daily Life*, pp. 33–35.

ing wooden handles; also bow-drills, polishing blocks of sandstone and wooden mallets. At first and for a very long period, the blades were copper, which later gave place to bronze and at a very late date to iron.

The saw may be mentioned specially, as it is of particular interest. Saws are of two kinds, the push-saw and the pull-saw, the former, which is the Western type, having the cutting edge of the teeth set away from the handle, the saw being pushed forward in use, while the latter has the cutting edge of the teeth set towards the handle, the saw being pulled. As is shown by Miss M. Lane, it was the pull-saw that was employed in ancient Egypt.[1] From numerous illustrations on tomb walls and from four tomb-models of carpenters' shops, three in the Cairo Museum [2] and one in Copenhagen,[3] it is seen that the wood to be sawn was tied in the vertical position to an upright post and cut from the top downwards, which is the most convenient position for the pull-saw in contrast to the horizontal position of the wood when a push-saw is used. Also, the tip of the saw is shown pointing upwards, as would be the case with a pull-saw, and both hands are being used, which again is necessary with a pull-saw. Petrie stated [4] some years ago that the saw dates certainly from as early as the First Dynasty, as from this period there is a wooden coffin showing rough saw marks,[5] and just before the war Emery found seven copper saws in a First Dynasty tomb at Saqqara, which are the oldest and largest known up to the present.[6] The blades of these vary in length from 25.1 to 40 centimetres (9.8 to 15.7 inches). In the Cairo Museum there is from the end of the Third Dynasty a section of a trunk of a small tree found by Rowe, on which are ancient saw-cuts and which is labelled 'Section of a log which projected from the wall of the shaft leading up to the burial chamber of the pyramid of Sneferu at Medum'.[7] A small copper saw was found by Firth in a Second Dynasty tomb at Saqqara,[8] and Reisner found one of Old Kingdom date at Giza.[9]

The plane was unknown in ancient Egypt, the wood being smoothed with the adze and by rubbing with pieces of fine-grained sandstone, as is shown in certain representations and in the Eleventh Dynasty model carpenter's shop from the tomb of Meketrē.

With respect to the lathe Petrie says [10] 'There was no lathe cutting, even in Roman times; and it is curious that the rings on wooden legs of stools are all hand-worked in imitation of lathe turning'; and in an anonymous review, almost certainly written by Petrie, it is stated[11] that 'the early stool legs are not turned, but hand-worked, yet the pattern is obviously copied from turned work in the XIXth. dynasty. A small box (University College) is clearly turned, of the XVIIIth. or XIXth. dynasty . . .' Davies mentions the head of a walking-stick from the Eighteenth Dynasty, which

---

[1] M. Lane, *Ancient Egypt*, 1935, pp. 55–58.
[2] The model from the tomb of Meketrē, and Nos. J. 39129 and J. 45319.
[3] Cf. J. H. Breasted (Jr.), *Servant Statues*, pp. 50–52.
[4] W. M. F. Petrie, *Tools and Weapons*, p. 43.
[5] W. M. F. Petrie, G. A. Wainwright and A. H. Gardiner, *Tarkhan*, I, *and Memphis*, V, p. 26, Pl. XXIV.
[6] W. B. Emery, *Ann. Serv.*, XXXIX (1939), pp. 427–37.
[7] No. J. 57710.   [8] Cairo Museum: not numbered.   [9] No. J. 67596.
[10] W. M. F. Petrie, *Social Life in Ancient Egypt*, p. 153.   [11] *Ancient Egypt*, 1926, p. 55.

he calls a 'piece of turnery',[1] and refers to a stool leg of the same date which he states was 'turned in a lathe', because there is a pivot hole at the foot.[2] Legs ornamented with rings like modern turnery occur on a stool from the tomb of Tutankhamūn, but whether they are turned or filed has not been determined. Wainwright states [3] that 'In every direction in Graeco-Roman Egypt one is met by quantities of turned woodwork of every variety, forming the strongest contrast with Pharaonic Egypt. This sudden flowering of the craft, and the variety of the sizes and forms produced, seems to indicate the revelling in a newfound method of decoration. . . . This would imply that the turning lathe was a Graeco-Roman introduction into Egypt.' He discusses the stool leg cited by Davies and says that 'A close inspection of the piece leaves no doubt that during the process of manufacture it has been set in such a manner as to turn', and that 'for ease of manipulation and to ensure a more perfect roundness to the completed article, the wood seems to have been supported between points'. On the other hand, 'The shortness of the scratches and the fact that they run at angles to each other suggest that it was the file or sandstone that was moved rather than that the wood was spun against the cutter, as in a true lathe', and 'it seems probable that the work was not so much turned, in our sense of the word, as filed into shape.' 'Thus, this leg seems to have been made on a kind of proto-lathe, and it only remained for some genius to apply motive force to the piece of wood itself to produce a genuine turning lathe.' The archaeological evidence would suggest that this was a Hellenistic innovation, and the earliest representation of a lathe, in the tomb of Petosiris,[4] is of the fourth century B.C. However, the principle of turning had long been known in the bow drill, and the possibility of an earlier origin for the lathe cannot entirely be discounted.

Illustrations of wood working that may be mentioned [5] occur in a Fifth Dynasty tomb at Saqqara;[6] in a Sixth Dynasty tomb at Deir el Gebrawi;[7] in two Twelfth Dynasty tombs at Beni Hasan;[8] in four Eighteenth Dynasty tombs [9] and in two Nineteenth Dynasty tombs [10] in the Theban necropolis, as well as in several tomb-models of carpenters' shops, where the men are shown using miniature tools.[11] The processes shown include sawing wood tied to an upright post, rough dressing with the adze, polishing with sandstone blocks, the cutting of mortises with a chisel and the use of dowels.

---

[1] N. de G. Davies, *Five Theban Tombs*, pp. 5–6 (No. 8), Pl. XVII.

[2] N. de G. Davies, *Five Theban Tombs*, pp. 5–6 (No. 5), Pl. XVII.

[3] G. A. Wainwright, *Ann. Serv.*, XXV (1925), pp. 112–19.

[4] G. Lefebvre, *Le Tombeau de Petosiris*, III, Pl. X.

[5] Cf. P. Montet, *Scènes de la vie privée*, pp. 298–311; L. Klebs, *Reliefs, A.R.*, pp. 87–89; *M.R.*, pp. 113–16; *N.R.*, pp. 134 f.

[6] G. Steindorff, *Ti*, Pls. CXIX, CXX, CXXXII, CXXXIII.

[7] N. de G. Davies, *Deir el Gebrâwi*, I, Pls. XIV–XVI; II, Pl. X

[8] P. E. Newberry, *Beni Hasan*, I, Pls. XI, XXIX; II, Pl. XIII.

[9] N. de G. Davies, *Rekh-mi-rē*, Pls. LII, LIII; *Two Sculptors*, Pls. XI–XIII; *Nefer-hotep*, I, Pls. V, XXVII; *Puyemrê*, Pls. XXIII, XXIV.

[10] N. de G. Davies, *Two Ramesside Tombs*, Pls. XXXVI, XXXVIII.

[11] J. H. Breasted (Jr.), *Servant Statues*, pp. 50–52; H. E. Winlock, *Models of Daily Life*, pp. 33–35, Pls. XXVIII, XXIX; J. E. Quibell, *Saqqara, 1906–1907*, pp. 10, 75, Pl. XVII (4), pp. 11, 75, Pl. XVII (1, 3); C. M. Firth and B. Gunn, *Teti Pyramid Cemeteries*, I, p. 53; II, Pl. XXIX; J. E. Quibell and A. G. K. Hayter, *Saqqara, Teti Pyramid, North Side*, pp. 40–41, Pl. XXIV (2).

As early as the First Dynasty the Egyptians were able to carve wooden statues of near life-size,[1] and during the Old Kingdom wood working reached a high degree of skill, as is proved, for example, by the carved wooden panels with relief decoration from the tomb of Hesirē [2] and the six-ply wooden coffin from Saqqara,[3] both of Third Dynasty date; the Fourth Dynasty furniture from the tomb of Queen Hetepheres at Giza; [4] the Fifth Dynasty carved wooden doors from Saqqara [5] and the celebrated wooden statue known as the Sheikh el Beled.[6]

From the Middle Kingdom, examples of woodwork that may be mentioned are the immense cedar coffins and the cedar canopic box of Amenemhet;[6] the ebony and ivory caskets from Lahun,[7] and the wooden statue of King Hor.[8]

From the Eighteenth Dynasty there are the furniture (chairs, stools, and beds), coffins, boxes, gaming boards and other wooden objects from the tombs of Kha,[9] Yuya and Tuyu,[10] and Tutankhamūn,[11] as well as the bent wood chariots from the two latter tombs and that in the Florence Museum

It is often assumed that chairs are peculiarly Western, but this is not so, their origin being Eastern and possibly Egyptian, and from the Fourth Dynasty there is the chair (restored) from the tomb of Queen Hetepheres and the several chairs of excellent design and workmanship from the Eighteenth Dynasty tomb of Tutankhamūn.[12]

The Third Dynasty plywood coffin, or rather what remains of it, was discovered in an alabaster sarcophagus in a passage in the step pyramid at Saqqara. The sides, ends and bottom of the coffin (the lid is missing) consisted of six-ply wood, each layer being about four millimetres (0.16 inch) thick, from four to thirty centimetres (1.58 to 11.82 inches) wide and of various lengths. None of the pieces of wood was either broad enough for the height of the sides, nor long enough for the length of the coffin, and in order to obtain the necessary height, width and length, separate pieces of wood were joined together by means of flat wooden dowels, which were held in place with small wooden pegs. The different layers making the thickness were also pegged together, the various layers being arranged with the grain of the wood alternately in different directions, exactly as is done today in order to give strength and to prevent warping. At the bottom corners of the coffin the edges of the five outermost layers were bevelled, that is to say the joints were mitred, but the innermost layer had square (butt) joints. The bottom corners were strengthened inside by

---

[1] W. B. Emery, *Great Tombs*, III, p. 13.

[2] J. E. Quibell, *Saqqara, 1911–1912*, Pls. XXIX–XXXII.

[3] C. M. Firth, J. E. Quibell and J.-P. Lauer, *Step Pyramid*, I, p. 42; J.-P. Lauer, *Pyramide à degrés*, I, pp. 60–61; *Ann. Serv.*, XXXIII (1933), pp. 163–5; A. Lucas, *Ann. Serv.*, XXXVI (1936), pp. 1–4; *Empire Forestry Journal*, XIII, No. 2 (1934), p. 213.

[4] G. A. Reisner, *Boston Bull.*, XXV (1927), Supplement; XXVI (1928), pp. 76–88; XXVII (1929), pp. 83–90; XXX (1932), pp. 56–60; *History of the Giza Necropolis*, II, pp. 23–35. The present wood is entirely new, but only replaces old wood that had perished.

[5] No. J. 47749.   [6] Cairo Museum.

[7] A. C. Mace, *Ancient Egypt*, 1921, pp. 4–6; H. E. Winlock, *Treasure of El Lāhūn*, pp. 12–22.

[8] J. de Morgan, *Dahchour, mars–juin 1894*, Pls. XXXIII–XXXV.

[9] E. Schiaparelli, *La Tomba intatta dell' Architetto Cha*.

[10] J. E. Quibell, *Yuaa and Thuiu*.

[11] H. Carter, *Tut-ankh-Amen*, I–III.

[12] Cf. A. Wenzel, *Die Formen der altägyptischer Liege- und Sitzmöbel*.

separate pieces of wood. The outermost layer had a carved ribbed pattern which originally had been covered with sheet gold fastened in place with small gold rivets.

Certain features of Egyptian woodwork, namely joints, veneer and inlay, will be briefly discussed below, and one should also mention the bent wood construction of chariots, in which different woods were employed for specific parts. The use of wood in architecture has already been noted in connexion with building materials.[1]

Joints

Owing to the relative scarcity of timber suitable for sizeable straight planks, the ancient Egyptian carpenters developed a remarkable technique of 'patchwork' construction, joining together small or irregular pieces of wood by means of flat tongues or dowels, butterfly cramps, various forms of lashing and pegging, and occasionally in fine work by tongue and groove.[2] Nails were not used in woodwork until the Eighteenth Dynasty, though they were employed to fasten metal to a wooden core at least as early as the Old Kingdom.

Lashing and Pegging. One of the simplest and earliest methods of securing the joints of woodwork was by lashing them with thongs of hide or leather, narrow copper bands, or linen string. Leather thongs were used as early as the First Dynasty.[3] Timbers with holes for lashing, probably from wooden houses, were found at Tarkhan,[4] and lashed as well as pegged joints occur in the wooden coffins from the same site (Third to Eleventh Dynasties), which have been described and illustrated by Mackay.[5] Brunton [6] says of a coffin of the Seventh or Eighth Dynasty that 'The . . . corners were held together by ropes running round pegs placed in recesses in the thickness of the wood.' A few special examples of lashing (and in some instances also of pegging and of mitred joints) in the Cairo Museum include the reproductions of the wooden bed-frame and the gold-covered wooden canopy from the Fourth Dynasty tomb of Queen Hetepheres,[7] which have been lashed by Reisner with leather thongs on evidence obtained from the tomb; the huge wooden sarcophagus and the wooden coffin of Amenemhet (Twelfth Dynasty), which have mitred joints lashed with narrow copper bands (6 to 7 mm. wide and 0.6 mm. thick) and also pegged with wooden pegs, and an Eighteenth Dynasty wooden coffin from Deir el Medineh,[8] which has the joints pegged and lashed with linen string. The mortise lacing and secret mortise lacing used to join the planks of coffins have been described by Lallemand.[9]

---

[1] See p. 79.

[2] Cf. H. Lallemand, *B.I.F.A.O.*, xxii (1923), pp. 78–86; W. M. F. Petrie and E. Mackay, *Heliopolis, Kafr Ammar and Shurafa*, pp. 23–30, Pls. xxiv, xxv; E. Marx, *Antiquity*, xx (1946), pp. 127–33; C. Aldred, in *History of Technology*, I, pp. 684–703.

[3] W. B. Emery, *Hor-Aha*, pp. 63–64.

[4] W. M. F. Petrie, G. A. Wainwright and A. H. Gardiner, *Tarkhan, I, and Memphis*, v, p. 24, Pl. ix.

[5] E. Mackay, in W. M. F. Petrie and E. Mackay, *Heliopolis, Kafr Ammar and Shurafa*, pp. 23–30, Pls. xxiv, xxv.

[6] G. Brunton, *Mostagedda*, p. 101.

[7] G. A. Reisner, *Boston Bull.*, xxx (1932), pp. 56–60; *History of the Giza Necropolis*, II, pp. 23–35.

[8] No. J. 66869.

[9] H. Lallemand, *B.I.F.A.O.*, xxii (1923), pp. 78–86.

Mortise and Tenon Joints. These joints were used in the Hetepheres furniture (Fourth Dynasty);[1] to fasten on the arms of the Sheikh el Beled (Fifth Dynasty); in the Eighteenth Dynasty furniture of Yuya and Tuyu and Tutankhamūn respectively and in many other instances, being quite common even in the simplest construction.

Dove-tailing. This is exemplified in the Hetepheres furniture [2] (Fourth Dynasty); in a large box from the tomb of Tutankhamūn [3] (Eighteenth Dynasty); in the wooden framework of a tambourine [4] (Eighteenth Dynasty) and in a coffin from Thebes [5] (Eighteenth Dynasty). Petrie states [6] that dove-tailing is known in ivory from the First Dynasty.

Dowels. Flat dowels both of ivory and of wood were used in the First Dynasty,[7] and flat wooden dowels in the Third Dynasty for the plywood coffin already mentioned; also in the Fourth Dynasty Hetepheres furniture and in the tomb of Tutankhamūn, especially in the four large shrines that were outside the sarcophagus. Dowels were also regularly used in the construction of coffins and mummy cases.

Mitred Joints. These have already been mentioned as occurring in the Third Dynasty plywood coffin, and among the corner joints noted by Mackay in coffins of the Third to Eleventh Dynasties from Tarkhan were several varieties of mitre.[8] The seven types of joint distinguished were: (1) Square end; (2) Halving; (3) Mitre; (4) Shoulder mitre; (5) Double shoulder mitre; (6) Mitre housing; (7) Dovetail mitre housing. The majority were held with pegs driven diagonally through, though some were lashed in addition, and a few only lashed. Dovetail mitre housing is common in later coffins.

The joints of furniture were frequently strengthened with angular pieces of wood which may possibly have been grown to shape for the purpose.

Hinges similar to the modern type were used in some of the boxes from the tomb of Tutankhamūn, as well as in the 'camp bed'.

In addition to the publications of the furniture from the tomb of Queen Hetepheres and the early coffins from Tarkhan already mentioned, the constructional details of several other specimens of Egyptian woodwork have been described, notably the Middle Kingdom beds from Kerma,[9] the coffins of the Middle Kingdom and Intermediate periods in the Cairo Museum,[10] certain individual objects noted by Aldred,[11] and a group of coffins of the Hellenistic period.[12]

---

[1] G. A. Reisner, *Boston Bull.,* xxv (1927), Supplement; xxvi (1928), pp. 76–88; xxvii (1929), pp. 83–90; xxx (1932), pp. 56–60; *History of the Giza Necropolis,* ii, pp. 23–35.

[2] G. A. Reisner, *Boston Bull.,* xxv (1927), Supplement, p. 30.

[3] H. Carter, *Tut-ankh-Amen,* iii, Pl. xxxi (No. 370).

[4] Found at Thebes by A. Lansing, No. J. 66246.

[5] W. C. Hayes, *M.M.A. Bull., Egyptian Exped. 1934–1935,* p. 19.

[6] W. M. F. Petrie, *Royal Tombs,* ii, p. 39.

[7] W. B. Emery, *Hor-Aha,* pp. 63–64.

[8] E. Mackay, in W. M. F. Petrie and E. Mackay, *Heliopolis, Kafr Ammar and Shurafa,* pp. 23–30, Pls. xxiv, xxv.

[9] G. A. Reisner, *Kerma,* iv–v, pp. 212–20.

[10] P. Lacau, *Sarcophages,* i–ii.

[11] C. Aldred, in *History of Technology,* i, pp. 684–703.

[12] C. Watzinger, *Griechische Holzsarkophage,* pp. 25 f. (in particular pp. 63 f.); M. Cagiano de Azevedo, *Bollettino del' Istituto centrale del restauro,* xxix–xxx (1957), pp. 11–29.

Veneer and Inlay

The use of veneer and inlay is a common feature of Egyptian woodwork, articles made of inferior woods being covered with panels or strips of ebony and ivory. Inlay of ivory and different woods is present on a small wooden box from the First Dynasty tomb of 'Hemaka' at Saqqara,[1] and veneer of wood alone on another box from the same tomb.[1] The carrying chair of Queen Hetepheres (Fourth Dynasty) was veneered with strips of ebony in which gold hieroglyphs were inlaid,[2] and the caskets from Lahun,[3] and another casket also of the Twelfth Dynasty,[4] were covered with veneer and inlay in ebony and ivory. Veneer of 'cedar', varying in thickness from 1.5 mm. to 2.5 mm., was also used on the coffin and canopic box of Senebtisi (Twelfth Dynasty).[5] A toilet casket of Amenhotpe II is veneered with thin slips of ebony and has applied ornamentation in ivory,[6] and both veneer and inlay occur on furniture from the tombs of Yuya and Tuyu[7] and Tutankhamūn respectively. The thicker veneer (3 to 4 mm.) is held in place by small wooden pegs, while the thinner pieces and small strips are glued in place. Many of the boxes from the latter tomb are elaborately veneered and inlaid, particularly fine examples being the carved ivory inlay on a box bearing representations of the king and queen, and caskets veneered with strips of ivory, framing marquetry panels composed of thin slips of ebony and ivory.[8] Some details of panelling on articles of furniture from the tomb of Tutankhamūn have been given by Aldred.[9]

The inlaying of wooden objects, especially coffins and boxes, with coloured stones, faience and opaque coloured glass is very common from the Eighteenth Dynasty, examples being the gilt wooden coffin of Yuya; the coffin lid from the so-called 'Tomb of Queen Tiy' and the middle coffin, the throne and two chariots from the tomb of Tutankhamūn.

BARK

Bark was much used in ancient Egypt, particularly during the Eighteenth Dynasty, as a decoration for wooden objects, such as the compound bows, walking-sticks, fan handles, goads, a bow box and the axle of a chariot from the tomb of Tutankhamūn, and sticks, bows and chariots from other tombs. Hall says [10] 'the wood used in the construction of chariots was foreign . . . while the bark of the birch-tree served as a decoration. The birch bark, which must have come (if we rule Italy and Macedonia out) from Anatolia or North Persia, was apparently much admired, and was used to decorate sticks and staves, as also was cherry bark, which certainly came from Persia

---

[1] W. B. Emery, *Hemaka*, p. 41 (both described as inlay).

[2] G. A. Reisner, *History of the Giza Necropolis*, II, pp. 33-34.

[3] A. C. Mace, *Ancient Egypt*, 1921, pp. 4-6; H. E. Winlock, *Treasure of El Lāhūn*, pp. 12-22.

[4] Carnarvon and H. Carter, *Five Years' Explorations*, pp. 55-56; C. Aldred, in *History of Technology*, I, pp. 694-5.

[5] A. C. Mace and H. E. Winlock, *Senebtisi*, pp. 29, 33-34.

[6] C. Aldred, in *History of Technology*, I, pp. 686-7, 693.

[7] J. E. Quibell, *Yuaa and Thuiu*, Nos. 51109, 51110, 51113.

[8] C. Aldred, in *History of Technology*, I, p. 693.

[9] C. Aldred, in *History of Technology*, I, p. 692.

[10] H. R. Hall, *Cambridge Ancient History*, II, p. 424.

and the Caucasus region.' This identification as birch bark and cherry bark respectively was largely guesswork based on the appearance of the barks in question, though it may be correct, but so far as is known to me, only one expert examination has been made.[1] Schäfer thinks that the 'birch' bark employed in Egypt was the inner bark or bast and that it was probably obtained from Armenia.[2]

What is possibly birch bark of neolithic date has been found in the Fayum,[3] and a small roll of bark in the Cairo Museum is described in the register as 'Roll of Birch Bark'.[4] Petrie found at Athribis 'a curious chain made of long strips of bark, coiled round and covered with a vegetable paste . . .'[5] the date of which is unknown, but probably late. A bow of the Second Intermediate period, bound with birch bark, is in the Metropolitan Museum,[6] and birch bast was used for the binding of the Eighteenth Dynasty chariot in the Museum at Florence.[1]

SILICIFIED WOOD[7]

Silicified, petrified or fossil wood is wood the original substance of which has been removed by natural agencies and replaced by silica in such a manner that the structure of the wood has been preserved.[8] Silicified wood occurs plentifully in Egypt and is widely distributed,[9] being found near Cairo, in both the eastern and western deserts, in the Fayum and in Sinai. Although very hard, this material was employed occasionally for carving and a statuette of it from the late Eighteenth or Nineteenth Dynasty[10] is in the Cairo Museum and Petrie mentions a unique scarab of silicified wood, of Nineteenth or Twenty-fifth Dynasty date.[11] Grinders (hammer stones) and other tools of this wood are known from the neolithic period[12] and a worked fragment probably from the Badarian period.[13]

The genera and species of much of this silicified wood have been determined,[14] but

---

[1] U. Fasolo, quoted by G. Botti, *Aegyptus*, XXXI (1951), pp. 192–8.

[2] H. Schäfer, *Armenisches Holz in altägyptischen Wagnereien* (*Sitz. Preuss. Ak.*, 1931, pp. 730–42). Cf. G. Clarke, *Antiquity*, XV (1941), pp. 58, 59.

[3] G. Caton-Thompson and E. W. Gardner, *Desert Fayum*, pp. 88, 122.

[4] No. J. 48153.

[5] W. M. F. Petrie, *Memphis*, I, p. 15, Pl. LI (18).

[6] W. C. Hayes, *Scepter*, II, p. 29.

[7] Cf. J. R. Harris, *Lexicographical Studies*, pp. 178–9.

[8] Cf. M. M. Ibrahim, *Bull. Inst. d'Ég.*, XXV (1943), pp. 159–82; XXXIV (1953), pp. 317–28; N. M. Shukri, *Bull. Inst. d'Ég.*, XXVI (1944), pp. 71–75.

[9] The literature is too extensive to quote, cf. E. H. Keldani, *Bibliography of Geology and Related Sciences Concerning Egypt* (s.v. Petrified Forests); C. D. Sherborn, *Bibliography of Scientific and Technical Literature Relating to Egypt* (s.v. Forest (Fossil)).

[10] G. Legrain, *Statues et Statuettes*, I, pp. 55–56, Pls. LX, LXI.

[11] W. M. F. Petrie, *Scarabs and Cylinders*, p. 9; *Buttons and Design Scarabs*, p. 23.

[12] G. Caton-Thompson and E. W. Gardner, *Desert Fayum*, pp. 32, 87.

[13] G. Brunton and G. Caton-Thompson, *Badarian Civilisation*, p. 102.

[14] F. Unger, *Der versteinerte Wald bei Kairo*, 1858; Krauss and Schenk, quoted by Barron (*Topog. and Geol. of the District between Cairo and Suez*, p. 58); F. W. Oliver, *Trans. Norfolk and Norwich Naturalists Society*, XIII (1930–31), p. 176; A. C. Seward, *Leaves of Dicotyledons from the Nubian Sandstone of Egypt*, Geological Survey of Egypt, 1935; M. M. Ibrahim, *Bull. Inst. d'Ég.*, XXV (1943), pp. 159–82; XXXIV (1953), pp. 317–28; N. M. Shukri, *Bull. Inst. d'Ég.*, XXVI (1944), pp. 71–75.

it is unnecessary to quote them here, since none of the kinds of wood is known from historical times.

CHARCOAL

Charcoal, which may be dealt with conveniently in connexion with wood, was until comparatively recently, when it was largely displaced by paraffin oil (kerosene), the principal fuel of Egypt and it is still much used.

At one time charcoal-burning was extensively carried out in the eastern desert and in Sinai, in both of which localities it still lingers on, though to a very limited extent, and it is this industry that has been largely responsible for the destruction of trees in those districts.

Charcoal has often been found in connexion with ancient Egypt, for example in Badarian graves;[1] in First Dynasty tombs at Saqqara;[2] in two of the store rooms of the pyramid temple of Menkaurē (Fourth Dynasty)[3] and in early dynastic tombs at Naga el Deir,[4] and it is mentioned as being distributed to the masons who cut the corridors of one of the royal tombs in the Valley of the Tombs of the Kings.[5]

The making of charcoal was a natural outcome of the burning of wood, and the first deliberate making must have been very early in Egyptian history, though the date is unknown. The value of charcoal in the progress of civilization must have been enormous, for without charcoal any advance in metallurgy beyond the most primitive methods would have been difficult, if not impossible.

---

[1] G. Brunton, *Mostagedda*, pp. 8, 9.

[2] J. E. Quibell, *Saqqara, 1912–1914*, p. 15; W. B. Emery, *Hor-Aha*, p. 70.

[3] G. A. Reisner, *Mycerinus*, p. 238.

[4] G. A. Reisner, *Naga-ed-Dêr*, III, p. 157.

[5] On an ostracon (No. J. 33857) of Twentieth Dynasty date in the Cairo Museum.

Chapter XIX
HISTORICAL SUMMARY[1]

From what is known about a people, to trace their gradual growth from a primitive state to one of advanced civilization is a task for the historian, and I have no intention of trespassing in this matter, but I hope to be pardoned if I endeavour to piece together, very briefly and in a very elementary manner, the most important of the facts recorded and to give some little indication of their bearing upon the condition of the ancient Egyptians and upon their intercourse with other nations.

Ancient Egyptian history, like that of many other countries, may be divided roughly into a Stone Age, a Copper Age,[2] a Bronze Age, and an Iron Age, each in turn gradually giving place to the next. The distingushing feature of these several periods was not the mere employment of stone, copper, bronze, or iron, as the case might be, since each of these was employed in all the succeeding periods and was even known as a curiosity and occasionally used in the preceding period, but consisted in the use of the special material, after which it is named, for weapons and tools.

Up to the present time fossil remains of primitive man have not been discovered in Egypt, neither remains of the earlier stages of his development when he was merely the genus *homo* (who probably dates back to the end of the Pliocene period or the beginning of the Pleistocene period, possibly a million years or so ago), nor remains of the later and finished stage of his physical evolution after he had become *homo sapiens* (who is much more recent and possibly not more than fifty thousand years or so old).

The first inhabitants of Egypt of whom there is any knowledge were the Old-Stone Age or paleolithic people. Whence they came and the reason for their coming are unknown, but that they must have originated outside Egypt is manifest unless Egypt is 'the cradle of the human race', which is not suggested by anyone. Once in the country, however, abundant game and water and a pleasant climate would be sufficient reasons for their remaining. These earliest Egyptians date back from about 12,000 years ago to possibly about 30,000 years ago or earlier.

'The Pleistocene period during which Paleolithic Man hunted along the banks of the Nile and ranged over the surrounding hills and plateaus was a time of copious rainfall in Egypt. The dry wadis of the desert were running streams and the landscapes were pleasantly diversified with forest and grassland over which wandered troops of wild animals. Reaching far beyond its present bounds, the ancestral Nile flowed rapidly over a pebbly bed, augmented on its journey northward by a host of

---

[1] References previously given have not been repeated.

[2] To group the Egyptian Copper and Bronze Ages together and to call them both the Copper Age, or both the Bronze Age, as is sometimes done, is most misleading.

tributaries draining the surrounding country. The Nile of the present day is but "a dwindled shadow of the original river".' [1]

Neither the habitations nor the graves of these people, if they had either, have been discovered, only large numbers of characteristic stone weapons and implements (mostly flint and chert) that have been found in various parts of the country. With these their owners could hunt and fight, and paleolithic man must have been essentially a hunter, depending largely for food on the animals he killed, supplemented by certain fruits, seeds (cereal grain) and roots he found growing wild: he was, therefore, a wanderer and a food gatherer and not a food producer, which means that he was not yet civilized. Since pottery containers or animal skins for water had not yet been invented, paleolithic man could not go very far from his water supply and the range of his wanderings was, therefore, restricted.

The exact manner in which civilization developed in Egypt may never be known, but it seems probable that the first step towards it was taken when a community of the hunting paleolithic nomads (possibly at first only women and young children), driven almost certainly by a gradual diminution of rainfall and a gradual conversion of the hills and plateaus into desert, with a resulting scarcity of game, settled down temporarily near the Nile, or on the borders of the Fayum lake, and there discovered that a constant supply of the grain they were accustomed to gather in a haphazard manner, and which sometimes failed, might be assured by sowing, for almost certainly it was agriculture that first anchored man to one locality by making a permanent hunting life both unnecessary and impossible, thus paving the way for the arts and crafts that are essential to material civilization. All that would have been necessary to have started the ball of civilization rolling would have been for someone, either accidentally or intentionally, to have thrown ripe grain (barley or wheat) [2] on to a patch of mud left bare after the flood water of the river had subsided, and when the grain sprouted (which in Egypt would have been very soon after the sowing) to have realized that it was the direct result of the sowing and that never again need there be any shortage of food, since man had the power to grow it, and grain was a food that could be stored easily in a dry climate like that of Egypt without deteriorating.

But since seeds were falling regularly on the ground and germinating wherever there were plants, and so producing an object lesson in the elements of agriculture. the artificial sowing of seed may surely have originated independently in more than one place and, if so, the initial Egyptian sowing may not have been the first in the history of the world, as suggested by Professor T. Cherry,[3] but merely an independent repetition of what had been done elsewhere under different conditions. Even imported knowledge of grain growing, though improbable, does not seem absolutely excluded, since the paleolithic hunters may have been in touch with kindred in the north, or they themselves may have ranged as far northward as Palestine and Syria, the north-

---

[1] K. S. Sandford and W. J. Arkell, *Paleolithic Man and the Nile Valley in Nubia and Upper Egypt*, p. xv.

[2] Both barley and wheat have been found in Egypt from the neolithic period, millet not being known until the predynastic period.

[3] T. Cherry, 'The Discovery of Agriculture', in *Proceedings of the Australian Association for the Advancement of Science*, 1921.

east being the direction where other early civilizations arose. The probability, how-ever, is in favour of agriculture having been practised first in Egypt, since, as pointed out by Professor Cherry, nowhere else in the world do such favourable conditions exist. Thus, the Nile flood, which commences about the beginning of July, subsides in November, and seeds sown, either naturally or artificially, germinate after the summer is over, and so the young plants, which would be killed by the heat of the summer, are able to live and grow. In the case of Mesopotamia, the flood water of the Euphrates and Tigris arrives and subsides earlier than that of the Nile and the conditions for agriculture are, therefore, less favourable, since the young plants that sprang up would be scorched by the heat of the summer and would die.

With respect to the period when desiccation set in, Sandford states [1] that 'Complete failure of rainfall . . . seems to have started in Nubia and to have spread slowly north-ward along the Nile. The western plains and plateaus probably lost their surface run off in later Middle Paleolithic times . . .' 'The condition of absolute desert may be of late date near the Nile Valley. In Neolithic times there was a greater freedom of move-ment west of the Nile, especially in the north, than is now possible and crops were raised on ground now barren.' Sandford also says [1] of Upper Egypt in Middle Paleolithic times that 'No signs of desert-like conditions are to be seen' and that north of Qau 'There is no indication that the rainfall had failed in this part of the Nile Valley' and that 'Man could still wander at will at any rate between the Nile and the Red Sea, and westward beyond Kharga Oasis.'

The increase of population in Egypt ultimately and inevitably led to an extension of the natural irrigation system and land near the river not covered by the annual flood had water conducted to it by artificial channels. It is often assumed that agricul-ture commenced with artificial irrigation, but this would not have been needed until the settled population in any one district had outgrown the grain supply of the naturally-inundated land of that district, and a very long period may have elapsed between the earliest agriculture in Egypt and any attempt to extend artificially the area of cultivation.

It is suggested sometimes that agriculture may have originated from the practice of either burying wild grain, such as barley, in graves, or of scattering it on the sur-face of newly-made graves. Though plausible and attractive, this is very improbable with respect to Egypt. Thus, in the neolithic settlement at Merimda, although grain was placed on the body to serve as food for the dead person, there is no record of this grain showing signs of having germinated and, even if exceptionally some of it had commenced to grow, the chance of the young plants reaching the surface of the ground would have been very small. At later periods, too, grain was sometimes placed in graves, but it was usually, if not always, in receptacles, such as baskets or pots, where it had no opportunity of germinating. At Merimda the dead were buried, not in special cemeteries, but among the buildings of the settlement, that is to say on high, dry ground, and when later the burial was at a distance from the houses, in places set apart, these were never, so far as is known, in the inundated plain, but always on the edge of the dry desert, and in such cases any grain scattered on the surface of the graves would have stood a very poor chance of survival. It seems

---

[1] K. S. Sandford, *Paleolithic Man and the Nile Valley in Upper and Middle Egypt*, pp. 125–6.

improbable, too, that 'graveyard tillage', as it has been termed, could ever have led to an artificial irrigation system, such as is practised in Egypt and with which the early agriculture in the country seems inseparably bound up.

When once some of the nomad people had become settled in one place, even though at first only temporarily, needs would arise and could be satisfied that either were not felt before, or that were not previously capable of realization. Thus, shelters from the weather would be built, baskets and pots would be made as containers for grain and water respectively, sleeping mats would be plaited, clothing would be woven, food would be cooked, to the growing of grain would be added the growing of flax to make linen, and animals would be tamed and others would be bred in order to secure a constant supply of meat and skins, each advance, however, resulting in a loss of freedom, since hunting as a permanent whole-time occupation is incompatible with civilization as it does not leave any time for the development of arts and crafts. This is what actually did happen, the shadowy Old-Stone Age (paleolithic) people being succeeded [1] (possibly about 12,000 years ago) by the New-Stone Age or neolithic Egyptians, who until recently were as unsubstantial as their predecessors, though their stone weapons and implements were of a more advanced type and the flint industry of Egypt attained an excellence that has never been surpassed, or even equalled, elsewhere. Of these neolithic folk, settlements and cemeteries have been discovered during recent years,[2] which prove that, although still in the Stone Age, that is without any knowledge of metals, they were no longer merely food gatherers, but food producers and that they practised agriculture, domesticated animals, dressed hides, plaited baskets and mats, wove fabrics, made pottery, made bone as well as stone implements, made shell and stone beads and small stone vases, all of which connote some degree of civilization and a more or less settled mode of life. Hunting and fishing, though still carried on, gradually became of secondary importance.

Up to the present only a few neolithic sites have been excavated, of which the three principal are all near Cairo, one (in the Fayum) on a lake about fifty miles to the south-west, another (Merimda) [3] about thirty miles to the north-west near the west bank of the river, and the third (Helwan) [3] about twenty miles to the south, also not far from the river, but on the east bank. The so-called 'neolithic site' at Maadi near Cairo is not included, since according to the excavators 'The neolithic settlers at Maadi knew copper very well, and apparently possessed large quantities of it.' [4,5]

This neolithic existence, slowly and steadily improving all the time, continued for several thousand years and then gradually and automatically came to an end as metals became known and as their use increased, the beginning of the knowledge of metals possibly dating from about 5000 B.C., or some 7,000 years ago.

The use of metals (at the outset copper and gold) was naturally at first only very

---

[1] Traces of mesolithic culture have been found at Helwan and elsewhere.

[2] G. Caton-Thompson and E. W. Gardner, *Desert Fayum*; G. Caton-Thompson, *Man*, XXXII (1932), pp. 129–35; H. Junker, *Merimde-Benisalâme*, 1929, 1930; P. Bovier-Lapierre, *Congrès Int. de Géog., Le Caire, Avril 1925*, IV (1926), pp. 268–82.

[3] Cf. however, E. J. Baumgartel, *Cultures of Prehistoric Egypt*, I, pp. 120–2.

[4] O. Menghin and M. Amer, *Excavations of the Eg. University . . . at Ma'adi, First Prelim. Report*, p. 48.

[5] Cf. E. J. Baumgartel, *Cultures of Prehistoric Egypt*, I, pp. 121–2.

occasional and was confined to small articles of personal adornment, but later they were employed in greater quantity, gold always chiefly for ornament, and copper for weapons, tools and such household utensils as ewers, basins and dishes; silver and lead also became known, though they were not used to any great extent until a very late period.[1]

Although both copper and gold occur naturally in the metallic state, other things being equal, gold is the more likely to be discovered and used first, partly on account of its occurrence in the form of glittering and attractive yellow particles and partly because of its great malleability, since it is readily shaped into simple ornaments. In Egypt, however, although gold occurred plentifully in certain localities and native copper very rarely, copper objects have been found of earlier date than those of gold, but the evidence is as yet so scanty that this does not necessarily mean that copper was used first (though this may have been so), since the earliest gold may not have been buried, or, if it was, the graves may have been robbed.

It has been suggested that the earliest copper known was always native metal and in certain countries (notably North America) this was undoubtedly the case; but the use of native copper has not always led to the method of producing it from ore and in Egypt there is no definite evidence of native copper and no need to postulate either its existence or use, since a copper ore (malachite), from which the metal might have been obtained easily and from which it may be proved to have been obtained at an early period, was employed in large amount for painting round the eyes and for producing a blue colour in glaze, at a date not only as early as that of the use of the metal itself but probably earlier.

Malachite occurs in a number of different localities both in Sinai and in the eastern desert, in the latter of which no date can be fixed for mining before about the Twelfth Dynasty (about 2000 B.C.), but there is evidence of expeditions to Sinai as early as the Third Dynasty (about 2750 B.C.) which may have been either for copper ore or for turquoise (unfortunately it is not known which), and of the mining of copper ore in the Old Kingdom (about 2750 B.C. to 2480 B.C.) of which period copper slag, chips of ore, broken crucibles and an ingot mould have been found and, since malachite (possibly from Sinai) was employed in the Badarian and predynastic periods respectively, it seems feasible that mining (which at first would consist merely in the extraction of ore from surface deposits and only later of excavation) dates from these periods. Some slight confirmation of the early date of the Sinai mining is the occurrence of a small proportion of manganese in copper objects of both the middle predynastic period and also of First or Second Dynasty date,[2] which seems to indicate that the ore from which the metal in these cases was derived had been obtained from Sinai, where there are abundant deposits of oxides of manganese in close proximity to the copper ore. The object of middle predynastic date referred to is a large cast axe-head of copper weighing three and a half pounds, and if this were made from Sinai ore, then the copper industry in Egypt was already in an advanced state.

Since metallic copper may be produced from malachite by the very simple process

---

[1] Cf. E. J. Baumgartel, *Cultures of Prehistoric Egypt*, II, pp. 1–23.

[2] Probably manganese would be found in other ancient Egyptian copper objects if search were made.

of heating it under certain conditions in a wood or charcoal fire, it is highly probable that the first production of copper was by accident from this ore (the usual ore of surface deposits), the constant use of which would present innumerable opportunities for its accidental heating in such a manner that would produce a small quantity of the metal.

Coghlan states that, contrary to the usual idea, a camp fire, or 'hole in the ground' fire, would be unlikely to have led to the first accidental production of metallic copper, and he suggests that this may have occurred either in a pottery kiln, or in connexion with the making of glaze, which he seems to associate with glazed pottery. But glazed pottery is very late in Egypt, faience not being glazed pottery, and pottery kilns were not known in Egypt until some time after the discovery of metallic copper. Glazed steatite, glazed solid quartz, and glazed quartz frit (faience) were, however, known from a very early date, the glazing was probably carried out in a small closed chamber, or kiln, and the glaze was often a blue colour obtained from malachite, a copper ore, and all the conditions would thus have existed for the accidental reduction of the malachite to metallic copper. On the other hand, it is possible, as Reed has suggested and Coghlan now accepts, that smelting was not discovered in connexion with glazing, but as a result of the melting of native copper.

In the earliest graves in which copper has been found in Egypt, it was in the form of small primitive articles, such as beads, pins, rings and needles, and only in graves of later periods were there weapons and tools, that is to say, copper did not appear suddenly in a comparatively highly developed form as would be expected had it been imported, but all the stages of evolution from small and simple objects to larger and more complex ones have been found in proper sequence. This gradual increase in the amount of copper employed and the progressive improvement in the size and nature of the objects made, together with the very early use of malachite, might seem to indicate that copper smelting may have been of Egyptian origin, but Frankfort, while admitting the facts, does not admit the inference, pointing out that 'history is no matter of logic and comparative archaeology plainly proves . . . that the use of copper on a considerable scale was due to Asiatic initiative'.[1] That copper working was a Mesopotamian discovery has been maintained by several authorities, but it seems likely that its origins are to be sought even farther afield, in north Persia and in the regions immediately south of the Caucasus mountains between the Caspian Sea and the Black Sea, where copper ores are plentiful, and where there are ancient mines and slag heaps. Aitchison suggests,[2] probably correctly, that copper smelting was discovered in these regions during the latter centuries of the fifth millennium B.C., and that the knowledge spread thence to Anatolia and later to Mesopotamia and Egypt. A great deal, however, depends upon the correct dating of copper objects from different sources, about which there is still dispute, and in view of this it is not shirking the difficulty if the question of the origin of copper working is left unanswered for the present.

Closely following and consequent upon the use of copper tools in the late predynastic period was the wonderful stone vase industry, which reached its zenith dur-

---

[1] H. Frankfort, *Antiquaries Journal*, VIII (1928), p. 230, *n.* I.
[2] L. Aitchison, *History of Metals*, I, pp. 40–41.

ing the early dynastic period, and nowhere has there been found such a wealth of beautifully made, handsome stone vases as in Egypt, the stones employed including, not only the comparatively soft alabaster (calcite), but hard diorite, granite, quartz, rock crystal, greywacke ('schist') and volcanic rock. Literally thousands of these vases (mostly broken) have been found in early dynastic tombs and in the step pyramid at Saqqara, especially in the latter. In the Third and Fourth Dynasties and the dynasties immediately following came the phenomenal working of stone for building pyramid tombs and mortuary and other temples, and the oldest and largest stone buildings in the world belong to this date. The hard stone statues, too, of this period have long been a source of wonder and admiration on account of their excellence.

One of the great landmarks in the history of civilization was the discovery of bronze, which displaced copper for many purposes, the Copper Age gradually giving place to the Bronze Age. This alloy, which is a mixture of copper and tin, was first made in western Asia and was used in Mesopotamia about 1,000 years before the knowledge of it spread to Egypt. Although there may have been, and probably were, a few sporadic importations of bronze into Egypt, possibly even as early as the Fourth Dynasty, it was not in general use until about the Twelfth Dynasty (about 2000 B.C.) from which period tools and other objects of bronze are known, and the Middle Kingdom, therefore, may be considered as the beginning of the Bronze Age in Egypt. Bronze of this date was, however, made by mixing ores of copper and tin, and it was not until the Eighteenth Dynasty that the alloy was produced by mixing and melting together the two metals.

Whether bronze was ever made in Egypt, or whether the bronze objects found were fashioned from material imported into the country in the form of ingots, is uncertain, but since tin was known in Egypt in the Eighteenth Dynasty (a few objects of this metal and also a small quantity of artificial tin oxide from this period having been discovered) it seems probable that at least from this date onwards bronze was made locally from imported tin. At first the tin required was obtained from western Asia, possibly from near Byblos in Syria, but later this source of supply seems to have failed, probably because the ore became exhausted, and tin then reached the eastern Mediterranean from western Europe (Brittany, Cornwall and Spain).

The Bronze Age in Egypt lasted about thirteen hundred years and was succeeded by the Iron Age. Iron working, like bronze working, had its origin in western Asia and it did not become an Egyptian industry until more than 2,000 years after its discovery in Asia. The earliest iron objects found in Egypt are a few small beads of predynastic date, the metal of which has been proved by chemical analysis to be of meteoric origin and, therefore, not made by man. Although this was not the only instance of the utilization of meteoric iron by the ancient Egyptians, only one other is known, and from the predynastic period until the end of the Eighteenth Dynasty very few specimens of iron objects have been discovered in the country, of which several are probably of later date than that assigned to them by their finders, leaving only two, now iron rust, but once iron objects that have been tested and found not to be of meteoric origin. From the tomb of Tutankhamūn at the end of the Eighteenth Dynasty (about 1350 B.C.) there is an iron dagger (a gift to the king from western Asia) and a few very small typically Egyptian objects, almost certainly made in Egypt either from meteoric iron or from a small piece of imported iron, probably also a present from western Asia. After this there is a gradual increase in the number of iron objects known, but the first group of iron tools yet found dates from about 700 B.C., which may, therefore, be considered as the beginning of the Iron Age in Egypt.

The earliest iron smelting of which evidence has been found in Egypt was at Naucratis and Defenneh in the Delta, about the sixth century B.C., but the source of the ore dealt with is not known. Iron ores, however, were mined anciently both in the eastern desert (possibly by the Romans) and also near Aswan. It is possible that iron was worked in Nubia somewhat earlier than in Egypt, perhaps during the seventh century B.C.

The first production of iron was almost certainly an accident, possibly due to the use by mistake of iron ore in place of copper ore, and there cannot be any doubt that when first obtained the metal was treated in the same manner as copper and bronze in order to shape it, namely by hammering it cold, which naturally was found to be useless. This is likely to have happened many times until by chance the metal was hammered before it cooled, when partial success would have been obtained, and eventually it would have been realized that for complete command over the new metal it must be hammered while red-hot. Also, the only kind of hammer the Egyptians knew until late, apart from wooden mallets, was a stone hammer without handle, with which it would not have been possible to beat red-hot metal. The first iron, however, cannot have been much, if any, improvement over copper and bronze for weapons and tools, since it was less easy to work and it was not any harder than hammered copper and bronze and any cutting edge given to it by hammering would readily have become blunted. Somehow it was discovered eventually that if repeatedly heated in a charcoal fire and well hammered between the separate heatings and cooled by plunging it into water, iron would acquire a hardness superior to that of copper and bronze and it was only at this stage that it became of much practical use. This experience was gained before iron was known to the Egyptians, to whom iron smelting and iron working were probably taught by blacksmiths from western Asia or Greece.

One important material employed in ancient Egypt was a vitreous glaze, which was used in small amount during the Badarian period to cover objects of stone (steatite), and a little later, during the predynastic period, for coating both steatite and quartz, at which period, too, objects were made of powdered quartz (heated possibly with a small proportion of natron or salt to make the quartz cohere), and these were then glazed. It is to this glazed quartz frit that the name of Egyptian faience is given and the industry became an important one and reached a high state of development at an early date. Neither the glazing of stone nor the making of such an extraordinarily complex material as faience is likely to have been invented in more than one place, and it has generally been assumed that both originated in Egypt, since the Egyptian finds have appeared to have the priority of age, and nowhere was faience made on such a scale and in such perfection.[1] Recently, however, the problem of the origin of faience has been carefully reconsidered by Stone and Thomas,[2] who

---

[1] Cf. A. Lucas, *J.E.A.*, XXII (1936), pp. 141–64.
[2] J. F. S. Stone and L. C. Thomas, *Proceedings of the Prehistoric Society*, XXII (1956), pp. 37–84.

have examined the records of early finds in some detail. From the available evidence they conclude that both glazed steatite and faience made their first almost contemporary appearance in northern Mesopotamia during the fifth millennium B.C., and that from this centre the knowledge of the materials and their production was carried southward and to Egypt, at first by trade and then possibly by the Naqada II invaders. They have also outlined the subsequent spread of faience to the Indus valley and Anatolia during the third millennium, and its eventual distribution over the Near East and Europe in the first half of the second millennium.

A very important outcome of glaze was glass, which is merely glaze used as a separate material instead of as a coating on other materials. The evolution from glaze to glass, so far as can be judged from the known evidence, took a very long time, a likely reason for this being the conservatism of the glaze worker, who, like artisans of all ages and particularly of early times, would naturally have been averse to new methods and non-receptive of fresh ideas. Although glaze, while in the crucible ready for use, or even if it fell upon the floor, was glass, the worker would have been so occupied with glazing, and research so foreign to his nature that any experiments respecting new possibilities for his material would not have occurred to him and any development would have been delayed until there happened to be a glaze worker, with the special inquiring turn of mind that is so rare even today, and then some considerable time must have elapsed before the experience necessary for the manipulation of the material on the new lines could be acquired. Although doubtless originating, as suggested, as a development of glaze, glass making would soon have branched off as a separate industry.

The early history of glass and its country of origin are somewhat obscure, though it was almost certainly not an Egyptian invention, since glass making on a large scale was not practised until the New Kingdom. The scattered examples of glass that have been reported from earlier periods are all small and relatively insignificant, the majority probably accidental products intended as faience, a few perhaps imported, and others misdated. The sudden emergence of a flourishing glass industry and the production of vessels and other larger pieces at the beginning of the Eighteenth Dynasty is hardly consistent with these earlier finds and was almost certainly the result of outside influence. It is true that the extensive use during the New Kingdom of glass inlay for coffins, boxes, furniture and other objects appears to be typically Egyptian, but this has little bearing on the origin of glass, since the technique of inlaying with coloured stones had long been established in Egypt, and the new material was simply employed in imitation of the old.

Petrie and others have maintained that Syria was the home of glass making and that the outburst of glass working in Egypt in the early Eighteenth Dynasty was due to the introduction of Syrian workmen after the Egyptian conquests in Asia.[1] But, although glass making may have been a Syrian industry before about 1500 B.C. (as it certainly was much later during the Arab period when Tyre, Tripoli, Damascus and Aleppo were all noted for their glass), no proof of this can be found and no glass-making centres in Syria of such an early date are known, though this may be due largely to the fact that relatively few sites have been excavated.

---

[1] W. M. F. Petrie, *Descriptive Sociology, Ancient Egyptians*, p. 187.

With respect to the Indus valley civilization, it has been stated [1] that 'no true glass has yet been found either at Harappa or Mohenjo-Daro', though there is a material the outward resemblance of which 'to an opaque glass is very close' and which 'to the casual eye resembles an opaque glass', but 'the granular nature of its paste proves it definitely not to be glass'.

Beck,[2] among others, was of the opinion that glass making originated in Mesopotamia, and this seems inherently probable in that both glazed steatite and faience can be traced to this region and glass occurs in many forms on Mesopotamian sites from 1800 B.C. A lump of blue glass, now in the British Museum, found in Mesopotamia, 'which must be at least as early as 2200 B.C. and is probably older',[3] is not part of an object and, although as it now exists it is glass, it may possibly have been made as glaze, before glass was being used for separate objects. It was found by itself and no other glass is known from the same site. The finder says [3] 'There is of course nothing to show that this isolated fragment of glass was made at Eridu or in Mesopotamia at all—it might be an importation from Egypt. . . . This piece of glass may merely show that the invention had reached Babylon at least as early as 2200 B.C., though it certainly was rarely used there or we must have found examples of its use as inlay, etc., on the other sites of that period.' In the published description of 'The Royal Cemetery' at Ur by Woolley, glass is not mentioned in the Index, but in the chapter on beads it is stated that there are two instances of 'glass paste', whatever that may be, in both the predynastic cemetery and in the much later Sargonid period. The most significant find is, however, a small 'cylinder' of clear glass found at Tell Asmar and dated to the Agade period, about 2600 or 2700 B.C.[4] This is, in fact, a piece of glass tube of a type regularly used in manufacture and would appear to indicate that glass working was already established in Mesopotamia in the first half of the third millennium B.C.

Inventions that are generally admitted to be of Egyptian origin are the use of papyrus as a writing material, mummification and the mural painting in tombs and temples.

Although Egypt is somewhat isolated geographically and was still more isolated anciently, on account of the very considerable difficulties of communication that then existed, and although it was largely self-contained and needed no outside help for the necessaries and little for the luxuries of life, yet it was not cut off absolutely from the rest of the world, and two important examples of the result of intercourse between Egypt and its neighbours, namely bronze and iron, have already been mentioned. But, in addition to these, other foreign articles found their way into Egypt, though, until a late period, such imports were few in number, the greater proportion of the materials used being of local origin. Thus the building materials, brick, stone, mortar and plaster, were all local; glaze, glass and pottery (wherever they may have originated) were all made in the country from native materials; the metals gold and silver [5]

---

[1] E. Mackay, in Sir John Marshall, *Mohenjo-Daro and the Indus Civilization*, pp. 576, 578, 582.

[2] H. C. Beck, *Ancient Egypt*, 1934, p. 19.

[3] H. R. Hall, *A Season's Work at Ur*, pp. 213–14.

[4] H. Frankfort, *Iraq Excavations of the Oriental Institute, 1932–33*, pp. 56–58.

[5] Some silver was imported from the end of the Twelfth Dynasty, and perhaps very much earlier.

and their alloy electrum, as also the ores of copper and lead from which these two latter metals were produced all occurred in the country; the animal fats and beeswax were native products; the pigments were almost entirely naturally occurring materials, or were made from such materials; the precious and semi-precious stones employed, with two exceptions (jade, of which only very few examples are known, and lapis lazuli) were of local origin, as were also the ornamental and monumental stones (except obsidian); the textile fabrics were woven in Egypt and baskets, ropes and mats were made from fibres that grew in the country; the skins made into leather were local and most of the dyes with which the textile fabrics and the leather were coloured were probably Egyptian; and the foodstuffs (chiefly cereals, green vegetables, oil,[1] fruit, honey, meat and fish) were all produced in the country.

The principal materials imported into Egypt may now be considered, but especially those received up to the early part of the Eighteenth Dynasty, at about which period began a much greater intercourse between Egypt and other nations, largely as a result of the Egyptian conquests in Asia, the natural effect of which was a considerable increase in the import of commodities from abroad, which included a number of articles received as tribute or taken as the spoils of war.

The imports were almost entirely either from western Asia, or from Nubia and the Sudan, and to what extent materials were ordinarily received from the countries to the west of Egypt is not known, though this was certainly not an important source of supply.

The principal materials received from Asia before the beginning of the Eighteenth Dynasty, taking them in alphabetical order, were bronze, and possibly also tin for making bronze, from the Middle Kingdom onwards; lapis lazuli, continuously from predynastic times; oil, probably chiefly olive oil, from the early dynastic period onwards; resins and wood continuously from the predynastic period.

From about the middle of the Eighteenth Dynasty a number of new materials began to be imported into Egypt from Asia, the principal of which were copper, which up to about this date had probably been produced largely from local ores; iron in the form of a few small objects with probably also a very small amount of metal, the amount gradually increasing until iron began to be smelted in the country; orpiment and probably realgar during the Empire, as also varnish or varnish resins, the import of which latter continued until about the Twenty-sixth Dynasty, when it practically ceased.

The materials received from, or through, Nubia and the Sudan were chiefly ebony, gold, ivory, obsidian (the total amount of which was not great), ostrich feathers, leopard skins, fragrant gum-resins and fragrant woods. It is worthy of note that, so far as is known, there was not any material used in ancient Egypt until about the Eighteenth Dynasty that can be traced to India, though India and Ceylon possessed, among other commodities, precious and semi-precious stones and odoriferous resins and fragrant woods, materials that were in great demand in Egypt and that are of small bulk and easily transported. It is possible, however, that some of the fragrant woods mentioned in the Egyptian records as having been received from Punt may have been of Indian origin. From the Eighteenth Dynasty onwards the varnish resins

---

[1] A small amount of oil for special purposes was imported.

may have come from, or through India, and possibly at a later date indigo and, still later, certainly cotton.

To bring to Egypt most of the foreign materials enumerated Egyptian ships were trading both in the Mediterranean and the Red Sea, the former sailing along the coasts of Palestine and Syria to the port of Byblos, especially to carry the bulky timber from the Lebanons that could not be transported easily otherwise, and the latter down the Gulf of Suez and the Red Sea to the Somali and Arabian coasts; the Sudan and Nubian produce was carried by way of the Nile, which is a great natural highway passing through the country from south to north.

At a very early date the whole country, and particularly the desert, was scoured for useful natural materials, thus during the Old Kingdom, when the capital was at Memphis in the Delta, alabaster was quarried near Helwan; amethyst and other semi-precious stones were brought either from the eastern or western desert; a special diorite was brought from the western desert in Nubia; gold from Nubia; granite from Aswan; malachite and copper from the eastern desert and probably also from Sinai; natron from the Wadi Natrun; porphyritic rocks from the eastern desert; 'schist' from between Qena and Quseir and turquoise from Sinai.

Intercourse with other countries meant not only the import of foreign com-modities, but also the export of Egyptian commodities to pay for them, since at the time under consideration, coined money was unknown and barter was the only means of exchange, though values were reckoned in terms of copper, and pieces of gold or silver may have changed hands. Exactly what these exports were is not known, but among the objects the Egyptians had to offer were faience, glass, gold, jewellery, including precious and semi-precious stones, linen, papyrus and stone vessels.

But more valuable than the material objects exchanged was the knowledge given and received, a subject already touched upon, but any detailed discussion of which is outside the scope of the present book.

Appendix

CHEMICAL ANALYSES

MODERN EGYPTIAN GYPSUM [1]

							%	%	%
Gypsum (hydrated calcium sulphate)	...	...	...	...			75.4	85.2	89.9
Sand	...	...	...	...			7.6	3.7	2.1
Calcium carbonate	...	...	...	...			15.2	9.4	7.5
Oxides of iron and aluminium	...	...	...	...			1.0	1.0	0.5
Not determined	...	...	...	...			0.8	0.7	—
							100.0	100.0	100.0

ANCIENT EGYPTIAN LIME MORTAR (PTOLEMAIC PERIOD AND LATER) [2]

						%	%	%	%	%	%	%
Sand	...		29.0	30.6	38.4	25.4	23.8	27.4	8.8
Oxides of iron and aluminium	...	...	3.0	1.8	3.0	2.9	1.7	2.6	1.2
Lime	...		1.8	26.2	20.2	27.3	25.5	27.3	46.1
Magnesia	...		—	—	—	—	—	—	—
Carbon dioxide, combined with water, etc. ...			66.2	41.4	38.4	44.4	49.0	42.7	43.9
			100.0	100.0	100.0	100.0	100.0	100.0	100.0

ANCIENT EGYPTIAN LIME MORTAR (ROMAN PERIOD) [3]

					1 %	2 %	3 %	4 %	5 %
Sand	...	...	...	...	73.5	22.3	54.9	29.1	87.2
Oxides of iron and aluminium	...	...	...	...	3.7	7.5	13.3	4.0	1.5
Lime	...	...	...	...	10.1	33.9	14.6	34.7	5.9
Magnesia	...	...	...	...	0.7	1.8	3.2	2.1	0.4
Sulphur trioxide...	...	...	...	...	1.4	3.2	nil	0.9	—
Carbon dioxide, combined water, etc.	...	...	...	10.6	31.3	14.0	29.2	5.0
					100.0	100.0	100.0	100.0	100.0

[1] From Helwan. Analyses by A. Lucas. Cf. A. Lucas, *Ann. Serv.*, VII (1906), p. 5.

[2] R. Salmoni, 'Sulla Composizione di alcune antiche malte egiziane', *Atti e Memorie della Reale Accad. di Scienze . . . in Padova*, XLIX (1933), pp. 251–6. The method of presentation has been changed by me.

[3] Nos. 1–4. Analyses by A. Lucas. No. 1. Cf. A. Lucas, *Cairo Sc. Journ.*, I (1906–7), p. 82. No. 5. Analysis by L. P. Kinnicutt, quoted by H. H. Gorringe, *Egyptian Obelisks*, p. 169.

ANCIENT EGYPTIAN GYPSUM MORTAR [1]

	1	2	3	4	5	6	7	8	9	10	11	12	13	14	15	16	17	18	19
	%	%	%	%	%	%	%	%	%	%	%	%	%	%	%	%	%	%	%
Gypsum (hydrated calcium sulphate)	99.5	70.7	79.6	80.0	97.3	54.4	89.2	23.4	57.2	54.4	46.9	66.9	73.1	78.0	47.3	54.0	84.0	89.2	78.6
Sand	tr.	9.5	6.9	12.8	2.0	7.8	2.0	4.8	7.4	3.2	12.6	25.5	15.4	12.3	11.5	11.4	8.0	6.0	13.5
Calcium carbonate	—	8.0	3.5	tr.	—	26.6	tr.	58.0	30.4	39.5	37.1	tr.	6.9	4.3	38.6	32.3	8.0	4.8	3.7
Magnesium carbonate	—	1.3	tr.	tr.	—	tr.	tr.	3.8	3.8	tr.	1.3	0.8	1.6	2.1	tr.	1.3	tr.	tr.	0.8
Oxides of iron and aluminium	—	2.6	1.1	1.2	—	2.2	0.8	0.7	1.1	0.6	1.5	2.0	1.8	1.4	1.3	1.0	tr.	—	2.9
Not determined	0.5	7.9	8.9	6.0	0.7	9.0	8.0	9.3	0.1	2.3	0.6	4.8	1.2	1.9	1.3	—	—	—	0.5
	100.0	100.0	100.0	100.0	100.0	100.0	100.0	100.0	100.0	100.0	100.0	100.0	100.0	100.0	100.0	100.0	100.0	100.0	100.0

No. 1. From the tomb of Hetepheres (IVth Dyn.).

Nos. 2–5. From the pyramid of Khufu (IVth Dyn.).

Nos. 6–7. From the pyramid of Khafrē (IVth Dyn.).

Nos. 8–10. From the valley temple of Khafrē (IVth Dyn.).

Nos. 11–16. From the sphinx (IVth Dyn.).

Nos. 17–18. From the Mastabat el Faraun (IVth Dyn.).

No. 19. From the hypostyle hall at Karnak (New Kingdom).

---

[1] Analyses by A. Lucas.

Nos. 2–4, 6–15. Cf. A. Lucas, *Ann. Serv.*, VII (1906), p. 7. (Slightly adjusted. The original figures give 0.1 per cent more gypsum in Nos. 4, 7, 10, 13, and 0.1 per cent less in Nos. 6, 8, 15.)

No. 16. Cf. A. Lucas, *Cairo Sc. Journ.*, I (1906–7), p. 82. (Slightly adjusted. The original figures give 55.0 per cent of gypsum and 1.1 per cent of oxides of iron and aluminium.)

No. 19. Cf. A. Lucas, *Ann. Serv.*, II (1902), p. 180; VII (1906), p. 6.

ANCIENT EGYPTIAN GYPSUM PLASTER [1]

	1	2	3	4	5	6	7	8	9	10	11	12	13	14	15	16	17	18	19	20	21
	%	%	%	%	%	%	%	%	%	%	%	%	%	%	%	%	%	%	%	%	%
Gypsum (hydrated calcium sulphate) ...	68.5	67.1	78.2	76.7	78.1	75.9	83.0	78.1	74.4	84.8	66.3	17.0	75.9	39.8	40.5	42.7	45.0	36.9	15.5	83.3	34.6
Sand	12.0	11.0	10.8	13.0	11.0	11.0	17.0	15.0	15.0	9.0	16.0	10.0	14.0	15.0	30.0	25.0	36.0	27.0	17.0	14.0	27.0
Calcium carbonate [2] ...	19.5	21.9	11.0	10.3	10.9	13.1	tr.	6.9	10.6	6.2	17.7	73.0	10.1	45.2	29.5	32.3	19.0	36.1	67.5	2.7	38.4
	100.0	100.0	100.0	100.0	100.0	100.0	100.0	100.0	100.0	100.0	100.0	100.0	100.0	100.0	100.0	100.0	100.0	100.0	100.0	100.0	100.0

Nos. 1–2. From the 'Cache of Akhenaten' (XVIIIth Dyn.).

Nos. 3–12. From the tomb of Tutankhamūn (XVIIIth Dyn.). Cf. A. Lucas, in H. Carter, *Tut-ankh-Amen*, II, pp. 162–3 (Appendix II). Some of these specimens are of a grey colour owing to the presence of particles of unburnt fuel.

No. 13. Used as a cement to repair the lid of the sarcophagus in the tomb of Tutankhamūn (XVIIIth Dyn.) This was the principal cementing material, though there was also another cement in places consisting of a mixture of resin and powdered limestone. Cf. A. Lucas, in H. Carter, *op. cit*, p. 168.

Nos. 14–17. From the tomb of Seti II (XIXth Dyn.).

No. 18. From the tomb of Siptah (XIXth Dyn.).

No. 19. From the tomb of Setnakht (XXth Dyn.).

Nos. 20–21. From the tomb of Ramses XI (XXth Dyn.).

---

[1] Analyses by A. Lucas.
[2] With a small proportion of oxides of iron and aluminium.

ANCIENT EGYPTIAN GYPSUM MORTAR

	1	2	3	4	5	6	7
	%	%	%	%	%	%	%
Gypsum (hydrated calcium sulphate) ...	52.1	92.3	97.3	91.4	88.5	45.6	69.4
Anhydrous calcium sulphate	33.6	nil	—	—	—	—	—
Sand	6.4	1.3	1.1	4.8	1.4	10.3	2.7
Calcium carbonate	5.7	4.6	—	0.6[1]	4.7[2]	41.3	12.9
Oxides of iron and aluminium	2.0	1.7	1.2	1.5	1.5	1.2	0.6
Loss on ignition (moisture)	—	—	1.3	2.2	2.4	1.6[4]	13.4
	99.8	99.9	100.9	100.9[3]	100.7[3]	100.0	99.0

Nos. 1–2. From the 'bent' pyramid (IVth Dyn.). Analyses by Z. Iskander, *Ann. Serv.*, LII (1954), p. 272.

Nos. 3–5. From mastabas at Giza (IVth Dyn.). Analyses by Müller, in H. Junker, *Giza*, I, p. 90.

No. 6. From the pyramid complex of Sahurē (Vth Dyn.). Analysis by Rathgen and Brittner, in L. Borchardt, *Sahu-rē*, I, p. 80.

No. 7. From the steps of the New York obelisk (Roman period). Analysis by R. H. Richards, quoted by H. H. Gorringe, *Egyptian Obelisks*, p. 168.

ANCIENT EGYPTIAN GYPSUM PLASTER

	1	2	3	4
	%	%	%	%
Gypsum (hydrated calcium sulphate)	92.8	89.9	81.5	82.9
Sand	2.7	4.0	5.3	4.3
Calcium carbonate	tr.	1.6	9.5	9.8
Calcium phosphate	nil	0.4	—	—
Magnesium carbonate	—	—	0.6	0.8
Sodium chloride	0.7	0.6	—	—
Oxides of iron and aluminium	1.2	1.2	2.7	3.2
Loss on ignition (organic matter)	2.0	1.6	—	—
	99.4	99.3	99.6	101.0

Nos. 1–2. From the sarcophagus in the pyramid of Sekhemkhet (IIIrd Dyn.). Analyses by Z. Iskander, in Z. Goneim, *Horus Sekhemkhet*, pp. 35–36.

Nos. 3–4. From the pyramid of Khufu (IVth Dyn.). Sir Ed. Thorpe, *Dictionary of Applied Chemistry*, I, pp. 467–8; A. Lucas, *Ann. Serv.*, VII (1906), p. 4.

ANCIENT EGYPTIAN GYPSUM PLASTER [5]

	%	%	%	%	%
Moisture (loss at 100°C.)	1.0	4.0	0.4	0.2	0.2
Combined water	2.7	8.6	4.2	9.2	6.5
Silica and insoluble silicate	4.5	4.8	5.1	3.5	3.7
Oxides of iron and aluminium	0.8	1.3	0.7	0.6	0.5
Sulphate	35.3	34.5	33.9	31.3	34.4
Lime	40.4	34.3	40.7	38.8	41.2
Calculated Composition					
Gypsum (hydrated calcium sulphate)	60.0	58.6	57.7	53.3	58.5
Calcium carbonate	28.0	18.0	30.2	30.0	30.5

---

[1] Lime 0.7: Carbon dioxide 0.2.   [2] Lime 4.8: Carbon dioxide 2.1.

[3] Including lime left uncombined.   [4] Not determined.

[5] Plaster samples from El Amarna. Analyses by H. E. Cox, in J. D. S. Pendlebury, *City of Akhenaten*, III, p. 244.

ANCIENT EGYPTIAN MORTAR WITH ORGANIC ADHESIVE [1]

	%
Gypsum (hydrated calcium sulphate)	0.5
Insoluble, mostly silica	2.2
Calcium carbonate	93.7
Calcium phosphate	1.2
Sodium chloride	0.5
Oxides of iron and aluminium	0.2
Organic adhesive	1.3
	99.6

ANCIENT EGYPTIAN WHITEWASH [2]

	1 %	2 %
Gypsum (hydrated calcium sulphate)	1.5	9.6
Sand	11.0	32.0
Calcium carbonate, etc.	87.5	58.4
	100.0	100.0

No. 1. From the 'Cache of Akhenaten' (XVIIIth Dyn.).
No. 2. From the tomb of Seti II (No. 15, XIXth Dyn.).

PLASTER MOULDS FOR BRONZE FIGURES [3]

	%	%
Gypsum (hydrated calcium sulphate)	97.3	95.8
Silica	1.3	3.4
Calcium carbonate	tr.	tr.
Oxides of iron and aluminium	1.4	0.8
	100.0	100.0

[1] From the enclosure wall of the pyramid complex of Sekhemkhet (IIIrd Dyn.). Analysis by Z. Iskander, in Z. Goneim, *Horus Sekhemkhet*, p. 36. For a gesso plaster of essentially similar composition cf. W. B. Pollard, in J. E. Quibell, *Yuaa and Thuiu*, p. 80.

[2] Analyses by A. Lucas.

[3] Analyses by A. Lucas. Cf. C. C. Edgar, *Greek Moulds*, p. iii.

ANCIENT EGYPTIAN FAIENCE

Body Material (Ordinary Faience)

	1	2	3	4	5	6	7	8	9	10	11	12
	%	%	%	%	%	%	%	%	%	%	%	%
Silica	99.6	90.1	94.7	94.2	90.4	94.0	94.2	94.2	92.2	90.0	88.0	81.0
Alumina	}0.3	1.1	}1.4	0.6	0.5	1.8	0.6	1.9	4.9	4.0	6.0	13.5
Oxide of iron		2.7		1.6	0.9	0.9	1.6	0.3	tr.	—	—	1.0
Lime	0.3	2.7	1.7	1.7	0.5	2.0	1.7	1.6	2.1	2.0	3.0	3.0
Magnesia	—	—	1.8	1.8	0.1	1.1	1.8	0.1	tr.	0.6	—	tr.
Alkalies	—	2.7	0.4	—	2.8	0.3	—	1.1	}tr.	2.4	3.0	1.9
Not determined	—	0.7	—	0.1	3.0	—	0.1	0.8				
	100.2	100.0	100.0	100.0	98.2	100.1	100.0	100.0	99.2	99.0	100.0	100.4

No. 1. XIXth Dyn. Analysis by A. Lucas, Specimen of finely divided, white material.

No. 2. XIXth Dyn. W. C. Hayes, *Glazed Tiles*, p. 8, *n.* 36.

No. 3. XIXth–XXth Dyn. Analysis by A. Lucas. Specimen of coarse, yellowish-brown material.

No. 4. XXIInd Dyn. L. Franchet, *Céramique primitive*, p. 41; *Revue scientifique*, August 1907, p. 163.

No. 5. B. Boccolari, *Atti e Memorie dell' Accademia di Scienze . . . di Modena*, XII (1954), p. 212.

Nos. 6–8. W. Burton, *Journ. Royal Soc. of Arts*, LX (1912), p. 594. No. 7=No. 4.

Nos. 9–12. K B. Hofmann, *Z.Ä.S.*, XXIII (1885), p. 63; J. Llorens i Artigas, *Les pastes ceramiques i els esmalts blaus de l'antic Egipte*, pp. 21–22. Analyses by Hofmann, Salvétat, Laurent and Buisson.

FAIENCE BODY MATERIAL (NON-EGYPTIAN)

	%		%
Silica	98.64 [1]	Silica	95.68 [2]
Cupric oxide	0.27	Aluminium oxide	0.75
Aluminium and other oxides	0.29	Iron oxide	0.27
Calcium oxide	0.11	Calcium oxide	0.66
Potassium oxide	0.12	Magnesium oxide	0.24
Sodium oxide	0.08	Potassium oxide	0.25
Loss on ignition	0.55	Sodium oxide	0.30
	———	Loss at 110°	0.17
	100.06	Loss on ignition	0.55
			———
			98.87

[1] Faience found at Antioch on the Orontes. E. R. Caley, *Technical Studies*, VIII (1939–40), pp. 151–4.

[2] Faience bead from Dendra near Midea. G. Hägg, in A. W. Persson, *New Tombs at Dendra near Midea*, pp. 197–8.

ANCIENT EGYPTIAN FAIENCE

Glaze (Ordinary Faience)

	1	2	3	4
	%	%	%	%
Silica	92.9	75.6	74.5	75.6
Alumina	0.3	0.8	3.4	1.9
Oxide of iron	0.5	0.8		
Lime	0.8	3.8	3.9	3.7
Magnesia	—	0.7	—	0.6
Oxide of tin	—	nil	—	—
Oxide of lead	—	nil	—	—
Oxide of copper	1.1	1.8	2.1	1.8
Potash	0.5	10.7	10.2	10.4
Soda	1.6	5.5	5.8	5.6
Oxide of manganese	—	0.3	—	0.3
Not determined	2.3	—	—	—
	100.0	100.0	99.9	99.9

No. 1. Pale greenish blue: XIXth Dyn. W. C. Hayes, *Glazed Tiles*, p. 9, *n.* 38.

No. 2. Blue colour: Roman date from Dima (Fayum). Analysis by J. Clifford, F.R.I.C., for A. Lucas.

Nos. 3–4. Specimens prepared by Nicolini and Santini in imitation of typical Egyptian blue glaze. L. Nicolini and M. Santini, *Bollettino del' Istituto centrale del restauro*, XXXIV–V (1958), pp. 59–70.

ANCIENT EGYPTIAN FAIENCE

	Faience Variant D				Faience Variant E
	1	2	3	4	5
	%	%	%	%	%
Silica	92.3	93.9	94.4	95.3	88.6
Alumina	1.1	1.0	2.4	1.6	1.4
Oxide of iron	0.3	0.1	0.2	0.4	0.4
Lime	0.6	1.7	1.3	1.7	2.1
Magnesia	—	—	—	—	—
Alkalies	2.5	2.4	1.2	0.6	5.8
Oxide of copper	0.8	0.8	0.5	0.4	1.7
Oxide of manganese	2.4	—	—	—	—
	100.0	99.9	100.0	100.0	100.0

No. 1. Thebes: XXth Dyn.

Nos. 2–3. Saqqara: Saite period.

No. 4. Saqqara: Ptolemaic period.

Analyses by H. Le Chatelier, *C.R.Ac.Sci.*, CXXIX (1889), pp. 477–80. Cf. also J. Llorens i Artigas, *Les pastes ceramiques i els esmalts blaus de l'antic Egipte*, p. 41.

No. 5. H. Le Chatelier, *C.R.Ac.Sci.*, CXXIX (1889), pp. 387–8. Cf. also J. Llorens i Artigas, *op. cit.*, p. 34.

ANCIENT EGYPTIAN GLASS [1]

	Trans. XIIth	Yell. XIIth	Or.-yell. XVIIIth	Blue XVIIIth	Blue XVIIIth	Blue XVIIIth	Blue XVIIIth	Blue XXth	Blue XXth	Blue Persian	Blue Persian	Green XXth	? Byzant.
	%	%	%	%	%	%	%	%	%	%	%	%	%
Silica	68.3	68.0	59.0	60.7	59.8	59.9	60.3	60.1	58.7	57.9	58.0	60.4	60.1
Oxides of iron and aluminium	3.2	4.0	3.9	2.3	2.7	2.7	2.3	3.1	5.0	5.3	5.0	3.5	3.8
Lime	4.9	5.0	3.7	3.6	3.4	3.9	3.8	3.7	3.8	5.4	5.6	3.8	5.1
Magnesia	1.0	0.9	3.0	3.0	3.0	2.8	2.6	2.0	1.8	1.1	1.1	2.2	1.0
Potash	2.0	2.2	} 30.2					1.4	} 29.6			1.4	} 28.7
Soda	20.2	19.4		29.8	30.5	30.1	30.4	29.1		29.7	29.9	28.3	
Oxide of manganese	0.3	0.3	0.4	0.6	0.5	0.7	0.6	0.4	1.0	0.4	0.4	0.4	1.1
Oxide of cobalt	—	—	—	tr.	tr.	tr.	tr.	tr.	tr.	nil	tr.	tr.	tr.
Oxide of copper	—	—	—	—	—	—	—	—	—	tr.	—	—	tr.
	99.9	99.8	100.2	100.0	99.9	100.1	100.0	99.8	99.9	99.8	99.9	100.0	99.8

[1] H. D. Parodi, *La Verrerie en Égypte*, 1908. For some observations on these results, see A. Lucas, *Cairo Sc. Journ.*, III (1909), p. 24; F. R. Matson, *Journ. Chemical Education*, XXVIII (1951), pp. 82–87. The percentage of alkali reported in the glasses stated to be of the New Kingdom is high by comparison with that found in other examples of similar date. The date of the two specimens stated to be of the Twelfth Dynasty is doubtful.

ANCIENT ARAB GLASS [1]

	%	%	%	%	%	%	%	%	%	%	%	%	%	%	%	%	%
Silica	67.8	68.0	66.4	67.0	55.7	56.6	68.7	66.7	68.3	67.4	68.3	67.9	68.0	68.0	63.1	64.2	58.1
Oxides of iron and aluminium	4.0	4.2	5.1	5.0	8.3	8.0	2.2	5.4	3.3	2.7	2.1	2.9	2.6	2.1	0.6	3.0	7.4
Lime	2.9	2.6	4.7	4.2	4.6	4.7	8.6	7.4	8.7	8.1	8.0	8.3	8.1	8.2	3.5	5.0	4.9
Magnesia	0.9	0.9	1.4	1.1	3.3	3.7	4.2	3.5	3.2	4.0	3.7	3.7	4.1	4.2	—	nil	3.0
Potash	}23.5	23.4	22.6	21.7	25.1	24.0	2.9	3.9	2.5	2.6	2.5	2.5	2.1	2.7	}31.0	26.7	25.3
Soda							12.5	12.4	12.7	14.4	14.7	13.3	14.1	14.0			
Oxide of manganese	0.9	0.8	0.6	0.9	1.9	1.3	0.7	0.7	0.6	0.7	0.8	0.8	0.7	0.8	0.8	0.8	1.1
Oxide of cobalt	—	—	—	—	—	—	—	—	—	—	—	—	—	—	—	—	—
Oxide of copper	tr.	—	—	—	—	—	—	—	—	—	—	—	—	—	—	—	—
Oxide of sulphur	—	—	—	—	1.0	1.1	—	—	—	—	—	—	—	—	—	—	—
	100.0	99.9	100.8	99.9	99.9	99.4	99.8	100.0	99.3	99.9	100.1	99.4	99.7	100.0	99.0	99.7	99.8
	Blue	—	—	—	Blue	Blue	—	—	—	—	—	—	—	—	—	—	—

[1] H. D. Parodi, *La Verrerie en Égypte*, 1908.

ANCIENT EGYPTIAN GLASS [1]

	1	2	3	4	5	6	7	8	9	10	11	12	13	14	15	16	17
	%	%	%	%	%	%	%	%	%	%	%	%	%	%	%	%	%
Silica	61.7	59.6	50.9	62.7	62.4	64.1	62.3	51.4	62.6	63.9	63.2	65.9	68.1	60.8	64.7	60.3	67.3
Oxide of iron	0.7	0.4	1.1	0.8	0.8	0.5	0.6	0.8	0.6	0.7	0.5	0.8	0.7	0.6	0.8	10.0	0.5
Oxide of aluminium	2.5	3.0	2.9	1.5	1.0	1.3	0.8	0.9	0.8	0.7	1.0	1.3	1.9	2.2	2.8	2.6	2.6
Lime	10.1	10.6	10.3	9.2	9.2	7.0	10.1	8.4	9.3	7.9	9.1	9.1	4.2	1.5	7.1	6.5	6.8
Magnesia	5.1	4.4	4.5	4.5	3.1	3.8	4.2	2.5	4.4	4.2	5.2	3.7	1.3	1.5	2.1	1.2	1.9
Potash	1.6	7.4	19.0	20.3	2.8	2.8	—	1.9	2.8	0.8	0.4	0.6	1.9	—	—	0.5	—
Soda	17.6	14.9	}		18.1	19.3	19.9	17.2	18.2	22.7	20.6	18.0	18.9	29.0	20.4	18.8	20.4
Oxide of manganese	0.5	tr.	—	—	—	0.3	0.9	—	—	—	tr.	—	—	—	0.5	0.3	—
Oxide of copper	0.3	0.5	—	—	2.0	0.2	—	12.0	0.5	—	—	—	2.7	3.0	0.2	—	—
Oxide of lead	—	—	—	—	0.5	—	—	—	0.5	—	—	—	—	—	—	—	—
Oxide of tin	—	—	—	—	—	—	—	—	—	—	—	—	—	—	1.3	—	0.5
Sulphur trioxide	—	—	2.4	0.9	0.7	0.8	1.2	5.5	0.5	—	—	0.8	—	0.9	—	—	—
	100.1	100.8	91.1	100.1	100.6	100.1	100.0	100.6	100.2	100.9	100.0	100.2	99.7	99.5	99.9	100.2	100.0

	18	19	20	21	22	23	24	39	40	41	42	72	73	95	96	97	98
	%	%	%	%	%	%	%	%	%	%	%	%	%	%	%	%	%
Silica	58.5	59.1	55.6	66.3	66.0	68.5	67.5	72.3	70.6	65.9	71.2	67.8	62.5	67.8	62.7	62.9	67.0
Oxide of iron	0.9	1.6	1.3	0.8	0.3	0.9	0.1	0.5	1.0	1.0	0.3	1.1	1.7	0.9	1.1	1.3	1.9
Oxide of aluminium	5.0	3.6	3.5	3.3	2.5	3.9	5.0	1.2	1.2	1.4	0.8	4.4	1.6	3.2	3.8	2.6	2.5
Lime	10.7	9.8	8.4	7.1	6.9	9.9	10.3	5.2	6.5	8.4	8.6	4.0	5.6	3.8	8.8	8.9	7.8
Magnesia	3.4	3.1	2.7	1.5	1.4	1.2	0.8	—	—	—	tr.	2.3	4.2	2.9	3.3	5.5	4.9
Potash	7.6	6.4	2.8	0.4	1.0	0.2	0.1	—	—	—	—	2.3	2.2	2.1	2.1	1.9	1.8
Soda	9.0	10.3	12.2	19.3	20.3	14.8	15.4	20.8	20.7	22.3	18.8	13.7	17.8	16.1	15.2	12.8	10.1
Oxide of manganese	0.5	0.7	0.3	0.6	1.0	0.8	0.3	—	tr.	0.9	0.4	1.1	0.8	0.5	0.8	1.7	2.6
Oxide of copper	2.1	2.5	4.4	1.0	—	—	0.3	—	—	—	—	2.0	2.7	1.5	1.0	0.5	0.8
Oxide of lead	1.3	3.0	6.3	—	—	—	—	—	—	—	—	—	—	—	—	—	—
Oxide of tin	—	—	—	—	—	—	—	—	—	—	—	—	—	0.5	0.4	0.4	0.4
Sulphur trioxide	1.4	0.5	1.8	—	1.1	—	—	—	—	—	—	1.0	1.4	1.0	0.9	1.5	0.8
	100.4	100.6	99.3	100.3	100.5	100.2	100.0	100.0	100.0	99.9	100.1	99.7	100.5	100.3	100.1	100.0	100.6

Nos. 1–12, 72–73, 95–98. XVIIIth Dyn. The date of No. 72 has been questioned by F. R. Matson, *Journ. Chemical Education*, XXVIII (1951), pp. 82–87.

Nos. 13–22. 2nd–1st cent. B.C.

Nos. 23–24. Alexandrian.

Nos. 39–42. No date given. Quoted from Benrath, *Glasfabrikation*, 1875, p. 4.

Colours: Nos. 1, 2, 9, 13, 21, 23, 24, 72, 73, 95, 96, 98 Blue; Nos. 3, 4 Yellow; Nos. 5, 14, 40, 42 Green; Nos. 6, 15, 16 Black; Nos. 7, 97 Purple; Nos. 8, 18, 19, 20 Red; Nos. 10, 11, 22, 39 Colourless; No. 12 Honey; No. 17 Milk white; No. 41 Brownish.

Nos. 1–9, 13–20, 72–73 Opaque; Nos. 10–12, 21–24, 95–98 Translucent.

[1] B. Neumann and G. Kotyga, *Zeitschr. f. angew. Chemie*, XXXVIII (1925), pp. 776–80, 857–64; XL (1927), pp. 963–7; XLII (1929), pp. 835–8.

ANCIENT EGYPTIAN GLASS

	1 %	2 %	3 %	4 %	5 %	6 %
Silica	62.6	74.3	74.4	67.1	52.1	38.2
Oxide of iron	0.6	1.8	1.8	4.9	9.5 ⎫	2.1
Oxide of aluminium	1.5	1.0	1.0	1.2	11.8 ⎭	
Oxide of titanium	tr.	—	—	—	2.2	—
Lime	12.2	8.5	8.5	5.6	15.9	8.2
Magnesia	4.9	2.8	2.8	0.9	3.0	—
Potash	tr.	5.5	n.d.	12.2	1.7	0.6
Soda	17.2	3.6	n.d.	2.1	2.1	10.3
Oxide of manganese	0.2	—	—	1.4	tr.	0.1
Oxide of copper	0.7	—	—	—	—	5.4
Oxide of lead	—	—	—	3.7	—	32.6
Oxide of tin	—	—	—	0.6	—	0.7
Oxide of cobalt	—	2.9	2.8	1.0	—	—
Sulphur trioxide...	0.4	—	—	—	diff.	—
	100.3	100.4	91.3	100.7	98.3	98.2

No. 1. XVIIIth Dyn. Blue. W. E. S. Turner, *Journ. Soc. Glass Technology*, xxxviii (1954), p. 441; xl (1956), p. 168.

Nos. 2–3. No date given. Blue. Clemm and Jehn, quoted by C. R. Lepsius, *Les métaux dans les inscriptions égyptiennes*, pp. 26–27. Two samples from the same specimen.

No. 4. No date given. Blue. Clemm, quoted by C. R. Lepsius (as Nos. 2–3).

No. 5. ? Ptolemaic. Glass slag. H. N. Bassett, in A. de Cosson, *Mareotis*, p. 204. Loss 0.2 per cent.

No. 6. Roman. Opaque red. H. Jackson, quoted by J. N. Collie, *Transactions of the Ceramic Society*, xvii (1918), p. 383.

ANCIENT EGYPTIAN AND ARAB GLASS [1]

	1 %	2 %	3 %	4 %	5 %	6 %	7 %	8 %
Silica	64.06	66.98	66.27	66.27	63.53	58.38	69.25	69.43
Oxide of aluminium	3.51	2.13	2.71	0.92	2.25	0.78	1.22	0.69
Oxide of iron ...	1.71	0.50	0.85	2.12	1.27	0.53	3.01	0.69
Lime	8.56	10.45	9.02	9.59	10.12	5.88	6.86	7.95
Magnesia	2.73	4.27	2.03	2.40	2.05	1.51	1.94	2.23
Soda	15.47	14.32	16.12	10.48	14.31	16.70	13.66	13.99
Potash	1.25	0.51	0.82	4.11	3.25	14.37	2.73	2.31
Oxide of manganese	0.163	0.38	0.17	1.52	2.1?	1.18	0.294	2.17
Oxide of phosphorus	0.213	0.13	0.23	0.38	0.27	0.083	0.220	0.341
Sulphur trioxide ...	0.160	0.18	0.31	0.08	0.12	0.49	0.04	0.04
Chlorine	1.17	pres.	0.88	0.53	0.42	0.30	0.03	tr.
Oxide of titanium ...	0.08	0.09	0.12	0.14	0.10	0.14	0.10	0.06
Oxide of lead ...	0.012	0.05	0.05	0.14	—	—	—	—
Oxide of copper ...	0.005	0.01	0.13	1.31	0.08	—	0.68	0.06
Oxide of cobalt ...	0.55	0.075	0.29	—	—	—	0.155	0.002
Oxide of nickel ...	0.075	0.03	0.05	—	—	—	0.007	—
Oxide of tin ...	0.02	tr.	0.01	0.10	0.08	tr.	—	—
Oxide of antimony	0.05	nil	0.03	—	nil	—	—	—
Oxide of arsenic ...	0.006	0.003	0.01	—	—	—	tr.	0.005
Oxide of boron ...	—	—	—	—	—	tr.	—	tr.
Carbon dioxide ...	0.15	tr.	—	—	—	—	—	—
Water	0.27	0.10	0.05	0.07	0.11	—	0.05	0.10
Total	100.21	100.15	100.13	100.16	100.09	100.34	100.216	100.068
Less oxygen for chlorine	0.26	—	0.20	0.12	0.09	0.06	—	—

No. 1. XVIIIth Dyn. Blue.
No. 2. XVIIth–XVIIIth Dyn. Blue.
No. 3. XVIIIth–XXth Dyn. Blue. From Medinet Habu.
No. 4. XXth–XXIInd Dyn. Blue-green, translucent.
No. 5. XXIInd Dyn. Violet.
No. 6. Alexandrian, 3rd cent. B.C. Colourless.
No. 7 10th cent. A.D.
No. 8. 14th cent. A.D.
    Spectrographic analysis indicated the presence of other minerals, notably oxides of lithium and strontium, vanadium and silver.

ARAB GLASS FROM FOSTAT [2]

	%	%	%	%
Silica	71.2	70.5	66.3	49.4
Phosphoric anhydride	0.3	0.6	0.6	1.2
Oxide of iron	1.4	1.9 } 4.6	8.6
Oxide of aluminium	1.0	0.8 }	14.5
Lime	8.1	7.8	10.5	18.7
Magnesia	3.2	1.2	1.0	1.4
Potash	2.1	tr.	3.8	3.5
Soda	11.4	16.1	11.1	2.4
Oxide of manganese	1.2	1.1	2.4	0.3
	99.9	100.0	100.3	100.0
	Blue	Green	Green	Green

[1] W. Geilmann, *Glastechnische Berichte*, xxviii (1955), p. 148.
[2] Analyses by J. Clifford, F.R.I.C., for A. Lucas.

SAND [1]

	1 %	2 %	3 %	4 %	5 %	6 %
Silica	83.6	95.2	96.7	82.4	93.8	32.0
Oxides of iron and aluminium ...	1.3	1.9	0.6	1.5	3.6	0.7
Lime	12.0	1.9	1.9	8.4	0.7	35.0
Magnesia	1.2	0.1	0.6	tr.	tr.	2.2
Sodium chloride	—	—	—	0.2	tr.	0.4
Sulphur trioxide...	—	—	—	0.2	nil	nil
Moisture	1.6	1.0	0.1	1.2	0.4	0.6
Loss on ignition	—	—	—	6.6	1.1	29.6
	99.7	100.1	99.9	100.5	99.6	100.5

No. 1. From Karnak. No. 2. From the Fayum. No. 3. From Eshmunein. No. 4. From Giza. No. 5. From Aswan. No. 6. From Alexandria.

SAND[2]

	1 %	2 %	3 %	4 %	5 %
Silica	60.5	72.7	97.9	97.8 [3]	99.2
Oxide of aluminium	2.3	8.2	1.4	1.0	0.5
Oxide of iron	1.7	5.6	0.2	0.3	0.1
Oxide of titanium	0.4	1.2	—	0.2	—
Oxide of phosphorus	0.1	0.1	—	—	—
Lime	18.9	4.9	0.2	0.4	0.3
Magnesia	0.8	2.4	—	0.1	—
Oxide of manganese	tr.	0.1	—	tr.	—
Oxide of barium	nil	0.2	—	—	—
Potash	0.7	1.1	—	—	—
Soda	0.3	1.2	—	—	—
Sulphur trioxide	0.1	0.1	—	—	—
Moisture	0.4	1.0	—	—	—
Loss on ignition	13.9	1.6	—	0.1	—
	100.1	100.4	99.7	99.9	100.1

No. 1. From El Amarna. No. 2. From Luxor. No. 3. From Maadi (sifted and washed). No. 4. From the Fayum. No. 5. From Sinai.

[1] H. D. Parodi, *La Verrerie en Égypte*, pp. 25–27 (Nos 4–6. Analyses by A. Lucas). Cf. also W. E. S. Turner, *Journ. Soc. Glass Technology*, XL (1956), p. 281.

[2] W. E. S. Turner, *Journ. Soc. Glass Technology*, XL (1956), pp. 281, 300.

[3] By difference.

MODERN EGYPTIAN COPPER ORE

	1 %	2 %	3 %
Copper	3.1	36.3	48.6
Iron	25.8	—	—
Oxide of aluminium	2.4	—	—
Insoluble residue	55.4	—	—
Sulphuric acid	tr.	—	—
Nickel and zinc	nil	—	—
Lead	—	—	—
Sulphur	—	—	—
Not determined	13.3	63.7	51.4
	100.0	100.0	100.0

No. 1. Chrysocolla. From Wadi Samra (Eastern Sinai). Analysis by C. H. Desch. Kindly communicated by G. A. Garfitt, Honorary Secretary, Sumerian Copper Committee.

Nos. 2 and 3. From Wadi Araba (eastern desert). Analyses by Chemical Department, Cairo.

ANCIENT EGYPTIAN COPPER SLAG [1]

	%
Insoluble in acid	37.9
Copper	21.7
Lead [2]	38.0
Iron	1.9
Nickel and cobalt	tr.
Arsenic	0.5
Antimony, silver, bismuth	nil
	100.0

[1] From near Serabit el Khadim in Sinai. Analysis by J. Sebelien, *Ancient Egypt*, 1924, p. 10.

[2] The presence of such a large proportion of lead is very extraordinary and needs explanation.

ANCIENT EGYPTIAN COPPER OBJECTS[1]

No.	Object	Copper	Iron	Tin	Lead	Nickel, Cobalt	Arsenic	Antimony	Bismuth	Sulphur	Manganese	Not determined	Total
		%	%	%	%	%	%	%	%	%	%	%	%
1	Axe	97.4	0.2	tr.	0.2	1.3	0.5	tr.	—	—	0.1	0.3	100.0
2	Bangles	77.6	0.2	—	0.1	0.1	tr.	—	—	—	—	22.0	100.0
3	Tool	98.5	tr.	—	tr.	1.2	pres.	—	tr.	—	—	0.3	100.0
4	Dagger	99.5	0.1	nil	tr.	nil	0.4	—	nil	—	—	—	100.0
5	Model Knife	99.6	0.2	0.2	—	—	—	—	—	—	—	—	100.0
6	Chisel	93.2	tr.	tr.	0.1	—	0.1	—	nil	—	—	—	100.0
7	Adze	99.6	tr.	nil	—	—	0.4	tr.	—	tr.	—	—	100.0
8	Adze	99.5	tr.	nil	—	—	0.5	tr.	—	tr.	—	—	100.0
9	Pick	100.0	—	tr.	—	—	pres.	tr.	—	—	—	—	100.0
10	'Hook'	99.5	0.5	—	—	—	—	—	—	—	—	—	100.0
11	Amulet	77.0	6.5	—	—	—	tr.	—	—	—	—	14.5	100.0
12	Pipe	96.5	0.2	—	—	—	tr.	—	—	—	—	3.4	100.1
13	Model Tool	98.4	0.2	nil	tr.	—	0.3	tr.	tr.	—	—	1.1	100.0
14	Statue	98.2	0.7	—	—	1.1	—	—	—	tr.	—	—	100.0
15	Sheet	94.8	—	1.1	—	—	tr.	—	—	—	—	4.1	100.0
16	Axe	93.3	0.2	0.5	—	—	3.9	0.2	—	—	—	1.9	100.0
17	Strip	95.0	0.3	tr.	0.3	0.1	4.2	—	tr.	—	—	0.1	100.0
18	Sheet	87.7	—	tr.	—	—	—	—	—	—	—	12.3	100.0
19	Axe	88.9	—	0.2	0.6	—	5.6	0.7	—	—	—	4.0	100.0
20	Ingot	93.0	5.9	—	—	—	0.1	—	—	1.0	—	—	100.0
21	Axe	96.9	0.7	0.2	—	tr.	1.5	—	—	tr.	—	0.7	100.0
22	Mirror	90.8	tr.	0.1	tr.	—	6.4	—	—	—	—	2.7	100.0
23	Knife	96.7	1.2	tr.	0.6	0.3	0.8	—	0.4	—	—	—	100.0
24	Model Adze	98.4	0.5	tr.	—	0.3	tr.	—	—	—	—	0.8	100.0
25	Model Hoe	97.6	0.3	1.3	—	0.2	tr.	—	—	tr.	—	0.6	100.0
26	Model Yoke	96.8	0.1	1.8	—	0.3	tr.	—	—	0.3	—	0.7	100.0
27	Knife	97.1	0.4	0.2	—	—	2.3	—	—	—	—	—	100.0

No. 1. Middle Predynastic. Analysis by H. C. H. Carpenter, *Nature*, cxxx (1932), pp. 625–6.

No. 2. Predynastic. Analysis by C. O. Bannister, in R. Mond and O. H. Myers, *Cemeteries of Armant*, I, pp. 117–20. Also gold 0.1 per cent and traces of silver.

No. 3. Protodynastic. Analysis by C. O. Bannister (as No. 2). Also traces of gold and silver.

No. 4. Ist Dyn. H. Garland and C. O. Bannister, *Ancient Egyptian Metallurgy*, p. 34.

No. 5. IIIrd Dyn. Analysis by A. Lucas, in J. E. Quibell, *Saqqara, 1911–1912*, p. 40.

No. 6. Early Dynastic (Nubian). Analysis by C. O. Bannister, *Report of the British Ass.*, 1928, pp. 437–41. Also gold 4.1 per cent and silver 2.5 per cent.

[1] Note also three copper figurines (Middle Kingdom) containing 99.6, 98.1, and 97.9 per cent of copper respectively, H. R. Hall, *Liverpool Annals*, xvi (1929), pp. 13–16.

Nos 7–9. IVth Dyn. Analyses by J. H. Gladstone, *P.S.B.A.*, XIV (1892), pp. 223–7.

No. 10. ? IVth Dyn. Analysis by W. Flight, *Journ. Chemical Soc.*, XLI (1882), p. 142, No. VIII.

No. 11. Vth Dyn. G. Brunton, *Qau and Badari*, I, p. 69.

No. 12. Vth Dyn. Analysis by Rathgen, in L. Borchardt. *Sahu-rē*, I, p. 78.

No. 13. Old Kingdom. Analysis by J. H. Gladstone, in J. E. Quibell, *El Kab*, p. 4.

No. 14. VIth Dyn. (Pepi I statue). Analysis by C. H. Desch, *Report of the British Ass.*, 1928, pp. 437–41.

No. 15. XIIth Dyn. Analysis by J. H. Gladstone, in W. M. F. Petrie, *Dendereh*, p. 61.

No. 16. XIIth Dyn. Analysis by J. H. Gladstone, *P.S.B.A.*, XII (1890), pp. 227–34.

No. 17. XIIth Dyn. H. Garland and C. O. Bannister, *Ancient Egyptian Metallurgy*, p. 68.

No. 18. ? XIIth Dyn. Analysis by M. Berthelot, *Ann. Serv.*, II (1902), p. 162.

No. 19. ? XIIth Dyn. Analysis by G. B. Phillips, *Ancient Egypt*, 1924, p. 89; *American Anthropologist*, XXIV (1922), pp. 129–43.

No. 20. ? XIIth Dyn. From Bir Nasb, Sinai. Analysis by C. H. Desch, *Report of the British Ass.*, 1928, pp. 437–41.

No. 21. Pan-grave. Analysis by H C. H. Carpenter, *Nature*, CXXVII (1931), pp. 589–91. Cf. also G. Brunton, *Mostagedda*, p. 132.

No. 22. C-Group Nubian. Analysis by W. Böttger, in G. Steindorff, *Aniba*, I, p. 111.

No. 23. XVIIIth Dyn. Analysis by W. B. Pollard, quoted by H. Garland, *Journ. Inst. Metals*, X (1913), p. 330.

Nos. 24–26. XVIIIth Dyn. (Tutankhamūn). Analyses by C. H. Desch, quoted by A. Lucas, *Ann. Serv.*, XLI (1942), p. 146.

No. 27. XIXth Dyn. Analysis by Dr. Percy, quoted by J. H. Gladstone, *P.S.B.A.*, XII (1890), p. 229. Also traces of gold.

ANCIENT EGYPTIAN COPPER OBJECTS [1]

No.	Object	Copper	Iron	Zinc	Arsenic	Tin	Silver, Bismuth	Nickel	Lead	Sulphur	Sand	Not determined	Total
		%	%	%	%	%	%	%	%	%	%	%	%
1	Axe	98.0	—	—	—	—	—	—	—	—	—	2.0	100.0
2	Axe	98.1	—	0.3	tr.	—	—	—	—	—	—	1.6	100.0
3	Axe	100.0	tr.	—	—	—	—	—	—	—	—	—	100.0
4	Axe	99.6	—	—	—	—	—	—	—	—	—	0.4	100.0
5	Axe	97.2	—	0.3	—	—	—	tr.	—	—	—	2.5	100.0
6	Axe	99.0	—	—	—	—	tr.	—	—	—	—	1.0	100.0
7	Axe	98.3	—	—	—	—	—	—	—	—	—	1.7	100.0
8	Adze	99.9	tr.	tr.	—	—	tr.	—	—	—	—	0.1	100.0
9	Adze	97.6	—	—	—	—	—	—	—	—	—	2.4	100.0
10	Adze	97.7	tr.	—	—	—	—	—	—	—	—	2.3	100.0
11	Adze	99.6	—	—	—	—	tr.	—	—	—	—	0.4	100.0
12	Adze	97.0	0.5	—	—	—	—	0.4	—	0.3	—	1.8	100.0
13	Adze	94.2	2.5	—	—	—	—	—	—	—	0.4	2.9	100.0
14	Chisel	98.7	—	—	—	—	tr.	—	—	—	—	1.3	100.0
15	Chisel	98.0	tr.	tr.	0.3	—	tr.	—	—	—	—	1.7	100.0
16	Chisel	98.8	0.6	0.2	—	—	tr.	—	—	—	—	0.4	100.0
17	Knife	98.5	—	0.3	0.6	—	—	—	—	—	—	0.6	100.0
18	Bar	98.1	—	—	0.2	—	—	—	—	—	—	1.7	100.0
19	Bar	88.0	0.1	—	—	—	—	—	—	—	8.0	3.9	100.0
20	Chisel	97.7	0.5	tr.	—	—	—	—	—	—	—	1.8	100.0
21	Adze	98.0	tr.	tr.	tr.	—	—	—	tr.	—	—	2.0	100.0
22	Chisel	97.6	1.2	—	—	—	—	—	—	—	1.4	—	100.2
23	Chisel	98.5	tr.	—	—	—	—	—	—	—	0.3	1.2	100.0
24	Adze	58.0	—	—	—	—	—	—	—	—	20.0	22.0	100.0

Nos. 1–19 inclusive. Ist Dyn.
No. 20. IInd Dyn.
No. 21. VIth Dyn.
No. 22. XIIth Dyn.
No. 23. XVIIIth Dyn.
No. 24. Possibly XXth Dyn.

ANCIENT EGYPTIAN COPPER-LEAD OBJECTS

	1 %	2 %	3 %
Copper	69.4	74.6	68.2
Lead	22.2	21.3	22.8
Tin	1.8	0.9	0.9
Iron	—	0.3	4.7
Nickel, Cobalt	—	—	0.8
Arsenic	—	—	1.5
Antimony	—	—	0.7
Manganese	tr.	—	—
Not determined	6.6	2.9	0.4
	100.0	100.0	100.0

No. 1. Aegis. XXIInd–XXVth Dyn. D. Dunham, *Boston Bull.*, XXIX (1931), p. 109.
No. 2. Nail. XXVIth Dyn. G. B. Phillips, *Ancient Egypt*, 1924, p. 89; *American Anthropologist*, XXIV (1922), pp. 129–43.
No. 3. Figurine. Ptolemaic. W. Flight, *Journ. Chemical Soc.*, XLI (1882), p. 142, No. IX.

[1] Analyses by J. Sebelien, *Ancient Egypt*, 1924, p. 8.

ANCIENT EGYPTIAN BRONZE-LEAD OBJECTS

							1 %	2 %	3 %	4 %
Copper	...	...	...	...	...	...	49.3	73.7	82.2	72.0
Tin ...	...	...	...	...	...	...	4.5	4.8	2.0	5.0
Lead ...	...	...	...	...	...	...	24.8	19.2	15.8	22.7
Iron ...	...	...	...	...	...	...	—	0.2	—	0.3
Cobalt ...	...	...	...	...	...	...	—	0.8	—	—
Not determined	...	...	...	...	...	...	21.4	1.3	—	—
							100.0	100.0	100.0	100.0

No. 1. Tablet case. XXVth Dyn. M. Berthelot, *Monuments Piot*, VII (1900), p. 125; *Ann. Chim. et Phys.*, XXIII (1901), p. 11.

No. 2. Handle. Late. G. B. Phillips, *Ancient Egypt*, 1924, p. 89; *American Anthropologist*, XXIV (1922), pp. 129–43.

No. 3. Figurine. Ptolemaic. W. Flight, *Journ. Chemical Soc.*, XLI (1882), p. 143, No. IX.

No. 4. Vessel. Roman. A. Lucas, *Ann. Serv.*, I (1900), p. 288.

ANCIENT EGYPTIAN COPPER AND BRONZE OBJECTS [1]

No.	Object	Copper %	Tin %	Lead %
1	Beaker	93.0	4.5	2.5
2	Mirror disc	99.2	0.8	—
3	Mirror handle	100.0	tr.	tr.
4	Tweezers	96.6	2.3	1.1
5	Knife	100.0	tr.	tr.
6	Dagger	100.0	tr.	tr.
7	Razor	98.0	2.0	tr.
8	Mirror disc	99.0	1.0	tr.
9	Drill or awl	98.4	0.8	0.4
10	Ear of statue	99.5	0.5	—
11	Dagger	100.0	tr.	tr.
12	Dagger	99.0	1.0	tr.
13	Dagger	93.0	6.2	0.8
14	Axe-head	99.3	0.7	tr.
15	Mirror disc	100.0	tr.	—
16	Tang	100.0	tr.	—
17	Model axe-head	100.0	tr.	—
18	Model vase	99.3	—	0.7
19	Dagger	99.0	1.0	—

Nos. 1–11. From Kerma.

Nos. 12–16. From Naga-ed-Dêr.

No. 17. From Hu.

No. 18. From El Bersheh.

No. 19. From Rifeh.

---

[1] Middle Kingdom. Spectrographic analyses. D. Dunham, *J.E.A.*, XXIX (1943), pp. 60–62; cf. also p. 76.

ANCIENT EGYPTIAN BRONZE OBJECTS [1]

No.	Object	Copper	Tin	Lead	Antimony	Arsenic	Nickel	Iron	Zinc	Sulphur	Not determined	Total
		%	%	%	%	%	%	%	%	%	%	%
1	Rod	89.8	9.1	—	tr.	0.5	—	tr.	—	tr.	0.6	100.0
2	Razor	88.5	8.5	0.3	—	—	tr.	1.8	—	—	0.9	100.0
3	Figurine	91.9	6.3	—	—	—	—	—	—	—	1.8	100.0
4	Figurine	88.4	11.9	—	—	—	—	—	—	—	—	100.3
5	Bowl	85.8	3.5	8.5	—	—	—	0.2	—	—	2.0	100.0
6	Axe	85.9	12.1	0.8	—	—	—	—	—	—	1.2	100.0
7	Chisel	93.6	7.4	—	tr.	0.5	—	—	—	—	—	101.5
8	Chisel	96.4	2.2	—	—	0.4	—	—	—	—	1.0	100.0
9	Nail	94.8	4.6	0.3	—	—	—	0.4	—	—	—	100.1
10	Adze	89.8	3.1	—	tr.	0.3	—	—	0.4	—	6.4	100.0
11	Chisel	88.0	12.0	0.1	tr.	0.4	—	—	0.3	—	—	100.8
12	Axe	89.6	6.7	—	tr.	1.0	—	0.5	—	—	2.2	100.0
13	Axe	90.1	7.3	—	tr.	0.2	—	—	—	tr.	2.4	100.0
14	Axe	90.2	9.5	—	—	tr.	0.1	pres.	—	pres.	0.2	100.0
15	Adze	67.6	9.6	—	—	—	0.6	tr.	—	—	22.2	100.0
16	Sword	89.9	8.0	tr.	—	0.6	0.2[2]	0.4	—	—	0.9	100.0
17	Knife	94.0	5.9	—	—	—	—	0.1	—	—	—	100.0
18	Vessel	88.3	8.9	2.3	—	—	—	0.5	—	—	—	100.0
19	Figurine	87.1	6.3[3]	4.4	—	—	—	tr.	—	—	2.2	100.0
20	Fragment	92.0	6.5	0.8	—	—	—	0.3	—	—	0.4	100.0
21	Crab	90.7	8.1	0.3	—	—	0.1[2]	0.2	—	0.1	0.5	100.0
22	Bowl	80.8	13.1	5.1	—	—	0.5[2]	0.3	—	—	0.2	100.0

No. 1. IVth Dyn. Analysis by J. H. Gladstone, *P.S.B.A.*, XIV (1892), pp. 223–7.

No. 2. IVth Dyn. Analysis by C. H. Desch, *Report of the British Ass.*, 1933, p. 304.

Nos. 3–4. IXth or XIth Dyn. H. R. Hall, *Liverpool Annals*, XVI (1929), pp. 14–25.

No. 5. ? XIth Dyn. Analysis by G. B. Phillips, *Ancient Egypt*, 1924, p. 89; *American Anthropologist*, XXIV (1922), pp. 129–43.

Nos. 6–7. XIIth Dyn. Analyses by J. Sebelien, *Ancient Egypt*, 1924, p. 8.

No. 8. XIIth Dyn. Analysis by J. H. Gladstone, *P.S.B.A*, XII (1890), pp. 227–34.

No. 9. XIIth Dyn. Analysis by Z. Iskander, in F. Bisson de la Roque, *Trésor de Tôd* (*Cat. Caire*), p. 55.

Nos. 10–11. XVIIIth Dyn. Analyses by J. Sebelien, *Ancient Egypt*, 1924, p. 8.

Nos. 12–13. XVIIIth Dyn. Analyses by J. H. Gladstone, *P.S.B.A.*, XII (1890), pp. 227–34.

No. 14. XVIIIth Dyn. O. Montelius, *Alt. Bronzezeit*, 1900, p. 150.

No. 15. XIXth Dyn. Analysis by J. Sebelien, *Ancient Egypt*, 1924, p. 8.

No. 16. XIXth Dyn. (Seti II). Analysis by Rathgen and Brittner, quoted by M. Burchardt, *Z.Ä.S.*, L (1912), p. 61.

[1] For some earlier analyses, mainly of undated specimens, cf. E. von Bibra, *Die Bronzen und Kupferlegirungen*, pp. 94–95; F. Rathgen, in P. Diergart, *Beiträge aus der Geschichte der Chemie*, 1909, pp. 212–14; J. R. Partington, *Origins and Development of Applied Chemistry*, pp. 56–58, 71–72.

[2] Including cobalt.

[3] Including silica.

No. 17. New Kingdom. Analysis by Dr. Beck, quoted by E. A. W. Budge, *Archaeologia*, LIII (1892), p. 90.
No. 18. New Kingdom. Analysis by A. Lucas, *Ann. Serv.*, I (1901), p. 288.
No. 19. ? XXVIth Dyn. Analysis by J. H. Gladstone, *P.S.B.A.*, XII (1890), pp. 227–34.
No. 20. XXVIth Dyn. Analysis by G. B. Phillips, *Ancient Egypt*, 1924, p. 89; *American Anthropologist*, XXIV (1922), pp. 129–43.
No. 21. Roman. Analysis by F. A. Genth, in H. H. Gorringe, *Egyptian Obelisks*, p. 173.
No. 22. Romano-Nubian. Analysis by W. Gowland, in C. L. Woolley and D. Randall MacIver *Karanog*, p. 67.

ANCIENT EGYPTIAN BRONZE OBJECTS [1]

No.	Object	Copper	Tin	Lead	Antimony	Arsenic	Iron	Zinc	Sulphur	Not determined	Total
		%	%	%	%	%	%	%	%	%	%
1	Bracelet	76.7	8.2	5.7	nil	tr.	nil	nil	tr.	9.4	100.0
2	Vase	86.2	5.7	nil	—	nil	nil	nil	—	8.1	100.0
3	Bracelet	68.4	16.3	nil	—	nil	tr.	tr.	—	15.3	100.0
4	Hook	69.2	9.8	—	—	nil	—	—	—	21.0	100.0
5	Nail	85.0	1.0	—	—	—	—	—	—	14.0	100.0
6	Ring	77.5	9.7	nil	—	tr.	nil	—	—	12.8	100.0
7	Ring	16.2	75.7	1.0	—	—	—	—	—	7.1	100.0
8	Vase	76.8	15.2	nil	—	nil	nil	nil	tr.	—	100.0
9	Arrow-head	81.9	12.2	—	—	—	—	—	—	5.9	100.0
10	Statue base	77.9	5.0	nil	—	—	—	—	—	17.1	100.0
11	Arrow-head	68.1	5.9	—	—	—	—	—	—	25.0	100.0
12	Mirror	78.6	11.3	—	—	nil	—	—	—	9.1	100.0
13	Ingot	87.5	11.5	tr.	—	nil	nil	nil	—	1.0	100.0

No. 1. ? IVth Dyn.
No. 2. VIth Dyn.
Nos. 3–5. XIIth Dyn.
Nos. 6–7. XIXth Dyn.
No. 8. XVIIIth–XXth Dyn.
No. 9. XXth Dyn.
No. 10. XXIInd Dyn.
Nos. 11–12. Undated.
No. 13. Late (from the Serapeum).

[1] Analyses by M. Berthelot, in J. de Morgan, *Dahchour, mars-juin 1894*, pp. 138–42; *Ann. Chim. et Phys.*, IV (1895), pp. 555–71.
No. 13. Analysis by M. Berthelot, *Archéologie et histoire des sciences*, p. 16.

ANCIENT EGYPTIAN BRONZE OBJECTS [1]

No.	Object	Copper	Tin	Lead	Iron	Zinc	Total
		%	%	%	%	%	%
1	Situla	82.5	10.1	5.6	0.1	0.2	98.5
2	Handle wire	86.2	11.5	0.6	0.2	0.2	98.7
3	Cup	86.7	12.5	0.3	0.1	0.2	99.8
4	Shovel	92.3	5.5	1.1	0.2	0.2	99.3
5	Clamp	88.6	7.0	0.8	0.3	0.2	96.9
6	Clamp	86.5	8.2	2.2	0.2	0.3	97.4
7	Armour scale	88.8	5.8	1.6	0.3	0.2	96.7
8	Flute	92.4	4.6	1.2	0.3	0.2	98.7
9	Dish	87.4	11.3	0.2	0.1	0.2	99.2
10	Dish	92.3	6.3	0.5	0.3	0.5	99.9
11	Dish	69.0	4.7	23.6	0.3	0.6	98.2
12	Vase	81.2	10.2	6.6	0.1	0.5	98.6
13	Eye setting [2]	82.5	7.2	9.1	0.2	0.1	99.1
14	Ring [3]	66.1	8.5	24.3	0.2	0.2	99.3

ANCIENT EGYPTIAN BRONZE OBJECTS [4]

No.	Object	Copper	Tin	Lead	Iron	Zinc	Arsenic	Bismuth	Silver	Total
		%	%	%	%	%	%	%	%	%
1	Dish	88.9	10.1	tr.	tr.	tr.	tr.	tr.	—	99.0
2	Dish	92.8	7.1	tr.	tr.	tr.	tr.	tr.	—	99.9
3	Dish	95.5	4.5	tr.	tr.	tr.	tr.	tr.	—	100.0
4	Douche	95.0	4.9	tr.	tr.	tr.	tr.	tr.	—	99.9
5	Spout of douche	96.0	4.0	tr.	tr.	tr.	tr.	tr.	—	100.0
6	Enema	65–71	4–5	25–30	0.1	—	tr.	tr.	tr.	—
7	Tube of enema	95.8	4.1	tr.	tr.	—	tr.	tr.	tr.	99.9
8	Retractor [5]	92.1	6.6	0.9	tr.	tr.	tr.	tr.	tr.	99.6
9	Retractor [5]	95.3	3.3	1.1	tr.	tr.	tr.	tr.	tr.	99.7
10	Clamp	78.2	6.1	2.4	tr.	tr.	tr.	tr.	tr.	86.7
11	Clamp	71.1	6.1	3.1	tr.	tr.	tr.	tr.	tr.	80.3

[1] Objects from the Bucheum (Ptolemaic-Roman). Analyses by W. F. Brazener, in R. Mond and O. H. Myers, *Bucheum*, I, pp. 105–9. (No. 1 of somewhat earlier date.)

[2] Also traces of nickel.

[3] Also nickel 0.1 per cent.

[4] Objects from the Bucheum (Ptolemaic-Roman). Analyses by C. O. Bannister and R. Rigby, in R. Mond and O. H. Myers, *Bucheum*, I, pp. 109–13.

[5] Also traces of nickel.

ANCIENT EGYPTIAN GOLD OBJECTS

	1 %	2 %	3 %	4 %	5 %	6 %	7 %	8 %	9 %	10 %	11 %	12 %	13 %
Gold...	79.7	84.2	84.0	79.5	91.0	78.0	81.7	92.3	92.2	80.8	94.8	90.5	92.7
Silver	13.4	13.5	13.0	16.8	9.0	18.0	16.1	3.2	3.9	14.7	3.7	4.5	4.9
Copper	nil	nil	nil	2.8	tr.	—	tr.	nil	nil	4.1	—	nil	—
Not determined	6.9	2.3	3.0	0.9	—	4.0	2.2	4.5	3.9	0.4	1.5	5.0	2.4
	100.0	100.0	100.0	100.0	100.0	100.0	100.0	100.0	100.0	100.0	100.0	100.0	100.0

	14 %	15 %	16 %	17 %	18 %	19 %	20 %	21 %	22 %	23 %	24 %	25 %	26 %	27 %
Gold ...	90.0	82.9	85.9	83.5	81.1	96.4	82.3	72.1	89.5	99.8	81.3	90.6	81.0	80
Silver ...	—	16.6	13.8	11.7	11.4	1.9	14.3	17.2	11.2	—	5.1	0.9	1.9	15
Copper ...	—	0.5	0.3	tr.	—	pres.	1.5	13.1	nil	—	13.6	8.6	17.1	5
Not det. ...	10.0	—	—	4.8	7.5	1.7	1.9	—	—	0.2	—	—	—	—
	100.0	100.0	100.0	100.0	100.0	100.0	100.0	102.4	100.7	100.0	100.0	100.1	100.0	100

Nos. 1–3. 1st Dyn. Analyses by J. H. Gladstone, in W. M. F. Petrie, *Royal Tombs*, II, p. 40.

Nos. 4–5. IIIrd Dyn. Analyses by H. E. Cox, F.R.I.C., for A. Lucas. Cf. C. M. Firth and J. E. Quibell, *Step Pyramid*, I, pp. 140–1. In No. 5 the silver is estimated by difference, Cox giving 11.0 per cent.

Nos. 6–7. VIth Dyn. Analyses by J. H. Gladstone, in W. M. F. Petrie, *Dendereh*, pp. 61–62. Cf. also *Chemical News*, LXXXIII (1901), p. 13, where the percentage of gold in No. 6 is given as 77.9.

Nos. 8–9. VIth Dyn. Analyses by M. Berthelot, *Ann. Serv.*, II (1901), pp. 157–63; *Ann. Chim. et Phys.*, XXI (1900), pp. 202–4; *C.R.Ac.Sci.*, CXXXI (1900), pp. 461–3; CXXXII (1901), pp. 1282–6. The specimens are given as XIth Dyn. in *Ann. Serv.*

No. 10. VIIth–VIIIth Dyn. Analysis by H. C. H. Carpenter. Kindly communicated by the finder, Mr. G. Brunton. (Part of a bracelet from Matmar).

No. 11. XIIth Dyn. Analysis by Z. Iskander, in F. Bisson de la Roque, *Trésor de Tôd (Cat. Caire)*, p. 52. The gold contained traces of metals of the platinum group.

Nos. 12–14. XIIth Dyn. Analyses by M. Berthelot (refs. as Nos. 8–9).

Nos. 15–16. XIIth Dyn. Analyses by M. Berthelot, in J. de Morgan, *Dahchour, mars–juin 1894*, pp. 145–6; *Ann. Chim. et Phys.*, IV (1895), pp. 571–4.

Nos. 17–18. XVIIIth Dyn. Analyses by J. H. Gladstone, *Proc. Soc. Antiquaries of Scotland*, XXX (1896), p. 33. Two samples from the same specimen.

Nos. 19–22. XVIIIth Dyn. Analyses by W. B. Pollard, in J. E. Quibell, *Yuaa and Thuiu*, pp. 78–79.

No. 23. Persian period. Analysis by M. Berthelot (refs. as Nos. 8–9).

Nos. 24–26. Roman period. Analyses by W. F. Brazener, in R. Mond and O. H. Myers, *Bucheum*, I, p. 109. The percentage figure for copper includes all base metals.

No. 27. Determination by X-ray powder photography. A. Weill, *Revue de Métallurgie*, XLVIII (1951), pp. 97–104.

ANCIENT EGYPTIAN ELECTRUM OBJECTS

	1 %	2 %	3 %	4 %	5 %	6 %	7 %	8 %
Gold	80.1	78.7	77.3	78.2	72.9	67.0	71.0	75
Silver	20.3	20.9	22.3	21.1	20.5	25.0	29.0	22
Copper	—	—	—	—	pres.	8.0	—	3
Not determined	—	0.4	0.4	0.7	6.6	—	—	—
	100.4	100.0	100.0	100 0	100.0	100.0	100.0	100

Nos. 1–4. XIth–XIIth Dyn. Analyses by M. Berthelot, *Ann. Serv.*, II (1901), pp. 157–63; *Ann. Chim. et Phys.*, XXI (1900), pp. 202–4; *C.R.Ac.Sci.*, CXXXI (1900), pp. 461–3; CXXXII (1901), pp. 1282–6.

No. 5. XVIIIth Dyn. Analysis by W. B. Pollard, in J. E. Quibell, *Yuaa and Thuiu*, pp. 78–79.

No. 6. XVIIIth Dyn. Analysis by A. Scott, in H. Carter, *Tut-ankh-Amen*, II, p. 211 (Appendix IV).

No. 7. XVIIIth–XIXth Dyn. C. R. Williams, *Gold and Silver Jewelry*, p. 118.

No. 8. Determination by X-ray powder photography. A. Weill, *Revue de Métallurgie*, XLVIII (1951), pp. 97–104; C. Desroches Noblecourt, *Rev. d'Ég.*, VIII (1951), p. 60, *n.* 2.

ANCIENT EGYPTIAN SILVER OBJECTS [1]

	1 %	2 %	3 %	4 %	5 %	6 %	7 %	8 %	9 %
Gold	38.1	8.9	0.7	14.9	pres.	—	—	—	—
Silver	60.4	90.1	91.8	74.5	69.2	98.4	95.6	98.7	96.2
Copper	1.5	1.0	n.d.	—	pres.	1.3	3.5	0.9	2.1
Lead	—	nil	—	—	nil	—	—	—	—
Not determined	—	—	7.5	10.6	30.8	0.3	0.8	0.5	1.7
	100.0	100.0	100.0	100.0	100.0	100.0	99.9	100.1	100.0

	10 %	11 %	12 %	13 %	14 %	15 %	16 %	17 %	18 %
Gold	1.0	8.7	8.4	5.1	2.7	3.2	2.7	17.9	1.2
Silver	61.0	82.5	84.9	90.2	92.1	92.5	95.0	82.1	94.8
Copper	0.6	8.9	4.3	4.5	3.3	3.9	2.3	tr.	1.7
Lead	nil	—	—	0.2	tr.	0.5	—	—	0.2
Not determined	37.4[2]	—	2.4	—	1.9	—	—	—	2.1
	100.0	100.1	100.0	100.0	100.0	100.0	100.0	100.0	100.0

No. 1. Early Dynastic. Analysis by C. Friedel, in E. Amélineau, *Les nouvelles fouilles d'Abydos, 1895–96*, p. 274.

No. 2. IVth Dyn. Analysis by H. E. Cox, F.R.I.C., for A. Lucas. Cf. G. A. Reisner, *History of the Giza Necropolis*, II, p. 44.

No. 3. IXth Dyn. Analysis by H. C. H. Carpenter, in G. Brunton, *Mostagedda*, p. 111.

---

[1] Three analyses by A. H. Kopp, in H. E. Winlock, *Treasure of El Lāhūn*, pp. 73–74, are not included, since the original silver content of the specimens was probably much higher than the figures obtained.

[2] Chiefly silver chloride.

No. 4. XIth–XIIth Dyn. Analysis by M. Berthelot, *Ann. Serv.*, II (1901), pp. 157–63; *Ann. Chim. et Phys.*, XXI (1900), pp. 202–4; *C.R.Ac.Sci.*, CXXXI (1900), pp. 461–3; CXXXII (1901), pp. 1282–6.

No. 5. XIIth Dyn. Analysis by M. Berthelot, in J. de Morgan, *Dahchour, mars–juin 1894*, pp. 145–6; *Ann. Chim. et Phys.*, IV (1895), pp. 571–4.

Nos. 6–9. XIIth Dyn. Analyses by Z. Iskander, in F. Bisson de la Roque, *Trésor de Tôd* (*Cat. Caire*), p. 53.

No. 10. Pan-grave. Analysis by H. E. Cox, F.R.I.C., for A. Lucas. Cf. G. Brunton, *Mostagedda*, p. 132.

Nos. 11–12. XVIIIth Dyn. Analyses by W. B. Pollard, in J. E. Quibell, *Yuaa and Thuiu*, pp. 78–79.

No. 13. XVIIIth Dyn. Analysis by A. Scott, in H. Carter, *Tut-ankh-Amen*, II, p. 210 (Appendix IV).

No. 14. XVIIIth Dyn. Analysis by H. E. Cox, F.R.I.C., for A. Lucas. Cf. H. Frankfort and J. D. S. Pendlebury, *City of Akhenaten*, II, p. 60.

No. 15. XIXth Dyn. C. R. Williams, *Gold and Silver Jewelry*, p. 29.

No. 16. XXIInd Dyn. Analysis by Z. Iskander, *Ann. Serv.*, XL (1940), p. 581.

No. 17. 5th–4th cent. B.C. C. R. Williams, *Gold and Silver Jewelry*, p. 143.

No. 18. Early A.D. Analysis by H. E. Cox, F.R.I.C., for A. Lucas. Found at Qustul in Nubia.

Two other specimens of silver examined spectographically gave the following results:

			A	B
Gold	...	...	A few per cent	5–10 per cent
Copper	...	...	A few per cent	A few per cent
Lead	...	...	Less than 1 per cent	Less than 1 per cent
Tin	...	...	Trace	Trace
Nickel	...	...	Slight trace	——

A. XIIth Dynasty. From Tôd. Analysis by Dr. H. Kenneth Whalley, Gov. Lab., London, for A. Lucas. Cf. Nos. 6–9 above.

B. XXIInd Dynasty. From coffin of Sheshonq, Tanis. Analysis by Dr. H. Kenneth Whalley for A. Lucas. Cf. No. 16 above.

MODERN NATRON FROM THE WADI NATRUN [1]

	%	%	%	%	%	%	%	%	%	%	%	%	%	%
Sodium carbonate [2]	38.2	22.4	28.9	35.5	43.5	28.9	58.6	75.0	67.8	33.4	38.3	41.8	35.4	53.9
Sodium bicarbonate [2]	32.4	6.2	20.5	25.8	33.8	9.9	14.3	5.0	8.6	25.2	18.3	29.4	12.1	24.2
Sodium chloride	6.7	26.4	24.8	14.0	4.8	26.8	7.4	9.4	4.3	20.8	2.2	11.9	12.4	1.9
Sodium sulphate	2.3	39.3	5.8	3.0	3.3	27.4	1.3	1.2	0.8	6.1	tr.	3.4	29.9	tr.
Water, free and combined	16.5	5.6	12.8	13.1	13.1	6.9	4.3	3.7	1.9	11.6	10.1	11.2	10.2	20.0
Matter insoluble in water	3.9	0.1	7.2	8.6	1.5	0.1	14.1	5.7	16.6	2.9	31.1	2.3	tr.	tr.
	100.0	100.0	100.0	100.0	100.0	100.0	100.0	100.0	100.0	100.0	100.0	100.0	100.0	100.0

MODERN NATRON FROM EL KAB [3]

							%	%	%
Sodium carbonate [4]	...	...	...	...	...	...	13.6	13.3	11.0
Sodium bicarbonate [4]	...	...	...	...	...	...	9.5	2.0	1.5
Sodium chloride	...	...	...	...	...	...	54.6	12.3	57.3
Sodium sulphate	...	...	...	...	...	...	11.4	70.2	29.4
Water, free and combined	...	...	...	...	...	...	4.7	tr.	0.4
Matter insoluble in water	...	...	...	...	...	...	6.2	2.2	0.4
							100.0	100.0	100.0

ANCIENT NATRON FROM TOMBS AND REFUSE EMBALMING MATERIAL

	1	2	3	4	5	6	7	8	9
	%	%	%	%	%	%	%	%	%
Sodium carbonate [5]	36.9	9.2	16.1	10.7	94.0	35.7	84.7	73.8	18.4
Sodium bicarbonate [5]	8.3	6.3	10.7	11.9					
Sodium chloride	9.9	39.3	25.2	18.2	0.5	39.5	1.5	13.0	62.0
Sodium sulphate	33.9	13.2	27.8	12.4	5.5	24.8	13.8	13.2	11.4
Water, free and combined	5.6	6.8	8.7	19.8	—	—	—	—	8.2[8]
Matter insoluble in water	5.4[6]	25.2	11.5[6]	27.0[7]	—	—	—	—	
	100.0	100.0	100.0	100.0	100.0	100.0	100.0	100.0	100.0

No. 1. From near the tomb of Ipy at Deir el Bahari (XIth Dyn.). Analysis by A. Lucas. Cf. H. E. Winlock, *M.M.A. Bull., Egyptian Exped. 1921–1922*, p. 34.

No. 2. Found in a vase at Thebes (XVIIIth Dyn.). Analysis by A. Lucas.

Nos. 3–4. From the tomb of Yuya and Tuyu (XVIIIth Dyn.). Analyses by A. Lucas. Cf. J. E. Quibell, *Yuaa and Thuiu*, pp. vi, 75–77; A Lucas, *Cairo Sc. Journ.*, II (1908), p. 134.

Nos. 5–8. From the tomb of Tutankhamūn (XVIIIth Dyn.). Analyses by H. E. Cox, F.R.I.C., for A. Lucas. Cf. H. Carter, *Tut-ankh-Amen*, III, pp. 178–9 (Appendix II).

No. 9. From bags found in a tomb at Qurna (XVIIIth Dyn.). G. Schweinfurth and L. Lewin, *Z.Ä.S.*, xxxv (1897), p. 143.

[1] Analyses by A. Lucas. Cf. A. Lucas, *Cairo Sc. Journ.*, II (1908), p. 133.

[2] The sodium carbonate and bicarbonate, together with any combined water, constitute the natron proper, the other ingredients being impurities.

[3] Analyses by A. Lucas. Cf. A. Lucas, *Cairo Sc. Journ.*, II (1908), p. 134.

[4] The sodium carbonate and bicarbonate, together with any combined water, constitute the natron proper, the other ingredients being impurities.

[5] The sodium carbonate and bicarbonate, together with any combined water, constitute the natron proper, the other ingredients being impurities.

[6] Chiefly sand.   [7] A mixture of sand and sawdust.   [8] By difference.

ANCIENT NATRON FROM REFUSE EMBALMING MATERIAL [1]

	%	%
Sodium carbonate [2]	18.9	19.4
Sodium bicarbonate [2]	10.5	6.0
Sodium chloride	45.8	50.1
Sodium sulphate	14.4	16.2
Magnesium chloride	1.4	tr.
Silica	3.4	
Oxides of iron and aluminium	0.3	
Calcium carbonate	0.2	3.1
Magnesium carbonate	0.1	
Fatty matter	nil	0.1
Water, free and combined	5.8	5.5
	100.8	100.4

[1] Found in jars from a cache of refuse embalming material of the Saite or Persian period discovered at Saqqara. Analyses by Z. Iskander, *Ann. Serv.*, LIII (1956), p. 181.

[2] The sodium carbonate and bicarbonate, together with any combined water, constitute the natron proper, the other ingredients being impurities.

EGYPTIAN BLUE FRIT

	1 %	2 %	3 %	4 %	5 %	6 %	7 %
Silica	57.2	70.0	88.7	70.5	70	63.7	63.4
Copper oxide	18.5	18.3	2.1	13.0	15	21.3	19.5
Oxides of iron and aluminium	0.8	0.3	0.6	3.7[1]	1[1]	0.6	—
Lime	13.8	9.4	7.9	8.5	9	14.3	14.4
Magnesia	0.5	—	—	4.2	—	—	—
Potash	nil ⎱	⎱ 2.0	—	— ⎱	⎱ 4	—	1.2
Soda	7.6 ⎰	⎰	0.8	— ⎰	⎰	—	0.9
Moisture	1.6	—	—	—	—	—	—
	100.0	100.0	100.1	99.9	99	99.9	99.4

No. 1. XIXth Dyn. Analysis by A. Lucas.

No. 2. Analysis by J. K. Crow, *Ann. Serv.*, IV (1903), pp. 242–3.

No. 3. Analysis by W. J. Russell, *Proc. Royal Institution*, XIV (1893–5), p. 69, *n.*; *Nature*, XLIX (1893–4), p. 375, *n.*

No. 4. Analysis by Rammelsberg, quoted by C. R. Lepsius, *Les métaux dans les inscriptions égyptiennes*, p. 25.

No. 5. Analysis by Vauquelin, quoted by C. R. Lepsius (as No. 4).

No. 6. Analysis by F. Fouqué, *C.R.Ac.Sci.*, CVIII (1889), pp. 325–7; *Bull. Soc. fr. de Minéralogie*, XII (1889), pp. 36–38.

No. 7. Specimen prepared by Laurie, McLintock and Miles in imitation of Egyptian blue frit. A. P. Laurie, W. F. P. McLintock and F. D. Miles, *Proc. Royal Society*, LXXXIX (1914), pp. 418–29.

---

[1] Iron only.

CLAY[1]

	1	2	3	4	5	6	7	8	9	10	11	12	13	14
	%	%	%	%	%	%	%	%	%	%	%	%	%	%
Silica	34.8	33.0	56.1	55.5	59.6	58.3	58.8	55.0	55.9	42.9	45.0	42.6	40.7	43.1
Oxide of aluminium	}20.6	15.0	18.5	8.7	17.2		13.6		16.9}	}8.7	12.6	14.1	13.3	}14.8
Oxide of titanium			—	—		}20.7	1.3	}25.4	1.5		0.8	—	—	
Oxide of iron	6.1	8.1	9.0[2]	13.8	5.6		6.3		7.5	6.9	8.4[2]	5.8	5.7	15.7
Oxide of phosphorus	1.1	—	—	—	1.7	—	—	—	—	—	—	—	—	—
Lime	12.7	17.5	5.2	4.7	3.8	6.9	6.9	8.6	6.8	26.8	21.0	20.9	19.8	3.3
Magnesia	0.4	2.0	1.1	2.8	1.6	2.3	2.7	2.7	2.9	1.8	3.9	5.1	5.2	3.2
Potash	1.0	1.0	—	—	—	1.1	1.5	tr.	tr.	n.d.	tr.}	}1.4	}2.2	1.1
Soda	1.3	1.0	—	—	—	7.9	6.8	4.9	4.9	4.1	0.7}			2.3
Sodium chloride	1.0	—	—	—	1.3	—	—	—	—	—	—	—	—	—
Carbon dioxide	8.7}		4.5	—	—	—	—	—	—	—	—	—	—	
Sulphur dioxide/ trioxide [3]	tr.	}20.0	—	—	—	1.2	n.d.	1.3	n.d.	n.d.	—	—	—	}15.5
Water	12.7}		5.6	—	2.8	—	—	—	—	—	—	—	—	
Loss	—	—	—	12.2	6.8	1.4	1.2	1.8	1.7	n.d.	8.0	10.1	13.1	—
	100.0	97.6	100.0	97.7	100.4	99.8	99.1	99.7	98.1	91.2	100.4	100.0	100.0	99.0

No. 1. Pottery clay from Ballas. Analysis for A. Lucas.

No. 2. Pottery clay from Qena. Analysis by M. Y. Bakr, *Silicates Industriels*, XXI (1956), p. 517.

No. 3. Pottery clay, locality not stated. Analysis by Brongniart, quoted by J. Llorens i Artigas, *Les pastes ceramiques i els esmalts blaus de l'antic Egipte*, p. 20.

No. 4. Magical brick. Analysis by J. Yoyotte, quoted by Mlle. J. Monnet, *Rev. d'Ég.*, VIII (1951), p. 153, *n.* 2.

No. 5. Slip on interior of pot. Analysis by R. Mond, in T. E. Peet, *Cemeteries of Abydos*, II, p. 9, n. I.

Nos. 6–7. Two samples from used glass crucible (El Amarna). Analyses by W. E. S. Turner, *Journ. Soc. Glass Technology*, XXXVIII (1954), p. 441.

Nos. 8–9. Two samples from unused glass crucible (El Amarna). Analyses by W. E. S. Turner (as Nos. 6–7).

No. 10. Sample from slip layer of glass crucible (El Amarna). Analysis by W. E. S. Turner (as Nos. 6–7).

No. 11. Glass crucible (Memphis). Analysis by W. E. S. Turner, *Journ. Soc. Glass Technology*, XXXVIII (1954), p. 442.

Nos. 12–13. Pots of New Kingdom date. B. H. Stricker, *Oud. Med. N.R.*, XXIV (1942), pp. 92–93.

No. 14. Nile mud. Analysis by M. Y. Bakr, *Silicates Industriels*, XXI (1956), p. 517.

---

[1] Nos. 1–13 'Special' clay; No. 14 Nile mud.

[2] Including traces of oxide of manganese.

[3] Nos. 1–2 Sulphur trioxide; Nos. 6–10 Sulphur dioxide.

Glaze from Islamic Ware [1]

	%	%
Silica	47.5	74.0
Alumina	1.0	1.5
Oxide of iron	2.1	2.6
Lime	6.1	2.4
Magnesia	0.7	0.8
Potash	tr.	2.7
Soda	6.2	14.1
Oxide of tin	4.8	0.3
Oxide of lead	31.4	1.4
Oxide of manganese	0.2	0.2
	100.0	100.0

[1] From Fostat. Colours not noted. Analyses by J. Clifford, F.R.I.C., for A. Lucas.

Addenda

The following important studies were published or appeared in this country too late to be included in the body of the text.

E. A. M. Greiss and K. Naguib, 'An Anatomical Study of Some "Sedges" in Relation to Plant Remains of Ancient Egypt', *Bull. Inst.d'Ég.*, XXXVII (1956), pp. 235–71.

Cyperus Papyrus, C. rotundus, C. Schimperianus and *C. alopecuroides* are described, and instances of the identification of all but *C. rotundus* among ancient Egyptian materials are given. These identifications have, however, been published elsewhere (*Mém. Inst.d'Ég.*, LV (1957)) and are largely incorporated in Chapter VIII.

M. Z. Nour, M. S. Osman, Z. Iskander and A. Y. Moustafa, *The Cheops Boats* (Part I).

On pp. 29–57 Iskander discusses the various materials examined, including:

An adhesive paste used to cement the pegs joining the wood of the boat. This was identified as a mixture of ferric oxide (ochre) and a nitrogenous organic adhesive, possibly glue.

Mortar used in connexion with the blocks covering the cavity, some coarse and pinkish white, some fine and almost pure white. Ten specimens from five different positions were analysed, and all were found to consist mainly of gypsum (calcium sulphate), the pinkish specimens containing a higher percentage of the usual natural impurities.

Plant materials from mats and ropes covering the boat (examined by E. A. M. Greiss). Some fragments and a mat were identified as *Phragmites communis*, other mats as *Juncus arabicus*, ropes as *Desmostachya bipinnata*, and flat 'ribbons', some tied together as mats, as *Typha australis*.

Fragments of corroded metal, apparently the broken edges of tools used to dress the blocks. These were found to be essentially copper, with very little iron and small traces of lead; no tin was detected.

Staples used in the construction of the boat. One was examined and found to be copper, with small proportions of arsenic, iron and zinc.

Pigments on the limestone blocks and on the wood of the boat. Black quarry marks on the blocks were carbon black; red-brown quarry marks were red ochre, another red pigment on the blocks was red ochre and finely ground limestone, and a red on the wood of the boat was also red ochre; white pigment on the wood of the boat was gypsum; yellow quarry marks were yellow ochre.

Wood from the boat, and elsewhere. Two scraps from above the limestone blocks were identified as cedar and acacia. Six specimens of the woods used in making the boat were identified as follows:

piece from oar blade: probably *Ostrya sp.* (presumably *Ostrya carpinifolia,* hop hornbeam)

piece from board: *Juniperus sp.*

piece from beam: probably *Balanites aegyptiaca*

piece from oar shaft: *Cedrus sp.*

pegs: possibly *Acacia sp.*

part of a tongue: probably *Mangifera indica*

The various methods of pegging, pegging and lashing, lashing, and dowelling used in joining the wood of the boat are also described.

F. Schuler, 'Ancient Glassmaking Techniques: The Egyptian Core Vessel Process', *Archaeology*, XV (1962), pp. 32–37.

The author briefly reviews the different methods of fabrication that have been suggested for the polychrome glass vessels of the Eighteenth Dynasty and later, and suggests, as a result of experiments, that these vessels were in fact mould cast by a technique essentially similar to the *cire perdue* process.

A. F. Shore, *Portrait Painting from Roman Egypt.*

The materials and media of the Fayum mummy portraits and the technique of encaustic painting are discussed in detail on pp. 20–25.

A. Zuber, 'Techniques du travail des pierres dures dans l'Ancienne Égypte', *Techniques et Civilisations,* V (1956), pp. 161–80, 195–215.

After a short discussion of the metals available to the ancient Egyptians for tools, Zuber examines various representations of sculptors at work, from which he concludes that chisels and adzes of copper and bronze were only used in carving wooden statues and those of soft stones, while the hard stones were worked with implements of stone. This is confirmed by his examination of unfinished hard stone statues, which show no traces of the use of metal picks or chisels, but are pitted, as though violently eroded by sand—the result of working with stone tools. To prove that hard stones can indeed be worked in this way, Zuber has executed a small head in granite, using only flint implements, the whole operation, exclusive of polishing, taking only thirty-six hours.

In the second part of the paper the author discusses the method of extracting blocks, based on an examination of the traces of work that remain in the granite quarries at Aswan, and particularly on the unfinished obelisk. Many of the extant wedge slots and other marks date from the Saite period and later, when iron chisels were available, but traces of earlier work point to the use of stone tools. After some experiment, Zuber was in fact able to detach a block of granite using wooden wedges, the slots for which he cut with fragments of dolerite.

The article concludes with a study of the evidence for sawing and the use of the tubular drill, and a consideration of the technique of grinding out stone vases.

In addition to the above there has recently been published an important series of identifications of Coptic materials by Iskander (in *Le Monastère de Phoebammon dans la Thébaide,* III, pp. 59–71) which, however, I have as yet been unable to consult.

Corrigendum to p. 168 (D. GLAZED POTTERY)

The reference to 'glazed Greek pottery' in this connexion is misleading, since the surface layer of the ordinary black-figure and red-figure vases is not properly a glaze, and would be better described as a gloss. The relevant technical studies are reviewed in a recent article by Miss M. Bimson ('The Technique of Greek Black and *Terra Sigillata* Red', *Antiquaries Journal,* XXXVI (1956), pp. 200–4) who concludes that '*terra sigillata* red and Greek black are fundamentally the same; in both cases the gloss is obtained by painting or "slipping" the partly dried pot with a fine suspension of an illite clay containing a certain amount of iron. The ware may then be fired either to obtain *terra sigillata* red, when it is kept from contact with reducing gases, or to obtain Greek black if exposed to reducing gases; in each case the colour is due to an oxide of iron'. Cf. also M. Farnsworth and H. Wisely, *American Journal of Archaeology,* LXII (1958), pp. 165–73.

INDEX

I Materials and Techniques

Abrasives, 42–43, 66–67, 71–74
Acacia, bark, 37
  gum, 5
  pods, 34
  wood, 434, 439, 440, 442, 498–9
Acids, *see* Fatty acids
Actinolite, 397
Adhesives, 1–9, 498, 499
  in gilding, 231–2, 252
  miscellaneous and unidentified, 8–9
  in painting, 351–2
  in papyrus, 138–9
Agate, 386–7
Alabaster, 59–61, 391, 406–7, 413
  in inlaid eyes, 100f.
  powdered, 7, 324
  quarries, 60
  vessels, 421–3, 427
Albumin, 1–2, 4, 232, 352, 359
Alcohol, 10–12, 18, 24, 85–86, 359
Alcoholic beverages, 10–27
Alkali, in clay, 366
  in faience, 175, 177–8
  in frit, 341
  in glass, 184–7, 191
  in glassy faience, 165
  in glaze, 160, 169–74
Alkanet, 150
Alloys, 195–257
Almond, oil, 86, 87, 329–30, 442
  wood, 330, 440, 442
Alum, 257–9
  as mordant, 34, 36, 154, 258, 259, 303
  in mummification, 303
  as tanning agent, 34, 35, 258
Alumina, 175, 184–6
Aluminium, oxide, 73, 260
  salts, 303
  silicate, 73, 262, 367
Amazon stone, Amazonite, 390, 393, 405, *see also*
    Felspar, green
Amber, 234, 305, 386, 387–8
Ambergris, 87
Amethyst, 126, 388–9
Amethystine quartz, 402–3, 421, 423
Amphiboles, 397
Analyses, 469–97
  bitumen, 304–8
  bronze objects, 486, 487–8, 488, 489
  bronze-lead objects, 486
  clay, 496
  copper objects, 216, 483–4, 485, 486
  copper-lead objects, 485

  copper ore, 206, 482
  copper slag, 482
  electrum objects, 491
  eye-paints, 83–84
  faience, 474, 475
  frit, 495
  glass, 476, 477, 478, 479, 480
  glass, Arab, 477, 480
  glaze, 475, 497
  gold objects, 490
  gypsum, 469
  gypsum mortar, 470, 472
  gypsum plaster, 471, 472
  lime mortar, 469
  mortar with organic adhesive, 473
  natron, 267, 493, 494
  plaster moulds, 473
  resins, 317–19
  sand, 481
  silver objects, 491–2
  whitewash, 473
Anhydrite, 413, 415, 422
Animal products 28–40, *see also* Fats, animal
Ankerite, 412
Anorthosite-gneiss, 409
Antimony, 82, 195–9
  compounds, 82–84, 195–6
  in copper and bronze, 196, 198
  -lead compound, 82, 190, 196, 244
  in gold, 226–7
  metallic, 195
  ores, 195, 197
  oxide, 198–9
  plating, 197–9
  powder, 196–7
  sulphide, 81–82, 196, 197, 199, 245
Antimony-copper alloy, 198
Aragonite, 59
Archil, 150
Architectural decoration, 4, 156–7, 162, 163,
  232
Argun palm, *see* Palm
Arsenates, 234
Arsenic, compounds, 82
  in copper, 214, 216
  sulphides, 245, 348, 349, 363, *see also* Orpiment,
    Realgar
Ash wood, 429, 431
Ashes, *see* Plant ashes
Asphalt, 307–8
Azurite, 171, 203–5
  described, 210
  as pigment, 340, 351

II BOTANICAL AND OTHER TERMS

III Greek and Latin

IV EGYPTIAN

V AUTHORITIES CITED (Substantive references only)

VI Principal Sites and Finds

A CATALOG OF SELECTED
DOVER BOOKS
IN ALL FIELDS OF INTEREST

A CATALOG OF SELECTED DOVER
BOOKS IN ALL FIELDS OF INTEREST

CONCERNING THE SPIRITUAL IN ART, Wassily Kandinsky. Pioneering work by father of abstract art. Thoughts on color theory, nature of art. Analysis of earlier masters. 12 illustrations. 80pp. of text. 5⅜ x 8½.   23411-8 Pa. $3.95

ANIMALS: 1,419 Copyright-Free Illustrations of Mammals, Birds, Fish, Insects, etc., Jim Harter (ed.). Clear wood engravings present, in extremely lifelike poses, over 1,000 species of animals. One of the most extensive pictorial sourcebooks of its kind. Captions. Index. 284pp. 9 x 12.   23766-4 Pa. $12.95

CELTIC ART: The Methods of Construction, George Bain. Simple geometric techniques for making Celtic interlacements, spirals, Kells-type initials, animals, humans, etc. Over 500 illustrations. 160pp. 9 x 12. (USO)   22923-8 Pa. $9.95

AN ATLAS OF ANATOMY FOR ARTISTS, Fritz Schider. Most thorough reference work on art anatomy in the world. Hundreds of illustrations, including selections from works by Vesalius, Leonardo, Goya, Ingres, Michelangelo, others. 593 illustrations. 192pp. 7⅛ x 10¼.   20241-0 Pa. $9.95

CELTIC HAND STROKE-BY-STROKE (Irish Half-Uncial from "The Book of Kells"): An Arthur Baker Calligraphy Manual, Arthur Baker. Complete guide to creating each letter of the alphabet in distinctive Celtic manner. Covers hand position, strokes, pens, inks, paper, more. Illustrated. 48pp. 8¼ x 11.   24336-2 Pa. $3.95

EASY ORIGAMI, John Montroll. Charming collection of 32 projects (hat, cup, pelican, piano, swan, many more) specially designed for the novice origami hobbyist. Clearly illustrated easy-to-follow instructions insure that even beginning papercrafters will achieve successful results. 48pp. 8¼ x 11.   27298-2 Pa. $3.50

THE COMPLETE BOOK OF BIRDHOUSE CONSTRUCTION FOR WOODWORKERS, Scott D. Campbell. Detailed instructions, illustrations, tables. Also data on bird habitat and instinct patterns. Bibliography. 3 tables. 63 illustrations in 15 figures. 48pp. 5¼ x 8½.   24407-5 Pa. $2.50

BLOOMINGDALE'S ILLUSTRATED 1886 CATALOG: Fashions, Dry Goods and Housewares, Bloomingdale Brothers. Famed merchants' extremely rare catalog depicting about 1,700 products: clothing, housewares, firearms, dry goods, jewelry, more. Invaluable for dating, identifying vintage items. Also, copyright-free graphics for artists, designers. Co-published with Henry Ford Museum & Greenfield Village. 160pp. 8¼ x 11.   25780-0 Pa. $10.95

HISTORIC COSTUME IN PICTURES, Braun & Schneider. Over 1,450 costumed figures in clearly detailed engravings–from dawn of civilization to end of 19th century. Captions. Many folk costumes. 256pp. 8⅜ x 11¾.   23150-X Pa. $12.95

THE INFLUENCE OF SEA POWER UPON HISTORY, 1660–1783, A. T. Mahan. Influential classic of naval history and tactics still used as text in war colleges. First paperback edition. 4 maps. 24 battle plans. 640pp. 5⅜ x 8½. 25509-3 Pa. $12.95

THE STORY OF THE TITANIC AS TOLD BY ITS SURVIVORS, Jack Winocour (ed.). What it was really like. Panic, despair, shocking inefficiency, and a little heroism. More thrilling than any fictional account. 26 illustrations. 320pp. 5⅜ x 8½.
20610-6 Pa. $8.95

FAIRY AND FOLK TALES OF THE IRISH PEASANTRY, William Butler Yeats (ed.). Treasury of 64 tales from the twilight world of Celtic myth and legend: "The Soul Cages," "The Kildare Pooka," "King O'Toole and his Goose," many more. Introduction and Notes by W. B. Yeats. 352pp. 5⅜ x 8½. 26941-8 Pa. $8.95

BUDDHIST MAHAYANA TEXTS, E. B. Cowell and Others (eds.). Superb, accurate translations of basic documents in Mahayana Buddhism, highly important in history of religions. The Buddha-karita of Asvaghosha, Larger Sukhavativyuha, more. 448pp. 5⅜ x 8½. 25552-2 Pa. $12.95

ONE TWO THREE . . . INFINITY: Facts and Speculations of Science, George Gamow. Great physicist's fascinating, readable overview of contemporary science: number theory, relativity, fourth dimension, entropy, genes, atomic structure, much more. 128 illustrations. Index. 352pp. 5⅜ x 8½. 25664-2 Pa. $8.95

ENGINEERING IN HISTORY, Richard Shelton Kirby, et al. Broad, nontechnical survey of history's major technological advances: birth of Greek science, industrial revolution, electricity and applied science, 20th-century automation, much more. 181 illustrations. ". . . excellent . . ."–Isis. Bibliography. vii + 530pp. 5⅝ x 8¼.
26412-2 Pa. $14.95

DALÍ ON MODERN ART: The Cuckolds of Antiquated Modern Art, Salvador Dalí. Influential painter skewers modern art and its practitioners. Outrageous evaluations of Picasso, Cézanne, Turner, more. 15 renderings of paintings discussed. 44 calligraphic decorations by Dalí. 96pp. 5⅜ x 8½. (USO) 29220-7 Pa. $4.95

ANTIQUE PLAYING CARDS: A Pictorial History, Henry René D'Allemagne. Over 900 elaborate, decorative images from rare playing cards (14th–20th centuries): Bacchus, death, dancing dogs, hunting scenes, royal coats of arms, players cheating, much more. 96pp. 9¼ x 12¼. 29265-7 Pa. $11.95

MAKING FURNITURE MASTERPIECES: 30 Projects with Measured Drawings, Franklin H. Gottshall. Step-by-step instructions, illustrations for constructing handsome, useful pieces, among them a Sheraton desk, Chippendale chair, Spanish desk, Queen Anne table and a William and Mary dressing mirror. 224pp. 8⅛ x 11¼.
29338-6 Pa. $13.95

THE FOSSIL BOOK: A Record of Prehistoric Life, Patricia V. Rich et al. Profusely illustrated definitive guide covers everything from single-celled organisms and dinosaurs to birds and mammals and the interplay between climate and man. Over 1,500 illustrations. 760pp. 7½ x 10⅛. 29371-8 Pa. $29.95

Prices subject to change without notice.

Available at your book dealer or write for free catalog to Dept. GI, Dover Publications, Inc., 31 East 2nd St., Mineola, N.Y. 11501. Dover publishes more than 500 books each year on science, elementary and advanced mathematics, biology, music, art, literary history, social sciences and other areas.